The Ruins of the Reich

The Ruins of the Reich

The Ruins of the Reich

Travels in Germany Past and Present

Michael Geoghegan

First published 2020 by Leitmotif Editions
14 Frognal Gardens, London NW3 6UX

ISBN 978-1-9163893-1-1

A CIP catalogue record for this book is available from the British Library

Book design and copy-editing by Sally Osborn
Cover design and maps by Ian Moore
Cover photograph by the author
Typeset in Sabon by EditExpert
Printed and bound in Great Britain by Clays Ltd, Elcograf S.p.A.

For Brigitte, Klaus-Jürgen and Justine

"He (Hitler) used to say that if his Reich were, centuries later, to crumble, the ruins of our buildings would still testify to the strength of our will and the greatness of our belief."

Albert Speer, Architektur

"Valhalla, I am coming!"

Led Zeppelin, Immigrant Song

Contents

Memel

River Memel

Königsberg

Danzig

EAST PRUSSIA

POMERANIA

Marienburg

Allenstein

River Vistula

River Oder

River Bug

Breslau

SILESIA

St. Annaberg

Reichenberg

Myslowitz

Olmütz

MORAVIA

Znaim   Brünn

River Danube

Wien

AUSTRIA

GERMANY PAST

— · — · — · — · — · —

German Confederation 1815-1866

— — — — — — — —

Kingdom of Prussia

The Ruins of the Reich

The Ruins of the Reich

Prelude

The Hall of Liberation

Kelheim, Bavaria. A Saturday evening in mid-December. The cobbled streets of the Altstadt were gritted and rimed with a residue of snow. Mounds of icy slush were piled around the trees, fountains and statues of Ludwigsplatz. Townspeople were locking up their shops and rushing to their cars, hunched against the cold. The broad façades of the sixteenth-century houses surrounding the square were floodlit from below, their stepped or cello-shaped gables highlighted against the night sky. In the centre was a gilt Madonna atop a plague column and a statue of King Ludwig I of Bavaria inscribed with the epithet "Gerecht und Beharrlich" ("Just and Persistent"). His ermine robe was embroidered with Wittelsbach diamonds and in his right hand he held a partially rolled architectural drawing, which revealed the ground plan for an eighteen-sided building. He looked like Sean Connery. The eastern end of Ludwigsplatz was blocked off by the Weißes Bräuhaus, its ochre walls decorated with purple pennants, coats of arms and a Gothic inscription claiming this to be the oldest *Weißbier* brewery in Bavaria. To the west, Ludwigstraße disappeared below one of three medieval gateways which allow access into the walled centre of this *Residenzstadt*. Rising above the gateway was a tall maypole painted in blue and white helter-skelter stripes and adorned with beribboned cartwheels and metal figurines representing the tradesfolk of Kelheim – butchers, bakers, cobblers, cutlers, carpenters, glaziers, apothecaries and moneylenders. It was all very *altbayrisch*, visibly rooted in the traditions of the Catholic Church, the Bavarian monarchy, the beer hall and peasant folklore; yet it was also modern and affluent, with an undercurrent of aggression: in the background you could hear the deep-house sound-system thudding of boy racers who spent the evening cruising around the old town in their souped-up Audi A3s.

The focal point of Ludwigsplatz was the Café-Bistrot-Tagblatt, which was warm and noisy, full of country boys and girls. I found a table free in the main bar, which was decorated in a *fin-de-siècle* style with Art Nouveau posters by Chéret, Mucha and Toulouse-Lautrec. Bon Jovi and Bryan Adams were on the jukebox; Real Madrid versus Borussia Dortmund on the television. The girls flung off their fashionable sheepskin coats, revealing hints of multi-coloured thongs and unseasonably bronzed cleavages. Everyone was smoking. The boys were drinking peachy *Weißbier* from bell-bottomed glasses; the girls attacked baroque ice-cream confections or sipped *latte macchiato*.

I ordered a *Gourmet-Pfanne* – pork loin and *Allgäuer Spätzle* served in a frying pan – and a *Weißbier*. A rock poster behind me advertised an open-air concert in the Volksfestplatz by Bonfire, a band whose long hair and lived-in faces suggested a blues-rock group who've been gigging since the 1970s – a German equivalent of the Steve Gibbons Band, maybe? I realised I was beginning to make frequent eye contact with a girl sitting with her friend at a table opposite mine. She seemed to be fascinated by me on my own in a crowded bar, scribbling away in a notebook. She had a curved nose, dark curly hair pushed up into a crow's nest by a broad headband, and a laugh that exposed her upper gums. She was wearing an off-the-shoulder pullover which she had to keep tugging back into position. Like everyone she was chain-smoking, but her highly strung, bohemian air was at odds with the sturdy, *echt deutsch* countryfolk in the rest of the bar. Perhaps she was a student home for the winter break?

After another beer the eye contact became more intense. I was torn between flirting and watching Borussia Dortmund. They lost 2–1, to the delight of the local boys, all Bayern Munich fans. Once the football was over, the bar staff turned up the jukebox and started playing golden oldies. "Alice, Alice, who the fuck is Alice?" Only the Germans could take a glam-pop anthem from the early seventies, insert an expletive and take it to the top of the charts in 1995 – and still find it funny ten years later. In the end, in spite of a schnapps chaser, I didn't have the nerve to approach the girl's table and introduce myself, so I settled my bill and headed for the door. I noticed her biting her nails furiously as I left. Outside, the pubs were closing and the boy racers were revving up. I walked aimlessly around the Altstadt for ten minutes, returned to the

Café-Bistrot-Tagblatt and peered through the window – but the moment had passed, as they do.

above the gateway at the far end of Ludwigstraße, beyond the town walls, was the Michelsberg, a steep, wooded hill overlooking Kelheim. Pushing above the dark trees on its crest was a yellow, cylindrical edifice which looked like a Victorian gasometer. It consisted of two drums: an upper drum surrounded by a balustrade of Italianate columns, which rested inside a larger, lower drum, ribbed with vertical buttresses surmounted by a circle of stone figures. The building was floodlit from below and shone like a golden crown against the night sky. I imagined a giant finger and thumb reaching down from the stars to unscrew the top of the rotunda from its base, or to set the two drums rotating inside one another.

On the spur of the moment I decided to climb the Michelsberg. A barometer on the wall of the Ludwigs-Apotheke read minus 3 degrees centigrade, but I felt invigorated by several glasses of *Weißbier* and a *Malteser-Aquavit*, a potent cocktail of north and south German alcohol. Whistling the overture to *Die Meistersinger von Nürnberg*, I set off along Ludwigstraße, my gaze fixed on the Grail-like vision on the hill above me. Once outside the town walls, I crossed the Graben and followed a street bridging the frozen harbour that links the Danube and Altmühl rivers. I found a steep path leading up to the building, which was presumably a monument of some kind, and began to climb. It was a clear, starry night. A full moon shone in the east, illuminating the winding, icy path. The sounds of Kelheim and the industrial humming from the chemical plants fell slowly away. I felt like Parsifal ascending Montsalvat. As I neared the summit the shadows were gradually suffused with a golden light from the rotunda above. I could make out a circle of tall female figures, in classical robes, perched on the buttresses around the building. Each statue was holding a brick-shaped tablet. As the lower half of the monument came into view, I saw a ring of stone candelabra on three massive, snow-clad plinths. Above the portal was an inscription: "Den Teutschen Befreiungskaempfern – Ludwig I, Koenig von Bayern" ("To the German freedom fighters – Ludwig I, King of Bavaria").

I emerged onto a lawn encircling the monument. A silent midnight over the Danube, and this vast Bavarian pantheon towering over me like an arcane, mystical force. I walked through the snow, keeping outside the ring of floodlights which threw giant shadows from the goddesses. The stone maidens' tablets bore the names of German provinces, but they were situated so high up it was difficult to decipher them. I identified Austria and Prussia on either side of the portal. On my second circuit the words began to fall into place: Prussia, Hanover, Moravia, Saxony, Silesia, Brandenburg, Pomerania, Mecklenburg, Westphalia, Hesse, Thuringia, Rhineland, Swabia, Franconia, Bohemia, Tyrol, Bavaria and Austria. A litany of eighteen kingdoms, principalities, duchies, archduchies, electorates, margraviates and landgraviates, which read like a sacred ring of power. The circle of petrified Valkyries symbolised *das großdeutsche Reich*, that empire of the soul which has bewitched every Germanic despot from Barbarossa to Hitler.

Despite the imperialistic bombast of the monument, I felt a sense of nostalgia and mystery in the naming of these regions, as if I'd become aware for the first time of a Germany older and greater than the Bundesrepublik. The ring of names fused past and present, core and rim, melding the golden age of Germany's Gothic past and the baroque Holy Roman Empire with the Communist GDR and those pieces of ex-Germany lying on the fringes of central Europe like abandoned shards of metal around a bomb crater. German history often reads like a tragic myth, a never-ending sequel to the *Nibelungenlied*, a violent process of fragmentation and division. The arrangement of these eighteen territories in a circle, however, offered an alternative, albeit idealised, history: one of unity and completeness.

I felt vaguely confused by these feelings of *Sehnsucht* for a lost fatherland that was not my own, and troubled that I was entertaining thoughts of a rather reactionary nature; but, up in the woods at midnight in the embrace of a cold Danubian night, I felt the germ of an idea stirring. A circular itinerary. A journey into the past. A requiem for Germania, for the ruins of the Reich. I sat down on an icy bench to think this through. I would write a travelogue of eighteen chapters, one for each of the provinces on the tablets borne aloft by the stone maidens. I walked around the monument again, mapping out a route which would take me through the territories named on the tablets. Then, in the distance, I heard men's voices, amplified by the darkness. Suddenly the lights went out and the monument was a ghostly gasometer once more.

The following morning there was an icy crust on the cobblestones and the smell of hops over the Altstadt. The temperature had dropped to six degrees below zero, but you could bask in the pale sun where it shone on the apricot walls of the houses around Ludwigsplatz. I sat in front of the post office and read a notice about a forthcoming *Schlesierfasching*, the traditional *Eisbeinessen* (pork knuckle feast) of the local Silesian *Heimat* association. From the upper floor of the Stadt-Apotheke a wooden casement window hung over Donaustraße, full of coloured-glass medicine jars glittering in the sunlight. In the wall of the pharmacy was a stone tablet in Hebrew script. I read the dates 1249 and 1519, but there was no translation of its meaning. In one of the chemist's windows was a display of *Sterbebilder*, black-framed photographs of local men and women killed or missing in action during the Second World War. Each photograph was accompanied by a short poem which served as an epitaph. Kelheim lost four hundred and twenty-one of its sons and daughters during the war. Most served in the Wehrmacht, the Luftwaffe or the Marine. I scanned the faces, as if daring the display to include one SS man – and then I found him: Hans Durmann, a young soldier with cropped blond hair in a neat black uniform. His smooth face looked out without expression. His epitaph read: "No one has a greater love than he who lays down his life for his own people." Hans was a Rottenführer, a "gang-leader" in the SS-Totenkopf division. He was killed in January 1945. It didn't say where.

I continued along Donaustraße to the Donautor and crossed a car park to the Danube. The waterfront was deserted, the river swollen with snowmelt. Six pleasure boats were drawn up at anchor, waiting for the spring season to come round again. Outside the walls of the Altstadt was the Schleiferturm, a circular stone tower built in the fifteenth century from the remains of a ducal castle. It was now a memorial to the townspeople of Kelheim who died in the two world wars. Inside the tower were wreaths, candles and plaques carrying the names of the fallen. I cast my eye down a list of the battlefields of Galicia in the early years of the First World War. In front of the tower was a tall statue of a medieval warrior planted on a concrete plinth. Clad in doublet, hose and cloak, the soldier was a crude version of the Roland figure found in market squares throughout Germany. He clutched a pennant-shaped shield and a square-bladed sword, unsheathed and erect in his robotic fist. His stern expression, inflated pectorals and the porous concrete from which he had been sculpted were reminiscent of the Aryan statuary of Josef Thorak or Arno Breker. I scrabbled at the ivy behind his ankles, looking for a date to confirm the statue's National Socialist provenance, but found only the sculptor's initials. Hidden below the statue in a wall of frozen geraniums was a small stone with the inscription "Den Sudetendeutschen Opfern für das Selbstbestimmungsrecht" ("To the Sudeten Germans who sacrificed their right to self-determination"). To the Sudeten Germans who, like the South Tyrolean Germans, found themselves in a foreign country on the wrong side of the mountains following the Treaty of Versailles, a treaty which was supposed to embody the right of any ethnic group to national unity and political independence within its own state.

The Michelsberg, rising up behind the Schleiferturm, beckoned once again. First, I walked back to Ludwigsplatz and asked in the tourist office about the Jewish pharmacy and the Nazi statue. The woman behind the desk told me that the Hebrew tablet was the gravestone of a daughter of Rabbi Jesud, who died in Kelheim in 1249. There was also a stone relief depicting three Jews and a pig which had survived from the Middle Ages, but it was destroyed in 1945. This was the year the Roland statue was erected; however, the woman assured me it was post-Nazi, put up in the autumn of that year. She then sold me two guides to the Befreiungshalle (Hall of Liberation), the monument on the hill.

Seen from close up in the morning sunlight, the cylindrical exterior of the Befreiungshalle is a mosaic of irregular rectangles of orange, yellow, pink and cream paint, rather like a Dulux colour card. The monument resembles a large cake on three plinths, the hardened marzipan, greyed icing sugar and gutted candles left over from a wedding where the guests failed to arrive. Historically, this is more or less what happened. The Befreiungshalle was conceived by King Ludwig I of Bavaria as a patriotic temple to pan-Germanic unity following the struggle against Napoleon. Bavaria was to play the role of a benign, elderly relative hoping to broker a marriage between two superpowers, Austria and Prussia, in order to secure the future of the German dynasty. Austria and Prussia, however, had no intention of getting into bed with each other. Ludwig's dream of a new German empire, a successor to the Holy Roman Empire of the German Nation destroyed by Napoleon, disintegrated before the foundation stone of the monument had been laid.

Ludwig conceived the idea of the Befreiungshalle during a visit to the classical ruins of Tiryns in 1836, in the company of the architect Friedrich von Gärtner. The concept was also based on a Greek monument at Plataea, which listed the names of heroic Greek participants in the wars against the Persians. Ludwig's idea was to honour in similar fashion the

German "tribes" who fought against Napoleon in the series of battles which culminated in the victorious Battle of the Nations at Leipzig on 18 October 1813. The site above Kelheim was found in 1838. The location had national-historical associations, since there had been a prehistoric Celtic settlement on the Michelsberg whose walls are still visible in the woods behind the Befreiungshalle. The Michelsberg is also close to the Roman *limes*, the 500-kilometre wall built to protect the Roman Empire against the Germanic barbarians. The Befreiungshalle, appropriately, lies on the side of the barbarians.

The neoclassicist Gärtner, commissioned by Ludwig to design the monument, proposed almost a dozen projects. His first sketches were based on the Pantheon in Rome and featured a square, domed building fronted by a colonnade rising above a monumental staircase. In later sketches he surrounded the entire dome with a square colonnade on a massive plinth. In his final plan, a reproduction of which was hanging in my hotel, the Weißes Lamm, the monument had evolved into an eighteen-sided, neoclassical colonnade surrounding a galleried dome. None of Gärtner's projects was particularly innovative. They all harked back to historical models based on a combination of colonnade and dome.

In the end this was all academic, as in 1847 Gärtner died. Construction on the monument had barely started, even though the foundation stone had been laid on 19 October 1842, the day after the consecration of Walhalla, Ludwig's other nationalistic temple overlooking the Danube on the opposite side of Regensburg. This had been designed by the Bavarian court architect Leo von Klenze, to whom Ludwig now turned to continue work on the Befreiungshalle. A stricter neoclassicist than Gärtner, Klenze immediately attacked the "barocken, häßlichen, byzantino-italico, germaniko-gärtnerikoschen Formen des Baues" ("the ugly, baroque, Byzantine-Italianate, Germanic-Gärtneresque forms of the building") and promised to construct a monument "for our time", rather than something mixed and matched out of the past.

He succeeded. Discarding Gärtner's square colonnade and heavy dome, he also rejected the Grecian-Italianate forms of Bavaria's other nineteenth-century temples, such as Gärtner's Feldherrnhalle and Siegestor or his own Walhalla and Glyptothek. His finished design was an almost circular (actually eighteen-sided) tower surmounted by a shallow cone. Klenze's Befreiungshalle has no obvious architectural prototype. The guidebooks suggest the Pantheon in Rome, the Baptistery in Pisa or the Mausoleum of Theodoric in Ravenna. The answer, I think, lies in the simple, medieval Schleiferturm at the foot of the Michelsberg, whose proportions are almost identical to those of the Befreiungshalle. Klenze had found a German solution for a monument to Germany.

In 1848, the year after Klenze took over the commission, Ludwig I was forced to abdicate in favour of his son, who was crowned Maximilian II. The cause of Ludwig's abdication was a combination of his scandalous liaison with the Irish dancer Lola Montez and his belief in the divine right of kingship, a concept somewhat outdated in the revolutionary year of 1848. The Bavarian ministers no longer wished to budget for this anachronistic folly. The ex-king, persistent as ever, decided to finance the construction himself, and work resumed in March 1850. The shell of the building was completed in August 1860; the topping-out ceremony was held in October of that year; and the Befreiungshalle was officially unveiled on 18 October 1863, fifty years to the day after the Battle of the Nations it was originally intended to commemorate. (Eighteen is the symbolic number of the monument, reflected in its architectural construction. The eighteen-sided rotunda, supported by eighteen buttresses bearing eighteen allegorical statues, rests on three eighteen-sided plinths which support eighteen limestone candlesticks.) A celebratory anthem was sung at the opening ceremony, and speeches were delivered by military veterans of the Battle of the Nations. An epic poem was published in the *Regensburger Morgenblatt*, full of eulogies to Victory and Immortality, to German blood and German soil, to German youth and German strength, to the *Heldenzeit* and the *Vaterland*.

I entered the rotunda. The effect was breathtaking. The interior of the monument seemed twice the size of its exterior. Far above me was a huge dome, disguised from the outside. Around the base of the hall thirty-four winged Victories, personifying the German states which survived the Napoleonic Wars, gazed serenely across the marble floor. Like petrified angels playing ring o' roses, these fourteen-metre-high Valkyries linked hands to form a protective, inclusive circle mirroring the defensive, exclusive circle of stone handmaidens around the exterior of the monument. The goddesses of Victory supported a circle of fire-gilt shields bearing the names of seventeen victorious battles fought by German armies during the Wars of Liberation between 1813 and 1815, from Danigkow in Prussia to Brienne, Bar, Arcis-sur-Aube, Paris and Waterloo.

On the walls above the lower colonnade was a circle of eighteen marble plaques commemorating the aristocratic generals and field marshals who commanded the German forces: Prince Schwarzenberg and Count

Radetzky among the Austrian commanders; Blücher, Scharnhorst and Gneisenau among the Prussians. On the architrave above the upper colonnade, eighteen fortresses reconquered from Napoleon were emblazoned in letters of gold. Like the battles, these ranged from Prussian Danzig and Marienburg to Belfort and Auxonne in France. Above these inscriptions was the white and gold dome, divided into seven concentric circles, each subdivided into thirty-six coffers decorated with rosettes, oak wreaths and trophies. In the apex of the dome was an oculus, eight metres wide, which flooded the hall with natural light.

I climbed a spiral staircase to the upper gallery, hidden behind thirty-six double columns of polished granite known as Kelheim marble. From there I could read the inscription set into the marble floor below: "Moechten die Teutschen nie vergessen, was den Befreiungskampf nothwendig machte und wodurch sie gesiegt" ("May the Germans never forget why the War of Liberation was necessary, nor the means by which it was won"). I noted the archaic spelling of "Teutschen", a poetic yet linguistically fanciful attempt to identify the Germans with the ancient Teutons.

A second spiral staircase led to a gallery on the exterior of the concealed dome. Far below me I could make out the Schleiferturm and the apricot, vanilla and peppermint colours of the houses around Ludwigsplatz. Beyond the churches and breweries of Kelheim lay a scimitar of land which ran into the confluence of the Danube and the Altmühl. To the east, smoke from chemical factories dissolved in the skies above the Danube valley. To the north, the south-facing slopes of the escarpment above the Altmühl had been drained of colour by melting snow. To the south, the wooded, north-facing slopes above the Danube were in shadow, still covered by snow. Below them was the empty tract of an abandoned cellulose factory. All that remained were two sewage tanks which formed huge circles in the snow. I walked around to the other side of the gallery. To the north-west I could see the medieval castle of Prünn on a cliff high above the Altmühl. To the south-west was the Danube, coiling into a forested gorge and disappearing towards Swabia. On my way down from the Befreiungshalle I discovered an old slot machine which called itself a "Love-Thermometer". I put a coin in. It told me I was "schüchtern" (shy).

1

Swabia

Maultaschen and Bone Meal

My journey began on the Jahnufer, a promenade which runs along the Bavarian bank of the Danube, in Neu-Ulm. The glassy green waters dissolved into a cloudy swirl where an excavator was dredging silt from the river bed. The temperature had crept above zero, and a miserable *Schneeregen* drizzled from banks of grey cloud onto a straggle of pensioners walking their dachshunds beneath a row of bare chestnut trees. A bastion of red brick ran along the Donauschwabenufer on the opposite, Swabian bank of the river. Above it rose the Altstadt of Ulm: steep-pointed gables zigzagging over burghers' houses, some half-timbered in black and white, one painted in orange and white diamonds. Rows of dormer windows in their roofs were like eyelids that would close at night and open again at cockcrow, or – more appropriately for the season – like the flaps of an Advent calendar. The Butchers' Tower leaned back over the city, the rounded arches of its windows lending it the expression of an affronted notary in a painting by Carl Spitzweg. And over everything, over the former corn exchanges and salt warehouses and guildhalls of Ulm, soared the tallest church spire in Christendom.

Behind me stood the Edwin-Scharff-Haus, a concrete bunker dedicated to the work of the eponymous sculptor from Ulm who created a series of monumental figurative works during the first half of the twentieth century. One of Scharff's sculptures stood on the lawn in front of the museum. It was of two men joined back to back like Siamese twins: the front man had a diminutive head, tiny but prominent genitals and one arm raised but severed below the shoulder; the rear man was both armless and headless.

Was this an allegory of Germany's severance with the Third Reich? Or a symbol of Germany's post-war dismemberment and the Siamese-twin relationship between the Federal Republic and the Democratic Republic? Alas, nothing so pretentious – the sculpture was entitled *Men in a Boat: Fragment.*[1]

I wandered into the building. The café was closed and I couldn't see the entrance to the museum. I found myself instead in a convention for digital technology whose slogan, in English, was "For Innovative Materials, Procedures and Applications". Desperate for a coffee, I pretended to be a delegate and feigned interest in the latest smartphones and tablets from Germany's Silicon Valley. Refreshed, I ventured out once more onto the Jahnufer. The snow-rain had stopped and the clouds were breaking up, revealing patches of blue sky. A bell tolled twice to mark the half-hour and the sun came out over the Altstadt, illuminating the filigree masonry of the minster's three steeples.

Across the river on the Ulm shore stood another bronze statue of figures in a boat. This relief of a man, woman and child in a vessel welded to a tall Christian cross was mounted on a plain concrete obelisk. The monument was erected in 1974 in memory of the "Donauschwaben", the Danube Swabians – German settlers who set off from Ulm in search of a better life in the uncharted regions further down the Danube. Afflicted by poverty, famine, over-population or religious persecution in south-west Germany, over half a million emigrants were dispatched by their rulers to repopulate areas of Hungary devastated by the Turkish Wars. They joined soldiers and officers already garrisoned in the Banat, who had been encouraged to stay there by Duke Karl Alexander of Württemberg's promise of a *Moidle-Schiff*, a boatload of one hundred and fifty Swabian and Bavarian wenches who were shipped off downstream from Ulm in 1719.

Looking more closely at the obelisk, and reading the inscription on the back, I realised it commemorated not those Swabians who emigrated in the eighteenth century, but those who perished, or returned, exiled a second time around, during the Second World War and its aftermath. On the grass in front of the memorial was a wreath in the green and white colours of the Donauschwaben diaspora. It read: "Sixty years after flight and expulsion – Danube Swabians worldwide remember."

---

1   The complete sculpture of (three) *Men in a Boat* stands on a pedestal in the Rathausplatz of Neu-Ulm.

The Danube is the great conduit enabling the peoples of Europe to move from east to west. After the return of the Danube Swabians, the next wave of emigrants began in the 1950s, when guest workers from Turkey, Greece and Yugoslavia were encouraged to form the workforce for the new factories of the German "economic miracle". Another wavelet of refugees arrived in September 1989: ten thousand disillusioned socialists from the German Democratic Republic who took "holidays" in Hungary when the Hungarians relaxed their border restrictions with Austria. Crossing into Austria in their Trabants and Wartburgs, they puttered westwards along the autobahn towards the Danubian city of Passau. The flow continued throughout the 1990s as thousands of Banat Swabians and Transylvanian Saxons arrived, free at last to leave Romania following the fall of the Ceauşescu regime. Ethnic cleansing swept through Bosnia and Kosovo, releasing further waves of refugees to drift upstream towards the haven of modern Germany. In the summer of 2015, I stopped for a cup of tea in a service station on the Hungarian-Austrian border and got talking to a group of Syrians from Homs, refugees from a brutal war who were following the well-worn trail up the Danube towards a new life in Germany.

This ugly little monument with its ribbons lying trampled in the muddy grass; the plaques to extinct Danube Swabian communities affixed to the town walls; the river flowing remorselessly by – all this gave me a feeling of history as a fluid, messy process, a repetitive cycle of exile and return, disintegration and regeneration. This was a truer symbol of German history than the Befreiungshalle which, for all its solidity, symmetry and rootedness, represented a fantasy, a dream of an eternal Teutonic nation that never really was.

I left the Danube through the Schwabentor and found myself in the Fischerviertel, an old quarter of Ulm once inhabited by fishermen and tanners. This was the lower town, a jumble of half-timbered houses and alleys backing onto the twin arms of the River Blau as it rushed into the Danube below a frozen water wheel. Like artisans' quarters throughout Germany, the Fischerviertel is designer medievalism rather than the genuine article. The historic Altstadt was destroyed by British bombers in December 1944, and the present enclave of craftsmen's houses, cobbled streets and narrow bridges has been reconstructed ("sanitised", to translate the German term) as a double-glazed, solar-panelled replica of the golden age of the Holy Roman Empire. Some of the original buildings have been restored in immaculate white plaster, their wooden beams picked out in dove grey or burnt orange paint. Others have been razed and replaced by exclusive apartment blocks with steep gables and dormer windows in the medieval manner. It is a very German exercise in recreating the forms of the past in the high-tech, eco-friendly image of modern Germany. There are, of course, no fishermen or tanners left here any more, no dyers or weavers of fustian, a mixture of linen and cotton spun from local flax that made Ulm rich in the fourteenth century. They have been superseded by a new breed of artisans, antiquarians and entrepreneurs who restore and recreate artefacts – paintings, porcelain and furniture – rather than create new works; in turn, their galleries and upcycling workshops are outnumbered by the infrastructure of fish restaurants, cocktail bars, boutique hotels, estate agents, "business and life coaching" studios, nail bars and saunas needed to sustain them. I was particularly intrigued by a Barfußladen, a shop selling footwear for people who prefer to walk barefoot.

I crossed Neuer Straße and passed through the arcade of Richard Meier's bone-white, key-shaped Stadthaus into Münsterplatz. The cathedral spire loomed over a Christmas market of wooden stalls sparkling with fairy lights and festooned with branches from fir trees. Decorated with candles, bells and baubles, the stalls glittered with a thousand miniature glass models of teddy bears and reindeer, milkmaids and infantrymen, post-chaises and seafaring galleons. Mobile trailers opened up to reveal banks of gingerbread hearts or chocolate-coated fruits. Students, tourists and shoppers filled the aisles between the stalls, sipping *Glühwein* and hot punch from ceramic mugs, or munching sausages and bread rolls stuffed with pickled herring. The air was thick with the competing odours of burnt almonds, wine and cloves, grilled *Bratwurst*, scented candles and vanilla waffles. In the centre of the market was a tall Christmas tree above a manger which featured a life-size crib and real sheep, lambs and a donkey. Hidden rather incongruously behind the stalls at the southern entrance to Münsterplatz was a pair of bronze steles commemorating Hans and Sophie Scholl, the brother and sister who founded the White Rose resistance movement in Munich and who were executed by the Nazis in 1943. The Scholls grew up in Ulm, which was designated by the National Socialists as a "Hochburg der Bewegung" ("Stronghold of the Movement"), before moving to Munich, the "Capital of the Movement", where they studied and where they were to sacrifice their lives. Surrounded by stalls in the centre of the Platz was a medieval fountain, its base boarded up for the winter. Open to the elements was a pair of golden lions, back to back with intertwining manes, bearing the shields of the *Reichsstadt* and the black eagle of the Habsburgs.

The buildings around the western side of the square were constructed in the standardised, functional, neo-medieval style of postwar *Wirtschaftswunder* Germany. Their steep gables, picked out with Christmas lights, were Gothic in shape, but their façades were inlaid with glazed tiles and glass bricks and illuminated with neon signs. I took shelter from a light drizzle of *Schneeregen* beneath the colonnade in front of a row of shops and cafés. Each establishment displayed a modern version of the old craftsmen's guild signs above its door: a pair of gilt spectacles above the opticians, a bunch of gilt grapes above the wine merchants, a gilt cup of coffee with golden steam coiling into the air above the *Konditorei*. I lingered in front of a bakery selling rolls and pretzels sprinkled with rye, caraway and poppy seed and stuffed with cheese, *Speck* or onion. In the window of the Café Trösler next door was a display of crystallised fruit ladybirds and gingerbread dolphins, sugar "piccaninnies" astride marzipan canoes, chocolate piglets, chocolate dice, chocolate clocks and edible versions of anything associated with Ulm, from praline sparrows and toffee steeples to flying tailors and heads of Albert Einstein in marzipan and chocolate icing sugar. I resisted these temptations and went back to the Stadthaus for a bowl of *Kraftbrühe mit schwäbischen Maultaschen* (a strong broth with Swabian ravioli).

Sufficiently restored, I entered the cathedral. The interior was colder and darker than the square outside. Stone cold. Tombstones and flagstones and a musty chill which rose up through the stone. Pointed arches along either side of the nave like rows of spears. Wide dark aisles emblazoned with shields, visored helmets, skulls and crossbones. A row of stone warlords leaning grimly on their broadswords. Affixed high on the walls of the aisles were the crests and coats of arms of the great patrician families who ruled the *Reichsstadt*: the black eagles of the Schads, the crimson and gold shields and lyre-shaped helms of the Kraffts, the silver greyhounds and blue and red antlers of the Baldingers, the red swans of the Ehingers, the black and white coxcombs of the Schermars and the silver chalices of the Besserers; each emblem a tangled rosette of wreaths, plumes, bones, leaves, wings and limbs spilling over a silver halo that recorded in Gothic Latin the great achievements and exact time of death of the noblest members of each dynasty: most were burgomasters or parish priests of the city, rectors of its university, captains of its army or leaders of the Swabian League. Above them, below a canopy of Holy Roman Imperial banners at the far end of the north aisle, hung the insignia of their overlords, the skeletal, two-headed black eagle of the Habsburg über-dynasty.

Perched on the columns separating the north aisle from the nave were statues of the warlords whose deeds had shaped the destiny of Ulm: Charlemagne, founder of the Holy Roman Empire; Konrad III of Swabia, the Staufer king who reconquered Ulm from the Bavarian Duke Henry the Proud in 1138 and established the *Pfalz* as a Free Imperial City; Rudolf I, founder of the Habsburg dynasty; Christoph Duke of Württemberg, who secured Ulm and its cathedral for Lutheranism in 1559; and Gustavus Adolphus, the Swedish king who fought part of his peripatetic campaign of the Thirty Years' War from the city. Claudio Magris described Ulm as "the heart of German Holy Roman Empire nationalism". The black eagle of the Habsburgs is indeed visible all over the city – on fountains, on the walls of the Rathaus – but I would be inclined to nominate Nuremberg as the dark heart of German nationalism.

The choir stalls of the cathedral resembled Prime Minister's Question Time in the British House of Commons. Two opposing parties of life-sized figures carved in polished oak engaged in silent debate across the chancel. On one side were the oracles of ancient Greece, the sibyls of Phrygia, Hellespontina, Tiburtina, Cimmeria, Cumae, Libya and Delphos; facing them a formidable front bench of Virgil, Seneca, Ptolemy, Terence, Cicero and Pythagoras. Each poet, philosopher or soothsayer was clad in the height of Habsburg fashion: in wimples, ruffs and voluminous robes set off by tight braids or flowing wooden locks. The dialogue between the sexes would have been a formal, classical discourse transcribed and disseminated by the new-fangled printing presses, and catalogued in the library of Ulm founded by Dr Ulrich Krafft. Pythagoras strummed the strings of a lute; Ptolemy held a globe to his ear, listening to the music of the spheres; Phrygia caressed a rolled manuscript; Tiburtina read a half-opened book with her blind wooden eyes – each representing a delicately carved humanist response to the warlords who dominated the aisles.

The smaller carvings on the armrests of the choir stalls depicted the baser instincts of Renaissance man. An asylum of half-witted knaves in silly hats farted and belched, stared with goggle eyes and lolling tongues, or pulled faces at the pious philosophers opposite by forcing their lips wide apart with their fingers. Further down towards the altar these village idiots were replaced by an even more grotesque menagerie of apocalyptic creatures writhing and spitting: owls with vampires' teeth, dogs with their heads on back to front, gryphons swallowing their tails, salamanders, basilisks, chimeras and sphinxes.

I retraced my steps along the nave, past effigies of Bach, Luther and a console in the form of a beautiful medieval queen whose locks of hair metamorphosed into a swirling crown of stone tendrils. Two paintings on one column depicted gruesome scenes of appalling torture: in one, men drilled into the mouth of a female martyr; in the other, two men were at work disembowelling a male martyr by tightening a contraption of ropes and levers in order to extract his innards. At the head of the nave was twentieth-century Germany's Man of Sorrows: a bronze sculpture by Ernst Barlach of a beggar on crutches – a simple, compassionate expression of the universal feeling of defeat experienced by Germans during the period following the First World War and the Depression of the 1920s. In contrast to the Christian Man of Sorrows standing in a niche by the choir arch, there would be no resurrection for Barlach's beggar, nor any redemption for his people in the decade following his creation in 1930.

In his magical tale of the nixie Lau, the Swabian poet and storyteller Eduard Mörike rhapsodises about the Blautopf, a bottomless pool which is the source of the River Blau. It is "a wondrous spring" whose water is of "a beautiful blue colour almost impossible to describe". Sun was shining from a perfect azure sky as I approached. The pool was enclosed by cliffs and overhung with beech and chestnut trees whose branches dipped into the clear turquoise water. Birds were singing in the trees and the outflow from the Blautopf gurgled over a weir into a tributary of the Blau. Every now and then I heard a pop as a bubble of air from caves deep beneath the pool reached the surface and burst.

Mörike's fairy tale concerns Lau, a water sprite with long flowing hair and lilywhite webs, "softer than a poppy's petal", between her fingers and toes. She was a princess, wedded to a Black Sea merman, but banished upstream to Swabia for bearing stillborn children because of her melancholic disposition. Her mother-in-law tells her she will bear living children only after she has laughed aloud five times. So Lau languishes in the Blautopf, a benevolent yet mischievous spirit, occasionally seducing one of the local boys in a vain attempt to amuse herself. Eventually she is released from her spell by the good honest humour of Frau Bertha Seysolffin, landlady of the Benedictine abbey of Blaubeuren, in a series of incidents which, it has to be said, are not exactly side-splitting to the modern sensibility. She then swims off down the Danube back to her merman husband and, presumably, lots of baby mermaids. The subtext of Mörike's tale is that the supernatural can be tamed by the homespun Christian faith of the Swabians. I went off to church to experience this for myself.

There was a clapping of wings as a flock of doves soared into the sky from the red gables and green turrets of the abbey. A bell tolled the quarter hour as I entered the church and walked through the cloisters. A sundial hung on the wall above a barren herb garden, where little was flourishing on this winter's day except thistle and apothecary's rose. Motifs from the herb garden were repeated on the ceilings and walls of the sacristy and chapels. In the chancel were the carved oak offspring of the grotesques in Ulm Minster: half-men, weird women and village yokels pushing their fingers down their throats as if to taunt the Teutonic Christ hanging above the Late Gothic high altar. The outer wings of the altarpiece were closed and, in this position, depicted sixteen scenes from the life of a Swabian John the Baptist. The first portrayed him, clad in doublet and hose, announcing the coming of the Messiah from a village green surrounded by half-timbered houses and Friesian cattle, as rabbits and a poodle played in the foreground. In the final panel a wimpled Herodias, egged on by courtiers wearing codpieces and tights, pokes insolently at the Baptist's decapitated head with a knife, as if deciding whether she would prefer it boiled or roasted. The executioner turns away, carefully wiping his sword, as blood continues to spurt from twelve precisely symmetrical holes in the Baptist's severed neck. In the background are the castles and rocky outcrops of the Swabian Alb.

It was onto the Alb that I drove from Blaubeuren. Snowbound fields merged with the snow-heavy sky, enclosing me in an opaque world defined by dark lines of fir trees, isolated barns looming out of the mist, and the black road snaking through the white night. A series of icy hairpin bends brought me down into the town of Schwäbisch Gmünd, where I checked into the Hotel Einhorn. The unicorn was presumably the emblem of Schwäbisch Gmünd, since the name of the mythical beast, in both its German and English forms, was repeated on cafés, restaurants, print shops and chemists throughout the town. There was a statue of a unicorn at the entrance to the Stadtgarten. For my evening walk I followed a path through the snow-dusted lawns of the park towards a baroque sandstone column, inset with glass cases containing astronomical clocks, thermometers, barometers and sundials, surmounted by a golden weather vane in the form of Apollo driving a chariot. In the centre of the park was a coral-coloured rococo *Schlösschen*, built in 1780 by the burgomaster as a *Lustschloss* for his wife. Behind the little palace, in the forecourt of a modern Congress-Centrum, was a bronze bust of Gregor Mendel, a nineteenth-century Austrian monk who formulated the laws of heredity by cross-fertilising peas and beans. Mendel came from Brünn (Brno in Czech), the Moravian city whose German citizens were driven out after the collapse of the Nazi Protectorate in 1945. Many of them found their way to Schwäbisch Gmünd, which in 1953 became the *Patenstadt* (godfather town) of the expelled German community of Brünn.

I crossed the Graben between the Lazy Tower and the Five-Headed Tower and followed Ledergasse until I came to the Marktplatz, an elongated square of baroque houses, gold-painted fountains – and chemists. There were at least four chemists in the market square and there seemed to be one more in each adjoining street, reinforcing the impression that the Germans are a nation of hypochondriacs. The Marktplatz and the adjoining Johannisplatz were packed with the stalls of another Christmas market. Lights were strung around the gables of the surrounding houses and the windows of the Rathaus were illuminated like a neon Advent calendar. The smells of wood smoke and mulled wine mingled with those of roasted chestnuts and hot sauerkraut. This was a folksier, more artisanal market than the one in Ulm. The cobblestones were strewn with wood shavings and straw, and many stallholders were dressed in medieval costume in the style of the local Staufer dynasty, forerunners of the Holy Roman Emperors. *Staufer-Honig* (honey) was on sale, together with *Staufer-Senf* (mustard), Staufer gingerbread, Staufer whisky, *Staufer-Blut* (cherry wine) and *Staufer-Brand*, a lethal cherry brandy. Another stall was selling mugs of *Barbarossa-Trunk* and *Agnes-Punsch*. Blacksmiths were hammering out Christmas ornaments and glass-blowers were turning baubles, custom-made for visitors to the market.

On Sunday morning I went to church. Designed by Heinrich Parler, the fourteenth-century stonemason who began the construction of Ulm Cathedral, the Heilig-Kreuz-Münster of Schwäbisch Gmünd is a Swabian hall church, the first and largest of its kind. It has neither tower nor steeple; and the traditional internal configuration of nave, aisles and transept has been abolished in favour of a single space supported by twenty-two stone pillars. A choir sang anthems from the loft as several hundred, mainly elderly worshippers assembled. A large wreath of fir branches was suspended below the great arch at the head of the nave. Its purple candles matched the surplice of the priest, who was a man of colour, the first I had seen in Schwäbisch Gmünd. After Holy Communion I wandered around the chancel behind the high altar. In one of the chapels an illuminated triptych from the workshop of Dürer narrated the story of Saint Sebaldus of Nuremberg, seemingly the patron saint of prosthetic limbs, who healed the broken wrists of the supplicants kneeling before him, their incapacitated hands hanging uselessly from their outstretched arms. In the adjacent chapel, below a bicephalous Habsburg eagle, was a stone tablet erected by the Homeland Association of Exiled Germans from Moravia. It was dedicated "to the memory of our dead in Brünn and to the victims who fell on the difficult path towards their new homeland".

Following the service the parishioners filed out into Münsterplatz, their breath steaming in the cold air as they paused to greet one another. On the walls of the Prediger Friary was another memorial to the German refugees from Brünn. The former Gasthof Adler opposite the Prediger was now, predictably, a chemist, or, to be more accurate, an old-fashioned apothecary's shop, where carboys and retorts filled with mysterious liquids rested on dusty shelves above a matrix of wooden drawers containing pills, ointments, enemas, laxatives and prophylactics. The façade of the former inn was decorated with carved oak figurines of silversmiths, glass-blowers, watchmakers, priests and hunters; and above the door perched a ferocious golden *Reichsadler,* symbol of the National Socialist lust for power and conquest that ultimately resulted in those desperate columns of Danube Swabians and Sudeten Germans being driven out of their homelands.

From Göppingen I re-ascended the Swabian Alb, driving up through tunnels of snow-glazed fir trees whose branches were bent into parabolas under the weight of snow. Every so often a ridge of snow would detach itself from a branch and come crashing down on my windscreen. The roads became narrower as I climbed above the tree line, wheels skidding as I lost traction on the hairpin bends, into another opaque world of ski stations and sawmills looming out of the cloud.

In Münsingen I stopped for lunch in the Café zum Spond, an "Insider und Kult Café mit Flair". The "Flair" bit was pushing it – the café had all the flair of the typical German bar that caters for bikers, Goths (hence the

"Kult" reference maybe) and middle-aged men with dirty blond mullets who wear turquoise shell suits and hang out all day drinking beer, smoking and playing the gaming machines. There was possibly a subtle racist message in the "Insider" reference – a German equivalent of "No Dogs, no Blacks, no Irish". (No Turks, no Jews, no asylum seekers, perhaps?) The café was decorated with Southern Comfort pub mirrors, freebie beer mats and complimentary beer glasses from every brewery in Swabia and Bavaria. The clientele was kept in order by the watchful eye of the smoky-voiced landlady. And she served a mean goulash soup.

Several kilometres west of Münsingen, I turned off the road onto an unsignposted track leading up to a forested ridge, hidden from the road behind a thicket of pine trees. Schloss Grafeneck slowly revealed itself as I followed the track up into the woods. The apricot-coloured baroque hunting lodge perched on a high stone foundation as sheer as a cliff face. Near the top of the ridge the track bent in on itself and led back along an avenue of lime and chestnut trees towards the castle. Schloss Grafeneck was built between 1762 and 1765 for Count Christoph von Württemberg, on the site of a medieval fortress. It was bought in 1928 by the Samaritan Foundation, a Protestant association for the welfare of the physically and mentally handicapped. In October 1939 it was appropriated by the National Socialist regime, which began bussing in mental patients from various asylums in the *Gaue* of Baden, Schwaben and Württemberg-Hohenzollern.

Every week from January 1940, two or three grey buses arrived at Grafeneck in the early hours of the morning, each containing seventy-five new patients hidden behind its milk-glass windows. On arrival the passengers were led into a barrack halfway along the avenue, about three hundred metres from the castle. Here they were stripped of their clothes, measured, weighed, photographed and registered (to check whether the numbers already inked on their backs tallied with those entered in the card index at Grafeneck). There were a hundred straw-covered bunks in the barrack which served as a reception centre, but they were rarely used. Shortly after registration, the patients were led before a team of five people, one of whom was a qualified doctor, and given a cursory medical examination and a jab of morphine if they were behaving in a distressed manner. Told that they were going to be bathed, the patients were then led into a wooden outhouse disguised as a shower room. One of the doctors who regularly supervised the inspections (Dr Horst Schumann, Dr Ernst Baumhardt or Dr Günther Hennecke) proceeded to release a canister of carbon monoxide gas into the chamber, and closed the ventilators. The doors were reopened between thirty and forty-five minutes later; an unnecessarily long delay, as the gas took a maximum of twenty minutes to kill. The sticky, intertwined corpses were separated and dragged to a makeshift crematorium next door to the bus garage, where they were fed into two ovens. The wooden roof of this shed was eventually removed after it began to disintegrate due to the heat generated by the incinerations below. Anything that remained of the corpses was shovelled into a charnel house, where the bones were put through a grinder. The ensuing bone meal was mixed with ashes and poured into small urns, which were arbitrarily posted to those relatives who requested the mortal remains of their loved ones. Each urn was accompanied by a death certificate and a letter of condolence stating that the patient had died from pneumonia, angina or "breathing difficulties".

Grafeneck was "Site A" of Aktion T-4, the National Socialists' first experiment with mass murder. During the 1930s the Nazis had carried out a programme of sterilisation designed to halt the propagation of "life unworthy of life". The next stage in the process of improving the racial health of the nation was to kill off its diseased or useless members, those people who could never be re-socialised according to National Socialist principles. Hitler ordered a national programme of euthanasia in early 1939, but delayed its implementation until 1940 so it could be camouflaged by the war. A target of seventy thousand was set as the number of disabled people to be eradicated, a figure that included ten thousand children. The categories of those to be exterminated included not only the mentally ill and the physically incapacitated, but also homosexuals, prostitutes, chronic alcoholics and the workshy, all of whom were listed as "racially" unacceptable to Nazi society. One of the women murdered at Grafeneck, for example, was Maria Issler, from Edenkoben in Rheinland-Pfalz. She had eleven siblings and, after the death of their mother, took over the responsibility of caring for the family. She apparently suffered from nothing more than a short temper, an obsession with cleanliness and a disinclination to marry (all traits, incidentally, that she shared with her Führer, Adolf Hitler). "Heusel-Rain", a good-for-nothing prankster from Betzingen, was another clinically sane person who was killed at Grafeneck. He was a latter-day Till Eulenspiegel who lived with his parents, and whose practical jokes got up the nose of the local National Socialist authorities.

A total of 10,654 people were murdered between 18 January and 13 December 1940 in the wooden barracks outside Schloss Grafeneck – an average of 225 per week, or exactly three busloads of 75 each. The centre was shut down in December 1940, not because of any exterior pressure, but because all the handicapped and asocial persons within the area of its remit had now been killed. Job done, targets achieved, the doctors and nurses of Grafeneck were transferred to Hadamar or other T-4 killing centres, whilst the SS personnel (guards, administrators and the secretaries who typed out the fake letters of condolence) were drafted into Aktion Reinhard, where their expertise would prove invaluable running the new extermination centres in Belzec, Sobibor and Treblinka. Obersturmführer Christian Wirth, a Gestapo detective from Stuttgart who became the first commander of the Belzec concentration camp, and subsequently overall inspector of the entire death camp operation in Poland, started his killing career as head of administration at Grafeneck, where he supervised the first gassings. Only eight members of the one hundred staff who implemented the euthanasia programme there were ever prosecuted. At their trial in Tübingen in 1949, three of them were found guilty of crimes and given prison sentences ranging from eighteen months to five years. The other five were acquitted.

At the top of the ridge, at the far end of the avenue of trees whose leaves turned black during the course of 1940, a modern *Gedenkstätte* (place of memorial) had been built over the site of the gas chamber, crematorium and charnel house. Under a pentagonal wooden roof (the Fifth Commandment states "Thou shalt not kill"), an altar of blue granite stood in front of a stone wall, which had been cut through with a jagged tear to express the pain and violence done to those who suffered here. Beside the memorial was a book of remembrance listing the names of the invalids murdered here and an "alphabet garden", based on an old Jewish folk tale in which an illiterate man is asked by a scholar: "How can you pray when you have no books?" He replies: "I have no books because I cannot read or write. But I can recite the alphabet. I ask God to take my letters and form them into prayers." In the adjoining graveyard two hundred and fifty urns containing the ashes of a small number of the people gassed here lay beneath a pall of snow.

I arrived in Tübingen after nightfall and checked into the Hotel am Schloss, a half-timbered hostelry at the top of the steep, cobbled Burgsteige, just below the gateway into Schloss Hohentübingen. After Ulm and Schwäbisch Gmünd, I found yet another Altstadt of -*häusle* and -*gässle* a little tiresome. At least there was no Christmas market. Instead, an international chocolate fair had spread out its wares in the marketplace. Each tavern claimed to be the oldest in the city; each brewery claimed to brew the strongest beer; and every restaurant advertised several different kinds of *Maultaschen* and *Spätzle* (a tasteless, egg-based pasta). The remaining dishes on offer consisted of tripe, sour kidneys, blood sausage, meatloaf and lentil stew. The restaurant in my hotel helpfully provided a glossary of Swabian culinary terms; like every other word in the Swabian dialect, you place an *umlaut* over the final vowel of each word and add the suffix -*le*. In the end I decided to cross the Neckar and eat something French and *nouvelle* at Ludwigs Restaurant in the Hotel Krone.

Monday morning was crisp and cold. Students were ascending Burgsteige on their way to lectures in the Schloss. I followed them up to a small park on the bastion of the castle. Tübingen lay spread out below in the winter sunlight. The medieval houses and churches of the old town were clustered together on a saddle of land between two hills: Spitzberg to the west and Österberg to the east. To the south the Neckar, hidden behind a row of poplars, receded into a morning mist produced by plumes of smoke from the chimneys of office blocks and factories. The Vorstadt of Tübingen ran north along Wilhelmstraße, lined with the neoclassical Institutes of Botany and Geology. Beyond them lay clinics and libraries built in the National Romantic style of the *Gründerzeit*. Further out, on the edge of town where the vineyards began to rise towards the table-topped plateaux of the Alb, were the white, multi-storied hospitals, laboratories, art galleries, car parks and shopping malls of the modern age.

Tübingen has an olde worlde image of duelling societies and Romantic poets (of Hölderlin going insane in his garret above the Neckar); but it is also a city of the *Gründerzeit*, the period of growth during the Wilhelmine Empire when commerce, industry and (in Tübingen's case) education expanded, when the bourgeoisie, the factory owners and academic professors built their stately villas along tree-lined avenues below the vineyards surrounding the town. Once I had left the Altstadt and its *Studentenkneipen* behind me and started to climb Doblerstraße, the town began to feel almost Prussian: orderly, diligent, authoritarian. Doblerstraße bent around the forbidding, neo-Gothic Justice Palace and became Stauffenbergstraße, named after the young Swabian officer Claus Graf Schenk von Stauffenberg, who was executed after his failed attempt to assassinate Hitler in July 1944. Here were the residential clubs of the *Studentenverbindungen*, the student associations that colonised Wielandshöhe and the lower slopes of Österberg around the turn of the previous century. Each fraternity built its own villa on the heights above the Neckar, from which it flew a flag emblazoned with its monogram. A bronze plaque affixed to the gate of each residence announced the full name of the association, usually a Latinised version of an old German city, province, river, hero or tribe; a trait shared with football teams in the Bundesliga such as Arminia Bielefeld, Borussia Dortmund, Alemannia Aachen or Hertha Berlin. I passed the lodges of the Burschenschaft Germania, the Corps Borussia, the Academic Association Stuttgardia, the ATV Arminia ("Ar!"), the Landsmannschaft Ulmia and the baronial mansion of the Corps Rhenania. A green and pink striped flag flew above the house of Corps Franconia ("Fr!"); a crimson, gold and white banner fluttered over the lawns around the Jugendstil villa of the Verbindung Normannia; and a green, white and black striped flag flew over the highest villa, that of the Academic Association Guestfalia ("Gv!"). The student fraternities, originally known as *Burschenschaften*, were founded in an explosion of patriotism following the Wars of Liberation from 1813 to 1815. They were the first Germans to adopt the black, red and gold which later became the symbolic colours of liberal nationalism and German unity. Most of the student associations are now perceived as reactionary societies existing primarily to propagate an all-male, old-boy network and to preserve the archaic practice of duelling with swords. Membership of the student fraternities in Tübingen is now less than 2.5% of all students; their annual torchlight procession invariably ends in scuffles with leftist demonstrators. Shortly after my visit a local website reported the death of a twenty-year-old member of the Turnerschaft Hohenstaufia after a night of heavy drinking in his fraternity's clubhouse.

Scrawled on a garden fence near the top of Stauffenbergstraße were the words "Nazis in der Nachbarschaft!" ("Nazis in the neighbourhood!"). I didn't know whether the graffiti referred to the student associations, or whether there were more sinister forces lurking in Wielandshöhe. I reached the end of Stauffenbergstraße and took an alley up the slope of Österberg. Hidden inside a grove of trees at the top of the hill was a Kaiser-Wilhelm-Turm, one of many neo-Gothic towers erected throughout Germany in the 1890s in honour of the first Kaiser of the Second

Reich, who died in 1888. It commemorated not only the Kaiser himself, but also the golden era of the *Gründerzeit* which Wilhelm I symbolised. Its situation on the summit of Österberg afforded views north towards the Hohenstaufen ruins and south towards the castle of the Hohenzollerns. Its sponsors, the local Organisation for Improvements, proclaimed that it would be "a watchtower with a view from one side towards the home of the glorious Swabian imperial house, towards the memory of German greatness and splendour, of German chivalry and German song; and from the other side towards the Hohenzollern, the ancestral home of the dynasty on which the future of our people rests". The foundation stone was laid in the spring of 1890 and the tower, a white sandstone pylon thirty-six metres high with rusticated stones reinforcing its corners, arches and windows, was completed in July 1892. It is in a less than glorious condition today: its niches and windows have been bricked in and its turrets replaced by the aerial transmitters of the Südwestrundfunk television station.

Wherever there is a Kaiser Wilhelm tower, there is sure to be a Bismarck tower nearby. The student associations, who were the most ardent supporters of the Second Reich, liked to do things thoroughly. A more heroic figure than Kaiser Wilhelm, Otto Fürst von Bismarck was the embodiment of the national virtues of strength, order and discipline. His popularity grew after his resignation in 1890, reaching its apotheosis on his eightieth birthday in 1895. Bismarck statues and Bismarck towers sprang up throughout the land during the mid-1890s. His death on 30 July 1898 generated a mania of monument-building which culminated in over seven hundred projects, of which at least five hundred were completed. Deprived by the wishes of Bismarck's family of a single national mausoleum in the manner of Napoleon, student associations decided to build "fire columns" in homage to the Iron Chancellor in every German university town. These would echo the ancient Saxon custom of building a cairn or funeral pyre on the top of a hill to mark the final resting place of a fallen warrior. The Bismarck columns sponsored by the students were to be "schlicht" (simple) and "wuchtig" (powerful). They were to be built from granite in order to express the toughness of the German nation, and were to be constructed in a standardised form in order to express the unity that Bismarck had brought to the German peoples. Each monument was to be surmounted by a copper fire bowl, which would be set ablaze during the nocturnal torchlight ceremonies envisioned to take place beneath them on appropriate national occasions.

Paul Wallot, architect of the Reichstag in Berlin, was charged with organising a competition to find the best design for a standard *Bismarcksäule*. The jury convened on 21 and 22 April 1899, holding a traditional *burschenschaftlich* festival on the Wartburg above Eisenach to select the winner. The first, second and third prizes were all awarded to the twenty-six-year-old Wilhelm Kreis, an architect steeped in Valhalla, Nietzsche and Wagnerian lore, who, as a twenty-three-year-old student, had gained first prize in a competition to design the Battle of the Nations Monument in Leipzig, although his winning submission was never commissioned due to budgetary constraints. The winning project in the competition for the Bismarck column was Kreis's *Götterdämmerung*, a design that rejected the neo-Gothic turrets and arches of *Gründerzeit* architecture in favour of a simpler, pre-medieval, almost heathen cult object. Its cuboid tower was reinforced at each corner by massive three-quarter columns bound together by a heavy architrave. *Götterdämmerung*'s combination of square tower within four round columns expressed the dynamism of Bismarck's character. Stripped of all ornamental effects, the tower was an expressionistic symbol of his power, rather than a literal representation of his person. Kreis's winning design was replicated, and at least forty-seven Bismarck columns of the *Götterdämmerung* model were erected throughout Germany; including this one on the Spitzberg overlooking Tübingen, which was commissioned by local student fraternities in 1898 and completed in 1907.

However, the idea that these Bismarck columns would form a network of ritual sites, an "iconography of the Reich" sacred to the nation, never really took hold. They were caricatured during the years of their construction as bombastic symbols of an authoritarian regime; and with the onset of the First World War their fire bowls were dismantled and melted down for use as munitions. Some were later destroyed, particularly those that came under Communist control after the Second World War. Those that remain are deliberately neglected, allowed to crumble away beneath undergrowth, or left to the designs of marginals, neo-Nazis, skateboarders or graffiti artists as undesired but indestructible relics of a megalomaniac era which led to two world wars and the eventual destruction of the German Reich.

I drove south from Tübingen along the B27, past trees balled with mistletoe, orchards of frozen crab apples and streams where herons stood immobile on the banks. I soon caught sight of the neo-Gothic turrets and bastions of Burg Hohenzollern, glittering against a pearly sky through which the winter sun sent a tube of pale light. The castle sat astride the crest of the Zoller, a volcanic hill whose slopes were covered with frosted trees. I declined the lift offered by a minibus from the car park at the foot of the Zoller, and instead took a steep path up the hill. It was marked "Verboten" because of the danger of ice, but the temptation to transgress the officious German public safety regulations was, as usual, too great to resist. I joined the road again at the base of the castle and mingled with the minibus passengers as they corkscrewed their way up through a spiral of tunnels and drawbridges towards the courtyard of the Schloss.

According to the family tree painted on the walls of the Ancestral Hall, the House of Hohenzollern split into two branches in the twelfth century when Friedrich of Hohenzollern, Burgrave of Nuremberg, divided the inheritance between his two sons. The power of the southern, Swabian line diminished as its patriarchs kept dividing their territories between their offspring, and as Swabia itself fragmented into a patchwork of principalities, duchies, bishoprics, free cities and exclaves of Austria. Gradually the Margraviate of Baden and the Duchy of Württemberg emerged as the most powerful forces in south-west Germany, and were eventually united to form the modern state of Baden-Württemberg in 1952. What remained of the Swabian Hohenzollerns had relinquished their rights to Prussia in 1850; and in 1866 the head of the line, Prince Charles of Hohenzollern-Sigmaringen, decamped to Romania, where his descendants remained on the throne until King Michael abdicated in 1947.

The northern, Franconian line, by contrast, went from strength to strength: Burgraves of Nuremberg, Electors of Brandenburg, Kings *in* Prussia (since Friedrich III, although crowned in East Prussia, had no jurisdiction in Polish West Prussia), Kings *of* Prussia (after the First Partition of Poland in 1772) and Kaisers of the German Reich. With the forging of each new dynasty they almost invariably started the line again with a new Friedrich I; and then continued through a series of Friedrichs and Friedrich Wilhelms until they became emperors and settled on Wilhelm as their *nom impérial*. Rows of porcine, pomaded monarchs, self-styled Supreme Dukes of Silesia and Great Chamberlains of the German Empire, gazed down from the walls of the lugubrious castle chambers, interspersed with portraits of their spouses: dainty Bavarian or Saxon princesses who must have been squashed to a pulp whenever they were summoned to conceive the next Friedrich Wilhelm.

The most illustrious of the Friedrichs, Frederick the Great, was never pictured arm in arm with his spouse, Elisabeth Christine von Braunschweig-Bevern, who, in modern parlance, would be described as a "beard" – and who was discreetly retired to Schloss Schönhausen when Frederick ascended the throne. On my first visit to Burg Hohenzollern in the summer of 1991, the coffins of Frederick the Great and his father Friedrich Wilhelm I were lying in state in the Christ Chapel. They had been brought here by Prince Louis Ferdinand of Prussia in 1952. Their original resting places were in the Garrison Church in Potsdam, which was destroyed during air raids in the Second World War. After the war they were hidden in a salt mine in Thuringia, before being discovered by American troops and reburied in the Elisabeth Church in Marburg in 1946. Prince Louis Ferdinand intended that they should finally be laid to rest in the grounds of Sanssouci Palace in Potsdam, as Frederick himself had wished, but in the meantime the Iron Curtain had descended over Germany, cutting Potsdam off from the family home in Hohenzollern.

Post-war Germans went through a process of suppressing their national identity and forgetting their history. They became good Europeans in an attempt to atone for the horrors of National Socialism. However, the triumphalism surrounding reunification threatened the delicate balance between Germans' war guilt and their natural belligerence. There was a resurgence, particularly in the new eastern *Bundesländer,* of nationalism and *Rechtsradikalismus*. There was also a rehabilitation of Germany's Prussian heritage.

In the summer of 1991, Prince Louis Ferdinand was able to return his two ancestors to their desired place of rest in the grounds of Sanssouci. The re-interment of Frederick the Great, accompanied by a ceremony attended by a hundred thousand people, was followed by the re-dedication of the Neue Wache war memorial in Berlin and the re-erection of a monument to Kaiser Wilhelm I on the Deutsches Eck at Koblenz. These reburials generated much soul-searching in the German media as to whether the newly reunified nation should be commemorating its history in this way. It formed part of a wider debate over whether or not Germany could come to terms with its past. The Prussians were not proto-Nazis, but there were certain core values of Germanness (order, discipline, subservience to authority) that the National Socialists inherited from Prussian absolutism and developed into more extreme forms. The fear was that any rehabilitation of Prussian history could be interpreted as a step towards the eventual rehabilitation of the Third Reich. If Frederick the Great were to be accorded a state funeral, how long would it be before the non-existent remains of Adolf Hitler were laid to rest with full military honours? Unthinkable, of course, but that hypothetical scenario expressed the unease that many Germans felt about these new confrontations with their history. The danger was that Germany would come to terms with its past for the wrong reasons.

After emerging from the Christ Chapel, now empty of royal coffins, I walked out onto the west-facing terrace of the castle, where a line of bronze Friedrichs, Friedrich Wilhelms and one solitary Wilhelm stood leaning on their swords. They were gazing into the distance: at the pink and blue tresses of cloud drifting high above a pale sun setting over the snow-dusted slopes of the Black Forest; at a river of cloud marking the course of the Rhine; and at the violet escarpment of the Vosges on the horizon.

Everywhere was closed in Donaueschingen. It was 23 December and the town was in hibernation, waiting for things to pick up again after Christmas. The hotels Ochsen, Hirschen and Sonne were locked and shuttered. The Linde had a sign in its window announcing the hotel would be open during the festive period, but my bell-ringing and telephone calls failed to elicit a response. The Hotel Schützen was now an Indian restaurant. The Bären opposite was open, just. I checked in as its only guest. The corridors on the first floor were hung with photographic wallpaper making it seem like an autumn glade. Those on the second floor were poorly lit and disappeared into areas of darkness: I felt like I was in a David Lynch movie. My room was large, with a high double bed, a spacious walnut wardrobe and an antique bath resting on metal feet. Above the bed was a painting of a young *Fräulein* at her *toilette*, with pink nipples and a dusky bum cleavage.

Standing on a console in the hotel lobby was a two-foot-high wooden figure wearing a floral headdress. Its white suit was decorated with painted images of men and women. A fox's brush dangled like a ponytail down its back; and down its front a long red necktie reached to its knees. In one hand the figure held a basket of fruit and in the other a blue umbrella. It had a mask-like, quasi-oriental face with smooth features and a little moustache which curled up at the ends and made it resemble a female drag king, or the sickly, guitar-playing mountebank in Visconti's *Death in Venice*.

I crossed the street from the hotel to a restaurant which would not have been out of place in Hackescher Markt in Berlin-Mitte. The Egyptian red and yellow walls of Szenario were painted in a fashionably distressed manner, below a pseudo-classical "ruined" frieze around the cornice. Behind the zinc bar the *sous-chefs*, clad in black Khmer Rouge tunics and bandanas, prepared fillets of sashimi or seared tuna with a quinoa and mangetout salad, whilst waiters in aprons and pleated Italian shirts served the clientele. The latter consisted of one solitary man in a blazer and tie, three smart young couples and the local Turkish mafia, who devoted more time to whispering conspiratorially into their mobile phones than talking to each other or eating. The diners were seated at wrought-iron tables laden with baroque candelabra and glass bowls of olives. Above them hung halogen lamps suspended fifteen feet below a silver-starred ceiling. Tall bundles of dried reeds and gold-lacquered, pyramid-shaped wine racks were scattered among the tables. Playing discreetly in the background were the timeless hits of Phil Collins, James Blunt and Chris de Burgh.

After dinner I walked through the empty streets of Donaueschingen. At the Schützenbrücke I turned down an icy path along the bank of the River Brigach towards a baroque shooting lodge, which had been converted into a gallery for contemporary art. A sculpture composed of illuminated orange and turquoise neon strips had been installed in the centre of the river. It was a fine evening with a clear sky, a three-dimensional half-moon and an infinite quota of stars. The hedges of rosehip on the river bank were frosted with ice, like Christmas decorations, and the lawns of the Fürstenberg Palace across the river were a ghostly white. The path beyond the art gallery was unlit, and I turned back towards the centre of town. In Karlstraße I came across a larger version of the character I had seen on display in the hotel lobby. A notice beside the fountain explained this was Hansl, the "white fool" who mocked the rites and symbols of the church during the local *Fasching* carnival.

"Hier entspringt die Donau" ("Here rises the Danube"). It was the morning of Christmas Eve and I was leaning over the ornamental balustrade of a circular pool in the grounds of Schloss Fürstenberg. The water was clear and I could see coins glinting in the sand at the bottom. Surrounding me was a larger stone balustrade, surmounted by an allegorical statue of Mutter Baar (Baar being the area of gentle hills between the Black Forest and the Swabian Alb) and her child, the infant Danube. Affixed to the wall of the palace grounds above the pool was a stone plaque, erected in 1987 by the 14th Congress of the Bulgarian League of Human Rights, which commemorated "this grandiose river which links Bulgaria with the heart of Europe". It was written in Bulgarian, German, French and English. Not to be outdone, the Union of Romanian Anti-Communists had put up its own plaque, also in four languages: "Romania – Age-old Europe's Guard watches the Danube's Delta." It probably sounded better in Romanian. Since the fall of Communism in the early 1990s it seemed that every other south-east European state had celebrated its newly won independence, and the revitalisation of its post-Communist nationalism, by travelling to Donaueschingen and screwing a multilingual plate to the iron grille around the *Donauquelle*: the Croats in 1994 ("For over one thousand years the Danube, lovingly sung about in the Croatian anthem, has connected the Croatian people and their state with the great European family of nations"), notwithstanding the fact that the Danube flows for less than twenty kilometres through Croatia; the Hungarians in 1996; the Slovaks in 1998; the Serbs in 1999; and in 2000 the Japanese, who nailed a bronze *haiku* by Mokichi Saito to the wall overlooking the pool in order to commemorate the fifth anniversary of the partnership between the towns of Kammoyama and Donaueschingen. "The Danube, the great river. Searching for its distant source. Evening twilight in the valley" – this sounds pleasant in any language, even German, and apparently sends Japanese tourists jumping up and down and clapping their hands in glee.

Another plaque revealed that it was 2,840 kilometres to the Black Sea. But how? This was a pool of water in a park, fenced in by a wrought-iron balustrade. There was no river in sight. Where was the Danube? I listened clandestinely to a tour guide who explained that the Danube did originally run here, in between and parallel to the rivers Breg and Brigach, but when the Fürstenberg Palace grounds were redesigned in 1820 the swamp through which the Danube flowed was drained and dried up. The rivulet was diverted into an underground canal which now trickles into the Brigach, one hundred metres away. I looked again into the pool, having overheard that the source delivers up forty litres of water per second from the deep *karst* of the Alb. There was admittedly some movement from below, a force causing gentle concentric circles to ripple over the surface; and there was some overflow dribbling through a grate into a basin which, in turn, emptied into the underground channel – but it didn't seem to amount to forty litres per second. I followed the course of the channel through the park to the Brigach, where the "Danube" emerged out of a pipe below a neoclassical pavilion built at the behest of Kaiser Wilhelm II. But the Brigach was already ten metres wide and thirty kilometres long. It was all rather unsatisfactory – maybe a conceit dreamed up by the marketing people of Donaueschingen to counter the rival claims of Brigach and Furtwangen higher up in the Black Forest. Geographers now consider the confluence of the Breg and the Brigach in Donaueschingen to be the starting point (rather than the source) of the Danube. Anyone with a serious interest in this dispute should refer to Claudio Magris, who devotes the first fifty-four pages of his book *Danube* to the issue. Magris plumps for the Breg as the absolute source of the Danube, it being longer than the Brigach, although the Brigach is wider than the Breg at their confluence. The Fürstenbergs claim that both streams dry up during summers when there is little rain (which seems unlikely) and that the ornamental pool in their park is therefore the true source of the river. Local feelings over this matter still ran high, as someone had recently been around putting stickers over the *-quelle* (source) part of the official signposts directing you to the *Donauquelle*. Perhaps the last word should remain with Magris, who remarks that the Danube is actually a tributary of itself.

I crossed the Brigach and continued along the promenade I had begun to walk down the previous evening. To my right was an ornamental park of fountains and statues. Jays flashed through the trees and swans and herons paddled in the ice-free waters around the shore of a lake. The Brigach ran in a perfectly straight line, more like a canal than a river, until joined by the Breg flowing in from the south. The promontory between the two rivers formed a triangle of virgin snow surrounded by reeds and silver birches. In the centre was another allegorical statue of Mutter Baar and the infant Danube pouring water from a bucket. It was dedicated to the "lieben Heimatstadt" of Donaueschingen by Irma and Max Egon, to mark the occasion of their golden wedding anniversary on 19 June 1939. The two rivers merged and their conflux, now indisputably the Danube, flowed off beneath a dual carriageway into the escarpments of the Swabian Alb – towards Ulm and Kelheim, Walhalla and Vienna, the Batschka and the Banat, the Iron Gates and the Black Sea.

2

Bavaria

"Where in God's Heaven Is Hitler?"

I drove into the suburbs of Lindau on Midsummer's Eve. A rent boy in white jeans nodded to me from an empty bus shelter. I crossed the causeway to the island, where the streets were crowded, and parked in the Marktplatz. The waterfront was teeming with people, noisy with laughter and music. I tried a few hotels, but they were all fully booked. Their receptionists explained this was the weekend of the annual yachting regatta. A fit, bronzed man in the Hotel Helvetia offered to share his double room with me. I was taken aback by his generosity, until I realised he had an ulterior motive. I declined and reconciled myself to a long evening drive up into the Allgäu. On my way back to the car I noticed a little *Gasthof* and made one final enquiry after a room, expecting yet another negative response. The landlady disappeared into a back room and reappeared a few minutes later, saying she could squeeze me in. There was some joke, which I didn't quite catch, about two other guests, a British couple at the bar, having to sleep in the garden, but when I returned with my bags from the car the room was mine.

Minutes later I was sitting with a beer at a table on the terrace of the Hotel Reutemann, which overlooks the small port, watching one of the white steamers of the Bodensee Schiffsbetriebe emerging out of the sunset over Lake Constance. It negotiated the gap in the harbour wall between the New Lighthouse and a statue of the Bavarian lion – a transalpine cousin of Venice's winged emblem – before sliding into its berth among the yachts and pleasure boats moored beneath the Mangturm, a medieval lighthouse. I was reminded of the white steamer in Visconti's *Death in*

Venice, although here the soundtrack was not the *Adagietto* from Mahler's Fifth Symphony but the melancholy German laments "Muß i' denn" and "O du lieber Augustin", strummed by a guitarist working the promenade in front of the hotels. The busker's singing was politely applauded by genteel couples from Munich, strolling along the quayside in linen suits and floral dresses. An elderly gentleman with unashamedly dyed hair joined me at my table and began to make polite conversation. After a while it dawned on me that we were playing out roles from Visconti's film: he was Aschenbach, I was Tadzio. I took my leave and walked out along the breakwater to the lion.

Twilight descended over the lake. The Alps slowly merged with the sky into a blue nocturne, leaving visible only the dark shoreline of Bregenz and a pearl string of lights up in the mountains. Two circles of lamps around the neck of the lighthouse switched themselves on, flooding the harbour with shimmering gold. Rings of neon illuminated the upper storeys of the hotels along the waterfront. Threads of light bulbs woven into the trees flickered into life. Floodlights picked out the stepped gables of the Altstadt. Drumbeats and laughter from crowded restaurants floated over the water from the promenade, competing with boomboxed Goth rock from one of the jetties where the black-clad, henna-haired marginals were hanging out, whacking their snarling mongrels into order with carved Alpenstocks. In a park beyond the marina, stalls and tents were being set up for a funfair the following day. The smells of beer and sausages carried over on the warm breeze and fed out into the lake.

I picked my way back along the mole, squeezing between teenagers swapping text messages, box-shaped *Hausfrauen* trailing beer-bellied husbands, and a huge transvestite in a blonde wig, teetering on stilettos and attracting a stream of female admirers with his/her basso profundo voice. Back on the promenade, pressed between the quayside and the hotels, it was difficult to move. A row of solitary queens in pristine white shirts and nautical blazers had procured the best tables in the front row of the terrace of the Bayerischer Hof. A *Kuschelrock* band, playing "How Long?", "Love the One You're With", "In the Midnight Hour" and lots of Otis Redding, occupied the remaining space between the sausage stalls. Beyond the Bayerischer Hof was a Paulaner beer hall which had been divided into a number of clubby venues, with techno beats and strobe lights in the cellars, and chill-out house parties in the galleries. The ravers, glamorous in skimpy gold lamé tops, teased hair and the whitest of white trousers, spilled out onto the quayside, chin-chinning each other with their caipiranhas and Cuba libres.

Saturday morning was market day in Lindau and Maximilianstraße was thronged with shoppers and stalls. The oriel windows and painted gables of the medieval houses were adorned with coats of arms and gilt emblems of goldsmiths and apothecaries. Folksy homilies in Gothic script and murals depicting bears, nymphs, sailors, *Landsknechte*, archbishops and archdukes covered every façade. I wandered past the Meat Market, the Bread Arcades, Lemon Lane and the House of the Plough. Two little girls in traditional costume were engaged in a dance, hopping from foot to foot while banging their wooden spoons together. The Gasthaus zum Sünfzen, meeting place of merchants in medieval times, was decorated with a mural depicting soldiers, bargees and farmers brandishing swords, axes, trumpets and ploughshares. A bronze plaque announced that the frieze was painted "circa 1930", but the artist's signature, "Rupflin Niederdorfer 1939", betrayed its National Socialist origin. The inn's sign was a golden Star of David, the symbol of public houses in Germany during the Middle Ages.

In the peaceful Schrammenplatz, next to a turreted Thieves' Tower, I discovered the church of St Peter, one of the oldest buildings in the area around Lake Constance. It was built around 1000 AD and contains the only surviving frescoes attributed to Hans Holbein the Elder. It is now a memorial chapel dedicated to the dead of two world wars. In the centre of the brick floor lay a marble statue to the Unknown Soldier. Plaques on the walls commemorated the dead: those of the First World War in stone, those of the Second in wood; the latter included SS officers. There were two further plaques in memory of soldiers of foreign nationality who died in exile from their homelands; and one final tablet listing the names of victims of National Socialism. The last of these, Cäcilie Herzberger, died in Auschwitz in 1943.

From Lindau I drove east through the high pastures of the Allgäu to Sonthofen, where one of the three Ordensburgen of the National Socialists towers above the town. These elite schools for a future generation of racially pure Nazi functionaries took their name from the Deutscher Orden, the medieval Order of Teutonic Knights who subjugated the pagan Baltic peoples of ancient Prussia and established German colonies along the Baltic coast. Alfred Rosenberg, ideologue of the Nazis and himself a German Balt, advocated the idea of appropriating the ideals of the Teutonic Knights for National Socialism. The Knights were precursors of the National Socialists, the first Germans to pursue that *Drang nach Osten*, the urge to seek *Lebensraum* in the east. They had the same crusading zeal for territorial expansion that resurfaced with the modern Prussians and Nazis. Steeped in sacral mysticism and blood and soil lore, the history of the Teutonic Knights provided a template for the occult-racist theories of the SS.

Those students selected for the intensive course of indoctrination offered to future leaders of the NSDAP would spend one of the three years of their schooling at each of the Ordensburgen. Their education embraced sport, science and politics, but the real aim of the Party was to breed a new generation of Aryan technocrats, loyal to the Führer, who would carry forward the flame of the racial community. At the end of their studies the students would graduate as *Ordensjunker* (a title heavy with associations of Prussian discipline and sacrifice) or be known as "Adolf-Hitler-Schüler" (Adolf Hitler Schoolboys) – these schools were not for girls. They were then to spend an additional half-year at the original Ordensburg of the Teutonic Knights at Marienburg, south of Danzig, which was to have been redeveloped as a National Socialist college had the war not intervened.

The architectural style of the three Ordensburgen was based on the late medieval *Burg* (fortress), comprising several fortified buildings arranged around a central tower (*Palas*), topped by a belfry. Built from natural materials such as stone and wood, and located in isolated, romantic settings, the Ordensburgen were intended to reflect a heroic Germanic age which would be perpetuated by the supposedly eternal values of National Socialism. The severity of their form, their rigid planes and harsh, unpolished surfaces, were to stand as a metaphor for the nature of the education being provided to the students within, many of whom were being trained to kill or to run concentration camps in the belief that these were noble, heroic sacrifices to be performed in the service of the fatherland.

Sonthofen was the third of the Ordensburgen to be constructed in the mid-1930s. The first two, Vogelsang in the Eifel and Crössinsee in Pomerania, were designed by the Cologne architect Clemens Klotz. Sonthofen was planned by Hermann Giesler from Munich, who went on to design the "High School of the NSDAP", the most grandiose project of the Nazi educational system, which was to have been built on the southern shore of the Chiemsee. When completed in 1937, the Ordensburg dominated the rolling hills above Sonthofen and the Iller valley. It is now a high-security Bundeswehr training school, concealed from public view behind dense woods. Driving out to a swimming pool in the suburbs of Sonthofen was the only way to get a clear view of the tall narrow *Palas*, a cross between a medieval keep and a Romanesque abbey, as it rose above banks of trees on the crest of a hill.

Later that afternoon I arrived in Füssen and drove out to Hohenschwangau to visit the royal castles. The village was full of Japanese tourists with cowbells hanging from their necks, so I went for a walk around the Alpsee instead. At the far end of the lake was a swan's nest below a monument to Queen Marie of Bavaria. It was a secluded spot, inaccessible except by a rough path through the woods surrounding the lake. The queen's son, Ludwig II, spent his nights roaming the forests and mountains near Hohenschwangau, his boyhood home, and must have passed this way many times on his solitary excursions. At the other end of the Alpsee were the two royal castles: in the foreground on the left was Hohenschwangau, small and crenellated like an English manor house, gleaming pale gold in the early evening sun; on the right, halfway up a mountain, was the ivory palace of Neuschwanstein, whose tall, minaret-like towers rose like swans' necks above the forest. After completing my circuit of the Alpsee I went for a swim in the lake. It was cool and fresh, a mirror reflecting the evening sky, its surface creased only by the wakes left by the swans. While I was in the water the sky darkened dramatically. Heavy cloud from the south hit the alpine ridges around Füssen, and thunder reverberated from peak to peak.

I checked into the Schlosshotel beside the lake and, over dinner, watched the rain pitting the gravel path which led up to Hohenschwangau. A mist rose over the Alpsee. As I returned to my room shortly before midnight, lightning flashed across the window at the end of the corridor. The forests turned green, the sky whitened and forks of lightning blitzed down on the black silhouette of Neuschwanstein, reminding me of something I had seen earlier in the day. I realised that both the Ordensburg at Sonthofen and Schloss Neuschwanstein were modelled on the same prototype – that of the medieval Wartburg overlooking Eisenach. If the Ordensburg was a brutalisation of the medieval spirit, then Neuschwanstein was its romanticisation. They represented two sides of the same coin. Both were parodies. Neither was used for more than a couple of years for the purpose for which it was intended.

A portrait of Ludwig II hung on the wall of my room. It was painted in the mid-1860s, when the king was about twenty years old. He was a tall man with a large head made to seem larger still by a bouffant hairstyle which billowed out at the sides and back. The portrait revealed his soft, fleshy features, weak chin and big, dark eyes – a little boy dressed up in military uniform.

A hot Saturday in June is not the best time to visit the castles of Hohenschwangau and Neuschwanstein. The courtyards were full of sweating queues and guides screaming a babble of Ludwigian anecdotes in German, French, English, Italian and Japanese. I recalled my first visit to Neuschwanstein many years before, one March when the castle was entrenched in deep snow and hidden below cloud. Then I had been able to wander alone through the king's apartments, experiencing something of the shadowy, in-between world that Ludwig created, where the historical dynasties of the Wittelsbachs and the Hohenstaufens coexisted with the Wilkings and the Nibelungs, where Charlemagne and Barbarossa consorted with Lohengrin and Tannhäuser.

Today, however, I found my attention continually wandering away from tapestries and candelabra towards the guides themselves. The guide in Hohenschwangau was a tough-faced blonde in a dirndl; in Neuschwanstein a young man with a face carved from wood – broken nose, hoods under the eyes, chiselled lines from nose to mouth, thick cropped hair. Both had robust Bavarian accents. It came as a shock to hear the high temple of Decadence and the inner life of the keeper of the Grail recounted by the sons and daughters of local farmers. It intensified the feeling of vulgarity that the excessive ornamentation had already inspired. Not that the guides dwelt much on Ludwig's personality; in fact, their text skilfully avoided any mention of the king's homosexuality, or his insanity, and concentrated instead on the furniture. They repeatedly explained that all the extravagance and eccentricity was just a dream, a fantasy, nothing to do with real life; that Hohenschwangau and Neuschwanstein were not working residences – they were dream castles.

I found myself increasingly irritated by the guides' uncomprehending patter. Ludwig was anything but the *Märchenkönig* whose image is sold on a thousand beer mugs. He was a real man who was torn apart by the conflicting demands of his kingship, his religion and his sexuality; driven to paranoia by the crowned heads in Bad Ischl and the tax collectors in Munich. He wished only to be left alone. It was sad to see how this visionary king, for all his vulgarity and narcissism, had been reduced to a character in a comic-strip book (*King-Kini – The Fairytale King*) or the romantic lead in a sub-Lloyd Webber musical that denied him his true sexuality. The brochure for *Ludwig – the Musical* invites you to "Join in the Dream! *Experience* the tragic story of *Bavaria's dream king Ludwig II, through a touching* drama with *romantic* arias, *dreamy* waltzes, *magical* images and *humorous* dialogue".

I arrived at the shores of Lake Starnberg in pouring rain. I checked into the Hotel Schloss Berg and went to a restaurant beside the lake for dinner. I remembered from my A-level studies the opening lines of *The Waste Land*: "Summer surprised us, coming over the Starnbergersee / with a shower of rain". April may have been the cruellest month, but June was the wettest in these parts. The rippled steel surface of the lake reflected the denser grey of the low sky. The opposite bank, dotted with the villas of Eliot's *echt deutsch* faded aristocrats, appeared one-dimensional, like a long, narrow peninsula with nothing behind it except an infinite expanse of water and sky. I ordered a main course of roast duck, dumplings and red cabbage and sat back in the comfortable, traditional restaurant. My fellow diners were elderly couples: the men dressed in C&A suits, sensible shoes and toupees; their wives in pastel twinsets set off with L'Oréal silk scarves. The room next door was host to the reunion dinner of a *Studentengesellschaft*, and every so often a group of young men dressed in formal suits, coloured sashes and those nineteenth-century Prussian flat-peaked caps would emerge for a cigarette on the terrace in front of the restaurant. I looked in vain for any sign of the duelling scars that were once the prerequisite of membership of these student societies.

The greys turned to blues as night fell, and the western bank of the lake disappeared into cloud and water. I went out onto the jetty and watched a pleasure steamer, a floating nightclub, cruising up the centre of the lake towards Starnberg. The keyboard riff from Van Halen's "Jump" reverberated briefly over the lake, and then all was silent again.

Early next morning I walked around the perimeter wall of Schloss Berg, the miniature palace that was one of Ludwig II's favourite residences, before it became his prison. The Schloss is still in the possession of the Wittelsbach family and is inaccessible, although they allowed Visconti to shoot the final scenes of his 1972 film *Ludwig* in the grounds. I took a path through the trees down to the lake, which resembled a sheet of lead.

This must have been the path that Ludwig would have taken, arm in arm with Dr Gudden, on the evening of 13 June 1886.

The king was taken directly from Neuschwanstein to Schloss Berg on the night of 11–12 June. The castle had been converted into an asylum, with bars over the windows and peepholes in the doors. There is a scene in Visconti's film where Ludwig, finally believing he is alone, is mortified to find that his guards are observing him through a peephole; he stands against the wall so he is out of their view. Every precaution was taken to ensure that Ludwig did not kill himself, so there were no knives or forks laid at the table or cords to open the curtains. The grounds of the palace were patrolled by half a dozen policemen. During the afternoon of 13 June, Whit Sunday, Ludwig had a late lunch which he washed down with a mug of beer, five glasses of wine and two glasses of arrack. At 6.45 pm he set off with Dr Gudden for a walk along the shore of Starnberger See. Neither of them returned. Their bodies were discovered later that night in the shallow waters of the lake. How the two men died remains a mystery.

Rain dripped from the trees onto the beech mast and slippery roots along the path. Wind bent the reeds and water lapped at the pebbles on the shore. I tried to imagine the turmoil of thoughts which must have been raging through Ludwig's mind moments before he died. It was an inelegant end to a life that was to have been lived as a work of art. A wooden cross in the water marks the fatal spot. The Queen Mother had an ugly neo-Byzantine votive chapel built on the hillside overlooking it. All the signposts direct you to the votive chapel, but most people come to see the cross in the lake.

I continued my walk along the shore of Starnberger See until I came to a signpost which gave directions to a "Bismarckturm". I followed a path up through rain-sodden woods until I emerged into an open space on the slopes above the lake. The tower was a heavy, aggressive monument to the ruthless Prussian, set among the rolling hills of Bavaria, barely a stone's throw from a shrine to the Dream King who represented the antithesis of the Iron Chancellor. This monument was not one of Wilhelm Kreis's *Götterdämmerung* monoliths. It was in the shape of an antique trophy, a squat tower surmounted by an imperial eagle rising above a square colonnade set upon a massive plinth. A spiked helmet above a set of knuckle-dusters, embellished with bronze plaques and stone reliefs. On the northern face of the tower the mother-figure Germania spread a protective cloak over four children who symbolised Bavaria and her three satellite provinces: Franconia, Swabia and the Palatinate. Jugendstil heads representing War and Peace decorated the eastern and western sides of the tower. A tablet built into the plinth declared: "We Germans fear nothing in the world except God."

Inside the colonnade, a ring of stone infants joined hands with each other. They symbolised the unification of Germany in 1871, which included the incorporation of Bavaria into the Reich. Above their heads a belt of shields represented the individual provinces of Germany, in a manner which recalled the stone tablets raised aloft by the handmaidens around the Befreiungshalle constructed fifty years earlier. I compared the differences between Ludwig I's vision of Germany in 1848 and the reality of Bismarck's Germany of 1898, the year the tower was unveiled. Bavaria, Hesse, Mecklenburg, Saxony and Prussia were represented here, as they were on the Hall of Liberation; Swabia had been split into Baden and Württemberg; Franconia had been assimilated into Bavaria; and Silesia, Brandenburg, Pomerania, Westphalia and the Rhineland had been absorbed into Prussia. The eastern kingdoms of Austria, Bohemia and Moravia had disappeared from the German map, as the *großdeutsch* (Holy Roman) empire monumentalised by Ludwig I had contracted into Bismarck's *kleindeutsch* Prussian-dominated Reich. On the other hand, Alsace and Lorraine were now German territories again, following their annexation during the Franco-Prussian War of 1870–71. The Hanseatic city-states of Hamburg, Lübeck and Bremen now merited their own emblems. So too did the Principality of Anhalt, the Duchy of Braunschweig and the Counties of Oldenburg, Waldeck, Schaumburg-Lippe, Schwarzburg and Altenburg, all of which were small enclaves that, as late as the 1890s, preserved a measure of independence from Prussia within the German Reich.

At the top of the steps up to the colonnade was a bronze plaque inscribed in timeworn Gothic script and decorated with busts of six famous Germans: Charlemagne, Otto the Great, Friedrich Barbarossa, Albrecht Dürer, Goethe and Beethoven. At the foot of the steps a second plaque explained that the monument had been conceived and funded by the Bismarck-Verein in Munich, "a union of patriotic men dedicated to preserving the immortal memory of the first Chancellor of the German Reich, Otto Fürst von Bismarck". Beside this plaque were the faint remains of some graffiti from the 1990s: "Tausche 100 Kohl gegen einen Bismarck" – I'll swap a hundred (Chancellors) Kohl for one Bismarck.

Iarrived in Munich on the evening of the farewell dinner for David Connolly-Smith, the racing journalist, punter and proprietor of the Anglia English Bookshop who, after thirty years in the book trade, had decided to sell his business to his German competitor Words'worth. The dinner was held in the Osteria Italiana in Schellingstraße, a restaurant in the traditional Italian style decorated with frescoes depicting Mediterranean life. I arrived late, noticing that everyone else had got dressed up for the occasion, the women in silk blouses and the men in suits and ties. I had merely put my best shirt on. I sat down in the place kept for me between my friend Judith, from the publisher W. W. Norton, and Bärbel from Words'worth. The waiters served me with a pear and prosecco-based aperitif and we shared a selection of delicious antipasti: carpaccio, caprese, crostini.

David reminded me that this restaurant, known in the 1920s as the Osteria Bavaria, was Adolf Hitler's favourite watering hole during the period after his release from Landsberg jail. He held court in the oak-panelled back room in which we were now dining. The writer Oskar Maria Graf described Hitler and his cronies Heinrich Hoffmann, Rudolf Hess, Hermann Göring, Ernst Röhm, Georg Strasser and Heinrich Himmler thus: "The man sat there with a few of his paladins, sat there looking ill at ease in a civilian suit and unbelievably dull, even when he occasionally lowered his guard and raised a laugh... Whenever Hitler looked over to us, his eyes would flare up, betraying a vindictive hatred towards us *intellectuals*." Graf was not the only regular of the Osteria Bavaria who felt intimidated by the presence of these thugs: many other members of the radical chic intelligentsia of Schwabing moved to another *Lokal*.

I chatted to Bärbel and several of David's former colleagues. The wine flowed abundantly and new courses kept arriving. Towards the end of the meal I went to have a look at the alcove where, in the 1930s, a more couth Hitler came to take tea with Unity Mitford. Gawping like a drunken Nazi-tourist at the startled diners there, I was eventually asked by one of the waiters to return to my table. Apparently, the current proprietors do not like to be reminded of their former clientele.

Outside the restaurant, in that state of garrulous inebriation that style journalists used to call "gurning", I made an appointment to see a buyer at amazon.de the following day (which I had to cancel due to a hangover), invited Judith to accompany me to the Granta Best of Young British Novelists launch party the following week (which I subsequently forgot about) and told David that I was writing a book about places associated with National Socialism (which was both premature and arrogant, as he knew much more about Munich during the Third Reich than I did). A colleague from a British book wholesaler helped me to negotiate the Munich U-Bahn system and I eventually found myself back in the vicinity of my hotel in Thierschstraße, in the Lehel area where Hitler, incidentally, lived from 1920 to 1929 in a tiny room with a linoleum floor. Not wishing to give up on the evening just yet, I went to the Roosevelt, a bar in Thierschplatz which claims to serve the largest selection of rums in the world. I ordered an espresso, which neither helped me to sober up nor reduced the alcohol level in my body. Staggering back to my hotel, I realised I had spent an evening in Hitler's restaurant wearing a brown shirt.

Twelve hours and several cups of tea later I was sitting on the steps of the Glyptothek, beneath a sky of Wittelsbach blue which matched the colours of the Bavarian flags hanging limply in the morning heat. I was watching a model pose for a fashion shoot on the lawns of the Königsplatz. The three Grecian temples gracing the square provided an elegant backdrop to a new collection of classic evening dress from one of Munich's top couturiers. Two art galleries, the Glyptothek and the Collection of Antiquities, face each other across the lawns. Commissioned in 1809–10 by Crown Prince Ludwig of Bavaria, they house his collections of Greek and Roman sculptures, ceramics, bronzes and jewellery. The western end of Königsplatz is dominated by the pylon towers of the Propyläen, a triumphal arch modelled on the gateway to the Parthenon. Along the eastern end is a row of trees.

Ludwig I conceived Königsplatz as a ceremonial space that would glorify the fledgling monarchy of Bavaria, which had been promoted from electorate to kingdom a few years earlier in 1806. The three buildings were erected between 1816 and 1860 under the supervision of Leo von Klenze, the architect who completed the Befreiungshalle. Like Klenze, the crown prince was a fervent Hellenist who looked to ancient Greece for inspiration; not only for the architectural designs of his buildings, but also for the cultural ideal of promoting art as a moral force. The Königsplatz was to be a sacred place, a temple precinct where the citizens of Bavaria would come to worship the cult of aestheticism and immerse themselves in the noble forms of classical antiquity.

Hitler, on the other hand, had more affinity with the Romans and their pursuit of a pan-European military empire. He was more intent on constructing massive buildings which conveyed the power of the Party and its Führer. Nazi architecture was one of intimidation rather than enlightenment. The National Socialists first moved into the up-market neighbourhood of Königsplatz in 1931, when they transferred their Party headquarters to the Palais Barlow at 45 Brienner Straße, which they renamed the Brown House. Two years later the Party became the government, and Hitler Chancellor of the Reich. Plans for a single new office building in the grounds of the Brown House were swiftly inflated into an imperial project which would transform the entire square into the "Acropolis Germaniae" of the new Reich. Two identical office blocks, a "Führerbau" and a "Verwaltungsbau" (administration building), were to be erected along the eastern end of Königsplatz. Between them were to be built a pair of "Ehrentempel", neoclassical shrines to commemorate the sixteen National Socialist "martyrs" killed in the shoot-out following the beer-hall putsch of 9 November 1923. These consisted of two square, open, pillared halls, graceless parodies of Grecian temples or Schinkel's pavilions. Inside each shrine was a sunken crypt in which were laid out eight coffins containing the mortal remains of the Nazi "blood witnesses". Each crypt was surrounded by blazing fire bowls and guarded by the "eternal watch" of the SS. In the days following the unveiling of the Ehrentempel, the *Völkischer Beobachter* and the illustrated magazines of the day published spreads of photographs which used artful contrasts of light and shade to show off the dramatic geometry of the shrines. As a finishing touch, the lawns of Königsplatz were paved over with twenty-two thousand granite slabs, each measuring exactly one metre by one metre – ideal for precision goose-stepping, and a neat way of concealing the scorch marks left by the book burnings earlier that year.

The "Acropolis Germaniae" was intended, like the Reich itself, to last for a thousand years. It lasted for less than twelve. The Ehrentempel were blown up in 1947; the Verwaltungsbau became a US-administered Central Collecting Point for reclaimed art treasures stolen by the Nazis; and the Führerbau served as a US Information Center before it eventually became the Bavarian State Music School. Königsplatz was used as a car park until 1987, when the city decided to replant the lawns and restore the square to its nineteenth-century elegance. A row of trees was planted along the eastern end of Königsplatz, screening the National Socialist buildings from the square and thus completing the restoration of its unblemished, pre-Nazi state.

Although still in use as cultural administrative buildings, the Führerbau and Verwaltungsbau are now grimy and unkempt, out of keeping with the majority of Munich's civic buildings, which are continually being cleaned and refurbished. Maybe the city authorities hope the pair will slowly disintegrate of their own accord. Their granite cladding stained by damp and pocked by bullet holes, they stand in sad denial (or unintended confirmation) of Speer's Theory of Ruin Value, which states that the greatness of a civilisation shall be measured by the grandeur of its ruins. Some of the building's entrances have been closed off, their steps overgrown with weeds. The turquoise and gold quasi-swastika mosaics in the coffered ceilings of the porticoes are crumbling away. I noticed blank spaces where the *Hoheitssymbole*, the Reich eagles, once hung above the Führer balconies.

I felt a chill descend as I entered the lobby of the Music School. It was an austere place for Bavaria's young musicians to study. The floor was paved with marble of a livid oxblood hue, veined with white like meat. Iron grilles supported the banisters of a staircase up to a colonnaded gallery on the first floor. Walls, columns and pilasters were clad in urinous marble. Bulbous light fittings clung like cockroaches to the ceiling. The skylight was a grid of metal and frosted glass. The square pillars surrounding the hall aligned clumsily with the architraves they supported. A pair of dusty rubber plants at the base of the staircase did little to soften the harshness of the Lichthof. Isolated busts of Brahms, Beethoven and Wagner served only to reinforce the impression of stony severity. The atrium of the former Führerbau was like a Roman bathhouse without the pool. Something else was missing, too.

I walked along the Wandelhalle, a long corridor between the former Congress Room and Hitler's private offices. I caught glimpses through giant doors of empty, soundproofed rooms with high ceilings, tall windows and parquet floors. It was in the toilets that I came closest to feeling the spectre of the Nazi regime as a tangible presence. German toilets, at the best of times, have a cold, faecal smell, as if no amount of disinfectant will erase the aroma of excrement. (Maybe this has something to do with the Germans' obsession with defecation. German slang employs anal terms such as *Scheiße, Arschloch, beschissen, Verarsch Dich*, whereas French or Anglo-Saxon slang is more evenly distributed between defecatory, urinary and copulatory images.) The lavatories on the first floor of the Führerbau – white-tiled, grey-painted, cold and sterile – were no exception. You could smell the Third Reich. On my way out, I realised what else was missing: I was in a music school, but I couldn't hear any music.

I went for a lunchtime beer in the garden of the Park-Café, built in the mid-1930s in a National Socialist neoclassical style on the site of the former Glaspalast exhibition hall. I sat among office workers enjoying a liquid lunch in the hot, still air. Set into the wall of the café were the stone heads of three Aryan women, their hair braided in porous travertine. The interior was decorated in an early 1970s style with orange plastic discs, lava lamps, strobe lights and brown leatherette sofas. In the centre of the Old Botanical Garden, redesigned in 1936 by Hitler and Paul Ludwig Troost, was a fountain surrounded by a low wall similar to the one around Königsplatz. From the middle of the basin rose a muscular Neptune, sculpted in 1937 in a Nazi-baroque style by Josef Wackerle, who also sculpted two horsemen for the Olympic Stadium in Berlin. In 1954 Wackerle was awarded the Prize for Visual Arts of the City of Munich; the jury argued that his statue "was not considered to evoke Nazi imagery". The fountain was empty in the summer heat, and Neptune rode on a sea of cigarette butts and discarded fast-food containers as the down-and-outs barbecued chicken and drank beer around him.

On the far side of the garden was the Justice Palace where Hans Frank, "Reichskommissar for the Coordination of Justice in the Provinces and for the Renewal of the Rule of Law", held sway; and where Christoph Probst and Hans and Sophie Scholl, members of the White Rose student group who had distributed anti-Nazi flyers within the university and daubed "Down with Hitler" on the Feldherrnhalle, were sentenced to death and guillotined later the same day in February 1943.

I walked back through the moneyed, corporate quarter of Munich, between once-Jewish department stores and a "Kunst-Block" of art dealers. A flame in a bronze cage in the centre of the Platz der Opfer des Nationalsozialismus (Square of the Victims of National Socialism) reminds one that the post-modern block of the Bayerische Landesbank, on the far side of Brienner Straße, was once the headquarters of the Gestapo in Munich. The final section of Brienner Straße is exclusive and expensive, lined with the showrooms of Cartier, Chanel, Lalique, Cerruti and Mercedes-Benz; and *Konditoreien* serving *Kaffee und Kuchen* to blue-rinsed, face-lifted *Hausfrauen*. Brienner Straße debouches into Odeonsplatz, a baroque concerto of elegant ochre, yellow and cream buildings. To the left is the sgraffitied Renaissance wing of the reconstructed Residenz; to the right is the Theatinerkirche – both buildings routinely painted during 1913 and 1914 by the struggling watercolourist Adolf Hitler.

Between the palace and the church is the Feldherrnhalle, a grim replica of the Florentine Loggia dei Lanzi, a military war memorial erected in 1841–44 by Friedrich von Gärtner between the splendours of the Wittelsbach monarchy and the Catholic Church. Guarded by two lions, the cavernous hall contains isolated statues of two Bavarian field marshals (Johann Tilly and Karl Philipp von Wrede) and plaques to the Bavarian dead of the two world wars. In the 1920s the Feldherrnhalle became the first sacred site of the National Socialists, for it was here that the beer-hall putsch of 1923 disintegrated into a bloody shoot-out, creating the first sixteen Nazi "martyrs". When Hitler came to power in 1933, he ordered a bronze plaque glorifying his "victorious" fallen comrades to be mounted on the wall below the eastern arch of the Feldherrnhalle. Topped by an eagle and swastika, this was the first shrine to National Socialism. This holiest site of the Movement was guarded by SS sentinels, who expected all passers-by to extend the *Hitlergruß* in honour of the dead heroes. Many *Münchener* took a detour along Viscardigasse, behind the Feldherrnhalle, in order to avoid having to salute them. The obligatory "Heil Hitler" in passing the monument also applied to passengers in buses and trams travelling down Theatinerstraße. "Hold tight please. Now, all together, one, two, three... *Sieg Heil!*" The monument to the National Socialist movement was spontaneously demolished by local citizens in June 1945. The damaged Feldherrnhalle became a post-war symbol of German shame and a rallying point for Communist-inspired anti-Nazi demonstrations in the late 1940s. Nevertheless, the Feldherrnhalle still exerted a fascination for latter-day neo-Nazis. The banners were raised again below its arches to mark the funeral of Rudolf Hess in 1987, and one could occasionally see the outline of a scrubbed-out swastika on the wall where the plaque to the "Alte Kämpfer" used to hang.

Nowadays the Feldherrnhalle is cold and gloomy, streaked with rust and stained with grime. Facing northwards up Ludwigstraße, it seems to draw all the chill and shadow in the atmosphere into its arches, leaving the rest of Odeonsplatz to bask in the sunshine. The Theatinerkirche to its right is split between light and shade: the blade of shadow that traverses its façade intensifies the rich orange of its sunlit part. The orange theme is reprised in the colour of the walls and arches, on the opposite side of the square, that link the Residenz with a range of jewellers, fashion boutiques and auction houses (Tiffany, Versace and Sotheby's) which back on to the Hofgarten. Cream taxis draw up in the centre of Odeonsplatz, and Wittelsbach-blue buses drop their passengers off at a U-Bahn station marked by illuminated signs of the same sky-blue colour.

Later that afternoon I returned to the State Music School for a Beethoven concert (the *Coriolanus* overture, Piano Concerto No. 1 and the *Eroica Symphony*) performed by the Marienbad Symphony Orchestra under the baton of Willy Merz from South Tyrol. The concert was performed in the space that was once the Congress Room of the Führerbau, now a run-of-the-mill auditorium. The music was undistinguished and I was glad to get out of the building while it was still light. I walked up Arcisstraße towards Schwabing and found myself, more by accident than design, in the Schelling-Salon, ordering a beer and a pair of *Weißwürste*, which arrived five minutes later in a bowl decorated with the blue and white fusils of the Wittelsbachs, with two lions' heads for handles.

The Schelling-Salon was founded in 1872 and is the oldest Viennese café-restaurant in Schwabing. It has also served as a billiard saloon throughout its history: Karl Marx, Lenin, Rainer Maria Rilke, Bertolt Brecht and Franz-Josef Strauss are among those who came here to play "the silent game". Adolf Hitler was a regular, but spent his time arguing about politics rather than playing billiards, and was eventually black-balled by the establishment for overstretching his credit. It was here, too, that Goebbels drowned his sorrows after being jilted by his first great love, Anke Stalherm. Most of the space is now taken up by pool tables, but there is one corner of the saloon which remains much as it was in the 1920s: dark panelled walls; gloomy paintings of sunsets and Prussian generals; yellowing certificates celebrating the reunion of army recruits (the class of '23 back together again in 1942); barrel tops painted in the blue and white lozenges of Bavaria; ancient photographs of "Germania" men's societies from the *Kaiserzeit*. Smoke curls upwards from the table of the Jewish chess club and from benches where the bohemian debris of Schwabing drink brown wheat beer or the new *Aventinus*. Working men tuck into *Zwiebelfleisch* with bread dumplings.

It was dusk when I left the Schelling-Salon, the sky illuminated by a chalky light. I walked south down Barer Straße. The block bordered by Schellingstraße and Barer Straße was being redeveloped, and the temporary walls erected by the construction company were plastered with posters put up by the Nationale Offensive Front, an organisation with a postal address in Dierdorf in Rheinland-Pfalz. Its slogan read "Deutschland uns Deutschen" ("Germany for us Germans"). The imagery was a mixture of neo-Nazi and neo-Stalinist motifs (swords, laurel wreaths, cogs, ears of corn) and the typography a similar blend of fascist and communist styles (yellow Gothic script against a red background). The group was targeting the same constituency of disaffected, working-class Germans as the National Socialists were in the 1920s. Most of the posters had been torn down by students; and the Nationale Offensive, an organisation with a clandestine membership of five or six hundred people, has since been banned by the Federal Government. However, all these neo-Nazi groups simply reconstitute themselves under a new name as soon as they are banned. Shades of Weimar in the 1920s.

As the evening was still young and I fancied another drink, I decided to go to a beer garden. I set off for the big one by the Chinese Tower in the middle of the English Garden. I arrived there at around half past ten, after stumbling around the unlit park, continually finding myself intruding on closed twilight societies of alcoholics, junkies or homosexuals. There were some two thousand people seated on the benches around the pagoda and beneath the surrounding trees. The first serving-point I tried had only wimpy half-litres of wheat beer left. I tried the next one, which had *Helles* sloshing out of a barrel into one-litre tankards travelling around on a conveyor belt. I picked up a full *Maß* and transported it with both hands to an empty place at a table beneath the fairy lights. I went back to the serving-point for something to eat. The cold food had been packed away and most of the hot food had gone too. The vendor asked me if I wanted some spare ribs. I accepted his offer, as that was all that was left. He cut half a pig from a spit, chopped it up with a hatchet and emptied a canister of paprika sauce over it. "Das ist ein bissl viel für mich," I ventured. "Don't worry," he replied. "You'll find plenty of people to help you." I stumbled back to my table clasping a blackened roast pig on a plate with two lemon-scented wipes clamped between my teeth. The surface of the trestle table was a mess of spilt beer, *Leberkäse* rind, pretzel crumbs, gristle and fat. All around me elegant *Münchenerinnen* in summer frocks were tearing chunks of pig off the bone with their teeth, the juice running down their chins onto their pearl necklaces.

I chewed my way through one of the ribs and felt satisfyingly full. There were nine left, but I surreptitiously swiped a few onto the ground, attracting a small pack of dachshunds. I was beginning to wonder how the management coped with last orders and closing time when there were two thousand drinkers still on the premises. The answer soon came: they switched the lights off. At this point a solitary man started to sing incoherently – "O meine Herren" and something about Bavaria – while waving his full tankard around in the air. A squad of men and women in lime-green T-shirts came around and began to confiscate the glasses. At 11.10 pm the lights came on again and a maudlin silence fell over the section of the beer garden where I was sitting. I noticed that a different section was still serving, so I lumbered over there for another *Maß*. At 11.25 pm the solitary man started singing and waving his beer around again. Two moustachioed guys in uniforms and peaked caps carrying batons wandered around looking threatening. I couldn't work out whether they were US military policemen, the beer garden security staff or a couple of heavy macho clones looking for their friends in the park.

I drove towards Berchtesgaden through torrential rain. The car skidded about on hailstones which fell like bullets of ice on the cobbled roads. I saw nothing of the Chiemgauer Alps except muddy streams pouring onto the road and an occasional glimpse of dark, rainswept mountains with clouds stuffed into their ravines. The bends in the road were buttressed by roughly hewn walls of dark stone. I wondered whether these had been built to assist Hitler's supercharged Mercedes-Benz as it careered between Berchtesgaden and Munich. The further I drove into the Berchtesgadener Land, the more I felt as if I were travelling into an older, darker corner of Germany. Even the names on the signposts (Schwarzeck, Schwarzbach) hinted at a blackness up there in the mountains and forests.

At the *Zimmernachweis* on the edge of the town, opposite the National Socialist-built railway station and post office, I stopped to make a hotel reservation. A French couple asked me if I knew where "le château de Hitler" was. I explained that the Berghof was destroyed in 1945 and then, on an impulse, phoned the Hotel zum Türken, a guesthouse in Obersalzberg situated next door to the Führer's former residence.

I drove up the steep, winding road to Obersalzberg and parked beside the entrance to the underground bunkers below the hotel. I recognised the landlady, Frau Ingrid Scharfenberg, from a previous visit thirteen years earlier. She let me into the hotel, which was warm and musty and smelled of cigars. The lobby was dominated by a painting, three metres square, of a scything peasant, which may well have hung in the National Socialist House of German Art in the 1930s. There were books about Hitler and Eva Braun on sale in reception, and the walls were covered with aerial photographs of Obersalzberg which pointed out the sites of the Haus Göring, the Haus Bormann and the Berghof. At dusk I stepped out onto the balcony of my room. The storm clouds had drifted away and

Berchtesgaden was hidden under a thick mist which was creeping slowly up the mountainside and would shortly envelop Obersalzberg. The hotel closed its doors at six in the evening and the alpine citadel of the Third Reich was silent. I had the impression that I was the only guest. A wind blew up and I felt that I could sense the presence of evil still haunting the place. To my left, from woods that have grown over the ruins of the Berghof, came a sudden screeching as a small animal or bird was killed in the darkness.

That evening I drove down into Berchtesgaden and parked in Franziskanerplatz. On the bastion overlooking the valley was a porous stone fountain guarded by a bronze eagle. Berchtesgaden is a hilltop town, a second-division alpine spa resort which seems to appeal to tourists from the former GDR, who come here in search of Hitler and the Third Reich. That apart, there is not much to do here except walk up and down the two main streets, examine the folksy kitsch in the shop windows and sit in a beer garden listening to an accordion band playing *Heimatlieder*.

I found a free table on the terrace of the Gasthof Watzmann. The first thing I did was to sweep aside the clutter that decorates the table of every German restaurant: the vase of dried or fabric flowers, the wrought-iron candle holder, the wooden stand into which the various menus are slotted, the wire stand holding the beer mats, the triangular plastic holder advertising the host's wine of the month, the beer mug containing the cutlery and serviettes, the ashtray, the cruet keeping in place the salt, pepper, mustard, toothpicks and that *Mäggi Gewürze* stuff the Germans like to sprinkle on their food. Having created a space in which I could eat, I ordered a *Bauernschmaus*.

My meal arrived, a cholesterol overdose of sauerkraut, bread dumplings, sausages, mashed potatoes and fatty cuts of roast pork, boiled pork and smoked pork garnished with horseradish. For dessert I had a choice between yeast dumplings or apple strudel. After finishing the meal, I ran through the predictable exchange with the waitress: "Hat's geschmeckt?"

"Ja, danke."

"Haben Sie noch einen Wunsch?"

"Nein, danke."

"Einen schönen Abend wünsche Ich Ihnen noch."

"Gleichfalls."

The post-prandial formalities are as formulaic as the weather reports or the travel information on German radio stations. Then I got a surly look from the waitress for not rounding the tip up to the required amount. I held on tightly to my unfinished glass of beer: they don't like you to hang around once you've settled your bill and they've said goodbye to you.

I wandered around the streets of Berchtesgaden. The shops were all *Stüberl* selling *Tracht, Loden* or carved wooden figurines which glorified the peasantry and the Catholic Church. There was a South Tyrolean wine and fruit grocer, and a confectioner with a display of *Mozartkugeln* from nearby Salzburg. Other shops were devoted to the retail of dried floral arrangements, lace doilies, lederhosen, wrought-iron candelabra or cruets, and meerschaum pipes with porcelain bowls decorated with images of mountain goats. The Marktplatz was overhung with blue and white Bavarian bunting. On the walls of the Gasthof Neuhaus at the far end of the square was a row of twenty noticeboards, each framed within a wooden casement. I walked along them, reading the latest news about the 114th *Gaufest* of the local *Schützen* (riflemen's) association, who were photographed in football team formation, dressed in lederhosen and plumed hats; the "nature friends"; the veterans' and soldiers' associations; the beekeepers' union; the choral society; the alpinists' club; the animal protection society; the 1883 gymnastic and sporting association; the Christian Socialist Union; the Sudetendeutsche Landsmannschaft, which was organising an excursion to the Egerland; and the Bund der Vertriebenen, an association for Germans exiled from the lost territories of Silesia, East Prussia, Pomerania and the Sudetenland who refused to recognise that these lands were no longer German.

The following morning I set off from the Hotel zum Türken for a walk around Obersalzberg. The area above the hotel had been utterly transformed. On my previous visit there had been a grassy clearing surrounded by trees enclosing the site of the former SS barracks, gymnasium and garages, below which were the remains of an underground shooting range. Now there was an enormous clay hole like an open-cast mine. The road leading up from the hotel had been closed off. The hill I had roamed on my previous visit, in search of the ruins of the chalets of Göring and Bormann, had been sealed off by a steel fence manned by security guards. A luxury hotel was in the latter stages of completion on the hillock known as the "Göring Hill". The ruins of the SS's servants' quarters to the west of the hole in the ground had been razed, a bus station and souvenir shop built over them. Beyond this I expected to see a reconstruction of the

Platterhof, which was a "people's hotel" within the Obersalzberg complex where the more affluent citizens of the Reich could spend a privileged night close to their leaders. The Platterhof was badly damaged in a bombardment of Obersalzberg on 25 April 1945 by Lancasters of the Royal Air Force, but was reconstructed after the war as a rest-and-recreation centre for US servicemen and their families stationed in Bavaria. Renamed the Hotel General Walker, its whitewashed chalets, trimmed lawns, marble terraces and the great panoramic window of the Skyline Room overlooking Berchtesgaden gave an impression of how the Berghof would have looked during the Third Reich.

Hitler first came to Obersalzberg during the winter of 1922–23, when he stayed with his mentor Dietrich Eckart in the Pension Moritz. During the mid-1920s he returned whenever he was able to, taking a room in the Deutsches Haus in Berchtesgaden in order to complete work on *Mein Kampf*. In 1928 he rented Haus Wachenfeld in Obersalzberg and invited his half-sister Angela Raubal and her daughter Geli to come and keep house for him. After seizing power in 1933 he bought the house, which he renamed the Berghof, and started moving his Party colleagues into the surrounding chalets. Rudolf Hess took charge of the process of buying up the neighbouring farms and guesthouses and evicting the owners, some of whom had lived in Obersalzberg for hundreds of years. Four hundred farmers and hoteliers were forcibly expelled. Reichsleiter Bormann completed the transformation of an idyllic alpine farming community into a high-security zone of barracks and guardhouses, which also contained a sports hall, a cinema, a kindergarten and luxury chalets for the National Socialist elite. Hitler, Bormann, Göring and Speer owned houses in Obersalzberg. Goebbels never lived here, but stayed occasionally in the Bechsteinhaus, which had been requisitioned from the family of Berlin piano manufacturers. The complex was surrounded by a 27-kilometre fence and guarded by thousands of SS. Beneath the slopes ran a subterranean network of bunkers which connected the villas of the leaders and contained emergency living quarters for Hitler, Bormann, Eva Braun and Hitler's physician Dr Morell. Photographs of Obersalzberg during the Nazi reign depict a neat enclave of whitewashed buildings which looks more like a Black Forest sanatorium than the nerve centre of the Third Reich.

The Hotel General Walker, too, had now been demolished and a car park built over its outbuildings. All that remained was the Skyline Room, its windows boarded up. Beyond the remains of the Platterhof, over the

site of the SS's tennis courts and mini-golf course, yet another car park
had been laid. I began to wonder what the point was of erasing all traces
of the Nazis from Obersalzberg and then building car parks for people to
come and visit what was no longer there.

I walked down a path through a gully in the woods towards the ruins
of the Berghof. I remembered the shell of the Hoher Göll guesthouse,
known as "Hitler's guesthouse" but actually used as an office and guesthouse by Bormann. Hitler's more prominent guests were accommodated
on the outskirts of Salzburg in Schloss Kleßheim, a baroque palace converted between 1938 and 1942 into a neoclassical residence more fitting
for Mussolini and Hitler's other state visitors. On my previous visit the
Hoher Göll was the last intact, albeit derelict, building in Obersalzberg
which had survived from the Nazi period, as the Platterhof and the Hotel
zum Türken had been destroyed and later rebuilt. I noticed queues outside
the ruined guesthouse and, once nearer, realised it had been rebuilt as a
documentation centre. It now dawned on me that Obersalzberg had been
"heritaged". All the ruins that were part of the original Nazi complex had
been pulled down or dug over and, instead, you had a Nazi theme park,
a sanitised, politically correct museum which showed you photographs
and video films of the buildings that now lay beneath the new car parks.
I could understand what the Bavarian authorities were doing. They were
trying to discourage the Hitler-tourists and souvenir hunters and provide a
more dispassionate interpretation of Hitler's life and crimes than the cosy,
humanising images contained in the "Adolf Hitler and Eva Braun" books
which were, hitherto, the staple souvenir for tourists to Obersalzberg. But
did they need to erase the authentic ruins of the Reich in the process? I
believe that historical sites, however evil they may be, should be left as they
are. Actual ruins convey a tangible sense of atrocities committed within the
time frame of our collective memory; documentation centres push these
crimes back into a "history" for which we no longer feel any responsibility.

So, what remained of the Berghof itself? I continued down the gully in
the woods until I came to a clearing where its massive foundation walls
still stood, partially hidden in the undergrowth. On my previous visit I
had stumbled almost by accident on the remaining fragments of Hitler's
home. I remember crawling through a window in the shattered foundations into what must have been a garage, where I found myself ankle deep
in murky water. It was dark, but I could make out some recent graffiti on
the dank walls: "ᛋᛏ and ᛋᛋ – we're still alive", "Jewish cocksuckers get
back to the desert", "The Führer lives on in our hearts".

I climbed up and down the slopes above and below the foundations of the Berghof. The cratered forest was littered with fragments of crumbling masonry, the twisted bases of iron poles or piping, and rusting metal brackets embedded in pieces of concrete. I came across a stone wheel, two metres in diameter, covered in moss and slime mould, which must have been hurled from the Berghof during the bombardment. It had crashed down the slope and come to rest for the next sixty years against a tree trunk. I looked for the garage whose windows I had crawled through thirteen years earlier, and eventually realised they had been cemented over. I discovered I was not alone. Two burly Americans had arrived, accompanied by a skinny youth in a *Deutscher Fussball-Bund* shirt, a neo-Nazi guide perhaps, who wished me a good morning as I passed. The Americans took photos of the rubble and tried to prise a piece of rusted piping out of the soil. I felt angry with them, as if they were desecrating an unholy site. I felt it was permissible to come here in order to reflect on the banality of evil, on the genocide planned on the patio of the Berghof; but unacceptable to come here, disturb the soil and cart off bits of metal to be sold as souvenirs on neo-Nazi websites in middle America.

Frau Scharfenberg greeted me when I arrived back at the Hotel zum Türken. I asked her about the large hole in the ground above her hotel. She told me that this area of Obersalzberg had been sold in 1999 to the Bavarian State Bank, which wished to erase all traces of National Socialism from Obersalzberg. It had excavated the field above the hotel and removed the underground rifle ranges of the SS, but had not yet worked out what it intended to fill the hole with. The "Göring Hill" had been sold to the Intercontinental hotel chain, which is reported to have pledged that it will no longer allow "Nazi-tourism" on its site. Frau Scharfenberg tut-tutted over these developments and told me they should have left things as they were. I was inclined to agree with her.

I went for one last tour around the perimeter fence of the Intercontinental building site, wading waist high through wet grass. On my previous visit this had been an area of open pasture overlooking the valleys around Berchtesgaden. I remembered the tinkling of cowbells and a carpet of edelweiss and cornflowers over the sodden fields. There were also bomb craters, pieces of exploded masonry and shards of rusting metal. I recalled finding the stump of a flagpole raised by the Allies after the bombardment of "Göring Hill". The Reichsmarschall had chosen the prettiest site in Obersalzberg for his own chalet, which had a swimming pool and a shingle roof weighed down with rocks in the traditional Upper Bavarian manner. Now there was just a flight of broken steps and a cellar full of water. Not a stone remained of the house of Reichsleiter Bormann, the overlord of Obersalzberg, the man responsible for the construction of the complex and ensuring its smooth organisation. I remembered the yellow warning signs posted all over Obersalzberg – "Einsturzgefahr – Betreten verboten" – and how they were ignored by the Hitler-tourists who swarmed over the area as if on an orienteering course. They squelched around in the muddy debris of the Thousand-Year Reich, yelling to each other over the meadows:

"Hey, Hansi, Göring's over here!"

"Have you found Bormann yet?"

"Where in God's heaven is Hitler?"

As I left, I bought myself a couple of illustrated guides from the bunker museum adjacent to the Hotel zum Türken: *Obersalzberg in the Third Reich* and *Adolf Hitler and Eva Braun in Obersalzberg*. *Hello!* magazines for Nazis.

(All this has now gone. The InterContinental Berchtesgaden Resort, a luxury hotel with a Michelin-starred restaurant, an award-winning spa and a heliport for VIP guests, was opened in 2005. In 2014 its ownership transferred to the Kempinski chain. Built over "Göring Hill", in a horseshoe shape following the contours of Bormann's glasshouses, the hotel's panoramic windows offer spectacular views of the Kehlstein and Hoher Göll. I went for a coffee there on a recent visit to Obersalzberg. The lobby and bar area were chic and understated in a modern take on the Neue Sachlichkeit style of the late 1920s. Elegant businessmen and politicians reclined on cream leather sofas and brown silk cushions, conferring discreetly over smoked glass coffee tables supported on boles of pine. I couldn't help thinking that this was the new Berghof.)

Viewed from the Mariahilf pilgrimage church high above the banks of the River Inn, the city of Passau appears to float on water. The magnolia-pink church of St Michael, the coral Herberstein Palace, the white, green and pink Florentine Jesuit College and the buttercup-yellow Alte Residenz – these and many other grand episcopal buildings line the promenade of the Inn, their bright colours reflected in the water. Above them the cathedral of St Stephen, the largest baroque building north of the Alps, straddles the spine of the peninsula like the bridge of a ship, steering the floating city into the confluence of the Inn, the Ilz and the Danube. The *Dreiflüsseeck* is the prow of land where Passau slides gracefully beneath the merging waters of the Inn and the Danube. The clay-coloured Inn, flowing swiftly down from the Tyrol, is the broader, deeper, stronger river. The bottle-green Danube, a clear broth to the soup of the Inn, meanders in from the Lower Bavarian plain. From Mariahilf you can see the separate colours of the two rivers for miles downstream. At first the swirling Inn overwhelms the Danube, which narrows to a thin stream hugging the northern bank. Gradually the Danube asserts itself as the two rivers merge and flow around the first bend into Austria.

I walked along the Inn promenade as far as the Schaiblingsturm, a medieval tower leaning out into the river. The sun danced on the water, sending waves of light across the Italianate façades of the buildings. The graffiti scrawled on the stone embankment was remarkably literate: "Death to the Pope", "Ulrike, red flower, you were the best", "The punishment of the liar is not that nobody believes him, but that he can no longer believe anyone else" (George Bernard Shaw), "Fear goes only after death". Thankfully there was no anti-Jewish graffiti. Passau is an ultra-Catholic town with a long history of anti-Semitism back to 1476, when the Jewish community was murdered or driven out of town for alleged crimes involving the desecration of consecrated hosts. Adolf Hitler lived here for three years, although that fact is probably incidental as he was a toddler at the time.

Elsewhere on the walls of Passau, the Danube Swabians are depicted in a little baroque mural on a house near the Ortspitze, paddling their red and white tarpaulined "crate" past Passau on their way to Pannonia in 1752. A plaque marks the spot where Princess Elisabeth of Bavaria, Ludwig II's cousin, took leave of her homeland and set off on her bridal journey to become Empress of Austria. The medieval emperor Ludwig the Bavarian and his four margraves are painted on the front of the town hall. A red wolf, the emblem of Passau, decorates the façade of the Oberhaus fortress which overlooks the Danube side of the city. Below the wolf is an enigmatic date written in large Gothic script: the second numeral is in the form of the remembrance ribbons that we now wear in our lapels to show solidarity with sufferers from AIDS or cancer. It turns out to be the 4 in the year 1499.

A colossal mural inside the banqueting hall of the Rathaus illustrates the entry of Kriemhild into Passau. Kriemhild the Nibelung spent the last night of the German leg of her journey here. Like Princess Elisabeth, she bade farewell to her Teutonic homeland in Passau, before proceeding further downstream towards a royal wedding in Vienna. Both queens led tragic lives and met with fateful ends: Kriemhild slaughtered amid the mayhem in Etzel's hall; Elisabeth assassinated in Geneva by an Italian anarchist. Also in the painting of *Kriemhild's Entry into Passau* is her uncle Pilgrim, a bishop of Passau who accompanied his niece on the first leg of her bridal journey to the court of King Etzel. Bishop Pilgrim ruled between 971 and 991, the period during which *Das Nibelungenlied* is set. One of his successors, two hundred years later, was Wolfger von Ellenbrechtskirchen, Bishop of Passau from 1191 to 1204. It is generally acknowledged that Wolfger was the patron of the anonymous poet to whom the epic is ascribed. *Das Nibelungenlied* was written between 1200 and 1203, possibly in Passau itself. The poet certainly knew Passau, for he mentions the Benedictine nunnery, Kloster Niedernburg, which lies near the confluence of the Inn and the Danube. The convent contains the tomb of a third queen, Gisela, the daughter of a Bavarian count. She too travelled downstream, to marry Stephen, the first Christian king of the Magyars. After Stephen's death in 1038 Gisela of Hungary returned to Passau, where she became the abbess of Niedernburg. Her remains were exhumed in 1995, before being reburied in April 2000 in a stone tomb in the chapel of the convent, surrounded by wreaths left by Hungarian pilgrims.

Whereas the Inn, flowing between the Mariahilf pilgrimage church and the Jesuit colleges, reflects Passau's spiritual timelessness, the Danube promenade, noisy, transient and commercial, expresses the city's temporal worldliness. Below the crenellated walls of the Oberhaus fortress a long line of pleasure cruisers was moored. At the far end, furthest away from the town centre, were the Ukrainians: the *Dnepr*, registered in Ismail on the edge of the Danube delta, and the *Wolga* from Odessa. Their crews had sent their passengers off into the city for the evening and were busy emptying the bilges, hosing down the decks, taking crates of drink on board or having a quiet smoke. In front of the Ukrainians were the sleek Austrian boats of the DDSG, the First Danube Steamship Company. Their passengers were embarking aboard the *MS Mozart* for a fifteen-day cruise that would take them across the Black Sea to Odessa and Kiev. On the deck of the Bulgarian *Rousse*, a cocktail-bar waitress in a red two-piece and peroxide blonde hair was taking a coffee and cigarette break. Next to the *Rousse* was the *Rákóczi* from Budapest, a raffish boat with fairy lights on deck and a smell of cheap *raki* emanating from midships. The prime berth alongside the quay was taken up by the luxurious *Switzerland*, a one-hundred-metre-long floating hotel registered in Basel. Beyond the pleasure cruisers was the sleazier world of barges and commercial boats. A Bulgarian barge from Ruse, empty oil drums littering its deck and the crew below watching a video, was under discreet surveillance from a police BMW cruising slowly among the shadows below a flyover. I wondered what they were looking for – contraband cigarettes, drugs, arms? Illegal immigrants, more likely. I had crossed the Danube in Kelheim, Ulm and Donaueschingen, but this was my first real port, my first whiff of piracy and trafficking.

By the Ortspitze, at the tip of the peninsula, was a flagpole bearing the colours of the Danubian lands, the states to which boats had to pay tolls. For forty-five years the same nine flags fluttered here in the breeze: Germany, Bavaria, Austria, Czechoslovakia, Hungary, Yugoslavia, Romania, Bulgaria and the Soviet Union. Now, three of these had changed. The red stars of the monolithic, multiethnic federations of Czechoslovakia, Yugoslavia and the Soviet Union had been taken down and replaced by the "new" nation-states of the 1990s: Slovakia, Serbia and Ukraine. The changing of the flags was a reminder that the atavistic forces of nationalism have proved stronger than the imposed structures of communism; that the history of nations often goes in circles rather in a straight line.[2]

This tongue of land is as far as Germany goes. The flagpole represented the end of solid, Teutonic Bavaria and the beginning of *Mitteleuropa*, that nostalgic cliché which stretches from Linz, just around the bend downstream, to Pannonia, Ruthenia and Bessarabia. This is where Germanic certainties end and a world of shifting allegiances, the turbulent legacy of the old empires of the Habsburgs and the Ottomans, begins. This is where the Danube proper starts. The river flows across Swabia and Bavaria, but as a stream, a tributary, a backwater away from the mainstream of German history and culture.

Germany's great river is the Rhine. Only here in Passau, where the Danube's volume is doubled by the Inn and the Ilz, does the river itself begin to define the territory through which it flows.

---

2 The flagpole has since disappeared from the Ortspitze. During my last visit to Passau I asked a fisherman who had removed it. "Die Stadt," he replied. "Why?" He shrugged.

3

Tyrol

Marksmen without Muskets

Criss-crossed by trolleybus wires, Maria-Theresia-Straße curves around the Annasäule, a column commemorating the liberation of Innsbruck from occupation by Bavarian troops during the War of the Spanish Succession. It narrows into Herzog-Friedrich-Straße, which bends in turn around the core of the Altstadt. The arcaded street is lined with tall Gothic houses fronted by three- or four-storied oriel windows which bulge outwards, giving the street a fluid, rippling effect – vertical waves of multicoloured stone pierced horizontally by the wrought-iron emblems of famous inns: the Golden Eagle, the White Cross, the Red Eagle and the Golden Rose, hosts to Montaigne, Mozart *et père*, Goethe, Metternich, Paganini, Heine and Ludwig I of Bavaria. The view down Herzog-Friedrich-Straße, which now also takes in the neo-medieval insignia of McDonald's hamburgers and Palmers lingerie, culminates in a frescoed Gothic oriel capped by the fire-gilt copper tiles of the Golden Roof, glittering in the sunlight below the snow-veined mountains rising above the city. At the far end, by the River Inn, is a bronze statue of Andreas Hofer, leader of the Tyrolean peasant army in the struggle against Napoleon, and symbol of the Tyrolean will for freedom and unification.

Overlooking Innsbruck from the south, Bergisel is the site of Hofer's skirmishes against Napoleon's French and Bavarian troops. There is now a complex of monuments to commemorate Hofer and the *Schützen*, his musketeer followers. A statue of Andreas Hofer in the grounds of Bergisel was unveiled by Kaiser Franz Joseph I in 1893 and portrays the Tyrolean freedom fighter in a stern, patriarchal posture, rendered more imposing by his beard of flowing curls and wide-brimmed hat. He is flanked by two spitting eagles, ferociously defending the plinth of the statue on which two shields are mounted, one bearing the single-headed eagle of the Tyrol and the other the double-headed eagle of Austria. A plaque at the base of the monument spells out the war cry of the *Schützen*: "For God, Emperor and Fatherland."

The paintings in the former Schützenhaus dedicated to the Tyrolean "Kaiserjäger" portray Hofer in a less heroic light. His beard is straight and woolly rather than imperiously permed, and the nose and cheeks of his apple-round face are the flushed red of a convivial landlord. His portly girth is strapped into the red waistcoat and green tunic and braces of the Tyrolean national costume, his waist held in by a broad leather belt hung with rosaries and embroidered with enamel images of saints and folksy emblems of the Tyrol. The two obligatory accessories are the *Loden* hat and the rifle slung over his shoulder. Hofer's Tyrolean uprising was a belt-and-braces insurrection. Armed with pitchforks, maces and hunting rifles, the local farmers scored two notable victories, liberating Innsbruck twice during 1809 from the French and Bavarian allied forces; but without help from the defeated Austrian army, they were unable to resist Napoleon's third and final attempt to suppress the Tyrol. Hofer and his lieutenants were betrayed, captured and executed in Mantua in 1810. The museum contains a sacred hall of honour to the memory of the Tyrolean dead. This is the repository of the *Tiroler Ehrenbuch*, seventy-five leather-bound volumes listing the Tyrolese sacrificed during the struggle for independence from 1796 to 1813 and during the two world wars. On the wall is a painting entitled *Verlorene Heimat* (Lost Homeland), which symbolises the Tyrol after its partition in 1919. Against a background of storm clouds, a naked hero is shackled to a mountain peak, the red eagle of the Tyrol draped lifelessly across his lap.

The Tappeiner Weg cuts down through the vineyards above Merano. I walked for miles in a subtropical paradise, between bushes of jasmine, hibiscus and yucca which perfumed the warm air. On every bend in the path I muttered a languid "Grüß Gott" to elderly, white-flannelled Bavarian couples gazing over the spa town, which had almost disappeared beneath a canopy of trees. Only the big public buildings were visible: the Kurhaus, the bell tower of the Pfarrkirche, the grand hotels. Villas were submerged below avenues of chestnut and cedar, drowned under magnolia and lilac. Mountains swept down on all sides to the valley of the Adige (Etsch), on which floated a carpet of apple blossom. On a nearby crag was Schloss Tirol, the historic seat of the pre-Habsburg counts of Tyrol. This was the heartland of the medieval county, the capital of Tyrol until 1363.

Eventually the Tappeiner Weg winds down through gardens of honeysuckle and oleander, populated by tiny lizards and snakes, to the promenades lining the Passirio (Passer). The Winter Promenade is on the sunny side of the river, the Summer Promenade on the shaded side. In its heyday Merano was famed as a winter spa. Its guests sought to escape the snowbound cities of Munich, Vienna and St Petersburg, hoping for a cure for their tuberculosis or other pulmonary infections. The first guests arrived in 1836 following a cholera epidemic in Vienna. Nowadays most visitors come in the summer, leaving Merano to a handful of elderly German convalescents during the winter. I was here in April, when the air is fresh and warm, but before the tramontane invasion of Teutonic hypochondriacs has begun.

The Wandelhalle, a pavilion of painted wood, lies on the Winter Promenade. Here you can rest on its green and cream benches beneath paintings of mountains and lakes, shaded from the sun by rose bushes and spirals of wisteria around the wrought-iron arches. You don't need to do anything more strenuous than read today's edition of *Dolomiten*, the local German newspaper; or you can just sit, listening to a distant waltz and watching the river flow by below the palm trees. In the evening you can repair to the terrace of the Wandelhalle Café and sip the house cocktail (Aperol with fresh grapefruit juice) while munching through a bowl of mini pretzels; or smoke a cigar and watch the last shafts of sunlight illuminate the mountain peaks.

Empress Elisabeth of Austria first came here in the winter of 1870–71 and it was her seal of approval that elevated Merano (or Meran, as it then was) to its status as the second most fashionable spa, after Karlsbad, of the Habsburg Empire. "Sissi" is now immortalised in white marble in a *giardinetto* on the Summer Promenade. She sits upright in a cushioned wicker chair, daydreaming as she takes a break from a novelette. The index finger of her left hand still marks the page where she has left off reading. Her hair is braided into a circular crown. Someone has placed a bunch of pansies in her marble lap; but someone else has chiselled off the tip of her nose. During the following season Sissi brought her husband Emperor Franz Joseph to Meran, and the next thirty years saw every triple-barrelled archduke or baroness from Central Europe, every "kaiserliche und königliche" civil servant, every German burgomaster from Limburg to Lemberg descend on the spa. Franz Kafka, who died in 1924 from tuberculosis, came to Meran in 1920 and wrote his *Letters to Milena* here. Stefan Zweig and Heinrich and Thomas Mann also recuperated here. Richard Strauss and Franz Lehar on occasion conducted the orchestra of the Kurhaus. The Jugendstil concert hall, surmounted by statuesque Muses which, when they were unveiled in 1914, caused offence to Meran's visitors on account of the "dubious contortions of their limbs", and the Stadttheater, a slice of Viennese Secessionist *Sachertorte*, are the grandiose symbols of Meran's Indian summer. Four years later the Austrian Empire had been dismembered and Meran, like Karlsbad, found itself in a foreign country.

I had to force myself to make a leap of the imagination every now and then in order to remind myself I was actually in Italy. The medieval Laubengasse through the centre of Merano is quintessentially German: a narrow street overhung with Gothic gables and oriel windows. The parallel Freiheitstraße (or Corso Libertà) is equally Germanic, its multi-coloured façades stuffed with geraniums; but the promenade along the river is a modern Italian *passeggiata* with marble banks and pavement cafés. I spent the evening drifting between *Weinstuben* and *Gelaterie*, listening to equal amounts of German and Italian spoken on the streets and in the bars. I ate *Jägerschnitzel* with roast potatoes, fried onions and a crispy circular *Schüttelbrot* studded with rye and caraway seeds, but was offered a cappuccino or espresso to finish. The oompah band in the restaurant played *Heimatlieder*, but the bill came with *pane e coperto* added. I noticed that the proprietors' names above shops, and the posters in their windows, were predominantly German, but all official signs were bilingual. As in any area of linguistic sensitivity, many of the bilingual signs had been defaced by graffiti. The older monuments were encased in reinforced glass to protect them against vandalism, but even this measure provided an invitation for self-righteous nationalists to shatter or break the glass. It seemed that both sides were as guilty as each other in this respect. On the Tappeiner Weg I came across a marble tablet in memory of Kurarzt Dr Tappeiner, on which someone had smashed the glass over the Italian version of the inscription. In Sandplatz in the centre of the town there was a statue of a Madonna, erected in 1801 to thank God for sparing Meran from the Napoleonic invasions of 1797 and 1799 which swept down the Eschtal. The German inscriptions on the statue were protected by glass, but that had not prevented someone from having a go at them. The text of these inscriptions referred, incidentally, to the French invaders as "Neu-Franken", as if the French were a subspecies of the real Franks, namely the Germans.

The evening swirled to its end outside Café Bruno on the Passeggiata Lungo Passirio. The pavement café was packed with shaven-headed teenage conscripts, reminding me of many all-night Italian train journeys; except that these young soldiers were speaking thickly accented German. A party at one table was dressed in chic Armani with Gucci accessories, whereas their neighbours at the next table were in *Loden* with feathers in their hats. The landlord of my hotel had explained to me (in German) that the population of Merano was two-thirds German and one-third Italian, but that it seemed even more German because of the influx of German tourists. He added, jokingly, that no self-respecting Italian would dream of coming here for a holiday. I felt that German and Austrian tourists must enjoy their visit because it made them feel both at home and abroad simultaneously. The Italian inhabitants, on the other hand, must feel at times like strangers in their own country. As if on cue my waiter arrived, a caricature Italian with slicked-back hair, black silk shirt and pointed shoes.

"Buona sera."

"Grüß Gott."

I ordered a coffee. He nodded and added "Deutsch", somewhere between a question and a statement. I thought he was referring to my nationality until he returned with the beverage, which was a "German coffee", diluted with revolting condensed milk.

Bolzano, capital of the province of South Tyrol, feels at first like a larger version of Merano. Wooded mountains sweep down from all sides around the city. The focal point of the Altstadt is Waltherplatz, named after the German troubadour Walther von der Vogelweide. With its asymmetrical pointed tower, the Gothic Pfarrkirche Maria Himmelfahrt is an amalgam of the Nikolaikirche in Frankfurt and the Frauenkirche in Nuremberg. The diamond-shaped tiles on its roof are reminiscent of St Stephen's Cathedral in Vienna. But the grand hotels flanking the square, in faded Alpine hues of grey and green, could just as easily be in Lugano, Trieste or any other city on the northern rim of the Italian-speaking realm;

and the ochre- and coral-marbled banks are modelled on those in Milan and Turin.

The statue of Walther von der Vogelweide in the centre of the square is the symbol of German Bolzano (Bozen). The *Minnesänger*, born in one of the surrounding valleys, was Germany's greatest medieval lyric poet. Although primarily known for his courtly love poems, some of his verse touched upon political themes: he supported, in particular, the supremacy of the Hohenstaufen dynasty against papal opposition. The monument to Walther, in the German National Romantic style and surrounded by lions, swans and lyres, was erected in the latter part of the nineteenth century when the Austrian Empire, including the whole of the Tyrol, was in its pomp. When the Italian Fascist government took power in South Tyrol, its removal was inevitable. In 1923 Ettore Tolomei, the Fascist senator of Alto Adige (as Südtirol was then known), advocated its removal and replacement by a statue of Drusus, the Roman general who colonised Rhaetia, as the Alpine region was referred to in pre-Imperial Roman times. Mussolini dissuaded Tolomei, dismissing Walther as a minor medieval poet. "Comparing his work to Dante's", the Duce said, "is like comparing the Pincio [one of the Seven Hills of Rome] to the Himalayas. The removal of the statue would cause a general uprising. And that is not worth it." Mussolini and Tolomei instead transferred their energies into constructing a Fascist Victory Arch, which commemorated Italy's victory over Austria and its annexation of South Tyrol. In the end, the rapid Italianisation of Bolzano during the inter-war years forced the government to remove the statue of Walther von der Vogelweide in 1935. The poet was not restored to the square he gave his name to until 1981.

The main street running through the heart of the old centre of Bolzano is named, like its counterpart in Merano, the Laubengasse (Street of Arcades). The long, narrow thoroughfare is overhung with pitched roofs leaning over the upper stories, almost meeting each other to form a tunnel. At its midpoint Laubengasse crosses Obstplatz, another narrow street of tall, vanilla and cream houses perched above arcades. Goethe reportedly stopped here to buy some peaches during his journey to Italy. German has the edge over Italian in the names above the shop fronts, although most are bilingual (*Pasticceria~Konditorei* or *Juwelier~Gioielleria*). As in Merano, the language on the street is a seemingly equal mixture of soft, sibilant German and guttural Italian. I found myself scanning people's faces and clothes, trying to work out whether they were Italian or German. Then I would eavesdrop on their conversation to find out if I had guessed correctly or not. Or I would find myself the object of the game: the waitress in a café on Waltherplatz took my order in German; but the waiter who served my coffee addressed me in Italian. I had lunch in the Weißes Rössl, a restaurant which was German to the core, right down to the heart shapes carved into the chair backs. Its oak-panelled walls were covered in antlers and Tyrolean hunting scenes. Dressed in embroidered dirndls, the waitresses served *Gröstl* and *Speckkraut* accompanied by foaming tankards of local *Helles*. A young man at a table next to mine asked me something in German. I didn't understand immediately, so he repeated the question in Italian. By then I realised what he wanted, so I replied – in German. It seemed that everyone in the old city centre was effortlessly bilingual and didn't mind in which language you spoke to them; in fact, they took pains to reply in the same language, even if it was not their native tongue. It was all rather wonderful, especially for someone like me who was neither German nor Italian, but was relatively proficient in both languages. I did notice, however, that there was not much intermingling between groups of Germans and groups of Italians. This would become particularly apparent in the evening, when the young Italians would come across the river to party in the bars along Obstmarkt (or Piazza Erbe, as they would call it), whereas the Germans preferred the more sedate surroundings of Waltherplatz.

After lunch I retraced my steps up Laubengasse and into Museumstraße. I noticed a subtle change of mood as Italian slowly replaced German as the dominant language. The transformation was complete when I reached the bridge over the River Talfer (or Talvera, depending on which side you live) and saw the white marble Victory Arch of the Italian Fascists rising to meet me from the far side. Crossing from the bilingual Altstadt of Bozen to the Italian "new city" of Bolzano feels like crossing a national frontier, without going through any customs formalities. You enter directly into the Piazza della Vittoria, designed by Mussolini and Tolomei as a Fascist forum built to surround the triumphal Victory Arch. The arch is mounted upon a broad plinth of steps in the centre of the square. It has fourteen columns in the form of lictorial bundles, the symbol of Italian Fascism. At the top of each column is an axe, each blade facing menacingly outwards. The axe heads are embellished with wolves, eagles and lions. The frieze above the arch is decorated with a dynamic relief of a winged Victory, sculpted at the moment of full tension as she shoots an arrow upstream (towards Austria). The arch ostensibly commemorates the Italian victory over Austria in the First World War, but is essentially a symbol of Italian

Fascism set provocatively in the centre of what was, in 1928, a predominantly German city. The inscription across its architrave, stretched between helmeted heads leering down like gargoyles, reads "HIC PATRIAE FINES SISTE SIGNA. HINC CETEROS EXCOLUIMOS LINGUA LEGIBUS ARTIBUS" ("Plant the standards here at the border of the fatherland. From here we have given to others civilisation in language, law and the arts"). Originally it was intended to read "HINC BARBAROS..." ("From here we have given to barbarians..."). The final insult to the German population was that the Fascist arch was built over the site of an uncompleted monument to the Second Kaiserjäger Regiment of the Austrian Army.

Inside the cage-like structure of the arch is a bronze statue of Christ Resurrected and marble busts of Cesare Battisti and two other Italian "martyrs". Battisti, a geographer from Trentino and a deputy in the pre-war Austrian parliament of the Tyrol, enlisted in the Italian army when Italy declared war against Austria in 1915. Captured by the Austrians and subsequently hanged as a deserter, he became a heroic symbol of Italian irredentism. However, the presence of his statue here in Bolzano has a certain irony, in that Battisti wished for only Trentino, the Italian-speaking part of the old Tyrol, to be incorporated into Italy. He believed that the province of Bolzano, the German-speaking part of South Tyrol, should remain German-Austrian. Battisti supported the division of the Tyrol along the ethnic, linguistic watershed of the Salorno Defile, midway between Bolzano and Trento, rather than along the geographical watershed of the Brenner Pass. So his memory is now enshrined in Bolzano, in the "annexed" German South Tyrol, on soil he believed should never have been Italian in the first place. In fact, in 1987 the Italian President Cossiga was requested by representatives of all political parties in South Tyrol, with the exception of the liberals and the neo-fascist MSI, to have the statue of Battisti removed. They felt his presence in the Fascist arch to be a falsification of his ideals; that the monument was not worthy of Battisti.

In a park behind the Victory Arch I came across another relic of Fascist Italy: a Roman column commemorating thirty-two South Tyrolean soldiers (both German and Italian speakers) who sacrificed their lives "for the Empire of Rome in Spain, Libya and Abyssinia". The date on the column read "16 E.F." (year 16 of the Fascist Era).

The modern, Italian half of Bolzano radiates out from Piazza della Vittoria. The main thoroughfare is Corso della Libertà, formerly named the Corso IX May in celebration of the founding of the Fascist Empire in 1936 following the occupation of Addis Ababa. Its hard-edged, geometrical arcades are a subconscious extension of medieval Laubengasse; its chrome and glass cocktail bars a joyless echo of the *Weinstuben* on the other side of the river. The Fascist authorities planned to destroy the German Altstadt and build their giant, marble-clad colonnades over Laubengasse. In 1938 the two buildings forming the bridgehead on the "German" side of the river – the offices of the INA insurance company and those of the South Tyrol Savings Bank – were rebuilt in a rationalist style with curved, marble façades. In November that year Galeazzo Ciano, Mussolini's son-in-law and Italian Foreign Minister, recorded in his diary: "The appearance of the city is transformed from Nordic to Mediterranean. In ten years or less it will be difficult to recognise in Bolzano the Bozen of earlier times." Mussolini's regime failed and Laubengasse was spared. Yet eighty years later, the savings bank still sports its bas-reliefs of eagles and Fascist standards.

Corso della Libertà leads to Piazza Mazzini, once the Fascist Piazza Impero, a cisalpine version of Stalinist Dresden or Warsaw, equally anachronistic in its brute monumentality. Corso Italia sweeps down through the Italian administrative area towards the apartment blocks of the Italian residential districts and industrial zones on the edge of the city. It was originally planned as a Fascist boulevard and, on Piazza del Tribunale, you can still see a pair of Fascist buildings facing each other, a pairing reminiscent of the Führerbau and National Socialist Verwaltungsbau on Munich's Königsplatz. The forbidding concave façade of the Palace of Justice, supported by square stone columns and decorated with Latin invocations to Justice and Hierarchy, complements the convex front of the Palace of Financial Offices. The latter, a severe, rationalist office block, was built as the Casa del Fascio, the Fascist Party's provincial headquarters. A bas-relief running the length of its façade illustrates the rise of Fascism, from the March on Rome to the apotheosis of Mussolini. Il Duce, on horseback, dominates the centre of the frieze, his right arm raised in the Fascist salute. The inscription reads: "Credere, Obbedire, Combattere" ("Believe, Obey, Fight"). The year is E.F. XX. It is as if the Finanzamt in Munich still depicted Hitler careering across its portals in his supercharged Mercedes.

(On a more recent visit to Bolzano I found the façade of the Tax Office hidden beneath a web of netting and scaffolding. Rather than removing the Fascist frieze, the local authorities have decided in the end to "neutralise" its message by covering it with a stone band engraved with a quotation from Hannah Arendt – "No one has a duty to obey" – in the three languages [German, Italian and Ladin] of South Tyrol.)

Irecalled a previous visit to Bolzano, twenty years earlier, during which I had noticed several official signs announcing that the Piazza della Vittoria would be closed to traffic that evening because of a "manifestazione". I checked the local papers, both the German *Dolomiten* and the Italian *Alto Adige*, and discovered that the demonstration would be on behalf of the *Schützen*, the contemporary followers of Andreas Hofer and supporters of South Tyrolean nationalism. They were commemorating the seventy-fifth anniversary of the death of teacher Franz Innerhofer, the first German victim of Italian Fascism. He was shot on 24 April 1921 while attempting to get two children out of the way of a Fascist parade. The *Schützen* were to assemble that evening at the Ansitz Stillendorf, the house where Innerhofer was killed, and march through the Altstadt to the Victory Arch, where they would lay a wreath of barbed wire, the "crown of thorns" that traditionally symbolises South Tyrolean suppression. They had also prepared a sign which would explain, in five languages, the real meaning of the Victory Monument; and two street signs which they would hang over the official "Piazza della Vittoria" signs, symbolically rechristening the square "Franz-Innerhofer-Platz" as a memorial to anti-fascism.

I arrived at the Ansitz Stillendorf, in the old centre of Bolzano, at 7.30 pm. Most of the *Schützen* were still in the pubs. The nearest bar was a chic cocktail lounge where the manageress, boasting of achieving her "Jahresumsatz" (her turnover for the year) within the next half hour, was dispensing glasses of beer to crowds of men wearing side whiskers and knee breeches. In an ironic twist, the *Schützen* greeted each other with the old Bavarian word "Pfürte", whereas real Bavarians in a Munich cocktail bar would yell "Ciao". Between 7.30 and 8 pm the *Schützen* gradually assembled in the streets leading into a small square in front of the Ansitz Stillendorf. Each unit arrived in formation, as if they had marched straight down to Bolzano from their mountain villages. Soon there were between five hundred and one thousand men, and a handful of pale girls in dirndl dresses with lace shawls and aprons, their hair braided in the traditional German manner. The men and boys were dressed in their finest Tyrolean national costume – brown, red or green *Loden* tunics, leather knee breeches, white woollen socks and black buckled shoes. Underneath their tunics they wore red waistcoats criss-crossed with green braces, on which were pinned ribbons and medals. Everything was held in place by thick leather belts, decorated with pins and brooches in the images of Andreas Hofer, the edelweiss of the South Tyrol People's Party or the red eagle of the Tyrol. The crowning glory of the costume was the hat. The Italians sarcastically referred to the *Schützen* as "plumed hats". Each unit had its own distinctive headgear, from the basic green or black felt hat with a single black-and-white plume to an array of tassels, ribbons, peacock feathers, flowers or sprigs of trees. Some of the men looked as though they were carrying wedding bouquets on their head. Their gnarled, weather-beaten faces, rosy cheeks, baroque moustaches, thick beards and side whiskers brought to life all those paintings in Bergisel of Andreas Hofer and his followers or, more disturbingly, those by Oskar Martin-Amorbach, Thomas Baumgartner and other "Blood and Soil" painters whose works used to hang in the Haus der Kunst in Munich during the Third Reich.

On the stroke of 8 pm, when the parade was due to begin with a minute's silence, Italians all around the old city started honking their car horns; but the *Schützen* were still assembling and were not disturbed by the protest. I wandered off to inspect the "Franz-Innerhofer-Platz" street signs, which were correctly bilingual, and the multilingual placards, which gave a German interpretation of the Victory Monument. The placards explained that the arch was the symbol of "a Fascist mentality", of "Italy's colonial subjection of South Tyrol", of "intolerance towards ancestral German culture". The Latin description over the arch was described as "a daily affront to the German population of South Tyrol".

By 8.15 pm the *Schützen* were all present and correct. According to their sashes, most had come from the province of South Tyrol itself, but several units had also been bussed in from Trentino and from the Austrian Tyrol. The *Schützen* described themselves officially as a "cultural organisation", but drew themselves up in military rank, had "officers" and a "commandant", and marched in uniform. They had all the attributes of a people's militia except the most obvious one. *Schützen* literally means "marksmen" – but these men carried no rifles. They must have left them at home.

As dusk fell the *Schützen* stood to attention while their commandant, Richard Piock, spoke in a low, proud voice of the sacrifice of Franz Innerhofer, of the subsequent decades of intolerance and nationalistic hatred, and of the "only living Fascist monument in Europe: that constant provocation to the German population of South Tyrol". His speech became a panegyric to the Germanness of South Tyrol: "deutsch war, deutsch ist, deutsch bleibt." At the same time, he was careful never to refer to the "Italians". The march was an "anti-fascist" demonstration, the Victory Arch was a "Fascist" monument and the *Schützen* were an "anti-fascist" organisation. After Piock had finished, the *Schützen* fell into silent prayer, uninterrupted this time by Italian klaxons. Then softly, like a roll of approaching thunder from the surrounding mountains, they began to sing the opening verse of the Tyrolean anthem: "Zu Mantua in Banden…", a hymn to Hofer which ends in a chorus of "Es ist *ein* Land Tirol". I focused my attention on a short fellow with a barrel-shaped body directly in front of me. He was so short that he had to crane his neck skywards in order to see anything. In this position he looked as though he was lifting his face towards the heavens. He sang in a clear tenor voice, like he was experiencing something mystical. For the first time I became aware that concepts such as patriotism, *Heimat*, love of your land, roots, the heartland, could mean something more profound than base nationalism.

The *Schützen* set off on their torchlight procession through the Altstadt of Bolzano, preceded by the barbed wire "crown of thorns" they were to lay in front of the Victory Monument. They marched in absolute silence. Only the pounding of a thousand feet and the beat of drums could be heard. Torchlight flickered across the faces of hundreds of men as the *Fackelzug* moved solemnly through the arcaded Laubengasse. Even as a detached observer, I found the experience moving. The fire and the drumbeat summoned forth powers which went deep into the soil of the land and far back into a distant past. Sadly, the procession did not pass off without an element of racist aggression. Two teenage skinheads, wearing Dr. Martens and bomber jackets with "Ein Tirol" ribbons stitched to their chests, followed the *Schützen*, shouting to bystanders that the "Franz-Innerhofer-Platz" signs should be in German only, rather than in both languages, and flashing Nazi salutes at anyone who looked Italian.

In spite of the two yobs, the march proceeded in a dignified manner along Museumstraße towards the bridge over the River Talvera which separates the Altstadt from the modern Italian city. I could hear whistling in the distance. As the *Schützen* reached the Piazza della Vittoria on the far side of the bridge, all hell let loose. Thousands of Italians were waiting for them, crowded into the bridgehead in front of the Victory Monument, held back by scores of *carabinieri*. "Italia, Italia", "Scheiße Austria", "Buffoni, bastardi"; jeers, whistles, and fascist salutes from the little knots of MSI rowdies who led the chanting. Those German onlookers who applauded the *Schützen* were jeered at ("Fascisti") by the Italian neo-fascists. Like the monument itself, it was all getting confusing. Italian neo-fascists were calling Germans "fascists", while the German *Schützen* who, while not fascists in any literal sense nevertheless recalled the *völkisch* "Blood and Soil" elements of National Socialism, were holding an "anti-fascist" demonstration in commemoration of an "anti-fascist" martyr. The two factions, both of which contained particles of fascism, self-righteously played the anti-fascist card for all it was worth. The real issue, of course, was Germans against Italians. Only the politicians on either side pretended otherwise. The "anti-fascist" line was, for both sides, a convenient alibi. For the *Schützen,* "anti-fascist" was a euphemism for "anti-Italian". For the Italians, "fascist" equated with "German". On this side of the river the gloves were coming off and the euphemisms were being discarded in favour of football-terrace racism.

Torches still flaming, the *Schützen* formed up in ranks in front of the arch. Solemn and silent, they seemed rapt in their own version of folk mysticism, oblivious to the taunts hurled at them by the MSI. The *carabinieri* strutted theatrically between the two factions, in a pretence of holding the neo-fascists at bay. A posse of glamorous female undercover agents rushed around, talking self-importantly into walkie-talkies. The Germans laid their wreaths of barbed wire on the steps of the square and hung their placards and symbolic street signs on the steel fence surrounding the monument – to shouts of "Stick them up your arse" from some of the Italians. It was all quite theatrical and, in spite of the abuse, not particularly threatening, somewhere between a football match and a medieval pageant. I don't think anybody expected any violence. There were certainly a handful of extremists present, but this was not Sarajevo or Londonderry. Until that evening I had been struck by how harmoniously the two communities coexisted. As someone who looks more Nordic than Mediterranean, I'd been treated in a perfectly friendly manner in the Italian part of the city, although I'd been careful to speak only Italian in the bars along Corso della Libertà.

By 9.10 pm the ceremony was over. The *Schützen* had made their symbolic stand. They broke ranks and dispersed towards a fleet of coaches waiting for them at the rear of the square, retaining their order and discipline as if unaware of the abusive chanting from sections of the Italian onlookers. The Italians continued to yell and mill around for half an hour, kept in check by a ring of *carabinieri.* When the Germans had disappeared, factions of Italians started to argue among each other: generational disputes between young, hard-line neo-fascists and their elders, who regarded the violence of the neo-fascists as playing into the hands of the "anti-fascist" stance of the *Schützen*. Eventually the ring formed by the *carabinieri* was breached and the German signs were torn down and thrown around. In an attempt to disperse the crowd, the Italian police stage-managed an incident. A blond, Saxon-looking young tough suddenly hurled himself towards the neo-fascist group shouting "Deutschland, Deutschland über alles" and "Italian wankers" in a poorly disguised accent. He was hustled away by plain-clothes agents before the MSI had a chance to get their hands on him. The agents then retired to a patrol car to share a cigarette and a joke with their "provocateur". The Italian press had got its story and its photographs. It could report a bit of "German provocation" in tomorrow's *Alto Adige*. Everyone was now happy and they slowly drifted away, until the next anniversary of Franz Innerhofer's killing, when the same, stagey drama can be re-enacted all over again.

4

Austria

Loden Green, Habsburg Yellow, Danube Blue, Nazi Brown

I was sitting at a window table in the breakfast room of the Hotel Wolfinger, high above the Hauptplatz of Linz. The room was furnished with Biedermeier commodes, dressers, tea chests and grandfather clocks, all beautifully inlaid with rosewood, walnut and mother-of-pearl. A piano sat in one corner with the score of *Lohengrin* resting on its stand, waiting to be performed. The walls were hung with reproductions of paintings by Degas and cartoons from old satirical magazines like *Simplicissimus* and *Kladderadatsch*. Heavy gilt-framed mirrors leaned at acute angles. The shelves of the cabinets were decorated with Viennese ball masks and pieces of antique glassware, meticulously colour-coordinated so that blue plates merged into turquoise vases which in turn coalesced into green wine glasses, and so on. In another corner was an ancient Rockola jukebox, its needle arm poised for eternity over The Sweet's *Poppa Joe*. The breakfast buffet on the long central table was not particularly copious; in fact it was the antithesis of the "eat as much as you can" abundance offered by German hotels – the two slices of salami and three remaining squares of processed cheese were already beginning to curl up at the edges in anticipation of being fought over by the breakfasters.

The Hauptplatz below me, a long rectangle encased within tall, ornate houses, more baroque than Biedermeier, felt closed off from the rest of the city; like an intimate drawing room lined with antique furniture dusty with the patina of age. The upper storeys, painted in faded pastels (Loden green, Habsburg yellow, Danube blue and Nazi brown), leaned over their supporting colonnades like a line of old wardrobes resting on casters.

The coral-pink Rathaus, streaming with red-and-white-striped national pennants, disgorged a wedding party which blared and hooted its way through a gap between a pair of blue and grey buildings at the Danube end of the square. A tramcar trundled in from the Nibelungenbrücke, halted before the town hall and disappeared, as if exiting stage right, into the Landstraße, a narrow high street of Mozartian façades overhung with a web of tram wires and suspended street lights, blocked off at the far end by the Ursulinenkirche. Over the rim of the Hauptplatz peered the towers of the city's other churches: the garlic-domed belfry of the parish church of Maria Himmelfahrt; and the green and white Jesuitenkirche, the former cathedral where Anton Bruckner was employed as organist between 1856 and 1868.

In the centre of the square the Dreifaltigkeitssäule, a baroque plague column erected in 1723, rose above the Saturday-morning flea market. The pillar was a literal representation of the plague, a stone coil of pus oozing excrescent cherubs and serpents. At its apex, eighty-five feet high, the Holy Trinity radiated golden rods of light over the trams and trestle tables of a *Trödelmarkt*. In the market I discovered some old issues of the National Socialist monthly art magazine *Kunst dem Volk*, published in Vienna by Hitler's photographer and art adviser Heinrich Hoffmann. One, a special edition published in April 1943 to celebrate the Führer's birthday, was the first publication to announce plans for Hitler's monumental New Gallery in Linz. It included colour plates of some of the confiscated art works that would form the basis of the collection: Rembrandt's *Hendrijke Stoffels*, Leonardo's *Leda with Swan*, Brueghel's *Hay Harvest* and Rubens' *Pan and Nymph*, for example. There were also plates of many of Hitler's favourite nineteenth-century German painters: Moritz von Schwind, Adolph von Menzel, Hans Thoma and Hans Makart. The journal ended with an article entitled "Künstler sehen die Heimat des Führers" ("Artists view the Homeland of the Führer"), illustrated with watercolours of Hitler's birthplace in Braunau, his schoolhouse in Fischlham, his parents' house in Leonding and the Adolf-Hitler Stammhaus in Walterschlag. The text evoked the bucolic "Blut und Boden" spirituality of the Upper Austrian landscape and celebrated the "Volksgemeinschaft" (national community) that also bred Adalbert Stifter, Franz Grillparzer and Anton Bruckner. Published in October 1943, the second magazine was dedicated to Karl (spelt with an *echt deutsch* K rather than the more usual C) Spitzweg, Hitler's "favourite painter". It included an original insert, printed on orange wartime paper, apologising for the distribution of the September issue being delayed due to unforeseen "kriegsbedingte" (war-related) difficulties. It signed off with a "Heil Hitler!"

I also bought three propaganda postcards from the 1930s, all illustrated by the same artist, Ernst Kutzer, a *völkisch* Arthur Rackham. The first was a fitting epitaph to my experiences in the Tyrol. Against a background of Alpine peaks, two sturdy *Schützen* (one a spitting image of Andreas Hofer) grasped a shield bearing the red Tyrolean eagle. In an orange tree above them hovered a Roman (SPQR) ghoul brandishing a sword whose blade had metamorphosed into a snake. The legend below read "Auf Wiedersehen!" and the message was clear: "Italians out of the Tyrol!" On the back of the postcard was the verse:

So lang Andreas Hofers Geist   (As long as Andreas Hofer's spirit
Die Alpen noch umweht,   Holds sway over the Alps,
Bleibt ganz Tirol ein harter Fels,   Tyrol will remain a solid rock,
Der nicht zu sprengen geht.   Never to be broken.)

The second postcard represented the Austrian "family" (a worker, farmer, teacher, soldier, mother and two children) standing grim-faced on top of a hill overlooking Vienna. Its message exhorted the citizens of the Republik Deutsch-Oesterreich to pull together and follow the example of their German *Vaterland*. The "German-Austrian" republic was at the time riven by fighting between the Schutzbund and the Heimwehr, the respective paramilitary organisations of the Social Democrats and the Austro-Fascist government. The third card was pure *Anschluss* propaganda: above the slogan "Oesterreich zum Deutschen Reich" a massive figure of Germania, her right hand raised in an unequivocal "Heil", clutched the barefoot waif Austria to her ample bosom. They stood together on a rock which formed an imaginary promontory between the Rhine and the Danube, encircled by a Wagnerian vision of Germanic oaks, dragons and dwarves. The poem on the reverse of this card read:

Große Stunde, die ich meine,   (Great hour of destiny
steig empor und werde Licht!   Rise up and become light!
Daß sich Stamm dem Stamm vereine,   That tribe may unite with tribe
bess're Heimat weiß ich nicht.   I know of no better homeland.
Haß der Welt und Sklavenschande   The hatred of the world and the shame of
heißt das Leid, das uns geschah.   Slavery were the woes we suffered.
Nimm dein Kind vom Donaustrande   Embrace, Germania, your child
an Dein Herz, Germania!   From the banks of the Danube!)

At eleven o'clock the glockenspiel on the Feichtinger Haus chimed a melody, apparently from one of Bruckner's symphonies. The baroque houses glittered in the sun. I wandered down the gentle incline of the Hauptplatz towards the Danube, reading the memorial tablets on the buildings as I passed. The plaque on the pair of blue and grey neoclassical buildings forming the bridgehead between the Hauptplatz and the Danube read: "Errichtet nach Pläne von Roderich Fick 1940/3" ("Built by Roderich Fick 1940/3"). Although they blended convincingly (to my untrained eye, at least) with the baroque houses round the rest of the square, these administrative buildings were, in effect, the work of Linz's most famous amateur architect, Adolf Hitler. They are the only surviving relics of Hitler's grand dream of transforming his "Jugendstadt" into a metropolis dedicated to the cult of the Führer – a Teutonic Paris or a Florence-on-the-Danube. The buildings themselves are now occupied by the local tax office, a use which echoes their original function as the Oberfinanzpräsidium of the National Socialist Gau Oberdonau.

The Nibelungenbrücke over the Danube is also of National Socialist provenance, first opened to traffic in 1940. The original design of the bridge included granite statues of Hitler's favourite Nibelung heroes – Siegfried, Kriemhild, Gunther and Brunhild – but their realisation, like many of Hitler's other Wagnerian fantasies, was overtaken by "Götterdämmerung" before they could be completed. The sculptor Bernhard Graf Plettenberg was, however, able to create plaster mock-ups of two of these statues in order to decorate the unfinished bridge when the Führer visited Linz in 1940. Today the bridge bears a less triumphal message: a marble plaque commemorating the tens of thousands of Sudeten Germans driven from their homeland in 1945 by the Czechs, whose journey into exile ended as they crossed the Nibelungenbrücke into Linz. I stood on the centre of the bridge and surveyed the murky green waters of the Danube as they drifted slowly down from Passau, beneath the Schloss, between arcades of chestnut trees and a promenade of lawns sloping gently down from the Brucknerhaus concert hall. On the left bank were apartment buildings and a fairground; on the right bank a sculpture park and the glass block of the Lentos Kunstmuseum, which glows in purple neon at night and sparkles in the rain. The first chimneys of Linz's huge chemical works were visible around the bend downstream. Above them, a panoramic view of the rolling hills and baroque churches of Upper Austria, a landscape that the young Adolf Hitler loved to sketch before he became obsessed with the architecture of power.

In the evening I had a ticket for a performance of Bruckner's Symphony No. 9 in the Neuer Dom. Hitler's plans to remould Linz in his own image included a Bruckner Festival Hall, which would have held an annual celebration of the works of his favourite symphonic composer. Given Hitler's taste in architecture, it is not difficult to understand his love of the music of Bruckner, whose symphonies are often described as "cathedral-like structures", monumental "blocks of sound" that begin and end abruptly, surrounded, like sculptures, by empty spaces of silence. Bruckner himself described his music as "sonic architecture". There are of course passages of tremulous beauty and sublime serenity, but their main characteristic is power, a brassy, rhythmic, elemental force which generates a sense of awe in the listener. The first movement of the Ninth opened with a brief shimmering of strings followed by a Wagnerian motif on the French horn, underscored by pairs of drumbeats reminiscent of Siegfried's Funeral March. The opening themes developed into a crescendo of sound which reverberated around the cathedral within three minutes of the opening bars, as if Bruckner could wait no longer to unleash the climax of the symphony. The formal, elderly audience sat rapt in concentration through the long first movement, which consisted of repeated patterns of lyrical melody that ebbed and flowed like waves over a night sea, continually threatening to break but always subsiding at the last moment – until the final shattering climax. At the end of the unfinished symphony, after the "wrath of God" and the "vision of Hell", after the last tremolo of the coda had died away, there was a long silence. As the symphony is dedicated to "the dear God", and as the performance took place in a cathedral, with the audience facing the altar and the orchestra behind them, many in the audience were unsure whether it was appropriate to applaud. Many were awed by the experience. The silence continued until a first, hesitant handclap exploded into a standing ovation.

After the concert I went for a coffee on the Promenade in the Café Traxlmayr, Linz's traditional Viennese-style coffee house, a chaotic jumble of rickety tables and grubby velvet banquettes shrouded in a warm fug of cigarette smoke. I'd been there eighteen months previously, when I stopped overnight in Linz on my way to spend Christmas with my brother and his family in Budapest. I'd gone to the Traxlmayr for a *Glühwein*, which was served in a funnel-shaped jug. I remembered swapping experiences of living in a foreign country with a *Linzerin* who worked as a nurse in Hackney, and who now spoke in a bizarre Austro-Cockney accent.

I pushed my way through the heavy drapes hanging from a semi-circular rail above the door and was shocked to find that the café had been transformed, smartened up, and was no longer the bohemian, *mittel-europäisch* haunt I remembered. The nicotine-stained ceiling and walls had been painted a pristine white, around whose edges ran a frieze in a geometrical pattern reminiscent of a row of swastikas. The tarnished gilt mirrors had been polished so brightly their Jugendstil floral motifs were now visible once more. The net curtains from the Habsburg days had been taken down and the once-crimson banquettes reupholstered in a silver-grey fabric. The revolving wooden newspaper stand had been replaced by a brass magazine rack. The small circular marble tables had survived, as had the chandeliers. Arranged around the walls was a gallery of water-colours of old Linz, of the type Adolf Hitler used to paint.

The serving staff negotiated their slow, truculent circuits over the parquet floor, bearing their little oval silver trays laden with "big brown", "little brown", "prolonged" and "mixed" coffees (no flavoured skinny lattes here yet). The waiters were dressed in grease-stained tuxedos and bow ties; the waitresses in frilly white blouses, pinafores and black sandals strapped around white socks. The main room was filling up with concert-goers winding down with a beer or an *Obstler* after the rigours of Bruckner. I listened to the clink of glasses on the marble tables, the rattle of pearl necklaces and the swish of sequinned stockings as women arranged their gowns over the banquettes. After last orders the concert-goers began to leave and the café fell into a hush. I heard the click of billiard balls from an adjoining room, reminding me of the Schelling-Salon in Munich, which also doubled as a billiard hall. Hitler must have frequented the Café Traxlmayr too, during his adolescence in Linz, since he often went to performances of Schiller's plays and Wagner's operas in the Landestheater at the far end of the Promenade. It occurred to me that Linz's most infamous son, himself a lifelong coffee-house philosopher, might have approved of the café's neoclassical makeover.

Perched on a hill outside Linz, the village of Ansfelden is dominated by the yellow church where Anton Bruckner senior was the organist. Anton junior was born in the house below the church on 4 September 1824. A stone plaque on the wall of his birthplace describes him as a "Tondichter" (tone poet) rather than a "Komponist" (composer). This epithet is particularly appropriate for Bruckner. It also illustrates an Austrian predilection for pithy, old-fashioned Saxon compounds in cases where the

Germans have introduced Latin-based words into the language. In Austria you may still spend the afternoon reading a book in a *Bücherei* rather than a *Bibliothek*, or the evening watching a film in a *Lichtspielhaus* instead of a *Kino*. Afterwards, in a restaurant, you would eat *Paradieseier* (paradise eggs) rather than *Tomaten*, or *Erdäpfel* (earth apples) instead of *Kartoffeln* (potatoes).

Bruckner lived in Ansfelden until 1845, when he moved to the Augustinian abbey of Sankt Florian to begin his first job as a schoolmaster. He later became organist of the abbey church, where the solemn, religious, chord-dominated aspect of his work was nurtured. I followed the route Bruckner would have taken from Ansfelden to Sankt Florian, up through the forests and meadows that inspired the nature-mysticism in his music. His *völkisch* religiosity was exploited by the National Socialists: a passage in one of the editions of *Kunst dem Volk* I bought in Linz waxed lyrically about how "Anton Bruckner's symphonies grew out of this (Upper Austrian) landscape which illuminates the view of the pilgrim as he roams, lost in admiration, over undulating fields, and looks up into the white snowfields towards the high altar of God."

The composer's tomb lies in a crypt beneath the great gold and white organ of the abbey church of Sankt Florian, beside a pyramid of skulls from a nearby mass grave dating from Carolingian times. Another wedding had just finished as I arrived at the church, and the altar and pews were decked with white, yellow and orange lilies, matching the colours of the frescoes and columns around the baroque nave. Outside, a brass band was playing for the wedding guests assembled in front of the church. The master of ceremonies, wearing a porkpie hat streaming with white ribbons, led the guests, in their finest silk or best maroon blazers, away to the adjoining monastery, where they regrouped around the lawns and fountains of the courtyard, beneath the Empire yellow of the grand imperial-episcopal staircase and cloisters.

The road from Sankt Florian wound back down through Enns towards the Danube. I crossed the river and followed the B3 upstream along a causeway above the *Auwald*, with the river on my left and the quarried hills of Upper Austria on my right. A right turn led me up through the hamlet of Langenstein-Mauthausen, through a belt of woods, past scattered farms and out onto the highland above the Danube valley. I came to a halt below the grey stone walls of Austria's "mother" concentration camp. It was early Sunday morning and there were already tourist buses from the Netherlands and the Czech Republic parked among lines of cars from all over Europe. I walked through an entrance gate in the exterior wall into a lower precinct lined with garages and storehouses. A right turn took me up a flight of steps to the gates of the inner camp.

I entered a long parade ground like a wide street, lined with green wooden huts, rising into the distance until it was cut off by the barbed wire of the perimeter wall. The impression was one of rigid, symmetrical order; of straight lines where nothing was out of place; of emptiness, silence – cleanliness almost. This sanitised, neutral perspective, this non-image of absence and separation, gave a false impression of what the camp would have been like when in use: an inferno of noise (lorries unloading, shouted commands, barking dogs, gunshots, the shrieks of prisoners); the smell of thousands of unwashed people living and dying on top of each other; the stench of putrefying corpses; smoke, fire, rain, dirt, mud – a place of chaos and disorder night and day. The neatness of the remains of the camp, whether viewed as a museum or as a memorial, has its dangers in that it encourages us to believe that the people killed here were at least killed in a clean, efficient, orderly manner.

Halfway along the right-hand side of the parade ground were two low, whitewashed buildings. In the small yard between them stood a narrow chimney, its lower half in stone, its upper half in red brick. In the basement below was a corridor of tiny cells forming a jail within the jail, where political prisoners were interrogated and troublesome inmates held in solitary confinement, awaiting execution. Leading off this corridor was an *Umkleideraum* (changing room), a cell where prisoners were led for a "medical inspection". Here they were stripped of their prison rags and given a cursory oral examination. Those with gold teeth or gold fillings had a red cross chalked on their chest or back. They were then herded into an underground chamber, the size of a small bathroom, lined with heating pipes and with shower heads fitted into its low ceiling. Eighty prisoners were crammed in at a time. The iron door was slammed shut and locked by an iron wheel. Zyklon B was pumped in through a small duct just below the ceiling. The gas took between ten and twenty minutes to kill. The mopping-up process lasted substantially longer: eighteen hours were required to separate, remove and cremate the corpses and to clean and ventilate the chamber. The hot water pipes and shower heads were for real, as the gas was only effective in warm conditions and the showers were used to clean out the blood and excrement left behind.

Adjacent to the gas chamber was a little suite of rooms dedicated to alternative methods of annihilation. In a tiny "surgery" the "patient" was placed upright against a measuring rule and shot in the back of the neck through a hole hidden in the rule. Other prisoners were hanged from a girder suspended above the same room. I wondered, but did not have the nerve to ask the guide, whether there was any hierarchy of death, whereby "good" prisoners were shot or hanged rather than gassed, or whether the means of liquidation were random, depending on what was available at any given time. The corpses were loaded immediately into two ovens in an alcove of the room. Those chalked with red crosses were dumped into a morgue next door until the "surgeons" in the dissecting room had time to come and rip the gold out of their teeth or draw off any tattooed skin. They were then loaded into a third oven, in a cell off the dissecting room, which fed into the same chimney as the ovens in the "surgery". In their spare time the SS doctors used the dissecting table – a stone slab with a thin drain running down its centre – to experiment with fatal injections. One of them used to saw off prisoners' heads, which he would embalm in order to decorate his colleagues' living rooms.

All this activity, which accounted for a substantial proportion of the 122,766 murders perpetrated in Mauthausen, took place in a complex of rooms which – changing room, gas chamber, execution cell, morgue, dissecting room and three ovens all included – took up no more space than an average hotel suite. There was no space, let alone time, for the condemned prisoners to contemplate what was happening to them or prepare themselves for death. The entire process was carried out with breathless speed and industrial efficiency. One moment you were going to have your height checked, and a few hours later your ashes were being tipped into the Danube or spread as grit over the cobblestones of the parade ground.

The majority of prisoners in Mauthausen, however, were worked to death in the quarry adjoining the camp. Most of the killing took place not in the quarry itself but on the overhanging cliffs and on the "staircase of death" leading down into it. Those prisoners who were pushed or thrown from cliff tops to the floor of the quarry were known as "parachutists". Those who died on the steps were "dominoes". As a column of forced labourers made its way down the steps, the guards at the top would push the last row forward so that each row fell upon the row in front, crushing those at the foot of the steps. On their way back up, laden with blocks of granite, stragglers would be beaten unconscious, and the rocks they were carrying would crash down on the rows behind them.

There are 186 roughly hewn steps from the camp to the quarry, but the steps you walk down today have been refashioned for tourists. The original steps were bigger and rougher. Now the quarry is a silent, grim reminder of death: murky pools of stagnant water lie at the feet of sheer cliffs, overlooked by a solitary watchtower and the jagged memorials erected by the governments of Poland, Israel and the former GDR. "O Deutschland, bleiche Mutter!" reads the last, in lines taken from Bertolt Brecht: "Wie haben deine Söhne dich zugerichtet, dass du unter den Völkern sitzest, ein Gespött oder eine Furcht!" ("O Germany, pale mother! What a mess your sons have made of you that you sit among the nations as a laughing stock or a fright!").

I discovered the Dichterstein (Poets' Stone) in the depths of winter as I drove back from a family Christmas spent in Budapest. I had come across its existence in a book I had bought in an antiquarian bookshop in Vienna entitled *Deutschland, Deutschland über alles* written by Marie Therese Hug, Princess of Prussia and a great-niece of Kaiser Wilhelm II. Published by DSV-Verlag, an imprint of Verlag Gerhard Rautenberg, a German publisher specialising in revisionist nostalgia, the book was an illustrated guide to German nationalism and, in particular, to the "lost territories". The chapter on Austria contained an illustration of a wood-cut of the Dichterstein, but there was no mention of the monument in the text. The caption read: "Another symbol of the German character of Austria: the Dichterstein in Offenhausen." The woodcut depicted a monument in the shape of a low circular wall broken into four overlapping quarter-circular sections (think of a swastika with curved hooks). In the centre of the circle were two square pillars, each the height of a man.

I set off in search of Offenhausen, turning off the Linz–Passau auto-bahn west of Wels and heading into the snowbound hills. The Dichterstein soon came into view, a grey stone circle standing out against the snow below a belt of dark pine trees. I parked my car in front of a map of the village, which made no mention of the monument, and took a narrow alley below the eaves of two farmhouses towards an icy track zigzagging up the side of a hill.

Guarding the steps that led inside the Dichterstein were two millstones, carved to resemble ancient shields, on which were inscribed the names of Goethe and Schiller. Inserted into the walls of the stone circle were hundreds of slate-coloured bricks, each bearing the name of a German or Austrian writer. I had never heard of any of the first few names I read. I walked around in the snow outside the circle and gradually began to recognise some familiar names: Nietzsche, Storm, Raabe, Rilke, Mörike, Hölderlin, Fichte, Kleist, Droste-Hülshoff, Walther von der Vogelweide, Karl May, Georg Trakl, Dietrich Eckart, E.T.A. Hoffmann, Klopstock, the Brothers Grimm, Lessing, Wagner, Fontane, Hauptmann, Hans Sachs, Stifter, Eichendorff, Grillparzer, Hebbel, Grimmelshausen, Luther.

The bricks seemed to be inserted at random: there was no obvious chronological, alphabetical or stylistic sequence, or any attempt to order the writers' names according to their degree of fame. I wondered whether there was any occult pattern understood only by initiates into some arcane literary circle. On the whole, the names on the bricks represented the conventional pantheon of German men of letters. There were, nevertheless, a couple of surprises: Karl May was a purveyor of penny-dreadful westerns – then I remembered that he was a favourite of Adolf Hitler. Dietrich Eckart was not a name one would normally associate with the great and good of German literature: euphemistically described as a "Bavarian nationalist poet", he is more commonly remembered as the composer of the SA's Storm Song *Deutschland Erwache!*, as the editor of an anti-Semitic broadsheet *Auf gut deutsch*, as the proprietor and first publisher of the *Völkischer Beobachter* and, above all, as the mentor of the young Hitler.

My next reaction was to try to think of any famous German writer whose name had been omitted. A process of elimination led me very quickly to Heinrich Heine, Germany's greatest Romantic poet. But wasn't he Jewish? I thought of Kafka, but as a Bohemian Jew he probably disqualified himself as neither strictly German nor strictly Austrian, in addition to being non-Aryan. Then there was the question of dating the monument. All the writers whose names I recognised were dead by 1926, with the exception of Gerhard Hauptmann, who died in 1946, although he was well into his dotage by the "cut-off" date of 1926 I had arbitrarily hit upon. Kafka, however, died in 1924, so it was clear that his name had been omitted on grounds of race, nationality or ideological unsuitability. I wondered whether Hugo von Hofmannsthal and Stefan George, who died in 1929 and 1933 respectively (before Hauptmann), had been omitted as too "degenerate". Hofmannsthal was an Austrian, a "humane conservative", and would therefore have had a strong claim to be included in this "circle of honour". Maybe he was too closely associated with the autocratic aesthete Stefan George, initially a disciple of Aryanism in a literary, Symbolist sense, before he became disillusioned with the brutal reality of National Socialism and left Germany in 1933. And where was Thomas Mann, twentieth-century Germany's greatest man of letters? Having made a mental note of those celebrated writers whose names had been excluded from the memorial, I then made a written note of three obscure wordsmiths, picked at random, whose names had been included. When I arrived home, I looked up their names in my *Duden-Lexikon*. The literary careers of Hans W. Ehrler and Ernst Wichert had not been recorded for posterity in the encyclopedia. I did, however, feel a twinge of perverse satisfaction on discovering an entry for Peter Rosegger (1843–1918): "Austrian writer. Novels about woodcutters in his Styrian homeland, with pedagogical intentions: *The Writings of the Forest Schoolmaster (1875)*; folkloristic tales from his youth: *Waldheimat (1877)*; and lyrics in Styrian dialect." How *völkisch!*

Carved on the faces of the steps leading into the stone ring were a number of "Stichwörter" (literally, "stab-words") – key words or slogans. None of these bore any particular relevance to the supposedly poetic theme of the Dichterstein. Translated into English they read: "Work Ennobles", "Allegiance and Sacrifice", "Fatherland", "Mother Tongue", "Devotion to the Homeland", "Ancestral Honour", "National Unity", "Purity of Kinship", "Joy in Action", "Consciousness of the Race", "Tranquillity of German Folk Traditions" and so forth. So what on earth was this place? What was a monument to German writers doing on a hill in the middle of nowhere in Upper Austria? Was it the grave of some eccentric failed poet of nationalist tendencies? An occult henge for literary Nazis? A miniature version of the Reichsehrenmal Tannenberg? Maybe a local librarian wished to ingratiate himself with the new regime, hoping to be rewarded for his efforts with a post in the Reichs Ministry of Culture? The language of the *Stichwörter* consisted not only of *völkisch* terminology such as "Vaterland", "Heimat", "Volk" and "Muttersprache", but also of words like "Ahnen", "Sippen", "Art" and "Einsatz" which had specific National Socialist meanings; and the manner in which these slogans had been cut into the stones reminded me of Sachsenhain, Himmler's grove of fake dolmens near Verden in Lower Saxony. Then there was the presence of Dietrich Eckart, an unequivocally National Socialist writer. The whole concept of a pantheon of great (and not so great) Germanic writers being commemorated on Austrian soil seemed like a celebration of the *Anschluss*: a monumentalisation of how Austria is inseparable from Germany; how its writers spring from the same blood and the same language as their German brothers – just as my *Anschluss* postcard from the flea market in Linz depicted the waif of Austria smothered in the bosom of Mother Germany.

What made the Dichterstein seem particularly sinister was a wrought-iron arch over the entrance to the circle, inscribed with the words: "He who betrays the spirit betrays his people." It resembled the grilles bearing the slogan "Arbeit macht frei" arching over the entrances to Dachau and Auschwitz. The arch must have been added later, as it is not illustrated in the woodcut in the book which led me to the monument in the first place. I looked again for a date. Was the Dichterstein pre- or post-Third Reich? Did it anticipate or celebrate the *Anschluss*? There were plaques acknowledging the work of the stonemasons who had carved the shields bearing the names of Goethe and Schiller, and of the smith (Walther Haberl from Carinthia – born 1908, died 1984) who had forged the arch. There were other tablets with some awful verse extolling the suffering of poets; but nowhere was there any indication of what the monument was, or when it was built. This only made me more suspicious that it was an authentic National Socialist shrine and that the post-war authorities had deliberately obliterated all reference to its origins.

I noticed a memorial stone on the ground between the two square pillars in the centre of the circle. I hacked away at the ice to try to decipher an inscription that might unlock the secret of the Dichterstein. I was not helped by the fact that it had been chiselled in heavy, impenetrable Gothic script. Eventually it revealed a name (Joseph Hietz), but no date. Hidden in the trees to the right of the Dichterstein was another stone pillar with two runic symbols on its plinth. Of the five names inscribed on its column, one was Guido List, an Austrian Wotanist, swastika-worshipper and progenitor of Aryan master-race theories. List was one of the founders of the Germanen-Orden, a quasi-Masonic, anti-Semitic society which, in 1918, evolved into the Thule Society, based in Munich, whose members included Dietrich Eckart, Rudolf Hess and Alfred Rosenberg; and whose newspaper, the *Münchener Beobachter und Sportblatt*, eventually became the National Socialist mouthpiece, the *Völkischer Beobachter*. In order to extend its influence, the Thule Society set up its own political wing, the German Workers' Party, whose third public meeting on 12 September 1919 was attended by Adolf Hitler.

I left the Dichterstein as puzzled as when I first came across it in the Princess of Prussia's book. Maybe she knew nothing about it either? It certainly bore the crude, ugly hallmarks of Himmler's "sacred realm": an amalgam of the occult, the literary, the racist and the uncanny – particularly under several layers of snow and ice with a biting wind howling through the forest behind it. I resolved to find out more about the monument, but I never did. Of all the (presumably) National Socialist sites I was to visit, the Dichterstein remained the most mysterious.

I drove from Vienna down to the Burgenland on Ascension Day. Bundesstraße 50 meandered through the "white villages" of the region: Oberpullendorf, Piringsdorf, Bernstein, Stadtschlaining. Each village consisted of a long street of low, rustic houses punctuated by oak gates leading into farmyards where grain was stored and wine pressed. Each house had a pair of storks clattering their bills in a nest of straw on the chimney tops. I stopped for a coffee in one of the villages, sitting by a pond beside a parish pump with an inscription in Hungarian. A family of Romanies, in their Sunday best, rattled past in a pony and trap.

I turned off the B50 towards Oberschützen, a village hidden in a valley of strip-farmed fields and terraced vineyards. I followed the tracks of a preserved steam railway into the village from a *Märchenwald*. The main street of gabled, single-storey houses was deserted, its shutters closed against the midday heat. I sat in the shade outside the only café, but nobody came to serve me. At the head of the street was an obelisk of roughly hewn local stone in the shape of a pylon. This was once the "Burgenlanddenkmal", erected in 1931 by a local student association to commemorate the tenth anniversary of the new Austrian province, transferred from Hungary by the Treaty of Saint-Germain in 1919. In its original incarnation it was capped by a square copper fire bowl and resembled an ur-Germanic sacrificial stone. The local newspaper described it as a "declaration of the German character of the youth of the Burgenland". *Der Anschluss*, the Viennese organ of the Austro-German People's Union, called it "an expression of hope for the future common German Fatherland". A tablet on the back of the monument read "Towering stone – remind future generations that they are the eternal guardians of Germany". The wrought-iron Gothic inscription on the front of the stone proclaimed "Germany our Fatherland", until the provincial government decided this was overstating the case and ordered the slogan to be toned down to "German for all time".

At a ceremony in the spring of 1938, the Burgenlanddenkmal, decorated with a wreathed swastika and surrounded by Nazi banners, was renamed the "Anschlussdenkmal". Afterwards the local committee for the upkeep of the monument convened and decided the obelisk was not grand enough to commemorate Austria's "homecoming into the Reich of Adolf Hitler". They resolved to erect a new, larger monument, a shrine which would become the focal point of the Third Reich in Austria; "a memorial to true *Deutschtum* on the eastern border of the Reich"; "a holy place of the nation, the first in the liberated Ostmark". The village elders commissioned the Graz architect Rudolf Hofer to design the new monument, which would be built on a more dramatic site, overlooking Oberschützen and the surrounding valleys. Hofer, like his more illustrious peer Albert Speer, was inspired by the Reichsehrenmal Tannenberg, whose octagonal composition of towers and walls formed a blueprint for many National Socialist "holy sites". Hofer's original sketches for an octagonal monument were eventually pared down to a square *Ehrenhof* surrounded on three sides by a pillared arcade. The final design, approved by the committee, was of a square temple, open to the skies, with a colonnade of three arches on each side. Within the temple stood eight "fire pylons", concrete pillars supporting braziers to illuminate the monument at night, creating the desired aura of blood and sacrifice that appealed to the pagan fantasies of the National Socialists. The centrepiece was a gold-painted *Reichsadler*, over two metres high, clutching an oak-wreathed swastika in its talons. The eagle's wings were half opened in a defensive posture and its look was directed towards the south-east, as if guarding the border of the new Reich against its Slavic foes. The stone plinth on which the eagle was mounted bore the legend "Ein Volk! Ein Reich! Ein Führer!"

The foundation stone of the new Anschlussdenkmal was laid on 7 August 1938 in the presence of the regional governor of the Burgenland and deputy Gauleiter of Styria Tobias Portschy, who, like many of the Nazi top brass in south-east Austria, came from the village of Oberschützen. (Portschy was a lawyer and amateur "racial scientist" whose inflammatory pamphlet entitled *Die Zigeunerfrage*, "The Gypsy Question", I had seen on display in the museum at Mauthausen, where thousands of Austrian Roma and Sinti were exterminated.) The official consecration of the new monument took place on 21 May 1939 and was presided over by the Gauleiter of Styria, Siegfried Uiberreither. The ceremony was accompanied by a sports display from the Hitler Youth and the League of German Girls, and a theatrical production of *Frankenburger Würfelspiel*, a pseudo-historical drama penned by Eberhard Wolfgang Möller of the Nazi Propaganda Ministry. A plane flew low over the hill and successfully dropped a wreath into the centre of the monument.

I walked down to the centre of Oberschützen where there was a painted wooden map of the village. A conventional symbol indicated a monument on the outskirts of the village on the road towards Oberwart. I followed the road and soon discovered the Anschlussdenkmal on the top of a hill overlooking the village. I was surprised to find that it still existed. In Germany an explicitly National Socialist monument like this would have been demolished, as were the Ehrentempel on the Königsplatz in Munich, whose basic structure the Anschlussdenkmal resembled. The fire pylons and eagle had naturally been removed and the Nazi slogan erased from the central plinth. There was no evidence that the monument was being used as a neo-Nazi shrine. In fact, the graffiti spray-painted on the pillars of the colonnade was commendably anti-fascist – "Racism kills", "Nazis out!" – and the local community had erected a plaque in commemoration of the fiftieth anniversary of the end of the Second World War, which read: "May this place be a reminder to us today and in the future. Against dictatorship, against violence, against racism. For democracy, for peace, and for the preservation of human rights."

It seemed at first a remote place for the National Socialists to build their only "Weihestätte" (sacred site) in the country, as the southern Burgenland is as far away from Germany as you can get in Austria. But when I considered other communities on the edge of the German-speaking world (the South Tyrolese, the Sudeten Germans and the East Prussians, for example), I realised that inhabitants of the outlying reach of the empire were probably in greater need of the centrifugal pull of the Reich than those closer to home. Liberated in 1921 from Hungarian hegemony, the ur-Bavarian *Burgenländer* quickly became "more German than the Germans"; certainly more pro-German than their Austrian compatriots, who wished at all costs to preserve the independence of their new republic. The Burgenland was therefore fertile soil for the propagation of National Socialist ideas. The village of Oberschützen and the nearby town of Oberwart became centres of National Socialist activity during the late 1920s and 1930s. Oberschützen in particular became a Nazi "Hochburg": almost all the Party functionaries who administered the Burgenland came from the village. The 1934 prohibition in Austria of the National Socialists served only to intensify the "brown revolution" in the local area.

The most conspicuous absence from the monuments of Oberschützen was, of course, Austria. None of the inscriptions on either the Burgenlanddenkmal or the Anschlussdenkmal made a single reference to Austria. It was as if the *Burgenländer*, those in Oberschützen at least, went from Hungarian fiefdom in 1921 to the German Reich in 1938 without passing through the Austrian Republic. In Oberschützen there were no "Kruckenkreuze", the old crusaders' cross adopted by the Austro-fascist Fatherland Front in the 1930s; nor were there any of the double-headed eagles of the old empire and monarchy, peering in both directions from beneath the architrave of the monument. Here there was just a single golden *Reichsadler* set squarely in the centre of the peristyle of the Anschlussdenkmal, with wings like sharks' fins and talons the size of grappling hooks – a symbol of the loyalty of the *Burgenländer* to the greater Reich; of contempt for republican Austria; and of aggression towards outsiders: "One people! One empire! One leader!"

5

Moravia

Sinfonietta in Purple and Green

I returned to Vienna and the following day drove east to Bratislava where, for the first time on my journey, I spent a night in a city which had belonged to neither the Holy Roman Empire nor the German Reich. In the morning I headed north, stopping in Malacky, where I spent my last Slovak crowns[3] on a cup of coffee. Turning left at Holič and driving towards the Czech border, I noticed a police car hidden behind a row of trees as I approached the customs post. I eased my foot off the accelerator and halted at the white STOP sign painted across the road. I waited there for thirty seconds and then glanced back at the passport official. He ignored me, so I put the car into first gear and inched forward, all the while looking back at the official. He waited until I had changed into second gear before pulling out a whistle and summoning me back to the STOP sign. After leaving me waiting for a further minute or two, he ordered me out of the car and marched me into a guard room, where we had a mutually unintelligible argument about our differing interpretations of the STOP sign. I claimed I had stopped at the sign, waited for a reasonable period, was not specifically bidden to wait any longer, and was therefore free to proceed. His argument, as far as I could ascertain, was that I was to remain at the STOP sign until he had ceased ignoring me and decided to attend to me. He was in a particularly officious mood, further aggravated once he realised I had no crowns left to pay the fine he produced after much triplicate form-filling and rubber-stamping. I made

---

3   This was before Slovakia joined the eurozone on 1 January 2009.

it clear that the contents of my wallet amounted to fifteen euros, which he was welcome to keep if we could bring this matter to a swift conclusion.

Once these bureaucratic niceties had been completed, I left Slovak territory and proceeded through the no-man's-land of woods and water meadows between the Slovak customs post and the River Morava, which forms the border between Slovakia and the Czech Republic. A pair of grey pipelines snaked along the edge of the forest. Latticed concrete tracks disappeared into the trees. A metal wheatsheaf, shorn of its Socialist greeting or valediction and riddled with bullet holes, leaked rust into its framing concrete plinth. Small white studs of concrete were set into the banks on either side of the river, in case the two formerly confederate nations decided to invade each other. Suspended over the Czech customs area were large signs depicting a red cross and a bolt of lightning superimposed over the figure of a man standing on top of a lorry: a warning to Polish lorry drivers that they would be electrocuted by power lines if they stood on top of their rigs. The Czech customs officials waved me straight through and I headed towards a quartet of red-and-white-striped chimneys spewing plumes of pink smoke into the blue sky above Hodonín.

I parked in T.G. Masaryk Square between a vanilla-coloured baroque church and a Jugendstil town hall. A band of tattooed, leather-pouched neo-hippies had set up a medieval craft fair in the gardens of the square. They were selling bearskins, hand-blown glassware and hand-carved wooden trolls, hammering on anvils and staging knockabout jousts to the accompaniment of dulcimers and flageolets. Národní Street was lined with crumbling nineteenth-century houses converted into shops: the dowdy stockings and glittery tops in the window of Česka Moda were beginning to fade in the sunlight; and the flyblown yellow plastic sunblind over the window of Česka Knigy prevented one from reading the titles of the books in dusty stacks inside. The more enterprising Vietnamese markets were doing a brisk trade in trainers, sandals, flip-flops and shell suits. In my brash Western way, I inadvertently pushed in to use a cash dispenser without realising people were queuing on the pavement behind me. My subsequent apologies in English were met with a resigned indifference, as if the Czechs expected me, a Westerner, to barge to the front. To compensate for my misplaced assertiveness, I went and sat meekly in a café on Národní Square – and the waitresses ignored me.

Leaving Hodonín behind, I drove north through a hilly landscape of yellow and brown chargrilled fields. Weedy vineyards alternated with strips of stubble strewn with pumpkins, wilting sunflowers, shreds of torn plastic and discarded bottles. Clumps of wasteland full of thistles and bracken rose out of the unkempt countryside. Concrete tracks led through fields to disused enclosures of corrugated iron surrounded by rusting barbed-wire fences. I struggled with an unwieldy analogy between the fresh green meadows cropped like pool tables and the roads delineated by trim white lines that I had left behind in Austria, and how they paralleled the air-conditioned, double-glazed, four-star hotel in which I had stayed in Vienna; and the coarse, soiled Moravian hills that were a foretaste of the smoky, sweaty hotel room in which I would doubtless find myself on my arrival in Brno.

The capital of Moravia lay in a bowl of smog beneath a bruised evening sky. The smells of smoke, drains, chemicals and two-stroke petrol grew more pungent as I drove through the suburbs. Lampposts hung like insects' antennae over streets lined with billboards, rusted ČSAD bus shelters and endless walls of prefabricated concrete. The traffic flow led me in confused circles around a series of cobbled open spaces criss-crossed by tramlines – around a bus station, a railway station and a Tesco. The supermarket was a Soviet-era concrete bunker rather than the postmodern brownfield mall one would find in the Home Counties. I eventually breached the defences of the one-way system and found myself in an *Innenstadt* resembling a provincial Vienna circa 1973. I parked in front of the Hotel Slavia, just off the former Ringstraße. An imposing receptionist wearing a severe white blouse with a peroxide-dyed bouffant checked me in, before passing me on to a young porter with a lank pudding-bowl haircut in a matching suit and tie of electric blue. He accompanied me from the polished marble of the lobby, via an antiquated lift with collapsible doors, to the fourth floor. The walls, carpets and padded doors of the hotel corridors were decorated in various shades of brown and smelled of stewing meat and leeks. The bathroom suite of my attic room was a particular shade of orangey brown that gave me a Proustian moment, provoking a memory from my childhood that I couldn't quite place.

From my window on the top floor of the Hotel Slavia, a provincial, poor man's version of the Hotel Sacher, I surveyed the Habsburg skyline of Brno. On a hill to the left was the Gothic Cathedral of Peter and Paul; on a hill to the right the baroque fortress of Špilberk. In the city below were churches with squashed onion domes or needle-sharp spires, palaces with urn-laden cornices and balconies supported by carbonised caryatids – a cityscape built in the 1890s whose inhabitants lived in the 1970s. A stratum of Socialist Realism lay over all the *Viennoiserie* like a layer of grime. The outlines of dismantled hammers, spades and sickles disfigured the pediments of grandiloquent Historicist ministries. Half-erased slogans ran around the façades of museums and workers' organisations. The concrete bunker of an all-purpose shopping mall lay in the shadow of the concrete block of the Premier Hotel International. Lumpy, angular statues squatted on threadbare lawns. Two Romany lads were begging in the car park below, scaring off the customers to such an extent that one couple returned to move their car somewhere else, despite having given the boys three lots of coins. As I dropped off to sleep, to the accompaniment of the grind and whine of tramcars on Husova, it dawned on me that the colour of my bathroom suite was that of butterscotch Angel Delight, a delicacy from the early 1970s.

The waitress glared at me as I arrived for breakfast the following morning. It was getting late (ten minutes to ten) and I was not affiliated to a group. The faux-Viennese breakfast room was illuminated by chandeliers of white plastic globes within oblong brass cages. Each cage held six globes, but in none of them did all six globes work simultaneously. I was still looking for a pattern in the malfunctioning lights when my breakfast arrived: four different combinations of salads accompanied by cold rice, cold pasta, strips of luncheon meat and tomato sauce. The bread roll disintegrated when I tried to cut it. The serviette disintegrated when I opened it; just like the toilet paper in the bathroom had. The tea was undrinkable.

After breakfast I wandered around the city centre, through market squares crowded with shoppers. The streets reverberated with shock waves from pneumatic drills laying new tram lines. I walked down Česka and Veselá towards Freedom Square. Austrian establishments (Julius Meinl coffee shops, Palmers lingerie stores, Raiffeisen banks) were interspersed with old-fashioned, wood-panelled chemists, jewellers and bookshops, and kiosks run by Vietnamese immigrants selling cigarettes, magazines, currency and lottery tickets. The most imposing shops were the chrome, glass and black steel emporia built in the late 1920s by Bat'a, "shoemakers to the world", as symbols of the modernist utopia of the young Czechoslovak Republic.

To escape the heat and noise of the city, I ascended the winding streets of cafés and pasta bars above Zelný trh (the former Cabbage Market) up towards the cathedral. A marble obelisk flanked by four golden lions stood on the terrace of the Denis Orchards, one of the old bastions of the city. On its base was a pair of bronze allegories of Trade and Industry, which once embellished a statue of Emperor Joseph II outside the former

German House on Moravian Square. Erected in 1818, the obelisk commemorated the Battle of the Nations at Leipzig and the triumph of the German nations over Napoleon. The German inscriptions were removed in 1918. Below, red trams screeched along Husova Boulevard, past neoclassical galleries and libraries, past the red brick Protestant church and the neo-Gothic hall of the Brünner Turnverein, the former German Gymnastics Club. Southern Brno lay spread out in concentric circles, from the flaking pink and ochre Habsburg villas in the centre of the city, to the suburbs of modernist tenements built during the inter-war years of the First Republic. Beyond them rose the high-rise tower blocks of communist Czechoslovakia, reaching up into the forested hills around the city.

Nineteenth-century Brno (Brünn in German) was a predominantly German city known as "Austrian Manchester" or "Moravian Manchester". It was the centre of the woollen industry in Central Europe and the hub of the industrial revolution within the Habsburg territories. Civic activity was dominated by liberal German business associations and German cultural associations – cycling clubs and choral societies as well as the Gymnastics Club. In 1910 the population of Brünn consisted of eighty-one thousand German speakers and forty-one thousand Czech speakers. After the birth of the Czechoslovak Republic in 1918, many outlying towns were incorporated into the city, and the Moravian capital metamorphosed from a small bourgeois German city into a large Czech workers' conurbation. Initially the two communities continued to live and work together. Brno remained a bilingual city where members of both communities spoke each other's language (the Germans' hard dialect was called *Prienerisch*). Nevertheless, German Brünn was gradually displaced by Czechoslovak Brno, and many Germans emigrated during the 1930s. Those who remained at the end of the Second World War (about twenty-six thousand women, children and pensioners) were forcibly rounded up by workers from the Zbrojovka arms factory in the early hours of the morning of 30 May 1945. They were assembled in the Cabbage Market and driven "like a herd of cattle" towards the Austrian frontier. During the march at least two thousand people died from hunger, thirst or typhus, or were raped or shot by their handlers. Many of the survivors eventually found their way to the "new Brünn" of Schwäbisch Gmünd in the Swabian Alb.

Inside the white Secessionist waiting room of the railway station travellers sat on marble plinths, perusing the timetables which revolved slowly inside tall brass cylinders. The station had been renovated to mark the

one-hundred-and-fiftieth anniversary of the Brno–Vienna main line. I had
a coffee in the restaurant, a large room decorated with creamy pilasters
and architraves gilded with Art Nouveau locomotive wheels. I had to listen to a song by the Eurythmics and breathe the odour of fried onions,
neither of which was a particularly pleasant experience. It seemed as if
every tram route in Brno converged on the open space in front of the
station, and the harsh metallic cacophony of screeching iron wheels soon
proved even less pleasing to the ear than *Sweet Dreams (Are Made of
This)*. The Czechs are by a long way the most prolific tram passengers
in Europe. An average distance of 830 kilometres per year is travelled by
each Czech, placing them way ahead of their nearest rivals the Austrians,
who travel an average of 350 kilometres per annum by tram. A five-storey-
high canvas screen with a blown-up image of André Agassi and Steffi Graf
looked down over the tram junction, an advertisement hoarding on behalf
of T-Mobile, emblematic of Germany's corporate re-colonisation of the
Czech lands in the post-Communist era.

I followed the tramlines around the old Ringstraße until I reached the
swathe of parkland between Rooseveltova and Koliště. Overlooking the
park is the Mahen Theatre, a stately neo-Renaissance building with an
imposing loggia and pediment crowned by statuettes of Orpheus, Dionysus
and the Nine Muses. Designed by the Viennese architects Fellner and
Helmer and designated the German Theatre of Moravia, it was completed
in 1882 and had the distinction of being the first theatre in Europe to
install electric lighting. In 1918 it came under Czechoslovak directorship
and was renamed the Theatre on the Trenches, after the fortified ditches
over which the Ringstraße had been laid in the mid-nineteenth century.
Local German theatre companies were at first permitted to perform their
productions on Monday and Tuesday evenings. However, cultural and
linguistic tensions began to run high, and in 1920 there was a riot when
a crowd of Czech nationalists forced their way into the foyer and interrupted a German production of *Carmen* because they disapproved of a
guest appearance by the Russian bass Yuri Baklanoff. Under the patron-
age of the National Socialist Protectorate of Bohemia and Moravia the
roles were reversed, and Czech companies were allowed only Monday
and Tuesday evenings on which to stage their repertoire. After the Second
World War it became the Janáček Theatre – until the new Janáček Theatre
was completed in 1965. It was then renamed after Jiří Mahen, a nationalist playwright, poet and newspaper editor who had worked there as a
repertory adviser.

Commanding the upper spaces of the park, the new theatre dedicated to Moravia's national composer is difficult to miss. Constructed in a style that could politely be termed International Totalitarian, the colossal monolith features a heavy attic roof, rectilinear pilasters and tall, narrow windows, all reminiscent of the National Socialist edifices of Munich and Nuremberg. The concrete sculptures and bronze reliefs flanking the entrance portal are in a Socialist Abstract idiom and must once have glorified some long-forgotten principles of heroic Communism. A statue of the composer, clad in a bronze overcoat, gazes over a stone forecourt of military proportions that now seems like a metaphor for the pretentiousness and ineptitude of Socialist urban design: marble flagstones that have cracked open, revealing jagged veins of tarmac beneath them; a marble fountain empty of water into which rubble has been tipped; rusted six-pronged flagpoles devoid of flags; floodlights without light bulbs; a low enclosing wall that is slowly crumbling to pieces. Václav Havel remarked that it will take another two generations before the footprints of Communism can be wiped away.

It is difficult to connect this neo-functionalist monolith with the music of Leoš Janáček. The composer was inspired by Czechoslovak patriotism and Slavic folk songs and dances. His operas were a folksy riposte to the Germanic dramas of Wagner; his *Sinfonietta* a joyous urban retort to the lush symphonic landscapes of Brahms, Bruckner and Mahler. The *Sinfonietta* was written for a Sokol gymnastics festival in 1926. It was dedicated partly to the English music critic Rosa Newmarch, and partly to the Czechoslovak Armed Forces. The dynamic opening fanfare of drums and trumpets expressed the soul of the new Czechoslovak man: "the contemporary free man, his spiritual beauty and joy, his strength, courage and determination for victory". The work celebrated the transformation of the streets and landmarks of Janáček's native city from oppressed Habsburg Brünn to liberated Czechoslovak Brno. The composer wrote in a lyric pamphlet entitled *Moje Město* ("My City"):

I once beheld the city in miraculous transformation. My disgust for the gloomy town hall and hatred for the hill in whose bowels once I screamed with pain disappeared; and with it my disgust for the street and that which went on there.

A bewitching halo of freedom illuminated the city, reborn on the 28th October 1918.

I gazed over it: I belonged to it.

The sound of victorious car horns;
and a glorious stillness from the monastery in Úvoz.
Night shadows and the breath of the green hills.

And dreams of the city's expansion and of its grandeur gave birth to my
Sinfonietta –
A hymn to my city of Brno!

The hill that filled Janáček with such hatred was the Špilberk, the symbol
of former Austrian oppression that overlooks the centre of Brno from the
west. The Špilberk fortress was originally a medieval castle built during
the age of the Přemysl dynasty. In the eighteenth century it was enlarged
into a baroque stronghold, which became a notorious prison where
common criminals languished for years in its dank casemates, shackled together, even as they slept, on sloping wooden boards. Hungarian
Jacobins, Italian *carbonari* from Lombardy and Veneto, and Polish insurgents from Galicia and Sandomierska were among the political prisoners
of the Habsburg monarchy confined in the upper storey of a high-security
prison wing added in 1800. From March 1939 to July 1940 the Špilberk
served as the headquarters of the Gestapo in Moravia. Austrian antifascists from the Mikulov region who defended the Czechoslovak borders
against the Wehrmacht in 1938 were incarcerated here; as were Liberal
Democratic politicians from Brno, members of the Moravian branch of
the Organisation of National Defence, and Czechs from Kladno arrested
in retaliation for the shooting of a German police reservist. Communist
resistance fighters and organisers of illegal border crossings were tortured
in the cells. A small museum in the Špilberk includes among its exhibits the
badges of political prisoners held by the Gestapo in the halls of residence
of the University of Brno in the suburb of Kounic. There are fragments
of bullets picked up from the execution yard at Kounic, and stocks found
in the Faculty of Law building in Veveří Street. From the Špilberk itself
there are handcuffs, bullwhips, metal truncheons, yellow stars forcibly
worn by Jews, a rubber stamp used to certify "of Aryan racial origin" and
a miniature gallows that served as a plaything on the desk of the Gestapo
official responsible for court martials. The final exhibit is a book bound in
human skin from the concentration camp of Buchenwald entitled *Feinde
des Volkes* ("Enemies of the People").

I drove down into Olomouc from the E462 expressway. All the city's lampposts and tram poles had been painted purple, and the railings that fenced off the tramway reservation in the centre of the road were a chemical green colour normally associated with shampoo or disinfectant – as if some paint had been left over from the days of the planned economy. Banks of suburban high-rise flats gave way to peeling ochre Habsburg townhouses as I approached the foot of Havličkova and arrived in the centre of Olomouc. I checked into the Hotel Gemo on Třída Svobody (Freedom Avenue), the boulevard around the old centre. Like Brno, it echoed to the screech and groan of Tatra T-3s negotiating a triangular network of tramlines forming the junction of Havličkova and Třída Svobody. The hotel was a new four-star establishment with tasteful furnishings, air conditioning, soundproofed windows, vanity packs and other mod cons. The one drawback was that the central heating was on full blast and could not be turned down by the knob on the radiator. The prospect of trying to sleep on a hot August night in sauna conditions, with a tram interchange in the boulevard outside, filled me with dread; but I decided, correctly as it transpired, to trust that the hotel would switch the heating off later in the evening.

I wandered back up Havličkova to look at a war memorial on the edge of the parkland that had been laid over the city's former fortifications. It was a Memorial of Liberation in honour of the Soviet Army, which occupied Olomouc on 7 and 8 May 1945. On a stepped plinth, the fifteen-metre obelisk was a twentieth-century version of the baroque plague columns adorning the cities of Central Europe; a monument of thanksgiving to the new religion of Communism which had replaced the old religion of Catholicism. Instead of the traditional scrolls of Latin religious texts there were bronze inscriptions in Cyrillic script to the "fallen heroes of the Soviet Army" affixed to the base of the column, and a factory-produced red neon star surmounted the pillar in lieu of the Holy Spirit. This was apparently the first monument to the Red Army to be erected in Czechoslovakia. It was commissioned at short notice from the Bohemian architect Jaroslav Kovář and unveiled in July 1945 to cries of "Long live the great, wise Stalin, father and teacher of all oppressed peoples! Long live Dr Eduard Beneš, great friend of the Soviet Union!"

As dusk fell I recrossed Třída Svobody and entered the Upper Square. Horní Náměstí was a large asymmetrical space with the town hall in its centre. Coloured floodlights illuminated the walls of the Renaissance *radnice* with a purple-pink glow. A quartet of golden spheres glittered atop the pinnacles clustered around its spire. To my left was the sand-stone Column of the Holy Trinity, the tallest plague column in the Czech Republic, which rose thirty-five metres in an organic, almost faecal moun-tain of saints, martyrs, bishops and cherubs. Scattered around the square were fountains and statues celebrating the history of the city, from its founder Julius Caesar to a bronze turtle bearing the imprints of the city's coins, seals, stamps and charters on the verdigris of its shell. The *náměstí* was enclosed on all sides by a palette of primrose, salmon, olive and grey townhouses, built in every architectural style of the Habsburg Empire, from Gothic to Jugendstil. A solitary police car was hidden in the shad-ows of the black steel walls and chrome-framed windows of Bat'a.

On the south-western side of the square was a cream building with a pediment inlaid with shields and flowing ribbons above its Renaissance façade. This was the municipal theatre, home to the Moravian Philharmonic Orchestra. A tiny noticeboard fixed to its door announced forthcoming productions of a comic operetta by Karel Novak; a musical based on the life of Edith Piaf; Janáček's *The Cunning Little Vixen;* and something unidentifiable by Goethe. Gustav Mahler had been appointed *Kapellmeister* of the Philharmonic in 1883. I found it difficult to imagine the manic, intense Mahler surviving for long in the provincial backwater of Olmütz, as the city was known in the days of the Empire. Mahler was twenty-three years old at the time, a young bohemian with a head full of Wagner. Arriving with long dishevelled hair, the beginnings of a straggly goatee and a horn-rimmed pince-nez perched on his "very prom-inent nose" (according to the local baritone Jacques Manheit), his initial appearance shocked the staid musicians of Olmütz. Without introducing himself, he launched into his first rehearsal of *Les Huguenots.* Several hours later the choral singers walked out, hoarse, exhausted and in tears, refusing to work any longer with the young tyro. During the interval of his public debut two days later, members of the orchestra complained they couldn't follow the maestro's directions because he repeatedly covered his face with his hands. Mahler explained that his pince-nez kept falling off his nose, so he attached it to his head with a black ribbon. This only served to make things worse, as the musicians found themselves unable to concentrate on their playing, so amused were they by their conduc-tor's ridiculous appearance. After the performance Mahler was invited, to the dismay of the orchestra, to the nearby Goliath Restaurant. To the derision of the beer-swilling, pork-loin-eating musicians, he ordered a glass of water and a bowl of spinach; apparently he believed that being a strict Wagnerite entailed being an equally strict vegetarian. Mahler's driven, autocratic style earned him the dislike of the local press as well as the disdain of his musicians. He in turn was frustrated by the insensitivity and lack of talent of the orchestra, likening his tenure in Olmütz to that of "the finest horse harnessed to an ox cart". He refused to perform the operas of Mozart and Wagner, believing they would be desecrated by the "poor folk" of his orchestra. Instead, he restricted their repertoire to the works of Verdi, Bizet and Meyerbeer. Mahler doubtless raised the standards of the Moravian Philharmonic during his brief spell with the orchestra, but it was clear that he was destined for wider horizons. Three months into his stewardship he was, much to the orchestra's relief, packed off to Budapest.

I tucked into a meal of roast duck and red cabbage on the terrace of the Pivnice Opera in Upper Square. The other diners were a Yorkshire couple and a quartet of women from Liverpool. Afterwards I walked around Dolní Náměstí, the adjoining, lopsided Lower Square, where the locals sat drinking beer on the steps around fountains and statues of Neptune, Jupiter and Mercury. I continued through silent, unlit, cobbled backstreets towards Náměstí Republiky, passing a dark, blistered building on Ulice Mahlerova that bore the faded German legend "Café-Restaurant Bergmann". A pack of feral dogs lurked in the shadows behind another stationary police car. Ulice 1. Maje led into the episcopal quarter of Jesuit churches, collegiate schools and university faculties that bear testimony to the staunchly Catholic history of Olmütz, an anti-Hussite, anti-Reformation, anti-Semitic city whose Jewish gravestones were recycled as flagstones for the new seminaries of the Jesuit era. The core of medieval Olmütz juts out in a promontory over the River Morava, crowned by Saint Wenceslas Cathedral and the Romanesque Přemyslid Palace, where Wenceslas III, last of the Přemyslids, was murdered in mysterious circumstances in 1306. Olmütz remained the royal capital of Moravia until 1641 when, in contrast to Brünn, it was sacked by Swedish troops during the final stages of the Thirty Years' War. The rebuilt city enjoyed a renaissance during the mid-eighteenth century when Empress Maria Theresa, in her role as Margravine of Moravia, visited to consecrate the Column of the Holy Trinity. In 1848 the Imperial Court descended on Olmütz to escape the bourgeois revolution in Vienna; and the new emperor Franz Joseph I was crowned in the Archbishop's Palace at the end of that year. Two years later the Punctuation of Olmütz between Austria and Prussia breathed new life into the failing German Confederation, the Greater Germany

espoused by the Bavarian King Ludwig I. This explains why the Kingdom
of Bohemia and the Margraviate of Moravia are commemorated on the
tablets surrounding the Befreiungshalle, which was completed around the
same time in the 1850s.

I returned to Upper Square just before 10 pm to hear the astronomical clock chime. The original fifteenth-century clock, a complex cos-
mological symbiosis of Classical and Christian elements, was destroyed
by a grenade during the final days of the Second World War. It was not
beyond restoration, but a year later the Communist-controlled Office
for the Preservation of National Monuments in Brno instructed the city
council of Olomouc to rebuild a completely new clock "in the spirit of
the present era" (in other words, to get rid of the old bourgeois German
Catholic clock). The current ensemble of astronomical clocks and lunar
medallions that represent the twelve months of the year was designed by
Karel Svolinský and unveiled on 9 May 1955 in what was then known as
Stalin Square. It is a curious mixture of Czech folklore and Soviet-inspired
Socialist Realism set into an apse filled with gold-painted mosaic like a
Byzantine iconostasis. Below the clocks are the heroic figures of a worker
in blue overalls clutching a spanner and a white-coated chemist analysing
a retort full of green liquid. At the top of the apse is a relief depicting three
noblemen on horseback clad in the traditional Moravian costume of flat
beribboned caps and billowing mutton-chop sleeves. Below them is a procession of noblewomen in ruffs and dirndls bearing a garlanded canopy,
beneath which a margravine reclines on a bed of cushions. The sixteen
marionettes rotating on the stroke of each hour include musicians, factory
workers, a commissar wearing a smart powder-blue suit and trilby, and a
pair of gymnasts in those high-waisted floppy, white flannel shorts worn
by Soviet-bloc sports teams in the 1950s. I half-expected the glockenspiel
accompanying their gyrations to play *The Red Flag* or the *Internationale,*
but the audience was treated to some forgotten folk melodies instead. A
little golden hen in the centre of the apse told the time.

In a small square below the brooding Church of Saint Maurice was a
lounge bar with banks of televisions transmitting the Italian-style erotic
variété shows which have become the staple diet of broadcasting in the
newer countries of the European Union. On the terrace outside, Czech
teenagers chatted and flirted quietly over a caffé latte. The relaxed ambience was disturbed only by a table of four German men with booming
voices and death-rattle laughs who seemed determined to flaunt their
beery, vulgar Germanness. I returned to Upper Square for a coffee and

becherovka outside the Café Corso. I felt suddenly very tired, experiencing for the first time a sense of alienation in a place where I could not speak the language. I bought a packet of Czech cigarettes, which only served to make me feel worse. At the table next to mine sat a skinny young Oriental woman dressed in a grey top, blue jeans and white stilettos. She was reading a tourist brochure and flicking through snapshots on her camera. She yawned a lot and seemed oblivious to everyone around her. I wondered whether she was a Chinese tourist who had lost the rest of her coach party and was marooned in Olomouc. Or a Japanese guide catching a few minutes to herself in the middle of a hectic schedule? Or the daughter of a local Vietnamese shopkeeper? I was tempted to ask her, but felt she would think I was trying to chat her up; which wouldn't have been far from the truth. An overwhelming desire for intimacy made me feel even lonelier. I decided it was time to return to my overheated hotel room.

D riving from Vienna on another occasion, I beheld Znojmo lying sprawled above slopes of vineyards on the next ridge of hills. Silhouetted against the late afternoon sun, its spires and turrets still formed the same townscape as that illustrated (as German Znaim) in a copperplate engraving from *Merians Topographie* of 1650. The illusion was marred, however, as I approached the town. Billboards along the road advertised rooms at the Moulin Rouge, the Venus House or the Pink Panther, at prices starting from 39 euros; presumably the price of the subsequent sexual transaction was negotiable. The cheaper prostitutes, buxom, swarthy Romany women with peroxide-dyed hair, stood by the roadside or sat glassy-eyed and cross-legged in bus shelters. Sex supermarkets such as The Erotic House or World of Sex catered for a less personal erotic thrill; and when the Austrian punters had exhausted their libido, they could fritter away their remaining euros at the gaming machines in the *Spielotheken*. A pungent smell of two-stroke petrol mingled with woodsmoke emanated from rows of prefabricated apartment blocks, each built from identical corrugated concrete panels to which identical corrugated plastic balconies had been appended. An all-purpose shopping mall shaped like a concrete shoebox was in front of the Hotel Dukla. Neon signs flashed up lottery numbers from the windows of newsagents and tobacconists. The residents of the flats stood around clutching plastic bags while they queued for buses or waited to cross the road, seemingly oblivious to the venality in their midst.

The main road twisted upwards into a mini-Ringstraße with pock-marked *fin-de-siècle* buildings on one side and scruffy parks containing empty fountains and statues of unremembered Socialist poets on the other. The deserted market square, Masarykovo Náměstí, drifted down towards a German *Mariensäule,* a baroque column "renewed during the glorious reign of Emperor Franz I of Austria in 1823, which offers gratitude for the deliverance of Znaim from the fires and plagues of 1679 and 1687". The town hall had a copper spire rotated at a forty-five-degree angle to its Gothic tower, each gallery of the spire surmounted by a quartet of tur-rets topped by golden globes. Cars drove over the potholed streets with painstaking slowness and exaggerated care, signalling right or left even when following the bends of the main road. I discovered why when I was pulled over by the police on the outskirts of Znojmo for exceeding the urban speed limit. The fine was one thousand crowns, which I did not have; I had stopped in Znojmo to change money, but had failed to locate a working cash dispenser. Thanks to the Slovak customs official, I had no euros either. I offered them my remaining twenty-five pounds, the sterling equivalent of the fine, but they weren't interested. Amazingly, they issued me with a payment slip and asked me to pay the fine at the next available post office, once I had purchased some Czech currency.

I took a left turn at the top of a hill and set off on a drive around the edge of the Czech Republic. My intention was to travel through the area known in German as the Sudetenland, from Znojmo in southern Moravia to Liberec in northern Bohemia. The term Sudetenland needs to be used with a degree of care (not in the presence of Czechs, for example), since it has German nationalist and specific National Socialist connotations. The word originated from the Sudeten Mountains that form part of the geo-graphical border between Poland and north-eastern Bohemia. The phrase "Sudeten Germans" was first coined by a hiking instructor named Franz Jesser at the beginning of the twentieth century. It gradually came into popular usage to denote the German-speaking communities of Bohemia, Moravia and Silesia who inhabited the mountainous rim around the Czech lands, together with isolated linguistic islands such as Iglau (Jihlava in Czech, where Gustav Mahler was born). It acquired a political mean-ing on 28 October 1918, when the First Republic of Czechoslovakia was founded. The *Sudetendeutsche* reacted immediately by announcing the integration of their disparate, isolated territories into the new Austrian republic of Deutsch-Österreich. This, however, was not a geographically viable option unless Austria formed an *Anschluss* with Germany, which at the time was forbidden by the peace treaties. In spite of Woodrow Wilson's stated principles of national self-determination, the Treaties of Versailles and Saint-Germain confirmed the existing historical borders of the Bohemian and Moravian crownlands and ignored the claims of the Sudeten Germans, who thus found themselves a chain of minority communities strung around the fringes of the new Czechoslovak state.

And so Sudetenland, a geographically incorrect term that deliberately created a false impression of a homogenous, joined-up *Volk,* came into its spurious existence, illustrated on German maps (the Czechoslovaks refused to countenance its actuality) as a grey penumbra around the Czech-speaking territory. Its official political existence began on 1 October 1938, when the Wehrmacht occupied the German-speaking administrative areas of Czechoslovakia. In April 1939 the National Socialist authorities perpetuated the misnomer by creating a "Gau Sudetenland" as an integral part of the German Reich, thus keeping "German" Sudetenland separate from the rest of Czechoslovakia. The latter was designated a Reich Protectorate (in much the same way that the Mafia "protects" the people it bullies) or, in the case of Slovakia, a "friendly" puppet state. According to the books and maps printed in Germany by publishers who specialise in revisionist literature about Silesia, East Prussia and the Sudetenland, it is just possible to travel around the present Czech Republic, from Znojmo to Liberec, within the borders of the former Sudetenland, those being the German "borders of 1938" to which German revisionist historians like to adhere.

I set off west along empty, bumpy roads, hogging the Austrian border. It was early evening and a single layer of pearly cloud remained in the sky. Tractors and combine harvesters were the only other traffic, and the air swam with corn dust that settled on apple trees along the roadside. The road wound up through forests to the vertiginous castle of Vranov, and then continued into upland pastures. In the distance I could make out a strip of fallow land studded with trees and watchtowers, which marked the former control strip on the Czechoslovak side of the border. Beyond the woods along the actual border I could see the mills and silos of the Austrian Waldviertel. In Czech villages like Uherčice and Rancířov, villagers congregated in low houses along the banks of streams, forming makeshift open-air pubs by placing chairs together in vegetable plots on either side of the stream. The road ran in detours around backstreets where storks clattered along rooftops. Derelict castles and palaces bore witness to the German and Austrian aristocrats who had ruled these lands for centuries, until their estates were confiscated by the state in the land reforms of 1919, or until they were finally deported in 1946. I paused briefly by a roadside shrine to the Virgin Mary engraved with a dedication in German to the memory of Karl and Maria Melzer, who died in 1927. The fields on either side of the road were littered with concrete pillboxes, now disused and overgrown – the ruined legacy of Communist paranoia.

In Slavonice I parked in the marketplace, a long triangle overlooked by a Florentine bell tower. It was surrounded by *fin-de-siècle* German buildings (the Hotel Stark and the former Zuckerbäckerei Kosarek) and older Peasant Baroque houses with crenellated parapets and false gables shaped like the fingers of a hand. In the centre of the *náměstí* was a statue of St Florian, patron saint of brewers, coopers, chimney sweeps, soap boilers and Austrians. The fountain around the statue was engraved with the golden rose of the Rosenberg dynasty, which ruled southern Bohemia from the thirteenth to the sixteenth centuries. (Slavonice was histori-cally in Moravia, but the boundaries of the new Czech Republic have placed the town in the administrative *okres* of Jindřichův Hradec, tech-nically in Bohemia.) Several houses in the square had sgraffitied façades, whereby parts of the outer layer of grey, brown or blue stucco had been scraped away to reveal lighter plaster beneath, creating a *trompe-l'oeil* effect as if the buildings had been built from bevelled stone blocks in the Florentine manner. Some of the houses in the upper square behind the church were covered with elaborate sgraffiti that depicted scenes from the Old Testament, Ovid's *Metamorphoses* or folksy medieval tales. Arranged in square frames across and down the façades, they resembled a cartoon strip illustrated by Dürer with captions in High German Gothic script. The dusky glow from Slavonice's feeble street lamps served only to inten-sify the artifice of these façades: exteriors became interiors, pasted onto house fronts like Mannerist wallpaper.

I decided to stop and eat on the terrace of the Hotel Arkáda. All the dishes on the menu included *porek,* and I sheepishly asked a married couple sharing my table if they could explain what this was. They not only translated the word into English as "chopped leek" (I should have guessed from the pervasive smell), but started to chat to me in my own language. This was my first proper conversation with Czechs. I had begun to feel invisible, a non-person who could be seen only by policemen and prostitutes. This was not just because of my linguistic shortcomings, but because of a growing feeling that the Czechs, a morose people at the best of times, regarded foreigners with an antipathy that manifested itself in sullen resentment. One talks of the melancholy of the Portuguese or the fatalism of the Belgians, but the Czechs seem to sleepwalk through their lives in a lethargic somnolence that sometimes borders on idiocy (on two occasions Czech drivers reversed their cars into mine without bothering to look in their rear-view mirrors). This is understandable in the light of their history: they suffered "three hundred years of darkness" under Habsburg rule, followed shortly afterwards by the "collective humiliation" of Nazi invasion and Soviet oppression. In his book *Postwar*, the historian Tony Judt describes Czechoslovakia as "complicit in its own defeat" in 1938, 1948 and 1968. Its inability to react to outside aggression and its acceptance of defeat is described as "normalisation". The Czechs are Europe's born losers. Twenty years after the Velvet Revolution, and fifteen years after separation from Slovakia finally gave them their own nation-state, they still seem to suffer from a condition that their former president Václav Havel termed "post-prison psychosis" – an inability to think or act for themselves.

This has not been helped by the re-colonisation of the country by Germans and other Europeans as a cheap tourist destination. Unlike most other European nations, the Czechs still regard foreigners as a necessary nuisance, a source of revenue to be grudgingly tolerated rather than embraced. Waiters, hotel receptionists and others whose profession it is to make money out of foreigners can scarcely bring themselves to acknowledge their presence. I was often reminded of my first visit to Prague in 1986, when the empty restaurants had "Reserved" signs on all the tables because it made no difference to the staff whether they had any customers or not. Three decades and one revolution further on, the situation has changed little. Twenty-first-century Prague has become an overpriced shopping-mall-cum-theme-park dispensing fake Baroquery and second-hand Bohemiana to undiscerning international visitors. The tourists patronise the city's waiters and hotel staff, who in turn behave obsequiously to their clients and charge them ten euros for a cup of substandard coffee. The result is a pitiful collusion between the condescending and the sycophantic. Prague and international tourism deserve each other. Even in the provinces the Czechs appear unable to shed a long-standing inferiority complex. They seem resigned to being second-class citizens within their own country.

So it was with a sense of relief that I talked to the couple from Prague in the Náměstí Míru in Slavonice. We didn't discuss anything controversial: we just chatted about work, families, food, the weather – but it made me feel visible again and restored my belief that Czechs could have minds of their own and treat foreigners as their equals. After the meal it was too late and I was too inebriated to travel further, so I took an attic room in the Hotel Arkáda. I was three floors above the kitchen, but I could still smell the leeks.

Ifirst came across Telč while flicking through the pages of a history of European urban planning in the Shakespeare and Company bookshop in Vienna in the mid-1980s. The book contained a fold-out panoramic photograph of a row of twenty-five houses built over the arches of a colonnade along one side of the town's market square. Each house was painted in a different colour; each one was unique in the structure of its façade. I can't recall the precise architectural style it represented (Rustic Renaissance or Peasant Baroque, maybe), but it was the most enchanting place I had ever seen.

I drove there the next day, crossed a dyke over the ponds that surround the old centre, walked through the Lesser Gate and entered Náměstí Zachariáše z Hradec, the main square, shaped like the blade of a scythe. The buildings on the south-western side disappeared around a convex curve. Those on the north-eastern side tilted back and forth above the undulating flagstones of the colonnade I had seen in the photograph. The house fronts were painted in pastel shades of apricot, lilac, buttermilk, magnolia or Wedgwood blue, offset by pink and white pilasters and dripping with golden tassels. Stone acorns and pyramids, gilt trophies and globes teetered precariously on gables in the form of violins, fingertips, candlesticks or lobster tails. Three of the houses resembled toy fortresses, their stucco façades painted in an imitation of ashlar bricks. One rose high above the others like a four-storey Georgian townhouse. Most had tiny windows in the shape of bells or ox-hides set into their eaves, from which their residents, if there were any, could peer down into the square like gingerbread figures from cakes coated with marzipan.

The square itself was deserted. A few Škodas, one in the brown-and-white livery of the Milicie, were parked on the cobblestones in front of the Černý Orel (Black Eagle) Hotel, which served me with a chicory-based "coffee". I walked beneath the colonnade below the multi-coloured houses. Their blistered stucco and cracked plaster served only to augment the decaying beauty of this otherworldly place. There were a few shops below the arches which sold "Alimentation", "Hardware" or "General

Goods", but they had no customers. I felt as if I had stumbled on a town that had been bypassed by the twentieth century because no one knew of its existence.

My second visit to Telč was in August 1990, the first summer after the Velvet Revolution. I was with my girlfriend on a trip around some of the areas of Central Europe that had recently become more accessible. We stayed the first night near Koblenz with one of my employees, a tall, blond Anglo-German man who was an expert on Prussian and Napoleonic military history and who had an undeserved reputation as a closet Nazi. Our second night was spent in the Gewandhaus in Dresden, a hotel that was superior by the standards of the former GDR, but spartan by those of the west. We slept in separate cots in a whitewashed cell-like room, divided by acres of parquet flooring. I recall the Hotel Monopol in Wrocław as gloomy and smelling of drains. In Kraków we stayed two nights in an Orbis concrete block. I was enjoying myself: it was the first time I had had the opportunity to travel freely to Saxony, Silesia and Slovakia without having to apply for visas or submit itineraries to the authorities weeks in advance. We had spent three previous holidays in Eastern Europe, driving down the Dalmatian coast through Kosovo, Macedonia and Bulgaria towards Istanbul; trips Candy claimed to have enjoyed too. We had also travelled together to Prague and Budapest during the darkest times of the 1980s. Nevertheless, Candy's idea of a proper holiday was shopping in New York or clubbing in Ibiza: being holed up in a Gothic grand hotel in the Tatras, having eaten nothing for a week except stringy meat and greasy potatoes, was not her idea of a good time. With hindsight I realise this was her "holiday from hell", but at the time I was blissfully unaware of this.

From the Tatras we drove down into Moravia and ended up in the Černý Orel in Telč. We took a room at the front of the hotel, looking out over one of the most beautiful squares in Europe. We were the only guests, however, and the gregarious Candy was clearly beginning to feel miserable. After yet another dinner of braised beef, boiled cabbage and soggy potatoes, we went for a moonlit walk through the *staré město,* there being nothing else to do. We sat by the Saint Margaret Fountain and, in an attempt to cheer her up, I proposed marriage. It was not a particularly dramatic proposal: there was no bouquet of roses or ring proffered on bended knee, no accompaniment of minstrels. In my self-absorbed way I assumed that the peeling, neglected charm of Náměstí Zachariáše z Hradec provided an appropriately romantic setting for the occasion.

Candy accepted my proposal in a mildly surprised, rather non-committal way, and we returned to our hard, single beds in the Černý Orel.

Next morning Candy asked me whether I had intended to propose to her in Telč. "Sort of", I replied; and that was the beginning of the end of our relationship. We spent two or three days in a *Gasthof* in the Bavarian Forest, but by this stage Candy had lost interest in me and in Central Europe and spent her time with her head in a novel. On our return to London we went through the motions of going as a couple to friends' weddings, and even held our own engagement party in a wine bar in Primrose Hill; but, if truth be told, our relationship lay dead and buried by the fountain in Telč. When I suggested Albania as our next holiday destination, she swiftly started seeing someone else.

Twenty years later I am back in Telč, and still single. The town is now a UNESCO World Cultural Heritage site, a tourist trap, a staging post on the day-trip, coach-party circuit. Although few tourists stay overnight in the Černý Orel, the path up Na Baště, over the dyke, through the Lesser Gate, into the market square and out through the Greater Gate is as well trodden as that between Old Town Square and the Charles Bridge in Prague. The Peasant Renaissance houses have been restored and sanitised, and now function as painted dolls' houses with Punch and Judy gables for the delectation of the sightseers. The dusty, state-run shops have been converted into juice bars and internet cafés. On a bandstand in the centre of the square, a group plays Moravian folk music through distorted loudspeakers. Souvenir sellers and environmental activists battle for the day-trippers' euros. The combination of fake vernacular tradition and global concern cannot fail to appeal to the twenty-first-century Eurotourist. I go for a walk around the back alleys and wonder whether I will ever again have the chance to get married.

6

Bohemia

Melancholy Squared or Nostalgia Twice Removed?

Somewhere west of Telč I crossed an invisible border between the former margraviate of Moravia and the erstwhile kingdom of Bohemia. I stopped for a coffee in Café Dvorak on Náměstí Přemysla Otokara II in České Budějovice, before heading south along the banks of the Vltava and up into the hills surrounding Český Krumlov. I parked in front of the Penzion Onyx and found the owner, a Yorkshireman named Peter. On my way up the stairs I passed two young women wearing long, tan-coloured dresses chattering to each other in Polish. In the master bedroom on the first floor, I met the men with whom I would be sharing the room for the next few nights. Craig was a self-obsessed, sex-addicted insurance man from Luxembourg who had arrived with Richard, a camp young Englishman from Mannheim with a saucy laugh. Flavio was a drinking companion from London, a balding, pot-bellied Italian who spoke fluent English, but at such speed and so heavily accented that nobody could understand a word of what he was saying. Uwe was a Mephistophelean German with swarthy, saturnine features. His cropped, bullet-shaped head, concealed behind dark glasses, was an image I had seen a thousand times in my rear-view mirror on the autobahn. He was a forty-year-old school-boy with a coltish enthusiasm for the German national football team (we were in the middle of the group stages of Euro 2008) and a booming voice that exploded every so often into the riff of "Smoke on the Water" (we had tickets to see Ritchie Blackmore's neo-Renaissance band playing in the Brewery Meadows on our final evening in Český Krumlov). After washing and changing, I went downstairs with these four insalubrious individuals to the terrace in front of the *penzion* where we met the rest of the company, including the two Polish girls from the stairs and Trish and Antonia, posh totty from the Home Counties. Trish was dressed in white satin as Queen Elizabeth I of England, her sister in black velvet as Mary Queen of Scots. The two Poles were both named Agnieszka. At first we attempted to distinguish one from the other by calling them Agnieszka A and Agnieszka B, but this was soon abandoned as nobody could remember which was A and which was B. The petite, doll-like Agnieszka with the mop of blonde hair eventually became known as Barbie.

We were assembled in Český Krumlov for the Festival of the Five-Petalled Rose, an annual celebration of the town's golden age in the late Renaissance period. Unfortunately, I had arrived too late to procure myself a costume, and the two pairs of tights I had brought with me from England were to remain unworn. Most of the rest of the group were in sixteenth-century garb: the men as cavaliers of the Rožmberk court dressed in velvet tunics, slashed breeches, white ruffs and cuffs, bipper-ty-bopperty hats and suede bootees; the women as ladies of the court in gowns embroidered with gold brocade or blouses with puffed sleeves. Nevertheless, with Craig's leer, Richard's camp giggle and Barbie's *décolletage*, we looked more like the cast of *Carry On Krumlov* than a company of noble lords and ladies.

Once we had finished the beer, *becherovka* and slices of smoked boar laid on for us by Peter and his Czech wife Daniela, we made our way to the town centre, passing below the Budějovice Gate into Latrán, a cobbled street which winds down to the Vltava. The upper floors of the houses on Latrán were sgraffitied with the golden roses of the Rožmberks and alchemistic and cabbalistic symbols; the English mountebank Edward Kelley, peddler of elixirs of life and philosophers' stones to the court of Emperor Rudolf II in Prague, later found service at the court of William of Rožmberk in Český Krumlov. The lower floors of the former burghers' houses were now craft shops or grocery stores whose windows displayed baskets of giant salamis, tins of Darling or Friskies pet food, show-cards for Tic-Tac mints and aerosol sprays of artificial whipped cream. At the foot of Latrán we crossed the wooden Barber's Bridge over the Vltava and ascended Radniční Ulice until we arrived in Náměstí Svornosti in the centre of the Old Town.

The square was packed with revellers attired in doublet and hose, swirling cloaks and tricorn hats. Serfs and wenches queued at stalls purveying beer, mead, *slivovice,* spiced sausages and hunks of pork from roasting spitted pigs. Jugglers, fire-eaters and sword-swallowers mingled with the crowds as they paused to admire Lenka, the Snake Woman from Prague, or the Goat Man, a *commedia dell'arte* mime artist. Flames from hundreds of hand-held torches flickered around a plague column in the centre of the square. On a stage in front of the town hall, dancers and swordsmen performed a fiery re-enactment of the Celebration of the Rose of 1589, when William of Rožmberk commanded the lords of southern Bohemia to assemble in Český Krumlov for a tournament at which they would pay tribute to their overlord. The official opening of this year's festival was announced by a fanfare of trumpets from the windows of the *radnice,* whose walls were covered with emblems depicting the rose of Český Krumlov, the lion of Bohemia, and the coats of arms of the Austrian Eggenbergs and German Schwarzenbergs, the two dynasties which inherited the town from the Rožmberks. Through the smoke and flame I could make out a hideous escutcheon on which two ravens pecked at the eyes in a Turk's severed head.

Those of our party who were in costume went off to the castle courtyard to join the procession that would wend its way through the town at 10 pm. Craig, Flavio and I remained in the market square, drinking beer and holding an increasingly inebriated conversation about the relative charms of the two Agnieszkas; Craig was clearly becoming besotted with the blonde one. We watched the torchlight procession of drummers, musketeers and lords and ladies bearing the banner of the rose as it passed through the square. Afterwards we sat on the terrace of a restaurant by the Vltava opposite the Clad Bridge. The walls of the castle rose on cliffs sheer above us. The night sky was illuminated by rings of light from its floodlit tower.

After the meal we discovered a Bar Horor (sic) in Masná Ulice, whose cellar bar was decked out with fake cobwebs, plastic bats and woodchip coffins. The waitress, a female Marilyn Manson with a face caked in white foundation and smudged with kohl-rimmed eye shadow and black lip gloss, kept up a relentless supply of beer and *slivovice*. All I remember of the rest of the evening is a *frisson* of genuine horror as one of the winged rodents in the ceiling started to flap its wings and turned out to be a real bat that had been trapped behind an overhead cable; a jukebox from the 1970s on which I recall selecting Nazareth's "Broken Down Angel"; and Craig dragging Barbie off into an alcove in order to worm his way into her favours. It must have been 4 am when we re-ascended Latrán. Revellers in dishevelled doublets or dirndls were staggering back to the suburbs. Romany rent boys lurked in shadowy doorways. Richard wistfully remarked that he wished he knew a few words of Czech so he could go and talk to them. I suggested he should just get his dick out.

I awoke the next morning after six hours of fitful sleep interrupted by the sound of five other drunks lying on their backs and snoring like swine. After a late breakfast on the terrace of the *penzion*, I joined the rest of the party for a restorative brunch of coffee and mojitos in the lower courtyard of the castle, by the former salt-house that functioned as the headquarters of the local Gestapo during the period when Český Krumlov (Krumau, or Krummau, as the town was known in German) was incorporated into the Nazi Gau of Oberdonau. The building later served as the offices of the municipal *Milicie* during the Communist era. Above the courtyard soared the sixteenth-century castle tower, a round keep whose Renaissance murals had been restored to their former lustre. The *trompe-l'oeil* effects painted on the lower section of the tower created the impression it had been hewn from massive blocks of yellow ashlar. The upper section of the tower was decorated with shells and heraldic symbols painted in coral and ivory colours. Above the circular ambulatory was a quartet of turrets topped with golden spheres. The tower rose above the castle like an ornate German drinking *stein*.

I sleepwalked through a guided tour of the castle: through the Wenceslas Cellars and the Renaissance chambers of the Rožmberks, who ruled here from 1302 to 1602; through the baroque Hall of Mirrors of the Eggenbergs from Styria (Eggenberg beer is the local brew in Graz as well as in Český Krumlov) who resided here at the invitation of Emperor Ferdinand II from 1622 to 1719; through the salons, theatres and Masquerade Hall of the Franconian Schwarzenbergs, who inherited the estate in 1719 and remained lords of the manor until 1941, when their domain was confiscated by the National Socialists on account of their anti-German activities. This was in spite of the impeccable German credentials of the family: Karl Philipp Prince of Schwarzenberg and Duke of Krumau was commander-in-chief of the armies that defeated Napoleon at the Battle of the Nations in 1813, and is duly commemorated by a plaque on the architrave of the Befreiungshalle. Between 1602 and 1622 the castle was the property of the Habsburg Emperor Rudolf II, whose insane, illegitimate son Don Julius of Austria was sectioned there between 1605 and 1608. During that period Don Julius took a young woman named Markéta Pichler, daughter of a local barber, as his mistress. He abused her repeatedly, one night beating and slashing her before throwing her body from the castle window. Her defenestration was not fatal, because she landed on a dung heap and managed to crawl back to her family home. Don Julius forced her to return to him by imprisoning her parents. The night after her return he beat her, cut her body into pieces and threw those from the window of the castle. He later collected her body parts, wrapped them in linen and had them solemnly buried. Don Julius is reputed to have died in the castle at the age of twenty-three, a stinking, depraved, ulcerous wretch. His body has never been found. Beyond the upper reaches of the castle are the Mannerist and Rococo gardens laid out by the Eggenbergs at the end of the seventeenth century. The lower *parterre* is adorned with golden statues and fountains of nymphs, tritons and frogs; the upper park contains the *pièce de résistance* of communist Krumlov – an open-air theatre with a revolving auditorium set on a circular disc which spins the audience round at a thirty-degree angle to the ground.

I rejoined my companions for the Tournament of the Rose, held in the Brewery Meadows by the Vltava. The field was thronged with spectators, many in costume, enjoying a spectacle of jousting, falconry, axe-throwing, crossbow-shooting and a re-enactment of the historical tournament of 1589, when five regional barons were invited to joust in a contest whose winner would earn the right to play a game of occult chess with Lord William of Rožmberk. The winning knight would be represented by Gottfried, Grand Master of Manifold Magic, who would pit his wits against Lord William's representative, the fabled alchemist John Dee. To the consternation of the audience, the jousting tournament of 2008 was won by a guest team from Sulmona in Italy, who unseated all the local Knights of the Rose. I spent most of the tournament supine on the greensward beneath the shade of an apple tree, nursing my hangover. I was dimly aware of a pair of *chevaliers* attired in chain mail wooing a couple of Bohemian maidens by swapping mobile phone numbers. As I recovered, I noticed I had an admirer of my own, a comely wench who was attracting my attention by repeatedly crossing and uncrossing her bronzed thighs, revealing a pair of white knickers beneath her leather skirt. Sadly, I was in no state to respond to her inducements. One of the Agnieszkas eventually rescued me from my torpor by bringing me a thick black sausage full of garlic and an unidentifiable cocktail of fizzy turquoise alcohol.

While the rest of our company returned to the Penzion Onyx to change into their codpieces for the evening, I escorted Agnieszka (the other one, not Barbie) to the market square to watch the final group match of Euro 2008 between Turkey and the Czech Republic. We found an upstairs bar on the corner of the square, a dimly lit saloon with wooden benches and soft-porn posters on the walls. I expected the local fans to demonstrate some patriotic fervour, but not even the prospect of their national team playing for a quarter-final place in the continent's most prestigious football tournament seemed to excite the morose Czechs, who watched the match in grim, pessimistic silence. They must have had a premonition of the result: with fifteen minutes remaining the Czech team was 2–0 up, only to capitulate to the Turks' three late goals – Europe's losers, as always. As we emerged from the gloom into the market square, a quartet of young German men marched out of a side street chanting "Deutschland, Deutschland über alles" – their national team had beaten Austria to win through to the quarter-finals. Uwe was not among them.

Agnieszka and I walked up Horní ulice to the five-star Hotel Růže for drinks. We sat on the terrace of the former Jesuit College, overlooking the fires of the neo-hippies who had set up camp in the town park on the other side of the river. The terrace was empty, but the waiter was reluctant to serve us, informing us the tables were reserved for a party later that evening. We explained we would just like a quick aperitif, if that wasn't too much trouble. Agnieszka ordered her eighth mojito of the day and got stuck into her second packet of cigarettes. I ordered a Campari. Wrong choice: Agnieszka was served with a large tumbler overflowing with fizzy Mexican cocktail; I got a centimetre of vermouth. Agnieszka proceeded to tell me about a swimming expedition that she, Uwe, Craig and her namesake had embarked on that morning. They had driven twenty-five kilometres to Lake Lipno, where she and Uwe had changed into their bathing costumes and gone for a swim. When they returned to the shore, Craig and Barbie had disappeared with the car "to go snogging or shagging or something", as Agnieszka delicately put it. It had turned cold and started to rain, and Uwe and Agnieszka were left freezing in their swimwear, trying to hitch a lift back to Český Krumlov. At this point in the narrative Agnieszka disappeared into the hotel, returning some ten minutes later with her hair let down, some newly applied lipstick and a twinkle in her eye.

At 8 pm we assembled on the terrace at the rear of a restaurant on Horní that afforded a spectacular view of the floodlit castle. Unfortunately, the setting wasn't matched by the food. I resisted the temptations of pork loin or pork knuckle and ordered the safer option of *Wiener Schnitzel*. It duly arrived one hour later, an inch-thick slab of deep-fried breadcrumbs with a sliver of veal-like meat buried in the middle, accompanied by tiny portions of stodgy dumplings and damp cabbage. Having drunk my fill of beer the previous evening and during the afternoon's football match,

I ordered a glass of wine. Wrong choice again. In the 1980s Austrian viti-culturists caused a scandal when it was revealed they cut their wine with a chemical used to manufacture anti-freeze. Czech wine tastes as if it has been adulterated with Novichok. This may be why the Czechs have the highest per capita consumption of beer in the European Union, an average of 185 litres per person per year. This in turn probably explains why the Czechs are so morose. However, any lingering disappointment at the gastronomy was quickly forgotten at midnight, when the firework display that closed the festival began. We rushed to the parapet of the terrace to marvel at the kaleidoscopic pyrotechnics exploding over the castle, illuminating the Renaissance murals of the cliff-top citadel. I noticed Craig shepherding Barbie off to a quiet corner, a tentative hand tugging at her waist.

Over breakfast the next morning Uwe announced he was going to spend the morning at a concert of choral music in the monastery of the Order of the Knights of the Cross with the Red Star, and the afternoon watching a chess game between the alchemist and the occultist that was to be contested in the castle gardens using human chess pieces. The rest of us were to go rafting on the Vltava. Barbie then revealed that she couldn't swim and opted out. This put Craig in a quandary: he didn't want to "lose quality time with Barbie", as he put it, so he also pulled out. We drove twenty kilometres south of Český Krumlov and embarked on the two inflatable rafts we had hired. We paddled back downstream towards the town, between woods and meadows, derelict cement works and paper mills, below cracked oil pipes and rusting factory bridges. I hummed the opening bars of Smetana's symphonic poem in praise of the river. To my surprise, Flavio provided a baritone counterpoint. Trish and Antonia regaled us with all twelve verses of "Green Grow the Rushes, Ho", an arcane mixture of Christian catechism and astronomical mnemonics. After an hour and a half of rowing we stopped in a clearing below a cliff for beer and cigarettes, then discovered that Český Krumlov lay just around the next bend of the river. After beaching the rafts, we met the rest of the party in the lower courtyard of the castle for a farewell drink. Uwe was missing. In spite of his claim to have gone to matins like a good Catholic boy, he had been spotted during the afternoon handing out business cards to young women. Craig was in avuncular form; Barbie looked somewhat sheepish. It wasn't difficult to guess how their "quality time" in the *penzion* must have unfolded. Richard jokingly asked Craig whether they should stop near the border to pick up some prostitutes on the way home. "I don't need to now," Craig replied.

I had one more visit to make. The Egon Schiele Art Centre is housed in the former town brewery on Široká ulice. A small collection of the artist's works is exhibited in the long, cross-beamed galleries of the building. Schiele first visited Krumau, his mother's birthplace, in May 1910. The following year he rented a house overlooking the Vltava (or the Moldau, as it was then known) with his model-turned-lover Wally Neuzil. Between 1910 and 1912 he painted a series of six visionary townscapes entitled *Dead City*. In these paintings Schiele isolates blocks of houses in Krumau (the crescent of buildings around Na Ostrově, or the rows of houses sloping up from the river to the market square, for example), painting their walls in luminous smudges of orange and yellow gouache and applying a green or brown metallic sheen to their steep roofs. These compressed blocks of houses are cut off from their real surroundings, framed within dense midnight-blue oil paint which represents the river flowing into the night sky. Isolated from any external reality, the town floats as if in deep space. There are no human figures in Schiele's Krumau. The Dead City paintings, like Fernand Khnopff's drawings of Bruges-la-Morte, create a townscape of the soul, an allegory of abandonment, emptiness and isolation.

Schiele frequented Caffé Fink in Latrán, where he attracted a small coterie of local youngsters enthralled by his bohemian lifestyle. The café mounted small exhibitions of his less offensive works. He and Wally hoped to settle in Krumau, but the narrow-minded citizens of the town took issue with their non-marital status and with Schiele's licentious behaviour. They took particular offence at his employment of pubescent girls as models, and their consequent exposure to the "pornographic" drawings in his studio. Many of Schiele's works were explicitly sexual, pornographic in form if not in intent. In some of the sketches exhibited in the Art Centre, the only coloured part of the work is the model's outstretched labia, a gash of scarlet or purple paint like an inflamed wound, behind which the rest of the body – the pelvis, the breasts, the head – is merely suggested by a charcoal line. Whether these works count as art or pornography (or both) is a matter for art historians or arbiters of public taste to decide. They have little erotic impact: the viewer is shocked rather than aroused. If anything, they convey the artist's fear or horror of the vagina. One specific incident, when a neighbour's daughter posing naked for Schiele was accidentally observed by another neighbour's daughter from her overlooking garden, caused particular offence. Schiele was arraigned as a "danger to public morality" and his resident's permit was rescinded.

He nevertheless returned several times during the following years, staying at the hotels Zur Stadt Wien or Zum Goldenen Engel, and continued to paint semi-real, semi-imaginary townscapes of Krumau. His later works, however, were more prosaic than his visionary pre-war paintings. He left for the final time in June 1917, returning to Vienna where he succumbed at the age of twenty-eight to the epidemic of Spanish influenza sweeping through Europe in the autumn of 1918.

"Heil Kaiser! Heil König!" Franz Joseph I – Emperor of Austria, Apostolic King of Hungary and Bohemia, of Dalmatia, Croatia, Slovenia, Galicia, Lodomeria and Illyria, King of Jerusalem, Grand Duke of Tuscany, Cracow and Transylvania, Duke of Lorraine, Salzburg, Styria, Carinthia, Carniola and Bukovina, Margrave of Moravia, Duke of Upper and Lower Silesia, of Modena, Parma, Piacenza and Guastalla, of Auschwitz and Zator, of Teschen, Friuli, Ragusa and Zara, Princely Count of Habsburg and Tyrol, of Kyburg, Görz and Gradisca, Prince of Trent and Brixen, Margrave of Upper and Lower Lusatia and Istria, Grand Duke of the Duchy of Serbia, Count of Hohenems, Feldkirch, Bregenz and Sonnenberg, Lord of Trieste, Cattaro and the Windic March – arrives in Lingolsheim in a fanfare of imperial and royal pomp and circumstance. The scene is depicted in one of the engravings that hang on the walls of U Zlaté Koule, the National Restaurant in Mariánské Lázně. The dining room is decorated with still lifes, bucolic paintings of the Bohemian peasantry, yellowing posters from the spa's Edwardian heyday, grandfather clocks and carriage lamps. Suspended from beams in the ceiling are a zither, a French horn, a wind-up gramophone, a stuffed pheasant, a samovar, a doll's house and an assortment of milk churns. In a dark corner an antique violinist plays a slithering melody to the accompaniment of a plodding pianist. Genuine Russian caviar (on crushed ice) is available at 3,950 crowns per 56 grams, ten times more expensive than any other dish on the menu, which is printed in the four standard languages of Marienbad: Czech, German, English and Russian. But the Russians don't come here any more: they go to London, St Moritz, Forte dei Marmi or, if they aren't part of the super-rich oligarchy that has siphoned off the country's remaining wealth, to Karlovy Vary. The only people who still visit Mariánské Lázně are the elderly in coach parties from Cottbus or Magdeburg; which is how I, arriving at eight-thirty on a Friday evening

in mid-August and expecting to find the spa fully booked, find that I have
the pick of the grand hotels at prices I can dictate myself.

I checked into a suite on the fourth floor of the Hotel Pacifik, a yellow
and white establishment the size of Vienna City Hall at the head of Hlavní
třída, the boulevard that runs up the slope between the hotels and gardens
of the spa. Feeling too scruffy to grace the hotel bar with my presence, I
walked out into the cool after-rain air of the evening. Mariánské Lázně
was deserted. The outlines of a famous spa were present – theatres, casinos, pump rooms, the turrets and domes of grand hotels – but there was
nothing to fill them in; only absent, disembodied spaces that I had imagined would be peopled by lustful *comtessas,* gangs of Russian *apparat-
chiks* or, at the very least, corpulent Bavarian tourists. The spa colonnade,
a genteel curve of cream cast-iron arches and coffered oak ceilings that
was reconstructed in the 1970s, smelled of boiled leeks and was as quiet
as a subterranean grotto, partly because the flooring was covered in grey
linoleum.

On the dot of 9 pm I heard the "Va, pensiero" theme from Verdi's
Nabucco strike up in the distance. Following the sound, I found a small
crowd gathered around a fountain in Skalník Park. Three circular jets of
water shot up from the spring, coloured red, white and blue by floodlights. Loudspeakers hidden within the base of the fountain issued synthe-
sised versions of The Greatest Schmaltzy Hotel Lobby Hits of All Time:
the opening bars of Tchaikovsky's First Piano Concerto; the "Fate" theme
from Beethoven's Fifth Symphony; Mozart's *Eine Kleine Nachtmusik;*
some Vangelis, Morricone and that piano tune by Richard Clayderman
that drove everyone to distraction in the 1980s. It was, at least, a relief
to come across some other people. I would otherwise have sunk into
Marienbad's fabled melancholy: the melancholy that W.G. Sebald evokes
when his sexually inhibited alter ego Austerlitz takes his *Lebensgefährtin*
Marie to the spa and cannot bring himself to make love to her; when
the mouse-grey nylon-coated hotel porter who escorts the couple to their
rooms almost expires on the stairs; when the waiter in the Město Moskva
café offers Marie a Cuban cigarette as if it were a Habsburg crown jewel;
when the gardens of the spa dissolve into a labyrinth of white mist into
which the guests disappear.

Melancholy squared or nostalgia twice removed? All spa towns are
melancholy by definition, for they evoke a glorious imperial past of
German kaisers, Russian boyars and Victorian crown princes which no
longer exists. Western European spas have undergone a slow graceful

decline: in Baden-Baden the ghosts of Brahms, Kafka, Turgenev and Dostoyevsky have been swept away by the table-dancing wives and girl-friends of English footballers. Eastern European spas lost their residue of glamour during the period of the Cold War, when their grand hotels were turned into recreation centres for trade unionists from the Soviet Union. But in post-Communist Europe the Russian proletariat no longer arrives in its hundreds of thousands; and neither the faded gentry nor the bohemian intelligentsia of Germany and Austria has returned to Marienbad. In Mariánské Lázně nostalgia for the golden age of the Edwardian era is overlaid by nostalgia for the cheap but cheerful years of the workers' revolution. Mariánské Lázně is beyond melancholy: it is moribund. Once the remaining wrinklies from the former GDR have passed away, who will visit the spa apart from a few oddballs like me in search of some *mitteleuropäisch* cliché; or misguided fans of Alain Resnais who have interpreted the title of his famous film (described in the *Time Out Film Guide* as "obscure, oneiric") too literally?

At 10.30 pm Mariánské Lázně is dead. The hotels have closed for the night. A solitary taxi waits outside the Café Opera of the Hotel Zvon. Inside the café a trio of geriatric couples are creaking around in erratic circles to the sound of a deafening *Schlager* band. In the "Disko" of the Hotel Jalta, a shabby first-floor café, inebriated Germans continue to drink beer and *becherovka* to the accompaniment of Shakin' Stevens. At 11 pm they are thrown out. A man in a white tuxedo waits for a trolley-bus, which arrives, silently, on time. The rest of his drinking companions totter over Hlavní třída and disappear into the shrubbery. I survey the statuary above my hotel balcony. A nymph is perched insouciantly on the cornice, her legs dangling over the architrave, one arm bent at the elbow as she cups a hand to her ear, straining to hear the waltzes and chink of champagne glasses of the *belle époque* of her youth. The rain comes down again, obliterating everything.

Iawoke the next morning to a patter of rain on the lead balustrade outside my room and the strains of Beethoven's *Moonlight Sonata* emanating from the singing fountain. I opened the French windows and stood on the balcony in my monogrammed bathrobe. In the soft light of the morning I saw that the hundred-year-old nymph, to whom I had blown a goodnight kiss before retiring to bed, was made of lead too, her knees and elbows eaten away by rust and her lap full of soil. I gazed down at the line of grand hotels that rose in a wall of *kaisergelb* up the slope of Hlavní. Each appeared to be trying to outdo its neighbours in the quantity of urns, cherubs and garlands of acanthus leaves encrusted on its façade. Golden emblems crowned their rain-soaked roofs: a globe on the Polonia; a Gorgon's head on the Bohemia; a reclining sea god on the Neptun; a chariot drawn by snarling lions on the Chopin; a bell on the Zvon. Lawns shimmering with dew ran off from Hlavní, flowing around exotic bushes, shrubs and beds of orange, red and purple flowers. Above the gardens rose the towers and domes of churches, colonnades and assembly rooms; and beyond the spa, above the red-brick Kaiserturm in the rain-green Kaiserwald, a shroud of pewter cloud loured over the spruce trees of the Bohemian Forest.

The spa colonnade smelled of vanilla and woodsmoke. A leaden sky filtered through the windows of its arches, failing to illuminate the pharmacies, porcelain shops and *oplatky* stalls lining the interior of the arcade. The reason the flooring was covered with linoleum suddenly became apparent: the guests were all in wheelchairs. Wrought-iron *Litfaßsäulen* advertised afternoon-tea concerts in the Central Spa or the Casino Social House to the accompaniment of Suppé's *Light Cavalry Overture* and melodies from *The Merry Widow* or *The Gypsy Baron*. Mineral springs issued forth from the Pavilion of the Cross Spring, whose colonnades were embellished with busts of Dr Johann Joseph Nehr, the "medical father" of Marienbad, who founded the spa in the year 1808. The cold mineral water had an aftertaste of rotten eggs. The warm water was smooth and pleasant to taste, even when imbibed from a plastic cup sold at a Communist-era price of three crowns rather than from one of the more elegant porcelain beakers with long curved spouts that German tourists purchase as souvenirs of their visit.

In Goethe Square the bronze statue of the poet seated in a chair is a replica, a gift from the Heimatverband der Marienbader Stadt to replace the original statue looted by the Nazis as they retreated at the end of the Second World War. Goethe stayed in Marienbad in 1821 and 1822, collecting minerals in the surrounding hills and preparing a herbarium of the local flora. He returned in 1823 in the entourage of his patron Carl August of Weimar. They resided in Klebelsberg Palace, where the seventy-four-year-old poet wooed the nineteen-year-old Ulrike von Levetzow, eldest daughter of Amalia Levetzow, mistress of the Austrian minister Klebelsberg. After the girl's departure to Karlsbad,

Goethe composed the *Marienbader Elegie,* a love poem to the object of his desire:

> Am heißen Quell verbringst du deine Tage,
> Das regt mich auf zu innerm Zwist!
> Denn wie ich dich so ganz in Herzen trage,
> Begreif ich nicht, wie du wo anders bist.

> (You spend your days at the hot spring,
> Which stirs me to innermost strife!
> For however much I hold you in my heart,
> I cannot grasp how you are somewhere else.)

The former Klebelsberg Palace is at the centre of a sumptuous crescent of marzipan-coloured imperial hotels around Goethovo náměstí. Later in the nineteenth century it was transformed into the Hotel Weimar and during 1904 and 1905 it was renovated in order to provide a fitting summer residence for King Edward VII of England, who stayed in the hotel every year from 1903 to 1909. This was the age when Marienbad was the playground of royalty: when Edward VII entertained the French Prime Minister Clemenceau, the Imperial Russian envoy Izvolskij, King Fuad of Egypt, Shah Muzzefir Eddin of Persia, the Renaults and the Vanderbilts. The Hotel Weimar was later renamed The King of England in honour of its royal guest. After the Communist coup of 1948 it became the more prosaic Hotel Kavkaz (Caucasus), suffering the same fate as many other hotels in Mariánské Lázně which lost their aristocratic, international names (Broadway, Balmoral, Sanssouci, Buen Retiro, English Court, King of Bavaria) and were Sovietised as the Hotels Ural, Jalta, Moskva, Leningrad and Sevastopol. The hotel is currently unnamed and untenanted, although a German plaque above its royal balcony still commemorates the fact that Albert, son of Queen Victoria, sojourned here in 1899 as Prince of Wales and returned each summer as King Edward VII of England. The refurbished Hvězda Hotel next door has reopened for business, its façade supported by a chain gang of Viennese caryatids bent double by the weight of history on their shoulders. Four stone eagles perched on the towers of the Hvězda wait like vampires for fresh blue blood.

I walked back through Skalník Park, past the restored colonnade of the Caroline Spring; past the "artistic fountain" that consists of a mass of bronze tentacles writhing out of a white marble basin in the shape of an enormous vulva; past *Litfaß* columns announcing *thés dansants* to musical excerpts from *Hello Dolly, My Fair Lady* and *West Side Story*. By the roundabout on Hlavní at the foot of the park was a forty-foot iron spike surmounted by a heroic figure holding a flaming torch. The Russian inscription on the plinth below had been erased, but the official guidebook explained that "the memorial should have reminded the part that the Soviet Army had played in the liberation of Czechoslovakia in the World War II". The grammatically subtle "should have" referred to the fact that western Bohemia was actually liberated by General Eisenhower's forces, who halted fifteen miles west of Prague in order to allow the Soviets the propaganda victory of liberating Czechoslovakia. A new memorial, a stone that survived forty years of Communism in the undergrowth of the gardens, commemorates the real liberators of Mariánské Lázně on 6 May 1945. It was unveiled by US ambassador Shirley Temple Black on 26 April 1990.

I entered the café of the Hotel Polonia (once the luxury New York Hotel that provided kosher meals for its Jewish clientele) through a cloud of cigarette smoke, and sank into one of its high-backed velvet banquettes. Gilt-framed mirrors covered the opposing wall from floor to ceiling, set at a slight angle so that the interior of the café ran off in both directions in myriad, ever-diminishing reflections of itself. Canned saxophone melodies drifted around columns of blood-veined marble on which sat plaster busts of enigmatic Jugendstil *femmes fatales*. Barefoot gypsies were smoking and drinking black coffee at one table. At another a huge woman in an electric-blue housecoat sipped a tiny cocktail of a matching blue. The nicotine fug coiled around a single revolving display case of dry strudels and up into an alcove decorated with a painting of Edward VII, arriving in Marienbad on 16 August 1904 in a fanfare of imperial and royal pomp and circumstance. He is greeted by Franz Joseph I, Emperor of Austria, Apostolic King of Hungary and Bohemia etc., etc.

My first visit to Karlovy Vary was with the aforementioned ex-fiancée, en route to Prague for an Easter weekend during the literally dark days of the Communist era. We arrived after nightfall and turned off the main highway into an unlit boulevard that appeared to lead towards the centre of the spa. I caught sight of two policemen in the mid-distance and drove over to ask them for directions. They promptly confiscated my passport and fined me for driving down a street that was apparently prohibited to non-authorised traffic. But how were you supposed to know that, given there were no streetlights to illuminate the road signs? I felt I had been tricked – and not for the first time. During the late 1980s I was stopped so many times for spurious offences by Czechoslovak traffic policemen that I eventually caught on to the fact that they stopped all cars with foreign plates as a matter of principle, and fined their drivers in order to augment their own salaries. I learnt that the golden rule was to argue your corner with them before handing over your passport. I got so annoyed with this practice that on one occasion, having been stopped for driving legitimately around Wenceslas Square by a pair of rookie cops, I let fly with such a torrent of abuse in German (they had addressed me in broken German since I was driving an Audi with German plates) that they turned white with shock and saluted me before waving me on.

After our run-in with the local constabulary, Candy and I found the authorised approach road into Karlovy Vary, which involved driving up into the hills beyond the town and then winding back into the centre of the spa. In Communist times the Grand Hotel Pupp was the only place in town, an establishment catering to a mixture of tour groups from the Soviet Union and Germans with a taste for a bit of luxury and vice on the cheap. We arrived there to find a scrum of would-be guests around the reception desk. Through a combination of persistence and bribery (I inserted a ten mark note between the pages of my passport and thrust it under the nose of the receptionist), I managed to procure a double room in the *dépendance* of the hotel, which I believe was called the Hotel Moskva in those days. After unpacking, we went to the cocktail bar to revive our spirits and struck up conversation with a spinster from Düsseldorf, who took a perverse delight in pointing out the call girls positioned at strategic intervals around the bar. She clearly enjoyed a vicarious thrill in being part of this louche scene; maybe it compensated for a barren social and sexual life back home in the Rhineland. There was also a dearth of restaurants in socialist Karlovy Vary, and I recall we ended up eating pizza in a discotheque. The Pupp is now way out of my league: tarted up with a veneer of Russian glitz, it attracts guests with corresponding taste, mainly Mafia types from beyond the Bug with shaven heads and shiny suits. This time I found myself on my own in a back room of the dingy Hotel Jessenius on Stará Louka.

I kick-started Sunday morning with a wimpish caffé latte – little more than a glass of milky foam – on the sunlit terrace of the Café Elefant.

I wandered up and down the double promenade on either side of the river Teplá, inhaling the saline smells from thermal springs and admiring the Jugendstil stained-glass heads above the Three Moors House, where Goethe resided on nine of his thirteen visits to Carlsbad (or Karlsbad, as Karlovy Vary was previously known). I took photographs for tourists and avoided making eye contact with anyone of venal intent, either the rent boys who loitered beneath the colonnades of the pump rooms, or the Slavic girl reclining lasciviously with her skirt hitched up on the parapet outside the Hotel Pupp. (If Mariánské Lázně recalled Thomas Mann's *The Magic Mountain,* Karlovy Vary, in its cosmopolitan babel of languages and promise of sexual adventure, evoked a twenty-first-century *Death in Venice.* Unlike the hypochondriac Kafka or the pleasure-seeking Goethe, the patrician, ascetic Mann seems to have avoided the decadent Bohemian spas.) French and Italian tourists in elegant casual wear rubbed shoulders with coach parties from Poland and Hungary who, overdressed in synthetic suits and blingy accessories, looked cheap and self-conscious by comparison. A party of giggly, pink-headed Brits, the East Midlands Choral Society here to perform *Zadok the Priest* in the Maria Magdalena Church, marched up and down Stará Louka brandishing their long-spouted spa beakers as if they owned the place. And then there were the Russians, who actually do own most of Karlovy Vary, arriving on daily flights from Moscow to enjoy the "Russian massage" advertised in many establishments. A cursory inspection of the hundreds of memorial tablets and plaques adorning the façades of the spa's hotels and villas reveals a line of distinguished Russian visitors: Peter the Great, Gogol, Turgenev, Pavlov, Tolstoy, Khachaturian, David Oistrakh, Yuri Gagarin, the Cold War warriors Leonid Brezhnev and Aleksei Kosygin and, finally, Mikhail Gorbachev. The municipal guidebook, nevertheless, states that "after the year 1945 the sanatorium [of the Imperial Spa Hotel] was put at the disposal of patients from the former Soviet Union. Since November 1989 the sanatorium has been open to an international clientele again"; which rather pointedly suggests that Russians didn't qualify as "international clientele".

After taking a dozen separate group photographs for an Italian tour party on the steps of the Sprudel Colonnade, I began to tire of balneological sightseeing and walked away from the spa along the Goethe Promenade upstream of the Pupp. I followed the Teplá, stopping at intervals to peruse the gold-inscribed marble tablets erected by convalescents successfully cured of their metabolic ailments by a spell of treatment in Karlsbad: a Frau Jungmann from Prague in 1895–96; one Archimandrit

Mitrofir from Sinaia in Romania in June 1928; Doctor of Philosophy Carl Theodor Hoefft from Hamburg in the "Kriegsjahr 1915"; Josefine Buchwald from Budapest who, in June 1927, was moved to pen an ode in gratitude to the curative qualities of the spa:

> Mein Karlsbad!
> Wohlbefinden bietet manche Quelle
> Aus der Erde triefend Urgestein
> Aber nur an diese heiligen Stelle
> Fand ich Heilung meiner Gallenpein.
> Sei gepriesen edle Göttergabe
> Die der Krankheit schwere Keime bricht,
> Sprudle weiter aus dem Felsengrabe
> Segenspendend an das Sonnenlicht!

> (My Karlsbad!
> Many a spring gushing from the primeval rocks
> Of the earth offers wellbeing;
> But only at this sacred place
> Did I find relief from the agony of my gall bladder.
> Praise be to this noble gift from the gods
> That crushes the heavy seeds of illness;
> O bringer of benediction, keep on bubbling
> From the rocky tomb into the sunlight.)

And here's Goethe again, in the shape of a white marble bust of the poet above a plaque alluding to the "good times" he enjoyed in Carlsbad during a sojourn at the Park Hotel Pupp. Not to be outdone, Schiller has an entire shrine dedicated to his memory. Erected in 1909 at the height of the Jugendstil fashion, it is a semi-circular sunken temple built around a marble altar. A pair of fearsome open-jawed snakes coils around the balustrades towards two shrieking Greek masks flanking a bas-relief of the poet's head. The titles of his greatest plays run vertically up the columns of the shrine, intersecting with horizontal quotations from his most celebrated poems:

> Nichts würdig ist die Nation, die nicht
> Ihr alles freudig setzt an Ihre Ehre.

(Worthy of nothing is the nation
That does not joyfully devote itself to its glory.)

A young girl appeared out of nowhere and gave me a quizzical look as I passed the Umeric Art Gallery further along the Goethe Promenade. She was a skinny teenager in a white cardigan, torn jeans and trainers, her hair done up in a bun. She proceeded to walk along the path parallel to mine through the gardens known as Dorothea's Meads. I wondered what you did, where you did it, how long it took, how much it cost. This was 11.30 on a Sunday morning and, apart from me and the young girl, the gardens were empty save for some little old ladies and mothers pushing their children in buggies. Did she have a room at the Pupp or at the Hotel Richmond across the river? Or did you just disappear into the woods above the gardens? She sat down on a bench fifty metres further along the path I was following. I pretended to be gay and flounced off down the sloping lawn to inspect a statue of Beethoven.

The composer was sculpted like a musical Lenin, his right fist clenched, his left hand clutching the lapel of his greatcoat and his head deep in composition. Beyond Ludwig was a Japanese Zen garden, a gift from Karlovy Vary's twinned spa of Kusatsu. It was laid out as a Yin and Yang map of Eurasia, with Europe as the Island of Man and Asia as the Island of Woman. In the centre were two boulders which, according to the guidebook, "emitted positive energy". A group of Russian tourists had taken over the garden. Two of them were hugging the energy-transmitting boulders while two others rubbed their backs up and down the other stones. The rest of the group had fallen asleep on the adjacent benches. I noticed the waif-like prostitute resuming her beat from Dorothea's Meads back towards the Hotel Pupp. She parked herself on a bench outside the art gallery, which meant I had to walk past her again on my way back to the spa. She was not unattractive, and I was beginning to entertain impure thoughts. It was time to leave Karlovy Vary.

I headed north into the Ore Mountains, stopping in Osek for a beer in a pub opposite a Cistercian monastery. Beneath the peeling plaster of the tavern's walls I could make out its former German name, "Zur Weissen Rose", and the date 1754. Little had changed in the intervening years: lampshades like ladies' bloomers were suspended on chains over the tables; the oak-panelled walls were covered with dried flowers and stags' skulls.

Leaving route 27, I took a vertiginous road that wound up the hillside in a series of hairpin bends, passing through hamlets of black-and-white half-timbered cottages where goats munched the lawns and hens careered across dusty yards. I emerged above the treeline onto uplands of tussocky grass, thistles, gorse bushes, small conifers and silver birch trees. Below me the opencast mines cut into the blighted plains of northern Bohemia resembled the bunkers of a gigantic golf course. Ahead of me plantations of wind turbines covered the green hills of Saxony. I caught a glimpse of an abandoned East German watchtower.

The configuration of the border crossing had changed utterly since my first transit here one cold October evening in 1985. I was travelling from Braunschweig, via Weimar and Prague, to Vienna. It was my first visit to Czechoslovakia and there had been a misunderstanding about visa regulations during the course of a telephone conversation with Čedok's London office, the upshot of which was that I arrived in Zinnwald at 4 pm without an entry visa into Czechoslovakia. In those days it took several hours for both sets of border officials to process the few cars that were authorised to make that particular crossing, and it was already dark by the time it came to my turn at the GDR exit control. I still possessed the mandatory twenty-five East German marks that one was obliged to purchase on entry to the German Democratic Republic. There had been nothing worthwhile to spend them on during my twenty-four hours there, as the Hotel Elefant in Weimar had insisted on payment in hard currency. I naively assumed that I could exchange them at the border, but that notion was met with incomprehension by the stone-faced East German officials. They advised me to spend the money at the "duty free" shop on their side of the border. I trotted off there with my twenty-five Ostmarks, but the shop sold only state-produced alcohol (East German vodka and slivovitz), which I knew from previous experience to be undrinkable, useful only as lighter fuel or anti-freeze. I decided to pocket the Ostmarks illegally and keep them for later visits to East Berlin, where I could at least spend them on Melodiya LPs or one of those obscure Estonian novels published by Aufbau-Verlag. (In the event I still had twenty Ostmarks left when the Wall came down and they became worthless.)

I spent the next half hour sitting in a freezing car in the no-man's-land between the East German and Czechoslovak customs posts. My lack of an entry visa caused a further delay when it finally came to my turn at the Czechoslovak control point. At first the Czechoslovak officer refused me entry. However, I had now left the GDR and would not be able to return there. I facetiously suggested that I could drive along the control strip between the two fences until I reached Austria. I wasn't sure whether he understood me, and he was certainly not amused. He eventually relented, permitting me to purchase a visa for the exorbitant sum of one hundred US dollars, more than three times the amount it would have cost me had Čedok advised me correctly in the first place. The next problem was unforeseen. Earlier in the trip I had been working on a stand at the Frankfurt Book Fair and had agreed to take several boxes of my employer's books back to its London office in the boot of my company car. The Czechoslovak officials recoiled with horror when they opened these boxes, summoning a superior officer who, judging by his uniform, was a political commissar. Many of the books were innocuous but the boxes did contain, for example, an illustrated edition of Siegfried Sassoon's war poetry with a photograph of a British (imperialist) regiment on the dust jacket; a travel book by Anthony Bailey with a map of an undivided Europe and images of the Berlin Wall on the cover; a paperback edition of a play by David Hare with an illustration of Stalin on the front; and a copy of George Steiner's *The Portage to San Cristobal of A.H.* with a large swastika on the cover. The commissar ordered me to transport the boxes into his office, where he inspected every one of the books, checking for religious, imperialist, capitalist or anti-Communist material. The excuse I gave him that I was transporting Faber and Faber's exhibition copies from the Frankfurt Book Fair to its London office, but just happened to be taking a detour through Czechoslovakia and the GDR, was laughable; although I was in fact on my way to some legitimate business appointments in Vienna. He eventually gave me authorisation to take the books with me, having first inspected my hotel reservations in Prague and Vienna. He was still clearly suspicious, and decided to check the audio cassettes in my car, fast-forwarding and playing random excerpts from *For Your Pleasure* and *Diamond Dogs*. Fortunately, he was not sufficiently informed to realise that David Bowie's album *Diamond Dogs* was based on George Orwell's anti-Soviet satire *1984*. I had been stationed on that freezing ridge on top of the Ore Mountains for five hours by the time I was allowed to proceed; and it was midnight when I arrived at the Zlatá Husa hotel in Wenceslas Square, paranoid that I was being followed and that my room was bugged (which it almost certainly was).

After revisiting the scene of my first encounter with Czechoslovakia, I drove back down the E55 towards Teplice. At each bend in the steep road were a number of wooden shacks selling the usual tat – plastic gnomes, cheap alcohol, contraband cigarettes – and sex, loads of it. Each kiosk had an anteroom with a glass front where a row of scantily clad girls would twitch and jerk in a pitiful go-go routine at the approach of a vehicle with foreign (i.e. German) plates. They didn't seem to have many punters this afternoon – a couple of articulated lorries with the cab curtains drawn, maybe? In Dubí, at the foot of the hill, the E55 ran down through a long street of dilapidated houses whose ground floors had been converted into brothels that resembled red-light fast-food joints. In each window half a dozen girls were squeezed together, gyrating lasciviously at the few passing motorists. Other nightclubs, "dancings" or non-stop go-go bars were set back from the highway in bungalows, in front of which girls sat on rows of plastic chairs sipping coffee and smoking cigarettes. Unlike the discreet prostitutes of Karlovy Vary, these girls were dressed for immediate action, in leotards, halter tops and thongs, or exotic gypsy carnival costumes. Other girls, shabbier and meaner, sat in the rusting skeletons of ČSAD bus shelters or crouched in lay-bys.

A long flyover at the foot of the hill bisects the city of Teplice. All that you see from the E55 are the top storeys of decaying *fin-de-siècle* townhouses, red-and-white-striped chimney stacks and the more desperate of the roadside prostitutes. In spite of its former German name Teplitz-Schönau (Schönau means "fair meadow"), the Teplice of my imagination was a grim industrial city corroded by toxic air. Coming off the flyover, a diversion took me around several blocks before depositing me back on the E55 heading back up the hill towards the German border. A second attempt led me past a restored *Gymnasium* in a Saxon neo-Renaissance style and into Zamecké náměstí. Castle Square formed an attractive ensemble of white churches and neoclassical buildings that gleamed in the evening sun. In the centre – between the Schloss and the House of the Golden Sun – stood the tallest baroque plague column in Bohemia. Coal dust had corroded its once golden sandstone, and acid rain caused by sulphur dioxide emissions from opencast mines had eroded much of its finer detail. In the English Garden that surrounded the castle I caught sight of the statues of two distinguished gentlemen dressed in frock coats. Surely not Goethe again? There must be more statues of the poet in the outlying reaches of Bohemia than there are in his native Germany!

After checking into a room at the Hotel Prince de Ligne, I found a table on a wooden terrace outside the House of the Golden Cross and, quite literally, weighed up my options for dinner. According to the menu the "Smuggler's Schnitzel" and the "Castle Baron's Spit" (chicken, bacon and onion roasted in oranges) both tipped the scales at 200 grams, whereas the "Little Tears" (chicken in cheesy batter) weighed in at a meagre 150 grams. A side dish of French fries provided an additional 150 grams and a hunk of bread an extra 50. A horseradish relish would augment the total weight of the main course by a further 7 grams. A post-prandial coffee was also measured at 7 grams, although its accompanying cream mixer was, confusingly, calculated at 11 millilitres. A glass of beer included, my meal came to a grand total of 414 grams and 511 millilitres. The prices seemed almost incidental.

Czar Alexander I, the Austrian emperor Franz I and the Prussian king Friedrich Wilhelm III met at the House of the Golden Cross on the eve of the Battle of Kulm on 30 August 1813. The ensuing defeat of Napoleon's army by the Holy Alliance founded in Teplitz prepared the ground for the final victory of the Battle of the Nations at Leipzig two months later. Kulm is one of the battles commemorated in the Befreiungshalle, as is the Austrian general Hieronymus, Count of Colloredo-Mansfeld, who led the allied forces on that day. This was the age of Teplitz-Schönau's heyday, when the spa was known as "le petit Paris" or the "salon of Europe". It was not only the first Bohemian spa, a predecessor of Marienbad, Karlsbad and Franzensbad, but the oldest known healing spring in Europe; Celtic brooches and Roman coins have been discovered in its disused springs. Saxon electors started coming to Teplitz-Schönau in 1550, followed by Polish kings, Empress Maria Theresa and Czar Peter the Great. During the nineteenth century Teplitz-Schönau attracted all the usual suspects: Goethe, Beethoven, Chopin, Liszt, Wagner – the artistic playboys of their age.

Beethoven arrived at the House of the Golden Sun in Lázeňská Street at 4 am on 5 July 1812, after mysteriously missing an appointment with Karl August Varnhagen von Ense arranged for 3 July in Prague. Over the following two days the composer wrote a series of passionate letters to an anonymous "Immortal Beloved", which were despatched to "K". Presumably he missed his appointment in Prague in order to enjoy a tryst in Karlsbad with a married woman, possibly Josephine von Brunsvik or Antonie von Brentano. Two weeks later Beethoven met Goethe in Teplitz-Schönau: this was the only recorded meeting between the two titans of German culture. They were walking together in the Kurgarten when they encountered the entourage of Marie Ludovica, consort of Franz I of Austria. The worldly courtier Goethe bowed respectfully to the empress, but Beethoven refused to acknowledge her, believing that his God-given genius should not be held in subservience to earthly authority. After that they never spoke to each other again. Goethe wrote that (Beethoven's) "talent amazed me; but alas he is a totally unrestrained individual who may not be wrong in finding the world detestable, but in doing so certainly does not make it any more enjoyable either for himself or for others".

After dinner I turned down Lázeňská, a street of neoclassical houses painted in shades of blue and green. At the far end a modern red-brick building ran in a bridge across the street. I was transfixed by the clean elegance of its architecture: it struck me that this was the first post-modern building I had seen since leaving Austria. After days spent walking streets of crumbling baroque and Jugendstil or concrete Soviet-era modernism, this was the architectural equivalent of being unexpectedly served a dish of *nouvelle cuisine* after a diet of goulash, dumplings and leeks. The *raison d'être* of the post-modern building became evident when I reached the end of Lázeňská and came upon an extensive Kurgarten of lawns, fountains, pavilions, ornamental lakes and an arboretum, surrounded by the peeling yellow wings of the Beethoven Sanatorium and its new red-brick extension.

What took my breath away, however, was the sight of the lawns of the Kurgarten covered with hundreds of black creatures; an image which spontaneously brought to mind a flock of large crows. Once I had recovered my breath, I realised that the garden was filled with hundreds of Muslim women, sitting or squatting on the lawns. They were clad from head to toe in black *jilbabs,* grey *hijabs* wound around their heads and throats, many wearing the *niqab* that concealed everything except their eyes. It was an astonishing sight; like being transported on a magic carpet from Bohemia to Bahrain – or finding oneself in a Habsburg *haj*. I couldn't work out why women from oil-rich Gulf States would descend on Teplice for their cosmetic surgery when they could presumably afford to go to Baden-Baden or South Korea. Were they from Iran or Afghanistan and could only afford a low-budget cure? Or were they, like the students from Vietnam, Cuba and Libya who still gravitate to the ex-Communist states of

Europe, ideologically committed to patronising non-capitalist countries? But why choose smog-enriched Teplice over the more obvious and healthier attractions of Mariánské Lázně or Karlovy Vary? When I returned to the hotel, I asked the receptionist why there were so many Arab women in Teplice but, like most Czechs, she was unwilling to engage in unnecessary conversation with a foreigner and made a dismissive remark about "the Arabs who own all the spas".

The route south towards Prague wound over the České Středohoří hills before dropping into a lignite haze produced by the Lovochemie petrochemical works. Fields of cabbages stretched along both sides of the straight road from Lovosice towards Terezín, an eighteenth-century fortified town in marshland at the confluence of the Labe and Ohře rivers. The air was dry and fetid. On one of the bastions surrounding Terezín two men were trying to dampen down a fire that had flared out of control in the parched grass of the glacis. I drew up outside the Park Hotel, which once served as a dormitory for the SS staff who administered the former ghetto of Theresienstadt. A mouldering neoclassical pavilion stood isolated in the Brunnenpark, where a woman was walking her pet Chihuahua. A man in a vest lingered over a coffee outside the hotel. Otherwise the square was deserted, fallen leaves from the previous autumn scattered over its untended lawns. I went to sit down in the park, but none of the benches retained their wooden beams: they were empty concrete brackets ranged uselessly along the gravel paths which cut broken patterns through the gardens. A smell of petrol fumes emanated from lorries and buses crawling lopsidedly along the two sides of the square, which used to form the main road from Teplice to Prague before the D8 motorway was built. I had driven through Terezín several times, usually at night when the unlit town was shrouded in shadow and mist. The first time would have been immediately after my five-hour ordeal at the border crossing on top of the Ore Mountains; and I remember shuddering with horror as I negotiated the cobblestones of this seemingly abandoned town with its appalling memories – if, indeed, anyone remained to remember its history.

In the side street Zizkova, once the Postgasse, two girls were delivering junk mail. This struck me as slightly pointless as nobody seemed to live in the faded ochre buildings of the former Bodenbach Barracks, which were once used as an assembly point for processing new arrivals to the ghetto and deportees to death camps in the east. The windows of the terraced houses were hidden behind rusted iron grilles, and the archways between the blocks led into courtyards where rows of wheeled metal dustbins lined up among the rubble. Two road sweepers had abandoned their task of cleaning the potholed surface of Muskolní Street, once the Hauptstraße, and were sitting down for a smoke against the walls of the former Dresden Barracks, above whose entrance the faded legend "Kaiserliches und Königliches Zeughaus" was still visible. The only shop in the street sold Bohemian crystal. It must once have been a café, as beneath its contemporary grime I could make out the Czech words "Vinarny-Kavarna" and, under them, the ghostly outline of the old German lettering "Sodawasser und Limonade". Above the shop a net curtain twitched.

Along Pražská Street was another park, a desiccated space of stubbly lawns, empty concrete sandpits and rough-hewn statues of Czechoslovak resistance fighters who died in the struggle against fascism. Building L414 (like Mannheim, the streets of Theresienstadt were laid out in a grid pattern and were designated either by an L for "Langstraße" or a Q for "Querstraße") was the seat of the fortress headquarters during Theresienstadt's original incarnation as an imperial Austrian barracks. It later served as the SS headquarters from 1941 to 1942, after which it housed a post office where parcels sent to inmates of the ghetto were inspected and distributed, and from where prisoners sent their own letters and postcards. These were routinely franked with a date several weeks after they were posted in order to disguise the fact that many of the senders had subsequently been deported to Auschwitz. Otto Sgall, for example, sent a postcard to his sister Ruza in Wildenschwert in the Protectorate of Bohemia and Moravia, complaining: "Am healthy, but why are you all ignoring me?" The card was franked with the date of 25 March 1944, by which time Herr Sgall, far from being healthy, had been suffocated to death in a gas chamber. An official stamp on the card requested the recipient to reply "in the German language only" to the Reichs Union of Jews in Germany at Iranische Straße 2, Berlin N65.

Opposite the former Hohenelbe Barracks was a third park, smelling of drains, in which a plaque commemorated the anti-imperialist hero Gavrilo Princip who, with his fellow Serb assassins, was the most notorious prisoner incarcerated by the Austrians in the Small Fortress outside the main fortifications of Theresienstadt. I followed the sound of a bell from the tower of the Church of the Resurrection and found myself in the marketplace, a large open space surrounded by a double row of lime trees.

On the corner of the square, opposite building L410 in whose basement musicians of the ghetto rehearsed Verdi's *Requiem* and Smetana's *The Bartered Bride,* was the Bazar antiques shop familiar to readers of W.G. Sebald's *Austerlitz,* in which the author not only describes in detail the contents of the shop's window display, but also inserts photographs of the shop front into the text of the novel. Sebald's fictional alter ego ponders the existential nature of the items he surveys, the unspoken understanding being that some of those goods would have belonged to Jews imprisoned in the urban concentration camp. For the record, the bric-a-brac on display in the windows of Antikos Bazar at the time of my visit included Czech and Polish military tunics, Meissen figurines of two young women baring their nether regions, a yellow washbasin of early 1970s vintage, a long-stemmed pipe with a porcelain bowl inscribed with the name František Dvořák, a pewter plate engraved with a relief of Dr Eduard Beneš, Habsburg swagger sticks and US Army flak jackets. There were china figures of two Jews, one holding a menorah and one a Torah, and a stained nightshirt with the name "Hans Lauter 1941 Augburg (sic)" stencilled over the breast; but it was not for me to surmise whether these were authentic relics of the ghetto, or unrelated items displayed in the window to give tourists the impression they might be purchasing a genuine memento of the concentration camp.

In 1943 and 1944 these premises did sometimes function as a shop within the ghetto, selling back clothes and underwear to inmates from whom they had been confiscated in the first place. The shop functioned commercially during the cynical propaganda campaigns choreographed by the SS to "beautify" or "normalise" Theresienstadt whenever a delegation from the International Red Cross was due to inspect the ghetto. Before each visit, thousands of elderly or infirm inmates were deported to Auschwitz. The remaining prisoners were persuaded to play exhibition football matches, perform concerts and cabarets, frequent the temporarily opened "cafés" and "stores", and generally circulate around the freshly painted town looking happy and healthy in order to give the Swiss and Danish delegates the false impression that Theresienstadt was a pleasant spa town where Jews were "permanently settled". The deception worked: the Red Cross delegate Maurice Rossel was taken in by the charade, reporting in July 1944 that Theresienstadt was a "final destination" facility, from where Jews were not deported elsewhere. In fact, between 28 September and 28 October 1944, a further 18,402 Jews left Theresienstadt for Auschwitz, of whom only 1,574 survived.

Idrove down from the forested hills of the Lužické hory into a bowl of derelict factories and gently decaying German villas. Sweeping off the E442 into Liberec, I was pulled over by a policeman for driving the wrong way down a one-way street. I kicked up a fuss, explaining I was following signs for the "Centrum". There was admittedly an orange cross taped over the last sign for the "Centrum", and there were a couple of "No Entry" signs, but it was not absolutely clear to which section of the street they applied. I made a bit of a spectacle, dragging the policeman off to inspect the taped-over sign and providing the local populace waiting at bus stops with some *Schadenfreude* (if they used the German word). But I knew I had committed an infraction. The fine was one thousand crowns. I tried the "I don't have any local currency" dodge, but was ordered to follow the policeman to the Grand Hotel where I changed some euros, paid the fine and checked into a single room.

A white stucco edifice adorned with Jugendstil lions' heads, the Grand Hotel Zlatý Lev (Golden Lion) offered cut-price Viennese elegance. Completed in 1906, the hotel was officially opened by Emperor Franz Joseph I on the occasion of a Bohemian-German trade fair. For a brief period it was one of the top hotels of the Austro-Hungarian Empire. In the autumn of 1918 it functioned as the seat of the "German-Bohemian" government, a short-lived union of the German-Bohemian provinces with the new republic of Austria. Both presidents of the Czechoslovak Republic, T.G. Masaryk and Dr Eduard Beneš, stayed here when they visited Liberec. I was shown to a room with a view over a rhubarb-and-custard-painted Schloss. The minibar was empty and the bathroom lacked essential items such as shampoo and bath foam; although there was a stack of wafer-thin paper sheets on which to clean your razor, and sachets of artificial "cotton wool" with which to remove your make-up. The white towels were of a synthetic material which smeared rather than dried your skin. In the bar downstairs I sank into a plush Viennese armchair beneath a partially lit chandelier. The wood-panelled walls of the lounge were decorated with jagged mosaics of coloured glass. Three-day-old German newspapers swung from a wooden rack. Two girls in a corner shot me a questioning, venal glance. There were no bar staff.

The town hall of Liberec towers over Náměstí Dr E. Beneš. Its grey stone neo-Renaissance façade of arches, balconies, towers, spires and

turrets soars to a height of sixty-five metres. Built between 1888 and
1893 to a design by the Viennese Franz Neumann, architect of the Wiener
Rathaus which it resembles, it is a symbol of the wealth and civic pride
of the former German Reichenberg, once the second city of Bohemia
and the most northerly outpost of the Austro-Hungarian Empire. Like
Brünn, Reichenberg's prosperity was built on the textile trade. The first
cloth guilds were founded in the sixteenth century. General Wallenstein,
who purchased Reichenberg in 1622 and incorporated the town into his
Duchy of Friedland, boosted the cloth industry by employing its weavers
to produce uniforms for his army. Reichenberg's heyday as the metropolis
of northern Bohemia was in the 1890s and 1900s, when its grand civic
buildings were built and when it hosted an annual trade fair equal in
importance to those of Frankfurt and Leipzig. The rights and privileges of
Reichenberg were embodied in the copper figure of a knight that bestrode
the highest turret of the town hall until 1952, when it was replaced with a
red star. The Communist emblem was replaced in turn with a lion, symbol
of the new Czech Republic; although this has subsequently been removed
and there are plans to restore the city's knight to the crown of the spire. In
front of the town hall is a bronze memorial in the shape of a tank track,
which commemorates the deaths of nine citizens of Liberec killed during
the invasion of Czechoslovakia by Warsaw Pact forces in 1968. In the
centre of the square there was once a Jugendstil fountain designed by the
Bohemian-German Franz Metzner, who also sculpted the figures in the
Hecker Crypt of the Monument to the Battle of the Nations in Leipzig. It
was installed in 1926, but removed and presumably destroyed in 1945.
Now there is only a manhole cover with the inscription "Paul Scheider,
Reichenberg" to remind one this was previously the Altstädter Platz of a
German city.

I took a seat on the terrace of one of the cafés that spilled onto the
square from beneath a colonnade of pink and green houses. The tables
below the sunshades were occupied by parties of burly Saxons, dressed in
curtain-patterned summer shirts from Karstadt or Hertie, drinking copious amounts of local beer and *Sekt*. The waiters were numbed by the
German custom of never buying rounds of drinks: each individual in a
group of ten or twelve pays for his or her own drink. During my long wait
to attract the attention of one of the waiters, I found myself eavesdropping
on a conversation between an elderly American gentleman with a thick
German accent and a sulky black-clad Goth teenager who I assumed was
his grandson. The grandfather was recounting his experiences of being

driven out of the Sudetenland by Czechoslovak militia in 1945, but the boy looked as though he would rather be back at home in Illinois, playing air guitar to his Slipknot albums.

Sloping down from Dr E. Beneš Square towards the Ještěd shopping centre was Pražská, the main shopping street of Liberec. I walked down between kebab joints, casinos for German tourists and "fashion" boutiques selling beige velveteen flares and men's matching shirt and tie sets individually wrapped in cellophane. The Ještěd mall, now leased by Tesco, was a Lego-style construction of lurid orange glazed-brick hexagons mounted on lurid orange glazed-brick octagons and held in place by stairwells and walkways of chocolate-brown corrugated iron. Tatra T-3 tramcars creaked and ground their wheels around the shopping complex, picking up passengers from the globular tram station surrounding the mall. Militiamen swaggered around in black uniforms, peaked caps and dark glasses, caressing their long rubber truncheons.

I decided to avoid the Saxon hordes and dine at a Czech restaurant. The only establishment I could find was the Kavárna Pošta in the square behind the town hall. I peered through its windows, noticing there were more waiters than diners, which always makes me feel self-conscious; but I was intrigued by its seedy elegance and wandered in as casually as possible. I was seated at a table in the centre, a single chandelier hanging precariously above me. I stared at multiple reflections of myself in the skewed mirrors that covered the walls. The gilt and stucco Jugendstil allure of the dining room was somewhat undermined by its threadbare tablecloths, a noisy fridge behind the bar and a row of free-standing display cabinets, each of which contained a single tray of sticky cakes, a line of three empty beer bottles and six cans of a popular soft drink. I observed the Kafkaesque formalities of ordering a meal: first, the *maître d'hôtel* presented me with a Czech-language menu on which I could recognise only *biftek* and *porek*; second, an ankle-socked waitress placed my cutlery with an exaggerated formality; then, a callow, unsmiling youth took my wine order; finally, a second waitress translated on auto-pilot the Czech menu into German, making a show of apology as every dish I selected was "unavailable" on tonight's menu. I ended up with a gristly *Pfeffersteak* that could easily have come from a horse. It was submerged in peppers and leeks, possibly to disguise its equine flavour. Midway through the meal a band dressed in matching brown Crimplene suits appeared on a makeshift stage to entertain me and the two other guests with deafening medleys of Beatles songs, grinning at me as they must have been informed

I was English. The two other guests, a thin woman and a fat woman who sat in a dark corner flicking cigarette ash over their table, turned out to be prostitutes, who took turns at sashaying over to my table to proposition me as I sat eating my leeks.

I strolled back to the Zlatý Lev with that tingle of excitement at the prospect of the sort of illicit sexual encounter one anticipates in any Central European grand hotel. The two girls from the hotel bar had transferred themselves to a sofa in the lobby, and their eyes lit up at the sight of an inebriated male Westerner reeling in. However, the uniformed receptionist, who had earlier sympathised with my run-in with the police, decided she would practise her English on me, telling me she had acquired a job as a nanny in Lincolnshire and asking me what I knew about the exotic city of Scunthorpe. She became so flirtatious I began to wonder whether she was on the game too. As I made my way towards the lift, the hotel manager tiptoed out of his office and discreetly enquired whether I would like a girl for the night. By the time I reached my room I was half-expecting a couple of call girls to come leaping out of the empty minibar.

7
Silesia

Chavskis and Choolygans

The noxious smell of a chemical factory. An out-of-town shopping mall – IKEA, Obi, MediaMarkt, McDonald's, Tesco, Auchan, Kentucky Fried Chicken – that could be anywhere in globalised Europe. A motorway intersection. A cobbled boulevard bisected by a tramway reservation, overgrown with weeds. Rows of trees screening off high-rise apartment blocks from the main thoroughfare. A Russian military cemetery guarded by tanks and gun carriages poised on angled plinths. A colossal roundabout, once known as Hindenburgplatz, now named Square of the Silesian Uprising. Prussian villas, neo-Gothic churches, mock-Tudor barracks. Disused tramlines in the asphalt. *Litfaßsäulen* on street corners. A railway bridge. A square of Stalinist office blocks. A canal that was once a moat encircling the old centre of German Breslau, now Polish Wrocław. I crossed a bridge over the Odra and saw my destination, the Hotel Park Plaza, glowing green and yellow in the dark like a giant BP petrol station.

The *rynek* on a Saturday night. Testosterone-charged teenagers pushing and shoving as they parade around the town hall in boisterous groups, peeling off into the cafés and bars on the square. Girls dressed to kill in white jeans and pink tops, faux leather blouson jackets and denim miniskirts, peroxide-blonde hair piled and layered into feathers and tufts, gold lamé accessories and bronzed cleavages. Rowdy shaven-headed chavskis clad in sportswear, baseball caps and camouflage trousers, chanting football songs, hunting in packs. The kids who were on their own were prostitutes, moving discreetly with the flow of the crowd, eyes darting from left to right in search of foreigners with money.

The maître d' of the Dwór Polski (Polish Court) restaurant stood, hands clasped behind his back and legs astride, surveying the tables of his establishment. Smug and thuggish, he may once have been an operative in the UBP secret police who has reinvented himself as a capitalist entrepreneur. He wore a square-cut beige suit whose arms and legs were too short, a beige sleeveless pullover and a thickly knotted silk tie. You could hear the abacus whirring inside his crew-cut skull as his steel-rimmed eyes scanned the ratio of occupied to empty tables on the terrace in front of him. I sat down at one of the unoccupied tables, but nothing happened. After fifteen minutes I followed the example of another couple of would-be patrons and moved to the restaurant next door. The Karczma Lwowska (L'vov Tavern), a similarly old-fashioned, traditional Polish establishment, offered a choice between burning beefsteak, Leopolitan herring, Old Polish *bigos* with ribs, chicken fillet with smoked sheep's cheese and garlic butter, grilled chicken wings *à la devil,* or tripe with fried dumplings and Leopolitan horseradish. While I was wondering which Leopold the Leopolitan[4] dishes were named after, a waiter approached and plonked a basket of bread and a bowl of goose fat on my table. "This is grease… and this is bread," he told me with a patronising smile. I selected smoked pork ribs at 7.50 zlotys per 100 grams, accompanied by 200 grams of potatoes *à la shoemaker's wife* and 120 grams of Jewish salad with a hint of coriander and lots of pepper. I wondered whether the goose fat was going to be charged by the gram. For dessert I settled for the "exclusive ice cream rainbow" rather than the Galician poppy cake, and had tea with jam of roses (200 millilitres of tea and 30 grams of jam of roses) to wash the meal down. At least I was getting served.

Sunday morning and the *rynek* was ablaze with sunshine. The tall, gabled buildings along the western side of the square reflect the age when the city was Habsburg Presslaw. The House of the Seven Electors, the House under the Blue Sun, the House under the Golden Sun, the House under the Griffins and the House of the Golden Cup are the former residences of the Fuggers, bankers from Augsburg, and the Thurzós, prelates and philanthropists from Kraków; of patricians such as Heinrich Rybisch, Thomas Rehdiger and the von Keltsch family; of Archduke Albrecht II of Silesia, King Władysław IV Vasa of Poland and Emperors Ferdinand I and Rudolf II of Austria. Prussian Breslau, by contrast, has been all but erased

---

4   In fact, Michael Moran's book *A Country in the Moon* notes that Leopolitan refers to the city of L'vov (L'viv) in Ukraine.

from the market square. An equestrian statue of Frederick the Great was removed and buried in 1944, then later melted down and replaced by a Perspex fountain. That of Friedrich Wilhelm III, on whose pedestal was inscribed his appeal "An Mein Volk" ("To My People") issued in Breslau in 1813 to exhort his subjects to take up arms against Napoleon, was removed and replaced in 1956 by a statue of the Polish dramatist Aleksander Fredro which had been transported from L'vov after the war. A statue of the Prussian field marshal Gebhard Leberecht von Blücher, hero of the Napoleonic Wars (and duly commemorated on the architrave of the Befreiungshalle), once stood in the centre of the adjacent Salt Market, its pedestal inscribed with the patriotic slogan "With God for King and Homeland". It was removed after the war, replaced by an obelisk celebrating the fifteenth-century Catholic inquisitor John of Capistrano, whose apocalyptic sermons encouraged the citizens of Bohemian Vretslav to unleash a wave of pogroms against the city's Jewish community, forty-one of whom were tortured, sentenced to death and tied to stakes in the market square, where their flesh was removed with red-hot tongs and thrown into frying pans.

Most of the buildings surrounding the *rynek* are reconstructions, since 70% of German Breslau was destroyed during the siege of the city between February and May 1945. The surviving structures were demolished on the orders of the Polish United Workers' Party, partly to provide bricks for the reconstruction of Warsaw, and partly out of a vindictive desire to eliminate any remaining traces of German culture from the new Wrocław. The replica baroque houses now around the square still looked new and clean, their red, yellow, green and pink façades shining in the sunlight like artificially coloured sweets. The Sweets Market, incidentally, where honey, figs, pineapples and gingerbread were traded, lay on the northern side of the square. The southern frontage, known as the Side of the Golden Cup, was devoted to beer drinking: here were the taverns, the Świdnica beer cellar and the brewery Under the Golden Jug. The Green Pipe Side at the eastern end of the market square was dominated in the early twentieth century by the Barasch Brothers department store, an Art Nouveau emporium opened in 1904 and now known as Feniks. In its German days the store's entrance led through a graceful, five-storey, glass-plated arch into a winter garden filled with exotic plants and tea rooms. The shop was surmounted by an illuminated globe, which was demolished after being struck by lightning in 1929. The affluent Side of the Scale at the western end of the square functioned as the Wool Market until its weighing house was pulled

down in the mid-nineteenth century in order to make way for the New
Town Hall. A ten-storey savings bank on the south-western corner of the
rynek is the only surviving building of an ambitious scheme to modernise
the centre of Breslau in the early 1930s. Its southern façade looks over the
Salt Market (once known as Blücherplatz), which also traded in fish, furs,
honey and wax. It is now decked with flower stalls which provide discreet
cover for cruising rent boys.

The city's council buildings, a Gothic Town Hall built in the Middle Ages
and a neo-Gothic New Town Hall built in the 1860s, occupy the centre of
the *rynek*. In the vestibule of the Townsmen's Hall is a German replica of
the first recorded map of Habsburg Presslaw, painted by Georg and Barthel
Weihner in 1562 to celebrate the coronation of Maximilian II as King of
Bohemia. Busts of eminent Wratislavians line the hall, among them Carl
Gotthard Langhans, superintendent of Prussian construction in Silesia and
architect of the Brandenburg Gate in Berlin; Adolph von Menzel, patriotic
German painter of the Frederician era and, like Carl Spitzweg, a favourite
of Adolf Hitler; and Gerhart Hauptmann, author of the Naturalist drama
The Weavers. Hauptmann survived National Socialism and the Second
World War, only to find himself dying, in the spring of 1946, in his native
Silesia – in a country that was now foreign. The Soviet authorities wished
to be rid of him, and the German authorities had offered to relocate him
to Dresden; but the playwright insisted on remaining on his native soil.
He intended to make one final appeal to the German people – for hope,
courage and solidarity – but he lost consciousness before he was able to
address his compatriots. His last words were a despairing "Bin Ich noch in
meinem Haus?" ("Am I still in my house?"). The grand, star-vaulted ceremonial chamber on the first floor of the town hall is adorned with heraldic
symbols of the city in its many guises: as capital of the Duchy of Silesia;
as one of the three great cities of the Bohemian crown; and as a northern
outpost of the Habsburg Empire. Piast eagles, Silesian eagles, Habsburg
eagles and Bohemian lions are mounted on stone portals or carved into the
marble floor. The figure of John the Evangelist, patron of the city council,
and the head of John the Baptist, patron saint of the city and province, are
engraved on a padded steel door leading from the council chamber to the
council offices. The black raven of the Hungarian king Mátyás Corvinus,
who ruled Silesia from 1469 to 1490, decorates a crowned shield set into
the tympanum of the door. The walls of the Grand Hall are hung with tapestries into which have been woven the German names of the towns and
cities of Lower Silesia – Brieg, Troppau, Oppeln, Liegnitz, Breslau.

The life of the Wratislavian priest Dietrich Bonhoeffer is commemorated by a bronze sculpture, in the form of a kneeling man, in the courtyard of the Church of Saint Elizabeth on the north-west corner of the *rynek*. The Protestant theologian was born in Breslau in 1906 and hanged in the concentration camp of Flossenbürg in 1945, after a lifetime of resistance to National Socialist policies of euthanasia. The western wall of the restored Gothic church is now covered with memorial tablets to Poles – soldiers, miners, peasants and boy scouts – killed by Soviet or Polish authorities for anti-Communist activities. These memorials have all been erected since the collapse of Communist dictatorship in 1989. Many refer to Poles murdered in Galicia and its capital Lwów at the end of the Second World War. Polish Lwów (later Soviet L'vov and now Ukrainian L'viv) is Wrocław's *doppelgänger* city. It was Poland's south-eastern metropolis in the same way that Breslau was the south-eastern *Metropole* of Prussia. Both were, for many centuries, northern outposts of the Habsburg lands. Polish Lwów and German Breslau were both destroyed in the war, their populations expelled and driven west. As Poland's borders moved to the west, displaced Poles from Lwów were transferred west to fill the empty city of Breslau and reinhabit the ruined properties abandoned by displaced Germans who, in turn, had been moved west beyond Germany's receding border with Poland. Hundreds of thousands of Polish "repatriants" (a misleading term invented by the Polish Communist authorities which gave the impression that the eastern Poles were reinhabiting lands that had previously been Polish) were forcibly relocated from Lwów to Breslau at the end of the war, shunted around in cattle trucks for weeks on end and left to fend for themselves once they arrived in the ruins of Breslau, now renamed Wrocław.

I crossed Most Pomorski and walked along the north bank of the Odra in the shadow of the former offices of the Polish United Workers' Party (PZPR). The grimy monolith ran for four hundred metres in a convex curve of grey concrete, its walls featureless except for hundreds of square windows and the occasional circle or rectangle of raw brick where a piece of Communist insignia had been torn out. On reaching its furthest point, I turned around the back of the building into Max Borna Square (named after one of Wrocław's Nobel Prize-winning physicists), a secretive space overlooked by lampposts shaped like twin antennae, with necklaces of grey-painted loudspeakers. Then I walked back along another quarter-mile of monotonous grey concrete, barred windows and tangled coils of barbed wire.

Upstream of the PZPR headquarters, the Odra diverges into four streams around five islets. In pre-war Breslau these were the domains of churches, monasteries, libraries and the villas of the rich. Most were destroyed in the final months of the siege of Fortress Breslau. On 4 May 1945, after the war had ended in most of Europe, the German general Hermann Niehoff moved his headquarters to Sand Island in the middle of the Odra. The explosions that were set off, when the mines and munitions stored there caught fire, sent the whole area up in flames, including a collection of three hundred thousand books that had already been rescued once from the university library. In the immediate aftermath of the war the remaining German inhabitants of the islets – teachers, doctors, clerics, choirmasters, librarians and their families – were terrorised by gangs of Polish Communist thugs. The remaining contents of their churches and libraries were looted and graves were dug up as robbers scoured corpses in search of gold teeth. The islands have now reverted to sandbanks of scuffed parks where men fish and defecate. A few isolated ruins of Prussian tenements stand sentinel over areas of untended wasteland. The random presence of surviving buildings and the contiguous absence of destroyed buildings; the roads that lead nowhere and the streets that have lost their names; the sluices, weirs and rusted girder bridges; the brick embankments that corset the oily river; that sense of a place which was once the centre of somewhere, but has now been abandoned – all this was reminiscent of that desolate swathe of Berlin along the banks of the Spree during the Cold War.

I followed the sound of trams rumbling across an ageing yellow girder bridge that led over the Stara Odra towards the suburb of Szczytniki (known as Alt-Scheitnig in German times) and the exhibition grounds dominated by the Jahrhunderthalle, built for the Centennial Exhibition of 1913. Like the Befreiungshalle above Kelheim, the Jahrhunderthalle (Centenary Hall) was built to commemorate the German Wars of Liberation against the forces of Napoleon; more specifically, the proclamation "An Mein Volk" issued by King Friedrich Wilhelm III in Breslau in 1813. The exhibition hall was one of the first monumental public works of modernism. Built in concentric circles that diminish in size as they get higher, the Jahrhunderthalle was likened at the time of its construction to a layered cake or a hatbox; from a distance it resembles a secular Aghia Sofia. Time has not been kind to the building: its concrete walls are cracked and stained by damp, window panes are missing. A cladding of ivy that covers its lower storey lends it an air of antiquity: it seems now like some Byzantine greenhouse or gasworks.

In contrast to its brittle, stepped exterior, the interior of the Jahrhunderthalle is breathtaking, seemingly twice the size it appears from outside. A dome of reinforced concrete soars over a circular arena, sixty-seven metres in diameter. The dome rises to a height of forty-two metres, supported by thirty-two concrete ribs resting on eight immense arches. Its raw concrete is not pretty; but the rhythm and dynamism of its curved ribs and arches, and the concentric circles of light formed in the dome, are awe-inspiring. Bruno Taut wrote at the time that the Jahrhunderthalle represented a "cathedral of the future". The architect of the hall, Max Berg, planned to commission Oskar Kokoschka to decorate the interior with murals and stained-glass windows, so that it would glitter with colour, but municipal funds ran out at this stage.

The Jahrhunderthalle formed the centrepiece of the Centennial Exhibition of 1913. The exhibition grounds were laid out in a "total environment" that included a pavilion of funerary art, a "Rheingold" winery, an open-air restaurant, the pavilion of the Silesian Artists' Association and an artificial lake enclosed by a pergola. A Four-Dome Pavilion designed by Hans Poelzig exhibited a reconstruction of Breslau, as it was in 1813. The Centennial Exhibition was officially opened on 20 May 1913 in the presence of Prince Wilhelm, heir to the imperial throne. A contemporary photograph illustrates thousands of dignitaries swallowed up in the enormous dimensions of the hall, paying homage to a giant Iron Cross. (The institution of the Iron Cross was founded during the Wars of Liberation, and was also celebrating its centenary.) The cultural highlight of the Centennial Exhibition was the première of Gerhart Hauptmann's *Festspiel in deutschen Reimen* ("Festival Drama in German Rhyme"), a symbolic re-enactment of the struggle against Napoleon. Directed by Max Reinhardt with a minimalist *mise-en-scène,* this was a utopian drama conveying a clear political message that could be understood by a mass audience of ten thousand people. Combining words and music with the futuristic backdrop of the Jahrhunderthalle, it provided a spectacle on the scale of Wagner's *Gesamtkunstwerk* – a modernist take on *Die Meistersinger von Nürnberg.*

The outbreak of war did not unduly affect the new hall. Trade fairs began there in 1917, and in November the following year the inaugural meeting of the new *Volksrat* (People's Council) was convened below its dome. An organist played the *Marseillaise* as Max Berg proclaimed to the assembled audience of union leaders, soldiers' councils and Social Democrats that the Jahrhunderthalle was a "cathedral of democracy" for the "quiet revolution" that had taken place in Germany. In June 1929 a model housing estate was added to the exhibition grounds as part of a *Wohnung und Werkraum* ("Dwelling and Workplace") architectural exhibition. A successor to Stuttgart's model settlement of Weißenhof built in 1927, *WuWA* showcased new projects by Hans Scharoun and other Silesian architects working in the style of Neues Bauen. The modernist houses have survived in good condition, despite the fact that Scharoun's Apartment Building for Unmarried Persons and Young Married Couples was later used as a brothel by the SS. The booklet relating the history of the Centenary Hall glosses over the 1930s, revealing only that "industrial fairs dominated the use of the exhibition ground. However, sport events and circus performances were also held there." So, no Nazi rallies, then? Breslau was the "brownest" city of the Third Reich, its citizens loyal and vociferous supporters of National Socialism. Hitler addressed a rally of thirty thousand supporters in the Jahrhunderthalle as early as September 1930. He returned to "Adolf Hitler's Most Faithful City" for a speech in April 1932; and again, in March 1933, for a victorious post-election rally. The Feast Day of the National Socialist Singing Union was celebrated below the cupola in June 1937; and the following year the Führer attended the Twelfth German Sport and Gymnastics Festival and a mass ceremony to commemorate the 125th anniversary of the Iron Cross.

The exhibition grounds survived the Second World War and the siege of Breslau relatively unscathed, despite the fact that a hard core of SS soldiers barricaded themselves in the Jahrhunderthalle rather than face surrender. The flat roof of the entrance forum was destroyed, leaving the needle-thin concrete pillars with nothing to support, as they remain today. The Centenary Hall was renamed the People's Hall (Hala Ludowa in Polish) and a ninety-six-metre steel spike was erected in front of it to symbolise the new Polish-Communist spirit of the site. From July to October 1948 an Exhibition of the Recovered Territories showcased "The Prehistory of Slav Tribes in Central Europe: The Return of Poland to its Piast Path", "One Thousand Years of Polish-German Struggle" and "The Exclusively Polish History and Culture of Silesia". Like the use of the word "repatriant", these were disingenuous slogans coined by the post-war Polish authorities in order to give the new citizens of Wrocław a spurious sense of belonging.

In 1948 the People's Hall hosted some of the events of a portentously named "International Congress of Intellectuals in Defence of Peace", which attracted to Wrocław figures such as Max Frisch, Paul Eluard, Luis

Aragon and the "Communist poster boy" Pablo Picasso, all of whom embarrassed themselves by vindicating Stalinist cultural policies through their presence at the conference. In the 1950s and 1960s the People's Hall functioned as a venue for mass sporting and musical events. Photographs displayed in the vestibule record that an army ensemble from the People's Republic of China performed here in 1959; followed by Paul Anka and Tom Jones in 1963; and Marlene Dietrich, twice, in March 1966. The European Basketball Championships took place in the hall in October 1963. The celebrations of the fiftieth anniversary of the October Revolution were held in 1967; and in 1970 the twenty-fifth anniversary of the "Liberation of Wrocław" was commemorated. The highlights of the "70-ties and 80-ties" (to quote the captions below the photographs) were concerts given by Iron Maiden, Leonard Cohen (a singer of Polish Jewish ancestry), People's Diva of the Soviet Union Alla Pugacheva, and Procol Harum (one wonders whether they retitled their greatest hit "A Redder Shade of Pink" for their Socialist audience). In the spring of 1978 there was a "presentation of culture of the people's democracy countries", photographs of which reveal pop groups bearing a visual resemblance to Middle of the Road or The Brotherhood of Man gyrating beneath a cluster of "psychedelic" balloons stencilled with the names of such groovy cities as "Moskva" or "Warszawa". The interior of the People's Hall was renovated in the mid-1990s in preparation for the International Eucharistic Congress of June 1987, presided over by Pope John Paul II. Since then the hall has functioned as an arena for boxing contests, lottery draws, folk dance performances, university entrance examinations, basketball matches, the "Nekropolie" (a "Fair of Cemetery Arts") and "foul (sic) and poultry exhibitions".

I left Wrocław on the Feast of the Assumption, a public holiday. Red and white flags hung in the still air on every street corner. Cemeteries were packed with people laying flowers. I headed south-west towards Wałbrzych, a town formerly known as Waldenburg, which in German means "Forest Keep". However, any notions I might have entertained that Wałbrzych would be a pretty little romantic town with a castle hidden in a forest were quickly dispelled. The first sign I passed extolled the delights of "Night Club Ewa"; and thereafter the graffiti scrawled over walls and tenements grew increasingly menacing: "MKS" (in support of an Inter-Enterprise Strike Committee founded by Lech Wałęsa in the Gdańsk shipyard); "Śląsk!" (Silesian separatists); "Górnik Choolygans (sic)"; and, in German, "Juden Raus!" Once past the signs marking the municipal boundary, route 35 continued beneath a succession of inverted U-shaped gas pipes into a seemingly endless valley whose slopes were pockmarked with defunct pitheads and abandoned factories. Below the chimneys, lines of grimy apartment blocks rotted away along streets that were little more than rutted dirt tracks covered with an oily film. There were no pavements along the main road, just a zone of slurry where the road petered out and the tenements started to grow, as if at random, out of the charcoal-textured earth. I caught glimpses through archways into greasy back yards where teenagers congregated: boys with cropped or shaven heads and scabby, pinched faces; undernourished girls in bleached denim. Their fathers and uncles, men in vests with bloodshot eyes and puffy grey skin, leaned out of cracked windows drawing slowly on cigarettes; or squatted, clutching bottles of beer, in disused quarries converted into used-car lots. Packs of feral dogs, cats and chickens careered blindly across the road. Mothers and grandmothers waited in derelict shelters for buses which were incongruously smart and modern, painted in a green and yellow livery that reminded me of the buses from Wolverhampton that ran past the scruffy housing estate in Bloxwich where my grandmother lived in the 1970s, which is now in a similar state of dereliction.

Several larger public buildings indicated I was approaching the centre of Wałbrzych. On the left was the tower block of the Hotel Sudety, whose hundreds of pairs of unwashed net curtains and spunk-encrusted eiderdowns could tell a thousand tales of visiting colliery executives or trade union delegates and the sleepless nights they endured, anaesthetised by Pay-TV and minibar vodka. To the right was the bronze monolith of the police headquarters (formerly those of the UBP secret police), whose shiny, reflective surfaces hid a multitude of more desperate ordeals. I passed a cluster of old Prussian churches and schools, their red-brick walls concealed beneath a century-old layer of soot that had now carbonised and was peeling off like strips of wallpaper. The windows of a former German *Gymnasium* in Plac Kościelny shone from its blackened façade with a dull light, like the eyes of miners emerging from a shift at the coal face. After several kilometres A. Mickiewicza Street began to climb out of the valley and I realised I must have missed the town centre, or passed through it without noticing. It started to rain and I turned back.

The *rynek* of Wałbrzych was an oasis of colour and elegance amid the charred corrosion of the rest of the town. The buildings around the square had been restored and repainted. Tubs of geraniums were stuffed into window boxes like swabs of bloody cotton wool. Baroque town-houses such as the House under the Atlanteans, the House under the Anchor or the House with Three Roses – lemon, pink and pigeon-blue mansions fronted by colonnades, caryatids and gilt medallions – reflected Waldenburg's heyday as a centre of the linen industry in the eighteenth century. Nineteenth-century Waldenburg became the hub of the Lower Silesian coalfield. After the Second World War the region was of such importance to Polish industry that Polish labourers employed by the Nazis, who would normally have been sent to labour camps in Siberia, were re-employed by the Soviet authorities. Polish miners returning from exile in Belgium and France were drafted to Wałbrzych; and ten thousand German workers, who would otherwise have been expelled from the new Polish state, were encouraged to remain in the town to keep the mines in operation. Wałbrzych remained a mining town until the 1990s, when "new social and economic conditions" (the loss of Silesia's captive export market in the Soviet bloc) forced the surviving collieries to close down. A new Toyota plant has provided employment for many of the former miners, but has not entirely alleviated the poverty and unemployment that are all too evident in the town.

The *rynek* had recently been relaid with new cobblestones that formed pink and grey swirls across the square. Flagpoles, wrought-iron lottery kiosks and small pollarded trees stood around its edge. In the centre was a circle of wooden benches where people sat waiting for a fountain to shoot upwards in a jet of spray every few minutes. One man was moaning to himself, clutching his liver in pain. As it was a public holiday, the cafés and shops around the square were closed. The only establishment open was a Chinese restaurant at the end of a gloomy passageway. I entered it, and went through the formalities of checking in my jacket in the cloak-room, being shown to a carefully laid table by a young waitress dressed in a kimono, and being presented with a menu (in English as well as Polish) and a hot towel. I was delighted to receive these small, home-from-home comforts; but when I placed my order for a single cup of tea and noticed the involuntary look of disappointment on the face of the waitress, I felt a pang of guilt.

I left, rather shamefacedly, returning to the *rynek* where I ordered a hot dog from a hole-in-the-wall stall. The vendor asked me in German what "in God's name" I was doing in Wałbrzych. I replied that I had come here in search of a mausoleum built by the Germans during the Third Reich. There was a photograph of it in one of the National Socialist art magazines, *Die Kunst im Dritten Reich,* which I had bought in the flea market in Linz. The photograph illustrated a square temple of white brick with a single band of darker granite that ran around the waist of the building. Two low extensions ran off at either end, culminating in elevated plinths. The only opening in the walls was a narrow slit, just tall and wide enough for a man to enter, set into a Romanesque portal in one side of the mausoleum. The photograph in the art journal emphasised the strong, spare lines of the memorial by setting it against a dramatic backdrop of distant hills and a menacing sky. According to an article by the critic Carl Meissner that accompanied the photograph, the mausoleum (or cenotaph, to be more precise, as it was literally an "empty tomb") was commissioned by the National Welfare Office for German War Graves in memory of the one hundred and seventy thousand German soldiers who sacrificed their lives on the Eastern Front during the First World War, "for the honour of the dead heroes, the forerunners of the Third Reich", as Meissner wrote. The article attributed the design of the cenotaph to Wilhelm Kreis and the sculptor Robert Tischler. In fact, it was exclusively Tischler's project, but he was no doubt inspired by the Bismarck Towers and Reich memorial sites designed by National Socialism's foremost "proto-Germanic" architect. The mausoleum was constructed between 1936 and 1938 and is listed in *Bauen unterm Hakenkreuz,* the bible of National Socialist architecture, as "condition unknown". I doubted whether it still existed. As a symbol of German imperialism and Nazi aggression, it would probably have been demolished by the Communists after the war. My map of the Wałbrzych district, however, indicated a "mausoleum" marked in the middle of a wood on a hill above the town. The smaller-scale plan of the centre of the town revealed this monument to be a square with an interior courtyard.

I set off, more in hope than expectation, following a blue "tourist trail" (tourists? In Wałbrzych?) that led up J. Pilsudskiego Street, through allotments on the slopes above the town and into a wood. Reaching the top of the hill, I was astonished to find that the German temple was still there – straddling the centre of a clearing like the remains of a medieval keep. Although crumbling into ruin and damaged where the Reichs insignia had been torn out, its white-brick exterior remained intact. The two low extensions disappeared into the undergrowth which now surrounded the former cenotaph. I felt as if I had stumbled on something forbidden; a relic of the past that should by rights no longer exist. I walked around the memorial, listening for any sound from within, daring myself to enter. The narrow entrance had been partially blocked by a concrete barrier, but it wasn't difficult to clamber over. I wondered what would await me inside – the ghosts of Wehrmacht soldiers? Or a group of neo-Nazis holding a barbecue?

The interior of the mausoleum was open to the skies, like the Ehrentempel adjoining the Königsplatz in Munich or the Anschlussdenkmal above Oberschützen in the Burgenland. It was overgrown with weeds and this-tles. Some large stones in the centre had been scattered around a circular area of ash that looked as though it was now used for nocturnal drink-ing sessions, or for something more sinister. The inner courtyard of the cenotaph was originally paved with stones laid around a central column, which was decorated with sculpted lions and four caryatids supporting a fire bowl. The cloisters around the courtyard, each consisting of five arches opening out into the central area, were now blackened by fire and resembled the charred temples painted by Anselm Kiefer. The flooring in the corners of the arcades had collapsed, revealing a network of sub-terranean chambers below the mausoleum. The crypts were now full of rubbish, broken bottles and chunks of masonry that had fallen from the ceiling of the colonnade. This was a true ruin of the Reich – a German temple built by a German architect that embodied the Nazi ideals of her-oism and sacrifice and celebrated the Nazi cult of death – which had been neither destroyed nor sanitised into a memorial to the victims of National Socialism. It had simply been abandoned, left to rot away in a foreign country.

The second of Tischler's Silesian monuments, built at the same time as the cenotaph above Waldenburg, was a memorial to commemorate the Freikorps counter-insurgency in Upper Silesia in May 1921; to honour in particular the fifty-one fallen "heroes" of the Battle of Annaberg on 21 May that year. Tischler's memorial was designed "to blaze forth like a shining beacon from the night of suffering of the German people". The monument was a low, circular, fortress-like bunker of enclosed walls fortified by ten projecting buttresses. Its prototype was the Castel del Monte, the medieval fortress of Emperor Friedrich II, whose towered octagonal structure also influenced the Tannenberg Mausoleum built in East Prussia in the 1920s.

The foundation stone of the Freikorps Mausoleum was laid on 28 August 1936 on a rocky plateau on top of a cliff, seven or eight hundred metres below Annaberg, one of the most sacred shrines to Polish Mariolatry.

On arriving at Góra Swietej Anny (Annaberg, or Saint Anne's Hill), I parked my car and wandered around the deserted chapels and shrines that criss-crossed the wooded hill. It was the morning after Assumption, and the Franciscan monastery and its surrounding calvaries had a hung-over air. On returning to the car I was accosted by a rough-faced man reeking of alcohol, who explained he had been "looking after it" for me, and threatened to punch a hole in it unless I "rewarded" him (this, at least, seemed to be the gist of his argument). As I was the only visitor to the basilica, it was difficult to fathom what or whom the car needed protection against. I tried to ask him if he knew where the *Thingstätte* (thingstead) or the site of the Freikorps Monument was, but he then threatened to punch a hole in me. I walked up to the village and found a signboard with a pictograph of a monument painted on it. I followed a residential street into a broad avenue paved with granite slabs. The avenue opened out onto a plateau paved with stone, on which a new memorial stood.

The Freikorps Mausoleum had been blown up in 1946 and its site razed. The monument the Poles had put in its place resembled a giant nursery table. Clad in silvery *ersatz* marble, the Monument to the Silesian Uprisings, built in 1955, consisted of four square legs linked by narrow horizontal bridges. A series of reliefs had been etched into the legs of the monument, but there was no explanation of which events they referred to. One depicted a row of warriors thrusting their spears into an invisible enemy: the date of this battle was given as 950, fourteen years before the Polish state was deemed to have been founded. A second frieze depicted a group of people being driven from their homes: the date of this expulsion was recorded as 1934, a time when this area of Upper Silesia was a stable part of National Socialist Germany. It was unclear whether these figures represented German oppression of Poles or Polish liberation from Germany. Slogans extolling peace in three languages – "POKOJ", "MUP" and "FRIEDEN" – were engraved on the architrave of the monument, and the inner walls of its four towers were decorated with the obligatory hammers, sickles and figures of robotic warriors. A fire bowl resting on a stone altar perpetuated the iconography of totalitarianism – one dictatorship exchanged for another.

At the foot of the cliffs below the monument was a former Nazi *Thingstätte*. Named after the Old Norse word for a tribal council, the

Thing movement was founded in January 1933, under the aegis of the Reichs Association for German Open-Air and People's Theatre, as a propaganda instrument for National Socialism. As part of the process of nationalising the masses, a number of open-air, semi-circular amphitheatres based on the ancient Greek model were built. These were cultural places of assembly to complement the paramilitary rally grounds under construction in Nuremberg. The rows of terracing around the edge of the arena were now overgrown and had disappeared into the encroaching forest. Three of the four shields around the pedestal of the flagpole had been dismantled; only one (presumably Polish) eagle remained. A broad flight of steps at the eastern end of the former *Thingplatz* descended into a sunken grove from which a mysterious hexagonal tower with an anchor carved into its walls loomed out of the trees. Built between 1934 and 1936, and abandoned two or three years later, these ruins of the Third Reich have merged with the natural structure of the forest. Indestructible, they will probably last for the one thousand years of the Reich – and will confirm Albert Speer's Theory of Ruin Value.

The Polish monument, the plastic eyesore on top of the cliff, is unlikely to last that long. Since the fall of the Berlin Wall, such socialist-patriotic memorials have become an embarrassing reminder of Poland's recent totalitarian history. Its anti-fascist, anti-German rhetoric is now redundant in Poland's post-Communist, pro-European renaissance. Both the Communist monument and the Nazi amphitheatre are white elephants which the authorities in the provincial capital of Opole are unwilling and unable to support; they have apparently applied to a German environmental agency for financial assistance. Apart from a handful of old-fashioned, anti-German, anti-European nationalists, members of the Union of the White Eagle or Polish National Rebirth, few Poles now visit the monument or commemorate the anniversary of the Third Silesian Uprising. The only people I encountered there were half a dozen members of a Silesian family, half of whom spoke in German and half in Polish.

North of Zabrze I could no longer stand the relentless roar and grind of heavy lorries on route 88, and turned off the main road into the city which was once named Hindenburg in honour of the victorious German field marshal; and which in 1939 was chosen as the *Gauhauptstadt* of National Socialist Upper Silesia. I found myself bumping along Ulica

Wolnosci, a long, straight avenue which led towards the centre of Zabrze. Rehabilitated Tatra T-3 tramcars purchased from the Czech Republic glided through the knee-high grass and weeds of the central reservation. Articulated Ikarus buses emitted clouds of acidic fume as they pulled out to overtake lopsided trucks struggling along in first gear under top-heavy loads of coal. A ribbon of soot-blackened two-up, two-down miners' cottages ran alongside the road, interspersed with crumbling Prussian tenements, many of which had collapsed, leaving vacant lots filled with mounds of broken bricks and strips of peeled wallpaper. Isolated tower blocks from the Socialist period reared up out of wasteland created by the closure of exhausted mines. The smell of bitumen, sulphur and the taste of coal dust hung over chimneys, railway sidings, slag heaps and the rusting wheels of disused pitheads. I watched a skinny, drugged-up teenager dressed in fake leopard-print pants tottering along a cobbled pavement in a pair of battered stilettos, passing in front of a grimy wall on which had been daubed "Piast Gliwice. Całz Zycie" ("Piast Gliwice, we'll support you ever more").

George Best wrote in one of his many autobiographies of a town "whose name I wouldn't like to attempt to pronounce". Manchester United were beaten 1-0 by Górnik Zabrze in the second leg of their successful European Cup campaign of 1968. Two years later, Górnik reached the final of the European Cup-Winners Cup, where they were beaten 2–1 by the other Manchester club. I wondered whatever happened to Górnik (their name literally means "miner") as I approached the centre of Zabrze. The *rynek* was an X-shaped slope criss-crossed by tramlines and surrounded by shops with generic names such as *Delikatesy*, *Apteka*, *Sklep Popularny* (people's shop) or *Spozywcze* (general store). A small selection of eels and sardines was on display in the *Ryby* (fishmonger), but most of the produce consisted of cans of pilchards and fish paste piled in pyramids behind the counter. A few cutlets lay on metal trays behind the windows of the butcher's; strings of sausages and salami hung from meat hooks; tins of meat paste and Polish spam were arranged in rows on the shelves. The *Friseur* offered its customers a "pedicure", a "henna" and a "tipsy" – the latter presumably meant having your highlights done, rather than enjoying a vodka-fuelled session with the hairdresser.

Icontinued my journey towards the heart of the GOP (Górnośląski Okręg Przemysłowy, or Upper Silesian Industrial Region). Zabrze merged into Ruda, which segued into Nowy Bytom, which fed into Chorzów. I abandoned any attempt at map reading and followed tramlines, travelling vaguely eastwards, orientating myself by the slag heaps and cooling towers that filled the empty spaces between these mining towns, which all coalesced with each other like the suburbs of some great metropolis that always lay over the next horizon. Eventually I reached Katowice, arriving in a garden suburb of high-rise apartment blocks. I joined the DTŚ (Drogowa Trasa Średnicowa), the trans-regional highway connecting the towns of the GOP. The traffic ground to a halt at the Rondo, a vast roundabout where the DTŚ intersects with Avenue W. Korfantego, which runs south into the centre of the city. On the far side of the roundabout was the Spodek, a "multi-purpose arena complex" in the shape of a flying saucer. A space-age version of Wrocław's Jahrhunderthalle, the Spodek is famous as a venue for international ice-hockey matches and rock concerts. It was built in the 1960s above a coal waste dump site classified as "2A", which indicated "medium mining damage with a possibility of local cave-ins". The authorities verified its structural soundness by marching three and a half thousand army conscripts into the building and measuring the vibration they caused. This was nothing compared to the vibration produced by ten thousand heavy metal fans headbanging to the hard rock of Deep Purple, Iron Maiden, Metallica and Pearl Jam; but the Spodek has survived. In fact, it was a nearby exhibition hall that collapsed in January 2006 because of the weight of snow on its roof, killing sixty-three pigeon-fanciers who had assembled for a fair. In front of the Spodek was the Monument to the Silesian Uprising, a semi-abstract heroic mass seemingly hewn out of anthracite. The three wings of the monster represent the three uprisings of 1919, 1920 and 1921. Like its counterparts in Opole and Góra Swietej Anny, the monument creates the disingenuous impression that the "Silesian" insurgents were Polish fighters defending their homeland against German aggression; correctly speaking, these are monuments to Polish insurgencies against German Silesia.

I turned down Avenue W. Korfantego, named after Wojciech Korfanty, leader of the "Silesian" insurgents. The boulevard was lined with grim, twenty-storey concrete blocks, former Orbis hotels built in the 1960s when Katowice was remodelled as a showcase for Communist urban planning. The damp-stained walls of the Hotel Katowice, Hotel Silesia and Hotel Polonia were illuminated by checkerboards of lugubrious light emanating

from the occupied rooms. Each of the hotels must have contained at least
four hundred rooms and I wondered who occupied them, since Katowice
was not exactly coach-party territory. A tramway ran along the centre
of the boulevard, fenced off by kilometres of red-and-white-striped railings which prevented one from crossing the road except at prescribed
pedestrian crossings situated at intervals of five hundred metres. As I
approached the railway station, I realised that I must have passed through
the *rynek* without noticing it, the central square of Katowice being just
one in a sequence of fenced-off roundabouts surrounded by tram stations
and prefabricated tower blocks.

Ulica Uniwersytecka, the street leading to my hotel, wound around
several office blocks doubling as university faculties. It was used by prostitutes: one a woman *d'un certain âge* dressed in a fluffy white twinset
and matching pillbox hat; the other in skinny jeans, low-cut top and
leather blouson. Neither was short of punters. The Novotel turned out
to be another ex-Orbis hotel with a makeover and a price to match. A
gallery of boutiques ran around the lobby, selling amber jewellery and
"folk art" paintings resembling psychedelic vaginas. The bar was full of
German businessmen and Ukrainian prostitutes, which went some way
to answering my earlier question about who occupied hotel rooms in
Katowice. The call girls, dressed in business suits and crisp white blouses,
were smarter than the executives; one of them had brought along a laptop
and was busy tapping away on her keyboard in order to hook in one of
the German technophiles.

After a coffee and a vodka, I went up to my room and leant out of the
window – "up on the eleventh floor, watching the cruisers below", so to
speak. The skyscrapers receded into the misty night sky. Katowice was not
a real city in the European sense. It had little historical continuity. It was
founded in the industrial revolution as German Kattowitz, then ceded to
Poland after the plebiscite of 1921, in spite of its overwhelmingly German
population. After the war it was renamed Stalinogród in honour of the
Soviet leader. Reverting to a Polish version of its original name in 1956,
it was reconstructed as a model Socialist city and flourished in the 1970s
during the false dawn ushered in by Eduard Gierek, a former miner from
the city, who rose through the ranks of the Upper Silesian *nomenklatura*
to become First Secretary of the PZPR in December 1970. Gierek presided
over the Polish "Great Leap Forward" – years of reckless spending that
had bankrupted the nation to the tune of twenty-three million dollars by
1980. Now that its coalfields, automotive plants and iron and steel works

are in decline, following the demise of Communism, what will the future hold for this unreal, unstable non-city? Will it collapse into disuse like its coal mines – or will the trans-regional highway and the new A4 motorway transform Katowice and the GOP into a Silicon Valley, a blue-chip centre for service industries and IT companies? To find the answer, follow the German businessmen (metaphorically speaking, unless you want to end up in bed with a Ukrainian prostitute).

Mysłowice lies ten kilometres east of Katowice, on the old eastern frontier of Silesia, close to the "Drei-Kaiser-Ecke" where the empires of Germany, Russia and Austria-Hungary once met. I parked in the market square to look at a map of the town, but there was no indication that Mysłowice had ever been anything but Polish. Lying just within German territory, Prussian Myslovitz was a frontier town of customs officials, railway workers, cigarette smugglers and people traffickers. Some 43% of the population were German, 43% were Polish; the rest were mainly Jewish. German was the *lingua franca,* although Polish, Yiddish and *Wasserpolnisch* – a mixed Polish-German idiom used by coal miners of both races to communicate with each other – were also spoken. Catholicism was the predominant faith, even among Germans. There was a Greek Orthodox church on the Russian side of the river, and several synagogues. The nearest town on the Austrian side of the border was the Polish-Jewish *shtetl* of Oshpitsin (Oświęcim), a centre of orthodox and Hasidic Judaism, whose population was 55% Jewish in 1910. Będzin, the nearest town on Russian soil, boasted a population that was 77% Jewish. The snakeheads of one hundred years ago smuggled emigrants from Serbia, Romania, Slovakia and Ruthenia into Myslovitz, where they were enrolled in the Deutscher-Feldarbeiter-Zentralstelle, an assembly point for German agricultural labourers. The wooden barracks in Myslovitz were built to house two and a half thousand immigrants, but by 1910 the number of Eastern Europeans seeking to register as migrant workers in Germany had grown to one hundred and fifty thousand. The influx reached a tipping point in 1915, following the Russian advance, and new barracks had to be built in neighbouring Austrian Oświęcim in order to contain the overspill.

I took highway 79 out of the centre of Mysłowice, travelling east in the wake of one of the ex-Berlin Bussing double-decker buses now plying their trade in this former outpost of the Prussian kingdom. I crossed the Black Przemsza River, which marked the end of the German Reich, and parked in a housing estate that was once part of the Russian Empire. I crossed a second bridge over the White Przemsza and walked along a levee on the southern bank of the river, which was formerly territory of the Austro-Hungarian Empire. A concrete pillbox lay hidden in undergrowth at the back of some allotments below the levee. The White Przemsza must have been named many years ago: it now consists of an opaque sludge that eventually soups into the even murkier Black Przemsza, from where the confluent river, formerly the border between Germany and Austria-Hungary, flows southwards to join the Vistula north of Oświęcim.

This was the geographical centre of *Mitteleuropa,* a meeting of the waters where, in 1815, after the remains of Poland had been obliterated by the Third Partition, the three great Central European powers aligned themselves with each other. When the German Reich was founded in 1871, the confluence of the two streams became known as the "Dreikaiserreichs-Ecke", the spot where three empires met. Philatelists of the early 1900s could purchase a souvenir postcard in Myslovitz depicting the portraits of Kaiser Wilhelm II, Kaiser Franz Joseph I and Czar Nicholas II; cross the Black Przemsza to buy a one heller stamp in the Austrian village of Jendzor; cross the White Przemsza to buy a one kopek stamp in the Russian hamlets of Niwka or Modrzejów; and recross the Black Przemsza to Myslovitz, where they could buy a five pfennig stamp from the Reichspost and post the card, franked in three different empires, to any destination within the German Reich, safe in the knowledge that it would arrive promptly the following morning.

After the Treaty of Versailles and the Upper Silesian plebiscite of 1921, the confluence of the two rivers lost its significance, becoming a meaningless spot where two backwaters met in the suburbs of an anonymous Polish town on the edge of the Upper Silesian coal and steel belt. If it has any resonance today, it symbolises the weakness of those overstretched, multi-ethnic empires that, by the end of the nineteenth century, had become wracked by irredentism and warmongering. As I stood on the river bank, trying to decipher a Polish sign which probably meant "No Trespassing on the Railway Lines", I found it hard to imagine that these streams and embankments had ever been German or Austrian, let alone Russian.

Above my head three girder bridges crossed the river, carrying railway lines from Katowice towards Oświęcim and Kraków. Between them stood the broken piers of the fourth and fifth bridges. I climbed onto one of these, which appeared to be disused: the planks underfoot were rotten; the metal plates between the sleepers had corroded; and the rails ran off into undergrowth on the "German" side. I was halfway over the bridge, taking a photograph of two fishermen on the tip of the "Russian" spit of land, when I heard the sound of a train approaching. For a few heart-stopping moments it occurred to me that this bridge could still be in use (after all, the trams plough along city streets through voluminous undergrowth). The roar of the train grew closer until it emerged out of the woods... on the adjacent bridge. I clambered down hastily and walked back along the embankment on the "Austro-Hungarian" side of the river.

It took me half an hour to cross a set of traffic lights in the centre of Nowy Bieruń. Heavy lorries were arriving in all directions, creating an olfactory cocktail of tar, petroleum, rubber and gas. I turned left at the lights and followed highway 44 through a landscape of slag heaps and cornfields until I reached a bridge over the Vistula. A concrete sign, whose paintwork had eroded, welcomed drivers coming from the opposite direction to the Voivodship of Śląsk (Silesia). Another sign announced that Bieruń was twinned with the idyllic Swabian town of Gundelfingen. A track built from prefabricated concrete plates led away along the western bank of the oleaginous brown river. On the far side of the Vistula was the Voivodship of Małopolskie (Lesser Poland), Habsburg Galicia from 1772 to 1918, and the municipal district of Oświęcim, better known in its German form, although it was not generally known as Auschwitz until the National Socialists extended the *Gau* of Upper Silesia eastwards, incorporating the area around the town into the *Reichsgebiet* in 1939 in order to exploit the rubber factories and oil refineries there.

The outer perimeter fence of Auschwitz-Birkenau concentration camp would have run through the woods less than two hundred metres from the opposite bank of the river. I had reached the point at which I had to decide whether I would go there or not. I was exploring the ruins of the Reich, and this was the biggest and most horrifying ruin of the Third Reich. But, according to the inscriptions around the Befreiungshalle, I was to write about Silesia; and Silesia ended here on the left bank of the Vistula. And in any case, who was I to contemplate writing about something beyond human comprehension?

After a few minutes of pondering, I slipped the car into gear and crossed the bridge, soon passing the Hotel Glob and the railway station. Auschwitz I, the original camp built as a barracks for the Polish Army, was small and claustrophobic, bustling with coach parties. I had a coffee and followed the tourist trail. You enter the barrack blocks and look at the exhibitions devoted to the different social and ethnic groups who were murdered here. You stand in front of huge glass cases (as if you were in an aquarium) and observe waves of dead hair, mounds of shoes (you wonder why they are all single, rather than tied together in pairs) and stacks of empty suitcases (you examine the names and addresses neatly stencilled in white lettering on the sides of the cases, and try to match German names to places now in Poland or the Czech Republic). You peruse the registration cards each prisoner had to fill out on arrival at the camp, recording their personal details and physical characteristics. You notice that all new arrivals describe their nose as "gerade" (straight), and you feel ashamed at finding that funny as well as heart-rending. And all the while you know that this is just a prelude, a foretaste of the horrors to come.

Just as the thousands of paintings in the Louvre lead to the *Mona Lisa*, all the photographs, exhibits, electric fences, cells and execution yards of Auschwitz I lead inexorably to the crematorium and the process of killing. After queuing to enter the gas chamber, you and the scores of other tourists look at the floor, at the walls, at the ceiling, at the vents in the ceiling and, self-consciously, at each other. You measure the size of the chamber and try to work out how many people would have been crammed into the space at one time (probably ten to twenty times as many as are permitted to enter as tourists) and how long it took to die (about the same amount of time you spend in there as a tourist). Then you enter the adjacent chamber and observe the four brick ovens and their semi-circular metal doors. You notice the stretcher-like trays that slide on and off the brick hearths in front of the ovens, and the little trolleys that stand in front of the hearths. You measure the width of the rails leading to the hearths, and compare them with the width of the rails disappearing into the ovens. You peer into the front of the ovens, and then you peer into the rear of the ovens, and you try to see what is inside the ovens, and you look upwards again at the chimneys – and you know that this is the culmination of something awesome, the most refined process of something (like alchemy or particle physics) that humanity has been striving for centuries to perfect; and you just about understand how it works; and you more or less know why it happened; but the fact that it did happen is still too terrible to contemplate.

The scale of Auschwitz II (Birkenau) is, by contrast, overwhelming. Once I had passed through the strangely symmetrical yet asymmetrical gatehouse, walked along the platform where the selections took place and examined the shattered ruins of crematoria II and III, I found myself walking alone, far from the proprietorial, flag-waving Israeli tour groups, along paths through stands of silver birches towards the perimeter fence. It was a dull, neutral day. Filtered through a translucent canopy of cloud, a weak sun intensified the greenness of the grass. The turf was closely cropped, mown to a smoothness that was unusual in Poland, carefully manicured around pools of murky water and empty depressions in the ground, which were once pits where corpses were incinerated in the open air when the process of gassing was running faster than the five crematoria could keep up with. The enormity of the flat, rectilinear spaces of the camp contrasted with the tiny size of these pits and pools. How could so many hundreds of thousands of human beings be reduced to such a small quantity of matter it could be fitted into these miniscule depressions? Once again you contemplate the alchemy that transmuted so many tons of living flesh and bone into such infinitesimal particles of ash or vapour.

On returning to the car park, I felt guilty at attempting to record my feelings about Auschwitz-Birkenau. My immediate reaction was to cease writing my planned book about Germany, the one you are reading now about *The Ruins of the Reich*. I felt ashamed of the levity with which I had approached the Third Reich, treating it as if it were a cultural-historical period like the Baroque. I realised that all the artefacts about which I had written (and was to write) so enthusiastically – the buildings of Paul Ludwig Troost and Wilhelm Kreis; the sculptures of Arno Breker and Willy Meller; the Osteria Bavaria and the Königsplatz; the Maifeld and the Zeppelinfeld; the Dichterstein and the Sachsenhain; the Ordensburgen and the *Gauforen*; the Anschlussdenkmal and the monuments above Wałbrzych and below Annaberg – all these were the expression of a brutal despotism which led, ultimately, to a few stagnant pools of water, a field of ruined chimneys, and the ghosts of one million Jews murdered in this godforsaken place just off the map of the German Empire.

8

Prussia

"Do You Take Credit Cards?"

The information panel below a display of silverware in the historical museum of the town hall of Gdańsk read: "After the incorporation of Prussia to the Polish kingdom (1454) Gdańsk became the main exporter of metal goods into the country." It didn't really make sense: perhaps it meant "the main importer ... into the country", or possibly "the main exporter ... out of the country". In any case it was slightly disingenuous in its implication that Prussia ceased to exist in 1454. The Teutonic Knights lost Royal Prussia (West Prussia including Danzig) to Poland in that year, but retained Ducal Prussia (East Prussia), albeit as a Polish fief. Danzig was never particularly Prussian in the first place: although predominantly German-speaking, it was for much of its history an autonomous, mercantile, Dutch-Hanseatic port city. The hub of the Baltic shipbuilding industry and the northern European grain trade, Danzig flourished during its Golden Age from 1580 to 1650, attracting Flemish sculptors and architects such as Abraham van den Block and Hans Vredeman de Vries. They and others constructed a rich, ornate city of courts, armouries and granaries in the style of the Dutch Renaissance.

I climbed the bell tower of the Cathedral of the Blessed Virgin Mary until I reached a rickety platform perched seventy-six metres above the city. The former *Rechtstadt* (Danzig adopted Lübeck Law in 1261) was laid out below in a grid of parallel streets of reconstructed burghers' houses – like a post-communist Lübeck or a Delft without the canals. Immediately to the south of St Mary's the rebuilt Flemish spire of the town hall soared above Długi Targ, the drawing room of Gdańsk. Embellished with Polish eagles and Prussian unicorns, its courts housed the merchants, guildsmen and aldermen of the city. Beyond the Green Gate at the eastern end of the square was the former Speicher-Insel, an island on which once stood three hundred brick granaries – the storehouses of the Free City's wealth. Only one and a half warehouses now remained standing, isolated ruins amid a wasteland of shattered walls and cellars. On the far side of the Motława canal were the oil refineries, tankers, railway sidings and scrap yards of post-war Gdańsk, a rusting landscape of girder bridges, gantries, chimneys and gas pipes that snaked over the streets and canals of the city's industrial zone. Residential Gdańsk stretched westwards, from tenements in the inner city and Prussian villas in the woodland belt to high-rise post-war apartment blocks looming over the foothills of Kashubia. To the north the Motława wound around shipyards where scores of green cranes hung doubled up, unemployed.

I descended the four hundred steps of the bell tower of the world's largest brick church. The plain, whitewashed nave was the size of a football pitch. During the period of martial law in the 1980s it regularly held over twenty thousand worshippers. The walls around the chapel devoted to the Lithuanian Our Lady of the Gate of Dawn were covered with plaques commemorating Poles killed in the war – fighting for the Allies in Arnhem and Tobruk, or murdered in Auschwitz. The cathedral was blitzed in the war, its tower turned into a chimney of flame and its flagstones torn up by Russian soldiers looting the tombs in search of gold teeth. The reconstructed side chapels have been repainted with images of the sadism of female martyrdom: the Chapel of the Eleven Thousand Virgins depicts the handmaidens of Saint Ursula being ravished by the Huns of Cologne; and a triptych in Saint Dorothy's Altar portrays the unfortunate saint submerged up to her neck in a cauldron of oil, while her Roman inquisitor pours a ladle of the boiling liquid over her head. In the final wing of the triptych her breasts are torn from her body with burning tongs.

As dusk fell, I walked from my hotel on Wyspa Spichrzów back into the centre of Gdańsk. I crossed the Green Bridge, between stalls selling sweets, trinkets, sandals, pelts, model sailing ships and cut-price amber jewellery, and turned off along the waterfront of the Motława, past houses and taverns which once formed the Lange Brücke of German Danzig. Perched like a bird of prey on a pair of brick towers, the Great Crane threw its hooded shadow over the canal. Built at the height of Danzig's grain wealth in the fifteenth century, the blackened wooden superstructure of the crane became one of the emblems of the Prussian kingdom: like the Holstein Gate in Lübeck or the Brandenburg Gate in Berlin, its image was printed on stamps and banknotes of the German Reich. Like every other building in Gdańsk, the present structure is a post-war reconstruction. So too is the Green Gate, above whose arches are the four coats of arms that embellish all the gates of the city: the crests of Royal Prussia, Hohenzollern Prussia and Poland, and the city's own symbol – the Jagiellonian crown and two crosses of the Teutonic Knights rising in a vertical formation reminiscent of the three crosses of Amsterdam. Once the official residence of Polish monarchs when they visited the city, the Green Gate latterly housed the offices of Lech Wałęsa. From his study the former electrician could look down over the throngs of citizens pouring through the gate on their way to the bars of the "old" city.

In Długi Targ two Ukrainian accordionists competed with a Russian brass quartet for the crowd's attention. I went for a beer in one of the boisterous bar-restaurants now occupying the baroque mansions on raised terraces along the northern side of the square. A quartet of young Italian men were chatting up local girls with a theatrical display of rolling eyes, fingers brushing elbows, entreaties of "ciao bella" and some dreadful abuse of the English language. It was too embarrassing to stay and eat there, so I returned to the waterfront and turned through St Mary's Gate into Ulica Mariacka, a narrow street leading back towards the cathedral. Street lamps shed a weak light over the smoky façades of rebuilt burghers' houses. The merchants of seventeenth-century Danzig lived on the upper floors of these tall, Flemish-style mansions, their apartments reached by flights of steps which formed bridges over basement workshops where craftsmen sculpted amber into the shapes of trees, animals and seafaring galleons. The delicately cut resin jewellery of contemporary artisans glittered from stalls along the pavements of Mariacka. I sat at a table outside a restaurant and ordered lemon soup with chicken and celery, followed by Russian *pierogi* washed down with bitter, amber-coloured Żywiec beer. After the meal I went to the Cico chill-out lounge in the lee of the cathedral's walls. I found myself unwittingly making eye contact with two bronzed creatures of the night – one blonde, one raven-haired – whose dresses were so scanty they could barely take a drag of their cigarettes or a sip of their cocktails without exposing their underwear. I ordered a coffee and asked the waitress whether *Goldwasser* was nice. The famous local *schnapps* was concocted in the sixteenth century by the Dutch distiller Ambrosius Vermöllen in vain pursuit of an alchemical panacea. "It's the sort of drink that only Germans like," she replied – which more or less answered my question. I ordered a glass anyway. It was surprisingly pleasant – like a dry Cointreau – and left lees of gold dust in the bottom of the glass.

I drove south-east on route 7 over the Vistula delta. The polders known in German as Großer and Kleiner Werder were reclaimed from the sea in the fourteenth century and later settled by Mennonites fleeing persecution during the Counter-Reformation. Friesian cattle grazed on low fields of barley, maize and sunflowers. Storks paddled through the irrigation canals and drainage ditches that bisected the fields. Rusted cars lay submerged in thickets of reeds. Swallows darted across the highway, dive-bombing like Stukas. The road was congested with lorries, tractors and car transporters. I tried to keep out of the grooves worn into the tarmac by heavy lorries and drive fast down the centre of the highway, praying that other vehicles would move onto the hard shoulder to make way for me. But oncoming vehicles were adopting the same tactic; and what started out as a pleasant drive over the delta turned into a nerve-wracking cycle of accelerating, overtaking, swerving and braking over the corrugated road surface.

I crossed the Vistula and turned off route 7 towards Malbork, known in German as Marienburg. The minor road wound through villages of crenellated Brick Gothic barns and half-timbered farmhouses. Gardens of summer flowers luxuriated behind wheel-shaped painted iron fences. Flutes of cloud cruised through the skies like a flotilla of U-boats. The immense landscape extended for hundreds of kilometres on all sides. Before long the steep red-brick roofs of Marienburg rose up from the plain. I parked on the banks of the River Nogat, a sluggish tributary of the Vistula which once formed the western border of the German province known as East Prussia. Sprawled between water and sky, the orange-red brick walls and keeps of the riparian fortress stretched for several hundred metres along the Nogat, their witches' hat turrets and peeling battlements reflected in the placid surface of the river. Slopes of worn grass spilled out from beneath the arches of the Mostowe Gates. Oak and ash trees filled the moats and courtyards of the reconstructed stronghold. Above them towered the steep roofs and serrated gables of the High Castle and the Grand Masters' Palace.

I crossed a drawbridge over the dry moat and entered the High Castle through a series of arches and gateways. Tiers of red-brick cloisters enclosed a Gothic courtyard. A well in the centre was surmounted by the figure of a pelican feeding its nestlings with its own blood. The courtyard reminded me of Burg Hohenzollern, almost a thousand kilometres away in Swabia. The Hohenzollerns acquired Marienburg in 1772 as a result of the First Partition of Poland. They allowed the castle, which had enjoyed a relatively stable period of three hundred years as a Polish royal residence, to fall into disrepair. In 1799 the Prussian architect Friedrich Gilly published an album of engravings of Marienburg, accompanied by an ode to the castle written by Maximilian Schenkendorf from Königsberg. This persuaded the Prussian king Friedrich Wilhelm III to place a conservation order on Marienburg and begin work on its restoration. By 1871 the castle was fully restored, the Gothic fortress enhanced by gardens and terraces adorned, like Burg Hohenzollern, with statues of Prussian monarchs. The National Socialist architect Clemens Klotz pursued a six-month project to convert the castle into a fourth Nazi Ordensburg; Marienburg was after all the original Ordensburg of the Deutschorden (as the Teutonic Knights are known in German) on which the elite schools of Vogelsang, Falkenburg and Sonthofen were modelled. The war on the Eastern Front, however, overtook any plans to remodel Marienburg, and the fortress suffered extensive damage in 1945. The second phase of restoration was still, at the time of my visit, in progress. The medieval Church of Our Lady, the sacred heart of the Teutonic Knights' mysticism, was only halfway to full restoration. In the dry moat below the church was the burial chapel of Saint Anne, where three mighty stone slabs marked the (now empty) tombs of Grand Masters Dietrich von Altenburg, Heinrich Dusemer and Heinrich von Plauen. In the open section of the moat were the graves of four more Teutonic Knights and other tombstones brought to Marienburg from Danzig in 1910, including those of several seventeenth-century Mennonites.

Finally, I ascended the Klesza Tower, the crowning point of the High Castle. From the battlements the surrounding land opened up in all directions, a green-gold patchwork of cornfields at different stages of ripening. Avenues of trees marked the lines of roads and canals. A train rumbled across a girder bridge over the Nogat on its return journey to Gdańsk. Shadows of low, tubular cloud slid over the fertile terrain like the ghosts of all the armies that had marched over these lands during the last millennium.

Halfway up the hill of Grunwald is a fragment of a wall of large, rough-hewn stones. The stones are the remains of a Grunwald Monument unveiled in Kraków in 1910 to commemorate the five hundredth anniversary of the battle. Grunwald is the site of the Polish Agincourt, the battle that changed the balance of power in Prussia. Lithuania had expanded during the fourteenth century, and in 1385 Grand Duke Jogaila converted to Christianity and married the twelve-year-old Polish queen Jadwiga, uniting the two nations in an eastern European commonwealth. In 1410 the Polish-Lithuanian forces advanced northwards into Prussia, stronghold of the Teutonic Knights. The two armies met at Grunwald on 5 July 1410. The Teutonic forces under the command of Grand Master Ulrich von Jungingen were lured into woods and marshes, where they were surrounded by Lithuanian cavalry. After routing the Germans, the victorious Polish army marched on Marienburg and began the negotiations that culminated in western Prussia passing into Polish sovereignty. The Teutonic Order abandoned Marienburg and retreated northwards in order to consolidate their new power base in Königsberg.

The battle was fought within a triangle of land between the villages of Grunwald, Stębark and Łodwigowo (Grünfelde, Tannenberg and Ludwigsdorf in German). Poles celebrate the Victory of Grunwald, whereas Germans refer to their defeat as Tannenberg.

In August 1914 the German Army was losing the war on its Eastern Front. Field Marshal Paul von Hindenburg, veteran of the Austro-Prussian and Franco-Prussian Wars, was summoned out of retirement to rally the German troops against the invading Russians. Between 24 and 30 August a battle was fought over a large terrain of forests and plains to the south of Allenstein. This proved to be the turning point of the war. In September 1914, Hindenburg and his chief of staff General Erich von Ludendorff stabilised the Eastern Front and restored order in East Prussia. The decisive battle around Allenstein (Olsztyn) and Hohenstein (Olsztynek) was first referred to as Tannenberg in a dispatch from Ludendorff on 28 August. The great German victory and the masterful leadership of Hindenburg were conflated into a myth of national heroism to which the name Tannenberg was applied; thus erasing the memory of the defeat of the Teutonic Knights by the Slavic forces of Władysław Jagiełło and the Lithuanian Grand Duke Vytautas, and reclaiming the name for the victory of a German army over Slavic forces five hundred years later.

The idea of building a monument to the victory of Tannenberg was first mooted at a rally on 31 August 1919, held near Hohenstein to commemorate the fifth anniversary of the battle. Six years later a Tannenberg National Memorial Association was founded in order to fund and supervise construction of the monument. Chaired by the anti-republican monarchist General Major Hans Kahns, the association announced a competition to design the new memorial. Wilhelm Kreis submitted a project entitled "Tann" ("Pine Forest"), a star-shaped, fortress-like structure on a raised mound, which prefigured his later National Socialist "Totenburgen". The jury favoured a monolithic cenotaph submitted by the East Prussian Kurt Frick, architect of the new exhibition halls in Königsberg. In the end they awarded the commission to the partnership of the brothers Walter and Johannes Krüger from Berlin. Entitled "Gode Wind" ("Fair Wind" in medieval German), the Krügers' initial design featured a medieval fortress in the form of an octagon of low, defensive walls punctuated by eight tall, crenellated towers. The ring of towers enclosed a grove of trees, within which rose the statue of a lion. (The stone lion already existed, having been erected on the site in 1924 as a memorial to Hindenburg's 147th Grenadier Regiment.) The symbiosis of arcane octagonal structure, unusually low walls and exaggeratedly high towers lent the Krügers' design an air of unreality. Silhouetted against an expressionist explosion of sunlight, the towers in their drawing resembled a caricature of a castle, a child's vision of a crusaders' fortress, or the backdrop to a silent film. The architect Dieter Bartetzko claimed it replicated the castle created for Fritz Lang's film *Nibelungen*. Bruno Möhring, the most severe critic of the Krügers' blueprint, described their project as "a low-point of taste, a laboriously thrown-together work ... an inauthentic castle in an oriental style inappropriate for Germany ... a fake, mendacious Romanticism ... a *Spektakelstück*" – a slur against which the Krügers initiated legal proceedings. The Association of German Architects accused the Krügers of plagiarising the medieval fortress of Smederevo, although the brothers professed to no prior knowledge of the Serbian stronghold.

The shell of the building was completed by September 1927, in time for the celebrations to mark the eightieth birthday of Hindenburg, who had in the meantime been appointed Reichs President. On the morning of 18 September 1927 the pristine building rose from the empty plain around Hohenstein like a modern Stonehenge. Contemporary photographs illustrate a monument that seems archaic, like a prehistoric stone circle; mysterious, like a "magic space" for occult rituals; and sinister, its low walls and high towers prefiguring the architecture of concentration camps that would follow in the next decade. Powerful yet paradoxical,

Tannenberg was reactionary in its structure but expressionist in its detail. Its walls were patterned in variegated colours of red, blue and purple clinker. The etched brickwork at the corners of its towers resembled that of the expressionist-Romanesque churches being built by Dominikus Böhm across northern Germany at the same time. The glass-fronted galleries capped by flattish turrets of patinated green copper owed a nod to modernism. Yet the tiny arches and windows in the walls were old-fashioned Romanesque; and the towers were embellished with intimidating patterns of upright, unsheathed gilded bronze swords that harked back to a more bellicose age.

I set off from Tannenberg I, scene of the Teutonic Knights' defeat, towards the site of Tannenberg II, where five hundred years later the Prussians would reclaim the name, transforming it into a symbol of German victory. Driving through tunnels of birch and chestnut trees, I arrived back at route 7 and headed north through forests towards Olsztynek, the former Prussian town of Hohenstein. On the outskirts of the town I turned off the highway at a sign for the Hotel-Restaurant Tannenberg and parked in a circular area below the hotel. There were some ruined walls surrounding the car park, but the circle was too small and too close to the road to be the site of the Hindenburg Mausoleum. I entered the woods behind the hotel, walking in ever-increasing circles in search of the fabled monument. I came across the graves of two German soldiers hidden in the undergrowth, both marked with rough wooden crosses inscribed with the date 1914. I walked along the top of a low stone wall that curved into the trees, but my path was cut off by a wire fence marking the perimeter of an institution of some kind. The rear of the wood opened out into an area of uncultivated grassland. I climbed onto a dyke, but found nothing that indicated the site of an octagonal monument. I made one final circuit of the wood before returning to the car, having decided to abandon my search for Tannenberg.

Fastening my seat belt, I realised I had dropped my sunglasses while clambering along the stone wall behind the wood. I walked back through the trees, but failed to find the glasses. I decided to make one last attempt to locate the site of the monument, following a track which led up to a levee of raised ground before dropping into a circular depression on the far side. In the centre of the bowl were the charred remains of a bonfire, which reminded me of the mausoleum above Wałbrzych. I took a different path back to the rim of the depression and walked around the edge of the sunken area. I began to notice I was treading on fragments of broken brick and splinters of sandstone, granite and marble. The circular path dropped into a narrow gully, whose side revealed the top half of a brick arch embedded in a wall of sand. This was recognisably one of the arches built into the foundations of the monument, which were later covered by a grass embankment. Following the circular path, I came upon a substantial section of clinker masonry, lying on its side but still intact; and then a corner of brickwork, the base of a tower perhaps, still embedded in the ground. The inner angle of the corner could have been that of an octagon. I continued around the rim of the depression and gradually the shape of the octagon fell into place. I walked in straight lines until I was no longer treading on bricks. When the bricks gave out, I bore to the left until I found another straight line of shattered bricks. It seemed I had found Tannenberg.

Reichs President Hindenburg died on 2 August 1934. Reichs Chancellor Adolf Hitler announced a *Trauerfeier*, a ceremony of mourning for the hero of Tannenberg, which was held four days later. Albert Speer had the towers of the monument draped in black and covered with giant Iron Crosses. "Flags of smoke" rose from fire bowls; anthems were sung; and Hindenburg was inducted into the pantheon of German warrior-heroes with Hitler's words: "Dead commander, go now to Valhalla." After the ceremony, Hitler decreed that Tannenberg should be reconfigured as a shrine to the dead Field Marshal. The focus of the monument was transferred to a crypt, in which the sarcophagi of Hindenburg and his wife Gertrud von Beneckendorff were to lie, beneath a porphyry statue of the warlord standing bare-headed, clad in a long military greatcoat. A study of melancholy rather than heroism, Friedrich Bagdons' sculpture seems, in retrospect, to embody the defeat of Germany, rather than its victory on the Eastern Front.

The Soviet Army reached Tannenberg in January 1945. One of the first Russian soldiers to capture the monument described it as "a stone pustule of German arrogance". They blew up the mausoleum and two of the towers and looted any remaining decorative elements. The sarcophagi of Hindenburg and his wife had been spirited away two days earlier, transferred to a salt mine in Thuringia and buried in Marburg after the war. The fabric of Tannenberg disappeared over the next forty years. Bricks from the monument were dismantled and used to reconstruct local buildings destroyed in the war. Granite slabs from the courtyard were torn up and recycled for new Soviet monuments and parade grounds in Olsztyn.

Post-war Germany had no place for the Hindenburg cult nor for the reactionary, neo-pagan architecture of Kreis, Tischler and the Krügers. East Prussia was now under Soviet-Polish administration and all traces of German culture were erased. The Krügers' *pièce de résistance,* the (now literally) missing link between the great neo-Romanesque monuments of the Second Reich and the arenas and Ordensburgen of the Third Reich, stood for less than twenty years. Hindenburg had less than ten years to rest in peace in his native East Prussia. All that remains of Tannenberg is a fragmented trail of broken bricks hidden beneath the waist-high grass of a circular dyke. The site of Tannenberg now resembles the sort of ur-Germanic earthwork the Nazis tried so hard to fake. I made one more circuit of the buried octagon before driving into Olsztynek. The tourist office was closed, but a red circle on a map in the window confirmed I had found the site of the Hindenburg Mausoleum. In the centre of the market square was a massive statue of a crouching lion – the only survivor of German Tannenberg.

A signpost on route 51 on the outskirts of Olsztynek indicated "Kaliningrad 153 kilometres" – my next overnight stay. I bypassed Olsztyn and drove north through Warmia, stopping for coffee and a packet of chocolate biscuits in a courtyard outside the great square Brick Gothic castle of the Bishops of Warmia in Lidzbark Warmiński. The last Polish place before the border was Bartoszyce, a scruffy town behind a tall Prussian gate with sixteen blanked-out windows and five limestone fingers set into its red-brick tower and gable.

It didn't take long to leave Poland: an official inspected my vehicle documents and took a cursory look in the boot of the car. As I drove into no-man's-land, I took out my camera to take a surreptitious photograph of the Russian border post I was about to encounter. I had passed through here seven years earlier and remembered it as a muddy enclosure pitted with deep troughs of stagnant water through which it was impossible to drive in anything other than first gear. I had been travelling to Kaliningrad with my brother and, as far as I can recall, we were the only travellers to pass through the Polish-Russian border post during the hour it took to process our documents. I recalled a young female official in loose green overalls, her long blonde hair spilling from beneath her oversized peaked cap; and a dashing male official, dressed in military fatigues, who was confused by the fact that the Russian Embassy in London had come up with two different transliterations (ГЭГАН and ГЭЙГАН) of our surname. He was also wary of the fact that we were travelling to Kaliningrad by car, no doubt suspecting we wished to sell the vehicle there illegally. I had to fill out a lengthy document listing its details, which I was to present to the authorities on our exit from the Kaliningrad *oblast*.

As I steadied my hand for the clandestine photograph, I was astonished to find that the farmyard-like compound of seven years earlier had been replaced by a smart new complex of blue-and-white-striped cabins. Orderly lines of cars and lorries waited to be processed by a team of officials in neatly pressed uniforms. The accession of Poland and Lithuania to the European Union in the intervening years had presumably increased the flow of traffic into and through the Kaliningrad *oblast*. I was apprehensive, because I had forgotten to bring my driving licence with me and had neglected to take out any additional vehicle insurance for driving outside the EU. I also had a couple of books about Kaliningrad's previous incarnation as German Königsberg, which may not have pleased the Russian officials.

The initial customs check was carried out by an officer with a hatchet face and a severe bun who could have been the offspring of Rosa Kleb or Tamara Press. It wasn't particularly thorough or intrusive, and there seemed to be no ideological concern about revisionist literature. The subsequent process of form-filling lasted about forty-five minutes. With the assistance of a grizzled officer who reeked of alcohol and whose only foreign language was broken German, I filled out passport, customs, currency and vehicle declaration forms before being despatched to an office that had just closed for a regulatory half-hour tea break. I joined a queue of Polish and Lithuanian truck drivers until the office reopened, and presented my papers to a woman with an indecently low-cut spangly top. The documents were transferred to another office, and I watched as my personal details were transliterated into Cyrillic script (my name condensed to ГЭГАН МАЙКЛ РОЙ) and typed on triplicate sheets of green-bordered tissue paper, one copy of which I was to retain and submit to the authorities on my exit from the *oblast* within a maximum of three days. Once the bureaucratic formalities had been duly completed, I reported back to the mirrored-glass customs booth, where I was asked the purpose of my visit to Kaliningrad. "Turism," I replied. An officer asked me to open the boot of the car. I braced myself for a lengthy search through my luggage. Instead, he bade me a curt "До свидания" and I was free to proceed, with neither driving licence nor valid motor insurance, into Russia.

Dark clouds were gathering as I entered the Kaliningrad *oblast*, a region closed to foreigners until 1989. It was only 8 pm, but I was now on Eastern European Time and had lost an hour of daylight. I drove through a tunnel of oak trees and soon reached Bagrationovsk, a town once known as Preußisch Eylau. In a spinney off the main road I caught a brief glimpse of a neo-Gothic monument, a Prussian cross flanked by two field guns, which commemorated a battle fought here on 7 and 8 February 1807, when Napoleon's *Grande Armée* was halted by a Russian army assisted by a small Prussian force led by Lieutenant-General Anton Wilhelm von L'Estocq, to whom the monument was raised in 1856. Despite one of the greatest cavalry charges in military history, Napoleon's army was unable to overcome the Russian-German forces. The only outcome of this inconclusive battle was a field of bloodstained snow strewn with the frozen corpses of between twenty and twenty-five thousand soldiers.

The road north towards Kaliningrad continued through barren wastes of tarnished grassland, a landscape depopulated after the war and never re-cultivated since. I passed through villages of ancient cottages and dilapidated cubic housing blocks, whose inhabitants sat drinking beer in bus shelters along the unlit highway. Derelict collective farms and caved-in Prussian barns loomed out of the dusk. I overtook a solitary car, full of customs officials still wearing their tall peaked caps, which was travelling at the regulatory speed of seventy kilometres per hour. I was then held up by a herd of white cows which had strayed onto the road. As I approached Kaliningrad the rust-coloured plains were covered with semi-cylindrical hangars, the debris of a disused military airfield. In spite of the reduction in size of the garrison, the Kaliningrad *oblast* remains one of the most heavily militarised regions of the Russian Federation. These corrugated iron hangars, however, covered with vegetation to camouflage them from the air, seemed to be abandoned.

Entering the suburbs of Kaliningrad, I was seized with a mild panic similar to those I had experienced on arriving in L'vov, Kiev and Kharkov by car on previous journeys. Russian road signs rarely direct you towards the city centre – maybe the hub of commercial activity is too bourgeois a concept? I missed a left fork to Lenin Prospekt because I failed to decipher the Cyrillic lettering of the road sign in time. A U-turn was out of the question: the tarmac had subsided over the decades, leaving manhole covers and disused German tramlines exposed several inches above the surface of the road. There were no white lane markings or red stop signs. Cars, taxis, lorries and articulated buses careered over the streets, cutting up or boxing in the disorientated driver until all the traffic ground to a halt in order to negotiate the exposed tramlines at the next road junction. With neither driving licence nor valid insurance, I was unwilling to take any risk that might cause an accident. At length I recognised an old Prussian tollbooth which stood isolated like a witch's gingerbread house on the banks of the River Pregolya. I bore left and followed Ulitsa Bagrationa, which must have taken me over Lenin Prospekt without me noticing it. I then recognised Brandenburg Gate, one of the six remaining Prussian gateways that surround the inner city, and veered left through one of its neo-Gothic arches. Having driven in a circle, I found myself in a traffic jam in front of a railway station, but was unsure whether it was the North or South Station. I turned left at the next junction, a manoeuvre which actually put me on Lenin Prospekt, travelling in the correct direction, but at this stage I was blissfully unaware of that. I recalled Lenin Prospekt as a long, straight boulevard, whereas this street curved around several open squares. Against my better judgement I executed a U-turn around a statue of Lenin, which should have alerted me to my whereabouts, and proceeded to drive back down Lenin Prospekt in the wrong direction. I soon realised that this time I was heading for the docks. I performed a second U-turn and returned to the railway station. While queuing again at the traffic lights, I deciphered a street sign as Lenin Prospekt and followed the road I had been on ten minutes earlier. Lenin Prospekt eventually opened out into the long boulevard I recalled from my previous visit, and, in the distance, I recognised the lights of my destination, the Hotel Kaliningrad.

The Soviet-era monolith had undergone a superficial facelift since my stay seven years earlier, but the lobby was still decorated in a familiar palette of functional browns and utilitarian greys. From the absence of activity it seemed I was the only guest they were expecting. I had taken the precaution of booking a business-class suite at the rear of the hotel, as I knew from experience that the tiny, sweaty tourist-class rooms at the front look out over the noisiest traffic intersection of the city. The view from the rear of the hotel was less spectacular, the car compound of the hotel and a poorly lit estate of low, peat-coloured apartment blocks on bare, mud-caked lawns. Seventy years earlier the same view would have encompassed the Paradeplatz and Königsgarten of Prussian Königsberg, replete with statues of Kant, Schiller and King Friedrich Wilhelm III.

I returned to the lobby to ask the receptionist if I could park my car in the hotel compound. She pointed me in the direction of a couple of security staff. The elder of the two was a heavily built man with a drinker's face, dressed in a grey suit two sizes too small for him. Neither he nor his underling spoke English or German and they assumed from my miming that I wanted to order a taxi or hire a car. They led me over to two prostitutes drinking coffee in the empty bar, who spoke passable English and successfully interpreted my request. The underling returned to the car with me and escorted me on a circuitous route, which first required a 270-degree turn around the anarchic intersection in front of the hotel. Two successive left turns led us bumping over the potholed avenues of a dark housing estate towards the protected compound at the rear of the hotel. When we returned to the lobby, the senior security employee, who reminded me of the former Soviet football coach Valery Lobanovsky, winked in the direction of the two call girls and mimed a pair of big breasts: "Девочка?"

I changed money at a cash machine in the brand-new Kaliningrad Plaza shopping mall and multi-screen cinema complex which had shot up since my last visit to the city. The continuation of Lenin Prospekt, heading north-west towards the North Station, was once the Steindamm of Prussian Königsberg, an elegant thoroughfare of *Gründerzeit* banks, department stores and coffee houses. It is now a six-lane highway of revving Audis and BMWs, most of them rebuilt in Poland from German wrecks and sold illicitly to the *mafiosi* of Kaliningrad. When not racing each other, the young hoods park their vehicles on the pavement and sit menacingly behind smoked windows, scanning the crowds from behind dark glasses, alert to any potential for making a fast buck or propositioning one of the young women who parade the streets, dressed and coiffed as if auditioning for a role in an Abba tribute band. These young men and women constitute the *nouveau riche,* semi-criminal overclass of Russia. The huge underclass shambles along the same pavements: spotty, undernourished, clad in market-stall denim, clutching cans of beer.

There were no bars or cafés on Lenin Prospekt: the only place to sit and drink was a tiny beer garden of trestle tables resting on a yard of baked mud. I joined a queue at the kiosk which supplied the tables, but it took half an hour to get served. On reaching the front of the queue it became evident why it moved so slowly: the waitress was using an abacus to add up the prices. When my turn finally came, I pointed to a cold beer from the refrigerator, paid for it with my new roubles and squeezed onto a table next to a teenage girl and a conscript on a blind and rather silent date. I flicked back the ring of the beer can and raised it to my lips, but nothing emerged. The beer was frozen solid. I queued for another twenty minutes to replace the frozen beer, which the waitress was most reluctant to do. She said something which sounded like: "You queued for half an hour to buy the beer, so you can ******* wait another half hour for it to thaw out." I eventually managed to get a liquid beer and returned to the table with the sulky couple. The conscript shortly got up to join the queue to buy another beer. His date scribbled a quick note on the back of his beer mat and disappeared into the night.

I sat and watched the Kaliningraders pass by. Every one of them was clutching a bottle or can of the local brew, swigging from it as they walked. It occurred to me I should have followed their example and bought a beer from one of the numerous kiosks lining the boulevard. Serious beer-drinkers congregated in a small park below a statue of Mother Russia and binged in the dark, leaving every litter bin crowned with a diadem of empty bottles; or, like the Germans, smashed their bottles on the ground once they were finished. Affluent beer-drinkers patronised a German-style beer garden sponsored by Beck's which had been set up along Ulitsa Teatralnaya. Here they could sit at white plastic tables, walk on green nylon grass and watch German hip-hop videos on a giant screen. The imported beer was more expensive, but tastier and chilled to the correct temperature. It also served tiny portions of pizza. A woman at an adjacent table, dressed in grey tights and a frumpy turquoise satin jacket and skirt, made eye contact with me. Sadly, my deficiency in Russian prevented our conversation from progressing any further than my asking her for a light for my cigarette. Back in my hotel room I was obliged to listen to some enthusiastic foreplay from the room next door. Prostitutes habitually turn on the television in order to muffle the sounds of their congress. Sure enough, the television soon came on, a music channel broadcasting some bland contemporary R&B. I drifted off to sleep trying to distinguish the "oohs" and "aahs" of the soul warbling from the moans and groans of the couple having sex.

Next morning was grey and overcast. A relentless drizzle descended over the long viaduct of Lenin Prospekt; over the empty spaces that used to be the Kneiphof and Lastadie of Königsberg; over a plaza of broken concrete that was once the seat of the Teutonic Knights and the second residence of the Prussian monarchy. The site of the former Reichsbank was now occupied by a fifteen-storey House of the Soviets. Construction work on this top-heavy monolith started in 1967, but was halted when cracks appeared in its walls and the building began to sink. Its engineers were forced to acknowledge that their architectural *pièce de résistance,* the skyscraper intended to glorify the authority of the Soviet Union, was too heavy to stand on an area of sandy marshland which had been tunnelled under since the Middle Ages. When I visited Kaliningrad in 2000 the building was a derelict shell, too big to dismantle, too dangerous to develop. It has since been fitted with windows and faced with blue and grey panels, but remains unused. The "King's Castle" tourist information centre in the hotel lobby exhibited a scale model of a plan to transform the area into a business park which would incorporate a Hanseatic Trade Bureau and a Russian-European Friendship Centre.

Queues of trams and *marshrutki* crawled over the viaduct, bringing in labourers and office workers from the southern reaches of the *oblast.* Buses were painted in the liveries of their former employers, the municipal authorities of Dortmund, Mannheim, Bremen and other West German cities. One MAN single-decker still displayed the destination "Hamburg-Billstedt" on its indicator. I crossed a section of the stagnant, brown River Pregolya that was once known as the Hundegatt (Dog's Strait) where, in pre-war Königsberg, hundreds of boats would have been moored, delivering goods to storehouses and selling *Colonialwaren* to crowds gathered on the quays. The twin arms of the Pregolya are now walled in by concrete embankments and empty parks. I recalled the similar cityscape of Wrocław, where the Odra flows around the abandoned islets of former Breslau; which in turn had reminded me of the Spree as it flows through the area of no-man's-land in the ruined centre of Berlin. All three former Prussian capitals, now separated from each other in three different countries, share a common topography of neglected islands and deserted riversides in their old German centres.

I descended a flight of steps to the island once known as Kneiphof. This was the oldest part of Königsberg, a warren of half-timbered merchants' houses, furniture shops and warehouses that led to the Gothic cathedral at the far end of the island. The brick cathedral, the only surviving building of medieval Königsberg, now stands in isolation at the end of an avenue of trees. A roofless shell for decades, the Königsberger Dom is being rebuilt. One tower has a new gable, the other has a new spire, clock and bell, all donated by German benefactors. A new roof has been fitted and the west front has been restored to its characteristic Prussian façade of red brick inlaid with vertical limestone stripes.

I was admiring a statue of Duke Albrecht of Brandenburg-Ansbach, last Grand Master of the Teutonic Knights and founder of the Albertina University of Königsberg, when an ancient gentleman emerged from the bushes and informed me, in German, that the statue was a replica. That was obvious: everything in Königsberg was destroyed in the firestorms of the war, including the fabled Amber Room stolen by the Germans from the Catherine Palace at Zarskoje Selo. I thanked him nevertheless for this information and asked if he was an original German *Königsberger*; he was about the right age, and had a bullet hole in the side of his skull. He replied he was a White Russian. I explained that I was English, not German. He told me that Kant's mother (we were standing by Kant's mausoleum) was Scottish, and pointed me in the direction of a monument in the form of a standing stone commemorating the life of a nineteenth-century evangelical theologian named Julius Rupp. A bronze relief set into the memorial was a copy of the original relief sculpted by Rupp's granddaughter Käthe Kollwitz, who was born and raised in Wilhelmine Königsberg before moving to Berlin in 1891. Engraved on the stone were the words "Wer nach der Wahrheit, die er bekennt, nicht lebt, ist der gefährlichste Feind der Wahrheit selbst!" ("He who does not live according to the truth that he professes is the deadliest enemy of truth itself!") – an inscription that could be read as an ironic commentary on Communism, but one which survived forty years of the Soviet Union. As well as Kant, Rupp and Duke Albrecht, there was also once a statue of Walther von der Vogelweide on the lawns around the cathedral. Smaller and more gnomish than the monument to the *Minnesänger* that graces the Waltherplatz of Bolzano at the opposite end of the German-speaking world, the statue of Walther was vandalised in 1993 and moved to a safer location in the courtyard of the university.

The monuments to Rupp and Kant were popular destinations for newly-weds to come and have their photographs taken. As I crossed the former Honigbrücke over the channel connecting the two arms of the Pregolya, I passed one of these wedding parties. The bride wore a ravishing dress of ivory silk, although her *décolletage* was more appropriate for pole dancing on the hen night than for the wedding itself. I was stopped on the bridge by a wolfish young man who, for three euros, offered me postcards and DVDs of German Königsberg. On the southern bank a wall of concrete apartment blocks ran for half a kilometre towards the neo-Florentine House of Seamen, the former Prussian Stock Exchange, now stripped of its blue and white Russian stripes and restored to its natural stone exterior. On the far side of Honey Bridge banks of housing blocks stretched away over the site of the old synagogue and the marshy expanse of the former Stadt-Wiesen. A banner across the top of one block proclaimed: "We congratulate our beloved city!" Emblazoned over images of one of the Prussian gates coloured in the white, blue and red stripes of the Russian Federation was the slogan "750 Years of Kaliningrad". The city celebrated its 750th anniversary in 2006, but the suggestion that it has been white, blue and red Kaliningrad for seven and a half centuries is stretching credibility.

I recrossed the river at the High Bridge and followed Ulitsa Bogdana Chmelnizkogo, a residential street which cut through the southern part of the city. On the steps of the former Catholic Church of the Holy Family (now the concert hall of the Kaliningrad Philharmonia), I encountered an elderly German couple who had spread out their replica map of 1930 Königsberg and were looking in vain for the street where the parents of one of them had lived before the war. The map showed a ladder of parallel streets named after Prussian warlords (Moltke, Blücher, Bismarck and so on) which had long since disappeared. The entire suburb of German streets was destroyed in the war: post-war housing blocks had erased the topography of pre-war Königsberg. To the south of the church was a paved park laid with flower beds. In the 1930s it was named Soldauer Platz and there was a monument to the SA in its centre. That was replaced after the war by a white concrete sculpture of banners rippling in the breeze that represented Polish-Soviet Friendship-in-Arms. The hammers, sickles and eagles of the Communist monument have since been dismantled, now that the Poles and Russians are no longer friends.

I crossed Kalinin Prospekt into South Park and followed the sound of a military brass band practising for an open day of some kind. Volunteers were loading trestle tables with bottles of beer and fizzy pop and erecting a marquee in the national colours. In the mid-1930s an "Ostpreußen" sports arena was built in the German Südpark, known at the time as Horst-Wessel-Park. After the war the Russians dismantled an ice rink which formed part of the sports arena and transported it to Moscow. The green space was renamed the Cultural and Recuperative Park of the Fortieth Anniversary of Komsomol; and Horst Wessel was replaced by busts of Lenin and the heads of some stern Red Army soldiers, which crown a sculpture shaped like a four-bladed metal sword that shoots up from a concrete plinth. "ВЛКСМ 1945 АЛРЕЛЪ МЧЖЕСТВУ-СЛАВА! МОДВИГУ-ВЕЧНОСТЪ! ГЕРОЯМ-ВЕССМЕРТИЕ!" ("Glory to the Komsomol legions of April 1945! Immortality to our heroes!")

The clock over the entrance to the South Station confounded me: it was an hour ahead of Eastern European Time and, for a moment, I wondered whether I had been on the wrong time since arriving in the *oblast* the previous evening. I entered the marble concourse of the station. In 1929 this was the most advanced railway terminus in Europe, the first to raise a cantilevered glass roof over its platforms. Trains arrived from Berlin, Breslau and Warsaw. Now they depart to Moscow, Kharkiv and Saint Petersburg, operating on Moscow Time, as explained by the caption "Moskovskoye Vremya" below the clock in the departure hall, which was also one hour ahead of Eastern European Time. The last Reichsbahn train from Königsberg departed for Berlin on 21 January 1945, overcrowded with desperate refugees. The service was resumed on 1 January 1991, but was subsequently axed again in 2009. I went into the station restaurant, but it smelt of boiled vegetables. There were a number of stalls outside and at one of them I ordered an unpleasant coffee-like beverage and a miniscule salad of pickled herring and onion rings. I took the snack into a marquee, where a party of women were bawling at each other over a bottle of vodka. They started to sing and the noise became unbearable. I went outside and sat in the drizzle.

The rain lashed down as I set off down the long stretch of Lenin Prospekt. I sheltered briefly in a coffee bar on the intersection with Ulitsa Bagrationa, sitting in a window where I had a view along the avenue. The pavement was lined on one side by booths selling flowers and on the other by an endless chain of clothes shops displaying every conceivable garment, from blue-dyed fake-fur coats for large women to miniature grey worsted suits for little boys. A bookshop I visited sold nothing in English, and only a handful of guides for *Ostalgie*-tourists in German. I bought a copy of the replica map of 1930 Königsberg that the couple searching for their parents' home had been perusing.

When the rain abated, I resumed my walk down Ulitsa Shevchenko (formerly Junkerstraße) and along the banks of the former Schlossteich towards the Upper Lake, where I bought a beer and some dried fish from a stall below the arches of the Roßgärter Tor. I took refuge from another shower in the Central Market, whose halls were filled with a cornucopia of glossy apples, melons, cherries, apricots, nectarines, kumquats, tomatoes, aubergines and cucumbers. Counters were piled high with red, green, orange and yellow peppers. Baskets of figs, dates, cashews and pistachio nuts spilled into the aisles. Women queued for salami, smoked fish, cheeses, biscuits, tea and coffee at booths around the edge of the central hall. In the yards outside, peasants from the countryside stood under umbrellas proffering plastic bags stuffed with onions or garlic; or squatted in the mud holding up jars of blackcurrants, blueberries, redcurrants and gooseberries. Mounds of yellow chanterelles were laid out on pages of soggy newsprint. In the clothes market many stalls sold a variety of garments (jeans, shirts, socks, pullovers) in exactly the same colour – predominantly beige or a bleached blue.

When I was here in 2000, Ploshchad Pobedy (once Hansa-Platz and for a brief period Adolf-Hitler-Platz) was a bleak open space of tarmac and cobblestones, used mainly as a car park. A statue of Lenin presided over its north-eastern corner, on a colossal plinth pierced with empty flagpoles like a row of knitting needles. Seven years later Lenin has been removed and Victory Square has been transformed into a plaza which combines the heroic pathos of the Communist era with the tasteless opulence of the new Russia. In preparation for the city's 750th anniversary celebrations in 2006, the square was relaid with gleaming granite flagstones and fountains of polished oxblood marble. In the centre of the square an imperious obelisk, on a plinth embellished with bronze reliefs depicting St George slaying the dragon, commemorates the dead of the Great Patriotic War. Overlooking the new Russian square is the Cathedral of Christ the Redeemer, completed in 2006 for the anniversary celebrations. Enclosing a capsule of soil from Moscow, the foundation stone of the church was laid on 23 June 1996 by President Yeltsin, accompanied by Metropolitan Cyril of Smolensk and Kaliningrad. The cathedral now soars seventy-eight metres above the site of the former German Baltic Exhibition Grounds, a glistening octagon of white marble walls, glass arches and golden domes. Constructed in a traditional Russian Orthodox style, with a nod to post-modernism, it is the second largest church in Russia after the equally post-modernist Cathedral of Christ the Saviour in Moscow. Yet the white monster with its golden baubles looks ill at ease in Kaliningrad – an anachronistic piece of olde-worlde Kievan Rus deposited in the middle of this harsh, gritty, Germanic city.

The same impulse to graft a new Russian identity onto Kaliningrad was evident on Mira Prospekt (Peace Avenue), the boulevard leading west from Victory Square. Its gardens were once rich in statues of Prussian kings and kaisers of the Reich. Now there is a statue of Peter the Great erected, like the Victory Column, for the 750th anniversary of the "Russian" city. The statue, in a romantic-heroic pose, stands on a plinth of the same liver-coloured marble as the fountains and obelisk in Victory Square. The czar's flowing bronze cloak is engraved with tiny double-headed eagles, which echo the golden crest emblazoned in the pediment of the candy-floss façade of the High Command of the Russian Baltic Fleet, in front of which the statue is placed. A strapping young woman stands rigidly to attention, shoulders back and elbows out, as her husband takes her photograph in front of the statue. Opposite the Russian czar is the German poet Friedrich von Schiller (ШИЛЛЕР, as he is known here), whose statue, unlike those of kings and kaisers, survived the war. The graceful bronze originally stood on the corner of the Königsgarten in front of the university and opera house, and was transferred in 1936 to its present site in the gardens of the former Hufenallee. It was saved from destruction by a Soviet officer of a literary bent who persuaded his troops to respect "the German Pushkin".

Parked by the kerb in front of Schiller was a jet black Chaika, limousine of choice of the *nomenklatura* of the Communist Party. The chauffeur leant against the bonnet, smoking a cigarette, while the wedding party he was driving posed under umbrellas for photographs in the ornamental arcade of a small park at the intersection of Mira Prospekt and Ulitsa Teatralnaya. The theatre the latter name refers to is the old Königsberger Schauspielhaus, a Wilhelmine edifice once inscribed with Schiller's words "Ewig jung ist nur die Phantasie" ("Only imagination is forever young"). Destroyed in the war, it was rebuilt in the 1960s with the addition of a neoclassical portico in imitation of the Bolshoi Theatre in Moscow. Feeling wet and hungry again, I took shelter below its columns and ordered a "mixed fish starter" from the Theatre Café. Half an hour later I was served a tiny prawn cocktail. Struggling to conceal my disappointment, I asked the waitress for some bread. She returned fifteen minutes later with a single slice, meticulously divided into thin fingers.

I continued west along Mira Prospekt, passing the cosmic loop of a Soviet monument to the three great cosmonauts of Kaliningrad: Alexei Leonov, the first man to walk in space; Viktor Patsayev, one of the crew of the ill-fated Soyuz XI mission who suffocated in space because of a faulty valve; and Yuri Romanenko, who completed a ninety-six-day space flight in the 1970s. At the end of Mira Prospekt, I took a right fork followed by a left turn into the former suburb of Amalienau – and at last found Prussian Königsberg. Untouched by the war, the tree-lined avenues of *Gründerzeit* villas, Swabian chalets and Franconian mansions survive in a state of glorious dilapidation. There were gladioli in the gardens, eyelet windows beneath the eaves, iron boot scrapers outside rustic doors, faded escutcheons on peeling walls. One house was "erbaut i.J.1936"; another was named "Landhaus Ruth". This was now the domain of the new rich of Kaliningrad. Oligarchs and *mafiosi* have rebuilt old villas or built new mansions in a post-modern approximation of neo-Gothic, albeit surrounded by electronic gates, security guards and surveillance cameras. On one side of the former Luisenplatz were the remains of tank traps and pillboxes. The other side had recently been renamed the Skver (a direct transliteration of the English word, even though the "square" was actually circular) of Russian-Byelorussian Friendship. Courting couples canoodled on the new benches, stubbing out their cigarettes on little trays fitted in characteristic eastern European style to the new litter bins. A red marble slab in the centre of the manicured lawns celebrated the links between Belarus and the Kaliningrad *oblast*. The fences of gardens surrounding the *skver* were decorated with the crests of Minsk, Brest, Hrodna, Vityebsk, Mahilyow, Homyal and other cities of the former Soviet republic which is now, like Kaliningrad, a loyal satellite of its Russian patron.

First Coffee is a smart coffee lounge in a restored mansion on Ulitsa Epronovskaya. Like most trendy establishments in eastern Europe, its interior featured wall-to-wall plasma televisions broadcasting Fashion TV. Café society from Zagreb to St Petersburg believes that observing a conveyor belt of catwalk models is more entertaining than watching a football match or a pop video. I ordered a pot of Earl Grey and sat at a table next to a large group of Russians with broad round heads, glossy black hair, thick noses and swarthy skin, who were clearly not of Baltic origin. The census of 2010 recorded an official population in the city of Kaliningrad of 401,649 (broken down into proportions of 87.4% Russians, 3.7% Byelorussians and 4.0% Ukrainians), most of whom are descendants of the 200,000 Russians introduced into the region after the German population was expelled in 1946. However, it is claimed that there are an additional 100,000 re-settlers from Armenia, Azerbaijan and Chechnya who have not registered with the authorities, and who are using Kaliningrad as a staging post to emigrate to Western Europe.

I found myself reflecting on the identity of this mongrel city. Although the trains run on Moscow Time, Kaliningrad does not look or feel particularly Russian to an outsider. The *oblast* is too small; the city, with its lakes and parks and red-brick churches, is too European. The Kaliningraders, however, have forged an identity of their own: first as good Soviet citizens, and latterly as loyal Russian nationalists. There is no question of any lingering German identity: less than 1% of the population is ethnic German, and most of those are Volga Germans transferred to the *oblast* from other regions of the USSR in the 1980s. In spite of the cranes, wharves and tankers visible downstream along the Pregolya, the Kaliningraders of today are not a seafaring Baltic people like those of Riga or Gdańsk: most are immigrants from the steppes of European Russia or, like the group at the next table, from the Caucasus. Like the Russians of Vladivostok or Murmansk, the Russians of Kaliningrad exist on the outer reaches of the vast motherland, in a European exclave some six hundred kilometres at its nearest point from the Russian "mainland". Kaliningrad is "Russia outside Russia" in exactly the same way that Königsberg was "Germany outside the Reich". The destiny of the city is and has always been that of the exclave: a bastard, unloved adolescent of a city handed down through history by generations of warring, abusive parents.

I snatched ten minutes' sleep in my hotel room before returning to the café on the fourth floor of the Kaliningrad Plaza. I was hungry, but had no idea where to eat. I needed something more substantial than last night's sushi or the tiny portions of pickled herring, dried fish or prawn cocktail I had snacked on through the day. None of the restaurants listed in my *Merian* pocket guide seemed to exist any more, and the only place I had noticed which served a decent meal was First Coffee. Looking out again at the damp, empty concrete wastes of Kaliningrad I felt tired, lonely and depressed; a long way not only from my natural home but also from the adopted *Heimat* I had decided to travel around on that magical evening in Kelheim.

I wandered back up Lenin Prospekt towards Victory Square and turned along Sovetsky Prospekt. I found an English-style pub decked out in nautical fashion called The Francis Drake or The Lord Nelson or something similar, where I ordered an imported beer. The only food it served was the ubiquitous local snack, which looked like deep-fried, salted pigs' ears. On my way back to Victory Square I dropped into a cellar restaurant named Traktir Razgulyay. The manager asked whether I had a reservation and looked me up and down rather venally, presumably to assess whether I was worth the bother of serving or whether it would be easier for him to claim that the tables were all reserved. I was reluctantly seated at a table with four Italian tourists and served vodka, smoked fish (again) and *Jägerschnitzel* (the Russians in these parts use the German word). The establishment was decorated in a rustic manner with dead animals' heads and painted straw doilies. The dance floor was overflowing with a wedding party gyrating to the sound of a live band playing *Schlager* (the German word again). A metal detector around the door of the restaurant bleeped as a quartet of gangsters arrived, checking in their handguns at the *vestiaire* before being obsequiously shown to the table they had clearly booked in advance. Later in the evening one of the men put his hand down his moll's dress and squeezed her breasts, leering drunkenly as his friend took a celebratory snapshot on his mobile phone.

I walked back to Pobedy Ploshchad, even more despondent. In a vain attempt to raise my spirits I bought a packet of German cigarettes and a can of Beck's and sat on the steps of the monument to the Great Patriotic War. I reflected again on this city with its two histories and its two cathedrals: one old, Gothic, Prussian; the other new, Byzantine, Russian. Which church will symbolise the city in a hundred years' time? Will the city still be named after a Bolshevik in the twenty-second century? Will it become an extra-territorial free trade zone, a sort of Russian Hong Kong; an honorary member of the European Union; an independent fourth Baltic Republic? Or will it turn into a "European dead-end zone"; a hole in the Schengen fence; a vacuum waiting to be filled by the *mafiosi* of eastern Europe? My guess is that Kaliningrad will probably muddle along as it has done for the last few decades – as an awkward, neglected leftover from both the German Reich and the USSR. An ex-Prussian exclave, an ex-Soviet exclave; a city with a Protestant past and an Orthodox future; a city where statues of Kant and Schiller rub shoulders with those of Kalinin and Lenin; an *oblast* pulled by Europe into the future and dragged by Russia into the past. It may slide, like Moldova, into a Ruritanian oblivion, stifled by Poland and Lithuania; or it may be the flashpoint that starts the next world war. As the Russian Deputy Prime Minister Sergei Ivanov announced in July 2007, "If US-backed missile defence systems are deployed in Poland, we will deploy nuclear missiles in the Kaliningrad *oblast*."[5]

Back in my bare suite at the Hotel Kaliningrad, I found it impossible to sleep. Having snoozed for ten minutes earlier in the evening, I was now wide awake; and the incident in the restaurant had left me feeling aroused. I opened the windows and watched the mysterious comings and

5   In 2016 Russia did just that, deploying an unspecified number of nuclear-capable Iskander-M missiles in the Kaliningrad region.

goings of night owls in the estate to the rear of the hotel. In the end I could stand the loneliness no longer, threw on some clothes and took the lift down to the hotel reception.

The lobby was empty save for a solitary man drinking at the bar and two young women sipping coffee at a table. I ordered a beer and lit a cigarette. After a couple of minutes, the man asked me where I was from. I explained I was staying for a couple of days in Kaliningrad, "on my way from Poland to Lithuania". He was a coach driver from Sweden. We were soon swapping stories of motorways, ferries and border crossings. He recalled the German motorway signs, now sadly disappeared since the ratification of the Oder–Neiße Line, which marked the distances to "Königsberg" from arbitrary locations on the West German autobahn system.

The young women glanced occasionally in our direction. I assumed they were part of the Swedish coach party or, since one of them looked Mediterranean, members of another tour group. After another round of beers, the Swede went off to find the toilet. One of the young women motioned me to their table and asked me to join them. I offered to buy them another coffee; or a beer, if they preferred. The Swede returned to the bar and joined us. We offered the girls cigarettes. Katya and Viktoria told us they were students at the university. As far as I can recall, Katya studied something to do with milk production. We chatted about the usual things – work, money, clothes, travel – comparing the opportunities in our respective countries. They told us they were saving up to go on holiday to Helsinki for two weeks. We bought another round of drinks and the conversation grew more flirtatious, with subtly coded references to age, partners, marital status and so on. The Swede and I were on the same wavelength and encouraged each other to open up and bare our souls in the Russian way. I felt Katya brush her arm against mine; then our knees touched. She was wearing a black trouser suit over a lacy black top which showed off her figure. She was warm, cuddly and fun to be with. Her friend Viktoria, the Italianate one, was more reserved, and I felt that she and the Swede had not bonded as spontaneously as Katya and I had.

The two girls left together to powder their noses and the Swede and I ordered another round of drinks. "Do we get to fuck these girls?" he asked, in a sing-song accent which made the question seem funny rather than crude. "If you want to, but you'll probably have to pay for it," I replied. "No, I could never pay for sex," he answered. He didn't need to: he had long blond hair, the face of a Viking warrior and the body of Thor... and he was a coach driver. We spent a few moments debating the rights and wrongs of the situation in which we were about to find ourselves; until Katya and Viktoria returned and we resumed our drunken flirting. I felt Katya's thigh pressing against mine and soon her hand strayed across.

"We can go to my apartment and drink champagne and have sex," she whispered. "It will cost a hundred euros."

"Do you take credit cards?" I replied.

Kaliningrad announced its outer limits in concrete letters twenty feet high. At some point along the orbital road I must have confused the exit signs in Cyrillic for Svetlogorsk and Selenogradsk and ended up on a minor road, travelling north through fields of brackish marshland, villages submerged in damp mist, hedges and trees bent by the wind. The endless expanse of the Russian steppe this was not. I felt hemmed in by this claustrophobic parcel of artificial Russia. Approaching Selenogradsk was disorientating: banks of apartment blocks rose out of the fields, and there were no signs to the centre of the town. It was supposed to be a seaside resort, once the "Königliches Seebad Cranz", but there was no sign of the Baltic.

I arrived at a square festooned with balloons and ticker tape where a crowd of parents and children had gathered to listen to a jazz-pop band. Policemen were directing the traffic into a diversion and I soon found myself driving aimlessly around potholed streets of rotting wooden villas and derelict brick churches, until I reached a dead end at the gate of a military barracks. I turned around and approached Selenogradsk from a different direction, eventually finding the high street, once known as Königsberger Straße. There were Soviet murals on the post office and the faded lettering of a former German off-licence – "Liköre–Wein–Ziemar GmbH" – over a general store. A sudden downpour emptied the square of the jazz band and its audience. Holidaymakers who had arrived for a weekend by the seaside huddled in doorways, waiting for the rain and wind to abate. In a park around the corner another small crowd had collected, listening to a band dressed in navy-blue suits and ties playing Russian *Schlager.* The *chanteuse,* a skinny waif in a sleeveless satin top, was fighting a losing battle against the elements. At the far end of the park the town disappeared into a blank space, which I deduced was the Baltic.

Grey waves roared in from the north, crashing against the sea wall. Spray bounced off the rocks like spittle. Horizontal gusts of rain lashed the promenade. There was no beach, only black rocks. The concrete carcass of a gutted building, an unfinished casino or a ruined amusement arcade, jutted over the empty promenade into the sea. Behind me was a wrought-iron pavilion where for one rouble you could buy a plastic cup and take the waters from a tap below a bust of a glum Königin Luise. Queen Louise of Prussia, consort of Friedrich Wilhelm III, was obliged to take her summer holidays in the godforsaken *Kurort* of Cranz in 1808 and 1809, when the Prussian court decamped to Königsberg after Berlin had been occupied by Napoleon's troops. Three tatty posters illustrating Hohenzollernstraße, the Hotel Königin Luise and the Königliches Seebad Cranz hung on the railings of a building site. I returned to the former Hohenzollernstraße and found a café-restaurant where the solitary wait-ress seemed intent on ignoring me. She took fifteen minutes to acknowl-edge my presence and a further ten minutes to come and take my order. I realised I would be there all afternoon if I ordered anything to eat, so I decided to have a coffee and a cigarette instead. The facial expression of the waitress made it clear she couldn't be bothered to serve a single cup of coffee, and my Russian was not up to explaining that I would have liked something to eat but was unimpressed by her sense of urgency. By now I had come to accept that Russians have no concept of service. In Germany you can simply take your custom elsewhere. In Selenogradsk there was nowhere else to go.

Except across the Curonian Spit to Lithuania. I reported to the toll-booth at the entrance to the 98-kilometre road along the causeway from Selenogradsk to the tip of the spit opposite Klaipėda. As far as I could recall from my previous visit seven years earlier, the toll was thirty-five roubles or some such insignificant sum, and I had retained a few hun-dred roubles in order to cover the cost. When confronted with my sign language requesting a ticket to cross the causeway, the woman in the tollbooth tapped into her calculator a sum of eight hundred roubles, an astonishing equivalent of sixteen pounds to drive the fifty kilometres of empty road to the Lithuanian border. I mimed shock and emptied my wal-let and my pockets of all my remaining roubles, which amounted to 570, making it clear this was all I possessed. The toll-mistress left her booth and consulted with the official who manned the barrier. Between them they agreed to waive the outstanding 230 roubles.[6]

---

6   I kept the brochure listing the various tariffs and showed it to my brother when I returned home. He concluded the fee of 800 roubles was correct, as there was a separate column of charges for foreigners. We had paid a much lower toll on the previous occasion because the official had assumed my brother was Russian.

Feeling cheated by the authorities I set off along the spit, and soon felt cheated by the landscape. The road led through a strip of forest (the former Königswald) of beech, rowan and silver birches. Neither the Baltic Sea on the left nor the Curonian Lagoon on the right was visible from the road. I drove cautiously: partly because this was an area of ecological fragility; partly because the police had been conducting random checks on motorists ever since I left Kaliningrad. It felt strange to be driving northeast in order to travel from Russia to "Europe"; which in turn made the "Russianness" of the Kaliningrad *oblast* seem even more fake. I stopped at a car park short of the border where hawkers sold amber washed up on the beach, and climbed to a vantage point on the sand dunes which afforded a view of the grey, choppy Baltic and a long scimitar of partly forested dunes.

At the border I panicked when I couldn't find the green-bordered sheet of tissue paper that served as my all-purpose exit document, eventually remembering I had stored it with my vehicle documents in the glove box. I watched through bronze-tinted windows as an official scrutinised my mugshot on her screen – an old photograph which had caused a rare moment of laughter from the receptionists in the Hotel Kaliningrad. I expected to spend at least forty-five minutes going through the entry procedure in reverse; but I was suddenly waved on and out of the *oblast* into an area of no-man's-land between the Russian and Lithuanian border posts. I felt a surge of elation on leaving this ugly, joyless European place that called itself Russia. I was tempted to take my hands off the wheel and applaud, as one used to do on leaving Soviet air space.

The Lithuanian customs post was a doddle. Five minutes and I was back in the European Union. The toll for driving through the Lithuanian half of the Curonian Spit was three euros, a more reasonable and more convenient charge, as motorists arriving from Kaliningrad would not yet have had the opportunity to purchase Lithuanian currency.[7] I turned off the causeway into Nida, a cute tourist resort on the lagoon of brown- and blue-painted fishermen's cottages converted into restaurants and souvenir shops. I purchased some *litas,* without having any idea how much they were worth, and put my watch back on Central European Time. The last

---

7   This was before Lithuania adopted the euro.

time I had travelled this way I had been caught out by not realising that Lithuania, east of Kaliningrad, was on Central European Time whereas Kaliningrad, to the west of Lithuania, was on Eastern European Time. On that previous visit in 2000 my brother and I had arrived in Kaunas, eaten out, gone to bed, got up, eaten breakfast and checked out of the hotel exactly one hour earlier than we had intended to do. This time I checked carefully the row of clocks on the rear wall of the tourist office which showed the current times in London, Kaliningrad, Vilnius, Moscow and Tokyo. Except that the current time in Vilnius was apparently 4.30 pm, whereas the current time in Kaliningrad was apparently 3.30 pm. Surely it should have been the other way around?

I took this up with a young man on the reception desk (it was a relief again to address people who automatically understood English). He assured me that the clock showing the Lithuanian time was set correctly, which certainly didn't tally with my previous experience. I had always regarded time and its corresponding zones as something immutable, like language or weather; not as something that was subject to change, like politics or currency. "And the time on the Kaliningrad clock is also wrong," I pointed out. "I know. I have just come from there. What time do you think it is in Kaliningrad?" He shrugged and replied, "I don't know." I felt doubly confused and ran to the bus station to check the clocks there. They all read 4.30 pm – Eastern European Time, the same as in Kaliningrad.[8] Once I had reset my watch to Eastern European Time, I repaired to a table on the terrace of the Pašiuré restaurant by the lagoon, where I had a delicious snack of smoked eel and potato skins sprinkled with cinnamon, washed down with a cold beer which didn't have to be defrosted first.

I walked north through the buckthorn and pine trees on the edge of the lagoon. On a high dune once named Schwiegermutterberg (Mother-in-Law Hill) stood the former summer holiday home of Thomas Mann. The writer and his family first visited Nidden in the summer of 1929 and were enchanted by the "primitive elemental character" of the Expressionist artists' colony. Mann had been awarded the Nobel Prize for Literature that year and decided to use the proceeds to build a holiday home in the village. The house, built in the vernacular style from wooden beams,

---

8 My hairdresser in London later explained to me that Lithuania changed from Eastern European Time to Central European Time in 1998 in an attempt to coordinate itself with Brussels: as a way of saying we are now part of Europe rather than the Soviet Union. However, it changed back to Eastern European Time in 2003 when the Lithuanians got fed up with it getting dark at three o'clock on winter afternoons.

with a thatched roof and a crossed gable tipped with horses' heads, was completed the following year. Mann spent three summers in the house overlooking the lagoon, during which he worked on the tetralogy *Joseph and His Brothers* and a number of essays, including his warning to the German people *Was wir verlangen müssen*. Written in the wake of SA pogroms in Königsberg during the Reichstag election of 1932, this polemic against terror and dictatorship advocated a new liberal democratic party to counter the rise of National Socialism. It had little effect: the following year Mann emigrated to Switzerland and never enjoyed the tranquil setting of his summer home again. After the *Anschluss* of the Memelland with the Reich in 1939, Mann's home was appropriated by the state and converted into a hunting lodge for Hermann Göring. The Reichsmarschall never used the cottage, although Albert Speer was occasionally seen there. It was destroyed in the war but painstakingly restored, against opposition from the Communist authorities, by the writer Antanas Venclova. In 1995–96 Mann's study and his family's bedrooms were reconstructed and the house opened as a museum. There are a number of photographs of the writer looking dapper, almost Cowardesque, in a tweed suit or double-breasted nautical blazer and white brogues, leaning on the chimney breast with a cocktail in one hand and a cigar in the other. A facsimile of an interview in *John O'London's Weekly* on 17 October 1931 records the author speaking of being "often mistaken for an Englishman".

The road along the Curonian Spit continued north through the village of Juodkrantė, before dropping to the right through hectares of burnt, deforested dunes to a jetty where a ferry transported cars over the channel connecting the Curonian Lagoon to the Baltic Sea. On the far side of the channel the wharves, cranes and container depots of Klaipėda, once the fourth largest port of the Soviet Union, stretched for thirty-two kilometres along the waterfront. Before it belonged to Lithuania or the USSR, the port was Memel, capital of the Memelland, the north-eastern frontier of the German Reich. As the first verse of the *Deutschlandlied* goes:

Von den Maas bis an die Memel,	(From the Meuse to the Neman,
Von der Etsch bis an den Belt.	From the Adige to the Belt.)

The strip of land on the far side of the River Memel (now known as the Nemunas) was German from 1252, when the Teutonic Knights built a fortress there and adopted the Lübecker Stadtrecht six years later, until 1918, when the Memelland was placed under the international jurisdiction of the Council of Ambassadors as part of Germany's punishment for initiating the First World War.

The ferry set off from Smiltynė across the channel to Klaipėda, performing an apparently unnecessary 180-degree turn as it did so, requiring all the cars to reverse off the boat when it docked at the far shore. This was a momentous crossing. Germany defines itself from west to east by its great rivers. One only arrives in Germany proper after crossing the Rhine: the Elbe (where American and Soviet troops joined up with each other at Torgau in April 1945) symbolises the old west–east divide; the Oder is the river where one crosses from Germany present into Germany past; and this last crossing of the Memel signifies the end of Germany past – the final frontier of the former Reich, and the furthest point on the journey I had commenced in Kelheim.

I checked into a small boutique hotel in a quiet side street near the docks. It was an oasis of luxury after the dreary, sleazy Hotel Kaliningrad and the chaotic bustle of the Russian city. I spent an hour leaning out of the window, savouring the peaceful cool of the evening. In a park opposite the hotel stood several tree trunks, carved into crosses, which commemorated bishops of Lithuania Minor – a strange combination of pagan and Christian symbolism, like Catholic totem poles. On Daukanto Street there was a monument to thousands of Lithuanian partisans and collaborators who were exiled to Siberia by the post-war Communist regime. Most died between 1946 and 1949; many disappeared into the *gulag* with no record of their death. In the centre of the Square of Lithuania Minor stood a statue of Martynas Mažvydas, a sixteenth-century scribe whose Protestant catechism was the first book to be published in the Lithuanian language. In the Soviet era the square was dedicated to the Red Army, who used it as a parade ground. At the southern end of Manto Street was the main square of the New Town, formerly Börsenplatz. The stock exchange which once stood there was destroyed in the war and the empty space that replaced it was renamed Lenin Square. A statue of the Communist divinity was unveiled in 1976, but survived for only fifteen years, dismantled when Lithuania liberated itself from Russian hegemony in 1991. The Borussia Monument, symbol of Prussian Memel, had a more chequered history. It was erected in 1907 to commemorate the centenary of the year in which King Friedrich Wilhelm III and Queen Louise, fleeing Napoleon's advance, relocated the Prussian court to Memel for a twelve-month period. The monument was removed in 1923, when Lithuania annexed the Memelland; was restored in 1938, when the Lithuanian authorities

lost control of the city to the National Socialists; and finally demolished
by the Soviet authorities in 1945. In 1970 an innocuous statue of a fisherman was placed on the site of the monument, in front of the Old Town
Hall which served as the residence of the Prussian royal family in 1807–
08. This small neoclassical building, with medallions of the royal couple
embedded in its beige walls, is now overshadowed by the Soviet-era Hotel
Klaipėda and a pair of post-modernist high-rise office blocks.

Bïržos Bridge, the former Börsenbrücke, was closed for repairs and
a temporary footbridge had been raised over the Danė, the river which
runs in a straight channel through the centre of Klaipėda. A three-masted
sailing ship was moored on the far bank. Built in Finland in 1947, the
Meridianas was assigned to Soviet Klaipėda for use as a nautical training
school as part of Finland's post-war reparations to the USSR. I continued
through the wide, empty streets of the neoclassical Old Town, uncannily
deserted for a Saturday night, until I arrived at Theatre Square, where I
ordered a beer from the only restaurant open and sat outside on my own.
On the far side of the square was the small theatre where a young Richard
Wagner opened the summer season in August 1836 as part of his nine-
month spell as conductor of the Königsberg Opera House. Wagner sailed
from Königsberg to Memel across the Curonian Lagoon, describing his
voyage as "one of the most melancholy crossings I have ever experienced".
His "unhappy sojourn" in the "desolate neighbourhood" of Memel was
only alleviated by the presence of his lover Minna Planer, whom he married in Königsberg later that year. Adolf Hitler arrived in Memel in more
triumphant fashion, storming off the battleship *Deutschland* at dawn on
23 March 1939 and proceeding in a motorcade through the streets of
the city to the theatre, where he was greeted by a "Heil" from thousands
of his compatriots holding banners declaring "Dieses Land bleibt ewig
deutsch" or "Wir danken unserem Führer".

In the centre of the square was the Simon Dach Fountain, surmounted
by a little bronze statue of Ännchen von Tharau. Simon Dach was a poet
and hymnist from Memel who was co-rector of the cathedral school in
Königsberg in 1637. He was enchanted by the demure teenage bride of a
friend of his and wrote the poem "Anke von Tharaw" in her honour. The
words were transposed into High German by Johan Gottfried Herder in
the eighteenth century and set to a melody composed by Friedrich Silcher
in 1827. Both the story of Ännchen and the folk song were handed down
through German popular culture. *Heimat* films based on her story were
released in 1935 and 1954; and the tune became a staple of German

songbooks, covered by scores of artists, including the famous bandleader James Last. The original statue of Ännchen was inaugurated in 1912 in honour of Simon Dach and became a symbol of the folksy piety of the *Memelländer*. It was replaced in 1939 by a bust of Adolf Hitler and disappeared during the war. In 1989 the Ännchen von Tharau Club, an association of exiled German *Memelländer*, decided to celebrate the fall of the Iron Curtain by recasting the statue and replacing it on the pillar in the centre of the fountain. The re-inauguration of the statue was held on 15 November 1989 before a multitude of local Lithuanians and German visitors assembled in the newly paved square in front of the renovated theatre – a communal celebration which healed wounds inflicted by fifty years of Hitler–Stalin tyranny.

The tranquillity of Theatre Square was shattered by the arrival of two white stretch limousines and a trio of black 4x4s, which roared into the empty square and disgorged a party of wedding guests into the cold, grey northern evening. Stilettos tottered over the cobblestones. Men in suits, tails and black trilbies adorned with white ribbons staggered towards the toilets of the restaurant, sucking desperately on their cigarettes. The bride and groom posed for photographs on the steps in front of Ännchen. On the banks of the Danė at the far side of the square stood a pair of half-timbered brick warehouses, the faded legend "Germania Speicher" still legible across their gables. One had been converted into a restaurant named Memelis, whose brewery emitted a pungent smell of hops. The menu in English (Lithuanian is an archaic language with distant links to Sanskrit, and a challenge to foreign linguists) offered "slightly smoked pigs' ears" (I prefer them fully smoked myself), "blue onions", a "could soup" (as opposed to a "couldn't soup", presumably) and "potato zeppelins". I washed my meal down with a mug of Juodasis, the brewery's own black beer, and joined the rest of the clientele outside for a post-prandial cigarette.

O n leaving Klaipėda the following morning it became evident why the centre was so deserted: everyone lived in high-rise apartment blocks on the edge of the city. I joined a queue of cars waiting at a level crossing for a train of fifty Russian container wagons to pass by on the single track southward, carrying supplies to Sovetsk (formerly Tilsit) in the Kaliningrad *oblast*. Road and rail traffic between Kaliningrad and the rest of Russia now has to cross EU territory, and it seemed as if a lot of Russian maritime traffic was being unloaded at Klaipėda and transported by train through this corner of Lithuania to the *oblast*. For the next hour, as I drove south-east along route 141, I played leapfrog with the double-headed Russian freight train. I would overtake it on the road, but would then have to wait at the next level crossing for it to catch up and trundle past me again. In Šilutė (formerly Heydekrug) the townspeople, in their Sunday best, were emerging from a neo-Gothic church over whose oak door were inscribed Luther's words "Ein' feste Burg ist unser Gott". This church is apparently the most important Protestant place of worship remaining in Lithuania, where some twenty thousand believers still adhere to the evangelical Lutheran faith.

I was driving through the Memelland, the sliver of land which formed the north-eastern and most distant march of the German Reich (the part which resembles the horn on the rhinoceros of Prussia). As in the Silesian plain or the Vistula delta, the landscape formed an immense expanse of woods and wheat fields. Avenues of tree-lined roads connected villages of red-brick schools and churches; Gothic tollhouses marked out the stages of my journey. The Russian freight train finally turned south towards Sovetsk, and at Smalininkai the Memelland petered out. For the first time since leaving Kelheim, I was finally in territory which had never been German. Almost immediately the landscape changed. The prim curves of the old Prussian byways, double-stitched by rows of oak trees, opened out into long, straight, traffic-free roads which ran for miles through dense pine forests parallel to the border with the Kaliningrad *oblast*. The few hamlets I passed were built from wooden cottages rather than brick houses. I crossed the River Nemunas at Jurbaikas and turned south towards Marijampole and the Polish border. Back in Poland I circumvented Suwałki and drove west along route 655 towards Masuria. The north-eastern corner of Poland around Suwałki belongs to the Podlaskie Voivodship, and the terrain is Slavic *puszcza* rather than German forest. I wondered when I would return to land that was formerly part of East Prussia. As if on cue, I passed a road sign announcing the Voivodship of Warminsko-Mazurskie. The composition of the asphalt changed and I dived at once into a tunnel of beech trees that continued for the next ten kilometres, by which stage I was in the Masurian heartland of lakes and forests. It was as if the Prussians planted rows of trees along their roads to impose their identity upon the landscape – as a way of marking their territory.

As I approached Kętzryn I noticed signposts leading to the "Wolfschanze" (Wolf's Lair), Hitler's forest retreat during the Second World War. I was directed to a parking slot and invited to join a tour group in the language of my choice: Polish, German, English or Russian. Quadrilingual signs advised visitors not to climb onto the bunkers, but it soon became apparent that the official guides tacitly encouraged sightseers to explore the ruins. Little remains of the conference barracks where the attempted assassination of Hitler took place on 20 July 1944. A group of Wehrmacht officers led by Klaus Schenk Graf von Stauffenberg concluded that Hitler was bent on destroying Germany once the tide of war had turned against him; that his personal defeat would be expressed in the annihilation of the nation. The explosives in a briefcase beneath an oak table that lunchtime killed four of the twenty-four officers and adjutants assembled in the room, but only shredded Hitler's trousers. The Führer was able to receive Mussolini later that afternoon, by which time the ringleaders of the plot were being rounded up. They would be executed the same evening in the courtyard of the General Staff Headquarters in Berlin.

I followed a path that wound through the woods past low concrete barracks, warehouses and stenographers' offices; past the shattered ruins of flak bunkers, water tanks and machine-gun posts; below the rusted remains of wires, clamps and hooks on which camouflage netting had been hung. The heavy bunkers of Göring, Bormann, Keitel and Hitler loomed out of the forest like broken ziggurats: too solid to be blown up, they had collapsed in on themselves, creating labyrinths of moss-coated cliffs and defiles which might almost have emerged organically out of the forest. The woods were rank with the smell of wild garlic and buzzing with mosquitoes which penetrated the dank, dripping corridors inside the bunkers. In winter, little warmth or light would have filtered through the tree cover or permeated the gloomy chambers inside the bunkers. It's no wonder Hitler became slowly deranged and addicted to a cocktail of narcotics and stimulants which poisoned his body during the two and a half years he spent in the Wolf's Lair. Having withdrawn from the world he was destroying, he gradually withdrew from his inner circle, taking dinner in the company of his secretaries and walking alone with his Alsatian Blondi. Hitler lost his passion for music and cinema, only emerging from his bunker to listen to reports on the war from his military commanders. He would then bark orders which often contradicted the advice he had just received from his Chiefs of Staff. The halcyon days of Obersalzberg

were lost for ever. Eva Braun never visited the place that General Jodl
described as "a cross between a cloister and a concentration camp".

The breakfast table of the Hotel Warminski was laden with a dozen
varieties of smoked meat and scores of sticky cakes. A Polish version of
"What Shall We Do with the Drunken Sailor?" blared from a pair of loudspeakers, followed by some martial music remixed to an acid house beat.
I smiled at the young waitress as I left; she responded with a stony glare.
I crossed the empty marble expanse of the lobby and set off down Ulica
Mickiewicza towards the centre of Olsztyn. I passed the neo-Gothic Church
of the Holy Heart of Jesus Christ, the tallest of the three Prussian churches
that tower above the city. Its red gables were striped with white vertical
indentations in the North German manner, and the pointed arches of its
doors and windows were braided with bands of green and yellow glazed
brick. Its spire rose above turrets, finials and gargoyles to a height of eighty-
three metres – seven metres higher than St Mary's Cathedral in Gdańsk.

Below the church was the intersection of Ulica Mikołaja Kopernika
and Aleja Marszałka Józefa Piłsudskiego, the administrative hub of the
province of Warmia and Masuria. On one corner stood the Regional
Administrative Court, a red-brick Wilhelmine pile, decorated with
friezes and escutcheons, which embodied the classical ideals of Prussian
absolutism. On another corner was the Provincial Government of the
Voivodship, a low concrete block the colour of egg custard with rows
of identical windows that characterised the more pragmatic, furtive
nature of Communist despotism. In the centre of the square opposite
stood a Polish-Russian monument built from the same *ersatz* marble as
the Silesian monument in Góra Swietej Anny. The pillar on the left was
carved with neo-constructivist images of tanks, submarines and missile
launchers. Sculpted into the right-hand pillar was the colossal figure of
a Red Army infantryman of Asiatic appearance. Like the monument by
the South Park in Kaliningrad, this was until recently a celebration of
Polish-Russian Friendship. Like its counterpart in the Russian *oblast* it is
now obsolete, its slogans of brotherhood dismantled. The former Square
of Polish-Russian Friendship is paved with flagstones removed from the
ruins of the Hindenburg Mausoleum. It is a forum of recycled German
nationalism and redundant Soviet militarism – currently used as a car
park.

I entered the Old Town through the restored fourteenth-century High Gate and walked down Staromiejska to the market square, where I sat at a table on the terrace of one of the café-restaurants at the head of the *rynek*. In the middle of the square was the Old Town Hall, a pair of reconstructed buildings connected by a colonnade beneath which florists, *delikatesy* and antiquarian booksellers spread their wares. The houses around the square were rebuilt in the 1950s in their original gabled forms, coated with a muddy plaster wash and decorated with angular Socialist Realist medallions illustrating cogwheels and ears of grain, symbols of the mechanised agriculture introduced to the region under Communist rule. A trio of swarthy Romany girls, teenage prostitutes with leathery skin and frizzy black hair in ponytails at the tops of their scalps, splashed in the fountain in front of the cafés; pouting and strutting, they flaunted their youthful energy and the wads of cash they had earned from passing lorry drivers on the long haul from Warsaw to Kaliningrad. The respectable German tourists on the café terraces tut-tutted and tried their best to ignore them.

In the evening I returned to the restaurant at the head of the *rynek*. I had an appetite for some hearty German food, and ordered pork knuckle and fried potatoes. But the *Schweineshaxe* was unavailable and I had to make do with *pierogi* again. As dusk fell, I had a strange sense of *déjà vu*; after a few moments I realised that Olsztyn reminded me of Liberec in Bohemia. Superficially there was something about the layout of the market square: the colonnaded houses along the eastern side, and the way the two main streets ran downhill, parallel to each other, from the foot of the square. Underlying that was something less tangible: an old-fashioned provincial melancholy. Liberec and Olsztyn, both cities in the north of the countries to which they now belong, share a double-layered nostalgia for a recent Socialist past and an older German history. Both cities also have magnificent neo-Renaissance German city halls. Like their Sudeten or Silesian compatriots, the Germans of East Prussian Allenstein were driven out by the advance of the Red Army or expelled after the war; replaced by immigrants from former Polish regions subsumed into the Soviet Union. A familiar history of war, exile, repression and stagnation haunted the Stare Miasto of Olsztyn just as it did the Staré Město of Liberec. At 9 pm a fanfare of trumpets sounded in unison from St Jacob's Cathedral to my left and from the castle tower on my right. The echo of the fanfares faded away on the soft evening air.

The next morning, I walked out of the centre of Olsztyn, following buses displaying the destination of Jakubowo, through suburbs of

Jugendstil tenements and rainbow-striped high-rise blocks. I reached a
park once known as Jakobsberg, site of the former *Kurhaus* of Prussian
Allenstein. At the centre was once a monument to a plebiscite held on 11
July 1920 to establish whether the people of Warmia and Masuria wished
to remain East Prussian, or transfer their allegiance from Germany to
Poland. The result was a humiliation for Poland, as 97.5% of the population voted to remain in East Prussia. The German monument commemorating the victory of the plebiscite was replaced after the war by a Polish
memorial in the form of a wall of white eagles bearing the inscription "To
the heroes in the struggle for national and social liberation in Warmia
and Masuria". "Struggle" against whom, "liberation" from what, one is
tempted to ask. As in Gdańsk, Elbląg, Kaliningrad or Klaipėda, the memory of German East Prussia (of Danzig, Elbling, Königsberg and Memel)
has been falsified or erased. Although not quite. I found myself staring at
a tiny iron fire hydrant cover embedded in a patch of lawn near the monument. It read "Gebr. Kühn. Osterode, Ostpr."[9]

9   "Kühn Brothers. Osterode, East Prussia."

9

≋

Pomerania

Nuremberg-on-Sea

I was sitting beneath the portico of the Old Town Hall in Szczecin, sipping a watery white wine and nibbling at a "tuna steak" that had come out of a tin. The Old Town Hall was "barockisiert" in 1677 and lost its original function in the 1870s when the New City Hall was built. The Old Town Hall was converted into shops on the ground floor, a furniture store on the first floor and a millinery on the second. It was destroyed by bombs in 1944, although it had since been restored to its fourteenth-century Gothic appearance, with horizontal stripes of red and green glazed bricks around the arches of its portico. It now serves as Szczecin's Jazz Café. The reconstructed baroque houses along the eastern side of Rynek Sienny, the former Hay Market, have been painted in bright reds and blues and now comprise a wine bar, a Thai restaurant, a Dutch pancake house, an English pub and several dental clinics.

Signposts describe this area of Szczecin as "Stare Miasto" (Old City), but this is a woeful misnomer: the half-dozen rebuilt historical buildings are surrounded by grimy, prefabricated apartment blocks thrown up in the 1950s. The Altstadt of German Stettin was flattened by carpet bombing on 17 and 18 August 1944, and the remaining bridges and towers were blown up by the Wehrmacht as they retreated in April 1945. In contrast to Wrocław or Olsztyn, there has been little attempt to reconstruct the pre-war centre of Szczecin. The area inside the old walled city is now an estate of housing blocks and scruffy parks roamed by mangy cats and stray dogs. Grey-skinned derelicts sit on benches, clutching their heads and flicking cigarette butts onto the worn grass. Wheelie bins over-flow with rotting rubbish that fills the evening air with the smell of ripe melons. Spooky lampposts with clusters of bulbs on stalks cast a sickly light over the cracked pavements and corrugated iron fences that sur-round a miasma of backyards. The few buildings surviving from Stettin's Renaissance era (the Maiden's Tower or the Loitz Merchant's House, for example) are isolated on patches of waste ground or hidden beneath fly-overs. The great Brick Gothic Cathedral of St James has been refitted with rectilinear windows framed in concrete, which look as though they've been recycled from a disused factory.

The castle of the princes who ruled the Duchy of Pomerania from the eleventh century until 1637 was rebuilt after the war in its original Rustic Renaissance style, with medallions resembling a set of Formula One rac-ing wheels along the top of each gable. A terrace at the rear leads into Plac Solidarność, where the former Gate of Prussian Homage stands isolated in the middle of a tramway junction. Resembling a baroque shoebox covered with bellicose statuary, this is one of two city gates built by the Prussians between 1725 and 1728 to commemorate their purchase of Stettin from Sweden. I walked up to Polish Soldiers' Square (once the Königsplatz of Prussian Stettin) and turned down Niepodległości (Independence Avenue). This was the Paradeplatz of the German city, a boulevard of grandiose civic buildings built at the time of the *Jahrhundertwende*: the Post Office, the Palace of the Landowners' Society, the Headquarters of the Prussian Police (later the seat of the Gestapo and subsequently that of the UB secret police). At the far end of Niepodległości was a modernist block built in the late 1920s that once housed the UFA Palast cinema and the DEFAKA (Deutsches Familienkaufhaus) department store. It is now an all-purpose shopping mall with an Empik bookshop on the third floor, where I bought a book of postcards of pre-war Stettin.

The former Neustadt of German Stettin radiates outwards from Plac Grunwaldzki, along wide avenues with central *allées* filled with flower beds, fountains and cafés. Sections of the tree-lined boulevards are paved with pink marble tombstones lifted from German and Jewish cemeter-ies. Children play netball and young men repair cars in gritty backyards. Magnolia trees grow from tenement forecourts. Change the street names back to their originals (Hohenzollernplatz or Kaiser-Wilhelm-Straße, for example) and you might almost be in a run-down area of Berlin-Kreuzberg – although the Poles prefer to compare their city centre with Haussmann's Paris. A dusty park led back to Plac Zwycięstwa, where the spires of two former German churches were silhouetted against a moonlit sky. Late shoppers were purchasing flowers and vegetables from street vendors and waiting obediently at traffic lights for the green man to appear and permit them to cross the empty streets.

Like many Prussian capitals, pre-war Stettin was a city of statues and towers. An equestrian Kaiser Wilhelm I presided over Königsplatz. In 1945 the square was renamed Polish Soldiers' Square. The imperial statue was destroyed and replaced by a Monument of Gratitude to the Red Army, which represented a Polish worker fraternising with a Soviet soldier beneath an illuminated red star. This monument was dismantled in 1992.

The only surviving Prussian tower was the Bismarck-Warte, a circular stone tower built by Wilhelm Kreis on heights overlooking the Oder in Gotzlow, a suburb north of the city. It was the result of a competition in 1910 to design a Bismarck Memorial Hall for the province of Pomerania. To be known as the "Denkmal des Ostens" ("Monument of the East"), it would stand above the Oder estuary, marking the frontier of the old Frankish Nordmark. Professor Kreis submitted a project entitled "Adlerhorst II" ("Eagle's Nest II"), which was unanimously awarded first prize. Work on the tower commenced in 1913, but was interrupted two years later by the war. The memorial was completed and opened to the public in 1921. Based on the sixth-century mausoleum of Theodoric the Great in Ravenna, the Bismarck Tower consisted of two cylindrical drums positioned one above the other. The upper rotunda was supported by a circle of stone buttresses on which were perched a dozen *Reichsadler* designed by the Berlin sculptor Hermann Hosaeus, who also sculpted a bust of Bismarck inside the mausoleum. Two circles of blind Roman arches ran below the architrave. Tiny window slits gave the tower the aspect of a defensive fortification. An uninspired neoclassical portico detracted from its solid, Romanesque simplicity. Contemporary photographs show the completed tower at the summit of a bare hill, commanding a view across the estuary. A few birch trees in the background lend an impression of monumentality. A photograph of the rotunda taken in the 1920s forms the cover image of the *catalogue raisonné* of Wilhelm Kreis's work, published in 1994 by Klinkhardt and Biermann.

I set off for the Bismarck-Warte from the obelisks at the foot of Chrobry Embankment (the former Haken Terrace), from the quay where ships of the pre-war White Fleet (*Freia, Hertha* and *Odin*) once moored. I followed tramlines northwards along the left bank of the Odra. To the west, post-war Szczecin stretched away towards Germany, mile after mile of identical nine-storey prefabricated apartment blocks. The cobbled road wound between scrap yards containing pyramids of coal and piles of rusting sheet metal. A matrix of cranes and gantries soared above the backyards of the Baltic Marine wharves. I caught sight of the crown of the Bismarck Tower high up in the woods as I passed the tram terminus at the city limits. I crossed a railway line and drove up a sandy avenue into a small estate of pre-war villas, some of which still bore the faint outline of German escutcheons on their walls. I climbed through a forested ravine until I reached the abandoned mausoleum at the top of the hill. Now surrounded by thick woodland, the tower was smaller than I'd imagined. The stone eagles had been dismantled from their perches, but otherwise the monument was intact. The entrance had been secured by a rusty iron door. I peered through the slats of the grille and could just make out a dark circular crypt within. There was a rustling sound behind me, and I turned to see a man hastily concealing some magazines in a plastic bag before slipping furtively away.

I followed routes 142 and 20 eastwards from Szczecin, through a landscape of forests, lakes and fields of wheat that rippled in the summer breeze. Fertile brown soil furrowed into potato fields undulated for miles across moraines deposited by Ice Age glaciers. Tractors threw up clouds of hay dust over cropped cornfields. Sandy tracks lined with rows of silver birch trees led off the highway towards half-timbered cottages around duck ponds behind thickets of reeds. Storks nested on telegraph poles or on the chimneys of ruined monasteries. Horses' hooves and the wheels of carts decked out for Harvest Festival clattered over cobbled lanes.

I was heading for Szczecinek, with the intention of visiting the former Ordensburg of Falkenburg, one of three elite colleges where star pupils from the Hitler Youth were schooled in the arts of the SS. Unlike Sonthofen in Bavaria or Vogelsang in the Eifel, little is known about Falkenburg. The encyclopedia *Bauen unterm Hakenkreuz* includes two photographs of the Ordensburg, which was built with wooden beams and thatched roofs in a rustic, vernacular style appropriate to the region. It locates the site of Falkenburg at "Crössinsee (today: Szczecinek, Poland)". I assumed that the big lake on the map just east of Szczecinek would be the former Crössinsee, so I drove through the town and approached the lake from the south. The first track I took petered out in a forest of reeds. I tried approaching from the west and ended up on a sandy path which led in circles through marshy woodland. There was no sign of any military installation.

Convinced that the Ordensburg was in the vicinity of Szczecinek, I drove back to the town and left the car in a car park behind the main street, ignoring the ubiquitous urchins who demanded euros for "looking after" the vehicle. I found a tourist information bureau in the market square and asked the incumbent, a pleasant young man with a bulbous head who looked like Matt Lucas from *Little Britain*, for directions to Falkenburg. He spoke neither English nor German and my request drew a blank. I wrote the words "Falkenburg" and "Crössinsee" on a sheet of paper, but they elicited no response. I proceeded to write "Nazi School", "Third Reich", "SS Castle" and "Polish military". I drew a large swastika, but got in reply only directions to a bunker on the outskirts of Szczecinek that formed part of the Nazi *Ostwall*. This was baffling: I was sure that Falkenburg was now, like Sonthofen and Vogelsang, a military base of some importance. We examined an atlas and found three places in northern Poland named Krosin, but none of them was situated near a lake. The young man made a few phone calls, then closed the office and accompanied me to the local museum – which had just closed. Back in the tourist office, I retraced my route from Szczecin in the atlas and, just as one of the friends he had phoned arrived, discovered a J.Krosino (Lake Crosin, or Crössinsee) to the east of Złocieniec, a small town I had driven through an hour before, which I remembered because the local fire brigade had been hosing down the tarmac of the streets to prevent heat bubbles forming, and because there were people squatting by the roadside selling honey, blueberries and blow jobs. The young man asked his friend if he recognised the name "Falkenburg". He replied "Złocieniec". "Falkenburg," I repeated. "Złocieniec," he answered. I put two and two together and realised that Złocieniec was the literal Polish translation of Falkenburg (both meaning "fortress of the falcons" in English). The friend went on to confirm that there was indeed a Polish Army base at Grotniki Drawskie, just to the east of Złocieniec, beside a Lake Krosin. *Bauen unterm Hakenkreuz* had got it wrong.

I thanked the two young men and began the drive back towards Złocieniec. I noticed the two pink towers of the Ordensburg rising above the trees as I drew near from the east. I couldn't believe I had failed to notice them when I drove from the west three hours earlier. I turned off the main highway along a road through a tunnel of elm trees to the gate of the camp, which turned out to be the headquarters of the Second Brigade of a Polish Army regiment. Like Sonthofen, it was now a high-security military base surrounded by wire fences, sentry boxes and patrolling soldiers. I parked by the main gates and took a surreptitious photograph of the compound in front of the camp, which was full of tanks and other armoured vehicles under camouflaged tarpaulins. The two square brick towers rose in the distance, tall and slim (medieval Bologna crossed with the Reichssportfeld of Nazi Berlin), but they were too far away to observe anything of the former Ordensburg below them. I followed a sandy track around the perimeter fence of the installation, arousing the suspicion of the armed sentries on guard. Eventually I arrived at the lake, where a wooden jetty ran for a further twenty metres above some reeds and lily pads. And that was as far as I could go.

I stopped in Czaplinek to phone the Hotel Stadt Berlin in Bad Heringsdorf (across the border in Germany) to tell them I was running late, as they had instructed me to let them know if I was going to arrive after 6 pm. They sounded slightly put out, but said they would wait for me. However, it was already six o'clock and it would take at least three hours to drive to Świnoujście on the coast and cross over to Germany. They asked me to arrive no later than 9 pm. I set off towards Drawsko Pomorskie, from where I turned north-west through Łobec, Resko and Płoty, taking the tight bends of the country roads too fast and cursing whenever I had to stop to allow a train to pass at a level crossing. At Parłówko I joined the main E65 running north from Szczecin, which was congested with lorries heading for the ferries at Świnoujście. I crossed the eastern stream of the Odra delta onto the island of Wolin, where a dual carriageway ran along a causeway above the lagoon. I picked up speed, overtaking columns of lorries. By a quarter to nine I was congratulating myself on approaching Świnoujście, assuming I had only to cross a bridge over the Odra and drive through the border into Germany. There was a delay because of a contra-flow system, which required a diversion onto a minor road through some woods. In the confusion I ignored a sign to the "Centrum" (of Świnoujście presumably, although I hadn't yet reached its outskirts) and followed the main stream of traffic back to the E65. I finally reached the Świna, the central channel of the Odra delta known in German times as the Kaiserfahrt. There were ferry terminals from where one could sail to Denmark or Sweden, but no bridge, no indication of how one reached Germany, and no sign of Świnoujście.

I drove up and down the docks in a mild panic, returned to the E65 and turned right, down the only road not leading back to the Polish mainland. I expected to drive immediately into the suburbs of Świnoujście, but instead of encountering the familiar rows of concrete apartment blocks, I found myself going along a winding road deeper into empty countryside. I lost track of where I was in relation to the river and eventually lost my bearings completely. I seemed to be driving south, whereas according to the map the only directions one could go were either west to Świnoujście or east back to the mainland.

I was about to turn around and retrace my route to the diversion when I reached a crossroads and another sign which indicated "Centrum". I turned right and the road led around a bend onto a car ferry. I boarded the vessel without considering its destination, as there was nowhere else to go. The boat set off on a diagonal course across the river. I collected my thoughts and took a closer look at my road atlas. I worked out that I was now crossing the Świna; that there was no bridge connecting the island of Wolin to the predominantly German island of Usedom (Uznam in Polish) on which Świnoujście lay (rather inconveniently, thanks to Stalin's arbitrary red lines); and that the ferry crossing was ten kilometres south of the town, requiring a ten-kilometre drive south from the E65, followed by a drive of equal distance north to Świnoujście after disembarking on the left bank of the Świna. None of this had been signposted: I had found the car ferry more through accident than design. It was perplexing that there were no road signs to "Germany" (or "Niemcy", in Polish) for the benefit of German drivers; and odd that I had not seen any cars with German plates.

After disembarking from the apparently free car ferry, I followed the traffic towards Świnoujście, turning right along Grunwaldzka when I reached the outskirts of town. The avenue led to a junction where a plethora of green road signs pointed in the direction of various destinations, but none of them, even to my limited understanding of Polish, suggested anything remotely connected to Germany, to the towns of Ahlbeck or Heringsdorf, to a customs post, a tollbooth, a border crossing, a frontier or any of the other terms or symbols commonly used to guide motorists from one country to another. I was growing increasingly irritated because it was now way past nine o'clock, it was getting dark, and I was keeping my hosts waiting.

I stopped and examined my German road atlas. There were two border crossings indicated on the map: one to the north-west of Świnoujście marked "pedestrians and cyclists only"; and one to the south-west, which appeared to be at the far end of Grunwaldzka. I performed a U-turn and drove back along Grunwaldzka, wondering again why there were no road signs to "Deutschland" or "Niemcy". The avenue became increasingly bumpy. I smacked the chassis of the car against two particularly protu- berant ruts. The road finally petered out altogether, disappearing into a row of residential front gardens. There was something in the woods ahead that resembled a frontier post, but it was unclear whether it was closed, disused or had never been completed in the first place; and in any case there was no access to it. I returned along Grunwaldzka and noticed a car with German plates. I tucked in behind it and followed it until it reached a square, with a post office and town hall, which was recognisably the centre of Świnoujście. The German car continued through an area of unlit parkland, before arriving in what seemed to be a completely separate town of Prussian villas and ice-cream parlours. I followed it along a crowded promenade until it came to a stop in a car park at the end of the road. I got out to read a hand-painted map and learned I had reached the pedes- trian border crossing at the north-western edge of Świnoujście. I drove up to the crossing, which was indeed for pedestrians and cyclists only. There was a red-and-white-striped pole across a cobbled road, which led tanta- lisingly into Germany. It was now a quarter to ten and I was within ten minutes' drive of the room I had booked in the Hotel Stadt Berlin in Bad Heringsdorf. I telephoned the hotel to explain that I was in Świnoujście, but had got lost and had not yet found the border crossing for automo- biles. The hotel asked me whether I was arriving by car or on foot, which I thought was a strange question, given I was still in Poland.

I inspected the map again and drove back through the dark Kurpark and the centre of Świnoujście, towards the one remaining road that could possibly lead to the frontier. Ulica Gdańska, however, led me in a series of ever-diminishing circles around a housing estate. I found myself back on Grunwaldzka at the traffic junction where I had decided to follow the car with German plates. I pulled over into a backyard and confronted the awful truth – there were no road signs to "Deutschland" or "Niemcy" because there was no border crossing for vehicles from Świnoujście to Germany. To reach my hotel in Bad Heringsdorf, ten kilometres along the coast, I would have to return to the car ferry and cross the Świna, drive back over Wolin to the Polish mainland, follow the E65 to Szczecin, cross into Germany south of Szczecin, drive north-west through Germany to Anklam, and then cross the German part of Usedom. That would take about five hours, and it was now 10 pm. I phoned the Hotel Stadt Berlin once again and tendered profuse apologies: "I had no idea there was no crossing for cars from Świnoujście; I drove here specially; it's *unglaublich*; maybe next time; I'm really sorry, I hope you can still sell the room I booked" – all the while racking my brains to recall whether I had given them my credit card details or not (I hadn't).

I sat back, lit a cigarette and had a quiet laugh at my misfortune. It was one of those moments when you realise you've been defeated by geopolitics. What had seemed a straightforward journey from Poland into Germany had become mired in the serpentine geography of the Odra delta and obstructed by barriers thrown up by the politics of the Cold War. It was 10.30 pm and I was marooned in a Polish seaside resort at the height of the season – with nowhere to sleep. Every *pensjonat* I tried was full. I went into one of the holiday-apartment blocks to ask for advice. To my surprise, they offered me a room. It was on the thirteenth floor and quite spartan. The regulation pair of twin beds and plywood furniture provided me with a pang of *Ostalgie* for student holidays I spent in the Soviet Union in the 1970s. They would not accept credit cards (justifiably, as the room was so cheap). I was thus required to make another two crossings of the Kurpark between Świnoujście spa and Świnoujście town in order to change money at a cash dispenser. I then had to find a guarded car park, as it was forbidden to park on the streets. It was almost midnight before I was free to go in search of a beer and some food.

The Promenada still reeled with sweaty, inebriated holiday-makers; young couples who would be middle-aged by the time they reached thirty; young women who were pregnant before they were twenty. Kebab parlours competed for business with junk-food outlets and stalls selling framed colour photographs of Pope John Paul II with a halo of amber chips glued onto an airbrushed sunrise. There were no cafés or restaurants, only heaving karaoke bars or greasy takeaways. I ordered an XXL baguette, which might have tasted vaguely of cheese and mushroom had it not been smeared with a snake of white gunk which tasted like synthetic whipped cream. I went to sit on the beach beneath a peach-coloured harvest moon suspended low over the Baltic. I watched a car ferry steering out of the port on an overnight crossing to Bornholm. I looked wistfully in the other direction at the two purple neon beacons illuminating Bad Heringsdorf, and at the sparkling lights of Bansin and Ahlbeck, the other *Kaiserbäder,* so near geographically yet so far out of reach. I bought another can of beer and a bar of chocolate to eradicate the aftertaste of the XXL abomination, and returned to the thirteenth floor of my hotel.

I was kept awake throughout the night by Polish football chants and the mewing of seagulls. At 5.30 am I got up and opened the window to watch day break over Świnoujście. A lingering odour of fried onions rose on the breeze from the jumble of *Kaiserzeit* villas and jerry-built holiday apartments below. A horizontal shaft of purple cloud pierced the yellow haze over the Baltic. A carpet of trees stretched west, beyond the German spas, towards Peenemünde, Greifswald and the mauve skies and ivory cliffs of Rügen.

Eleven hours and two hundred and seventy-five kilometres later, I arrived in the *Ostseebad* of Ahlbeck, less than two kilometres as the crow flies from Świnoujście. I might almost have been on another continent. Bad Heringsdorf, the middle of the three imperial spas, was a cluster of Prussian villas with filigree wooden balconies and verandas surrounded by manicured gardens in the English style. Busts in Italian marble of the grandees of the *Jahrhundertwende* stood to attention in beds of pinks and rhododendrons. Were it not for the two GDR-era *Plattenbau* towers of the Kurhotel and the Reha[bilitation]-Klinik, whose purple lights I had observed last night from the Polish beach, I could easily have imagined myself transported back to the 1890s, when the resort was in its Wilhelmine pomp.

I parked in Friedenstraße and strolled down to the pier head, where I ordered a smooth, creamy caffé latte *(latte macchiato* in German, unobtainable in provincial Poland) and an indecently large wedge of *Walnußtorte* with real whipped cream. The coffee arrived within two minutes, whereas the two fried eggs I had ordered for breakfast in Świnoujście had taken over three-quarters of an hour. Heringsdorf was quiet, comfortable, elegant, orderly, efficient, sophisticated and affluent. A genteel murmur of conversation ebbed and flowed with the swish of the tide against the sandy beach; music to my ears after the raucous Polish resort with its bawling children and chain-smoking parents. The German holiday-makers enjoyed a leisurely programme of paddling in the sea, sunning on the beach, *Kaffee und Kuchen* in a *Konditorei*, a sauna in one of the Wellness-Studios, some retail therapy in the luxurious shopping malls, and a cultural visit to a local museum. I walked out to the end of the pier, at five hundred and eight metres one of the longest in Europe. Hundreds of *Strandkörbe,* white wicker baskets that open up like clams to reveal a blue-and-white-striped seat snug for two people, lay scattered along the white sands from the pier of Bansin to the border beyond Ahlbeck. Świnoujście had disappeared beneath a belt of marine woodland.

Originally a fishing colony owned by Georg Bernhard von Bülow, Master of the Royal Forests, Bad Heringsdorf was named by King Friedrich Wilhelm III when he stopped here in the summer of 1820 after inspecting the fortress of Swinemünde (now Świnoujście). The king tasted a dish of *Matjes*, drank a toast to the success of the herring industry, and christened the village. During the *Kaiser-Zeit* the *Seebad* of Heringsdorf was developed by a joint-stock company established by the Reichstag deputy Dr Hugo Delbrück. His company built the Kaiser-Wilhelm-Brücke, in its time the longest pier in Germany, and connected Heringsdorf by rail to Swinemünde, and thence to Berlin. By 1910 the resort was attracting an annual influx of ten to fifteen thousand guests, who could walk, ride and cycle in the surrounding woods, or spend their wealth at the racetrack or in the spa's concert halls, dance palaces and casinos.

The social whirl of Bad Heringsdorf came to an abrupt halt when war broke out in 1914. The spa was turned into a sanatorium for wounded soldiers. The Russian writer Maxim Gorky stayed in Villa Irmgard from May to September 1922, recuperating from a pulmonary disorder. He commented on the thousands of "rachitic, scrofulous and short-sighted children" who inhabited the colony; orphans and foundlings "like old dwarves" who wore dark glasses "for old people" – "innocents paying for their fathers' sins". Gorky recorded in a guestbook that "in spite of all this, people will one day live together like brothers", unwittingly presaging the "fraternity" that would later exist between the German Democratic Republic and the Soviet Union.

Heringsdorf recovered its prosperity in the late 1920s, when the number of seasonal guests returned to pre-war levels. The resort advertised itself at the start of the 1933 season as a "wieder deutsches Seebad", implying that its previously high influx of foreign and Jewish guests was no longer welcome. The brochure read: "Green and white jewel box on the German Baltic coast; fairy tales of bright summer delight; joyful times for all in sun, sea and wind … colourful sandy beaches glistening in the sun, wood-crowned dunes, the joyful life of happy people, good music, beautiful women, fashion, sport, games and dancing. There is only one Heringsdorf! And now it is again what it was for decades – a German spa administered by nationally-minded men." In 1935 Jews were prohibited from visiting the Baltic resorts. Jewish inhabitants such as the banker

Gerson von Bleichröder, who owned Villa Diana in Heringsdorf, were dispossessed and expelled. The Social Democrat mayor was dismissed. As war approached again, the island of Usedom was transformed into a military *Sperrgebiet*. Flak batteries were erected along the beaches. Swinemünde was fortified. V-weapons were developed in nearby Peenemünde. Hotels and *Pensionen* were used for *Kinderlandverschickungen*, retreats for children from endangered cities. Towards the end of the war the hotels filled up with refugees from East Prussia or bombed-out cities such as Hamburg. The Hotel Miramare, however, was reserved for high-ranking Wehrmacht officers and the bodyguard of Hitler. Tens of thousands of refugees sought shelter on ships marooned in the harbour of Swinemünde; twenty-three thousand are believed to have been killed during a bombing raid on 12 March 1945 by six hundred planes of the British and American air forces, who may have mistaken Swinemünde for Peenemünde. As the Red Army approached, the community of Heringsdorf became increasingly nervous. The mayor dismissed his employees on 2 May 1945 and fled with local Gruppenführer on a lifeboat towed by a speedboat. The remaining Wehrmacht defenders jumped from the pier when it was strafed by Soviet fighter planes.

Once the Russians had settled in, they built a sanatorium and cultural centre for the Red Army on the site of a burned-out cinema. This was initially reserved for the Soviet military, but in 1950 it was handed over to the GDR. During the following decade Heringsdorf developed into an elite resort for the Central Committee of the SED, the upper echelons of the Volkspolizei and members of the FDGB (Holiday Service of the Trade Unions), a Communist equivalent of Strength Through Joy. By the 1960s Heringsdorf had become a people's resort which attracted sixty thousand privileged holiday-makers every summer, providing mass physiotherapy in the twin towers and mass callisthenics on the beach.

Heringsdorf was transformed in the 1990s, when families of the owners expelled by the Communist authorities in 1953 were free to return. The new pier was opened in 1995, with a pier head that contained boutiques, hairdressing salons, ice-cream parlours, restaurants and a mussel museum. At the entrance to the pier is a two and a half ton ball of Swedish granite revolving above a film of water. New hotels and shopping malls, a new *Kursaal*, a new casino and a new "subtropical bathing paradise" completed the post-*Wende* renaissance of Bad Heringsdorf.

One of the sights of Prussian Heringsdorf was its Bismarck-Warte, the second tallest Bismarck Tower in Germany. A chimerical structure with a neo-Romanesque base, a neo-medieval stone tower and a North German Brick Gothic crown, it stood on the Präsidentenburg overlooking the resort. A woman in the tourist office told me it was destroyed in the war, but there were plans to reconstruct it. I could however, if I wished, visit a National Socialist *Thingstätte* that was built in the woods above the spa in 1934 and was used for marches, solstice ceremonies and performances of dramatic works such as Kleist's *The Prince of Homburg*. I thanked her and asked why there was no border crossing for vehicles between Świnoujście and the German spas, explaining I had made a detour of two hundred and seventy-five kilometres to get here. She explained that Usedom was a conservation area with only two roads across the island; and that tourist traffic from Poland to northern Germany would create unimaginable congestion and pollution and destroy the delicate eco-structure. (Usedom is shaped like an open-jawed hinge, a triangular atoll of dunes and polders surrounded by two lagoons and the open sea.) The tone of her reply also suggested that the elegant bourgeoisie of Bad Heringsdorf did not particularly fancy being invaded by tens of thousands of Poles coming over for the day armed with packed lunches and bottles of vodka.[10]

I went off to look for the *Thingstätte,* driving up into the woods above the spa. I left my car in a clearing and found a wooden signpost indicating that the *Thingplatz* was located four hundred metres along a sandy track towards the north. After a while I came to a crossroads in the woods, but there was no sign of an amphitheatre or any rows of stone seating. I searched the four quadrants of undergrowth and cross-referenced my modern map against the facsimile of a Prussian map of Heringsdorf in the back of a historical guide to the town, which clearly showed the sites of both the *Thingstätte* and the Bismarck Tower to be more or less where I was now standing. I stopped a passing jogger and asked if he could help, but he knew nothing about these historical monuments. I apologised for interrupting his exercise. I walked a further four hundred metres until I came to a steep embankment running down towards the spa, but that didn't resemble an amphitheatre either. I retraced my steps and followed another sign to a "Steinerne Tisch", a stone table that the woman in the

---

10   Land border controls between Germany and Poland were abolished in 2007 (the year after my visit) when Poland joined the Schengen Area. Both the pedestrian crossing towards Ahlbeck and the frontier post at the end of Grunwaldzki were opened to vehicle traffic. In 2008 the railway line to Ahlbeck was extended over the border to Świnoujście. There are currently plans to build a road tunnel beneath the River Świna, which will connect Świnoujście with Wolin and mainland Poland.

tourist office had also mentioned as being of interest. I found this at the head of a ravine. It was a circle of concrete set around an oak tree with five stone cinema-like seats arranged in an arc around it. I had no idea what it was – presumably some Nazi ritual site, now covered with a coat of moss. A pair of discarded surgical gloves suggested the place was used for sexual practices of a deviant nature.

It was now 7.30 pm and I had booked a room for that night in a hotel in Sassnitz on the island of Rügen. I sat on the edge of the "stone table" and phoned the hotel to enquire whether it was possible to delay my arrival by one night, so I could stay in Heringsdorf as originally planned. The receptionist explained politely that I was perfectly entitled to cancel my reservation but, as they had my credit card details, they would charge me for the room whether I turned up or not. So I gave up on the hidden *Thingstätte* of Heringsdorf and set off along the coastal road towards Wolgast and the mainland of Mecklenburg-Vorpommern.

I reached Rügen at dusk, clanking over the Rügendamm on a low metal bridge, built during the Third Reich, which is now overshadowed by a new suspension bridge that soars and swoops hundreds of metres into the air above Stralsund. The sun glowed like a fireball on the flat horizon as I crossed a causeway between the boddens, the lagoons that perforate the island. At nightfall I arrived at the port of Sassnitz, which turned out to be a fish-processing centre rather than a seaside resort, and a run-down one at that, as the herring industry had declined by two-thirds since the fishing grounds left the jurisdiction of the GDR and were now subject to EU quotas.

I checked into the Rügen Hotel, a fifteen-storey ex-Socialist tower block that dominated the town. My room on the twelfth floor had an identical configuration to that of the previous night's hotel in Świnoujście: two single cots enclosed in wooden panels at either side of the room, twin bed-side tables, a separate vestibule with identikit wardrobe, everything in the shower room in the same position as it was in the Polish hotel. The difference was that this room had been renovated, re-plumbed, re-wallpapered and re-carpeted to Western standards, and cost three and a half times as much. The hotel restaurant had closed, but two *Gasthöfe* down by the waterfront were open late. I had a meal on the quayside of breaded plaice, fried potatoes, *Speck* and onion, washed down with a few crisp *Pilseners*. It was not only the most delicious meal I had eaten for weeks, but by far the amplest. No wonder the eastern Europeans are so thin.

I awoke in the morning to a bird's-eye view over Sassnitz. The town was the familiar random juxtaposition of buildings that had been renovated since the *Wende* and those that had fallen into disrepair. Many of the older buildings bore faded stencilled lettering from the Socialist era: "Mölkerei Genossenschaft" (dairy cooperative) or "Stubnitz Lichtspiele" over the entrance to the former comrades' picture palace. One suburban street was preserved as if in aspic from the GDR period, with multi-antennae lamp-posts and car-parking spaces painted at the prescribed diagonal angle to the kerb. From the breakfast room on the other side of the hotel there was a magnificent view over an iridescent Baltic. Car ferries were leaving the port of Mukran for Klaipėda, Rønne and Trelleborg. (Rügen was a Danish fiefdom from 1168 to 1325, and under Swedish sovereignty from 1648 to 1815.) To the south lay the dunes, boddens, mud flats, saltpans and woods of the island, flattened into each other in a land- and waterscape of ragged blue and green strips. To the south-east was the great sweep of the Prorer Wiek, a perfect arc of woodland bordered by blond beaches. Above the tree line I could make out the upper stories of the five-kilometre-long holiday camp built by the *Kraft durch Freude* (Strength Through Joy) organisation in the 1930s.

The name of the architect Clemens Klotz raised a laugh from the audience watching the video presentation. *Klotz* means "block", as in *Betonklotz* (concrete block) or *Klotz-Bau* (blockhouse), pejorative terms used to describe the monolithic architectural projects originated by the Germans during the Third Reich, and continued by their successors in the GDR. I was sitting in the documentation centre of the biggest *Betonklotz* of them all, the colossal holiday camp of the National Socialists, later used by the National People's Army of the GDR.

In the mid-1930s *Kraft durch Freude* submitted a project to build five identical holiday centres on the Baltic coast. One was planned for Timmendorfer Strand near Lübeck, a second at Kolberg (now Polish Kołobrzeg) and a third here at Prora on the Schmale Heide, a narrow strip of sandy heath parallel to the beach of the Prorer Wiek from Mukran to Binz. The land was procured from its owner Malte von Veltheim, Prince of Putbus, in an apparently amicable settlement arranged by Robert Ley, leader of the KdF's parent organisation the DAF (German Labour Front). Clemens Klotz, architect of the Ordensburgen at Vogelsang and Falkenburg, was commissioned to prepare a set of preliminary sketches for the new resort, designed to accommodate twenty thousand holiday-makers within an area of land five kilometres long and five hundred metres wide. Klotz presented his first sketches to Ley and Hitler on 5 September 1935. They were exhibited at the Party Rally in Nuremberg later that month.

In February 1936 the project was put out to tender, although Klotz's designs were already in favour at the highest level. The competition was organised by Albert Speer in his role as head of the Reich department Schönheit der Arbeit (Beauty of Labour). Eleven leading architects were invited to participate but Klotz, unsurprisingly, was awarded the contract to oversee the complex. He was obliged to incorporate the winning design for a monumental Festival Hall, submitted by Erich zu Putlitz, into his plans. The initial sketches by Klotz were modified many times between 1935 and 1939, but they consisted essentially of two wings of accommodation blocks, each of which stretched in an arc for two and a half kilometres along the head of the beach. Each wing contained four or five communal halls with cinemas, restaurants and a gargantuan swimming pool one hundred metres long and forty metres wide. The Festival Hall at the centre of the resort was to be surrounded by a ceremonial square, which would link an artificial lake in the woods behind the camp to the piers and landing stage on the beach.

The project became an important propaganda vehicle for the regime. Described in the National Socialist media as the "Seebad der 20,000" (as if its size were its main attraction) or the "Eldorado of the German Worker", it was the one national project where the Nazis could counter any criticism that they were focused exclusively on military aims. A model of the holiday camp was exhibited at the Paris World Fair of 1937 in order to allay international fears that the German Reich was concentrated on rearmament.

The foundation stone was laid on 2 May 1936, the third anniversary of the abolition of trade unions implemented by Robert Ley in 1933. The ceremony was attended by bigwigs of the NSDAP, DAF and KdF and thousands of ordinary Germans ferried in on free trains from the mainland. Then nothing happened for two years: the foundation stone stood in splendid isolation amid the buckthorn on the beach, while the eleven architects submitted increasingly grandiose plans for the German workers' week in the sun. (The architectural dilettante Hitler loved to pore over sketches and models, but lost interest whenever actual construction began, so it was in the architects' interests to continue feeding him plans and blueprints rather than start any work.) Nevertheless, once work did begin on the site in April 1938, it progressed rapidly. The quay walls and shells of the accommodation blocks were completed by the summer of

1939. Then war broke out and the construction companies were required elsewhere. A small workforce remained at Prora to oversee the completion of the accommodation units by prisoners of war and forced labourers from occupied Poland.

Each of the two half-completed sections of accommodation blocks stretched for two and a half kilometres to the north and south of the barely started Festival Square. Each wing was subdivided into four six-storey blocks which ran end to end, forming an arc of mud-coloured concrete of titanic proportions. Each of the eight blocks contained 1,250 accommodation units, identical cellular rooms measuring 4.75 by 2.2 metres – not unlike my hotel rooms in Świnoujście and Sassnitz. Each room had a sea view to the front. To the rear, each block was reinforced by ten stairwells which jutted out at right angles to the main arc; from the air the building looks like a gigantic toothed rack.

Stylistically, the Strength Through Joy holiday camp is functional modernism of a rather uninspired, old-fashioned kind – more Albert Speer than Le Corbusier. The German buildings of the 1930s it most closely resembles are Tempelhof Airport and the administrative offices built for firms such as Bayer, Krupp, Osram and, in particular, the IG Farben Works in Frankfurt am Main. In its sheer size, in the monotony of its identical, repetitive blocks, it resembles a military-industrial complex rather than a leisure resort. Its primary function was, of course, the industrialisation of recreation under the aegis of *Kraft durch Freude*. Its secondary, undisclosed function was to serve as a military hospital once the inevitable war started. No German worker ever got to enjoy a power-holiday on the Prorer Wiek. During the war the unfinished blocks were used as a school for trainee police officers, as a training centre for naval radio operators, as a military hospital and, as the war turned, as a refugee camp for Germans expelled from Pomerania and East Prussia or fleeing from fire-bombed cities such as Hamburg and Lübeck.

After the war Soviet troops were briefly deployed in those buildings that remained habitable. During the next two years the accommodation blocks were partially dismantled and much of the building material was shipped off to the Soviet Union. Local inhabitants plundered the storehouses and carried off tens of thousands of swastika-decorated knives and forks, towels and bed linen, manufactured for the tourists who never arrived. A section of the northern wing was demolished for safety reasons. In 1949 the new regime of the GDR examined ways of using the now derelict complex for social housing, particularly of refugees from East

Prussia, but nothing came of these projects. In 1956 the Red Army again moved into two intact blocks in the northern sector; and the NVA, the National People's Army of the GDR, requisitioned the southern sector.

Throughout the 1950s the area around Prora was heavily militarised. Up to twenty thousand soldiers of the Volksarmee – tank units, motorised divisions and parachute regiments – trained in the former holiday barracks. During the 1960s and 1970s the area was sealed off with barbed wire and surrounded by tank traps. In the 1980s one section of the southern wing was turned into the Walter-Ulbricht-Heim, a rest and recreation centre for the highest-ranking generals of the armies of the Warsaw Pact. Another section housed the secretive Otto Winzer Officers' High School. The OHS was an academy of the National People's Army that recruited and trained officers from foreign regimes sympathetic to the Soviet cause. Two rooms in one of the museums which have sprung up in the camp are devoted to photographs of soldiers plucked from Cuba, Tanzania, Nicaragua, Congo, Zambia, Zimbabwe, Palestine, Syria, Yemen, Afghanistan, North Korea, Laos, Vietnam, Cambodia, Ethiopia and Madagascar – all transported to this grim barrack block on the edge of the Baltic in the hope that the bracing climate and some Soviet indoctrination will inspire these hapless recruits to return to their native lands and lead their peoples in a global revolution that will bring down the crumbling edifice of Western capitalist fascism.

Other rooms in the museum have been reconstructed in the style of a *Kompanie-Klub* of the National People's Army. Mass-produced editions of the collected works of Marx and Lenin are shelved alongside yellowing copies of *Junge Welt* and *Neues Deutschland* newspapers: badges, playing cards and beer glasses celebrating the *Parteitag* of the SED are arranged along a plywood dresser. Artificial flowers and patterns of beer mats are pinned to the walls below banners proclaiming German-Soviet Friendship. Pennants from visiting *Ostblock* volleyball teams (Dukla, Spartak and Red Star) hang above photographs of Ulbricht and Brezhnev clasping each other in fraternal bear hugs. In pride of place is a framed copy of the "Fahneneid der NVA", an oath of loyalty to the flag of the GDR sworn by recruits to the National People's Army. Olive green uniforms of the Red Army and grey-green tunics of the NVA are decorated with hammers, sickles, wheatsheaves, compasses and red stars. Long-playing records of 1960s *Schlager* sit idly on the turntables of primitive record players. Radiograms and computers from the 1970s display a bewildering array of knobs and buttons marked with stencilled instructions in Latin and Cyrillic script.

After reunification in 1989, the People's Army relinquished control of the camp to the Bundeswehr. I watched a video of the final roll call and tattoo of one of the last battalions of the NVA to leave Prora. A thin line of relatives and civilian colleagues watched glumly from the edge of a rainswept parade ground as their comrades were demobilised. "Auferstanden auf Ruinen", the stirring anthem of the former GDR heard so often at Olympic Games during the 1970s and 1980s, was played for the last time.

The Bundeswehr abandoned the site in 1991 and the blocks, fenced off with barbed wire and surrounded by compounds of rusting anti-tank obstacles and derelict vehicles, fell into disrepair and were looted again. The Federal Republic, into whose possession the site had passed, had no idea what to do with this embarrassing National Socialist ruin. Like the Zeppelinfeld in Nuremberg, it is a listed building because of its historical associations; and as one of the largest buildings ever constructed in Europe, it cannot easily be dismantled. No government organisation or private company came up with a strategy that would recognise the cultural significance of the building, or that would regenerate the site. Instead, the state began to sell off chunks piecemeal to small local businesses. The result is a hotchpotch of studios, ateliers, potteries, tea houses, coffee shops and a plethora of quirky *Ostalgie* museums: the Museum of German Boxing; the Museum of the Binz Fire Brigade; a collection of old cigars; motorcycles of the GDR; sewing machines of the GDR; scale models of the *Kraft durch Freude* ships *Der Deutsche*, the *Wilhelm Gustloff* and the *Robert Ley*; and three historical museums which vie with each other in their claims to be the "official" museum of the Prora holiday camp. In the summer of 2000, an attempt was made to transform the camp into a techno clubbing venue – a Tacheles-by-the-Sea or a Baltic Ibiza. But the few hundred ravers who braved both the climate and the disapproval of the islanders were lost amid the miles of cavernous derelict spaces. Since then there have been several symposia at which creative minds from around Europe have gathered to discuss the potential of the Prora site – as a Baltic University, for example, or a waterfront housing development in the Dutch style – but no company has as yet put forward either the vision or the millions of euros required to regenerate the resort.[11]

---

11   In 2010 one of the blocks was purchased by a property developer from Berlin, who has refurbished the derelict units as luxury apartments. Wealthy Hamburgers and Berliners use them as holiday homes.

In spite of its colossal size, the former barracks is not easy to find. The only way of seeing the camp in its entirety is from the air. From the fifteenth floor of my hotel in Sassnitz I could make out the arc of the building's roof, perfectly aligned with that of the beach of the Prorer Wiek. At ground level the building is concealed from the both the road and the beach by a belt of trees. During the period of the GDR the road between Mukran and Binz was out of bounds, and few civilians knew of the existence of the military installation. There is a now a single yellow road sign directing you off the main road, through the trees and over a level crossing to the "ehemaliges KdF Seebad Prora" (the former Strength Through Joy seaside resort of Prora). And once you have arrived in one of the car parks you are disorientated by the abundance of signs advertising a multitude of amateur ateliers and unofficial museums.

I found myself walking along the rear of the southern wing of the camp, past relentless, repetitive blocks of oatmeal-coloured concrete, punctuated every fifty metres by a stairwell. At the thirtieth stairwell the blocks came to an abrupt end. I walked round to the front of the building, which was separated from the beach by a row of pine trees, and began the long return trek. After twenty minutes I arrived at the central section, where a tongue of concrete jutted over the sand and broom towards a bastion protruding over the beach into the sea. In the KdF brochures of the 1930s the quay was the focal point of the resort, where ships would drop anchor and holiday-makers would make their grand entrance from the landing stages to the Festival Square. The quay is now derelict, its steps covered with algae, its walls sprayed with graffiti.

A concrete ramp led inland towards an unfinished neoclassical colonnade, reminiscent of the Haus der Kunst in Munich. I walked a further five hundred metres north, through a tract of thistles and buckthorn covering the site of the unbuilt Festival Hall at the centre of the resort. The northern wing of the holiday camp curved into the distance. Much of it was still in the *Rohbau* (roughly finished) state in which it had been abandoned in 1939, and several blocks had been completely demolished. I set off along the rear of the northern sector, but soon became numbed by the unremitting banality of the architecture, intimidated by the concentrated, quasi-industrial nature of the planned resort. I turned through a tunnel between two of the blocks and stumbled on a beach that was more FKK (Free Body Culture) than KdF. I had read the National Socialist position on nudism in the historical guide to Bad Heringsdorf. In 1933 the Prussian Ministry of the Interior issued a regulation stipulating that "naked bathing in public is prohibited, and women may only bathe publicly if they are wearing a bathing costume that completely covers the breast and stomach on the front side of the upper body, that is securely tied under the arms, and that is fitted with a gusset and cut-off legs". This became popularly known as "the gusset decree".

I sat on the sand and wrote an imaginary postcard:

Dear Mutti and Vati

Weather is bracing and the sea is not the warmest. Wish you were here but, to be honest, I am not short of company. I rushed to the beach at 6.30 this morning to unroll my towel on the allotted 3m² of sand. Had breakfast in one of the communal halls. They have beautiful curved façades with a panoramic view of the beach. I had difficulty finding my towel again after breakfast, as there were 5,000 identical towels laid out in orderly columns and rows on the beach. I had stuck a little flag in the sand to identify mine, but everyone else had done the same – and they all used the same flag. At 9 o'clock we had callisthenics, spinning hoops around our hips and performing handstands. My neighbour was cross because I fell over onto his towel. I was just about to doze off when the Führer's voice boomed out of the loudspeakers, exhorting us lucky Strength Through Joy holiday-makers to ensure that "our leisure time was truly relaxing" as he needed "a people with strong nerves in order to…" I missed the end of the sentence when his voice became distorted. In the afternoon my roommate and I went to one of the community halls to play Bingo. The game didn't last long: 127 players got the winning number at the same time, so the prizes weren't up to much. Afterwards we bought sticks of rock that had little swastikas of liquorice running through them. In the evening we had a sing-song.

With fondest greetings from Nuremberg-on-Sea
Your dear son

10

Mecklenburg

"Not Everything from the Nazi Period Was Bad"

The centre of Rostock was flattened by Allied bombing in 1942, the area sloping up from the docks being particularly badly damaged. I walked up from Lastadie, the quay where ballast was loaded onto ships, and recalled the street of the same name in pre-war Königsberg. Badstüberstraße, Grapengießerstraße and Aalstecherstraße now form a housing estate of prefabricated apartment blocks constructed between 1983 and 1986, cleverly designed to reflect the colours and contours of the tall, gabled, Brick Gothic structures which stood here for centuries before they were destroyed. The main thoroughfare of central Rostock is Lange Straße, obliterated during the war. It was widened and rebuilt in the 1950s as a communist *Prachtstraße*, a showcase of Socialist urban planning. The architects constructed a Stalinist interpretation of North German *Backsteingotik*, erecting walls of apartment blocks in stripes of red brick and white limestone, capped with crow-stepped gables and punctuated by towers of red brick echoing those of the granaries on the wharves of the River Warnow. The walls of the five-storey apartment blocks were decorated with medallions depicting gannets, cormorants, plaice, cod, crabs, seahorses and jellyfish, their architraves inlaid with green-and-white-striped glazed bricks. The manner in which vernacular stylistic elements were successfully incorporated into a commanding Stalinist structure led to the Lange Straße of Rostock being hailed as the "schönste Stalinallee" of the GDR.

It has been smartened up since the *Wende*: flower beds and new tramlines have been laid, and six pairs of illuminated bronze steles mark the locations of former side streets. I walked through an arcade to Universitätsplatz, a triangle at the heart of the oldest university in mainland northern Europe – and the focal point of Rostock's café society. It is surrounded by grand baroque and neoclassical buildings: the Appeal Court, the Rostocker Hof hotel, the Ducal Palace and a bright orange Neue Wache. At the centre of the *Platz* is a statue sculpted by Johann Gottfried Schadow of Field Marshal Gebhard Leberecht von Blücher, victor of the Battle of the Nations and Rostock's most famous son. At the apex of the triangle is a circular "Brunnen der Lebensfreude", a fountain which once represented the joys of Socialism in the GDR.

On August-Bebel-Straße there is an office block built in the functional style of the 1950s that now serves as the Provincial Law Courts. Before the *Wende* it housed the offices of the regional administration of the Ministry for State Security of the GDR. Behind this block is Hermannstraße, the former site of Rostock's synagogue, from where one can enter a yard at the rear of the former Stasi offices. An anonymous block in this anonymous yard served as a prison for suspects awaiting interrogation by the Stasi. It is now a museum and documentation centre that records the history of the state security apparatus, and of its victims, in the former *Bezirke* of Rostock, Schwerin and Greifswald. The jail consisted of forty-six cells, on three floors, which could hold one hundred and ten prisoners at a time. A total of 4,872 detainees passed through the prison between 1960 and 1989, an average of one hundred and ninety-one per year. The cells had no windows: the only natural light was filtered through squares of glass brick. Ventilation was provided by a ten-centimetre slit in the wall. The only sounds penetrating the walls were the creaking of bolts, the clatter of food hatches and the monosyllabic commands barked by the guards. Exercise was restricted to four twenty-minute periods per week in the "tiger cage", a tiny yard with high walls and overhead grilles that was patrolled by a guard armed with a sub-machine gun. The regulations were strict and unequivocal: "If a prison officer enters the cell, the detainee must step immediately below the window; face turned towards the window, hands placed on the back, and may only turn around when spoken to by the guard." "During the night it is forbidden for prisoners to cover their face or hands." Transgression of these regulations led to a spell in a padded, sound-isolated cell or one of the "dark cells" in the basement where there was almost total sensory deprivation – except for flashlights which would be switched on at random to prevent the development of a regular sleeping pattern. Detainees in the "dark cells" were isolated in a hallucinatory netherworld of fears and fantasies, their only human contact the periodic session with their interrogators. This generated a dependency on their interrogators that the latter exploited in order to elicit or coerce the confessions they required. The ultimate punishment was the deprivation of these interrogations, leaving the prisoner alone in a nightmare of darkness and silence for days or weeks on end, believing they had been abandoned even by their torturers.

The detainees inside the Ministry for State Security (MfS) prison were not common criminals or suspects who had been charged with a specific crime. They were "political" prisoners who had been suspected of expressing an opinion, harbouring a wish, nurturing a secret desire. The most common of these was the wish to leave East Germany. As a member of the United Nations, the GDR signed the Helsinki Agreement at the Conference on Security and Cooperation in Europe on 1 August 1975, which guaranteed the basic right of any citizen to live wherever they wanted. However, the Socialist Unity Party (SED) applied so many qualifications to the right to emigrate to West Germany, or to any other non-Socialist state, that the "right" it had signed up to applied only to citizens of little further use to the regime, such as pensioners, invalids or divorcees.

One detainee was Klaus Ketzler, a *Fräser* (milling cutter) at the Diesel Motor Works in Rostock. He developed an antipathy to the policies of the regime during the 1970s, refusing membership of the SED and declining to cast his vote for the Party (in contrast to the 99.85% or 99.86% of the population who ostensibly did vote for the ruling party in the elections of 1971 and 1976, respectively). Ketzler came onto the radar of the MfS when it intercepted correspondence between him and a citizen of the United States. An initial OPK (Operative Personal Control) was instigated against him in 1975, by which time he was twenty-four years old. After subsequent measures were taken against him, he applied on 8 January 1980 for a permanent exit visa from the GDR. His application was rejected by the Department for Internal Matters in Rostock as "illegal". In fact, this decision had already been reached by the head of the department, in collaboration with the MfS, in advance of Herr Ketzler's application. A second OPK was instigated against him. A series of "discussions" with the MfS and "persuasive measures" carried out by other organs of the state failed to produce the desired result, and Ketzler was officially declared an "obstinate" applicant. He subsequently came into contact with other applicants for emigration who formed part of the Warnemünder Friedenskreis, a group whose hopes of permission to leave East Germany had been raised by the GDR's apparent commitment to the 1980 Madrid Protocol of the Conference on Security and Cooperation in Europe.

Another four years of ineffectual discussions with the Department for Internal Matters and the Ministry for State Security passed, and in 1983 Herr Ketzler decided to make his protestations public. He cut out a letter A (for "Ausreisewilliger") from white paper and pasted it on the front window of his apartment, illuminated by a burning candle. The next morning he was arrested, following a report from an "unofficial collaborator", and incarcerated in the MfS's detention centre in August-Bebel-Straße. He was subjected to two months of intensive interrogation, during which he admitted asking for assistance from relatives in West Germany through the channels of an international human rights organisation based in Frankfurt am Main. By means of postal surveillance and listening devices the MfS already had this information on file, but needed confirmation from the horse's mouth, so to speak, of a crime more specific than "a desire to leave the GDR". Herr Ketzler was sentenced to three years' imprisonment for "establishing connections hostile to the state" and transferred to a jail in Cottbus, where he spent six months. He subsequently served time in prisons in Brandenburg and Karl-Marx-Stadt before being accompanied by officers of the MfS to the German–German border, where he was released into the Federal Republic in exchange for a ransom of approximately one million deutschmarks in February 1985.

Another case was that of three teenagers, Dörte Neubauer, aged seventeen, and Ute and Gunnar Christopher, both aged nineteen, who expressed their antipathy to the regime by participating in a tiny, but not officially sanctioned, "Friedenswache" on 1 September 1985 at a Monument to the Victims of Fascism that the "post-fascist" GDR had thoughtfully erected in order to distance its own brand of fascism from the one that had preceded it. The MfS photographed the three teenagers at the Peace Watch. Two evenings later they were surreptitiously followed by Stasi agents as they wandered through the centre of Rostock in the early hours, daubing slogans "of a mostly pacifist content" on various walls. The MfS used the full arsenal of measures to prove the identity of the miscreants. Stasi agents secretly entered their homes and put bugging devices on their telephones. They took swabs of their body odour, which they stored in bell jars and trained their dogs to identify. They found a note scribbled by

Gunnar Christopher which read: "I have never been to New York, I have never been to Hawaii or San Francisco in torn jeans, I have never been to New York, I have never been really FREE." The three youngsters were arrested and detained in the prison in August-Bebel-Straße, where they were subjected to a series of interrogations. The protocol of the discussions with Dörte Neubauer records: "I would like to express that I am neither totally engaged politically nor completely uninterested in politics. I took part in the actions of 3.9.85 because some things about the GDR annoy me. I take a critical view of events around me. I absorb them and consider what is right and what is wrong. I weigh things up and extract conclusions which I then openly represent ... I do not find it good that you play around with our emotions in order to extract something." One of Gunnar Christopher's statements reads: "We were of the opinion that there are sufficient yea-sayers and fellow travellers in the GDR who accept the social conditions in the GDR without speaking out or questioning certain issues. We therefore came to the conclusion that we should demonstrate publicly to the citizens of Rostock that there are also people who think differently about the issues of freedom, expression and inequality that in our opinion exist in the GDR."

For expressing such opinions, the seventeen-year old Dörte was expelled from the medical faculty where she studied and rendered unemployed. The two older teenagers were sentenced to eighteen months' imprisonment: Gunnar in a jail in Cottbus; Ute in the notorious women's prison of Hoheneck which, like Colditz, was a former medieval castle on an isolated hill in Saxony. In 1951 Hoheneck became the prison for all female "political" detainees of the GDR. Over the next four decades the regime earned three and a half billion deutschmarks by selling these women to the Federal Republic. Ute Christopher recorded: "In winter it was particularly bad in Hoheneck. There was not a single tree in the yard; only cold and snow and everyone wore long black coats and black headscarves. It was dreadful – we were like a pile of old charnel-house women. Once Frieda and I decided to cut our hair short on one side, for which we were sentenced to twenty-one days' arrest. That was the time that was most difficult to survive. The heating was switched off for four of every five hours. It was the end of October and I shivered with cold in my thin smock." Gunnar and Ute both served approximately twelve months of their sentences before being expelled to West Germany in 1987. Dörte was finally granted an exit visa on 19 October 1989 – three weeks later she could have walked out of the GDR without one, like everyone else.

I emerged from the former MfS prison complex feeling soiled and paranoid, wondering how many of the good burghers of Rostock, pushing prams around the rose gardens or waiting obediently for the green man at the traffic lights, had been numbered among the 3,686 salaried staff or the 6,279 "unofficial collaborators" employed by the Stasi in the Rostock District. Eastern Germany suddenly seemed to be a society (if that is the right word) of sneaks, snitches, tell-tales, peeping Toms and knicker-sniffers, ruled by a humourless cadre of bullies and killjoys. I found it difficult to imagine that any save the most bone-headed members of the East German Volksrepublik spied on their colleagues because they believed they were helping to create a better society. Some "unofficial collaborators" may have got a furtive kick from being authorised to peer through their neighbours' net curtains; stand on street corners with a micro-camera concealed behind a rivet in their knapsack; or dress up as a hitchhiker in a fake leather waistcoat, peaked cap and rucksack, as recommended by the "masking catalogue" of the MfS, in order to engage in conversation Western tourists travelling through the transit corridors (who probably thought they had picked up a Communist rent boy). The secretive power of the "little man" is a particularly German characteristic that, allied to the Germans' prurience and sense of self-righteousness, created a powerful tool that could be exploited by those in authority. However, many "unofficial collaborators" were people who were already compromised in some way, and were blackmailed into working for the Stasi in order to escape punishment themselves.

Back in Universitätsplatz later that evening, I picked up a copy of the day's *Ostsee-Zeitung*. T-Mobile had fired the cyclist Jan Ullrich for doping; the stork population of Mecklenburg-Vorpommern had increased; German drivers were "taking their foot off the gas" in response to high fuel prices; and the Polish president Lech Kaczynski had criticised a planned Russian-German pipeline underneath the Baltic as "not in the interests of Poland", adding for good measure that "the relativisation of responsibility in Germany for the Second World War was not in the interests of Poland either". He was referring to the forthcoming opening in Berlin of an exhibition organised by the Bund der Vertriebenen about the German communities expelled from Pomerania, Silesia and East Prussia at the end of the war. A cartoon on the second page of the newspaper illustrated Angela Merkel receiving a letter from the Iranian president Mahmoud Ahmadinejad. When the Chancellor opens the letter, a cartoon Adolf Hitler jumps out, screaming "Die Juden sind an allem Schuld!"

("Everything is the fault of the Jews!") I found the cartoon neither politically correct nor particularly amusing.

The headline on the front page of the paper was "Schwerin breaks a taboo". An exhibition had opened the previous day in the Schleswig-Holstein-Haus in Schwerin featuring seventy sculptures by Arno Breker, one of the super-sculptors of the Third Reich. This was the first exhibition on German soil dedicated exclusively to "Hitler's favourite sculptor" since 1945. The official line presented to the media by the Head of Culture of the City of Schwerin was that the show was not an "*hommage*" to Breker, but a contribution towards the "ongoing critical debate about the art of the Third Reich". The Education Minister of Mecklenburg-Vorpommern, Hans-Robert Metelmann, added that the exhibition "should provide the impetus for a discussion about the seductiveness and disposability of art". In contrast, some thirty-four artists, gallery owners and historians from Mecklenburg-Vorpommern had signed a petition demanding the removal of the exhibition. One local painter, Ute Laux, had shown her displeasure by splattering the entrance to the gallery with ten of her own works, depicting fragments of women's bodies smeared in pigs' blood, representing the victims of National Socialism. According to Frau Laux the show was an "appreciation" of Breker, a tribute to an artist "who sold his soul", and an insult to the memory of greater sculptors such as Ernst Barlach who were persecuted as being "degenerate" by the Nazi regime. Heavyweight contributors to the debate included Klaus Staeck, President of the German Academy of Arts, who withdrew an exhibition of his own work due to be shown in Schwerin and questioned whether "one could hold a critical appraisal in this city", adding that Breker was "a monumental decorator of barbarism"; and author Günter Grass who, in a more measured response, noted that the public was "sufficiently adult" to make up its own mind about the exhibition, adding that "Breker's early works prove that he had talent; but he allowed himself to be corrupted by the National Socialists".

After checking into the Hotel Elefant in Goethestraße, I took a stroll through the streets just south of the centre of Schwerin. It was mid-afternoon on a Saturday and Heinrich-Mann-Straße was deserted: blocks of brown, grey and white town houses from the *Jahrhundertwende*; launderettes and corner-shop tobacconists; abandoned spaces. I crossed the main road at the foot of the street and took a path along the edge of the Burgsee. The first inhabitants of Schwerin I encountered were a six-pack of alcoholics, circling unsteadily around a park bench by the shore of the lake. I walked past them rather self-consciously; a little too self-consciously, it seemed, as I heard one of them slur to another: "Da ist ein schöner Kerl für Dich, Rudi." ("There's a nice bloke for you, Rudi.")

The Schloss rose up from the island separating Burgsee from the larger Schweriner See. Part *château du Loire*, part Swiss grand hotel, its pale gold pentagon of rounded towers and neo-Renaissance wings seemed to float on the surface of the lake. In an arch below a turreted dome, an equestrian statue of Duke Niklot commanded the forecourt of the castle. "Hier stand zur Wendenzeit eine Burg kampfbereit, die barg den Koenig Mistislav Held Niklot Lobedan. War dieses Hauses Ahn, befestigte die Stammburg brav." ("In the age of the Wends a fortress stood here that was held by Prince Niklot, hero of King Mistislav. He was the forefather of this house and bravely defended the ancestral castle.") Niklot was a chieftain of the Obotrites, one of the West Slavic tribes known as Wends. He fought against Henry the Lion, Duke of Saxony, who captured Schwerin in a mission to convert the Niklotings to Christianity in 1160. Although Niklot fell in battle, he is regarded as the founder of Mecklenburg. His son was enfeoffed and given Henry's daughter Mechthild as a bride. Their progeny founded the ducal dynasty of Mecklenburg-Schwerin in 1348. In 1815 Mecklenburg-Schwerin and Mecklenburg-Strelitz were united to form a grand duchy that survived until the collapse of the German royal families in 1918.

I walked around Schlossinsel. To the rear of the palace was a semi-circular colonnade from which flights of stairs and balustrades led up to an elevated *orangerie* decorated with statues of cherubs, nymphs and woodland deities; and down to a sunken courtyard of fountains and flower beds. I had an enchanting Moorish garden to myself as I looked out towards the green fringes on the far side of the lake. I resumed my solitary circumambulation of the island, recrossed the Schlossbrücke and walked up Schlossstraße towards the centre of Schwerin. In Puschkinstraße I found the Schleswig-Holstein-Haus, venue of the controversial exhibition devoted to the sculptures of Arno Breker. There was no sign of Ute Laux or her blood-spattered female body parts; presumably she had registered her protest on the day of the *vernissage* and decided to leave the exhibition to the prurient bourgeoisie, of whom there were a satisfactory number – a sign of life in Schwerin, at least. The first room of the exhibition contained a selection of the young Breker's works from the early 1920s. These were small-scale sculptures of the female body, a combination of the polished classicism of Aristide Maillol and the semi-abstract forms of Pablo Picasso. While studying in Düsseldorf Breker attended classes on architecture given by Wilhelm Kreis who, in 1925, commissioned him to create a monumental sculpture entitled *Aurora*, which was mounted above the central arch of Kreis's new art gallery and exhibition hall in the city. (In 2002 it formed part of a sound installation in which Aurora, covered with bindweed, spoke as Eva Braun.) In 1927 Breker moved to Paris, where he fell in with an artistic set that included Maillol, Jean Cocteau, Constantin Brâncuşi, Salvador Dali and Man Ray. He studied the works of Auguste Rodin, and his sculptures became more dynamic and expressive. The second room of the exhibition contained sculptures from this period, such as *Runner, Pleading Woman* and *Torso of Saint Matthew*, which are reminiscent of the knobbly, emaciated paintings of Egon Schiele. Breker sculpted several busts of Romanichel, a gypsy boy who hung around the Cocteau set; one of these was later displayed in an exhibition in occupied Paris in 1942 retitled *Study of a Head.*

In 1932 Breker was awarded the Rome Prize of the Prussian Ministry of Culture and sent to study for a year at the Villa Massimo in the Italian capital. Here he fell under the spell of the larger, smoother sculptures of Michelangelo. Two works from this period entitled *Pietà* were displayed in the exhibition in Schwerin. In the spring of 1933, Breker caught the eye of Reichs Propaganda Minister Joseph Goebbels, who travelled to Rome to inspect the works of the prize-winning sculptor. Impressed by the smooth monumentality of Breker's new works, he persuaded the sculptor to return to Germany, where "a great future" awaited him. In 1935 Breker set to work on a series of sleek, muscular sculptures with titles such as *Prometheus* and *Dionysus*, which expressed the racial ideal of his new patrons. The following year he was invited by the regime to enter a competition to design sculptures to provide a backdrop to the monumental sporting complex being created by Werner March for the Olympic Games of 1936 in Berlin. He was awarded a silver medal for the works *Decathlete* and *Victor*, two ten-foot-high sculptures modelled on real athletes, representing the male and female ideals of the master race. The sculptures were installed on plinths at either end of a colonnade along the façade of the House of German Sport, at the centre of March's German Sport Forum. A torso version of *Siegerin*, the female victor, was exhibited in the Schleswig-Holstein-Haus.

By 1938 Breker had joined the NSDAP and usurped the position of Josef Thorak as Hitler's favourite sculptor. The National Socialist Party rewarded him with a professorship at the High School for Fine Arts in Berlin and a studio in Dahlem. He was awarded a commission to design two bronze statues that would stand guard on either side of the entrance to the New Reichs Chancellery. Representing the two pillars of National Socialism, *The Party* and *The Army* were installed in the Ehrenhof of the Chancellery at the end of the year. A delighted Hitler remarked they were "the finest ever created in Germany". Thereafter Breker's sculptures, and the reliefs he designed for the mausoleums along the North–South Axis of Germania, became increasingly bellicose and grotesque, distorted body-builders that bore more resemblance to the lantern-jawed heroes of comic strips than to the real soldiers and athletes of Hitler's Germany.

The fourth and final room of the exhibition was devoted to works that "embody National Socialism". There were three pairs of statues: *Orpheus* and *Eurydice*, *Eos* and *Demut*, and *Wager* and *Wäger* (known in English as *Active Life* and *Contemplative Life*). This last pair of complementary sculptures was created for the Round Hall of the New Reichs Chancellery in 1938–39, but not cast in bronze in time to be installed. Once war broke out it was forbidden to cast works of art in bronze. Albert Speer later gave Breker permission to have them cast for an exhibition of his sculptures held in the Orangerie in Paris in 1942. *Contemplative Life* is a smooth, realistic representation of a young man with a handsome Anglo-Saxon face and a contemporary short back and sides hairstyle, who could pass for a member of the House of Windsor. Its companion piece *Active Life* is, by contrast, a sleek, muscular young god cast in a fey, mock-archaic pose, whose noble Roman face is surmounted by a mop of Grecian curls.

Removed from a National Socialist context, there was little that was intrinsically fascist, let alone disturbing, about the particular sculptures on display in Schwerin in 2006. Some of the later works such as *Wager* and *Demut* were explicitly heroic and monumental; but size and heroic gestures are not in themselves a prerogative of fascism. Breker himself was a convinced Nazi who confessed to being excited by his first sight of SA marching men. He and his family were on close terms with Albert Speer and his family. He entertained Heinrich Himmler and Joachim von Ribbentrop at the Jäckelsbruch estate on the outskirts of Berlin donated to him by Hitler. On 23 June 1940 he was one of the select few (along with Speer and Hermann Giesler) chosen to accompany Hitler on the Führer's triumphal dawn tour of a defeated Paris. Breker knew that his works supported and legitimised National Socialism; that his sculptures for Germania were the plastic equivalent of genocide. He knew that Jews were expelled from their homes by his friend Speer to make way for Berliners, whose houses had been demolished to create space for the Germania he had been commissioned to decorate. At the same time he was a committed Francophile, an artist who moved in cosmopolitan, Jewish and homosexual circles. He used his contacts to help fifty-nine people escape punishment from the Nazis. After the war he claimed that he was "just an artist", a naïve intellectual who was seduced by the luxurious lifestyle offered to him, in exchange for his talent, by a regime of whose brutality he claimed to be unaware. His reputation suffered because of his exclusion from the canon of European art history, and most of his works were destroyed; but financially he profited enormously during the post-war period by sculpting over three hundred busts of the great and good of German society, for each of which he charged fifty thousand marks.

Was Arno Breker a great artist? He was lionised by Cocteau; Dali called him "the greatest sculptor of the twentieth century"; Maillol referred to him as "the Michelangelo of Germany". A group of French artists on a tour of Germany in 1941 to inspect the art of "new Germany" were awed by the grandiosity and sheer size of Breker's work. His friend Cocteau remarked that "if the statues had an erection, we would not have been able to move". Phyllis Tuchman, reviewing an exhibition of German sculpture from the 1930s held in Leeds in 2001, praised Breker as "a four-star, albeit conservative, talent, as gifted in his field as film-maker Leni Riefenstahl was in hers". On the other hand, there are those, primarily non-artists, who believe that any painter, sculptor or architect who allowed his or her talent to be misused in the service of a criminal regime should no longer be recognised. The writer Ralph Giordano, for example, demanded in 2006 that Breker's sculptures in the German Sports Forum in Berlin should be dismantled and scrapped before the Football World Cup of that year.

On the evidence of the exhibition in Schwerin, Breker was a highly skilled, prolific but derivative sculptor. He began his career in a modernist style influenced by Maillol, with a nod to Picasso. He went through an impressionist period in imitation of Rodin, followed by a neoclassical phase where he copied Michelangelo. Under his National Socialist patrons, he discovered a talent for producing large-scale reproductions of classical archetypes, described by Susan Sontag (with reference to Breker's female figures) as "pin-ups, as strictly asexual as they are (in the technical sense) pornographic". After the war he created a production line of hyper-realistic, almost photographic likenesses of the famous politicians, artists and athletes of post-war Germany. Ironically, Breker was at his most original during his "heroic kitsch" period, when he produced the pneumatic warriors for which he is best remembered; but these are precisely the works that his critics denigrate on account of their subjugation of aesthetics to ideology.

What does the exhibition in Schwerin achieve? Some fear that the exhibition of any National Socialist art leads to a relativisation of the horrors of National Socialism; results in a rehabilitation of people who were the associates of criminals; or is an insult to greater artists who were persecuted by the Nazis. Others believe that the memory of National Socialism is central to German culture and that the Nazi period should be demythologised by displaying its art, so that people can make their own judgements on its quality; that exhibitions such as these are important documents of their age, rather than just a display of sculptures. And why does the bourgeoisie of Schwerin flock to the Schleswig-Holstein-Haus? Would they visit with such interest an exhibition of sculptures by Fritz Klimsch, Georg Kolbe or Richard Scheibe, to give three examples of Breker's contemporaries? Breker was an "Obernazi", and there is an element of prurience or voyeurism at being within touching distance of the works of a man who formed part of Hitler's inner circle. Some of the visitors probably felt they were breaking a taboo, in the same way the bourgeoisie of Munich felt they were doing something vaguely transgressive when they visited the exhibition of "Degenerate Art" in 1937. Art history has come full circle, and it is now Breker who is regarded as degenerate. When invited to comment, Grass declared it was "up to the public to visit the exhibition and judge for themselves whether Breker was a good sculptor or not". However, his words were lost on a group of "pseudo-anti-fascist" activists with links to an anti-globalisation movement who, several days later, wrapped four of the seventy sculptures in toilet paper and demanded the visitors leave the exhibition.

Grass's comments reminded me that much of the action in his novel *Im Krebsgang*, published in Germany in 2002 and in English, as *Crabwalk*, in 2004, takes place in Schwerin. The novel has a triple-stranded storyline that interweaves the histories of the National Socialist "martyr" Wilhelm Gustloff; the Slavonian Jew David Frankfurter, who assassinated Gustloff in 1937; and the Soviet submarine captain Alexander Marinesko, who sank the ship named after Gustloff. Wilhelm Gustloff was born in Schwerin in 1895. After rising through the ranks of the Nazi Party, he was sent to Switzerland as Landesgruppenleiter responsible for recruiting German and Austrian citizens living in Switzerland for the Party. Following his assassination in Davos, he was elevated to the status of the second most sacred martyr (after Horst Wessel) of the Third Reich. His body was buried with full military honours in a mausoleum on the southern shore of Lake Schwerin. The mausoleum was in the form of a concrete Ehrenhalle similar to those dedicated to the "martyrs" of the 1923 putsch on the Königsplatz in Munich. Figures of SA standard-bearers were sculpted into its columns; bronze plaques bearing the names of other Nazi "martyrs" were attached to its walls; and the mausoleum was surmounted by a jagged S-shaped victory rune. The monument was set in a memorial grove, surrounded by granite boulders on which cuneiform inscriptions were chiselled with the words "Lived for the Movement, Murdered by a Jew, Died for Germany". According to Grass, the mausoleum was dismantled by the Russians in 1949, and a GDR youth hostel was built over the site in the 1950s.

Launched in 1939, the *Wilhelm Gustloff* and her sister ship the *Robert Ley* were the pride of the Strength Through Joy fleet. However, their tour of duty as cruise liners sailing to Madeira, Pompeii or the Norwegian fjords was curtailed when war broke out shortly after they were launched. Requisitioned as a floating barracks and infirmary during the war, the *Wilhelm Gustloff* found itself on 30 January 1945 in the port of Gotenhafen (now Gdynia), laden with nine thousand wounded soldiers and refugees, five thousand of whom were children, fleeing the Russian advance in East Prussia. The ship left the port in driving snow and steamed north across the Bay of Danzig towards the peninsula of Hel, from where it was to sail west along the Pomeranian coast towards Flensburg and Kiel. Shortly before midnight it was torpedoed by an S-13 captained by Alexander Marinesko, and sank into the icy waters with the loss of almost all the women, children and invalids on board.

Grass fuses the historical strands of the novel with the contemporary story of a semi-autobiographical narrator, a deserter from East Germany now making a living as a liberal journalist in West Berlin. Born symbolically on the night of 30 January 1945, either on the *Wilhelm Gustloff* itself or on a rescue vessel (it remains unclear), Grass's narrator is drawn, during his research into the sinking of the vessel, to a neo-Nazi website www.Blutzeuge.de that, unbeknown to him, is hosted by his son Konrad under the name of "Comrades of Schwerin". Konrad in turn is drawn into a cyberspace relationship with "David", a young German pretending to be a Jew. The two young men eventually meet in the grounds of the youth hostel on the site of the memorial to Wilhelm Gustloff, where Konrad shoots "David" – a mirror image of David Frankfurter's assassination of Wilhelm Gustloff.

Crabwalk was the first novel by a respected German writer to address the great taboo of post-war Germany: the issue of Germans' own suffering in the final stages of the war. The novel's publication unleashed a slew of newspaper articles and illustrated features in Stern and Der Spiegel documenting the tragedy of the eleven million civilians from Silesia, Pomerania, East Prussia and the Sudetenland who were killed, raped or driven from their homes during the Russian advance. Since the publication of Crabwalk, the German people have felt less inhibited about acknowledging the violence done to them, without this necessarily diminishing their guilt for the crimes they perpetrated on others. The final sentence of Grass's novel, however, provides a chilling warning that German guilt for the Holocaust, as represented by "David", is in danger of being killed off by its opposite force, the right-wing revisionist radicalism and neo-Nazi violence symbolised by Konrad.

I set off from the Schloss in the early evening, crossing the bridge that connects the Burggarten with the Schlossgarten, a landscaped park in a baroque style which was being relaid with new lawns. An equestrian statue of Kaiser Wilhelm I rose in regal isolation at the head of a sceptre-shaped canal. I followed Franzosenweg, a path hugging the southern shore of the lake, threading its way between the back gardens of Jugendstil villas and the yachting clubs of the Mecklenburger bourgeoisie. After an hour's walk I reached the hostel, a nondescript, two-storey building in the standardised style of 1950s Germany, set within an acre or two of wooded parkland. I pushed open a wicker gate and wandered around, avoiding the stares of two teenage girls who probably thought I was a pervert attempting to peer into the dormitory windows. (I wondered whether Günter Grass felt as self-conscious as I did when he came here to do his research; or whether he booked an appointment in advance and arrived with a team of secretaries and photographers.)

There were indeed two fragments of a huge granite boulder, the size of a meteorite, on the lawn in front of the hostel. I discovered some Gothic lettering chiselled into the surface of the smaller fragment. By tracing the shape of the letters with my finger I could make out a Sig-rune, a Leben-rune and the words "...helm Dahl". The first syllable of the man's name was missing: maybe he was one of the forgotten National Socialist martyrs? I noticed a third fragment of the boulder, which had rolled away and come to rest against the wooden fence. The only letter I could find on this fragment was a "...g", possibly the final letter of "Bewegung" (Movement). Creeping as innocently as possible behind the bench on which the teenagers sat, I noticed the outline of a square foundation in a raised area of the lawn. There were a few broken bricks and in one corner a rusty metal reinforcing rod. This was all that remained of the mausoleum of Wilhelm Gustloff, a ruin of the Reich immortalised in literature as the site where the fictitious Konrad shot the doubly fictitious "David".

On Sunday morning I drove east from Schwerin along the B321, beneath a low canopy of grey cloud. In *Crabwalk* Grass's alter ego drives to the suburbs of Großer Dreesch and Neu-Zippendorf in search of a statue of Lenin that stood below an apartment block on Gagarinstraße, where his mother lived on the eleventh floor. The B321 broadened out into a dual carriageway between high banks of grassed slopes, like driving through a railway cutting. Following directions to Großer Dreesch, I turned off the highway and found myself in a huge housing project; a substantial town that would have been invisible to the uninformed traveller. I crossed avenues of identical eleven-storey *Plattenbau* housing blocks that extended in a grid pattern for several kilometres south of the main road. I found Lenin on the corner of Hamburger Allee (formerly Leninallee) and Plater Straße (named after the nineteenth-century Polish-Lithuanian revolutionary Emilie Plater). The bronze statue of Lenin, now green with verdigris, stood astride a jagged plinth whose tiles had begun to peel away. The inscription on the plinth read "The Land Reform Decree". Although twelve feet high, the statue, sculpted by an Estonian, was not a particularly awe-inspiring representation of the Russian leader: there was no clenched fist or jutting goatee. Hands deep in his raincoat pockets, he looked like a concerned father watching his son play football on a wet Sunday morning. This must surely be the last remaining statue of Vladimir Ilyich in Germany; possibly in Central Europe. The great statues of Lenin in Berlin, Kraków, Sofia and Bucharest (and Klaipėda) were removed in 1990 and 1991, and the squares they once dominated were renamed. Maybe this statue was overlooked because the authorities couldn't find the hidden town of Großer Dreesch?

I parked on the concrete slabs of a windswept square that served as an all-purpose "market area" for the particular housing estate I was in. Like the centre of Schwerin, it was deserted. Großer Dreesch was founded in 1972 as an estate of 4,829 prefabricated units designed to accommodate 14,000 inhabitants. Schools, supermarkets, a polyclinic, petrol station, swimming pool and printing works were added later in the decade. On its completion in 1983 it was acclaimed by the regime as "the new housing project with the nicest setting in the German Democratic Republic". Together with its neighbouring developments of Mueßer Holz and Neu-Zippendorf, it was home to 62,000 residents by 1989. The new town fell into decline after 1990 when its inhabitants emigrated to the West or moved into private housing, and the remaining residents had fewer children. New arrivals were mainly foreigners, or poorer people who could no longer afford rising rents in the cities. Many housing units remained empty. The amenities which were once a model of Socialist communal living deteriorated once they were no longer subsidised by the state. The new town suffered from truancy, drug abuse, racist violence and petty crime, social problems that were officially unknown in its Socialist heyday. A census of 2000 recorded an ageing population which had declined by 40% since 1989; and an unemployment rate of 23.6%. The names of the shops around the anonymous square betrayed the fact that price was an issue here: "Kik Textil Discount", "Tedi Top Euro Discount". The barber's shop advertised its services as "Top Trends für wenig Cents" ("Top Trends for a Few Cents"); Eddis Grillhaus offered doner kebabs for two euros, and pizzas for three. I returned to V.I. Lenin, alone on his plinth beneath the tower blocks, forced to contemplate the soulless, mass-produced "workers' paradise" he had created. Now surplus to requirements, I wondered how much longer he would survive.

South of Neubrandenburg I turned left off the main road and headed towards the Tollensesee. The road forked and I bore to the right along an unmade road which wound around some tithe barns until it reached the hamlet of Alt Rehse. I parked outside the entrance to an abandoned manor park, a former *Junker* estate that looked as if it had once passed into the hands of the National People's Army. Opposite was a white-washed village hall named the Dorfkrug, which had the date 1936 patterned in white bricks into the paving stones of its forecourt.

I walked along the sandy cobblestones of Lindenstraße, presumably named many years before the famous German soap opera of the same name. Below the lime trees was a row of identical two-storey cottages of red brick and black-painted beams. Each was built into the eaves of a steep thatched roof, below which an occasional satellite dish poked out discreetly. Double-glazed eyelet windows were framed with polished pine wood and looked out over balconies stuffed with tubs of geraniums. The gardens between the cottages contained hand-pumped wells with miniature thatched roofs. Pyramids of neatly stacked logs were piled between colourful flower beds and gaily painted wooden benches. It was a model village; a pristine reconstruction of the rustic idyll of pre-war Germany. Each cottage bore the name of a German city or province inscribed in runic lettering above the lintel of its front door: Haus Hamburg, Haus München, Haus Baden, Haus Schlesien, Haus Pommern, Haus Mecklenburg, Haus Heidelberg, Haus Hessen, Haus Württemberg, Haus Sachsen-Anhalt, Haus Sachsen, Haus Schleswig-Holstein, Haus Niedersachsen, Haus Bayern, Haus Dresden, Haus Westfalen, Haus Leipzig, Haus Rheinland, Haus Thüringen, Haus Kurhessen, Haus Kurmark. But, hang on... Kurhessen, Kurmark – these were not the names of traditional German provinces; these were names given to National Socialist *Gaue*. And what did the dates inscribed on the beams mean? Haus Baden was "built in Year 3", Haus Bayern opposite was "built in Year 4" – of the Thousand-Year Reich. This was a Nazi model village, preserved as if in mothballs since 1938 and hidden here in the rolling countryside of Mecklenburg. It had everything except swastikas.

Lindenstraße opened out into a village green. There was a hay wain, some rustic benches, a children's playground and a sturdy oak tree in the centre. Fallen sycamore buds lay sprinkled like amber over the greensward. On the far side was a duck pond surrounded by bulrushes and weeping willows, and a small restaurant with rustic tables set up on the grass outside. The only other people there were a Danish couple who had rented Haus Mecklenburg for a week's holiday. I was tempted by the "eels in aspic" chalked on a blackboard that served as a menu; that seemed appropriate, as the whole village appeared to be marinated in a toxic aspic. It reminded me of one of those films like *The Stepford Wives* where villagers living seemingly normal lives are in fact mutants subject to some time warp or alternative reality – in this case, National Socialism. The dense, humid atmosphere and low, heavy cloud heightened the sense of unreality. I was served by a woman who was only four feet tall, and

I immediately wondered whether she was the offspring of some horrific genetic experiment carried out in the 1930s. I was joined at my table by a wiry, bronzed man in a skin-tight cycling vest and a pair of skimpy denim shorts, who ordered red mullet, potato salad and a beer. He looked like "the only gay in the village", so to speak – although I wondered whether a Nazi village would have tolerated a token homosexual resident. I questioned him about the cottages and who now lived here, but he replied he was staying in a campsite by the lake and didn't know anything about the history of Alt Rehse. A plaque by the thatched gateway to the church recorded that in 1995 the *völkisch* idyll won a gold medal for the best kept village in Mecklenburg-Vorpommern, and a bronze medal in the national competition.

I made another circuit of the village, and this time I called in on Haus München, where the mayor Dr Wolfgang Köpp lived: he had a noticeboard on his fence advertising a book he had written about the history of the village. I was reluctant to disturb him, as he was enjoying a postprandial siesta with his wife and a couple of friends in the garden, but he seemed pleased to welcome a visitor and launched enthusiastically into a history of Alt Rehse.

The manor park originally belonged to Freiherr von Hauff, a distant relative of an aristocratic Russian family. In 1898 he built a small Schloss overlooking the lake, but his source of gold roubles dried up in 1917 following the October Revolution. His grounds were expropriated in 1934 by the SS in order to establish a secretive Führer School of German Doctorship, a centre of excellence for the most promising and ideologically committed doctors of the Third Reich – a kind of medical Ordensburg. Doctors, dentists, chemists and midwives from Germany and beyond were to be trained in the new disciplines of racial hygiene, hereditary biology and euthanasia. A complex of buildings in the half-timbered *völkisch* style, comprising hostels, lecture rooms, gymnasium, running track, abattoir and apiary, was constructed in the Schlosspark. At its centre was a communal hall built in the style of a Germanic *Thinghalle*. The campus was officially opened on 1 June 1935 in the presence of Rudolf Hess, Martin Bormann and leaders of the KVD, the German Association of General Practitioners. The Reichs Deputy declared: "With his effort, the doctor supports the National Socialist endeavour for racial purity." The acting director of the Führer School, Dr Peltret, continued with a discourse on the links between Judaism and tuberculosis: "Almost everyone harbours the tuberculosis bacillus: almost all nations harbour

Jews. Tuberculosis tends to affect weaker rather than stronger persons. The Jewish infection befalls only racially weak peoples." Approximately twenty-two thousand trainee eugenicists passed through the Führer School between 1935 and 1943, including a group of a hundred English medical students who were captured smiling for a group photograph on the steps of the *Gemeinschaftshaus*. The school was wound down in 1943 once the logical consequences of the students' education (euthanasia and genocide) had been satisfactorily completed.

The model village was constructed between 1935 and 1937, after the Führer School had been established, to accommodate not the medical trainees but the local peasants, who were transformed into a labour force to care for the upkeep and provision of the campus and its students. The farmers' original houses were torn down and replaced by the *völkisch* cottages which, so Herr Köpp informed me, were built incorrectly in the red-brick vernacular of Schleswig-Holstein and Lower Saxony, rather than in the traditional whitewashed plaster common to Mecklenburg. The only original house to survive was the Dorfkrug, which became the local pub and beer garden, and which was decorated with folksy *plattdeutsch* sayings chiselled into its oak beams. The *völkisch* vernacular architecture of self-contained, half-timbered cottages reflected the "Blood and Soil" ideology of the National Socialists. Alfred Rosenberg, who gave a course of lectures on racial purity at the Führer School, argued that the Aryans were a race of farmers and settlers – as opposed to the Jews, who were seen as a nomadic race. Hence the German *Volk* was expected to live for the next thousand years in rustic homesteads with thatched roofs. The idea of dating buildings from the inception of the Third Reich was a fad of Hess and Bormann, borrowed from Mussolini. Unimpressed by such numerological twaddle, Hitler banned this practice in 1938.

Wehrmacht reservists relinquished the Führer School to the Soviet Army without a fight on 30 April 1945. The Russians intended to blow up the campus and demolish the village, since it was a potent expression of Nazi architecture. But they never got round to it and eventually the original farmers were free to reclaim their fake village. The doctors' facilities and the former Schloss were converted into an orphanage for children exiled from lost eastern territories. In 1952 the site was taken over by the Institute of Physical Education of the GDR, and promising young athletes were trained there for success in the Olympic Games (it thus became a secret centre for steroid abuse rather than sterilisation). In 1955 the old manor park passed into the hands of the Volkspolizei and subsequently the National People's Army, who surrounded the site with barbed wire and installed anti-nuclear bunkers and the breeze-block barracks visible from the entrance to the park today. The Land Reform Decree of 1960 enabled the villagers to buy back their cottages from the state, and their families now appear to make a handsome living from renting out the restored properties to tourists during the summer.

The gates to the former Schlosspark were open and there was nobody manning the kiosk that was supposed to charge an entrance fee of two euros in a desperate attempt to raise funds for the upkeep of the now disused estate. I followed a straight avenue, bordered by lime trees, between the crumbling yellow barracks and administrative buildings formerly used by the National People's Army. The park was overgrown and deserted. The four half-timbered hostels built for the trainees in euthanasia lay abandoned in unmown grass on the slopes down to the lake. The communal hall where the doctors met to eat and entertain themselves was unlocked. I pushed open a door and entered a large, wood-panelled hall with four weighty, wrought-iron chandeliers suspended from the ceiling. There was a long table at the far side on which a pair of record decks and speakers had been set up; the standby lights were still switched on, which suggested the local community (or a neo-Nazi group) had held a disco here the previous night and had been too wrecked to switch off and pack up their equipment. I looked around the antechambers off the main hall: they were mainly toilets and shower rooms, bare and unused. The rooms upstairs were also empty, apart from one which, incongruously, contained an upright piano. I ascended another flight of steps to the attic, which was also bare: just wooden beams and wire netting in place of a floor. I expected at any moment to be apprehended by a janitor from the estate and asked why I was trespassing on private property – but no one came.

I returned to Haus München and Mayor Köpp to hand back the key he had lent me to the village museum. As Herr Köpp was also the curator of the museum, I didn't learn anything he had not already told me, but it was interesting to see photographs of the study group of English medics smiling for the camera on the steps of the communal hall, in between their lectures on racial genetics and *Volksheilkunde*. Herr Köpp was soon in full flow again, and I felt obliged to purchase a copy of the book he had written about the history of Alt Rehse. He bade me farewell with the ambiguous words: "Nicht alles von der Nazi-Zeit war schlecht. Einiges war ganz gut. Es ist nur, was sie davon gemacht haben." ("Not everything from the Nazi period was bad. Some of it was quite good. It just depends what they did with it.")

11

Brandenburg

"You're Wearing Grey Today, You're from Berlin I'd Say"

I turned off the B109 by a forestry depot and bumped in second gear along a rough track into the heart of the Schorfheide, a forest of beech, pine and oak trees growing out of the sandy soil of the Mark. As the forest grew thicker, I passed stacks of logs and an enclosure hung with a sign that read "Sauschwanzpossee" ("Pig Tail Possee"?). A boulder marked the distance to Carinhall as 1.2 km. I noticed the dull sheen of lakes through the trees on either side of the road. Reaching a small clearing, I parked the car. This was the Hirschplatz, the entrance to Hermann Göring's country estate, once presided over by a bronze stag modelled on one named Raufbold that the Reichs Master of the Hunt had shot in the Rominter Heide in East Prussia. An avenue of moribund chestnut trees led in the direction of a gatehouse in the distance. I followed a narrow trail into the woods towards the centre of Carinhall. The trees were in bad shape: silver birches with exfoliated bark, larches defoliated to the tips of their branches, oak leaves coated with white fungoid stains, chestnut leaves curled, yellowing and flecked with brown spots. The track continued through beds of harebells and clumps of nettles into the ruins of Carinhall. Nothing remained of Göring's retreat except a few circles of broken bricks, some chunks of masonry, depressions in the ground, rusted reinforcing rods and twists of piping from destroyed heating systems. I felt a blast of cold air from deep underground as I peered into the collapsed air vent of a bunker.

In a moment of Nordic nostalgia, Göring decided to name the hunting lodge after his first wife Carin Freiïn von Fock, a Swedish baroness who had died of tuberculosis in 1931. Two years later Göring revisited her ancestral home on the island of Lovö near Stockholm and laid a bouquet of red roses in the shape of a swastika on her tomb. Swedish anti-Nazis took exception to this and removed the wreath. Göring saw this as an excuse to exhume her body and return it to Germany. Carin's coffin left Lovö the following summer and was shipped via Stockholm, Trelleborg and Sassnitz to the railway station of Eberswalde, where it was received at 8.30 am on 20 June by the Reichsmarschall, accompanied by a military band. The coffin was placed on the chassis of a converted military vehicle and escorted through the villages of the Schorfheide, which had been garlanded with wreaths for the occasion. As the cortège approached Carinhall, the coffin was transferred to a horse-drawn gun carriage for the last few kilometres through the forest. On its arrival at the hunting lodge the coffin was met by Hitler, Goebbels and Himmler and borne on the shoulders of twenty soldiers to its final resting place above the shore of the Wuckersee. The military band launched into Siegfried's Funeral March from *Götterdämmerung*, followed by Luther's hymn "Ein' feste Burg ist unser Gott"; and the mortal remains of Carin Göring were laid to rest in a crypt specially built for her above the lake, surrounded by wreaths, fire bowls, oak trees and four red granite menhirs.

The first incarnation of Carinhall was built in the winter of 1933–34 in the style of a Swedish log cabin: a modest two-storey cottage, constructed from pine trunks and boulders, with a thatched roof. The ground floor was in the form of a Nordic hall decorated with rugs, wall-mounted antlers and a stuffed eagle. The study, bedroom and guest rooms of the Reichs Master of the Forest and Hunt were built into the eaves, the study dominated by an oil painting of Carin sitting in a meadow in the Bavarian Alps. After visiting Carinhall on 9 March 1934, Goebbels noted in his diary: "Inspected Göring's 'Hunding's Hut'. Hideous style. But glorious isolation. Lake, forest, melancholy. You feel good here."

During 1936–37 the log cabin was incorporated into a three-winged "summer palace" more appropriate to the requirements of the potentate, whose official posts now included those of Reichs Aviation Minister, President of the Reichstag and Prime Minister of Prussia; and who regarded himself as the unofficial Foreign Minister of the National Socialist state. The business wing of the new extension contained the private rooms of Göring and his family; Hermann slept alone in a four-poster bed below a lascivious painting by Werner Peiner of *Europa and the Bull*. His bedroom was connected to that of his new wife Emmy by means of an upholstered sliding door. The business wing also included a restaurant, bowling alley, shooting range, winter garden, Russian steam bath, two casinos, a gymnasium with a mechanical horse donated by the cosmetician Elizabeth Arden, and a train set with six hundred metres of electrified track with which Göring would play with his nephew Klaus. The Great Gallery of the central wing was furnished with antique vases, Persian carpets, Gobelin tapestries, Old Masters and a Gothic choir stall, most of which had been purloined from Jewish collections throughout occupied Europe. Behind the gallery was Göring's library, in which he had hung a wall map that showed no division between Germany and Austria. During a visit to Carinhall in September 1937, six months before the *Anschluss*, the Austrian Foreign Minister Guido Schmidt was horrified on being shown this map. Göring waved away Schmidt's protests in his avuncular way, telling him this was how the political landscape would soon look. Three weeks later Mussolini, on being shown the same map, remarked presciently that Czechoslovakia cut too deeply into the German Reich. The centrepiece of the central wing was the Great Hunting Hall, a reception room hung with paintings, tapestries, animal skins and trophies. The richly embroidered carpets across the polished stone floor concealed underfloor heating for the winter months. Scattered around the room were bulky armchairs and settees upholstered in leather and brocade, and standing lamps so hefty "one could fell an ox with them", according to Göring's translator. An organ was built into the eaves of the room, which were supported by oak beams engraved with runes and swastikas. At the western end of the hall an electrically operated window, equal in size to that of Hitler's in the Berghof, afforded a view over the Großer Döllnsee.

The "Lord of the Schorfheide" entertained his guests dressed in a leather waistcoat, lederhosen and riding boots, sometimes brandishing a spear as he rushed around like an excited schoolboy, showing off his pet lion cubs or his herds of elk and wild horses to the bemused assembly of foreign diplomats he invited to Carinhall. On one occasion Göring is said to have left a dinner party and returned dressed as Siegfried, pulling a pair of bison behind him on a chain. He then treated his stupefied guests to the spectacle of the bison mating. Göring liked to think of himself as "the last Renaissance man"; the memoirs of his guests, however, emphasised the vulgarity of their host and his hunting lodge. The American Under-Secretary of State Sumner Welles concluded: "It must be difficult to find an uglier building; or one more vulgar in its swanky pretentiousness." Another American guest, William C. Bullitt, commented on the potentate's width: "He has the proportions of a German tenor. His backside has a girth of at least one yard. In order to make his shoulders as broad as his hips he wears two inches of padding on either side. ... Apparently he always has a beautician with him as his fingers, which are as fat as they are long, have long, pointed and carefully painted nails; and his pink complexion betrays daily care. His eyes bulge wildly as if he were either suffering from swollen glands or is still using cocaine. His lips are small, like those of an underage child."

In 1939 Göring doubled the size of Carinhall by adding two additional wings. The new buildings, in an English manorial style, were laid out around a second courtyard, in the centre of which stood a replica of the Lion of Brunswick raised on a tall pedestal. Although elements of *völkisch* vulgarity remained, the ceremonial rooms of the new extension were designed in the ostentatious, mock-classical idiom favoured by the rich and powerful. The stucco ceiling of the Great Banqueting Hall was supported by marble columns. Renaissance tapestries framed in marble decorated the walls. Its electrically operated panoramic window now claimed to be the largest in Europe: Göring had trumped Hitler. Gold and Silver Cabinet Rooms led upstairs to a conference room where Göring received his General Staff. The new library was decorated with a medieval altarpiece and paintings by Cranach, many of them, again, plundered from Jewish collections. The basement of the library wing contained a cinema, two massage parlours, a swimming pool with underwater lighting that could alternate the colour of the water between blue and green, and a second train set twice as long as the one in the business wing.

Now at the zenith of his career, Göring shed his hunting leathers in favour of pseudo-military uniforms which he designed himself: wide-lapelled blue and yellow blazers with matching trousers, or double-breasted suits in white satin on which were pinned the medals of his various offices – he held a total of twenty-eight posts between 1932 and 1945. Prince Philipp von Hessen remarked that "if this continues, Göring will soon have to pin the medals to his backside"; it was rumoured that he did pin rubber medals to his bathing suit. Ribbentrop referred to him as "that Christmas tree". His appearance was enhanced by the discreet use of facial creams and powders, lipstick and other cosmetics. Although not as corpulent as he had been in the mid-1930s, the Reichsmarschall still had the soft, fleshy appearance of a lickerish uncle.

I followed hidden trails that led through the site of the obliterated Waldhof and descended a slope to the shores of the Großer Döllnsee.

A sudden wind ruffled the reeds and whipped up the waters of the lake. The sky turned a Wehrmacht grey. Rain pelted down, shrouding the trees on the far side in a pall of mist. On my way back to the Hirschplatz I encountered a man from Hanover who told me that he came here every year; and that each year the forest reclaimed more of the ruins, and the undergrowth concealed more of the depressions in the ground. Thunder cracked overhead. The rain became torrential. I sheltered in the car. Once the worst of the downpour had ceased, I walked towards the Wuckersee to look for Carin's crypt. There was nothing to see except the subliminal hint of a rectangular depression lying across the path to the lake. For some reason Göring failed to have his wife's coffin removed from the crypt before the Red Army arrived. The tomb and her coffin were broken into and ravaged. Carin's mortal remains were strewn around the wood and not discovered until 1947, when they were collected and reburied (minus head and feet) below the menhir that bore her family crest. Her bones were exhumed again in 1951 and cremated in Wilmersdorf, before her ashes were finally returned to Sweden and reinterred in the small cemetery in Lovö from where her body had been stolen some twenty years earlier.

I clambered down to the shore of the Wuckersee, where some broken bricks and chunks of red-black marble had tumbled into the shallows. It was here that in 1990 three statues by Arno Breker were dredged up from the floor of the lake; one of these was *Eos*, a sculpture I had seen in the exhibition in Schwerin. The rain stopped as abruptly as it had started. Sunlight dappled the leaves of the forest and flooded the Wuckersee with turquoise, colouring the rushes and trees in bright shades of green. Birds started singing again. Woodpeckers began to hammer through bark. I squelched through a mulch of beech mast and sodden twigs to the Hirschplatz, where a cloud of steam rose from the soaked ground, enveloping the car. I drove off down a Kastanienallee of moth-eaten chestnut trees towards a pair of tall stone sentry boxes engraved with oak leaves and crossed maces, the coat of arms of the Reichsmarschall. They marked a new ceremonial entrance to Carinhall built in 1942, by which time Göring had virtually disappeared from public life, withdrawing from the reality of total war into a morphine haze in the depths of the Schorfheide. Today, the two guardhouses were farmhouses where cockerels crowed and eggs were on sale at fifteen cents each.

I returned to the B109 and drove around the head of Großer Döllnsee to the Hotel Döllnsee-Schorfheide, a three-storey villa painted in shades of pink. The glossy brochures on display in reception noted that the "Herrenhaus" was built in 1934 in a "Tudor style". Advertising itself as a "Traum in der Natur", the hotel offered a "Wellness" programme in its "Traumzeit Body Lounge" that included massages, "Peeling", a milk bath, an "Aromasauna" and body packing in algae and herbs. Refreshed and detoxified, the guests could then enjoy the outdoor pursuits of cycling, rafting or Nordic walking.

The actual history of the hotel is somewhat less wholesome. Built in 1940 in a *völkisch* style similar to the first extension of Carinhall (not in 1934 in a Tudor style, as the brochures suggest), it was originally a guesthouse for Göring's international visitors. Surviving the war unscathed, it was used in the early years of the German Democratic Republic as a hostel for the FDJ (Free German Youth) movement. It later served as a guesthouse for the Staatsrat of the GDR and a country retreat for the elite of the SED. It was here on 12 August 1961 that the Politbüro nodded through the final details of "Operation Rose", the construction of the "anti-fascist protection barrier" around West Berlin. Ten years later Erich Honecker deposed Walter Ulbricht as First Secretary of the Central Committee of the SED in the same building. Ulbricht died here in 1973. Under Honecker's regime the state guesthouse welcomed foreign visitors such as Leonid Brezhnev, Andrei Gromyko, Alexei Kosygin, Wojciech Jaruzelski and Gustáv Husák. They were entertained with hunting parties every bit as lavish as those of Göring. Federal Chancellor Helmut Schmidt complained during a visit in December 1981 about the violet neon lighting in the conference room. He was told it was necessary in order to succour the cactus plants presented as a state gift by Fidel Castro.

I wandered out through Honecker's apartments to a genteel terrace at the rear of the hotel and sat in the sun with retired couples from Berlin and IT executives formulating business strategy. An impeccable waitress in a maroon uniform served me a pot of Assam tea and a Göring-sized slice of strawberry-yoghurt cake. Later I strolled down through a landscaped park to the lake, whose shore looked back towards the site of Carinhall. A gentle breeze rustled the reeds around the boathouse and bathing house: both were log cabins that originally stood in the shallows on the opposite bank of the lake. A photograph taken on 5 July 1935 shows Hitler, Göring and Emmy gazing out over the Großer Döllnsee from below the thatched eaves of the bathing house. A sign on the wall of the latter ordered today's "Hotel Guests Only" to behave with decorum: to keep quiet and keep their clothes on. In spite of the warning, one couple discreetly divested themselves of their bathing costumes and lowered themselves gently into the lake. The other residents, lying on their sun loungers, kept their noses in their magazines and pretended not to be offended.

I turned back along the B109 to the south, passing through forests of denuded trees. The road threaded its way through Groß Schönebeck, Zerpenschleuse and Klosterfelde, villages whose low houses and barns hugged the main street: neat gardens enclosed by prim iron fences; *Gasthöfe* with names like Weißen Hirsch or Zum goldenen Adler advertising "Deutsche Küche"; red-brick churches dedicated to Kaiser Wilhelm II; war memorials surmounted by Iron Crosses; florists and fire stations. Signs at the exit of each village informed me I was following the *Märkische Eiszeitstraße* (the "Ice Age Road of the Mark").

In the centre of the village green of Eichhorst was a wooden gateway beneath a thatched roof. Below the gateway stood a sandstone wall, on which was sculpted a charging bison. Chiselled in Gothic script below the animal were excerpts from the *Nibelungenlied* that extolled Siegfried's prowess at slaying bison and elk. An inscription on the rear of the wall read: "Once upon a time primeval big game laid their tracks through Germany's forests. Hunting was a test of courage for our Germanic forefathers. 1n 1934 a German big game park was established here. Bison and aurochs, elk, deer, wild horses, beavers and other creatures native to our homeland were to find a sanctuary which would serve coming generations as a living testimony of the richness of an animal kingdom before Germany was ruled by man." The Bison Monument was erected in 1934 and unveiled by the Reichs Master of the Hunt. Under pressure from the Communist authorities, it was dismantled in 1958 and buried in the Schorfheide. In the 1990s it was rediscovered, restored and reinstalled in the centre of Eichhorst. Its original inscription recorded that the monument had been commissioned by "Reichs Master of the Forest and the Hunt H. Göring", but at some stage this had been doctored, erasing the memory of the man who had been almost single-handedly responsible for reintroducing elk and bison to the Schorfheide.

Somewhere between Eichhorst and Wandlitz, I located a private road through woods to the secretive Bogensee. Duck-necked lampposts craned over the winding, potholed track. I parked in a clearing opposite a row of garages. Judging from the activity in the other parked cars, this was a lovers' rendezvous. A wooden signboard illustrated the layout of a campus of some kind. There were blocks named Haus Wien, Haus Potsdam, Haus Budapest and Haus Reggio Calabria. There was a sports centre, a Wiener Café, a *Kneipe* in the Landhaus and a Restaurant Bogensee. I walked in the direction of the lake, passing a football pitch enclosed within stone terracing overgrown with weeds. Up on my left was a low, one-storey villa in a *völkisch* style built around a forecourt. This was once the country retreat of Dr Joseph Goebbels. Sixteen thousand square metres of land around the isolated Bogensee were put at the disposal of the Reichs Propaganda Minister by the city of Berlin in 1936. The UFA film studio built a small house for its patron on the eastern shore of the lake as a gift to celebrate both his thirty-ninth birthday and the tenth anniversary of the *Gau* Groß-Berlin. "Ein Waldidyll," wrote Goebbels in his diary. Others referred to it as his "love nest". By 1939 he had outgrown the so-called log cabin and commissioned a larger "Waldhaus" for him and his family on the western shore of the Bogensee. His new three-winged villa contained twenty-one rooms, five baths and a cinema. The reception room at the rear of the house was fitted with air-conditioning and a trio of large, electrically operated windows (still apparently in working order) through which Goebbels and his guests could wander out for afternoon tea, served on a terrace with a scenic view over the lake.

In contrast to Göring's pleasure dome, Goebbels' villa was untouched by the war. It remains intact, locked and seemingly abandoned. Weeds are growing through the cracks in the paving stones, the lawns are unkempt and small fir trees planted around the forecourt are beginning to obscure the clean white lines of the villa. A crude sculpture from the Socialist era, of lovers embracing, stands in the centre of the courtyard. Peering through the front door I could see a pair of radiators encased in metal grilles and a row of brass light fittings on the walls of a corridor tiled in grey marble. The patio windows at the rear revealed an empty reception room below a heavy coffered ceiling. Radiators, wall lamps and oak doors surrounded a bare floor tiled with black and white squares in a checkerboard pattern. On the terrace were areas for morning coffee, afternoon tea and barbecues, each area with a steep tiled roof supported by oak beams. A joyless children's playground to the side of the villa looked like a later GDR addition, rather than one built for the Goebbels' ill-fated offspring.

After the war the secluded location of Goebbels' retreat provided an ideal home for a new Jugendhochschule established by Wilhelm Pieck, leader of the Communist Party in the Soviet Zone. This was an educational centre for the young elite selected to become future leaders of the Free German Youth (FDJ) and the Socialist Unity Party of Germany (SED). Students were indoctrinated in the dogmas of Socialism: Marxism-Leninism, dialectical materialism, the function of the SED and the role of the Communist Party of the Soviet Union. Like their pre-war counterparts at Nazi Ordensburgen, they were also trained in mental toughness and physical prowess. Wilhelm Pieck gave frequent lectures at the college during its early years from 1946 to 1949. The Third Session of the Central Council of the FDJ was held in the school on 21 September 1946 under the chairmanship of one Erich Honecker.

By the end of the decade, the requirements of the Jugendhochschule Wilhelm Pieck had outstripped the facilities provided by Goebbels' former *Waldhaus*. In 1951 the foundation stone was laid for a much grander complex of offices, seminar rooms, restaurants and accommodation blocks. The enlarged campus was designed in a Socialist Classical style by Hermann Hanselmann, chief architect of the Stalinallee in Berlin, which had been completed in 1953, two years before the inauguration of the Jugendhochschule. The new buildings surrounded a landscaped park of pools, gardens and statues which descended in a series of terraces from Haus Berlin at the head of the complex to the Wiener Café at its foot. Some four hundred students were enrolled each year in an intensive one-year course in the doctrines of Soviet-inspired Socialism. The college became a centre of excellence for international anti-fascism, welcoming delegates from Hungary, Poland, Bulgaria, Romania, Korea, Vietnam, Laos, Cuba, Nicaragua (in the person of President Daniel Ortega), Somalia and the Soviet Union. Cadres of students from the school were despatched abroad to represent the GDR at anniversaries of the October Revolution, or to participate in events such as the Komsomol Games and the Spartakiade of German-Soviet Friendship. One group of volunteers assisted the Volkspolizei in constructing the "anti-fascist protection barrier" around West Berlin. The secretive campus, known colloquially as the "Red Cloister" on account of its rigorous methodology, became obsolete in 1989. During the 1990s it was used occasionally for training recruits to the Federal Border Police or by civilian training organisations.

Since the turn of the century its buildings have fallen into disuse and the entire complex seems to have been left to crumble into oblivion. The grounds are owned by the Senate of Berlin, but it costs 250,000 euros per annum for minimal upkeep; and no organisation has offered to purchase an estate of Stalinist blocks hidden away in the depths of rural

Brandenburg. The site is slowly being reclaimed by nature: weeds, nettles and bindweed are encroaching upon the staircases, balustrades, fountains and statues; the walls of seminar rooms, lecture theatres and refectories are beginning to peel and fade. Only the ghosts of the FDJ, former alumni of the Jugendhochschule Wilhelm Pieck, now return on an annual visit to survey the ruins of their youthful idealism.

At a road junction on the approach to Wandlitz, a car in front of me with western German plates, impatient to turn right, rammed the car in front of it. A local man got out, inspected the damage to the rear of his Passat and exploded with rage: "Scheiße, Scheiße, Scheiße!" I circumvented the accident and turned down Thälmannstraße, an avenue of villas along the northern shore of Wandlitzsee. I checked into the Hotel Seeterrassen, a restored villa run by a gay couple which afforded a view over the ruffled, silver-grey surface of the lake. The restaurant served meals in a New German Cuisine style: I enjoyed an artfully arranged dish of pig's liver, asparagus and red cabbage. A Swedish-American family at the next table asked the waitress what the local sights were. "Well, there's Göring at Carinhall, Goebbels on the Bogensee, Honecker's Waldsiedlung just outside Wandlitz, or...," and here she paused to think of something exceptional, "there's the concentration camp at Sachsenhausen."

When I finished my meal, a solitary man who had been drinking at the bar asked if he could join me at my table. He muttered something about coming to the hotel once a week to talk to the guests. He said he was the owner of the nearby Café Nostalgie and that this was his night off. I asked him about Wandlitz, a bourgeois resort of villas spread along the fringes of the lake, depressingly empty on this damp, chilly July evening. He explained that 90% of Wandlitz belonged to Berliners, who owned holiday homes that they visited at weekends; 90% of Wandlitzers, by contrast, lived or worked in Berlin as there was nothing to do in Wandlitz. I guessed that he was on the pull and made my excuses. The waitress later apologised for his intrusion on my privacy. As night fell, I walked along a promenade between the gardens and jetties of the empty villas. I reached a Strandrestaurant where a few retired couples from Berlin were spread thinly around the café. I ordered a *latte macchiato* and a *Malteser* and sat by the window watching the grey clouds merge with the grey waters of the lake – until all was black.

Tuesday morning was brighter. A weak sun burned a hole through the pearly cloud cover. A breeze blew in from the lake, rippling the flags which hung over kindergartens. Shoppers pushed supermarket trolleys around car parks. I drove along Wandlitzchaussee in the direction of Bernau, following signs for the Brandenburg-Klinik. At some stage the road acquired an empty third lane, separated from the other lanes by a crash barrier. The turn-off for the Klinik led into thick forest, denser than the Schorfheide. I continued on Brandenburger Allee until the avenue came to a halt at a pair of heavy iron gates. On the other side of the gateway was the sanatorium, an exclusive complex of neurological, cardiological and orthopaedic clinics built during the 1990s in a light, post-modern style. The four main clinics – Haus Berlin, Haus Barnim, Haus Brandenburg and Haus Havelland – were set amid a landscaped park of lakes and gardens replete with fountains, sculptures, exotic trees and rare shrubs. Patients sat on benches, sunning themselves in front of the bandstand or the mini-golf course; nurses pushed wheelchairs beneath the trees; doctors and physiotherapists glided by, clutching charts in plastic folders. Surrounding the clinics was a network of streets named after German composers (Bachstraße, Brahmsstraße, Mendelssohnstraße, Offenbachstraße, Schumannstraße and Schubertstraße) that led to supermarkets, restaurants, hotels, banks, churches, schools, hotels, tennis courts and children's playgrounds. This was a complete, self-sufficient town hidden in the forest.

Before it was redeveloped into a sanatorium, the Waldsiedlung Wandlitz was the inner sanctum of the Politbüro of the SED. Following popular uprisings in the GDR in 1953 and in Hungary in 1956, the leaders of the Socialist Unity Party of Germany decided they needed somewhere more secure and secluded to live than their villas in the Berlin suburb of Niederschönhausen. The Waldsiedlung was built between 1958 and 1960 to house the highest officials of the Politbüro: Otto Grotewohl, Walter Ulbricht, Erich and Margot Honecker, Willi Stoph, Egon Krenz and Erich Mielke. The estate was surrounded by an outer fence of barbed wire on which signs announced to the outside world that it protected a game reserve. The inner compound was fortified by an iron fence and guarded by soldiers of the Felix Dzierzynski Regiment. The settlement consisted of a central clubhouse, swimming pool, cinema, restaurant, hospital, tennis court, shooting range and twenty-three detached houses. There were shops where the Politbüro and their families could spend East German currency on high-quality produce imported from West Berlin. My friend

Sara, who grew up in East Berlin, told me ordinary citizens of the GDR believed their leaders led a debauched life of orgies and drinking parties behind the high fence guarding their retreat; but it is more likely they spent most of their free time hunting in the Schorfheide. Honecker in particular was addicted to game hunting, often shooting as many as twelve stags a day. Like Göring, he would impress visiting heads of state with his proficiency with the rifle; numerous photographs exist of Honecker and his cronies standing proudly inside circles of dead boar and deer splayed out around them.

The homes of Honecker, Krenz, Günter Schabowski and their intimates were spread out along three avenues (Habichtweg, Bussardweg and Eichelhöherweg) deep in the wooded centre of the Waldsiedlung. They are unremarkable two-storey family houses built in the standardised style of 1950s Germany – but larger and no doubt more luxurious than the prefabricated apartment blocks ordinary "comrades" were allocated. They now serve as residential blocks for patients of the clinic. Parents sit with their children on the steps of the houses or lounge in deckchairs on the lawns, possibly oblivious to the fact they are living in the former houses of paranoid Warsaw Pact warriors. As I left the Waldsiedlung an ancient Wartburg clattered along the Kurallee, a relic from a forgotten, secretive world. It reminded me that the black Wartburg was the limousine of choice for Grotewohl, Stoph and Ulbricht, figures from black-and-white newsreels who would have been chauffeured to and from this impenetrable hideout in the forest. It dawned on me that the third lane of Wandlitzchaussee would have been reserved for these autocrats, enabling them to speed past ordinary traffic without needing to come into contact with the proletariat over which they ruled.

I returned to the B109 and headed south through the Bernauer Heide. A yellow sign announced the city boundary of Berlin, somewhat incongruously, as I was driving through fields of wheat and barley, past groves of conifers on sandy heath criss-crossed by irrigation canals. Gradually the terrain along the road became more urban – petrol stations, car showrooms, supermarkets (invariably either Lidl or Aldi). Metropolitan Berlin began in Buchholz where the trams turned around and where I caught my first glimpse of the television tower, a 365-metre-high syringe shooting up above the city. A viaduct led the B109 over swathes of S-Bahn tracks. The yellow and grey prefabricated housing units of Prenzlauer Promenade gave way to the townhouses of Prenzlauer Allee, solid buildings from the Wilhelmine or Weimar eras with rows of wrought-iron balconies and columns of square, three-storey oriels. I passed the silver orb of a planetarium and stopped for traffic lights at the junction with Danziger Straße, a street I vaguely remembered as Dimitroffstraße during the Socialist years. Renamed in 1950 in honour of the Bulgarian Communist who led the Comintern (and was charged by the Nazis for setting fire to the Reichstag), Danziger Straße reverted to its pre-war imperial name in 1995.

Traffic slowed to a halt beside the St Nicholas Cemetery, where Horst Wessel may or may not still be buried, with or without his head. (In 2000 a group named "Autonomous Gravediggers" allegedly dug up Wessel's skull and threw it into the Spree. The police, however, reported that the excavation was superficial, and it remains unknown whether the Nazi "martyr" is now with or without his skull; or whether his father's skull was stolen instead; or whether he was ever buried here in the first place.) Then I was skirting Alexanderplatz, in a permanent state of reconstruction judging by the yellow workers' cabins and blue water pipes that formed tubular bridges across the street. I had got used to the disappearance of the Ministry for Foreign Affairs of the German Democratic Republic, which had been demolished shortly after the fall of the Berlin Wall, but now the Palace of the Republic had vanished too. Storm clouds were brewing over the Forum Fridericianum as I crossed Liebknechtbrücke and Schlossbrücke. Trying to avoid a queue of traffic circumventing the Brandenburg Gate, I found myself in the wrong lane and had to turn back east along Unter den Linden. I turned right down Glinkastraße, then right again along Behrenstraße, where tourists sat eating sandwiches on the steles of the Holocaust Memorial. Once past the Soviet War Memorial, I raced through the Tiergarten, around the Victory Column and along Budapester Straße.

I checked in to the Sylter Hof in Kurfürstenstraße, a concrete block that must have been built in the 1960s and was now being refurbished. I requested a quiet room at the back of the hotel, but the clanging of scaffolding and the screech of machinery cutting through sheet metal in the rear courtyard proved unbearable. The art historian Karl Scheffler famously wrote: "Berlin is condemned to be eternally becoming, never to be"; and that is as true today as it was in 1910, when Scheffler wrote *Berlin – the Fate of a City*. I changed to a room at the front of the hotel, from where I had a view over the main street. Kurfürstenstraße runs through an "in-between" area that is neither old nor new, neither wholly residential nor wholly commercial. It is one of those areas of West Berlin that lost its sense of place when the city was divided; a street of hotels, restaurants, car rental offices, internet cafés and Polish *Delikatessen* that now caters for the transient and the unfulfilled. There are massage parlours, a "Kleine Nachtrevue" and a gay sauna which advertises itself as the "biggest erotic labyrinth in Berlin", featuring "S/M cabins" and a "dark area". As its name suggests, Kurfürstenstraße was an imposing street in Prussian Berlin, an avenue of Wilhelmine mansions that connected the Zoological Garden with the Potsdamer Station. The Sylter Hof was built on the site of the Judenreferat, the Reich Security Main Office Section IV B4, from where Adolf Eichmann supervised the expulsion and extermination of Europe's Jews. Before it was taken over by Eichmann, the building was occupied by the Fraternal Lodge, a society of Jewish freemasons. A memorial to the victims of the Judenreferat consists of two illuminated panels in a bus shelter outside the hotel.

In the 1920s Auguste-Viktoria-Platz was the centre of bohemian Berlin. Avant-garde writers and artists congregated in the smoke-filled halls of the Romanisches Café, the largest coffee house in Europe. Impressionists, Expressionists, Dadaists, novelists, poets, essayists, journalists, actors, playwrights, scriptwriters, producers, directors, cabaret artists – each had its own *Stammtisch*. Erich Kästner described the café as the "Waiting Room of Talent". Most of its habitués had been going there for years – and Talent had never arrived. They shuffled from table to table in pursuit of that chance encounter which would launch their career. In the 1930s those regulars who did have talent – Bertolt Brecht, Otto Dix, George Grosz, Erich Kästner, Friedrich Hollaender, Max Liebermann, Alfred Döblin, Stefan Zweig, Erich Maria Remarque, Hanns Eisler, Billy Wilder – found that their talent was a potential death sentence: they were too left-wing, too pacifist, too subversive, too "degenerate", too Jewish. Their books burned, their paintings destroyed, most fled Germany within a few years.

The sister-building of the Romanisches Café was the Romanisches Haus at the opposite end of the square. It housed the Gloria-Palast cinema, whose box-office hit in 1930 was a film called *The Blue Angel* featuring a song by Hollaender entitled "Ich bin von Kopf bis Fuß auf Liebe eingestellt", sung by a new star named Marlene Dietrich. Dietrich was too posh to drink in the Romanisches Café; and she too left Germany shortly afterwards. The third neo-Romanesque building in Auguste-Viktoria-Platz was the Kaiser Wilhelm Memorial Church. All three buildings were constructed in the 1890s at the height of the Wilhelmine obsession with Romanesque architecture as an expression of the true German style; as opposed to Gothic architecture which, since the Franco-Prussian War, was considered to be "too French". Of the three buildings, only the church survived the Second World War – just. Its ruined nave was demolished in 1956 and the fractured stump of its spire became the iconic image of West Berlin.

Renamed Breitscheidplatz, the square was the artificially created centre of the capitalist half of the city. Since reunification, the avant-garde pendulum has swung back to the east of Berlin, and Breitscheidplatz today is an unappealing concrete plaza with a smell of fried onions that emanates from the McDonald's, Kentucky Fried Chicken and Mövenpick takeaways that occupy the site of the Romanisches Café. The steps around the church and the "Wasserklops" fountain are the preserve of buskers, Romany beggars, caricaturists and hawkers who sell rubber spiders that "climb" up walls, or strips of fluorescent pink and green plastic that girls can braid into their hair.

I strolled down Kurfürstendamm, weaving my way between the glass display cases at regular intervals along the boulevard, each filled with elegant shoes, dowdy hats, antiquarian books or lumps of spray-painted concrete that purport to be fragments of the Berlin Wall. In the 1980s the display cases were used by prostitutes to mark out their territory. On summer evenings the girls, clad in leopard-print leotards, would lean against the vitrines. On winter nights, when slush was piled high in dirty glaciers along the pavement edge, they would prowl slowly around the glass cases, swaddled in ski jackets, ear muffs and moon boots. Punters now have to go to the far end of Kurfürstenstraße, where Ukrainian girls stand in lines outside the sex shops.

Named after a Prussian field marshal, Knesebeckstraße is one of those broad Berlin streets that have an air of indestructibility. Running straight as a die from Wilmersdorf to Charlottenburg, between tall trees and Wilhelmine townhouses, the street is wide enough for cars to park at right angles to the pavement. I recall returning to my car, after an appointment one November morning with the art bookshop Bücherbogen, to find that another vehicle had blocked my exit. I looked around helplessly and honked the horn. A resident on the ground floor of the adjacent building told me it was probably the woman on the top floor who had doubleparked. I raced up to the fifth floor of the apartment block, briefcase in hand, and rang the bell. The door was opened by a young woman with blonde hair wearing nothing but a silver bikini.

"Excuse me, the gentleman on the ground floor sent me up here. He thinks that your car may have blocked in mine." Even as I said this, I realised how foolish it sounded; as if a young woman would be driving around Berlin on a November morning clad in a bikini.

She smiled and said: "I think the gentleman below was playing a trick on you. But do come in anyway."

In Kantstraße I passed the Theater des Westens, a privately funded operetta house built in a gloriously eclectic style in the 1890s. Its basement was occupied in the 1930s by Friedrich Hollaender's Tingel-Tangel-Theater, a Jewish cabaret club where Hollaender's satirical song "An allem sind die Juden schuld" was performed; and where Marlene Dietrich sang the hits from *The Blue Angel*. In 1935 the Tingel-Tangel-Theater was closed down and the Theater des Westens reopened as the "German Music Theatre of the National Socialist Cultural Community", under the auspices of Robert Ley's Strength Through Joy movement. I was once accosted outside the theatre shortly after the fall of the Berlin Wall by a couple of double-denim-clad East German men who stank of beer. They asked me where they could find the "Teilweiber". After a pause for thought I guessed they were in search of a transvestite club, although it was an odd way of putting it. "Teilweib" literally means "part-woman". "Weib" is an archaic, pejorative word for a woman (the English word "wife" comes from the same Old High German root), so the expression was both doubly quaint and doubly demeaning. In any case I was unable to help them, not knowing at the time where the Lützower Lampe, where David Bowie used to hang out with Romy Haag, was located.

Zoological Garden station had changed little since I first arrived from Hamburg in 1974 on a Deutsche Reichsbahn train of green and cream carriages and a maroon Mitropa restaurant car. The glass and steel cage built over the elevated platforms in the mid-1930s to transport visitors to the Olympic Games of 1936 had been renovated; and the shopping mall at ground level had been refurbished since the administration of the station (and of the S-Bahn network) had been taken over from the East German Reichsbahn by the West Berlin public transit system in 1984, and by Deutsche Bahn ten years later. The urinous stone cladding on the walls and pillars of the mezzanine concourse still evoked the atmosphere of the station in the early 1980s, when it was administered by the Reichsbahn. The policy of neglect perpetrated by the East German network allowed the station to become a haven for rent boys, drug dealers and black marketeers – students from Cuba and Nicaragua who would come over for the day from Friedrichstraße. I remember once sitting in an alcove, perusing a copy of *The Sunday Times* for the latest football results from the

English leagues, and noticing a young Turkish lad with a mop of thick curly hair spreading his legs in a lascivious manner on the bench opposite mine.

The rent boys in tight white jeans and figure-hugging tops still haunt Zoo Station, as do the alcoholics and drug addicts, but the lines of skinny teenage girls in denim shorts that used to stand outside the rear entrance of the station have gone. I first saw the film *Christiane F – Wir Kinder vom Bahnhof Zoo* in Madrid, in the company of a tiny, stoned *madrileña* who had befriended me in one of the bars on the Plaza Dos de Mayo where one went to buy *chocolate*, a euphemism for marijuana. She later sent me 45s of her favourite New Romantic bands, whose titles she helpfully translated into English (*Maniobras Orquestrales en la Oscuridad*, for example, turned out to be Orchestral Manoeuvres in the Dark) and wrote me long love letters in Spanish about white knights on chargers rescuing damsels in distress. The Sound discotheque, where much of the drug-dealing action of *Christiane F* takes place, was in a side street close to the Sylter Hof. I remember going there some time in the mid-1980s and feeling disappointed that it was a rather ordinary club for suburban heavy metal fans. In fact there is a disclaimer at the end of the film making it clear that Sound was in no way associated with the "fictional" events portrayed in the film.

At around the same time I used to go jogging in the Tiergarten, running along the banks of the Spree, around the back of the Reichstag and then southwards, along a track which hugged the Wall, to Potsdamer Platz, where I would scramble up the steps of the viewing platform and survey the wide swathe of no-man's-land separating East and West Berlin. Once the busiest traffic junction in Europe, Potsdamer Platz was blasted to pieces in the war and then cut in two by the Wall. Streets still converged there, like the broken spokes of a wheel that has lost its hub. The only buildings that remained were the Weinhaus Huth and the Hotel Esplanade, both as isolated as the Königsberger Dom in post-war Kaliningrad. Below the viewing platform were a few stunted trees, some white railings and a row of kiosks that sold cigarettes and souvenirs to tourists. The entrances to Potsdamer Platz underground station were bricked up, tramlines broken off where they reached the Wall.

The death strip was a broad expanse, several hundred metres wide, of worn grass; green in summer, brown in winter. You could recognise the outlines of pre-war streets and squares – the ghost of a traffic island at the centre of Potsdamer Platz, the octagon of Leipziger Platz, the straight line of Voßstraße and narrower paths which once ran through the gardens of Hitler's New Reichs Chancellery. The visible details of the death strip were banal: lampposts, duckboards, tank traps like rows of white knucklebones, metal plates in the ground that concealed the apparatus of surveillance. In the mid-1980s the East Berlin border police erected two watchtowers and a new inner wall painted with white rectangles so that any figure or shadow would be immediately visible. On the far side of the inner wall ran Otto-Grotewohl-Straße, formerly Wilhelmstraße. Most of the former Prussian and Nazi ministries – the Foreign Office, the Reichs Chancellery and the Palace of the Reichs President, for example – had been destroyed in the war. But some had survived: Göring's Air Ministry was now the Socialist "House of Ministries"; Goebbels' Ministry for Public Enlightenment and Propaganda now housed the Volksrat of the German Democratic Republic; and the palace of the Kaiser's and subsequently Führer's Representative, once occupied by Rudolf Hess and Martin Bormann, was now the head-quarters of Margot Honecker's Ministry for Public Education. Below the viewing platform on the western side of the outer wall a Baader-Meinhof supporter had daubed the slogan "Es herrscht Terror in Deutschland". The real terror, however, lay in the view over the death strip – over the tripwires and dog runs and the tumulus of rubble above Hitler's bunker – towards the tower blocks of Leipziger Straße, which seemed as far away as Warsaw or Minsk. This was a panorama of (what was then, in the 1980s) evolving, unfinished German history; of Socialist totalitarianism built over the ruins of National Socialist tyranny.

The walls and watchtowers have long since gone. Germany is no longer ruled by terror. The gardens of Prussian palaces and chancelleries obliterated by the death strip have been given new life as the Ministry Gardens, an enclave of cutting-edge contemporary offices (models of sustainability built from slate panels and Nordic wood) that house the representations of seven of the federal states of reunified Germany. The northern section of the death strip has been overlaid by Peter Eisenman's Memorial for the Murdered Jews of Europe, 2,711 steles of grey concrete which undulate over the site of what was once Goebbels' Berlin residence. Weary tourists eat sandwiches or smoke cigarettes on the outer blocks. The inner blocks provide a playground for children who leap across the tops of the pillars, screaming with delight as they play hide-and-seek with their disoriented parents.

In the early 1920s, Mies van der Rohe created photomontages of glass skyscrapers that were intended to be built above Friedrichstraße. Those projects prefigure the glittering, sharp-edged towers that now rise above Potsdamer Platz in a post-modern panegyric to corporate globalisation – to Sony, Sky, Disney, Daimler-Benz, Deutsche Bahn, Marriott, Hyatt, Starbucks and McDonald's. I wondered what had happened to the Hotel Esplanade, one of the two isolated buildings which stood by the Berlin Wall for the duration of the Cold War. The *Belle Epoque* establishment patronised by Kaiser Wilhelm II was destroyed in the war, but its Kaisersaal and Palm Court were restored in the 1950s and became a venue for the socialites and black marketeers who frequented Potsdamer Platz before the Berlin Wall was erected. When Berlin was divided, the hotel was cut adrift from the city centre. Film directors found its isolation alluring: Bob Fosse and Liza Minnelli transformed it into the Kit Kat Klub of Weimar Berlin. Wim Wenders put Nick Cave and the Bad Seeds on the stage of the Kaisersaal for a cameo appearance in *Wings of Desire*, while fallen angel Bruno Ganz, shorn of his ponytail and creepy smile, discovers true love and the meaning of life (desire) with a French trapeze artist in the bar next door. The Hotel Esplanade I remembered from the 1980s had disappeared, its site obliterated by the towers of Deutsche Bahn and the Sony Center.

I recalled meeting a friend for a drink in the Esplanade some time in the late 1980s. We spent most of our time there arguing about whether the music playing from the loudspeakers around the mock-decadent Kaisersaal was Chopin or Liszt. I can't remember who was right. Afterwards we walked along the sandy path that followed the course of the Berlin Wall as it curved east towards the burned-out shell of the Martin-Gropius-Bau. The only other surviving building was the Weinhaus Huth, at the time either social housing or a squat. Its blackened walls were daubed with graffiti, rainbow flags and the black and red stars of anarchy and revolution. *Autonomen* trailing Alsatian dogs would charge tourists a handful of deutschmarks to have their photographs taken by the Wall. The elevated track of the Magnetbahn, an experimental monorail, ran on stilts over the rubble of the demolished Potsdamer Station. We crossed the site of Haus Vaterland, Kempinski's pleasure dome of the 1930s. In this "department store of restaurants" foreign tourists and visitors from the provinces could while away the afternoon in the Turkish Café, the Japanese Tea Room and the Wiener Café Grinzing, or eat pastries in the Hungarian Czardas. They could drink in a Wild West saloon, a Spanish *bodega* or a Löwenbräu beer hall. Afterwards they could dine in an Italian *osteria* or a rolling ship's galley; or they could eat turnips from Brandenburg in the Teltower Rübchen. The *pièce de résistance* was the Rhine Wine Terrace, where diners could tuck into *Sauerbraten* washed down with *Kölsch* to the accompaniment of a simulated thunderstorm over a panorama of the Rhine valley, complete with paddle steamers, ruined castles and the Loreley cliffs.

We turned right down Köthener Straße, another dead-end street where only two buildings survived the war: one a former showroom of the Buderus boilermaking company; the other the Meistersaal, a neoclassical concert hall from the late Wilhelmine era. During the 1960s and 1970s the Meistersaal's isolation made it an ideal location for a recording studio. In Hansa by the Wall Studio 2, David Bowie recorded the art-rock album *"Heroes"*. Harsh and histrionic, romantic and fragile, *"Heroes"* celebrates the bohemian West Berlin of the 1970s. In the following decade Bowie sold his soul to EMI for twenty million dollars. Now Potsdamer Platz has sold its soul to Sony.

I drove west along Heerstraße, the former military highway that during the Cold War became one of the four transit routes that connected West Berlin to West Germany. I turned off at Raußendorffplatz, by a bronze statue of a *Wrestler* cast by Hugo Lederer, sculptor of the colossal Bismarck Memorial in Hamburg. At the far end of Preußenallee stood *Der Sieger*, another heroic bronze statue from the first, Wilhelmine, decade of the twentieth century. Turning left by the *Victor* I followed Olympische Straße, crossed Olympische Brücke and parked in Olympischer Platz. At the head of the square was the Olympic Gate, the five rings of the movement slung between a pair of tall, slender stone pylons that counterpoised the horizontal sweep of the Olympic Stadium seventy metres further up the slope. The Bavarian Tower on the left was decorated with its original 1936 clock: the Prussian Tower on the right was once adorned with a sun wheel – a cross with curved hooks – but that was dismantled after the war. Inside the stadium grounds two symmetrical paths curved inside the perimeter fence, punctuated by *Siegerstelen*, stone pillars that represented each of the Olympic Games at which Germany had participated. Chiselled into the front of the steles were the names of every German gold medallist since 1896. Carved into the rear of the pillars were bas-reliefs illustrating the disciplines at which German athletes excelled; 348 extra names were added to the columns in 1998 when the German Olympic Committee decided to honour retrospectively those German medallists who had been victorious in the blue vest of the GDR.

Each path culminated in a pair of seven-metre-high statues cast in the porous white travertine stone beloved of early National Socialist sculptors (before the smoothness of bronze became a more appropriate expression of the purity of the Aryan body). Each of Karl Albiker's statues depicts a pair of naked athletes – robotic young relay runners or discus throwers – rapt in concentration as they prepare to unleash their power. At the far end of the stadium are another four faux-medieval towers, representing Swabia, Franconia, Saxony and Friesland, and two more statues, a pair of lumpy *Rosseführer* by Josef Wackerle cast in the same Graeco-Roman style as those of Albiker. The two *Horse Tamers,* muscular automatons with lobotomised expressions leading their ponderous steeds, were intended to symbolise the Führer Principle, the resolute leader guiding the docile mass of the people; but they look more like the robotic leading the idiotic.

The cumulative effect of all the pylons, steles and effigies that surround the Olympic Stadium was meant to forge a link between a glorified Graeco-Roman-Aryan past and an equally glorious German-Nordic-Aryan present – with Fritz Schilgen as the new Pheidippides, Schinkel's Altes Museum as the new Parthenon and the Third Reich as the new Sparta. Nowhere is this more explicit than in *Olympia: Festival of Nations,* the first of two films directed by Leni Riefenstahl that document the Summer Olympics of 1936. The opening credits of the film are "engraved" on a faux-marble, mock-classical frieze. Brooding skies reveal the ancient stones and heroic columns of the Parthenon. Marble figures of Greek victors dissolve into the bodies of German shot-putters and javelin-throwers. Myron's *Discobolus* metamorphoses into the German decathlete Erwin Huber, shot as a "living statue" in the same pose as Myron's Athenian athlete. The martial musical score becomes lighter and more playful as we encounter a trio of female German athletes, as naked as their ancient Greek prototypes, spinning hoops around their torsos and waving their arms at the sun. They dissolve into fire as the soundtrack becomes Wagnerian again; and out of the fire comes the German bearer of the Olympic flame, setting off from Mount Olympus and running a lap of the ancient Olympic Stadium before handing the torch to a relay of runners who cross seas and mountains through Bulgaria and Yugoslavia, follow the course of the Danube from Belgrade to Vienna, turn north via Prague and Dresden and finally arrive at the great new classical arena in Berlin.

German bells toll, German voices cheer as the flags of the Olympic nations are hoisted for the opening ceremony. A hundred thousand

German right arms shoot forth to hail the entry of the fifty-one competing teams, some of whom (Greece, Austria, Italy and France, for example)
return the outstretched Nazi salute as they march past the *Führerloge*.
Those that do are acclaimed with a roar of approval by the German spectators; those that don't are greeted with a ripple of polite applause. Leni
Riefenstahl's film cuts to the Brandenburg Gate where the penultimate
relay runner bears the Olympic Torch along Unter den Linden, decorated
for the occasion with eagles and swastikas on Doric columns. The runner hands the torch to Fritz Schilgen, a hurdler who had failed for the
third time in succession to qualify for the Olympic finals and who was
not a member of the NSDAP; but Riefenstahl deemed that his appearance and running style were easier on the eye than those of his more
successful colleagues. Schilgen ascends the Marathon Steps and ignites
the Olympic Tripod, which bursts into flame. Cannons fire, doves fly and
a choir dressed in Greek robes sings an Olympic Hymn dedicated to the
Führer by its composer Richard Strauss. There are dramatic shots of the
setting sun seen through the blaze of the Olympic Flame.

The sporting events begin the following day. A shapely Italian athlete
wins the women's 80 metre hurdles and executes a majestic Nazi salute
on the podium, providing Riefenstahl with a heaven-sent opportunity to
linger over the aesthetic appeal of Fascism. Hitler claps the fingers of his
right hand against the back of his left, which enables him to applaud and
salute simultaneously. In the final of the women's 4x100 metres relay the
German team is ten metres in the lead as it approaches the final hand-
over. Göring is pumping his huge arms up and down in support. Hitler is
gripping his knees with manic energy – and then the German women drop
the baton. The "English" team wins the men's 4x400 metres relay, one of
only four gold medals won by the decadent "old nation" of Great Britain.
The host nation, by contrast, wins thirty-three gold, thirty-one silver and
thirty-two bronze medals, although it should be noted that most of these
are won in disciplines such as shooting, fencing and weightlifting, or in
equestrian and gymnastic events, rather than in track and field athletics.
The men's high jump, long jump and most of the track events are won
by athletes of colour representing the USA, whom the stadium announc-
ers refer to unashamedly as "blacks". The start of the men's 800 metres,
for example, is announced as "Two blacks against the best of the white
races". Despite the "Negroes" running faster and jumping further than his
own Aryan athletes, Hitler enjoys himself so much that he declares that
the Olympic Games will be held every four years in Berlin – for ever.

On my visit storm clouds were brewing over the stadium, their grey-black luminosity intensifying the green of the Maifeld. Towering over the far end of the parade ground was the Langemarckhalle, a cavernous cenotaph commemorating the German dead of the First World War; specifically, the tens of thousands of young reservists killed during a suicidal attack on Allied lines in Flanders in November 1914. I took a lift to the top of its bell tower, from where there was a view into the amphitheatre now known as the Waldbühne. Constructed between 1934 and 1936 on the orders of Goebbels, the Dietrich-Eckart-Bühne (named after the "Poet of the Movement" and first publisher of the *Völkischer Beobachter*) was one of the largest *Thingstätten* built in Nazi Germany. Modelled on the ancient Greek theatre at Epidaurus (with a nod to the Hollywood Bowl, where concerts at the previous Olympic Games in 1932 had taken place), the amphitheatre could seat twenty-two thousand spectators in its open-air auditorium. The stage, a stepped stone terrace in front of a stone tower, was specially designed to perform the *Frankenburger Würfelspiel*, the dramatic staple of the National Socialist *Thing* movement.

Restored after the war, the denazified Waldbühne hosted open-air concerts and boxing matches. The venue closed for seven years in 1965 after fans of the Rolling Stones, angered by the brevity of the band's performance, clashed with police and caused four hundred thousand deutschmarks' worth of damage to the rows of wooden seating in the auditorium. They also smashed up the S-Bahn carriages waiting for them at the Olympic Stadium railway station. As the rolling stock of the S-Bahn belonged at the time to East Berlin, the authorities in the GDR took a dim view of this outburst of decadent Western rowdiness and used the incident as an excuse to clamp down on "beat" music and the youth subcultures that accompanied it. Walter Ulbricht, General Secretary of the SED, was moved to pronounce: "Do we really have to copy all the rubbish that comes from the West? I think, comrades, that we should put an end to the monotony of all this 'yeah, yeah, yeah' or whatever it is called."

The entrance to the Waldbühne is flanked by two blocks of white travertine stone with high reliefs sculpted by Adolf Wamper. The porous stone has not worn well, but the figures are still recognisable – powerful and vulnerable in their nakedness. On the left-hand wall two athlete-warriors brandish the Olympic Torch and one of the short, thick, square-bladed swords common in early National Socialist sculpture; on the right-hand wall two seductive muses, daughters of Franz von Stuck's *femmes fatales*, play sweet music on a lyre and proffer a sprig of oak leaves (and the promise of sexual favours, perhaps) to the two champions opposite.

I followed Friedrich-Friesen-Allee north-east, past hockey pitches, running tracks and the training grounds of Hertha BSC football club, until I reached the grounds of the former German Sports Forum, founded in the 1920s as the headquarters of the German Academy of Physical Education. At its centre is the Jahnplatz, an open space flanked by a Swimming Hall and a Great Gymnastics Hall. Between them is a T-shaped pool surrounded by bronze sculptures from the Third Reich: a bull and cow by Adolf Strübe, representing the strength and fertility of young German athletes; and an insolent *Reclining Athlete* by Georg Kolbe, which was regularly heaved into the swimming pool by British soldiers during parties at the High Command – and needed a crane to be hauled out again the following day. The eastern end of Jahnplatz is closed off by a tall stone colonnade that leads into the domed auditorium of the House of German Sport. The inscription across the architrave of the portico reads "Ewig mahnt von Anbeginn des Werden das heilige Wort Vollkommenheit" (which means something like "We are eternally reminded from the very beginning of our Being of the sacred word Perfection" – and probably sounds as pretentious in German as it does in English).

At the top of the monumental flight of steps from the lawns of the Jahnplatz to the colonnade is a pair of bronze statues by Arno Breker – *Zehnkämpfer* and *Siegerin*. The model for the female *Victor* was reportedly a nineteen-year-old athlete from Brandenburg named Erika Matthes who, in 1938, set a world record for the women's javelin with a throw of 47.80 metres at a meeting in Stuttgart. The record-breaking throw was never ratified: officially, because of a light following wind; unofficially, because "the truth was that her sexual status was disputed". There is no ambiguity about the gender of Breker's sculpture, which represents the victorious athlete in a comely, naturalistic manner. The smoothness of her pert breasts, muscular thighs and *mons veneris* is now covered by a patina of verdigris, but there is no question of Breker's *Siegerin* being anything other than female. By an odd coincidence the women's 800 metres final of the 2009 World Athletics Championships, held in the Olympic Stadium one week after my visit, was won by a South African athlete named Caster Semenya, who was widely perceived as potentially intersex, with levels of testosterone outside the regular female range, and who was subsequently required by the International Association of Athletics Federations to undergo a gender verification process.

Breker's *Decathlete* was modelled on Gustav Stührk, a young athlete from Lüneburg who had been studying at the German Academy of Physical Education. Breker was impressed by the young decathlete's ideal physique (1.82 metres in height and 80 kilograms in weight) and offered him five marks a day to model. On the first day of their collaboration the twenty-one-year-old stood naked for nine hours, in temperature of fourteen degrees centigrade, while the sculptor worked. His chilly ordeal was duly rewarded, as Breker's finished statue was awarded a silver medal in the Olympic competition for sculpture. A larger version was cast in bronze to stand on a plinth above the steps of the House of German Sport, looking down over Jahnplatz and the German Sports Forum. Rumour has it that the statue's genitals were reduced in size to avoid offending the Führer, who was famously sensitive on this issue, and who might otherwise have thought that the sculptor's admiration for his model had gone beyond aesthetic considerations. Breker and Stührk did indeed forge a friendship that survived the war. Meeting again in Donauwörth in 1946 Breker, who had got off as a *Mitläufer* at his denazification process, and Stührk, who although a member of the SS had served only six months in prison, resumed their relationship, the athlete living in the sculptor's attic, just as he had done before the war, and continuing to model for Breker – although the ensuing sculptures bore titles such as *Saint Sebastian* rather than *Victor, Leader* or *Harbinger*.

The sky turned to granite and rain strafed the streets of Charlottenburg's Neu-Westend. I drove back to Steubenplatz, where I sheltered in a Viennese café. After the deluge I headed north-west along Reichs Straße towards the centre of Spandau, where I turned north by the Wilhelmine-Baroque Rathaus. I followed Schönwalder Allee, a cobbled avenue that wound into the depths of Spandau Forest. It emerged from the trees by a narrow bridge that humpbacked over the Havelkanal – once the border between West Berlin and East Germany. The strip of marshland between the two arms of the canal would have been a no-go area separating the inner and outer fences of the "anti-fascist protection barrier". It has now been reclaimed by reeds and rushes: there is no longer any sign of the concrete tracks that would once have run along its centre. I turned down a single-track road that led to an area known as the Eiskeller, once an exclave of West Berlin that had been cut adrift on East German territory.

The name "Eiskeller" had nothing to do with the Cold War: this area of open heath on the western edge of Berlin was the coldest part of the city, and there was once an icehouse in one of its fields. The exclave of fifty-one hectares contained a handful of farming families who were connected to West Berlin by the narrow road along which I was driving, which in the 1960s was little more than a sandy track eight hundred metres long and four metres wide – nominally under the jurisdiction of the British Army. On Monday, 14 August 1961, the day after the city was divided, the twelve-year-old son of one of the farmers was arrested by an East German border patrol for allegedly straying out of the British sector (or off the British road) into the Soviet Zone. The British military authorities despatched thirty soldiers to the exclave, and henceforth Erwin Schabe was escorted to and from his school in Spandau by armoured car. The incident attracted notoriety as an example of the absurdity of the Berlin Wall. A propaganda magazine distributed in 1961 by the British Central Office of Information, for example, stated that "Erwin stayed home from school in fear". It later transpired that the boy had bunked off school that day in order to play, as usual, in the woods, not realising they were now out of bounds.

In the 1970s and 1980s those slivers of land that had ended up on the wrong side of the fence were exchanged for each other, in order to round off the border in a more practical manner. There was an area of empty heath, for example, belonging to the GDR, which curled around the inside of the hook of land formed by the Eiskeller and the road connecting it to West Berlin. At first a simple wire fence was erected along the northern edge of the road to the Eiskeller, stopping its inhabitants from straying into the Soviet Zone and preventing East Germans from straying into the capitalist Eiskeller. When the frontier was reinforced, the East German authorities saw no advantage in building a lengthy, serpentine section of walls and fences around the strategically worthless area of open fields inside the hook of West Berlin land; so the Berlin Wall was built straight across the southern opening to this hook of moorland – thus leaving several hectares of land that belonged legally to the GDR open to West Berlin. I remember walking through Spandau Forest in the 1980s, following the border, and arriving at a clearing where the Berlin Wall ran off to the west. Wooden signs announcing "You are now leaving the British Sector" marked the actual border; but you were free to cross the frontier and walk around a parcel of open heath, surrounded by watchtowers, that belonged to the Soviet Zone.

The narrow road through the fields of the Eiskeller doglegged to the south and then ran in a semicircle between West Berlin farmhouses and woods that belonged to East Germany, but had never been walled in. The road forked into two by a riding school and finally petered out near a small community of New Age hippies who had constructed a camp from some decommissioned panels of prefabricated concrete, and who made a living from selling half-litres of beer at one euro each to the few sightseers who ventured this far out to the city's margin. I parked the car and walked across a strip of sandy grassland that curved away into the distance. I sensed that I was close to the route of the Berlin Wall, but there was no longer any indication of where it might have been. It was extraordinary how such a complex and extensive structure had been so completely erased: presumably each small community along its path had diligently removed every man-made reminder of its existence – and nature had done the rest. In any case, the circular geography of the Eiskeller was so disorientating that I had lost all sense of direction and would not have known on which side I was, even if I had discovered traces of the border.

I got back in the car and drove in first gear along a rutted track that belonged to the Forestry Commission. After several hundred metres I turned right and found myself in the back streets of a dusty villa colony whose prim, gentle aura suggested I was in the former east. I retraced my route, stopping to ask a family from the Saarland, who were on a country stroll, whether they knew where the former border lay. They told me they were visiting their daughter, who was studying at the Free University in Berlin, and had no idea where the Berlin Wall used to be. On a notice-board outside the riding school I discovered a map that had been pinned up as part of a protest by the tiny community of the Eiskeller against a proposal by the Berlin Senate to build a new motorway through the area. I traced my route on the map and worked out I had parked the car in no-man's-land and had then driven south towards Falkenhagen, along what would once have been the control strip on the East German side of the border.

I drove south-west through the garden suburbs of Dahlem and Zehlendorf, passing Leni Riefenstahl's villa, Arno Breker's atelier and an idyllic estate of whitewashed cottages built in the 1930s as a *Kameradschaftssiedlung* for SS officers and their families. I turned off Koenigsallee and parked in the square Am Bahnhof Grunewald, where I bought a sandwich and a coffee from the café in the ornate little S-Bahn station. I sat on the terrace outside with all the "yummy mummies" (or whatever the German equivalent is) and admired the opulent, eclectic mansions of Berlin's *haute bourgeoisie*. The oppressive atmosphere of the morning had cleared and the afternoon sun beat down from a brilliant azure sky onto the balconies, gardens and roof terraces of Grunewald.

To the left of the station entrance a ramp of cobblestones sloped up towards a former goods yard of the pre-war Reichsbahn. A concrete wall, hollowed out in places with the inverted shapes of human forms, had been erected as a memorial to the fifty thousand Jews of Berlin deported from Grunewald S-Bahn station. Some preliminary deportations had already taken place from the Lehrter Bahnhof in central Berlin, but the Gestapo decided to carry out mass deportations from a more discreet location. Most of the wealthy, cultured Jewish families of Grunewald had emigrated in 1933, and the remaining German residents of Grunewald would have feigned not to notice the columns of poorer Jews being marched through their suburb on their way to the station. The site of Gleis 17 (Platform 17) lay neglected for decades after the Holocaust. A simple stone plaque in memory of the deportees was repeatedly stolen. In 1993 the management of the reunified Deutsche Bahn decided to use the rotting freight ramps as a facility for cleaning their high-speed trains. This finally pricked the conscience of the city authorities into commemorating their former Jewish community in a more appropriate manner; and in 1998 a monument was unveiled in the form of a series of metal gratings that run around the siding in between the two platforms from where Jews were loaded onto the transports. Each rust-encrusted grating is stamped with the date and destination of each transport, and with the approximate number of deportees on each train. The first departed on 18 October 1941, carrying one hundred Jews to the ghetto in Łódź. For the next twelve months regular transports carried around one hundred Jews at a time to ghettoes in Łódź, Chełmno and Riga, probably in standard railway carriages in order to disguise the deportations. From spring 1942 onwards you notice that more and more transports were destined for Theresienstadt; and in December 1942 there was a dramatic increase from one hundred to one thousand deportees at a time, heading directly to Auschwitz – presumably in cattle trucks. You notice from the dates that everyone involved – perpetrators, intermediaries and victims – took the weekends off. Young sycamore trees now grow along the siding of Gleis 17, forming a canopy of shade beneath the glare of sun on stone and metal. A red and yellow S-Bahn train rattles past on the parallel main line.

From Spanische Allee I crossed a bridge onto the island of Wannsee and turned into the avenue that runs along the shore of Großer Wannsee. No. 56–58 is a palatial mansion built in 1914 with a classically columned entrance porch reached via a circular driveway. There are cherubs on the cornices, statuary in the gardens and a beautiful view of yachts sailing on Großer Wannsee and thousands of sunbathers disporting themselves in the *Strandbäder* on the opposite shore of the bay. Marble pillars support the conference room where Reinhard Heydrich, head of the Reich Main Security Office (RSHA), chaired a lunchtime meeting on 20 January 1942. Heydrich spoke for one hour, addressing the fifteen assembled representatives of various government agencies responsible for the deportation of Jews from the German Reich. He updated them on the current position of the expulsions; reported on the number of Jews remaining in other European countries; and gave a lengthy reinterpretation of the Nuremberg Race Laws, a document that detailed the fine distinctions between Jews, Aryans and people of "mixed blood", both "first degree" and "second degree". During the course of his presentation the head of the RSHA advocated that "under proper guidance, in the course of the final solution the Jews are to be allocated for appropriate labour in the east. Able-bodied Jews, separated according to sex, will be taken in large work columns to these areas for work on roads, in the course of which action doubtless a large portion will be eliminated by natural causes. The possible final remnant will, since it will undoubtedly consist of the most resistant portion, have to be treated accordingly because it is the product of natural selection and would, if released, act as the seed of a new Jewish revival." After Heydrich's presentation the delegates discussed the issues and then, over glasses of cognac, conversed among themselves "off the record". During these conversations official terms such as "deportation" and "evacuation" were reportedly replaced by words such as "liquidation" and "extermination"; none of the delegates had misunderstood the purpose of the meeting. Eichmann's minutes of the conference summarised the content of these informal discussions thus: "In conclusion the different types of possible solutions were discussed."

In 1992 the Villa Marlier was reopened as a Holocaust Memorial. After an hour perusing the consequences of the 1942 meeting, I left the building with a sickening feeling. I walked out onto the lawn and took a deep breath by the shore of the lake. I got into the car and drove further around

Wannsee until I found a beach opposite the Pfaueninsel, where I stripped off and plunged into the Havel, as if to cleanse myself from the horrors on show in the exhibition. Then I remembered that Peacock Island was where Goebbels held a spectacular "Italian Night" to celebrate the grand finale of the Olympic Games of 1936. Between two and three thousand guests – kings, crown princes, ambassadors, athletes and film stars – were greeted by aisles of young women, dressed in white silk pageboy costumes and waving white wands as they escorted the celebrities across a pontoon bridge specially installed by pioneers from the Wehrmacht. Girls from the School of Physical Culture brandishing blazing torches performed a ballet below thousands of fairy lights shaped like butterflies strung from the branches of ancient oaks. Champagne flowed like water to lubricate the white-suited gentlemen and their elegantly attired wives or mistresses. The American ambassador William E. Dodd was appalled by the fireworks that sounded like artillery fire and by the spectacle of inebriated SS officers throwing up in the bushes. It is not recorded whether Heydrich was at the party.

As I lay on the sand, I recalled a summer's evening in the late 1980s when I jogged around the island of Wannsee. I remembered the low, bright sun gilding the Arcadian follies in Schlosspark Glienicke; remembered the view over Glienicker Lake to the merlons and turrets of a nineteenth-century steam-generating hall, extravagantly crenellated like a crusaders' castle, that lay at the foot of Babelsberg Park on the Potsdam side of the channel; remembered the watchtowers in the water, the wire fence across the lake and the wall disappearing into a wood, surrounding an East German hamlet of decaying Prussian villas marooned on the wrong side of Griebnitzsee – an exclave of the east in West Berlin, a mirror image of the Eiskeller. I recalled the Glienicker Brücke, a girder bridge over the Havel that marked the boundary between Potsdam and Berlin. The western and eastern halves of the bridge were (and still are) painted in different shades of green. The western half belonged to East Germany and had been officially designated in 1949 "Brücke der Einheit" (Bridge of Unity). Three years later the bridge was closed to civilians, manned by Russian soldiers and fenced off by red and white barriers. Its status as a symbol of division was reinforced by three spy swaps: the captured American pilot Francis Gary Powers was released in 1962 in exchange for the Soviet spy Colonel Rudolf Ivanovich Abel; twenty-three American agents held in Poland and East Germany were swapped in 1985 for one Polish and three Soviet agents arrested in the West; and on a freezing morning in February

1986, the Jewish-Russian human rights activist Anatoly Scharansky was exchanged, together with three Western agents, for five Communist spies.

I set off back towards the centre of Berlin. It was the late afternoon rush hour and vehicles were pushing in and cutting each other up along the dual carriageway that ran for mile after mile through the centres of Zehlendorf and Steglitz. Schlossstraße of Steglitz segued into Rheinstraße of Friedenau, which continued into Hauptstraße of Schöneberg, each high street an endless succession of supermarkets, *Asia-Imbiss* bars, Greek restaurants, tyre fitters, internet cafés and Turkish grocers. "Dum Dum Boys" Iggy Pop and David Bowie lived between 1976 and 1979 above a motor-spares shop at 155 Hauptstraße, while they recorded *Lust for Life* and *"Heroes"* at Hansa Studio by the Wall. Hauptstraße merged in turn with Potsdamer Straße, which added sex emporia and *Spielotheke* to the mix. I turned left at the Kulturforum and dipped into the Tiergartentunnel, emerging at the new Hauptbahnhof where I turned right into Invalidenstraße and, two hundred metres into Berlin-Mitte (once East Berlin), checked into Gates Hotel.

Later that evening I found myself walking south along Chausseestraße, past a building site where the demolished Stadium of World Youth was being redeveloped as the headquarters of the Federal Intelligence Agency. Scores of cranes were silhouetted against a horizontal stripe of translucent gold sky that was about to be crushed by darkening cloud. A violent wind whipped up fallen leaves and yellow buds, throwing up tornadoes of sand and dust from the street. I ran for shelter in a tiny Mexican *cantina* and ordered a *Berliner Kindl*. After the thunderstorm I continued down Chausseestraße towards Oranienburger Tor. This was a radically different city from the one in which I had spent the morning and early afternoon. Leaving the leafy suburbs of Dahlem and Grunewald for the mean streets of Berlin-Mitte was like being transported from Paris to Warsaw, or from Hollywood to Detroit. Instead of sleek buses, Tatra tramcars built in the 1980s rattled along the streets. The paving stones were cracked or holed. There were few trees and fewer gardens or parks. The *Kiez* was working-class, punk, DIY. The small number of people on the streets, returning home from work, wore plainer clothes and comported themselves in a more phlegmatic fashion than their western counterparts. East Berlin was muted and low-key; less self-conscious, less pretentious, less smug than the western half of the city.

I paused outside the Bertolt-Brecht-Haus, where a reading was taking place in the salon. Earnest literary types and ageing actors dressed in black filled the room. I sat at a table in a yard at the side of the museum which served as an alfresco restaurant. I was handed an incomprehensible Viennese menu offering *Erdäpfelsuppe* (potato soup), *Tafelspitz* (boiled beef in broth), *Paradeisersuppe* (tomato soup), *Wiener Backhend'l* (roast chicken), Schweinsstelze (pork knuckle), *Fleischlaberln* (meatballs), *Szegediner Gulasch* (sauerkraut goulash), *Surschnitzel* (pickled schnitzel), *Salzburger Beiried* (beef loin), *Wiener Schnitzel* (breaded veal), *Apfelkrapfen* (apple fritters), *Topfenpalatschinken* (sweet pancakes), *Salzburger Nockerln* (dumplings), *Kaiserschmarren* (pancakes) and some awful Austrian wine – Grüner Veltliner or Blauer Zweigelt. The menu explained that the cuisine reflected the tastes of Brecht and his wife Helene Weigel. (I had always assumed he was a laconic northerner, but apparently he came from Augsburg and adopted Austrian nationality in 1950.) Brecht and Weigel lived in the house in Chausseestraße from 1953 onwards, in order to be close to the Berliner Ensemble in the Deutsches Theater. I remember studying *Der Gute Mensch von Sezuan* for A levels, learning about *Verfremdungseffekte* (distancing effects) and dialectical materialism, but the play left me cold (as the *V-Effekte* were meant to, I suppose). For me, Brecht was the other half of Brecht/Weill. Too young for Lotte Lenya, I was introduced to Kurt Weill's songs through the modern, pop interpretations of Bryan Ferry ("September Song") and David Bowie ("Alabama Song" and fragments from *Baal*), before I discovered the divine Ute Lemper. I also remember attending a concert of Brecht/Weill songs performed by Marianne Faithfull in the Freie Volksbühne in Wilmersdorf in the 1990s. Although one should admire her courage in attempting this repertoire, in Berlin of all places, the 1960s icon was past her best. Her voice was all over the place (too slow, too deep) and failed to capture the spirit of the Weimar years. The booing grew louder: one man shouted "Singen können Sie auch nicht!" ("You can't sing either!") and stormed out in a huff.

Friday morning. Heavy cloud lay heaped over Berlin-Mitte, grey and full of bulges, troughs and protuberances; a reflection of sorts of the grey, lumpy cityscape below. I walked down Hessische Straße and Hannoversche Straße, between the university clinics below the Charité hospital. The pavements were unrepaired since the 1930s. Beggars lay in doorways along Friedrichstraße. The Weidendammer Brücke had been restored to its Wilhelmine glory, resplendent with wrought-iron Reich eagles and candelabra crowned by gilded suns. To the west, rhubarb-and-custard S-Bahn trains clattered over a girder bridge. To the east, the murky, green-brown Spree parted to either side of the domed Bode Museum.

Somewhere around here I once bought a novel entitled *Herbstball* by the Estonian writer Mati Unt, published by Aufbau-Verlag in 1983. Although I have never read it, I take it out of the bookcase every now and then and run my thumb over the thin paper dust jacket which illustrates a housing estate that could be anywhere in communist Europe, its inhabitants walking with heads sunk deep into their overcoats through a grey-green morning fog. It is the last remaining artefact I possess from the GDR: the twenty-mark note left to me after my ordeal in the Ore Mountains has disappeared, as has the East German flag I bought as a souvenir of my first visit to East Berlin, which I used for many years as a tablecloth. I looked in vain for the bookshop where I had purchased *Herbstball* twenty-three years earlier. As far as I could recall, it had been in the stretch of Friedrichstraße between the two theatres, the Admiralspalast and the Friedrichstadtpalast; but most of the old Prussian tenements with their old-fashioned, generically named shops have been demolished, replaced in the late 1980s by "posh *Plattenbau*" apartment buildings, or in the 1990s by post-modern retail blocks.

I entered Friedrichstraße station for nostalgic (or *Ostalgic*) reasons, in an attempt to relive the day trips I used to make to East Berlin in the 1980s. I remembered the sense of nervous anticipation as I sat on the wooden benches of the S-Bahn train as it crossed the border over the Humboldthafen, slowed and tilted as it negotiated the curve through the no-man's-land between the Charité and the Spree, ran behind the blank walls of some housing blocks, crossed the river and came to a halt below the steel and glass arch of the elevated station. I recalled the wall which separated the platform for western passengers, changing trains without entering East Germany, from the platform for eastern passengers travelling from East Berlin to East Germany; remembered the silent guards who stood, legs braced, staring at you with expressionless faces; the exit marked "Einreise in die DDR" which divided into four queues (for West Berliners, West Germans, citizens of "other countries" and transit passengers). I recalled the smell of sweat and cigarette smoke, the tense excitement as I awaited my turn at the checkpoint; the pale grey-green short-sleeved shirt of the official behind the glass screen; the angled mirror by means of which he or she could inspect the back of your head; the methodical stare that scrutinised every feature of your face from top left to bottom right; the flick through your passport and the metallic thud of the stamp; the slit through which you handed over five deutschmarks for a day visa; the buzzer that opened a grey metal door through which you could pass, having successfully negotiated the first rite of your passage from west to east. You would then queue at a counter to exchange the mandatory twenty-five deutschmarks for twenty-five smaller, chalkier DDR-marks (in Socialist Realist style, rather than the High Renaissance design of West German banknotes), before proceeding down a subterranean corridor, tiled in the same urinous hue as the walls of Bahnhof Zoo, towards a concourse patrolled by customs officers, who would stop and search you for "fascist" literature or punk cassette tapes. The last aluminium door would open and you would find yourself deposited on a damp Georgenstraße, accosted by black-market profiteers attempting to persuade you to exchange even more of your valuable Western currency for worthless *Ostmarks*. Of course, none of this exists any longer. The underground labyrinth of passageways and holding pens has been replaced by a shopping mall; the station's façade has been retiled in its original maroon expressionist brickwork; and only the slightly higher levels of platforms 4 and 5 remind you this was once a railway station where you changed worlds, not just trains.

As I left the station it was beginning to drizzle. The mass of grey cloud had thickened and darkened and was about to rupture against the angular roofs of the hotels and department stores towering above Friedrichstraße. I was desperate to find an establishment where I could drink a cup of coffee and sit outside to smoke a cigarette without being drenched by the imminent downpour. I tried Starbucks, but the queue was too slow. Tchibo was empty, but I would have to stand at a table outside in the rain. I paused to drop a coin into the lap of a Romany woman begging in the colonnade in front of the Polnische Apotheke, and decided to walk down Dorotheenstraße. Halfway down this street of rebuilt *Gründerzeit* ministries I experienced a sense of *déjà vu*: this was the street I recalled walking down on one equally grey morning in the mid-1980s, shortly after purchasing my copy of *Herbstball*. If I remember rightly, the street was then named after Clara Zetkin, a class revolutionary of the late nineteenth century and co-founder of the German Communist Party, whose image was printed on the 10 DDR-Mark banknotes of the time. The Clara-Zetkin-Straße of the 1980s was a desolate, fractured row of blackened façades, untouched since the firestorms of the Second World War. Isolated buildings stood amid empty plots of brick-strewn wasteland. At the end of the street was the Berlin Wall; nothing spectacular, just the sort of wall on which kids would chalk goalposts and kick a ball against, as I did as a boy growing up in a terraced street in Leeds in the 1960s. I remember standing on the corner of Wilhelmstraße (at the time named Otto-Grotewohl-Straße), the last side street before the Wall, thinking how surreal this was. I was inside the looking-glass world, behind the tarnished glass of the mirror into which West Berliners would occasionally look, seeing only a dull, drab, anachronistic image of their own city. Travelling to East Berlin "just for one day" was like entering a fictional world, a dystopia somewhere between *Alice's Adventures in Wonderland* (East Berlin was a place of wonder, after all) and *1984* (and it may literally have been 1984, as far as I can recall). I remember noticing Western tourists standing on a viewing platform (presumably behind the Reichstag), observing me as if I were a real East Berliner, which made me feel even more fictional.

I turned left towards Unter den Linden and found the eastern branch of Café Einstein, where I could sit outside below a waterproof awning, drink a *latte macchiato* and smoke a cigarette. The rain soon lashed down, blurring the rigid outlines of the monolithic Russian Embassy on the opposite side of the street. Cars with their headlights on swerved from Glinkastraße into Unter den Linden, drenching businessmen's suits and secretaries' summer dresses as they ploughed into troughs of rainwater formed by the uneven camber of the streets. The gale tore buds from the lime trees in the central promenade, leaving soggy mounds of yellow mush that nylon-caped tourists ground into the spongy gravel of the pathways. Globules of rain dripped from the edge of the awnings onto those patrons of Café Einstein who remained outside, flooding ashtrays and soaking newspapers until even the most committed smokers preferred to retire into the interior of the café and suffer from nicotine withdrawal, rather than brave the elements outside.

An hour later the grey clouds of the morning had disappeared and Berlin-Mitte was roasting under a clear blue sky. I found some shade on the terrace of a Turkish fast-food joint in Wilhelmstraße, and ordered a lunch of spicy meatballs and boiled potatoes. The café was full of office workers from the surrounding ministries and tourist guides taking a break from their "Third Reich Tours". On the opposite side of the street was the Peking Duck, a Chinese restaurant on the site of Palais Borsig, a Wilhelmine palace built in the 1870s on the corner of Voßstraße and Wilhelmstraße, which was later integrated into Hitler's New Reichs Chancellery. Hitler spent most of his years as Chancellor in the offices of the Old Reichs Chancellery, the baroque former Palais Radziwill-Schulenburg which he had inherited from Hindenburg in 1933, and which he described as "rotten" or "run-down", often complaining about the state of the toilets. A modern extension to the Reichs Chancellery had been added between 1928 and 1930, but this was not to Hitler's taste either. He remarked that it "looked like a warehouse or a municipal fire station". He did nevertheless have a "Führer balcony" fitted to its façade in 1935.

Hitler craved a chancellery that would be many times larger than the existing one, a seat of power which would reflect his new status as "Führer of the Greater German Reich". His protégé Albert Speer duly completed the project assigned to him within twelve months, unveiling the New Reichs Chancellery in January 1939 in time for the Führer's New Year reception for the diplomatic corps. From where I sat at the crossroads of Wilhemstraße and Voßstraße, the view down the latter would have been filled by the pale yellow and grey stone façade of the New Reichs Chancellery. Hitler and Speer's architectural projects were progressing beyond the early National Socialist Graeco-Roman style exemplified by Paul Ludwig Troost's House of German Art in Munich: their new *pièce de résistance* was a distended amalgam of German Baroque and Prussian neoclassicism – megalomania embossed with the stamp of Knobelsdorff and Schinkel.

Equally monolithic was the Aviation Ministry on the other side of Leipziger Strasse, designed by Ernst Sagebiel for Göring and the Luftwaffe. A paradigm of early National Socialist architecture, its severe stone façades, heavy stone cornices and repetitive stone-framed windows exude power, permanence and a suggestion of brutality. In contrast to the New Reichs Chancellery, the Air Ministry remained undamaged during the war and was denazified with minimum fuss: the roc-sized *Reichsadler* in Göring's Hall of Honour was dismantled, and Arnold Waldschmidt's military frieze was replaced by a mural glorifying the new German Democratic Republic that had been declared on 7 October 1949 in the state room of the building now known as the House of Ministries. After several enforced revisions, the new mural was eventually installed inside the colonnade in 1952. Assembled from thousands of glazed Meissen porcelain tiles, Max Lingner's *March of Socialism in the German Democratic Republic* depicts cadres of the new socialist state engaged in a variety of healthy socialist activities. Young women in the blue shirts of Freie Deutsche Jugend clap their hands in the air as they march behind a quartet of musicians playing guitars and accordions. A trio of fresh-faced children sporting the blue neckerchief of the Ernst Thälmann Pioneers leads the parade. At the centre of the mural are three men, representing a worker, peasant and party official, who shake hands and smirk as they congratulate each other on the successful construction of a wall, the irony of which they are at this point in their history blissfully unaware. A blonde-haired beauty in an immaculate white frock and blue-and-white-checked pinafore tosses a huge wheatsheaf under her arm and flirts with a tractor driver. Construction workers lay railway lines; steelworkers forge cylinders in a blast furnace; architects and engineers pore over the blueprint of a new factory; and at the far end of the mural a joyful family (Mutti, Vati and a single flag-waving blond male child) make their way along a Stalinist boulevard towards a stadium of cheering crowds.

The next incarnation of the former Air Ministry was as the post-*Wende* headquarters of the Treuhandanstalt, whose function it was to dismantle and privatise the collective farms and state-run industrial concerns of the GDR, thus rendering unemployed the children of all the happy workers and peasants celebrating the *March of Socialism in the German Democratic Republic* in 1952. The building became a symbol for East Germans of the capitalist takeover of their country, as abhorrent as it had been in its previous incarnations as a centre of Nazi or SED bureaucracy. Detlev Rohwedder, head of the Treuhand organisation, was assassinated by left-wing terrorists in 1991, and the building was renamed Detlev-Rohwedder-Haus in his memory. In 1999 the offices were refurbished and have since served as the Federal Ministry of Finance.

I found myself on Mohrenstraße, skirting Gendarmenmarkt where the high domes of the French and German Cathedrals rise on either side of Schinkel's Konzerthaus. Like Königsplatz in Munich, Gendarmenmarkt was paved over by the National Socialists in an attempt to transform it into a parade ground. Gardens, fountains and a statue of Schiller were removed; the national poet was not restored to the square until 1988. After crossing Schleusenbrücke, I sat down for a coffee on the terrace of the White Cube, a temporary café and exhibition space on the corner of the former Schlossplatz (or Marx-Engels-Platz, depending on which era you choose to remember it by). The empty space on the island between the two arms of the Spree had been newly laid with turf rolls. The afternoon sun brightened the artificial greensward, on which tourists unpacked sandwiches or skimmed Frisbees to each other. Pleasure boats cruised the Spree between the Marstall and the Berliner Dom.

For me, however, this area of Berlin-Mitte will always be 1974, the year I first came to Berlin and spent a day in the eastern half of the city. The Palasthotel, the Ministry for Foreign Affairs, the Palace of the Republic and other buildings from that decade have long since gone; as has that peculiarly austere atmosphere – the pungent smell of two-stroke petrol hanging in the air, and the feeling of being watched, even though there was hardly anyone out on the streets. The six hundred bronze-tinted windows of the Palasthotel would have glittered in the sun on a day like this. Opened in 1979, it was home in East Berlin to Brezhnev and Mitterand. It was demolished in 2001 and replaced by an SAS-Radisson Hotel. The Ministry for Foreign Affairs of the German Democratic Republic overlooked Kupfergraben, the western channel of the Spree. Built in the mid-1960s, it was a long, tall, narrow office block clad in vertical aluminium strips like the World Trade Center in New York. Resting upon a glass-fronted lower storey, it resembled a central heating radiator. I remember driving along Karl-Liebknecht-Straße in the mid-1990s, on my first visit to East Berlin since the *Wende*, feeling vaguely disquieted that something was missing from the urban landscape. I stopped the car and inspected the map, as I was sure that this was the correct location of the ministry. It had already been demolished.

The most conspicuous absence from the East Berlin cityscape was the Palace of the Republic. Built in the 1970s, it resembled one of those cumbersome radios of the period that you could tune to "Hilversum", "Luxembourg" or "Warsaw". Framed in white marble, its long façade of bronze mirrored glass, embellished with the state emblem of crossed hammer and compasses, used to hover over Marx-Engels-Platz, as if resting on a set of rubber studs. It was a multi-functional building, more cultural than political. The Small Hall served as the Volkskammer (People's Chamber) of the GDR, but the parliament of East Germany was relatively insignificant, meeting only a few times a year to rubber-stamp policies decreed by the Central Committee of the SED on the other side of Kupfergraben. The hexagonal Great Hall functioned as an auditorium for state galas, party congresses and a host of artistic events: musicals, television shows, folkloric dancing, symphony concerts, a "Festival of Political Song" and "Rock for Peace" concerts; in 1980 Tangerine Dream was the first Western group to play here. Three years later Udo Lindenberg, a politically engaged West German singer with a voice like Alex Harvey's, disobeyed the instructions he had been given and performed "Sonderzug nach Pankow", a song satirising the East German leader Erich Honecker. There were also cafés, bars, restaurants, theatres, a bowling alley and a discotheque with hydraulic dance floors that could be raised or lowered to different heights – presumably not while the clientele was on the glass floor bopping to Boney M.

I recall walking up the steps from Marx-Engels-Platz into the foyer of the Palace of the Republic one afternoon in the 1970s. I remember the bold colours and rough textures of Socialist Realist paintings hanging on the walls, the "Glass Flower" sculpture in the centre of the hall and the thousands of lamps suspended from the ceiling. East Berliners recall the Palace of the Republic as a popular venue where musical performances and fashion shows were held and people came to meet. I remember it as eerily empty, like an out-of-season hotel lobby or the china and glass department of a retail store on a Monday morning. In 1993 it was decided to demolish the Palace of the Republic: partly because of contamination from the asbestos cement that had been used to cover the steel girders of the building's structure; and partly because there was a ground swell of opinion in favour of rebuilding the Prussian Royal Palace that originally stood on the site. The dismantling of the building commenced in January 2006 and took three years, longer than the one thousand days it had taken to build the structure in the first place.[12]

I walked through the Nikolaiviertel, the prefabricated "Altstadt" of Berlin; folksy, beer-and-sausages medievalism works in some places, but not in the centre of Berlin-Mitte. In Gruner Straße I waited at the lights for the jaunty green man of East German pedestrian crossings to appear. I crossed the street in the company of scores of shoppers clutching plastic bags (in West Berlin they use trolleys). Alexanderplatz was agreeably post-Socialist, a wide expanse of grey-brown granite surrounded by old-fashioned modernist department stores and high-rise office blocks once known as the House of the Teacher, the House of Statistics, the House of Travel and the House of Electrical Industry. I sat on the crowded terrace of the Kaffeehaus am Alex and ordered a strong, cheap coffee, which was served promptly and without that slightly patronising "I'm so cool with my tribal tattoos and perfect breasts" attitude you get from waitresses in West Berlin. A pile of sleeping punks lay flopped over each other beneath the World Clock, oblivious to the breakbeats of b-boys arching and spinning around them. Ageless women in summer dresses

---

12 The Prussian Royal Palace has since been rebuilt on the site of the Palace of the Republic. Seams of a more palatable prehistory have been unearthed in order to conceal layers of a more toxic recent history. Prussia is rising again in an attempt to consign the German Democratic Republic to oblivion.

that could have been bought before the *Wende* spread their haunches over the rim of the Fountain of People's Friendship. Peripatetic purveyors of *Bratwurst* circulated in front of the Alexanderhaus and the Berolinahaus, the two department stores designed by Peter Behrens in 1929. After the war the rebuilt Alexanderhaus functioned as an "HO-Kaufhaus" (HO as in *Handelsorganisation* or trade organisation, the Socialist euphemism for that bourgeois activity known elsewhere as shopping). During the 1950s it was emblazoned with slogans such as "THE FIVE-YEAR PLAN IS THE CORNERSTONE OF THE REBIRTH OF OUR FATHERLAND".

Revived by the coffee, I wandered around the edge of Alexanderplatz, watching the reflections of clouds floating across the windows of the House of the Teacher, above a long belly-band of glass mosaic illustrating the communal paradise of "Unser Leben" ("Our Life") in the GDR of the 1960s. This panorama of happy, healthy, young and attractive teachers, parents and children performing useful communal activities was painted in a style somewhere between Diego Rivera and Enid Blyton, symptomatic perhaps of the infantile state in which the men in suits in the Council of Ministers wished to preserve their less privileged comrades. I spent some time trying to decipher the letters pasted onto three hundred windows of an office block overlooking the north-eastern side of the square. They appeared to spell out texts from the expressionist novel *Berlin Alexanderplatz* by Alfred Döblin, chronicler of the city during the Weimar years. They ended with the lines "Auf Wiedersehen auf dem Alex. Hundekälte. Nächstes Jahr, 1929, wird's noch kälter." ("Goodbye from the Alex. Frozen stiff. Next year, 1929, will be even colder.")

A grey evening sky sank over Berlin-Mitte. I sat drinking a beer outside one of the bars of Hackesche Höfe, watching the clouds thicken and blacken until they were punctured by the spike of the television tower. A summer storm exploded over the city, releasing a barrage of rain that volleyed off the asphalt at the junction of Rosenthaler Straße and Oranienburger Straße. Raven-haired Amazons in micro-skirts and bustiers that accentuated their pneumatic cleavages scattered for shelter, tottering over potholes in thigh-length red plastic boots whose platform soles put to shame those worn by David Bowie on the rear sleeve of *Space Oddity*. When the rain stopped, I crossed Hackescher Markt and followed the elevated Stadtbahn until it crossed the Spree and disappeared inside the Bode Museum. Slime glistened on the waterline of the museum walls. In Monbijou Park there was an open-air dance floor where middle-aged couples jitterbugged to Glenn Miller beneath chains of fairy lights that sparkled with droplets of rain. Perhaps this was a distant folk memory of Schloss Monbijou, where Queen Sophie Dorothea entertained Czar Peter the Great with *soupées* and masked balls.

Beyond the Berliner Ensemble was a row of restaurants with terraces spilling out over Schiffbauerdamm. Ganymed was a posh French brasserie frequented in the 1950s by Brecht and Weill, and in the 1970s by Bowie, Iggy Pop and Tony Visconti when they were slumming it in the east. Brechts was a Viennese restaurant serving New Austrian Cuisine at post-modern prices. I decided to eat in Ständige Vertretung, a beer hall transposed from the Rhineland to the Spree, replete with nostalgia for the days when the movers and shakers were in Bonn; when West Germany had only an isolated "Permanent Representation" in East Berlin, because it did not recognise the GDR as a foreign country. The walls of the restaurant were cluttered with every kind of *Ostpolitik* kitsch. There were photographs of Beuys, Lindenberg, Grass, Adenauer, Brandt (with Günter Guillaume peering over his shoulder), Schmidt, Kohl, Genscher, Scheel, Ulbricht, Honecker, Gysi, Brezhnev, Gromyko and Gorbachev – drinking, smoking, dining, cuddling, kissing, backslapping in an orgy of false bonhomie. There were film posters from the 1970s: *Deutschland im Herbst* or *Die Verlorene Ehe von Katharina Blum*; slogans such as "Deutschmark, Deutschmark, über alles", "Lieber von Kohl was erben, als mit der SED sterben" and "Vom Wessi lernen heißt siegen lernen"; and brass plaques engraved with "Botschaft der Deutschen Demokratischen Republik" or "Abschnittsbevollmächtiger (Section Representative) der Deutschen Volkspolizei". All of it made me feel nostalgic for that peculiarly earnest, humourless, grey-green Germany of the 1970s – the Germany of Beckenbauer, Fassbinder and the Baader-Meinhof Group – that I had experienced as an exchange student living with the Steffner family in a dormer town outside Düsseldorf during the Munich Olympics of 1972, and as a gap-year intern working for a book distributor in Hamburg two years later.

After a *Flammkuchen* and a *Kölsch*, I left the Ständige Vertretung and continued along Schiffbauerdamm until the river wound north between the Paul-Löbe-Haus and the Marie-Elisabeth-Lüders-Haus, government offices resembling giant washing machines or fridge freezers. The bridge between them formed the "Sprung über die Spree", the leap over the Spree uniting East and West Berlin and counteracting the National Socialist vision of a North–South axis. If Honecker had had his way, I would now be standing in the death strip; if Hitler and Speer had had their way, I would now be standing beneath the largest building the world had ever seen. For a moment I tried to imagine the dome of Germania's Great Hall floodlit at night, reflected in the inky waters of the Spree. Then I remembered that the river would have been diverted underneath the monstrous building. I followed the blue glow of the Hauptbahnhof, which rose to the north like a huge rock stage. The promenade along Schiffbauerdamm petered out into Kapelle-Ufer and the path gave out altogether when the Spree reached the Humboldthafen. I found myself at midnight in a dark field of long grass and cow parsley. It was utterly silent and nothing was visible for hundreds of metres around me, except a canal and a railway line. Geographically, this was the dead centre of Berlin. I was in the middle of the former death strip between east and west, at the junction of the riverine divide between north and south. It felt like the middle of nowhere.[13]

In the morning I drove east through Prenzlauer Berg, passing DIY theatres and corner *Kneipen*, below red-brick churches, breweries and water towers in the neo-Gothic style of the *Gründerzeit*. I parked in Danziger Straße and walked through Ernst-Thälmann-Park, a landscaped housing development of prefabricated high-rise apartment blocks built in the mid-1980s over the toxic site of an old Prussian gasworks. The masterwork of this "unprecedented architectural and aesthetic ensemble" was a bronze bust unveiled in 1986 of Ernst Thälmann, chairman of the German Communist Party from 1925 to 1933. The colossal sculpture of Germany's heroic anti-fascist stands on a plinth of Ukrainian granite at the centre of an empty parade ground along Greifswalder Straße. His open, manly face gazes into a future of permanent revolution which had only three years left to run. A clenched fist rises somewhat awkwardly from a non-existent arm. A bronze flag embossed with the hammer and sickle of the Communist Party ripples in a sculpted breeze behind him.

---

13   Ten years later this empty, ghostly area has been built over by the offices of PricewaterhouseCoopers, the Federal Ministry of Education and Research, and a mysterious Futurium which describes itself as a "laboratory for shaping the future" – rather ironic in this city so obsessed with its past.

His bronze nose was allegedly heated in winter to prevent melting snow forming icicles of snot that would detract from his heroic manliness. Had he not been murdered by the Nazis in Buchenwald, Thälmann would probably have become the first leader of the GDR. After that regime had been discredited, the monument to its Stalinist father figure was scheduled for demolition; but groups of leftists and East Berlin *Ostalgists*, desperate to preserve one of the few remaining icons of their life under Socialism, opposed its removal. The monument survived in the end because it was too heavy to demolish and too costly to dismantle. So Thälmann remains in this empty, rainswept plaza, an abandoned symbol of the strength and hope of Communism. The black bronze of the bust and flag is now soiled with a patina of verdigris and the granite plinth smeared with graffiti – crew tags and spray-painted flowers, butterflies and ejaculating penises – and one pitiful message: "Patrick, mein Sohn, lieb' Dich über alle. Nie wieder ohne Dich?" ("Patrick, my son, love you more than anything. Never again without you?")

Karl-Marx-Allee today has an air of abandonment. You can sit among the flowerbeds and read stone tablets on the walls of each apartment block which commemorate the "Stalin prizewinners" who constructed the boulevard (known until 1961 as Stalinallee), or admire the 1950s-style italic neon signs that advertise *Blumen, Strümpfe, Fleischwaren* or *Damen-Moden* above the shops at street level. But few people come here to shop, since Karl-Marx-Allee is a protected historical landmark that prohibits global retail brands from moving in and installing their logos. In any case there are no parking spaces, given that Stalinallee was built by a regime that regarded the automobile as a capitalist extravagance. You suspect that most of the apartments are inhabited by elderly residents who have lived here since the 1950s, unwilling to swap what was once a prestigious address for a more modern apartment.

I went for a coffee in Café Sybille, a former milk bar on Block C-South that has been restored to its 1950s Socialist splendour, furnished with simple wooden tables and chairs and decorated with wallpaper patterned with tipsy cocktail glasses and dancing ice-cream cornets. Glass cabinets around the edge of the café displayed artefacts from the early years of the GDR: coins, medals, propaganda posters from the National Reconstruction Programme of 1952, Stern transistor radios, Rembrandt television sets, Erika typewriters, Melamine dinner services, Bakelite hair dryers, tulip lamps, cocktail chairs and kidney-shaped Formica tables. There were booklets of unfolding postcards whose unnaturally red toning intensified the alien Russian idiom of Stalinallee; a calendar for the year 1962 that was withdrawn from sale because Stalinallee had been renamed; and, in pride of place, Uncle Joe's bronze ear. (The rest of his statue was melted down and recycled as animal sculptures in a zoo.)

Below the colonnade next to the café was the Karl Marx Buchhandlung. Once known as the "Devisenabwurfstelle", the state-run bookshop made a healthy profit for thirty years as the place where day-trip visitors from the west could use up what remained of the twenty-five East German marks they were obliged to purchase on arrival in East Berlin. It was now empty, having been forced to close the previous year due to post-*Wende* rent increases and the stagnation of Karl-Marx-Allee as a retail destination. All that remained was the green neon lettering above the shop front. I was reminded of the closing scene of the film *The Lives of Others*, in which the discredited Stasi officer Captain Wiesler recognises a novel in the bookshop window written by the author on whom he had been assigned to spy – and whom he ends up protecting. Wiesler enters the shop, opens a copy of the book and discovers that it has been dedicated to him – "to HGW XX/7, in gratitude". "Es ist für mich," he tells the disbelieving bookseller.

It occurred to me that I could go and see whether I had my own Stasi file, as the former headquarters of the State Security Service of the German Democratic Republic lay just a couple of miles further down Frankfurter Allee. I had no idea whether I had a file or not, but the possibility suddenly intrigued me. During the 1980s I had made several day trips to East Berlin and, when driving from West Germany to West Berlin, had occasionally strayed from the official transit routes in order to visit Magdeburg, Eisenach or Dresden. I'd been stopped and fined for speeding several times on the East German autobahn, had received a parking ticket in Wittenberg and had a nighttime encounter in a wood near Weimar with a couple of teenage motorcyclists who may possibly have been "unofficial collaborators" of the state security apparatus. On the other hand, I'd never been approached by spooks from either side of the ideological divide, which was slightly surprising as my job as a freelance European sales agent gave me licence to travel legitimately throughout Eastern Europe.

I drove through Frankfurter Tor and continued east towards Lichtenberg until I reached the fourteen-storey tower block once occupied by the General Reconnaissance Administration (the Foreign Intelligence Section) of the Ministry for State Security. I turned left into Ruschestraße and then right, below an arch formed by a bridge of office blocks disguised to resemble residential housing units. Driving into the courtyard at the centre of Stasi-Zentrale was like entering a time warp. The dilapidated administrative blocks were covered with layers of grime that had accumulated since they were thrown up in the early 1950s. A string of elderly men were hanging around the edges of the yard, smoking cigarettes and scrutinising everyone who arrived; former Stasi officers or "unofficial collaborators" waiting to see if anyone would turn up who might incriminate them. Building 1 was the central office from where Erich Mielke ran a network of agents and informers whose numbers had reached 270,000 by the 1980s. It was now an unofficial museum, run by an Anti-Stalinist Action Group of former dissidents, and was under threat from the federal government who wished to "sanitise" the site and turn it into a national "heritage" centre that would commemorate the victims of the Ministry for State Security.

I headed for the entrance to Buildings 7 to 11, which housed the offices of the BStU, the *Bundesbeauftragte für die Unterlagen des Staatssicherheitsdienstes der ehemaligen Deutschen Demokratischen Republik*. The interior of the Federal Commissioner for the Records of the State Security of the former German Democratic Republic was a typical German office building, furnished with grey-green linoleum flooring, colourless tiles, glass-brick partitions and mass-produced alloy fittings. There was an odour of disinfectant that seemed appropriate to its purpose. The receptionist was a ruddy-faced man with old-fashioned short-back-and-sides who looked like a former Stasi officer. I expected him to be abrupt and officious, but he turned out to be pleasant and helpful. I asked him if I could find out whether I had a Stasi file or not, at which the woman in the queue behind me snorted, gave a grisly laugh and asked why it had taken me twenty years to get around to coming here. "Maybe you have something to hide?" I was about to explain that I had only ever visited East Germany as an innocent British tourist when the receptionist handed me a form which I filled out in triplicate, listing all the addresses at which I had lived since my eighteenth year. I naively assumed that I could speak to someone who could inform me at the click of a mouse whether I had a file or not; but I had not reckoned with the thoroughness of German bureaucracy. The receptionist told me that it would take eight to twelve weeks to process my request, and that I would be informed by mail.

The first letter arrived two weeks later, informing me my application had been received, assigning me a reference number and instructing me not to make any written or telephone enquiries in the meantime, as my application would take some time to be processed. The second letter arrived four months later. It read (in German):

Dear Herr Geoghegan

You have applied for access to those files of the State Security Service of the former German Democratic Republic which may concern you. Our investigations into the records of the Central Office in Berlin and into those of the Berlin branches have revealed that you were registered by the State Security Service in a "VSH" (Preliminary Search and Reference) file. "Preliminary Search and Reference" files (VSH files) were kept under the jurisdiction of individual service units rather than filed centrally in the Ministry for State Security. In these files details were recorded and, if need be, updated about persons who were of interest for reasons of political security. The appropriate service unit of the State Security Service could thereby access information of interest to them at short notice. From our investigations into the files it has been established that a record was made by the HA (Main Department) II. The HA (Main Department) II was responsible for the uncovering of and defence against secret service attacks against the GDR ("Espionage Defence").

Reference: 011108/10 Z

A copy of the indexed card is attached for your information. As the card indexes of the various service units of the Ministry for State Security were not standardised, some of the notes and abbreviations used can no longer be correctly interpreted. I can however inform you of the meaning of the following abbreviations:

HA VI – The HA (Main Department) VI was responsible from 1970 for passport controls, for the protection, control and supervision of entry, exit and transit traffic, and for Interhotels and tourism.

OuT – Object Protection and Tourism

Apart from this indexed card no other files concerning your person were found. I would like to point out that this information relates to those files of the State Security Service that have been uncovered so far. It cannot be ruled out that further research may uncover more files relating to your person. Because of the high number of claims submitted I regret that I cannot inform each applicant personally about newly discovered files. In order to supplement the information contained herewith you may reapply to me at a later date using the above reference. Because a signature is required, you are requested to do this by handwritten letter rather than by e-mail.

With best wishes

Schulze

The attachment to the letter was distinctly underwhelming. There was no record of my excursions into East Berlin, my illicit wanderings off the designated transit routes through East Germany, my parking or speeding offences or my encounter with the two motorcyclists near Weimar. In fact, there was no suggestion that the Ministry for State Security considered me a person of any interest at all. Attached to the letter was a photocopy of a single index card listing my name, nationality, date of birth, passport number, occupation and the address of my employer. The spidery, joined-up handwriting on the back of the card read: *"HA VI / OuT v. 1.10.83: Tourist Aufenthalt v. 21-22.10.83. Weimar, Hotel "Elephant" gebucht."*

In the early evening I drove east along Landsberger Allee, a six-lane highway formerly known as Leninallee. To the north lay banks of monotone *Plattenbau* housing estates; to the south industrial wasteland, once the site of the central slaughterhouse of Berlin and of numerous VEBs, People's Own Enterprises that produced electrocarbon and manufactured menswear or ball bearings. Penny supermarkets, Sconto furniture warehouses and car dealerships lay isolated beneath a layer of low, rippled cloud. A flyover soared in an S-bend over Märkische Allee and descended into Marzahn, where the prefabricated apartment blocks increased in height and multiplied in density. In 1936 the rural village of Marzahn was used by the Nazis as a discreet location to keep the city's Gypsies out of sight during the Olympic Games. In 1971 the 8th Party Congress of the SED implemented plans to alleviate the housing crisis in East Berlin by building a new *Trabantenstadt*, a satellite town over the village; 91,400 apartments were assembled during the next fifteen years. I turned into Allee der Kosmonauten, where the apartment blocks towered up on every side. Dull yellow squares of light flickered above empty walkways, underpasses, car parks and playgrounds. There was nothing to do outside except wait for a tram.

I turned off Cosmonauts' Avenue into Biesdorf-Nord and discovered an older part of Marzahn, a villa colony from the 1920s. I parked outside the house of Hannes and Sara, two friends who were part of the group that had met in Český Krumlov the previous summer. I was visiting them to deliver a copy of *The Lives of the British Poets*, three weighty tomes in a slipcase, published by Oxford University Press, that cost £100 and

would have cost as much again to have sent by post. Hannes was a bib-
liophile from Freiburg im Breisgau who had converted the largest room
in their house into a library lined with a collection of German and world
literature in the finest editions – Folio Society, Everyman's Library, original
King Penguins, Library of America, Bibliophilen Taschenbücher – which
ran from Middle High German lays through Chaucer, Shakespeare, Goethe
and Schiller to the complete works of Tolkien. (Hannes ran Overland, a
science fiction bookshop in Kreuzberg, but made his living from writing
reviews of the latest science fiction novels for amazon.de.) Sara, an East
Berliner who was seven months pregnant, had prepared a supper of bread,
cheese and cucumber salad (Germans traditionally eat their main meal of
the day at lunchtime). I was ravenous, having eaten nothing since breakfast
except a doughnut with a hole in the middle that I had ordered in a *Stehcafé*
in Kreuzberg many hours earlier. (I had asked the waitress for a *Berliner*,
believing this to be the correct term, in this city of all places, for the doughnut I was pointing at. The waitress looked at me blankly, before correcting
me: "Das ist ein Donut.") Sara explained that a *Berliner* is a doughnut
without a hole in the centre; and that had I ordered a *Wiener* in Vienna or
a hamburger in Hamburg I would probably have been met with an equally
blank look. Hannes presented me with a copy of *Siegfried und Krimhild* by
Jürgen Lodemann, a modern German take on the *Nibelungenlied*. At 892
pages long, it looked as daunting as the original Middle High German epic,
but Hannes assured me I would find it rewarding.

I drove back along Landsberger Allee beneath a turquoise sky darkened by a triangle of low cloud, finned and tailed like a giant manta ray
gliding over the city. Back in Berlin-Mitte I wandered aimlessly down
Oranienburger Straße, feeling that peculiar combination of exhilaration
and loneliness you get when you're on your own in a foreign city at midnight on a Saturday evening. A crowd of sophisticates was spilling out of
the Postfuhramt, having attended the *vernissage* of a new Pierre et Gilles
exhibition. Prostitutes glammed up like Sigue Sigue Sputnik were stationed
on their platform boots between parked cars whose windscreens glistened
with rain. I was desperate to hear some music. Tacheles was too industrial
(I remembered going there in the 1990s when there were disused Trabants
ploughed vertically into the sand of the back yard and the white noise of
Mauersound pulsating off the walls of the windowless studios. Now it is
a vaguely subversive tourist trap threatened with demolition.) The lounge
bars on the other side of the street were too conventional, playing mainstream hits by Adele or Lady Gaga.

I was about to return to my hotel when I heard the demonic voice of a sozzled MC in a beer hall rasping out "Eins... Zwei... Drei..." There was a snatch of cocktail-bar piano (the aural equivalent of Dubonnet on ice) and a Wurlitzer lurched into "Happy Birthday to You". I recognised the opening sequence of Lou Reed's *Berlin* and crossed the street to a cellar bar named X-Terrain, where a barman in a bowler hat and black waistcoat, who resembled the late Gary Holton (lead singer of a band called The Heavy Metal Kids whom I remember seeing in support of Alice Cooper in a school gymnasium in one of those dormer towns south of Stuttgart in 1975), was dispensing drinks to a few night owls. What's more, you could smoke inside the bar. I ordered a glass of wine and listened to *Berlin*. The sombre orchestration, spectral choirs and Wagnerian tempo of the album create a chilling atmosphere over which the world-weary Reed recounts the story of an abusive relationship between two speedfreaks, ostensibly an American GI stationed in Berlin and the German mother of his children, but in reality more likely to have been based on the cocaine-fuelled set that hung out at the Factory or lived in the Chelsea Hotel in New York. (As far as I know, Reed had never visited Berlin when he wrote the album.) The couple's children are taken into care because of the woman's promiscuity and drug abuse. She cuts her wrists and the narrator is left with the bitter memories of their addictive relationship. (And, oh, those children's voices crying in the night.)

I lit a cigarette and reflected on how other glam rockers of the time had been inspired by Berlin: Bowie's outsider "heroes"; Iggy stumbling into town with "visions of swastikas in my head, plans for everyone". Bryan Ferry sang one verse of "Bitter-Sweet", a song from Roxy Music's fourth album, in German so camp that he could have been auditioning for a role in *Cabaret*. The lyrics were translated into German by Eveline Grunwald and Constanze Karoli, two fans whom Ferry met on holiday in the Algarve and who, at the singer's suggestion, stripped to their see-through underwear to provide the cover shot for *Country Life*. And then there was that song by Cockney Rebel, of which I can remember only the opening line, but which I have used anyway as the subtitle of this chapter.

12

Saxony

White Temple, Black Colossus

It was 11 November 1989, less than forty-eight hours after the fall of the Berlin Wall. I was driving on the autobahn near Hermsdorfer Kreuz. A young woman flashed her headlights as she overtook me; an expression of joy at her new freedom, I suppose. I stayed that night in the Hotel Newa in Dresden. It was a Saturday evening and the lobby was full of suited West Germans speaking urgently into clunky car phones. The first wave of capitalist entrepreneurs had arrived, eager to exploit the vacuum created by the collapse of the Communist state. I spent the Sunday morning leaning out of my hotel window, watching an ancient Ikarus 260 emitting black fumes as it spluttered up the slope behind the Hauptbahnhof towards the housing blocks of Dresden's Südvorstadt. The city centre was subdued, as if the Dresdeners had not quite taken in the significance of the events during the previous two days. I expected an air of celebration, maybe a street party; but there was just a ginger-haired man on a soapbox in Theaterplatz urging a small gathering of his fellow citizens to join him in a *Bürgerinitiative*, a "green-pink" coalition of environmentalists and progressive socialists that would counteract the old communists and the new capitalists. Most Dresdeners seemed to have stayed in bed – or gone to West Germany for the weekend.

Twenty years later I have a room in the Newa again, now a Pullman Hotel owned by the French chain Accor (although still named after a Russian river). This time my room is on the northern side, overlooking Prager Straße thirteen floors below. This former showpiece of Socialist Modernist urban planning has undergone some changes since I was last here. The statue of Lenin has been removed; a ceramic mural entitled "Dresden, City of Modern Industry, Science and Art, Greets its

Guests" has been dismantled; and the tin tack and puffball sculptures that once decorated its concrete fountains have disappeared. The Speeresque streetlamps have been replaced by slim glass steles, and the uneven concrete paving blocks by a smooth sandstone surface. Gone are the old *Selbstbedienungsgastronom* eateries and the *Schuh- und Lederwarenhäuser*, supplanted by Caffé Nero, Subway, Mango, Esprit and Salamander. The utopian vision of the Socialist "International Style" is still evident, however, in the housing block which runs for two hundred and fifty metres along the eastern side of Prager Straße; in the trio of identical hotel blocks (once Interhotel, now Ibis) that rise along its western side; in the aluminium-plated cylinder of the Rundkino cinema; and in the sole surviving sculpture from the Communist era, a prickly explosion of metal thorns which once represented the *Völkerfreundschaft* between Socialist Peoples' Republics. Glittering in the morning sun at the far end of the boulevard is the Centrum-Galerie, a new department store with a façade of retro-futuristic, diamond-shaped aluminium casings which replicates the frontage of the Socialist Centrum-Warenhaus it has replaced. Beyond the post-modern banks and shopping malls of the revitalised "Prager Zeile" is the skyline of the Dresdener Altstadt, the blackened spires and belfries of the Hofkirche, Kreuzkirche and Residenzschloss, all appearing much as they were when painted in the eighteenth century by Bernardo Bellotto, *dit* Canaletto, nephew of the Venetian painter. Interspersed with the gilt orbs and crosses of the baroque churches are the Wilhelmine domes of the Ständehaus and the Lipsius-Bau, crowned in turn by golden effigies of Fama and Saxonia. And towering above them all is the great bell dome of the rebuilt Frauenkirche.

I walked down Prager Straße and continued into Seestraße, a single block of apartments three hundred metres long constructed in a Stalinist version of the Dresden Baroque style. The flats overlooking Altmarkt rose six storeys high, their sandstone façades embellished with balustrades, parapets and tall casement windows. Cog wheels and wheatsheaves decorated the medallions set into the pilasters; steelworkers and ploughmen laboured in the bas-reliefs beneath the colonnade. At the entrance to the Café Prag stood a pillar of jade-coloured glass mosaics that depicted a quasi-oriental composition of herons, bulrushes and lily pads. Once the fashionable place to be seen in Socialist Dresden, the coffee house was locked and shuttered, a victim of capitalist market forces in the guise of Starbucks, Segafredo and McDonald's. The latter had hung its yellow arches in the colonnade beneath Haus Altmarkt, a tower block on the opposite side of Dresden's Old Market Square. Plastered in burnt orange and Saxon green, striped with cream pilasters and adorned with lunette windows, miniature obelisks and viola-shaped gables, Haus Altmarkt looked, to the untutored eye, as if it had been built in the 1740s by Matthäus Daniel Pöppelmann or his assistant Johann Christoph Knöffel, architect of the Altstädter Rathaus that stood here until it was destroyed in 1945. A curlicue of Elbe sandstone, however, revealed that Haus Altmarkt and its adjoining wing were "Erbaut MCMLV" – built in 1955. In the tympanum of the *Kopfbau* on the opposite side of the square a pair of lions rampant bore a shield inscribed with the dates "1206 1945 132+ 1956". The initial date referred to the year in which Dresden was first officially documented – "Acta sunt hec Dresdene"; 132+ 1945 denoted the night, 13 February, on which the city was incinerated, when the bodies of citizens burned alive in the firestorms were brought to the square and cremated in pyres in order to prevent disease spreading; and 1956 celebrated the completed reconstruction of the Altmarkt as a monument to the baroque fantasies of Stalin.

It was the weekend of the *Dresdner Stadtfest*. Crowds milled around a funfair in the centre of Altmarkt, playing table tennis, riding on merry-go-rounds or sunbathing on the sands of an artificial beach. Rows of children sat in front of stages, transfixed by clowns, marionettes and a pantomime Faust. Rustic stalls dispensed beer, smoked sausages, Mexican cocktails and Hungarian *Lángos*. And in a modern sandstone basin in the middle of the square were the sculpted outlines of molten human shapes through which pale water flowed, shimmering in the sunlight – a poignant reminder of the burning flesh piled high in the Altmarkt some sixty-five years earlier.

I crossed Wilsdrufferstraße and found myself in front of the Kulturpalast, a slab of 1960s Socialist Modernism deposited in the middle of all the real and fake baroquery of Dresden's Altstadt. Posters behind its glass façade advertised a summer repertoire of *Schlager* groups, tribute bands and a constellation of stars from yesteryear: Vicky Leandros, Howard Carpendale, Chris de Burgh and Michael Bolton, the latter now shorn of his mullet. Along one wall of the people's palace was a communist mural entitled "Der Weg der Roten Fahne" ("The Way of the Red Flag") in which Marx, Engels, Thälmann and Ulbricht made cameo appearances beneath the clenched fist and red flag of a strapping young East German wench.

I turned into Augustusstraße, which was lined with souvenir stalls facing the Fürstenzug, a frieze of twenty-three thousand tiles of yellow

Meissen porcelain that depicted an equestrian panoply of the dukes, electors and kings who ruled Saxony between 1127 and 1904. Coming from
the direction of Schlossplatz, I commenced at the back of the procession
with the side-whiskered architects and spiked-helmeted generals of the
penultimate King Georg, who ascended the throne in 1902 and died two
years later in 1904, the year the original painted mural was replaced by
the porcelain version. I followed the parade as it reversed through the
nineteenth century, *Pickelhauben* giving way to the plumed cockades of
the retinue of Anton der Gütige (the Kind) and the pomaded wigs worn by
the courtiers of Friedrich August der Gerechte (the Just), King of Saxony
from 1805 to 1827 and Duke of Warsaw from 1807 to 1813, the year
Saxon and Polish troops misguidedly fought on the side of Napoleon in
the Battle of the Nations. Following their defeat Poland languished for
a hundred years under Russian rule, while the northern half of Saxony
was annexed by Prussia. The two baroque characters on rearing horses
to the left of the defeated king were August III and his father August
II, Electors of Saxony, Kings in Poland and Grand Dukes in Lithuania,
Ruthenia, Prussia, Masovia, Samogitia, Kiev, Volhynia, Podolia, Podlaskie,
Livonia, Smolensk, Severia and Chernigov. August II, founder of baroque
Dresden and ruler of north-eastern Europe, was known as "the Strong"
on account of his prowess at, among other things, fox-tossing. He held
a contest in Dresden at which 647 foxes, 533 hares, 34 badgers and 21
wildcats were reportedly catapulted into the air. The king liked to show
off his strength by jerking the end of his sling with a single finger. He
could also have earned the sobriquet "the Lecherous", as he was alleged
to have sired between 365 and 382 children. His body is buried in the
Wawel Cathedral in Craców, but his heart is encased in a silver casket
in Dresden's Hofkirche. It beats again, according to legend, whenever a
pretty girl in a skirt passes overhead.

Continuing backwards in time, I came to Johann Georg I, Elector of
Saxony from 1611 to 1656. Although a Protestant, he lent his support to
the Holy Roman Emperor at the outset of the Thirty Years' War, but later
changed sides and supported Gustavus Adolphus. After the death of the
Swedish king, Johann Georg switched sides again but was defeated by
the Swedes, who proceeded to ravage Saxony just as they had devastated
Swabia. The floppy velvet hats and ermine cloaks worn by rival Catholic
dukes and Protestant electors of the divided province attest to compar-
atively peaceable times in the sixteenth century. Lucas Cranach painted
them all: grave Duke Georg der Bärtige (the Bearded), Electors Johann

der Beständige (the Steadfast) and Johann Friedrich der Großmütige (the Magnanimous), all swaddled in sable and fox fur – and Heinrich der Fromme, the pious one who converted the duchy to Lutheranism and modelled for Cranach in an outrageous red and yellow costume of darts, slashes, bows and pompoms. Like the Hohenstaufens and the Hohenzollerns, the medieval Margraves of Meissen and Electors of Saxony went through a phase of Friedrichs: in reverse order, Friedrich der Weise (the Wise), Friedrich der Sanftmütige (the Gentle), Friedrich der Streitbare (the Belligerent), Friedrich der Strenge (the Strict), Friedrich der Ernsthafte (the Serious) and Friedrich der Gebissene (the Bitten), the latter so called because his mother, Margaret of Germany, was so overcome with grief at having to flee her husband Albrecht der Entartete (the Degenerate) that she bit a piece out of her child's cheek. The House of Wettin recedes into the mists of the Dark Ages with the *Minnesänger* Heinrich der Erlauchte (the Illustrious), Dietrich der Bedrängte (the Oppressed), Albrecht der Stolze (the Proud) and Otto der Reiche (the Rich), until it reaches its beginning with Conrad the Great, Margrave of Meissen, Count of Groitzsch and Rochlitz, and Lord of Chemnitz and Naumburg. But this far back in time Dresden was a small Slavic settlement by a ford in the river, and Saxony was another country far to the north, ruled by Henry the Lion.

The flameproof tiles of the Fürstenzug were largely undamaged by the firestorms of February 1945. The new Communist regime had few qualms about cleaning up these glorified trappings of provincial feudalism: it needed anything it could lay its hands on to encourage tourists to visit the ruined city it had inherited. The GDR also inherited the ruins of the Frauenkirche. The magnificent church, known as "St Peter's of the North", had been reduced to two blackened stumps at either end of a mound of rubble after its columns had cracked in the heat of the firestorm, causing its dome to collapse twenty-four hours later. Fragments of the chancel and a stair-tower stood isolated from each other like ruins in a landscape by Caspar David Friedrich. The authorities designated the battered arches a war memorial, as they had neither the means nor the will to reconstruct the church. They paid lip service to its "restoration" by employing a couple of workmen to prevent the remaining structure from collapsing any further. The surrounding Neumarkt was left undeveloped. Cars parked where the rubble had been cleared. The Police Praesidium built itself a prefabricated annexe. I remember visiting the city shortly after the *Wende* and seeing long queues of Dresdeners snaking around this disused area as they waited to enter a bank. It must have been Sunday, 1 July 1990, the day currency union was implemented and East German citizens were permitted to exchange savings of up to four thousand East German marks into deutschmarks at a 1:1 rate.

Now the Neumarkt is one of the finest urban spaces in Germany. The mansions of baroque Dresden have been reconstructed and repainted in vanilla, ochre, coral and duck-egg blue: the Haus zum Schwan, the Haus zur Glocke, the Goldener Ring, the Hotel Stadt Berlin, where Chopin and Dostoyevsky used to stay; the Hotel de Saxe, resplendent in *kaisergelb*; the Salomonisapotheke where Friedrich Adolf Struve concocted the first artificial mineral water, whose fame spread from Königsberg to Brighton; the pale gold and white curve of the Köhlersches Haus, where Heinrich Schütz lived and worked as *Kurfürstlicher Oberkapellmeister* between 1629 and 1657. In the centre of the square are coal-black statues of Martin Luther and Friedrich August II, surrounded on this festive weekend by sunshades splayed out over the pristine cobblestones. The Frauenkirche soars ninety metres above the square, its golden sandstone pocked with small black squares where three and a half thousand pieces of the original stone have been restored and replaced in their original positions. The blackened arch of the north-west staircase remains charred, like scar tissue from a burn that will never fully heal. Although fundamentally a square structure, the body of the church appears multi-faceted on account of its great height and the exuberance of its bevelled corners and projecting porticoes, each of which is surmounted by gables, pediments, capitals and flowering turrets. Inside the Frauenkirche a three-quarter circle of wooden pews converges on a chancel that resembles a stage set for *The Marriage of Figaro*. Milky statues of prophets, apostles and angels emblazoned with gilt wings, crosses and harps float above the altarpiece. Corinthian columns of grey marble drip garlands of wheatsheaves and vine leaves. An oriole of golden sunbeams radiates from an eye of God wreathed in stucco clouds high above the organ. The eight pillars of brown and yellow marbled stone supporting the circular nave rise through four tiers of galleries faced with panels of pink, lemon and powder-blue marble – a palette of sugary colours that represents the sweetness and light of God's grace. High in the cupola is a green and gold simulacrum of heaven, where the evangelists have tamed the lion, the bull and the eagle, and consort with cherubim and seraphim on duvets of fluffy white cloud.

I walked out to Sankt-Petersburger-Straße, a boulevard laid out in the 1960s that cuts a swathe through what was once the eastern Altstadt of Dresden. Yellow trams swished along the central reservation past baroque nymphs and classical goddesses, charred statuary rescued from palaces destroyed in the firestorm and deposited rather incongruously in the grassy strip between the tramlines. I waited at the pedestrian traffic lights for the chunky red man with his stubby hat and outstretched arms to change into the jaunty green man with his single arm and hurrying legs. (The East German *Ampelmännchen* was such an iconic symbol of the Socialist state that the "new federal states" created in 1990 were allowed to keep him, rather than convert to the less distinctive West German traffic-light man.) It was hot, there was no traffic, and I felt quite stupid standing on my own at the edge of a three-lane highway waiting for the green man to appear. In order to cross the tramlines in the central reservation, I had to spend another two or three minutes repeating the same procedure. By the time I reached the three-lane highway in the opposite direction, I was sweltering in the heat and determined to cross the empty road whether the man was green or red. To my amazement the red figure facing me in the traffic light turned out to be female – a pigtailed *Ampelfrau* wearing a dress. I was so astonished by this example of political correctness, or positive discrimination, that I remained rooted to the spot until the red girl turned green and, pigtails flying, permitted me to cross. As I approached the next pedestrian crossing I was wilting in the heat generated by the treeless expanse of Sankt-Petersburger-Straße, and decided to cross the side street without stopping. Two women waiting obediently at the far side of the street looked at me in horror and disbelief. "Bleib, Mensch, es ist rot," said one. I rolled my eyes, told them I was a foreigner and muttered something about how we didn't need little green men (or women) to tell us what do in England.

Neue Herkulesallee led into Dresden's Großer Garten. A sculpture in the Socialist Realist style at the head of the avenue purported to represent some muscular workers raising a banner of some kind, but it had been so badly made that the concrete had disintegrated to the point of abstraction. Skateboarders hammered their plastic wheels into empty concrete basins that were once Socialist fountains. To my right were the sleek, clean lines of the German Hygiene Museum, a building designed in the late 1920s by Wilhelm Kreis.

The guiding spirit behind the museum was Karl August Lingner, a self-made millionaire of the Wilhelmine era who invented, among other things, a backscratcher for use in the bath and a mustard pump for the dining table. He founded the dental hygiene company Odol, still the leading brand of mouthwash in Germany. In 1903 Lingner organised an exhibition entitled "People's Illnesses and How to Fight Them", which consisted mainly of dozens of microscopes through which the public could, for the first time, view living bacteria. Eight years later he curated a much grander exhibition, devoted exclusively to the concept of hygiene. Held in Dresden's Großer Garten, the First International Hygiene Exhibition attracted five and a half million visitors. Drawn by the "all-seeing eye" designed by Franz von Stuck that advertised the show, they were led through rooms that displayed rows of microscopes and X-ray machines, anatomical models illustrating bone structure or digestive tracts, and painted wax *moulages* of body parts infected by syphilis or tuberculosis. The scope of the exhibition embraced not only health and hygiene but also biology, genetics, sport and anthropology. Visitors could explore a Japanese pavilion, a Red Indian settlement and an Abyssinian village – or they could inspect the sexual diseases displayed in "Galewsky's Chamber of Horrors". The centrepiece was a neoclassical pavilion devoted to "Der Mensch", where crowds thronged around a colossal statue of a finely toned Hercules – the embodiment of the virtues of health and cleanliness.

Following the success of the 1911 exhibition, a competition was announced in 1920 to design a permanent Hygiene Museum in Dresden. Hans Scharoun, Paul Bonatz, Hans Luckhardt and other modernist architects submitted expressionist visions of crystalline glass buildings, but nothing came of these initial projects because of the economic crisis of the early 1920s. The project was revived several years later and this time the call went out to Wilhelm Kreis, principal architect of the exhibition grounds in Düsseldorf, where the *GeSoLei* exhibition of 1926 devoted to health, physical education and social welfare had attracted seven million visitors. Kreis arrived in Dresden and laid the foundation stone of his new building in October 1927. The museum was completed within three years, in a style which combined Bauhaus modernism with the neoclassical monumentality of Kreis's earlier work. Its smooth white planes, circular windows and semi-circular balconies reflected the international modernist style of the time; while the tall square granite columns of its towering entrance hall expressed the German virtues of order, clarity and strength. Kreis insisted that the building "expresses higher aims than pure functionalism", describing his work as an embodiment of the "eternal values" of the German people.

Tables and chairs had been set up on the museum forecourt, opposite a statue of a muscular athlete caught in the act of throwing a ball,
a Wilhelmine allegory of health and strength. I sat beneath a sunshade
and ordered a coffee, but the heat from the midday sun reflecting off the
building's white exterior was so intense I had to take refuge inside the cool
grey marble foyer of the museum. Inside the exhibition I found a "transparent man", whose see-through body, moulded from a synthetic material called Cellon, revealed veins, nerves, organs and intestines painted
in primary colours. Displayed on a dais in a circular apse at the centre of
the museum, this was the highlight of the Second International Hygiene
Exhibition of 1930–31, a fair whose pavilions filled the Großer Garten
and remained there until 1933, when the National Socialists pulled them
down in order to lay the foundations of a new Gauforum. Visitors to the
Second International Hygiene Exhibition could admire a model hospital
and visit a model coal mine or a "hygienic farm". They could taste a
"radioactive chocolate", manufactured by the firm Burk und Braun from
Cottbus, which was designed to boost energy levels. In the evenings they
would be dazzled by *son et lumière* effects that illuminated the Chlorodont
Tower and the Glockenspiel Tower; or they could dine in the restaurant
below a mural painted by Otto Dix, which illustrated the construction of
the museum.

In 1932 a bronze statue of *Hygieia*, Greek goddess of health, was
unveiled in the courtyard. It was sculpted by Karl Albiker, creator of
the *Relay Runners* and *Discus Throwers* which would later decorate
the grounds of the Olympic Stadium in Berlin. The following year Dr
Bruno Gebhard, one of the museum's curators, took an exhibition entitled "Eugenics in New Germany" on a tour of the United States. In 1935
he curated an exhibition in Berlin called "Miracles of Life", which was
visited by Hitler and Goebbels. British geneticists attended the SS medical
centre in Alt Rehse in order to keep abreast of the latest developments in
racial hygiene. In Nazi Germany personal hygiene became a metaphor
for the health of the nation (the *Volkskörper*). The forced sterilisation of
"unhygienic" (or mentally handicapped) Germans led to the gas chamber
at Schloss Grafeneck.

As you proceed through the historical rooms of the Hygiene Museum,
the thought occurs to you that every life-affirming statistic produced by
the museum during the 1930s had its life-denying counterpart in the liquidation of Jews and other "bacilli" that afflicted the "healthy organism
of the German people". You realise that the increasing birth rate among

Aryan Germans during the 1930s (according to the chart you are reading) would have been mirrored by a corresponding increase in the death rate among German Jews during the same period. A photograph of a mobile "hygiene bus" that toured the German provinces in the 1930s, promoting various health campaigns (in this case exhibiting a collection of diseased livers as a warning against alcohol), seems wholesome enough; until you remember that similar buses functioned several years later as mobile gas chambers. And the Hygiene Museum itself was to have its antithesis in the Hygiene Institute of the Waffen-SS, established by Oberführer Joachim Mrugowsky to coordinate the appalling medical experiments carried out on prisoners in concentration camps.

The "white temple" was largely destroyed in the bombardment of Dresden, but rebuilt quickly after the war as a model for the city's regeneration. Sexual disease was the subject of the first post-war exhibition; young people under the age of eighteen were prohibited – and Wednesdays were for women only. In the 1950s the museum regained its status as a centre of excellence for medical research. Dozens of transparent men, women, horses and cows were manufactured and displayed, epitomising the health and medical progress of the new regime. The museum's annual calendar featured such paragons of health as Lenin, Stalin, Mao Tse Tung and Wilhelm Pieck. The hall in the restaurant where Otto Dix's mural had hung, before it was dismantled by the Nazis, was repainted by the young East German artist Gerhard Richter; until his artwork was in turn erased after his defection to the West. The new icon of the museum in the 1960s was Kundi, a cartoon Young Pioneer who appeared in comics and on television. Bearing a vague resemblance to ZDF's *Mainzlmännchen*, Kundi was the eyes and ears of the FDJ in the kindergarten, making sure that Socialist youth was not afflicted by dirty fingernails, smelly feet, runny noses, yellow teeth or waxy ears. Whether they are communist or capitalist, Germans dislike dirt or mess. They like things to be pure.

I returned to the Altstadt in the early evening and sat until dusk in the courtyard of the Zwinger Palace, beneath Venus-shelled capitals, carbuncled coronets and urns which erupted into a cornucopia of blackened stone fruit. Juno, Bacchus, Perseus, Andromeda and a priapic August the Strong frolicked with satyrs, leering fauns, pudgy cherubs and nymphs writhing in ecstasy as they flaunted their breasts and thighs beneath swirling strips of gossamer. (I later discovered that many of the nymphs were installed when the Zwinger was restored in the 1920s, a more permissive age than the High Baroque.) The buildings around Theaterplatz glowed in the bronze half-light, the Hofkirche an emblazed battleship, the Semper Opera House a great ark beached above the Elbe. In the centre of the square an equestrian King Johann reared high on a tall plinth. A rock band (ELO-lite) blared out from a stage near the Italienisches Dörfchen. The tramlines along Sophienstraße were covered with stalls purveying schnapps, nougat, waffles, marzipan, gingerbread and roasted almonds. Larger booths displayed toy soldiers, handmade jewellery, antique glassware, wooden mobiles, Indian scarves, Indonesian figurines and African masks. The air was perfumed with caramel, incense and wood smoke.

I followed the crowds onto Augustusbrücke, swept away in the throng. The sound of guitars, didgeridoos and tabla drums echoed from every parapet. Revellers swinging mugs of beer and bottles of schnapps blew lustily on plastic trumpets, adding to the cacophony. Football fans hurled empty beer bottles into the Elbe below. Above the bridgehead on the left bank, bungee jumpers threw themselves from a crane. A Ferris wheel rotated slowly over the water meadows on the right bank, where the lawns slide gracefully into the river. Beams of red, white and orange light rippled over the river's surface, reflections of streetlamps on the Carolabrücke two hundred metres upstream. Downstream the silver-black sheen of the Elbe curved into the night, beyond the dome and minaret of the Yenidze cigarette factory. I pushed back through the throng to the southern bridgehead, stopping to reclaim the deposit I had paid on a beer glass, before picking my way through the crowds on the steps of the Brühlsche Terrasse. I sat at a table outside the Vis à Vis Café, whose faux-baroque interior I remembered from my first visit to Dresden in 1986, on my way to the East German–Czechoslovak border and the aforementioned five-hour ordeal on the ridge of the Ore Mountains. A promotional flyer on the table persuaded me to order a grapefruit-flavoured *Weißbier*. Wheat beer traditionally tastes of apricot or peach, a smooth, sweet, creamy beer sometimes drunk with a slice of lemon to add a bit of fizz; but the additive of sour grapefruit was a mistake – it tasted like sugary vinegar.

Crowds of young women sporting bustiers, suspenders and coronets of inflated condoms cackled and squawked on the Terrassenufer below me. From a stage by the river a silver-haired singer in a purple bouffant shirt, and a pair of dress trousers too tight for a man of his age, belted out amplified versions of "Nessun Dorma" and the latest vernacular *Schlager*.

Moored beyond the stage were rows of ancient white paddle steamers belonging to the Weiße Flotte. On the far side of the river I could make out a larger stage in front of which a sizeable crowd had assembled, thousands of shadowy arms waving in the air in anticipation of a headlining act. I remembered Die Toten Hosen, Germany's premier punk band, performing a celebratory concert on the Königsufer when I was in Dresden two days after the fall of the Berlin Wall.

I wandered through a labyrinth of dark alleys behind the Albertinum and the Johanneum, below baroque arches, charred domes and tortured caryatids. I emerged once again into Schlossplatz, the cobbled square below the Hofkirche. In the centre was a statue of King Friedrich August I, restored in 2008 to the accompaniment of the same hymn Richard Wagner had composed on the occasion of the statue's original unveiling in the Zwinger in 1843. Clustered around its plinth were dozens of wooden stalls dispensing home-made wines from ten-litre glass jars: the evening air swam with a heady cocktail of fermented sloe, plums, cherries, oranges and blackcurrants flavoured with mint, sage, hemp, thyme and ginger.

I pushed my way back over Augustusbrücke to Neustädter Markt on the right bank, where crowds milled around the Goldener Reiter, an extravagantly gilded equestrian statue of August the Strong raised high on a heavy black plinth. Gold Latin script proclaimed the lustful monarch as King of Poland, Duke of Saxony and Prince Elector and Archmarshall of the Holy Roman Empire. The priapic king astride his rearing horse was another feudal-imperial symbol of baroque vanity that the Communist regime was happy to restore with gold leaf and present to the world as the centrepiece of its new suburb on the right bank of the Elbe. The Hauptstraße of Dresden's baroque Neustadt was renamed in 1946 the Straße der Befreiung (in commemoration of the city's liberation by the Red Army), but was left undeveloped until the 1970s. Its new manifestation as a Socialist *prospekt* lined with rows of state-run shops below mass-produced apartment blocks was unveiled in 1979, to mark the thirtieth anniversary of the founding of the German Democratic Republic. Tonight, however, the Hauptstraße was packed with food stalls and heaving with several thousand Dresdeners chewing candyfloss and toffee apples as they ogled a cabaret band of young women dressed as Marlene Dietrich, who were performing a high-kicking routine to a selection of numbers from *Chicago*. Tucked away from the crowds and oompah bands on Hauptstraße were quieter squares, where fairy lights were strung between circles of lime trees. I sat outside a Chinese restaurant below the neo-baroque spire of Pöppelmann's Dreikönigskirche, and listened to the strains of a gypsy violinist while the last pink tresses of the evening sky faded to Prussian blue.

As I negotiated my way back along Hauptstraße towards the Elbe, the spires and belfries on the far side of the river gradually came into view: the Hofkirche illuminated in silvery light and the Hausmannsturm of the Residenz in gold. As I reached Augustusbrücke the whole panorama of the Altstadt revealed itself, floodlit in silver and gold light: the crow-stepped gable of the Georgenbau, the double-canopied tower of the Ständehaus, the glass cupola of the Lipsius-Bau and the bell dome of the Frauenkirche. Downstream, laser beams zapped the Semperoper, the Zwinger and the Turkish dome of Yenidze. On the bridge it was impossible to move; it seemed as if the entire Free State of Saxony had gathered there. Thousands more thronged the water meadows below: shadowy groups drinking beer, grilling sausages, chanting songs and milling around the beer tents and funfairs. A few hundred metres away on Königsufer a major act was headlining the evening's musical entertainment. I couldn't hear the group because of the din made by all the other live bands, but I glimpsed a forest of fans in front of the stage punching their arms up and down to the beat. There was a brief pause, a moment of anticipation as the arms went still – and then the heavy, sinuous riff of Led Zeppelin's "Kashmir" kicked in. For a moment I wondered whether this was the real thing, whether Robert Plant, my second favourite singer, was performing live in Dresden unbeknownst to me (while I was sitting on my own eating Peking duck in the lee of the Dreikönigskirche). I pushed through the multitudes assembled on the bank of the Elbe, advancing ever closer to the main stage. The crowds grew thicker and I realised that thousands of music fans were singing and dancing in the darkness outside the fenced-off enclosure. In the end it was all rather an anticlimax: the headline act turned out to be Jan Delay and Disko no.1, a white funk-hiphop act from Hamburg.

To escape the crush I went for a coffee and a *Malteser* on the terrace of the Italienisches Dörfchen coffee house on the left bank of the Elbe. At 10.45 pm a siren pierced the night and the sky exploded with fireworks. Green and yellow starbursts, red comets and silver starfish rained down over the river, illuminating the bridge, which seethed like a living thing. Precisely fifteen minutes later the last glittering streamers faded away. Dresden applauded, and the police boat sounded its siren once more, in order to signal the end of the evening's festivities.

I was aroused from my slumbers by the pealing of bells: from St Nicholas's Church, from St Thomas's Church, by two jangles from the belfry above the Old Town Hall and by a pair of muffled chimes from a carillon on top of the Kroch Tower. I dragged myself out of bed and surveyed the view from the sixth floor of Motel One. Inside the hotel everything was turquoise. Outside, a veil of sleet drifted down over the centre of Leipzig. Strips of slush formed herringbone patterns across the car park below. Bare trees stood around a fenced-off square of waste ground. Blocks of grey housing units loomed over Reichsstraße. A lingerie shop advertised its wares via illuminated panels filled with lacy bras and panties, stretched over breasts and hips two storeys high. On the far side of the car park stood the Riquet Haus, topped by a Chinese turret. In the distance were the yellow pilasters of the Old Stock Exchange and the chocolate and cream gables of the Old Town Hall. Cranes hovered over Market Square, their beams shrouded in low cloud. *Schneeregen* muffled the sound of traffic on the Ring. I heard only the rustling of shoes over wet pavements as a few early Leipziger, dressed in grey and black, pinched faces hunched against the wind, made their way, plastic bags in hand, to the shops.

I breakfasted in the turquoise lobby, warmed by the digital flames of a virtual fireplace. Afterwards I ventured out into Nikolaistraße for a cigarette. The pavements were gritted and wooden poles leant against walls to prevent pedestrians from being struck by falling icicles. The Nikolaikirche loomed over the street, the three octagonal towers of its façade plastered in a colourless wash from the GDR period. After stubbing out my cigarette, I took shelter inside the church. In contrast to its drab exterior, the nave was painted in the colours of Paradise. Pink fluted columns supported white Egyptian capitals that sprouted forth into green palm fronds. The vaulted ceiling was panelled with diamond-shaped coffers stuccoed in rose pink and apple green, the hues of the Garden of Eden. I sat in one of the white-painted pews embossed with brass medallions which numbered the places to kneel and pray.

It was here that the East German peace movement began in 1982. The first protesters were members of evangelical youth groups who objected to the siting of Pershing II and CS-20 intermediate-range missiles in West and East Germany. Activists took the biblical image of swords beaten into ploughshares as their symbol. The peaceful dissent grew during the

1980s into a wider protest against the environmental destruction of East Germany. Leipzig in particular was badly affected by pollution from the surrounding brown-coal mines: one peace group from the Nikolaikirche organised a demonstration in the form of a funeral march for the River Pleiße, which had become a "cesspool". By 1988 the ritual of Monday peace prayers had grown in popularity and was attracting disaffected young people from the wider community. St Nicholas's Church became a haven of dissent against the broader issues in East Germany – civil rights, women's rights, human rights and the fundamental right to be allowed to leave the GDR. By the spring of 1989, over a thousand citizens were attending Monday peace prayers in the church, or holding candlelit vigils in the churchyard outside. Today the Nikolaikirchhof contains monuments to the peaceful revolution: a replica of one of Johann Carl Friedrich Dauthe's palm-fronded columns, and a bronze plaque set into the cobblestones of the square that commemorates 9 October 1989, the date which proved to be the turning point in the wave of revulsion felt by the people against their state. The plaque bears the imprint of the feet of some of the seventy thousand who marched on that Monday evening from the Nikolaikirche to the Ring, proclaiming "Wir sind das Volk!"

In Specks Hof, one of the turn-of-the-century trading courts that form the centre of Leipzig, I noticed the Connewitzer Verlagsbuchhandlung and remembered once meeting at the London Book Fair a young Anglophile bookseller from Leipzig who spoke impeccable English and had a fervent admiration for English literature. The upper floor of the bookshop was devoted to English books and I asked after Birgit (or Brigitte, for I couldn't remember her name on the spur of the moment). The assistant recalled a Brit, who had been one of the founders of the bookshop in the early 1990s, and who now lived in London. (Someone later told me that Brit was the real-life "love interest" in Nicholas Shakespeare's *Snowleg*, a novel which takes place in Leipzig in 1983 and 2002, before and after the *Wende*. I reopened my copy of the book and saw that the novel is indeed dedicated "To Niko and Brit".)

Running along one side of Specks Hof was Schuhmachergäßchen, a street of elegant, old-fashioned emporia that sold the kind of wines, cigars, jewellery and wedding dresses you would no longer find in Karstadt or Kaufhof. At the far end of the street was the Riquet Haus, a restored Jugendstil building with bands of gold and peacock-blue mosaic around its curved façade, and a pagoda-shaped turret on its roof. A Viennese coffee house was all that remained of the trading house Riquet & Co., established in 1745 to import tea and exotic wares from the East Indies. I passed below the elephants' heads that adorn the copper lintel above the entrance, sat in a wicker chair at one of the marble-topped tables, and ordered a *latte macchiato*. The oak-panelled beams were decorated with elephants' heads and enamel plaques advertising "Kakao und Schokolade". A brass till with rows of keys would have rung up prices in marks and pfennigs, had it still been in operation. The lush tones of a mid-nineteenth-century symphony (Brahms or Schumann) resonated around the café from loudspeakers hidden in the eaves of a stuccoed ceiling, above chandeliers also embossed with brass elephants' heads.

Two bronze lions sculpted by Johann Gottfried Schadow guarded the entrance to the Naschmarkt. As its name suggested, this was where sweets and candies were once sold. The Old Stock Exchange at the far end of the square was a toothsome building, a baroque delicacy covered in white stucco and yellow pilasters, like a cake coated with icing sugar and marzipan. Clad in frock coat and silk waistcoat, the young Goethe adopted a dainty pose atop his marble pedestal in the centre of the square. Below his bronze likeness were medallions commemorating Käthchen Schönkopf, his first love in Leipzig, and Friederike, daughter of his art teacher Adam Friedrich Oeser, founder of the Academy of Fine Arts in Leipzig and a leading exponent of early German classicism.

I followed the direction Goethe would have taken as he strolled towards Auerbachs Keller. The famous wine cellar is now inside the elegant Mädler-Passage, a Milanese-style arcade that runs through the Messehof. I wandered past Auerbachs Keller and the Mephisto Bar until I reached a glass dome above the intersection of the two galleries that make up the Mädler-Passage. At precisely 1 pm a glockenspiel chimed the melody of "Kein schöner Land in dieser Zeit", an evening song extolling the charms of Germany at the end of the Wilhelmine era. I was tempted to stop for a light lunch in the Kümmel-Apotheke, enticed by the idea that the dishes therein would be cooked with flavoursome caraway seeds, but the restaurant looked too formal for a quick snack. I retraced my steps until I stood between the bronze statues of Faust, Mephistopheles and a band of roistering students that announced the entrance to Auerbachs Keller. I discovered there were two establishments below the Mädler-Passage: the historical *Weinstuben* that is now an exclusive restaurant for trade fair executives on company expenses; and the Großer Keller, a cavernous wine cellar built in 1912 for the hoi-polloi. I descended to the latter and began to have a look at the murals on the walls, but was accosted by a pair of tall, blonde waitresses in maroon uniforms and politely ushered outside, once it became clear I did not wish to make a reservation for lunch.

I went instead to the Museum of Fine Arts, a glass bunker of vast proportions unveiled in 2004, which dominates Sachsenplatz. After a bowl of soup in the museum café I walked back along Katherinenstraße, past the Romanus Haus and the Fregehaus, restored baroque mansions that once belonged to eighteenth-century merchants. The Fregehaus was named after the financier Christian Gottlob Frege, a distant ancestor of Andreas Frege, lead singer of Die Toten Hosen. I passed through Barthels Hof, below the House of the Golden Snake, and came out on to the Dittrichring. Built between 1911 and 1913 for the Old Leipzig Insurance Company, the building on the corner of the Ring known as the "Runde Ecke" was occupied after the Second World War by the American Army. It later passed into the hands of the Soviet military before becoming the headquarters in Leipzig of the NKVD and, subsequently, the East German Ministry for State Security. It is now a museum devoted to victims of the Stasi.

Like the pages of a *noir* detective novel, the former cells of the Stasi HQ were filled with tape recorders, magnetic microphones and phone-tapping devices; forged passports, false number plates and rubber stamps with fake addresses; thermal radiation sensors, *Lichtsprechgeräte* (devices enabling agents to communicate by means of infra-red beams when telephone communication was not possible) and watertight canisters known as *Krebsen* (crabs) which could store reels of microfilm underwater in the event of a nuclear war. One cell was full of shelves of *Geruchsprobenkonserven*, vacuum-sealed glass jars containing a square of yellow cloth which had been surreptitiously impregnated with a suspect's body odour by concealing it below the suspect's chair during interrogation; the dogs of the Stasi were then trained to identify these and recognise the individual by the unique smell of their sweat. Another cell contained "masking disguises": wigs, rollers and hair nets; false moustaches or ponytails which could be applied with the aid of Mastix glue; and a "special product for very thin synthetic bald caps" named Glatzon, which came in a tin with instructions in German, French and English. There were handbags, rucksacks and jacket lapels fitted with micro cameras or wired for tape recording, and suitcases labelled "Araber" or "Baumann", neatly filled with the items an agent might need in order to impersonate an Arab (a prosthetic nose and false beard, for example) or a construction worker (a set of tools and a hard hat). The more mundane aspects of the Stasi's work had been reconstructed in grey-painted, linoleum-floored offices furnished with shredders, rubber stamps, filing cabinets, card indexes, hole punches and machines that looked like antiquated kettles with rubber tubes, which were used to steam open letters and reseal them. The one glaring omission was anything that resembled a computer. Maybe the budget of the MfS didn't run to such advanced technology – or perhaps the Stasi deliberately used old-fashioned methods in order to keep a high proportion of the populace employed in its service.

Some of the cells in the "Runde Ecke" were reserved for criminals awaiting trial or execution. Leipzig replaced Dresden as the central place of execution in East Germany in 1960. Eight years later the guillotine was superseded as the preferred method of execution by an "unexpected close-range shot into the back of the head". Most executions were for murder and other capital crimes, but the list of those executed in the jail in Leipzig's Alfred-Kästner-Straße included some whose crime was designated "Spionage" – political or financial espionage. One of these was Dr Werner Tecke, a captain in the MfS, who was executed on suspicion of selling state secrets to West Germany, in the wake of classified files relating to prominent Stasi officers being discovered in his apartment.

After supping on such horrors I needed a strong coffee and I repaired to the Arabian Coffee Tree (Zum Arabischen Coffe Baum), a baroque coffee house patronised in the 1830s by the composers Robert Schumann, Richard Wagner, Felix Mendelssohn-Bartholdy and Franz Liszt. Hector Berlioz also conducted at the Gewandhaus on many occasions, and may have accompanied Schumann and Mendelssohn to the Coffe Baum. One can speculate as to whether these illustrious musicians also visited Auerbachs Keller, as four of the five composers (Mendelssohn being the odd one out) wrote works based on the Faust legend. The coffee house had several cafés and restaurants spread over its four floors. I found a table in the Wiener Café on the second floor and sat for a while listening to the clink of coffee spoons and the strains of a Viennese waltz. I ordered a pot of Café Symphonie and a slice of Robert-Schumann-Torte, a creamy walnut cake which arrived with a white chocolate medallion stamped with the composer's portrait embedded in a whirl of walnut-flecked cream.

It was dusk when I arrived at Augustusplatz. Drizzle fell from low purple cloud. Yellow trams slithered across the centre of the square. A milky light shone from eight glass cylinders that covered stairwells to an underground car park. The floodlit muscles and scales of bronze Tritons, Nereides and hippocampi glistened in a neo-baroque fountain. Spherical chandeliers illuminated the foyer of the opera house, an unimaginative building in a late Socialist Classicist style. Raindrops sparkled on the anodised frames of its windows. The Leipzig Opera House opened in 1960 with a performance of *Die Meistersinger von Nürnberg*. Friedelind Wagner was the guest of honour in her grandfather's home town. I noticed that the stage director of the opera house was Peter Konwitschny, whose production of *Parsifal* I had seen in Munich several years earlier. At the opposite end of Augustusplatz was the new Gewandhaus, its great bronze roof raised like the shovel of a bulldozer. A huge ceiling fresco entitled *The Song of Life* illuminated the foyer of the concert hall. I went inside to escape the damp chill. Groups of parents were gathering, waiting to collect their offspring from a "Family Concert" that had started earlier in the afternoon.

In the evening I returned to the Mädler-Passage, pausing in front of Faust and Mephistopheles as I wondered whether to dine in Auerbachs' posh "Historische Weinstuben" or in the more popular Großer Keller. I decided to go for a drink in the Mephisto Bar while I made up my mind. I perched on a stool and ordered a *Mephisto Feuer*, a fiery, blood-red cocktail with a satisfyingly high alcohol content. Mephisto was a smart, pre-opera, *après-théâtre* piano bar, appropriately furnished in scarlet and black. On the walls were playbills and mementoes of various adaptations of the Faust legend: the score of a *Mephistopheles Polka*, for example, and photographs of different productions of Goethe's *Faust* dramas. Tables and shelves were decorated with bronze and marble statuettes of horned devils – one a female Mephisto with pendulous breasts and a splayed rump. On the dot of 8 pm a wall mirror lit up, illuminating an image of Gustaf Gründgens in his famous screen role as Mephistopheles. A devilish laugh emanated from above, and dry ice poured from the ceiling around the figure of a demon clasping a beer glass in his plaster hands.

The cocktail and the smoke-and-mirrors show had put me in the mood for some more Mephisto-kitsch, so I descended the stairs into the depths of Auerbachs' Großer Keller. The original wine cellar was founded in 1530, when Dr Heinrich Stromer from Auerbach in the Oberpfalz estab- lished himself as a vintner in Leipzig. His tavern became famous for its student clientele and for the legend of Faust's barrel ride, published in a popular chapbook entitled *Historia von D. Johann Fausten* in 1589. As a student in Leipzig between 1765 and 1768, Goethe would have heard the Faust legend while carousing in Auerbachs Keller. Years later he set a scene of his drama *Faust: Part One* in the wine cellar, thus immortalising the tavern. The joke at the time was that Goethe should have received a percentage of the takings from the wine cellar in perpetuity. The landlord did indeed present him with two bottles of champagne to mark the writer's birthday, a gift Goethe duly declared on his tax return (according to the history of the wine cellar printed on the back of its menu).

I ordered slices of roast boar with potato dumplings, red cabbage and mushroom fricassée, which I washed down with a green-stemmed goblet of *Spätburgunder*. After finishing my main course I wandered below the arched vaults of the Großer Keller. The wine cellar was rebuilt in 1912 and decorated with paintings in the historical-romantic, High Wilhelmine style of the age. The murals illustrated scenes from *Faust: Parts One and Two* ("The Witches' Kitchen", "Martha's Garden", "Auerbachs Cellar", "Valentine's Death", "Euphorion", "Faust at the Imperial Court" and "Faust's Monologue to Nature"), portraying Mephistopheles clad in scarlet cape, scarlet tights and a horned cap – a jester rather than a demon. In the alcove where I sat he was sidling up to three Japanese gentlemen dressed in embroidered kimonos: this painting was commissioned to commemorate a visit from one Mori Ogai from Kyoto in 1895. For dessert I had "iced Leipziger skylarks", a confection of ice cream, almonds and marzipan on a biscuit base accompanied by lemon mousse and raspberry sauce; a pudding that celebrated Goethe's time, when the culinary speciality of Leipzig was a pastry filled with real skylarks.

Posters tacked onto lampposts in the car parks to the south-east of Leipzig advertised a monument silhouetted in black against a scarlet background. The strapline read "Das Schönste der Welt" ("The fairest in the world"). I assumed this was meant with a degree of irony. The monument in question, the Völkerschlachtdenkmal (Monument to the Battle of the Nations), is colossal, powerful, rugged – but it's not pretty, by any stretch of the imagination. With the possible exception of the IJzertoren near Diksmuide in Flanders, it could be hailed as the ugliest memorial in Western Europe.

The approach to the Völkerschlachtdenkmal leads through a quartet of stone blockhouses in the form of ancient Egyptian mastaba tombs; dark and cold, they look like wartime air-raid shelters. Once through these bunkers you are in a hallowed precinct, isolated from the outside world by a double row of lime trees. A stone-rimmed basin stretches for one hundred and sixty metres towards the monument. This "Lake of Tears for Fallen Soldiers" is in the form of a trapezium, which gives it the illusion of being rectangular when viewed from ground level. On a clear day the monument would be reflected in the pool, but on this March morning the basin was encased in ice. Towering over the far end of the lake was the "Black Colossus", a mass of grimy, scabrous, rough-hewn granite blocks that rose almost a hundred metres above layers of walls, terraces and steps built up over a man-made hillock. In contrast to the tower, the dome of the monument had been cleaned, and its light brown sandstone glowed beneath the pale winter sun. Encircling the dome was a ring of twelve stone warriors, the Guardians of Freedom, distant cousins of the eighteen stone handmaidens who watch over the Befreiungshalle. The monument was originally intended to be capped in the conventional nineteenth-century manner by an Imperial crown and an Iron Cross, but its sponsors, the German Patriots' Association, insisted they would have none of the traditional ornamentation that glorified the church, the Chancellor or the Kaiser. And so the Völkerschlachtdenkmal was surmounted by a thick slab of porphyry, the screw head that holds the heavy bulk of the monument in place – or a sacrificial altar on which Germans can make burnt offerings to pagan gods.

I approached the base and stood on a terrace of broken flagstones, above a flight of steps leading down to the frozen water of the basin. The two lower walls at the foot of the monument culminated in a pair of stone Barbarossa heads: sunk in catatonic gloom beneath cobra-coiled Egyptian headdresses, their elongated beards swept down to form the parapet of each wall. At the centre of the high wall above me was a sculpture of an armour-clad Archangel Michael, brandishing a sword of flame as his chariot bears him across a nightmarish *Totenfeld* of skulls, corpses, serpents and dying horses. Barely discernible beneath the sulphurous grime were a pair of Jugendstil eagles and a quartet of angular Furies bearing the firebrands of war. "Gott mit uns" was the battle cry carved into the stone above this ghastly bas-relief.

A monumental staircase led to an elevated crypt, a circular chamber whose architrave rested on eight pillars carved into death masks; a sculptured henge of furrowed brows, aquiline noses and eyes closed in eternal sleep. Integrated into each sculpture was a pair of smaller statues of medieval warriors with grim heads bent in mourning, their armour-plated arms folded over tall, thick-bladed broadswords. A single wreath of irises lay in the centre of a floor of polished flagstones, green and grey and arranged in a cruciform pattern. Sepulchral music echoed around the crypt. A second flight of steps led to a circular Hall of Fame overlooking the crypt. Supporting the columns of the dome were four monstrous statues that embodied Bravery, Sacrifice, People's Faith and the Strength of Faith, the "characteristics of the German people during the Wars of Liberation". Each of these sombre, muscular titans weighed four hundred tons; the giant representing Strength of Faith cradled in his lap a boy whose flaccid penis alone was over a foot long. The pillars of the four arched windows that filtered a weak light into the Hall of Fame were etched with the figures of those bereaved by the deaths of the one hundred and ten thousand soldiers who lost their lives in the Battle of the Nations. Carved into the granite dome were three hundred and twenty-four equestrian sculptures, which formed an endless procession of knights disappearing into the gloom, symbols of the souls of the dead as they ascended towards Valhalla.

Although it commemorates the same Battle of the Nations as the Befreiungshalle, this monument in the suburbs of Leipzig bears little resemblance to its Bavarian counterpart. With its marble columns and winged goddesses, the neoclassical Hall of Liberation is a celebration of glorious generals and victorious battles – a luminous vision of a unified German future. The Saxon-Prussian Völkerschlachtdenkmal, by contrast, is a mausoleum that fetishises the Germanic cult of death. Heavy, solemn, doom-laden, it reeks of defeat rather than victory.

The inauguration of the Völkerschlachtdenkmal on 18 October 1913, the centenary of the Battle of the Nations, was a national celebration. Germans from all over the fatherland descended on Leipzig. The city was festooned for the occasion with bouquets of flowers, wreaths of pine leaves, Iron Crosses, Victory goddesses, busts of the Kaiser and eagles of the Reich. Fir trees trimmed into the shape of pylons were planted along Goethestraße. Banners in the black and yellow stripes of the House of Wettin hung from shops in Petersstraße. The Ury department store mounted a two-storey-high image of the monument over its façade. Eight pairs of Doric columns on blue plinths were erected in Augustusplatz. Fire bowls blazed through the night. The route to the monument was garlanded with flags, rosettes and pennants. The festival commenced on 16 October when gymnastics clubs, veterans' associations and civil servants of the Royal Saxon State Railway gathered for a "patriotic celebration". On the following day military bands were out in force as thousands milled around Leipzig's gargantuan railway station to catch a glimpse of the prominent guests. The list of VIPs included Prince William of Sweden, Crown Prince Franz Ferdinand of Austria, Grand Duke Cyril Vladimirovich of Russia and King Friedrich August III of Saxony.

At 7 am on 18 October a procession of five thousand sashed and sabred representatives of German student associations assembled in the centre of Leipzig and marched out to the Völkerschlachtdenkmal. At 11 am King Friedrich August greeted the guest of honour Kaiser Wilhelm II and his ostrich-plumed retinue at the station, from where they were driven in open carriages to the monument. A military band played Wagner's *March of the Grail Knights* as they joined ermine-robed princes and bishops beneath a ceremonial tent, adorned with Reichs eagles, that had been erected over the steps at the foot of the monument. A team of white-vested relay runners from the German Gymnastics Association arrived to greet the Kaiser. Forty-three thousand of the association's members had participated in a relay that connected the new symbol of national rebirth, this "mighty German cliff", with eleven other patriotic sites, including the Befreiungshalle, the Arminius and Kyffhäuser monuments, the Niederwald Monument to *Germania,* the monument to Ernst Moritz Arndt on the island of Rügen and the burial site of Bismarck at Friedrichsruh.

In the evening there was a royal banquet in the Gewandhaus, after which the Kaiser returned to Berlin. The remaining guests were free to remain in the concert hall and listen to a performance of Ernst H. Seyffahrt's cantata *Aus Deutschlands großer Zeit,* or repair to the New Theatre for a performance of Schiller's drama *Wallensteins Lager,* accompanied by Wagner's *Kaisermarsch* and excerpts from *Die Meistersinger von Nürnberg.* The official celebrations culminated in an illumination of Leipzig by candles and braziers that lit the city in "mystical flickering flames". The *Glühlampen* were so dazzling that the spectacle was repeated the following evening. A year later Germany was at war, which is what the Kaiser and the German Patriotic Association, sponsors of the monument, wanted all along. The consecration of the Völkerschlachtdenkmal was the last great hurrah of the Second German Reich.

This monument to the unity of the German nation became an inevitable focus of German nationalism and militarism. During the First World War it came to be a symbol of the "Schicksals- und Opfergemeinschaft" of the German people, that unique predilection the Germans have for regarding themselves as a "fateful" or "sacrificial" race. Nationalists viewed the war as a campaign that would "reawaken everything that was great, fair and holy" in Germany, that would strengthen the bonds of German unity that the Battle of the Nations had fostered in the first place. However, as the war on the Western Front became bogged down in trench and tunnel warfare that was neither fair nor holy, and as German casualties multiplied, the Völkerschlachtdenkmal rapidly lost its significance as a marker of the victory over Napoleon, and became instead a memorial to the German dead of the First World War – a symbol of sacrifice in the here and now.

The National Socialists reinforced the idea of the monument as a symbol of the heroic, sacrificial nature of the German *Volk*. The Völkerschlachtdenkmal was one of the principal altars of the Nazi cult of death, important to the ideologues of the regime because it commemorated not an individual (Kaiser Wilhelm I, Bismarck or Hindenburg) but the German people, that mythical-mystical concept of the *Volksgemeinschaft*. Adolf Hitler addressed the Saxon *Gauparteitag* from the steps at the foot of the monument on 16 July 1933. In June the following year, fifty thousand evangelical Christians assembled around the basin in a show of loyalty to National Socialism: Reichs Bishop Ludwig Müller's speech suggested that the Nazis' rise to power had been underpinned by the religious strength of the German people, a declaration that sat uneasily with the Nazis' perception of their movement as a "*völkisch*-mystical" cult in opposition to Christianity. In August 1934 a huge wreath was laid before the monument during a *Trauerfeier* to commemorate the death of Field Marshal Hindenburg. In October that year the Hitler Youth leader Baldur von Schirach lectured a torch-lit rally of eighty thousand *Pimpfe* on the ideals of duty and sacrifice. By the late 1930s the Völkerschlachtdenkmal was becoming a symbol of war once again. During the *Oktoberfeier* of 1937 and 1938, Wehrmacht guards stood to attention below the sculpture of Saint Michael – miniature replicas of the avenging archangel above them – as Gauleiter and Reichsführer thundered on about "military culture" and "never-ending struggle" below the sea of corpses on the frieze behind. And, inevitably, it came to pass that several years later the Monument to the Battle of the Nations was the site of funeral processions, as the dead of another war were mourned. The tower loomed like a giant tombstone over last rites, last posts and solemn requiems as Himmler, a thousand miles away in East Prussia, exhorted the surviving German troops to emulate their forefathers of 1813.

The Nazis' last stand in Leipzig was fought around the Völkerschlachtdenkmal. Oberst Hans von Poncet, Kampfkommandant of Leipzig, had holed himself up inside the monument with a remnant of three hundred soldiers and Volkssturm irregulars. On the evening of

18 April 1945 they shot at a passing convoy of US tanks. The Americans returned fire, but were beaten off. The Yanks regrouped and attacked the monument with 75mm and 115mm grenades, tearing chunks off the tower before they finally burst open one of the windows and exploded a grenade inside the Hall of Fame. The police chief of Leipzig had by this stage officially surrendered the city to the occupying forces; but the warriors in the monument fought on for one more day in a futile last stand that achieved nothing except a perverse adherence to the ideals of sacrifice enshrined in the monument. It was rumoured that the besieged troops eventually shot their Kommandant in order to end the senseless slaughter.

A final flight of three hundred and sixty-four steps led up a spiral staircase built into the walls of the dome. I emerged into pale sunlight, three hundred feet above ground. A terrace circled the crown of the monument, running above the ring of the twelve Guardians of Freedom, cartoonish statues with Desperate Dan chins and thick-bladed broadswords. I felt a rush of vertigo and had to clutch the railings. A fierce wind howling in from the east did little to allay my fear of heights. Eventually, I steeled myself to peer over the parapet and survey the view over the Leipzig Depression. The city lay to the north, its skyline of apartment blocks punctuated by the round tower of the New City Hall and the silver blade of the City Tower. To the south were escarpments formed from the slag of brown-coal mines. *Abraumförderbrücken*, huge mobile bridges-cum-conveyor belts, lay across the crests of slag heaps like the skeletons of ancient dragons. I bought a couple of books about the monument in the museum shop. The assistant wrapped them in a scarlet paper bag stamped with silhouettes of the world's most famous buildings – Big Ben, the Eiffel Tower, the Taj Mahal and the Statue of Liberty. Towering over them was the silhouette of the "Black Colossus" of Leipzig, the Völkerschlachtdenkmal. "Das Schönste der Welt" – irony presumably intended.

13

Thuringia

Beech Wood and Golden Meadow

It was a Friday afternoon in October 1986, and I was driving from Braunschweig to Weimar on the first leg of a journey through East Germany and Czechoslovakia to Vienna. I was stopped by the West German Bundespolizei for speeding through a contra-flow system as I approached the border crossing at Helmstedt. One hour later I was stopped by the East German Volkspolizei as I turned south off the official transit route. The fine in each case was twenty marks; deutschmarks and Ostmarks, respectively. The Bundespolizei insisted I pay the fine; the Volkspolizei let me off with a warning. It was dark by the time I approached Weimar. I was driving along an unlit road through a wood when I noticed a single light following me, the weak, flickering headlamp of an East German motorcycle. The headlight grew closer and started to flash me. I had done nothing illegal and did not feel apprehensive, but I was reluctant to stop as it was getting late. Eventually the motorcycle drew alongside me and flashed me repeatedly. I pulled over and two nervous teenagers emerged out of the darkness. They wanted to exchange money. I felt like helping them, but realised it was pointless. I had already exchanged my obligatory twenty-five deutschmarks into East German marks and knew there was nothing I could spend them on. It was also illegal. I would only be in East Germany for twenty-four hours, and if I could not account for my extra Ostmarks at the exit border I could be arrested. I apologised to the young couple and drove on. It occurred to me afterwards that they may have been Stasi agents trying to entrap me; but judging by the file I read many years later, the Stasi did not seem particularly interested in my stay in Weimar that autumn.

Weimar was silent and dark. A sickly yellow glow illuminated the empty streets. The smell of two-stroke petrol and smouldering brown coal hung in the air. I checked into the Hotel Elephant and was shown to a room on the first floor at the front of the inn. The wood-panelled restaurant was empty and the waitress was reluctant to serve me. I ate whatever she offered me: it was a way of using up my Ostmarks, after all. When I came to pay the bill, the waitress refused to accept East German currency and demanded payment in precious foreign deutschmarks. I queried whether she had the right to do this, but she replied quite firmly that this was an international hotel and that all transactions were in hard currency. After the meal I noticed a line of young people queuing to get into the cellar bar. I asked the receptionist what was on. She informed me there was a discotheque in the Elephantenkeller, but it was "for local residents only" and "forbidden to hotel guests". They clearly did not want a capitalist foreigner corrupting the local socialist youth by flashing deutschmarks around or getting into another argument about currency transactions.

The following morning I was woken at an ungodly hour by the sound of a crowd assembling in the marketplace in front of the hotel. A brass band struck up a march and loudspeakers broadcast a speech in a language I couldn't understand. Wearily, I pushed aside the curtain to find that a podium had been erected in front of the Rathaus to welcome a delegation of dignitaries from Rumania (as it was spelt at the time). According to the banner across the balcony of the town hall, this was a "Day of German-Rumanian Friendship and Fraternal Solidarity". But did it really need to start at eight o'clock on a Saturday morning?

Twenty-six years later, I woke at a more acceptable hour in the Hotel Amalienhof. From the terrace on the second floor I had a view over Wielandplatz. A bronze statue of the eponymous poet gazed over a small square bordered with beds of purple and yellow flowers. Pale water shimmered in a horse trough. A trio of tall streetlamps – spooky, five-pronged relics from the GDR era – craned over the junction with Steubenstraße. A clear blue sky shone over Weimar: over the Schinkelesque faculty buildings along Humboldtstraße; over the Jugendstil estate agents at the entrance to Frauenplan; over the heavy pink blocks of the *Gründerzeit*

savings bank; over the black tower of the Schloss and the trees in the Park an der Ilm.

I walked through Beethovenplatz into the park, following gravel paths around lawns sprinkled with daisies, buttercups and clover. Blackbirds and thrushes sang from red cedar and copper beech trees. There were flashes of blue as dragonflies danced between the branches of bay willows suspended over the green waters of the River Ilm. Butterflies flitted over molehill-speckled meadows on the other side of the stream. I caught fleeting glimpses through the trees of the Franz Liszt Music School, the Duchess Anna Amalia Library and the house of Goethe's platonic lover Charlotte von Stein. I passed a statue of Shakespeare reclining in a dandyish pose below a stone folly and walked through the ruins of the House of the Knights Templar, a neo-Gothic summerhouse destroyed during an air raid in 1945. At the edge of a Soviet Military Cemetery stood a white marble statue of the Abbé Liszt, *Kapellmeister Extraordinaire* of the Court Orchestra of Weimar from 1848 to 1861. Hidden between a white oak and a black poplar was a bust of his compatriot, the Hungarian national poet Sándor Petőfi. On a terrace above the Ilm was Duke Carl August's Roman House, a summer refuge designed for him by Goethe in the style of the antique temples the writer had observed during his Italian journey between 1786 and 1788. I went inside and sat in the Yellow Salon, decorated with gilded cornices and turquoise and gold *stuccolustro* panels framed by bands of ornamental birds, blossom and butterflies. In the adjacent Blue Salon, plaster *putti* representing Zeus, Hera, Hermes and Apollo fringed a portrait of the Duke's mother Anna Amalia, painted in Rome during her own Italian journey from 1788 to 1790.

I continued my walk across the pastures of the Ilm towards Goethe's Garden House. Like the Roman House, this was an expression of the classical synthesis of Art and Nature, a trellised cottage set in terraced gardens and orchards. The small, simply furnished rooms were wallpapered in a shade of green that matched the meadows outside. They were decorated with landscape paintings and the writer's own sketches and maps of Rome that served as visual aids as Goethe worked on the second part of his *Italienische Reise*. In the lower garden violets, pinks, pansies, marigolds and roses created a riot of colour around the lawns. Yellow sunflowers, purple gladioli and blue globe thistles two metres high lined a path leading to the Stone of Good Luck, a sandstone globe resting on a cube that the writer had erected as a monument to Agathe Tyche, the Greek goddess of Good Fortune. Goethe cultivated strawberries and asparagus in the garden, and swam in the Ilm. In the library he studied anatomy, biology, geology and mineralogy. He worked on Faust, Torquato Tasso and Iphigenie in Tauris and wrote the ballad Erlkönig and the poem An den Mond in the moonlight of his bedchamber. This was a life lived in harmony with nature and the cosmos; a world where Art, Nature and Science became one. There was romance too: whenever Goethe departed on his travels he would leave the keys to the Garden House with Charlotte von Stein, or with Carl August, so that the duke could hold discreet trysts with his own mistress, Caroline Jagemann.

I left the park and walked to Weimar's Historical Cemetery. The lower part of the cemetery was open parkland, a dozen or so wrought-iron crosses scattered over the lawns. White hellebore, red campion, liverwort and wood anemones flourished in the undergrowth beneath the cemetery walls. An avenue of linden trees led up a slope towards a Princes' Crypt, where Goethe and Schiller lay buried. The upper cemetery continued beyond the crypt, extending into the southern outskirts of Weimar – a dense network of stone crosses, marble tombs, obelisks and mausoleums mantled in ivy, moss and ferns beneath a canopy of poplar and cypress trees. I turned off the main avenue and discovered a birch grove, in the centre of which was a memorial resembling the Stone of Good Fortune in Goethe's garden. This Ehrenhain was marked with the initials VdN, which I took at first to mean "Vertriebenen der Nationen" ("Exiled of the Nations") and assumed it was another monument to Germans driven out of Silesia and East Prussia. On looking closer, I realised that VdN stood for "Verfolgten des Naziregimes" ("Victims of the Nazi Regime"). An inscription on the cube at the base of the monument commemorated "the unknown antifascist combatants of every nation". A row of stone tablets around the edge of the memorial grove bore the names of one hundred and fifteen men and women who had been massacred by the Gestapo in a nearby wood during the final stages of the war. An inverted triangle was implanted into the globe of the monument, painted red to signify the badge that political prisoners were forced to wear by their Nazi captors.

Back on the main avenue, I came across a detail of municipal gardeners who were tending the shrubbery around a monument that looked like a snake poised to strike. A nearby panel explained this was a memorial to the Märzgefallenen of Weimar. Designed by the Director of the State Bauhaus, Walter Gropius, the monument was unveiled in 1922 to commemorate nine workers killed by Reichswehr paramilitaries during a right-wing putsch two years earlier. Known as Frozen Lightning, the sculpture was composed of horizontal triangles of concrete, which over-lapped each other like plates of ice on a frozen sea, before rising and twist-ing, like concrete origami, into a bolt of lightning. The Socialist sculpture was deemed "degenerate" by the Nazis, and its vertical section was dyna-mited. The horizontal plates, which covered the graves of seven of the fallen workers, were left to recede into the undergrowth. The post-war Communist authorities restored the sculpture in 1946, but their recon-struction lacked the expressionist dynamic of Gropius's original.

The gardeners gathered around their orange van for a sandwich break. I followed a path which left the cemetery and climbed through the orchards and allotments of Silberblick, high on the southern slopes above Weimar. I came out on Humboldtstraße and sat in the garden of a housing estate built in a pre-war colonial style. After a brief rest I began the descent of Humboldtstraße, a long street lined with *Gründerzeit* vil-las and Jugendstil mansions that wound back down the hill towards the centre of the town. On a bend in the road I came across Villa Silberblick, a red-brick and stucco, German neo-Renaissance mansion. The words NIETZSCHE-ARCHIV were inscribed across a sandstone panel above its entrance. This was the pre-war home of the archive established in 1897 by Elisabeth Förster-Nietzsche to promote her brother's ideas and control his legacy. Closed by the Soviet military authorities in December 1945, Villa Silberblick reopened as a museum to the philosopher's works in 1991.

The doors were locked when I arrived. I went for a stroll around the garden, peering over the back wall to find out whether the adjacent Nietzsche Memorial Hall built by the National Socialists was still in use. It appeared not to be. When I returned to the front of the museum, several other visitors had arrived. We knocked on the door and were ushered in by the curator. The Art Nouveau dining room was lined with glass cases containing documents, manuscripts and newspaper cuttings relating to Nietzsche's life and work. The accounts ledger of his publisher recorded that *Also Sprach Zarathustra*[14] was reprinted at least once every year from

---

14   I remember struggling with *Also Sprach Zarathustra* as a teenager in the early 1970s. Like those of Hermann Hesse, Nietzsche's works were fashionable at the time, as they conveyed a search for the meaning of life dressed up as medieval fable or mythical parable, a combination which appealed to the counterculture. My interest in Nietzsche had been piqued by David Bowie who, around that time, was rumoured to have "dipped into Nietzsche" and was apparently seen around town with a copy of *Beyond Good and Evil* protruding from his jacket pocket. Several of his more disquieting songs from that period are imbued with the spirit of *The Supermen* and the *Homo Superior*.

1893 to 1907. Next to it was the frontispiece to the score of Richard Strauss's tone poem of the same title, dedicated to the philosopher in 1896. There were letters to Elisabeth Förster-Nietzsche from Mussolini (in Italian and German) and a photograph from 1932 of Hitler staring at a bust of Nietzsche. The stone Nietzsche stares back: it's a confrontation between two of the worst moustaches in German history. The restored library was lined with bookcases and furnished with beech-wood sofas upholstered in salmon pink. Art Nouveau pen holders and candlesticks glazed in ochre and cobalt decorated desks and shelves. Display cases contained photographs of Schopenhauer and Wagner, sketches and statuettes of Nietzsche and photographs of the *Burschenschaft* "Franconia" he belonged to as a student in Bonn. At the far end of the room, framed by windows shining with light from the garden, was a tall white marble herm sculpted by Max Klinger, its head distinguished by Nietzsche's high sweep of hair, his bushy eyebrows and the shaggy, matted growth on his upper lip.

Weimar in the 1920s was a city of "civil servants, pensioners and educated, middle-class bourgeoisie", a bastion of reactionary nationalism. In 1920 the Deutschnationale Schutz- und Trutzbund organised its first "Deutscher Tag", a gathering of *völkisch* and anti-Semitic associations, in the city. In 1926 the NSDAP held its Second Reichsparteitag in Weimar: its leader Adolf Hitler had recently been released from jail in Bavarian Landsberg, and Thuringia was one of the few states in which he was permitted to speak publicly. Fritz Sauckel was appointed Gauleiter of Thuringia in 1927, and he set out to establish Weimar as a cultural "Hochburg" of National Socialism. His aim was to forge a direct link between "Alte Weimar", that "beloved centre of German Classicism", and the "Neue Weimar" of the Third Reich, thus erasing the memory of the hated Weimar Republic in between. Hitler loved the city and often stayed at the Hotel Elephant during his long drives along the Munich–Nuremberg–Berlin axis. After the National Socialists came to power, Sauckel designated Weimar the "Stadt der Rassenreinheit" ("City of Racial Purity") and Thuringia as "Hitler's Schutz- und Trutzgau" ("Hitler's Protection and Defiance *Gau*"). He later instituted cultural events such as the "Week of the German Book", which ran regularly from 1934 to 1942, and "Great German Poetry Days", at which National Socialist bards assembled annually between 1938 and 1942.

The Nazi regime set out to stamp its authority on the public spaces of each of its *Gaue* by constructing a Gauforum – a self-contained complex of buildings that would represent the supremacy of the Party. Munich, Berlin and Nuremberg were already in the process of constructing new Party monoliths; and each of the remaining provincial capitals was to follow suit with a representative centre of its own comprising the offices of the Party, an assembly hall for the *Volk* and a parade ground for mass rallies. Sauckel was determined that Weimar should build the first Gauforum, a prototype that would provide a blueprint for other cities of the Reich. Hitler agreed, and in 1936 Hermann Giesler was awarded the commission to design the first National Socialist Gauforum in Weimar. On 4 July 1936, Hitler and Rudolf Hess arrived in Weimar to preside over the "first cut of the spade" performed by Gauleiter Sauckel in the centre of Carl-August-Platz in front of the New Museum. Work progressed rapidly over the next three years: the square was dug up and a residential area of one hundred and thirty-nine houses was demolished. By 1939 the first National Socialist Gauforum was almost complete.

Along the western side of the new Platz Adolf Hitlers were the Central German headquarters of the DAF (German Labour Front); along the northern side was the Haus der Gliederungen (the offices of various "limbs" of the Party, such as the SS, SA, Hitler Youth and League of German Girls); and along the southern side was the Reichsstatthalterei, the seat of the Governor and Gauleiter of Thuringia. Each block was one hundred and twenty-five metres long, three storeys high and contained two hundred and fifty rooms. Giesler's design followed the axial paradigm of National Socialist representative architecture – long, low office blocks in a symmetrical pattern around a central parade ground. The Haus der Gliederungen had a colonnade along its front, while the Reichsstatthalterei and the DAF headquarters had central porticoes in a crude neoclassical style. Doors and windows were framed in stone. The balconies, colonnades and lower-floor façades of each building were accentuated by a layer of travertine stone which stressed the monumentality of the forum as a whole. It was Hitler's idea to emphasise the Reichsstatthalterei by adding a bell tower to its western end. Designed in a pseudo-medieval style with "Führer" balconies and tiny embrasures, the tower was planned to rise to a height of sixty-three metres; but only three storeys had been built when war broke out.

None of the three wings of the Gauforum was ever used for its intended purpose. After the war the central parade ground was renamed Karl-Marx-Platz and the surrounding office buildings were occupied by the Soviet Military Administration. Their porticoes and balconies were hung with red stars and posters of Stalin and the heroes of the Great Patriotic War. Red banners proclaiming Communist slogans were unfurled along the upper façade of the former headquarters of the Gauleiter. A bronzed plaster statue of Stalin was unveiled at the head of the square, but it was so poorly made it was dismantled a year later. The buildings were later used for a variety of professional training purposes and were finally redeployed after reunification as the seat of the Regional Government of Thuringia.

The three completed wings of the Gauforum have recently been "sanitised", the former DAF headquarters repainted in a rich dark red and the two opposing office blocks in their original mustard yellow. A small museum has been opened in a corner of the Reichsstatthalterei which allows a glimpse inside the stump of the half-completed bell tower. In the base is an octagonal crypt where the banners of the "Martyrs of the Movement" would have been arrayed. An arched staircase in a faux-Romanesque style spirals up the walls until it comes to a stop at the level at which the tower was left unfinished.

I crossed Carl-August-Allee and entered Haus 2 of the Thuringian Provincial Administration, an office block which was once intended for the German Labour Front. The long, square corridors smelled of wax and disinfectant and were polished as smooth as glass. Their marble floors were red-brown and veined with white like meat. Their walls were panelled with travertine limestone, porous like pumice stone. I had the same feeling as I had experienced in the State Music School in Munich. The stark muscular architecture of the Third Reich had lost little of its potency.

I wandered back to Goetheplatz. Red and white buses pulled up in front of the Russischer Hof hotel and a neo-Renaissance post office. Two elderly couples were dancing to trad jazz beneath the medieval Kasse Tower. Built in the 1930s as a National Socialist Press House, the newspaper office on the corner of the square was a miniature version of the Gauforum, its walls encased in porous limestone. A banner on the Mon Ami Youth and Cultural Centre advertised a "Yiddish Summer" of Jewish dance, cinema and musical evenings. I couldn't help wondering who the audience for such a festival might be, but when I returned to Goetheplatz in the evening there was a score of (non-Jewish-looking) Germans standing around enjoying a cigarette during the interval of a performance of klezmer music. In the centre of the square was an empty stone slab, chipped at the edges and riddled with bullet holes. Carl Alexander, Grand Duke of Saxe-Weimar-Eisenach, once dominated the plinth, resplendent astride his steed in a cuirassier's greatcoat and spiked helmet. The

National Socialists dismantled the statue in 1938 as they intended to build a grandstand in the centre of Goetheplatz, and did not want the Grand Duke to steal their Führer's thunder during a march past of the SA or SS. The statue and its pedestal were moved to a less prominent position in Carl-August-Allee and the statue was melted down after the war. The plinth was unearthed and restored to its original site in 2001 to mark the one hundredth anniversary of Carl August's death. The juxtaposition of the bare stone slab without its statue and the festival without its Jews seemed somehow appropriate for this city which lives on its past; this city of museums, libraries, archives, monuments and cemeteries; this city of absence and memories – memories of the best of German culture and the worst of German history.

In the evening I returned to the marketplace and the Hotel Elephant. In 1986 I had no idea that I was a guest in a Nazi hotel. It was obvious now, from the design of the "Führer balcony" and the familiar rhetoric of hard travertine stone covering the walls of its ground floor. I entered the hotel. The lobby had been refurbished in a black and chrome Art Deco style, and was unrecognisable from the establishment I had stayed in before. The receptionist did not seem concerned about me, so I walked through to the rear of the hotel and up a flight of stairs to the first floor, trying to find the room I had occupied in 1986. The corridors of the upper storeys were like those of the Gauforum, the floors paved with polished "Deutsch-Rot" marble and the square-cut doors framed with thick limestone – the epitome of National Socialist chic.

In a gallery on the first floor was a small museum relating the history of the Haus Elephant. The hotel opened in 1696 and provided accommodation for the great writers and musicians of German Romanticism. Clara Schumann, Felix Mendelssohn-Bartholdy, Franz Liszt and Richard Wagner stayed here. Goethe and Schiller drank madeira in the Elephantenkeller I had been refused entry to. Adolf Hitler stayed here on twenty-six occasions between 1926 and 1933, using the premises as his unofficial headquarters in Thuringia. The pro-Nazi landlord would serve the Führer his favourite Weimar bread soup. Hans Severus Ziegler, director of the German National Theatre in Weimar, declared that the Haus Elephant played the same role as a retreat and restorative haven for Hitler as the Garden House had for Goethe. In 1937 Gauleiter Sauckel decided to tear down the seventeenth-century lodgings and build a new hotel for Hitler that would be "the most modern establishment in Europe", a model of "exemplary German design" which would be featured in German lifestyle magazines for years to come. Designed by Hermann Giesler, the remodelled hotel opened its doors on 5 November 1938 with a ceremony attended by Hitler and many of the Nazi top brass. The *Völkischer Beobachter* ran a special commemorative issue. Crowds assembled below the "Führer balcony" chanting:

> Lieber Führer, komm heraus,   (Beloved Führer, come on out,
> Aus dem Elephantenhaus.   Out of the Elephant House.)

Four days later those Jewish businesses that remained in Weimar had their windows smashed.

As dusk fell, I sat at a table outside the tavern Zum Schwarzen Bären and ordered a Thuringian speciality of *Rinderroulade mit Apfelrotkohl und Thüringer Klößen* – beef, cabbage and dumplings accompanied by a glass of *Köstrizer* black beer. I was still trying to work out which room I had slept in twenty-six years earlier. It had no balcony, so it couldn't have been Hitler's room; but it was on the first floor with a view of the town hall, so it must have been the room next door. After finishing my meal I went to the Residenz-Café for a coffee, followed by a nightcap in a lounge bar on Burgplatz. I returned to the Markt as the church bells tolled eleven. A chill summer breeze cooled the market square. Beams of lamplight glistened on the black cobblestones. Young men stood smoking in the dark by the Neptune Fountain. I heard laughter and music from inside the Black Bear Inn. Waiters were piling up chairs outside the Cranach House. Lights were on behind the windows of the Hotel Elephant. I watched as shadows moved over the bedroom walls: the ghosts of Liszt, Schiller – or Hitler.

The following day I drove up Ettersberg, the hill to the north of Weimar. I turned left at an obelisk and followed a road through beech woods along the crest of a ridge. I parked the car and walked into the forest. After a while I reached a narrow embankment, the course of an old railway line parallel to the road. I turned to the west and followed the ghost track. Soon I began to notice steel cylinders embedded in the undergrowth, steles which marked the mass graves of seven thousand prisoners of Soviet Special Camp no. 2, who died in Buchenwald between 1945 and 1950. The woods thinned out and there were rusted rails, pins and brackets, rotting sleepers and cracked blocks of concrete alongside the embankment. The single track opened into a sorting yard of sidings, ramps and platforms; although no rails remained. To the left were the ruins of the Gustloff II armaments factory that employed slave labour from the camp. The platforms were used to unload new arrivals and reload departing trains with prisoners who, through illness or exhaustion, were no longer required in Buchenwald. The departing trains would return to the railway station in Weimar, from where their loads would be resorted onto trains destined for camps in the east.

I followed a path through meadows strewn with poppies and clover towards a plateau on the top of the hill, where the SS camp administration once stood. Six barrack blocks remained in a quarter-circle around an avenue now used as a car park. A road known as the "Caracho Path" led past the sites of kennels, stables, a falconry and a zoo towards the gatehouse of the concentration camp. The wrought-iron gates marking the border between the SS precinct and the camp were inscribed with the words "Jedem das Seine" ("To Each His Due"). Surrounded by electrified fencing, concrete posts and watchtowers, the camp ran down the northern slope of Ettersberg, a vast tract of hillside covered with grey and brown stones. Rectangles of burnt copper slag marked the sites of barrack blocks where prisoners were interned. Oblongs of denser scree represented memorials to Sinti, Roma and Jews who died on this charred hill.

Conspicuous by its red-brick chimney, the crematorium lay below a watchtower on the south-east corner of the site. Like Mauthausen, Buchenwald was not an extermination camp, yet tens of thousands of prisoners died here: gypsies killed by lethal injections from doctors experimenting with typhoid vaccines; political prisoners strangled in the cellar of the crematorium; Russian prisoners of war shot in the back of the neck as they reported to medical staff to have their height checked. A total of 34,375 deaths due to illness or overwork were recorded. A further 12–15,000 transportees were dead on arrival from other camps. Corpses were piled onto wagons and taken to the yard, where they were tipped down a metal chute into a cellar, stacked up, and eventually hoisted up to the crematorium in a lift operated by a wheel in the cellar. Once in the crematorium, corpses were loaded onto six trolleys and trundled into one of six ovens, kept fired by a team of stokers stationed on a platform below the rear of the stoves. As at Mauthausen, the crematorium contained a post-mortem room with a dissecting table, where inmates with gold teeth would have their fillings ripped out. The surgeons recycled human skin to bind books and presented each other with gifts of human heads. By April

1945 the crematorium had exhausted its capacity, and corpses were being buried in circular mass graves below a Bismarck Tower on the southern slope of Ettersberg. After the last SS guards had retreated, bodies were left piled high in the back yard. The US military discovered them when they liberated the camp on 11 April 1945. They also found twenty-one thousand "shaven and toothless ghosts" – the survivors of Buchenwald.

After tramping around the hot, stony slopes of the concentration camp, I returned to the SS precinct for a bowl of *solyanka* in the museum café. Afterwards I walked up past the ruins of an isolation block where prominent prisoners were held captive in a barrack outside the camp. These special captives included the leading Social Democrat Rudolf Breitscheid and Princess Mafalda of Savoy, daughter of King Victor Emmanuel III of Italy. Both were killed in August 1944 when a British air raid on the Gustloff II armaments factory missed its target and dropped incendiary bombs on prisoners in the SS area of Buchenwald. I took a path into woods on the southern slope of Ettersberg. Crickets buzzed and butterflies and bees span in the warm air over glades threaded with daisies and forget-me-nots. Thrushes and blackbirds hopped over the ruins of bunkers and cellars that once lay beneath the garages and outhouses of the SS.

The path emerged near the crown of the hill, from where the view to the south unrolled back down towards Weimar. At the top was the Buchenwald Memorial, dominated by a tower visible from the A4 autobahn which I had always assumed was the actual site of the concentration camp. I thought it strange that the official monument to the victims of Buchenwald should be so separate from the camp itself, at least one kilometre distant on the other side of Ettersberg. The reason for this became clearer as I began to descend a monumental flight of steps, hewn from pink sandstone and black granite, which ran in a curve down the hill. Every twenty metres there was a tall stone stele engraved with a bas-relief illustrating the lives of prisoners in the concentration camp. A rhyming verse on the rear of each stone recounted the history of their suffering. The tableaux depicted inmates beaten by guards or strung from trees if they had disobeyed an order. By the fifth stele it became clear that the narrative had little to do with the tens of thousands of Jews, gypsies, homosexuals or Russian prisoners of war who died there. This, instead, was the story of the German Communists, the most powerful group of prisoners in Buchenwald. They had formed an International Camp Committee, a resistance group within the camp; and had also served as "Kapos", henchmen who brutalised their fellow prisoners on behalf of the SS guards. After the war it fell to former members of the International Camp Committee to document the crimes of the SS. The German Communists were naturally keen to rewrite the history of Buchenwald, emphasising the heroism of their resistance rather than their complicity in the suffering of other prisoners. On the penultimate stele the Communists rise up in revolt against the murder of their leader Ernst Thälmann, and in the final scene they topple their Nazi captors and liberate themselves – without any apparent assistance from the Americans.

At the foot of the stairway was the first of three ring graves, circular depressions in the ground marking the mass graves the SS dug to dispose of thousands of corpses that the overflowing crematorium could no longer process. Each of the three ring graves was surrounded by a circular stone wall, ten metres high and embellished with corbels and torch brackets in a pseudo-medieval manner. Stone tablets announced that the prisoners buried here were "antifascist resistance fighters and patriots from eighteen countries" – "fighters against fascism" rather than victims of Nazism. Connecting the three ring graves was a "Way of Nations" that curved in a broad terrace across the hill, punctuated by eighteen stone pylons, each engraved with the name of a nation whose "resistance fighters" had been killed in Buchenwald: Belgium, Bulgaria, Denmark, Germany, France, Greece, the Netherlands, Italy, Yugoslavia, Luxembourg, Norway, Austria, Poland, Romania, Spain, Czechoslovakia, Hungary and the Soviet Union. Each pylon was surmounted by a bronze fire bowl. The effect was reminiscent of Tempelhof Airport or the Zeppelinfeld in Nuremberg. The International Socialist *Ehrenhain* (memorial grove) then re-ascended the hill by means of a broad granite stairway towards the Tower of Freedom, a titanic campanile built in the mid-1950s from stone stockpiled by the Nazis to complete a "Halle der Volksgemeinschaft" in Weimar. At the head of the stairway was a bronze sculpture representing eleven survivors from the camp, a football team of heroic antifascists with the goalkeeper diving to his right. The bell tower pealed four dull, muffled chimes and the hot breeze flapped at a red and white plastic seal around the monument. I was alone on the hillside with the tolling of the bells.

It seemed to be the thing to do on a Wednesday morning in Erfurt to have a long, lazy breakfast. All the cafés in Hefengasse and Wenigemarkt offered a breakfast buffet. Nobody appeared to be in a hurry. The only concern was to find a table that would remain in the shade for the next hour or so, as the temperature had risen to thirty-seven degrees centigrade. After breakfast I wandered round to the Fischmarkt to have a look at the city hall. The Rathaus was a neo-Gothic building from the 1870s, fronted by a narrow, hunched portico that jutted forwards into the Fischmarkt. Abreast of the balcony were two empty niches that once contained statues of Emperors Friedrich I and Wilhelm I, the red-bearded and white-bearded Kaisers whose lives were conflated during the founding years of the Second Reich into a single personification of the German Empire. Their images were torn down when the Red Army occupied Erfurt and erased any symbols of imperial Germany. I entered the Rathaus and was allowed to visit the Festsaal on the first floor. The walls of the staircase to the upper floors were decorated with paintings in the Historicist style of the 1890s, monumental tableaux depicting the sagas associated with Erfurt and Thuringia: Tannhäuser swooning with lust in the embrace of Venus, then crossing the Alps as a penitent and expiring in the arms of angels fanning him with roses; the necromancer Faust conjuring up visions of Polyphemus and Alexander the Great for the delectation of Emperor Charles V, before ending up dead on a midden, having failed to redeem his soul; the bigamous Count Ernst von Gleichen frolicking with his two wives in a medieval "three in bed shocker"; and the more wholesome life story of Martin Luther, who studied philosophy and law at the University of Erfurt between 1501 and 1505, before entering the Augustinian Monastery where he was ordained as a monk in 1507.

I bought a tube of sun cream from a chemist in the Fischmarkt and sat in the shade of a tram shelter to apply it. The square was surrounded by sixteenth-century houses that glittered in the sunlight, their red and yellow façades embossed with friezes, corbels, pilasters and statuettes. Winged lions and gryphons capered over the gables of the Haus zum breiten Herd, while chubby muses (minus Calliope, for some reason) and the deities of Ptolemaic cosmology ran riot across the cornices of the Haus zum roten Ochsen. Like the obelisk in the centre of the Fish Market, both houses were capped by a statue of the "Römer", a local variant of the Roland figure found in the centre of many German towns; in this case the Roman warrior symbolised the autonomy of Erfurt before the city was subjugated to the Archbishopric of Mainz in 1664. The Sparkasse opposite me was built in the mid-1930s, in the style of the Neue Sachlichkeit, as an extension to the city hall. The stone frames of its tall, narrow windows were carved with astronomical symbols and its frontal projection was supported by six caryatids, glum figures in the fashions of the 1930s, who personified six of the Seven Deadly Sins. Lust was doing nothing more prurient than casting a wistful sideways glance at Vanity, who was powdering her face in a hand mirror. Anger was missing – or maybe anger was not regarded as a sin in Nazi Germany?

Running through the centre of Erfurt is the River Gera, its streams dividing and rejoining, flowing beneath elms and weeping willows, under wooden jetties built onto the backs of restaurants and bars; its waters fresh, cool and sufficiently shallow for girls to hitch up their skirts and wade across it. In 1472 the city built sixty-four houses across the river, constructing a bridge-street unique north of the Alps. The half-timbered Krämerbrücke is now rather twee, lined with shops selling hand-glazed pottery, hand-blown glass, hand-crafted jewellery, hand-made chocolates and hand-tooled shoes. A *Linkshänder-Laden* purveys a variety of scissors, peelers, mugs, cutlery, tin openers, corkscrews, rulers, pencil sharpeners, scythes, shears, planes, tape measures, watches, keyboards, computer mice, boomerangs and billiard cues to those of an exclusively left-handed bent.

In the evening I strolled down the Anger, once Germany's largest woad market, now Erfurt's main shopping street. I passed Luther, a bull of a man in voluminous bronze robes; and Bismarck, stiff and slight in a niche on one of the ornate houses that grace the street. I sat down to eat at a table outside the Gasthof zur Hohen Lilie on the eastern corner of the Domplatz, a huge square once used as a parade ground by the Prussian garrison stationed in the Petersberg citadel above the city. Two churches rise over the Domplatz, separated by "die Graden", a flight of broad steps descending from the Portal of the Wise and Foolish Virgins on the northern side of the Mariendom. The Late Gothic Cathedral of St Mary's thrusts itself over the Domplatz on a platform of arches. Its High Choir soars over the square, ribbed and toothed with buttresses and finials, statuettes and gargoyles. The High Gothic Church of St Severus on the opposite side of "die Graden" rises above an accretion of prelates' houses, each of its three towers surmounted by a needle-sharp spire in the Bohemian manner. I made the facile assumption that St Mary's Cathedral would be Catholic and the more severe Severikirche Protestant; but it transpired that both churches were Roman Catholic, a surprising revelation in this predominantly Protestant city. Erfurt was where Martin Luther studied and the earlier mystic Meister Eckhart preached, a city which embraced Protestantism during the Reformation. But it was later ruled for a hundred and fifty years by Catholic Mainz, and the two churches that dominate the city's skyline remain under the governance of the Holy See.

After dinner I sat on the banks of the Gera below the Krämerbrücke. I crossed to a tiny green island between the two streams of the river and walked through the gaps between the stone piers supporting the elevated street. I emerged in Wenigemarkt, a little marketplace where café tables and chairs were spread out beneath a canopy of chestnut trees. I sat in front of the Drogerie-Bistro, a chemist turned bar, and ordered a coffee and schnapps. The night was warm and I felt utterly relaxed; so relaxed, in fact, that instead of returning to my hotel at midnight, I ordered another drink and a packet of cigarettes, thus breaking the latest resolution to give up smoking I had taken on arrival in Weimar. A chapter of local bikers roared into the square, parked their machines around a fountain and pushed some tables together in front of one of the bars. They proceeded to order twenty cups of coffee. I noticed people entering a baroque house in Futterstraße and decided to follow them. There was a discotheque in the cellar and I paid a handful of euros to join the throng. While checking in my jacket in the cloakroom I inadvertently looped my arm inside the strap of a girl's handbag, which caused some consternation on her part and embarrassment on mine. Later in the evening I found myself crushed against a woman in a grey woollen dress, who slipped her arm inside mine and our hips touched. On the spur of the moment I couldn't think of anything clever to say to her in German, and the moment passed. I saw her again as I checked out of the cloakroom, and followed her out onto the street, watching as she walked away into the night.

I arrived in Eisenach in the early evening and checked into Haus Hainstein, a neo-Gothic villa high on the slopes above the town. I was shown to a corner room with a view of the Wartburg from one window and the Burschenschaftsdenkmal from the other. A golden cross on the tower of the Wartburg glittered in the setting sun. I went down to the hotel terrace to join the other guests: small groups of silver-haired West Germans clad in Ralph Lauren polo shirts and smart deck shoes, drinking Beck's or Bitburger Pils from fluted glasses; and an isolated quartet of East Germans wearing rock gig souvenir T-shirts and sandals, and drinking half-litres of a dark local brew. In the dining room a firm was holding its sales conference dinner. I ordered a *Bauernschmaus* of *Leberkäse*, fried egg and fried potatoes, and watched the swallows darting above the trees. The moon appeared, at first just a fingernail of gauze in an azure sky. The evening slowly darkened. Lights came on high up on the hill, flooding the Wartburg with an amber glow. A discotheque started up in the dining room and the sales conference delegates began to strut and twirl to the beats of Tom Jones, Chubby Checker and Olivia Newton-John. By midnight the moon had disappeared behind the Wartburg, leaving the golden palace on the hill beneath a deep indigo night sky. The stragglers in the discotheque were playing a drunken game of blind man's bluff, an excuse, no doubt, for the salesmen to grope the secretaries.

In the morning I walked up through the woods to the Wartburg, my feet crackling over dried beech mast and snapping fallen twigs. It was blisteringly hot on top of the hill. I passed below the fifteenth-century barbican and ascended the cobbled bailey to the nineteenth-century keep, where I bought a ticket for a guided tour of the castle. While waiting for the tour to begin, I stood on the battlements and surveyed the view over the ridges and gullies of the Thüringer Wald to the west of Eisenach, tracing the course of the old East German autobahn as it swept over the Karolinenbrücke viaduct, beyond the *Plattenbau* estates which once housed the employees of the VEB Automobile Works where the Wartburg motor car was constructed. The Volkspolizei used to lie in wait behind camouflage netting to film unsuspecting West German motorists who, impatient after queuing for hours to cross the border, would accelerate down the long incline, only to be pulled up at the next intersection and presented with a twenty-mark fine.

The guided tour of the Wartburg started in the bowels of the tall Romanesque *Palas*. The Knights' Hall and the Dining Room were medieval chambers, the former cross-vaulted by sandstone arches and the latter roofed with oak beams, both supported by a single central column whose capitals were carved with eagles and swans. On display in the Knights' Hall were the sword and shield of Konrad von Thüringen, a Grand Master of the Teutonic Knights, and the memorial slabs of Ludwig the Iron and Ludwig the Leaper, the latter the founder of the Wartburg in 1067. We passed through an arch below a grotesque tympanum depicting a dragon eating alive a knight in armour – breastplate, helmet, visor and all – and entered the neo-Byzantine Elizabeth Bower, a boudoir commissioned by Kaiser Wilhelm II as a memorial to his uncle Carl Alexander of Saxe-Weimar-Eisenach, the Grand Duke missing from the empty plinth in Weimar. The sparkling glass mosaics illustrated the worldly life of Elizabeth of Thuringia, daughter of King Andrew II of Hungary. Her birth in 1207 had been prophesied by the sorcerer Klingsor von Ungerlant (Hungary), and he duly brought her to the Wartburg as the child bride of Ludwig IV, Landgrave of Thuringia. After her husband's death in the Fifth Crusade she retired to a Franciscan monastery in Marburg, where she died at the age of twenty-four. Shortly thereafter she was canonised, and was later adopted by the Teutonic Knights as their secondary patroness (after the Virgin Mary). Much later she was immortalised by Richard Wagner as the redeemer of the poet Tannhäuser.

The tour continued through a medieval chapel on the first floor and into the Elizabeth Gallery, a corridor decorated with lyrical frescoes by the nineteenth-century painter Moritz von Schwind, which illustrated the spiritual life of the canonised landgravine. At the centre of the first floor was the Sängersaal, a Minstrels' Hall redesigned in the 1850s in an attempt to recreate the courtly atmosphere of the medieval Wartburg, where troubadours would gather to compete with each other in song. The walls were painted in patterns of spring green and autumn gold and decorated with friezes depicting squirrels and stags gambolling in rose bowers and groves of oak trees. At one end was a raised Minstrels' Gallery, hung with tapestries embroidered with texts by Novalis and Wolfram von Eschenbach. At the other end of the hall was the *Minnesängerschrank*, a Gothic cabinet ornamented with a triptych of paintings that illustrated scenes from Gottfried von Straßburg's *Tristan und Isolde*, von Eschenbach's *Parzival*, and the *Nibelungenlied* composed by an anonymous Danubian bard – the three ballads that provided the raw material for Richard Wagner's greatest operas.

A large mural on the interior wall of the Minstrels' Hall depicted the legendary "Sängerkrieg" of 1206 in which seven of the famed *Minnesänger* of the age (among them von Eschenbach, Walther von der Vogelweide and, representing Hungary in this early version of the Eurovision Song Contest, Klingsor von Ungerlant) perform in front of their patron, Landgrave Hermann I. The losing contestant is the upstart Heinrich von Ofterdingen, who offends the landgrave by singing the praises of the rival Babenberg court in Vienna. The hangman waits with his noose, but the troubadour is spared by the grace of Landgravine Sophie and the mediation of Klingsor, who persuades the landgrave to offer Heinrich a one-year stay of execution. In the background of Von Schwind's painting of the thirteenth-century contest are cameo portraits of Luther, Goethe, Schiller and Grand Duke Carl Alexander of Saxe-Weimar-Eisenach. The one figure missing from the fresco is Tannhäuser, the poet whom Wagner portrayed as the central character of his opera based on the Singers' Contest. It seems that Wagner got his dates wrong, or was just not that interested in historical accuracy: Tannhäuser's career as a wandering minstrel came several decades after the historical "Sängerkrieg" was purported to have taken place; and his redeemer Elizabeth of Thuringia had not yet been born. Wagner also removed Klingsor from the Singers' Contest and gave him a role in *Parsifal* instead.

We trooped through the Landgrave's Room and up a staircase to the Festsaal, the Knights' Hall that extends over the upper storey of the *Palas*. The fir-clad ravines of the Thuringian Forest were visible through triplets of arched windows in bays of powder-blue stone decorated with rings and diamonds, flowers of the field and medieval beasties. The wall at the far end glittered with red and gold bands intertwined in quatrefoil patterns around portraits of Landgraves Ludwig I, Ludwig II and their imperial ancestor Charlemagne; above each figure was an image of the temple of Jerusalem, their spiritual home. On the opposing wall the images of Landgrave Hermann I, his heir Ludwig IV and his saintly daughter-in-law gazed down from a screen of painted briars and thorns that curled and spiralled around gilded fields of roses and lilies. Hidden among the flowers were tiny crosses and orbs; and an echidna, a crowned half-woman, half-dragon, proffering a love potion in a golden chalice to the next questing knight to come her way. Suspended above the hall was a heavy wooden ceiling, its beams braided with gilded cornrows and its coffered panels engraved with the emblems of gaunt red eagles. Huge chandeliers in the shape of crowns threw a golden light over rows of rhubarb-coloured chairs that had been set up for the evening performance of the "Grand Romantic Opera" *Tannhäuser und der Sängerkrieg auf Wartburg* by Richard Wagner.

I walked back through the woods below the Wartburg and down steep, winding streets of Gothic villas, half-timbered and helmeted with turrets of black slate. In Pfarrberg I was stopped by an attractive young woman in a red top with a chic bob of black hair. She bade me good day. I had no idea who she was and stood there dumbstruck. She introduced herself as the receptionist from Haus Hainstein who had checked me in the previous evening. I apologised for not recognising her out of uniform and confirmed I had enjoyed my stay, but had not slept well because of the heat. She in turn apologised for the lack of air-conditioning in the hotel.

In the marketplace of Eisenach it was thirty-eight degrees centigrade. Cobblestones roasted in the heat. A gilded statue of Saint George slaying the dragon glittered in the sunlight in the centre of the square. A modicum of shade was provided by the Georgenkirche, a Gothic hall church with baroque end gables and a neo-baroque tower added in 1902. Luther's words "Ein' feste Burg ist unser Gott" were inscribed over the door of the church where he preached on his return from the Diet of Worms. Bach was christened here and sang in the church as a choirboy. Telemann composed cantatas during his brief tenure as cantor in Eisenach. I sat beneath one of the sunshades outside the Stadtcafé and ordered a light lunch of garlic bread and *Basilikumschaumsuppe*, a frothy basil soup which dissolved on the palate like champagne. The sun blistered the walls of the half-timbered Lutherhaus, the pink Rathaus and the Stadtschloss, one of Goethe's temporary residences. The town of Eisenach is close to the geographical centre of Germany and its architecture is an eclectic mixture of northern German Brick Gothic, central German *Fachwerkhäuser*, southern German baroque and East German prefabricated apartment blocks. Situated up against the old German–German border, its western suburbs within the five-kilometre restricted zone, Eisenach was of symbolic importance during the process of reunification. Willi Brandt addressed a crowd of thirty thousand here in January 1990, "formulating German unity", according to a plaque on the wall of the Rathaus. Eight years later Helmut Kohl brought Bill Clinton here. The American President spoke to a crowd of similar magnitude, declaring: "Do not underestimate what you, as free citizens, can achieve with your dreams." My own memories of Eisenach were of stopping off in the marketplace for a bowl of stodgy *Eintopf* in the grey, smoggy days of the 1980s. I wanted to ask the two women who shared my table what they remembered from those times, but they had more pressing issues – hairdressing appointments and school runs.

After lunch I walked up Lutherstraße towards the Bachhaus and its new, Frank Gehry-inspired extension, and then followed Johann-Sebastian-Bach-Straße as it climbed through a colony of slate-helmeted Wilhelmine villas with gardens ablaze with azaleas and rhododendrons. It was hot and quiet. An isolated peal of laughter from a back garden broke the silence, echoing around the hilly streets. Eisenach fell away below me as I came out onto the meadows of the Göpelskuppe. In front of me was the Burschenschaftsdenkmal, a monument to German nationalism forged by Wilhelm Kreis, the architect who had become a leitmotif to my travels. In a style similar to his Bismarck Towers, this was a tall, circular monument of nine columns bound together by a circular architrave. The columns represented the nine original *Burschenschaften*, patriotic student corporations founded during the Wars of Liberation, who held their first demonstration of national unity on the Wartburg in 1817. Their slogan "Ehre, Freiheit, Vaterland" ("Honour, Freedom, Fatherland") was engraved on the architrave below busts of Hermann the Cherusker, Charlemagne, Luther, Dürer, Goethe and Beethoven. The bell-shaped dome was encircled by nine stone eagles guarding the gateways to the cities of the Reich. A semi-circular colonnade of stone pillars ran behind the monument. In front was a flight of stone steps down to a Langemarck Memorial, added in 1933, engraved with the ghosts of fallen *Burschenschaft* soldiers rising from their graves.

I paid the three euros entrance fee and entered the circular vault. An opal light filtered through restored Jugendstil windows. The interior had been turned into a small museum, but there was little to exhibit other than the stone heads of Bismarck and his War Minister Roon, both of which lay disembodied on a stone bench. Nine bronze-coloured pilasters topped by Secessionist eagles led the eye up to a reconstructed fresco in the ceiling, a garishly painted depiction of Ragnarök, the final conflict between the Aesir and the forces of darkness – an ur-Nordic fable of cosmic destruction by giants, wolves and ravens:

> Schwarz wird die Sonne, die Erde sinkt ins Meer,
> Von Himmel schwinden die heiter'n Sterne.
> Glutwirbel umwühlen den allnährenden Weltbaum,
> Die heiße Lohe beleckt den Himmel.
>
> (Black is the sun as the earth sinks into the sea
> And the bright stars fade from the sky.
> Burning winds churn up the all-nourishing world tree,
> As raging flames lick the heavens.)

And all that remains is *Fimbulvetr* – eternal ice.

From Eisenach I drove north-east through golden-brown fields of wheat and rye. Combine harvesters blew clouds of corn dust across the roads. The Kyffhäuser range rose up on the horizon as I drove down the hill from Sondershausen. I caught a glimpse of the *Kaiserkrone*, the imperial crown on top of the Kyffhäuser Monument. At the far end of the ridge was the Panorama Museum, a ribbed cylinder rising above the trees.

I stopped in Bad Frankenhausen, where I had booked a room in the Alter Ackersbürgerhof, a converted farmhouse that was once a dwelling for ploughmen who had been granted citizenship rights and were permitted to reside within the town walls. I was shown to a granny flat, unchanged since the 1960s, and invited to join the other guests for a drink in the courtyard. I ordered a Thuringian wheat beer, lit a cigarette and sat back in one of the vine-clad bowers surrounding the yard.

The landlord and his wife were a taciturn couple, reserved in the manner of the generation who had been brought up as East Germans. The other guests were Dutch and more convivial. The landlord thought I too was Dutch, which was not unusual: many Germans find it difficult to believe an Englishman could speak passable German, so they assume I'm from the Netherlands. He asked me if I'd like a *Kalbssteak* from the barbecue. It seemed to be the only dish on offer, so I accepted. The veal was tough, and the lukewarm potato salad that accompanied it was not that pleasant either.

After supper I wandered into the centre of Bad Frankenhausen. The broad Anger and its surrounding streets were deserted. As in Sondershausen, Halberstadt, Gera, Schwerin and a hundred other towns in eastern Germany, it seemed that the citizens locked their doors, closed the shutters and retired for the night at 9 pm. I noticed a few traces of the town's GDR history – a disused "Haus der Dienste" and the ghostly lettering "Kurbad Drogerie" over a chemist – but it was the silent houses and empty streets that marked Bad Frankenhausen as a town with an East German past. Returning to the Anger, I found some people drinking beer and talking about dogs on the terrace of the Thüringer Hof hotel. Most of them turned out to be elderly tourists from western Germany, who told me that they liked to holiday in the east in order to escape the pace of life in the west and rediscover a quiet, dull Germany like the one they'd grown up in during the 1950s.

In the morning I drove up through the Diamanten Aue to the cylinder on the hill which housed the Bauernkriegspanorama, a painting one hundred and twenty-three metres in circumference, which depicted The Peasants' War of 1525. A staircase led from the foyer to a darkened gallery where I flopped down with the other spectators on one of the circular couches scattered across the centre of the rotunda. The colour, detail, complexity and sheer size of the painting made it breathtaking. I found myself in the middle of day and night, summer and winter, life and death; at the centre of a kaleidoscopic tumult of three thousand characters – nobles, clerics, patricians, guildsmen, artisans, soldiers and peasants. Werner Tübke's panorama is essentially a *theatrum mundi* of sixteenth-century Germany, painted in a Magical Realist style which owes much to Bosch, Brueghel and Grünewald. It depicts biblical and medieval figures such as Adam and Eve, Cain and Abel, a four-faced Whore of Babylon and a *Siebenlasterweib* (a heptamorphous female embodiment of the Seven Deadly Sins, with butterfly wings and crows' feet). An abundance of devils exhale their fetid scarlet breath around Golgotha, a Ship of Fools and an unfinished Tower of Babel. There are surreal images such as a bubble containing the flat earth and the eye of God; a blue cloud with the disembodied head of an Angel of Wrath at its centre; and a great blue transparent fish with the cosmos in its innards and a city swept away by flood in its egg sac. Tübke's monumental, preposterous *oeuvre* is unremittingly nihilistic, portraying a never-ending cycle of stupidity, venality and greed. Parched summer, barren autumn and icy winter roll into one other, each season populated by drunken peasants, lecherous clerics, obsequious burghers and incestuous aristocrats. Men are stabbed, beheaded, flayed alive, broken on the wheel or stretched on the rack. A hanged man has his purse cut before his corpse has stopped swinging. Emperors and popes throw dice for territory or cheat one another at poker. Rat-faced cardinals sell papal indulgences and a trio of noblemen perform unspeakable acts on a naked woman in a beer barrel. The portrayal of cruelty, avarice and superstition spins around and around, and then just starts again. Tübke's thesis is that there is no improvement in human nature: that civilisation is a cycle of violence and lust that repeats itself endlessly – a morality play from which nobody learns anything.

The pivotal scene is the Battle of Frankenhausen, a crucial struggle in the Peasants' War of 1525. The radical reformer and apocalyptic theologian Thomas Müntzer leads a rebellion of eight thousand peasants, miners and salt workers against an army of princes from Hesse, Saxony and Braunschweig and their *Landsknecht* mercenaries. The nobles offer free passage to the peasant army if it disbands and surrenders its leader. The peasants agree, but then Müntzer begins to preach and a rainbow appears in the clear blue May sky. Bad Frankenhausen has a reputation for aridity, and the rainbow is perceived as a symbol of divine intervention. The peasants hail their leader, attack the princes and are slaughtered. In the painting Müntzer stands alone and untouched at the vortex of the savagery, his flag lowered and a defeated expression on his face. Death plays the bagpipes on a nearby tree stump. Müntzer was later tortured and beheaded – and much later commemorated on the five-mark banknote of the GDR.

Below the wheeling armies is the only propitious scene in the panorama. Fenced off from the slaughter behind a grove of saplings is a Fountain of Wisdom, around which twenty representatives of the great and good of the early sixteenth century are assembled. At their centre is the triumvirate of Dürer, Cranach and Luther: Dürer fey and narcissistic, like a Renaissance rent boy, in slashed doublet with his chest bared and his long ringlets cascading from beneath a floppy hat; Cranach a rich, portly merchant of art; and Luther a dark, simian presence behind the other two. They are flanked by the cobbler-poet Hans Sachs, the sculptor Veit Stoß, the theologian Philipp Melanchthon, Erasmus of Rotterdam, Copernicus, Paracelsus, Johannes Gutenberg and Christopher Columbus; a pantheon of cultural grandees who personify the *Neuzeit*, the new age of Humanism and Reformation that was dawning just as the medieval age of feudalism and superstition depicted all around them was tearing itself apart. The Fountain of Wisdom, however, is a static tableau, at odds with the rest of the painting. The Wheel of Time turns another degree and chaos resumes.

The panorama is officially entitled *Early Bourgeois Revolution in Germany*, which suggests that it had some didactic purpose for the GDR. That was the intention, but Tübke insisted on the autonomy of his vision and refused to accept any interference from the cultural commissars in East Berlin. His finished work was regarded unfavourably by the regime and they despatched only Margot Honecker to the unveiling of the panorama in the rotunda they had constructed for its installation. Opened on 14 September 1989, the gallery was planned to show the world that East Germany was capable of great cultural as well as sporting achievements. But a few weeks later the Berlin Wall came down, and Tübke's apocalyptic carnival fell victim to the very wheel of time and cycle of history it described.

From Bad Frankenhausen I drove north, negotiating the hairpin bends up the southern slope of the Kyffhäuser hills. At the top of the ridge I turned right, along a road through a forest towards Burg Kyffhausen. I parked the car and followed a path to the ruins of the Unterburg, the lower castle which is the main surviving part of the medieval fortress that once stretched for six hundred metres along the crest of the ridge. Burg Kyffhausen was founded in the twelfth century as a stronghold to protect the Staufer *Pfalz* of Tilleda in the Golden Meadow below. It is not known whether the Hohenstaufen Emperor Friedrich I and his peripatetic court ever sojourned in Burg Kyffhausen, but over time the name of Barbarossa became closely identified with this particular castle and the hill on which it stood. A legend grew up around the figure of the sleeping king who would one day awake and restore Germany to its medieval glory. The myth gained particular currency during the period of romantic, nationalist movements in the nineteenth century. In 1817 Friedrich Rückert published a poem entitled *Der Alte Barbarossa* which specifically placed the dormant monarch in a cave beneath the Kyffhäuser ridge. By the middle of the century this myth had become the national saga of the German people.

In 1888 it was decided to commemorate the death of Kaiser Wilhelm I by erecting a series of national monuments to the victor of the Franco-Prussian War and founder of the Second German Reich. The grandest of these would be built on the site of Burg Kyffhausen at the tip of the Kyffhäuser forest. The prime motive behind building the monument in this location was to reinforce the theme of national re-awakening by conflating the military achievements of Wilhelm I with the myth of Barbarossa. In his proposal for the Kyffhäuser Monument, Dr Westphal, secretary of the German War Veterans' Association, proclaimed: "Here on the Kyffhäuser Mountain, beneath which, according to legend, Kaiser Friedrich the Redbeard awaits the restoration of the Reich; here shall Kaiser Wilhelm the Whitebeard arise and fulfil that legend." The Wilhelmine Reich would restore the glory and unity of the medieval Hohenstaufen Empire. The foundation stone of the new monument, designed by Bruno Schmitz, was laid on 10 May 1892 by the local satrap Prince Günther Victor von Schwarzburg-Rudolstadt. The tower was completed in 1895 and statues of Barbarossa and Kaiser Wilhelm, sculpted by Nicolaus Geiger and Emil Hundrieser, respectively, were installed the following year. The inauguration of the monument on 18 June 1896 was attended by twenty thousand war veterans, who marched up the hill and hung their banners over the walls and arches of the pristine monolith.

I followed a path through the trees on the northern slope of Kyffhäuser which overlooked the Golden Meadow, a plain of golden-green wheat fields stretching north towards the hills of the Unterharz and the blue, hazy Brocken, visible on the horizon. I emerged at length onto the broad Ring Terrace surrounding the monument, its gravel surface white-hot beneath the midday sun. I took shelter below the colonnade of the Barbarossahof,

whose pink sandstone arches lead into the Schlosshof, a grotto of roughly
hewn rocks, covered with green lichen, above which Barbarossa sits
enthroned on an ivory bench. His beard is a tangle of matted snarl, like
the roots of a great tree descending into the bowels of the earth. His right
hand clutches a sword and his right leg is cocked, as if ready to spring into
action should the ravens ever cease to fly around Kyffhäuser, thus releasing
the subterranean emperor from his catatonic spell. The neo-Romanesque
niche in which the slumbering warrior languishes is carved with serpents,
gryphons and death masks, an iconography that foreshadows that of the
Monument to the Battle of the Nations Bruno Schmitz was to build several years later. The tower of the Kyffhäuser Monument rises above the
Schlosshof, its eastern wall dominated by an equestrian statue of Kaiser
Wilhelm I, a moustachioed, side-whiskered, spiked-helmeted reincarna-
tion of the fabled king who presides over the grotto below him. The architrave of the tower is engraved with the slogan "Fuer Kaiser und Reich"
and with the names of the kingdoms, duchies, principalities and Hanseatic
city-states that constituted the German Reich at the *Jahrhundertwende*:
Prussia, Bavaria, Saxony, Württemberg, Baden, Hesse, Braunschweig,
Lippe, Anhalt, Alsace-Lorraine, Hamburg, Bremen, Lübeck, Oldenburg,
Schwarzburg and Schaumburg – an inventory of states which corresponds
more or less to that cut into the Bismarck Tower built around the same
time on the slopes of the Starnberger See; but which is radically different
from the vision of a Greater Germany commemorated by Ludwig I of
Bavaria on the Befreiungshalle fifty years earlier.

The National Socialists had little use for this monument to the
Hohenzollerns. Adolf Hitler paid a brief personal visit to Kyffhäuser on 2
October 1934, much to the consternation of Herr Brocke, a janitor who
was working in the kitchen below the monument when an SS guard burst
in and ordered him to open the barrier across the road to the tower. Knees
shaking, he found himself face to face with his Führer. Hitler clapped
Herr Brocke on the shoulder, shook his hand and looked into his eyes.
"A look I shall never forget; a look that penetrated deep into my heart,"
the janitor recounted, repeating the stock response of every ordinary
German who happened to be accosted by Hitler. The Führer returned to
Kyffhäuser in 1939 to lay a wreath below a statue of Hindenburg which
had been unveiled beneath the monument earlier that year. The gloomy,
musty Turmhalle inside the base of the Kaiser Wilhelm Monument was
redesigned by the National Socialists as a Hall of Honour, hung with reg-
imental banners and decorated with urns containing soil from Germany's

lost territories of West Prussia, Alsace-Lorraine and the Saarland. Bronze busts were installed of Wilhelm I, Bismarck, Moltke, Roon, Scharnhorst, Crown Prince Friedrich Wilhelm and Adolf Hitler.

After the Second World War the East German Ministry for People's Education vilified the Kyffhäuser Monument as "reactionary, militaristic" and "National Socialist". It recommended the removal of the *Kaiserkrone*, the destruction of the statue of Kaiser Wilhelm I and the permanent presence of flags of the German Democratic Republic and the Soviet Union. Even more radical were plans drawn up by the East German Finance Ministry, which proposed the demolition of the entire monument and its replacement by a giant steel sculpture in the Soviet style of a smith wielding a hammer, or a Ruhr collier conjoined with a Saxon milkmaid. During the 1950s and 1960s the decline in the monument's cultural and political significance was matched by a corresponding increase in its popularity as a tourist attraction. The figure of 163,000 visitors in 1953 rose to 319,000 in 1965 and had reached 335,000 by 1988. Most of the day-trippers, however, arrived in coach parties to drink the local beer and sample the "Barbarossa" schnapps; they would have had little idea of who Kaiser Wilhelm was. And so it remains in the reunified Germany of today – a scenic place to drive to at weekends and enjoy a stroll in the woods and a liquid lunch in one of the *Gasthöfe* below the monument. Legend has it that Barbarossa will rise again to save the German nation when the ravens cease to fly around Kyffhäuser. But I saw no ravens, and Barbarossa remains entombed in his grotto beneath the hill. Germany's hour of need is not yet at hand. Or maybe it came and went while he was asleep?

14

Hanover

The Last Swastika in Germany

To celebrate my return to western Germany I had *Teewurst* for breakfast – soft, fleshy pink wurst that tasted heavenly after the crumbling grey sausagemeat I had been served in Weimar and Eisenach. Breakfast finished at 9.30 am and all the hot food – the eggs, bacon and sausage – had been consumed by the time I arrived in the breakfast room of my small hotel in the suburbs of Goslar; I had forgotten how greedy the *Wessis* could be. Outside, the sun was shining from a clear blue sky. I sat in the hotel garden and smoked a cigarette. The neighbours were greeting each other over the fence as they hosed down their swimming pools for the weekend:

"Guten Tag, Frau Lucas."

"Guten Morgen, Herr Boedecker. Wie ist es, das allgemeine Wohlbefinden?"

Herr Boedecker's general feeling of wellbeing seemed to be in good order on this bright summer morning.

I set off towards the centre of Goslar, through streets of wood-panelled Wilhelmine villas with red and green sun wheels painted across their beams. The narrow lanes of the Oberstadt were lined with miners' cottages, half-timbered with black, brown or grey beams and roofed with slate tiles. Overlooking the Frankenberger Plan was the Kleines Heiliges Kreuz, a fourteenth-century almshouse criss-crossed with gold beams embossed with miniature coloured shields. In the centre of the square was a stone fountain ornamented with the crossed hammers of the local ore miners.

Tiny humped bridges led over the streams of the Gose and Abzucht into cobbled alleys of coppersmiths' cottages, many with scales of grey slate like the hide of a pangolin. Straw dolls were pinned behind lace curtains; doormats were woven with the words "Herzlich Wilkommen"; lintels and beams were inscribed with rhyming homilies picked out in gold lettering:

Ein frohlich Herz, ein friedlich Haus,
Daß macht das Glück des Lebens aus.
(A cheerful heart and a peaceful home
Make for a happy life.)

Schaffen und Streben ist Gottes Gebot,
Arbeit ist Leben, Nichtsthun der Tot.
(Strive and create is God's command;
Work is Life, Idleness Death.)

There was a wedding reception on the terrace of the Kaiserpfalz. Heart-shaped balloons danced in the breeze above tables laden with flutes of champagne. Guests in blazers and boaters or their best summer frocks spilled down the steps onto the lawn in front of the palace, to the consternation of some Goth youngsters sprawled beneath two equestrian statues of "Friedrich I Barbarossa" and "Wilhelm der Große". In spite of signs posted around the lawn to the effect that "The Consumption of Alcoholic Beverages on This Site is Strictly Forbidden", the *Gruftis* were swigging from cans of beer and spray-painting the pedestals of the statues with their tribal graffiti – "Evil Lady's [sic] of Darkness" or "Nazi Punks Fuck Off!"

The walls of the Kaisersaal inside the palace were covered with a cycle of monumental paintings which surrounded the hall. The murals were painted between 1876 and 1897 by Hermann Wislicenus, a professor at the Düsseldorf Academy who worked in the High Romantic style of Historicist painting championed by Moritz von Schwind and Julius Schnorr von Carolsfeld. His tableaux depicted the familiar tale of the Hohenstaufens and the Hohenzollerns: how Kaiser Wilhelm I assumed the mantle of Barbarossa and reunified the Reich that had fallen into disarray since the demise of the Hohenstaufen dynasty. The larger paintings illustrated key events in the Prussian-Protestant canon: Charlemagne chopping down the World Tree and converting the pagan Saxons to Christianity; Heinrich III towing the deposed Pope Gregory VI over the

Alps; Friedrich Barbarossa slaughtering the Saracens; and Martin Luther defying the Catholic Habsburg emperor at the Diet of Worms. Surrounding the larger murals were smaller grisailles depicting monks and minstrels; wintry landscapes symbolic of the bleak season Germany had endured between the fall of the Hohenstaufens and the rise of the Hohenzollerns; and scenes from the legend of Thorn Rose (Sleeping Beauty), who personified the catatonic spell under which Germany had slept during this period.

At the centre of the Reichssaal is the great arched mural illustrating the Imperial Proclamation of 1871, a grand operatic pageant which conflates Allegory, Myth and History into the apotheosis of the Second Reich. Side-whiskered and spiked-helmeted, Kaiser Wilhelm I and his heir Crown Prince Friedrich Wilhelm ride into the centre of the tableau, Kaiser Bill on a cross-eyed black stallion whose eye, according to the tour guide, follows you around the hall from whichever angle you look at it. To the right of the imperial duo are ranks of Hohenzollerns headed by Kaiserin Augusta, her sister-in-law Viktoria and her grandson, the future Wilhelm II. To their left is the Prussian General Staff, represented by Bismarck, Moltke and Roon. Almost lost in the crowd behind them is King Ludwig II, proffering his crown to the Hohenzollerns. This is poetic licence (or a deliberate falsification of history), since the Bavarian crown was never offered to the German Reich, and the Bavarian king was not present at the Imperial Proclamation. (The very idea of the Hall of Mirrors of Ludwig's beloved Louis XIV being sullied by ranks of goose-stepping Prussians would have been anathema to the Bavarian king – and he refused to attend the ceremony in Versailles.) In the misty firmament above the Hohenzollerns ride the spirits of Salian Heinrichs and Staufer Friedrichs: Barbarossa gestures pointedly towards Kaiser Wilhelm, as if to anoint his successor. In the foreground of the painting two medieval princesses – allegorical figures representing the reconquered duchies of Alsace and Lorraine – offer up models of the cathedrals of Metz and Strasbourg to the victorious Prussians. Below them sits Father Rhine, clad in a robe of river-green velvet: the Rhine is once again "that most German of rivers" after the recapture of the aforementioned duchies. By his side is a personification of the German Saga, a comely Brünhild who directs us to the open page of her story:

Und tritt der alte Kaiser aus seinem Schloss hervor,
Dann blüht die Dornenrose, das deutsche Reich empor.

(When the old emperor emerges from his castle,
The thorn rose flowers and the German Reich blossoms forth.)

A neo-Romanesque cloister leads from the Kaisersaal to the Chapel of
St Ulrich, the sole surviving building of the medieval Kaiserpfalz. From
the upper floor of the double chapel I gazed down on the sarcophagus
of Heinrich III, the eleventh-century Kaiser whose heart is locked in a
golden capsule in Goslar, but whose body is buried in the cathedral at
Speyer. Sepulchral music filled the chapel and echoed through the rooms
of the museum below the Kaisersaal. This contains a bronze throne commissioned by the anti-king Hermann von Salm, who had himself crowned
in Goslar by the Archbishop of Mainz during the Christmas festival of
1081; and a twelfth-century stone capital depicting two Jews, identifiable
by their conical *Kegelhüte*. One is attempting to milk a sow; the other is
riding bareback on a pig, lurching forward to stab the animal in its snout.
Presumably the juxtaposition of the dirty pigs and the dirty Jews was a
source of great mirth to the monks and minstrels of the medieval palace.

The centre of Goslar buzzed with the activity of a Wednesday morning
market. Stallholders had come from as far afield as Erfurt or Münster to
set up their vans in the streets and alleys below the towers of St Cosmas
and St Damian. They sold hand-woven shawls, wax candles in the national
colours of black, red and gold, and walking sticks with handles carved
into the shapes of pelicans or flamingos. Craftsmen sold jewellery, stamps,
mobiles and sundials made from local slate. Grocers purveyed almond
pastries and homemade jams, honeys, meads and spirits distilled from ber-
ries from the Harz Mountains. Two gypsies played fiddle and accordion
in the centre of the marketplace, by a medieval fountain surmounted by
a bronze eagle, symbol of Goslar's former status as a Free Imperial City.
Bells tolled from the towers of the market church and a carillon pealed at
midday from the roof of the slate-clad Kaiserringhaus. Ice-cream parlours
spilled into the square below the Gothic arches of the town hall and the
Kaiserwörth, the former guildhall whose coral-coloured walls were decorated with life-size wooden figures of Holy Roman Emperors, stiff and
formal with their orbs and sceptres. Below them were tiny, Gollum-like
figurines of *Dukatenmännchen*, common people captured in the everyday
acts of defecation or copulation.

Wisps of gauzy cloud floated in the azure sky as I drove west between Seesen and Bad Gandersheim. Farming villages lay in the low hills beyond wheat fields and orchards of apple trees. I felt at ease back in the west. Superficially there is no longer much difference between western and eastern Germany. The east is more exciting because it is young and raw and changing more rapidly. But the west is my comfort zone, where everything is as it should be, where "Alles ist in Ordnung". I stopped in Bad Gandersheim, a spa town known as "Roswitha-Stadt" on account of a tenth-century canoness and poet. A Kurpark ran along the valley floor, laid out with pavilions and ornamental lakes. I sat on the sun terrace of one of the thermal springs and ordered a coffee. Clinging to the hillsides above the spa were clinics, sanatoriums and a former training school for motor sport built during the Third Reich for the NSKK, a kind of Aryan Automobile Association. Built in the *völkisch* style of Nazi architecture, it now functioned as a "non-denominational bible school and faith centre".

I drove north in the direction of Hildesheim and then west towards Hameln, along roads bordered by fields of maize, potatoes and conical blue-green cabbages. A stone pillar on the outskirts of Latferde marked a "Hellweg". I followed the road as it snaked around the lee of the Bückeberg before emerging onto the north-western slope of the hill, from where there was a panoramic view of the River Weser as it meandered downstream towards Hameln and the forested hills of the Süntel further north. Immediately below me was a sloping field of closely cropped grass, split down the middle by a raised strip of longer grasses. The raised strip marked the "Weg durch das Volk", the "Path through the People" that Adolf Hitler ascended during the Reichs Harvest Festivals held on the Bückeberg from 1933 to 1937. In contrast to the Nuremberg Rallies, these were folksy, informal celebrations of "Blood and Soil" ritual during which Hitler presented himself as a man of the people, striding with a smirk on his face through a parting sea of farming families dressed for the occasion in lace shawls, bearskin hats, ribbons, bows and millinery that resembled bowls of plums, grapes or apricots balanced on the flaxen, plaited heads of Lower Saxon farm girls. Women strewed his path with flowers; children crept through lines of storm troopers to have their heads stroked by the Führer; men waved their pitchforks and cried "Heil!"

The first Reichs Harvest Festival was held on the Bückeberg on 1 October 1933. Half a million farming folk attended, crammed into the field between earth walls planted with loudspeakers and a palisade of swastika banners and imperial flags. A twenty-one-gun salute announced the beginning of the ceremony. A military band struck up the Badenweiler March and Hitler began his slow ascent of the "Führerweg", rising through the multitude of saluting peasants who thrust their children before him to be blessed. On reaching the grandstand at the top of the field, Hitler was received by Goebbels and presented with a harvest wreath by a female representative of the German farming community. As dusk fell, Hitler re-descended the "Weg durch das Volk" towards the "Deutschland Erwache" standards of the SA men massed around a platform at the foot of the hill. Albert Speer made his first attempt at throwing a "wall of light" around the rally, but on this occasion the floodlights he had borrowed from a film studio proved too weak, and the wind too strong, to create the desired effect: the vertical beams of light dissolved in the foggy night sky. The festivities ended with a firework display and the communal singing of the *Deutschlandlied* and the Horst Wessel Song.

The flagpoles, stairways and grandstands of the arena were disman-tled during the war. Only the upper grandstand, a smaller version of the *Ehrentribüne* at Nuremberg, survived. Some moss-covered fragments of its foundations remain, hidden beneath undergrowth at the top of the hill. The site of the lower rostrum has disappeared below a mound of rubble overgrown with brambles and compressed by layers of used car tyres. Only the raised strip of unmown grass over the "Führerweg" remains vis-ible, bristling with nettles and thistles and flecked with white cow parsley. The field itself is common ground and the entire site is now protected as a historical monument. I returned to my car and drove gingerly through the hamlet of Hagenohsen, down a steep avenue paved with rugged cobble-stones laid in 1933 to bring the motorcades of the guests of honour to the VIP rostrum at the top of the hill. I crossed the Weser on a girder bridge and parked by the railway station of Emmerthal, a tiny halt with an unusually large number of platforms. It was here that trains once brought a million visitors to the Harvest Festivals of the Third Reich.

I stayed overnight in Hameln, a dull town of post-war pedestrian pre-cincts and department stores. It was a Friday evening, but the town cen-tre was empty. The young people had been spirited away by the attractions of a pop concert in a local park. In the morning I bought a walking guide to the Süntelgebirge, a range of hills to the north of the town. Somewhere up there in the forest were the ruins of a Horst Wessel Tower, erected in 1935 to commemorate the National Socialist martyr killed in Berlin by Communist activists. Wessel's parents were farmers from the Hameln area and the Hohe Egge was chosen as the site of a monument to the young SA Sturmführer. The Krüger brothers, architects of the Hindenburg Mausoleum in East Prussia, were awarded the commission to design the Horst Wessel Tower. Their submission, a combination of medieval fortress and Germanic *Thingstätte* moulded into the cliffs and ravines of the natural landscape, was eventually cancelled by their nemesis Speer. A provisional memorial was erected instead, a simple sandstone stele eighteen metres high surmounted by a steel swastika rotated at forty-five degrees to the vertical. The martyr's name was inscribed in letters of iron on the base of the obelisk. The tower stood on the southern escarpment of the Süntelgebirge, from where its swastika was clearly visible from the Harvest Festival site. With the sun's rays at the right angle, the hooked cross would have glittered above the forest, describing an axis from the Süntelgebirge to the Bückeberg that represented Wessel's journey from martyrdom to immortality. The provisional monument was blown up on 20 April 1945 by American troops and reportedly destroyed. However, the website of a local cyclists' club provided instructions for a tour of the forest, which included a visit to the ruins of the tower.

I drove north from Hameln, parked in front of the Waldhof restaurant in the village of Unsen and set off along Wanderweg 4, following the instructions I had printed off the cyclists' website. The forest smelled of wild garlic and the air was heavy with impending rain. The path rose through woods of beech and oak; dead leaves carpeted the forest floor and piles of logs waited to be collected by woodcutters. Soon I was climbing through pine woods and glades covered with ferns, mossy boulders and the stumps of hewn trees. After two kilometres I found the site of a youth hostel built, presumably, at the time of the Horst Wessel Tower. All that remained was a stone hut at the end of a clearing, where I sheltered from a sudden downpour. When the rain abated, I crossed the clearing and followed a track through a grove of oak trees to a low, semi-circular wall encrusted with moss and lichen. This would once have been an observation point from where the Hitler Youth *Pimpfe* staying in the hostel would have enjoyed a panoramic view over the hills and valleys surrounding Hameln. Scraping off the lichen covering the stones, I discovered the remains of some *Frakturschrift* spelling out the names of villages and landmarks that were once visible from the observation point. I recognised Bellingen and Coppenbrugge.

So far, so good: I had followed the instructions on the cyclists' website and knew where I was on the map in the guidebook. Continuing to follow the instructions, I returned to the last fork in the path and followed a track signposting the Süntelturm. At some point there would be a disused quarry on the right and a trail off to the left towards the ruins of the Horst Wessel Tower. After climbing a further two or three hundred metres, I wandered into the forest on the left-hand side of the path, but found no discernible ruins of a tower. I returned to the path and continued uphill. After several hundred metres there was another fork in the path and a circular basin to the right, which might once have been a quarry. Again, I infiltrated the woods to the left of the path and clambered over boulders until I reached the top of the south-facing escarpment where, eighty years earlier, there would have been a view over Hameln towards the Bückeberg. I startled a deer and dislodged some rocks which bounced down the cliff face, but saw no stones which might once have formed part of a tower.

It was now pouring with rain again and I determined to continue uphill until I reached the Süntelturm at the top of the ridge. The tower was a circular, crenellated structure built in 1901. The café inside was full of hikers and mountain bikers, their damp clothes steaming in the heat of the small room. As I was ordering a coffee, the waitress noticed my annotated photocopies and asked if I was writing a thesis on the Süntelgebirge. I told her I was looking for the Horst Wessel Tower. Her colleague told me it no longer existed. It was "zerstört, Gott sei Dank. Es gibt hier keine Nazi-Dinge mehr" ("destroyed, thank God. There aren't any Nazi things up here any more").

"Completely?" I asked.

"Yes."

"When?"

"In 1945, after the Second World War."

I left it at that, as she was getting quite cross. Maybe she was fed up with Nazi-tourists looking for the ruins of the destroyed tower.

Restored by the coffee, I retraced my steps down through the rain to the crossroads. I identified which quadrant of the forest was most likely to contain the ruined tower and combed the woods above the cliff top. There were hundreds of moss-covered boulders lying on the forest floor or lodged halfway down the cliff face, but none of them looked as if they had been hewn by a stonemason into a shape which might have formed part of a monument. After half an hour of clambering up and down slopes, sliding down scree and hauling myself up again by the roots of trees, I gave up. I returned to the path and trudged back down to the Waldhof. By the time I arrived it was too late for lunch. I sat in my filthy boots among the stuffed foxes, stoats and pine martens decorating the half-timbered *Gaststube* and ordered a coffee and a slice of *Himbeer-Eierlikör-Torte*. Like the Bismarck Tower above Bad Heringsdorf, the Horst Wessel Tower had defeated me.[15]

I opted to drive to Hanover and have a quiet drink by the Maschsee to restore my spirits. I arrived there to find it was the first weekend of the Maschsee Summer Festival and the streets around the lake were jammed with motorists looking for a place to park. I noticed a vehicle about to vacate a space in a side street and accelerated towards it. But the car was parked in the opposite direction to the way I was driving, and in Germany it's illegal to park against the traffic flow. A car behind me was also cruising for a parking space and its driver raised his eyebrows as I pulled over to the left-hand side of the street and waited for the parked vehicle to pull out. I watched him as he drove to the end of the street, performed a five-point turn and drove back in the correct direction so he could park legally in the space which was in the process of being vacated. By that time, however, I had claimed the space for myself by parking in the "wrong" direction. The driver gave me a look of disgust and mouthed the words "Scheiß' Engländer" (or "Scheiß' Ausländer") as he drove past.

I walked through the Maschpark towards the lake. Copper beech trees lined the gravel path and weeping willows trailed their branches in the waters of the Maschteich. Ducks swam through water lilies on the surface of the pond and a flock of ravens descended on a sculpture by Henry Moore. The banks of the Maschsee were thronged with thousands of Hanoverians enjoying the sporadic sunshine of a cloudy Sunday afternoon. I bought a corn cob from one of the food stalls along the promenade. At the head of the lake was a tall stone pillar capped with a bronze statue of a *Fackelträger* ("Torch Bearer"), a personification of National Socialism with the torch of the movement in his left hand and his right arm outstretched in an imperial salute. Beyond the column a row of double-decker pavilions had been erected, each with its own themed cocktail bar – African, Cuban, tropical, colonial or Art Nouveau. One was

---

15   I returned to the Süntelgebirge two years later and found the ruins of the tower relatively easily, near the top of the cliff face. All that remained was a twelve-metre-long square pillar of moss-covered sandstone, lying in the undergrowth with its spine broken into two pieces. Some rusted spokes of a joist or bracket protruded from one end.

shaped like a toadstool; another a traffic cone. On the promenade below were jugglers, fire-eaters and dusty, black-cloaked musicians from Spain. A quintet of dancers dressed as cowgirls performed a go-go routine to the rhythm of KC and the Sunshine Band. I sat at a table on the upper deck of one of the pavilions, ordered an Aperol Spritz and watched the surface of the lake turn from grey-green to blue as the sun came out and sparkled on pedaloes, yachts, dragon ships and a gondola. After days spent in drab East German towns full of elderly tourists, it was exciting to feel part of normal city life once again. I was struck by how young and multi-ethnic the crowds were; something I had not experienced since leaving Berlin. A black gentleman in a tan suit smiled indulgently as his teenage girlfriend jigged up and down to the Seventies soul beats; and a quartet of Turks, dressed in silk shirts worn outside their trousers in an attempt to hide their huge bellies, puffed on cigarettes and shook each other's hands as they concluded a business deal.

I decided on the spur of the moment to visit Salzgitter. I knew nothing about the place except that it was the site of the Hermann Göring Works, the largest industrial complex of the Third Reich. It didn't look like a town on the map, more like a few isolated villages scattered over a large rural area; certainly nothing like the Ruhrgebiet or the Upper Silesian Industrial Region. I headed first for Salzgitter-Bad, where I turned up Erikastraße and found myself in an estate of houses built during the Third Reich. The Kniestedt-Mädel-Siedlung (like the Goebbels family, all the streets had old-fashioned girls' names – Hertastraße, Hedwigstraße, Hildegardstraße) was built between 1939 and 1941 to house several thousand coal miners drafted into the area to work in the new mines which would feed the Hermann Göring Iron and Steel Works. The houses were built on the slopes of the Hamberg to the north of Salzgitter-Bad: five thousand apartments in two-storied terraced blocks, plastered in military hues of green, khaki and grey and roofed with pink tiles studded with dormer windows. Some of the larger houses displayed carved red sun wheels and *sgraffito* murals of healthy or joyful National Socialist tableaux: a man and a woman planting a sapling; or a father returning from work to greet his wife and two children. A handful of pubs, shops, *Trinkhallen, Spielsalons,* florists, chemists and hairdressers supported the present community, mostly second- or third-generation Turks or recent Polish immigrants. The men wandered the streets with their dogs while their wives banged carpets or shook duvets from identical rows of square windows. Every tenth apartment sported a German flag in the window, as if to stress that these were Germans living here; and every third apartment had a "Zu Vermieten" (To Rent) sign in the window. The estate agent at the top of Elbestraße (once Horst-Wessel-Straße) had a poster in its window proclaiming "Hier will Ich leben!" – a sentiment more in hope than expectation. I couldn't find a café or an *Imbiss*, so I wandered into the *Stadtteiltreff NOW* and asked for a coffee. I wasn't sure whether it was a citizens' advice bureau or a youth club; but there were no other customers and the young woman was happy to serve me with a coffee for the princely sum of thirty cents.

I followed yellow road signs towards SZ-Engerode and SZ-Gebhardshagen, passing secretive mining communities, bucolic villages built during the Third Reich, now hidden from the main road behind a network of dykes. The road from SZ-Gebhardshagen to SZ-Barum ran through flat, open agricultural landscape where the only visible signs of industry were *Klärteiche*, artificial lakes once used to purify waste water from the mines, and terraced *Mülldeponien*, waste tips which had been built up over slag heaps. North of SZ-Heerte a massif of red iron ore rose out of the landscape like Ayers Rock, and in the distance were the smoking chimneys of a steelworks to the north of SZ-Watenstedt. At the entrance to an industrial site opposite SZ-Leinde an iron stele was embedded by the roadside. Metal plaques in German, French, English, Polish, Russian and Hebrew commemorated the victims of KZ-Watenstedt/Leinde. The words "Never to Forget Is the Secret of Reconciliation" were inscribed on the pillar in those six languages.

I turned into Industriestraße and stopped off in SZ-Watenstedt, an unprepossessing place with a tiny Dorfplatz, a closed *Stehcafé*, a Turkish market, an Anatolian sports and cultural centre, a recycling plant, a hostel for asylum seekers, some used-car dealerships, a pre-war police station and a network of backyards where men were unloading pallets and scaffolding from Turkish-registered lorries. Leaving SZ-Watenstedt, I accidentally entered the dual carriageway of Industriestraße in the wrong direction, becoming for the first time in my life a *Falschfahrer*, one of those idiots you're warned about on the radio who have somehow managed to gain access to the autobahn by driving up the *Ausfahrt* instead of the *Einfahrt*. I realised my mistake immediately, reversed cautiously around the bend back into SZ-Watenstedt and doubled back underneath the dual carriageway into the correct lane.

To the south of SZ-Watenstedt were the bus and truck factories of M.A.N. (formerly Büssing); to the east were the warehouses of IKEA Distribution; and to the north were the rolling mills of Salzgitter Flachstahl AG, formerly Preussag AG and, before that, the Reichs Works for Iron Ore and Steel "Hermann Göring". I turned up Eisenhüttenstraße and passed Gates 1, 5 and 6 of the smelting works. At their southern end they formed a seething mass of chimneys, blast furnaces, regenerators, gasometers, cooling towers, machine rooms, ore bridges, ramps and elevators. At their northern end were vast grey and orange hangars like the warehouses of a global logistics concern. The Central Administrative Building on the eastern side of Eisenhüttenstraße was a red-brick monolith, completed in 1939 for the Plenipotentiary of the Four-Year Plan by Ernst Sagebiel, architect of Tempelhof Airport and Göring's Air Ministry in Berlin. In its pediment was an empty plaque which would once have been embellished by the "Gö-Ring", the logo of the Reichswerke. The heavy base of the emblem symbolised the bedrock of German iron ore on which the works were founded; and the ring embedded in the base represented the incorporation of the employees into the embrace of the company. It looked like a mooring ring and was known colloquially as the "Göring-Schnuller" on account of its resemblance to a baby's dummy. A uniformed receptionist took exception to my parking in the company forecourt and taking photographs of the building, repeatedly getting up from her station behind a glass booth to stand in the window and stare pointedly at me.

The smell of chemicals persisted as I drove over a canal bridge towards SZ-Lebenstedt. To the south a giant conveyor bridge slumped across a slag heap. Across the fields to the north were the green iron headframe and winding gear of Schacht Konrad I, an iron ore mine which closed in 1976 and is currently being converted into a deep repository for radioactive waste. I entered Lebenstedt along a wide boulevard between banks of 1950s apartment blocks, and parked in front of the high-rise glass and steel Rathaus. I found myself in a 1960s new town of car parks, roundabouts and office blocks. The shopping precinct was a maze of treeless concrete plazas and parades of low, one-storey shops. Some were empty or boarded up. There were mobile kebab stalls and traders selling clothes on racks at five euros each. It reminded me of Bracknell, except the accents of the shoppers were Turkish, Polish or working-class Lower Saxon. I stopped to read the bronze plaques set into the pavement celebrating SZ-Lebenstedt's partnerships with its twin towns: with Staryj-Oskol, an iron ore city in the Russian Urals; with Créteil, a mosquito-ridden dormer town on the outskirts of Paris; and with Thamesdown, now more commonly known again as Swindon. At the centre of a plaza named In den Blumentriften (In the Flower Meadows!) was a marble and bronze "Tower of Labour", Salzgitter's modern equivalent of a plague column, a molten yet exquisitely detailed mass of pitheads, blast furnaces, miners, smelters, pit ponies, trolleys, slave labourers, concentration camp inmates, SS guards, hanged saboteurs and refugees from the East – a monumental sculpture relating the history of the conurbation from the founding of the Hermann Göring Works to their post-war dismantling, the closure of the coal mines and the modern expansion of the iron and steel plants.

Away from the town centre, SZ-Lebenstedt extended outwards along a network of radial boulevards named after lost German cities in Silesia and the Sudetenland – Gleiwitz, Kattowitz, Reichenberg (and Swindon). Inside each spoke of the wheel was a symmetrical web of terraced housing. The streets bore pastoral names such as Am Bauerngraben (By the Farmer's Ditch), Am Flachen Meer (By the Flat Sea), Am Moorgraben (By the Boggy Ditch), Steinackern (Stone Fields), Kälberanger (Calves' Meadows), Fasanenweg (Pheasants' Way) or Kornblumenstraße (Cornflower Street). While the names may have been bucolic, the houses were not. They were built in 1939 to house one hundred and thirty thousand iron and steel workers, drafted in from the Ruhrgebiet and the Upper Silesian coalfields, to man the foundries and blast furnaces and manufacture the millions of shells, grenades and tank parts required for the Blitzkrieg.

Walking through the suburbs of Lebenstedt today is like being in another country and another time. The rows of oatmeal-coloured terraced houses of Göring's *Trabantenstadt* are clearly more desirable than their identical counterparts in the former coalfields of SZ-Kniestedt or SZ-Gebhardshagen: here not a single apartment is available to rent or a solitary house for sale. But this is not the affluent modern Germany of "Vorsprung durch Technik". These are perfectly formed National Socialist housing estates of *völkisch* two-up, two-downs embellished with rounded arches, wooden oriels, folksy murals and colonnades on rough-hewn ashlars. The Third Reich is so tangible I would not have been shocked to see swastika flags hanging out of the windows. Ironically, hardly any of the current residents are German.

I stayed overnight in the Deutsches Haus in Braunschweig, an old-fashioned hotel with a grand staircase supported by columns of red porphyry and corridors lined with suits of armour. It was one of those hotels where the waiters clear away the breakfast buffet on the dot of 10 am, whether the guests have finished their meal or not. To escape their clutches, I took my cup of tea out into the Burgplatz, the heart of the old city – or what remained of it. Braunschweig once boasted the largest agglomeration of medieval *Fachwerkhäuser* in Germany, but 90% of its Altstadt was destroyed by incendiary bombs in the Second World War. The Veltheimisches Haus and the Huneborstelsches Haus on the northern side of the square have been restored, their half-timbered façades striped with beams carved into diamonds, rosettes, astrological signs and classical deities – and a bagpipe-playing ape. To my left was Burg Dankwarderode, seat of the medieval Dukes of Saxony. Like the Kaiserpfalz in Goslar, it fell into dereliction in the nineteenth century and was reconstructed in a neo-Romanesque style in the 1890s. Opposite me was the Braunschweiger Dom, the Romanesque-Gothic cathedral of St Blasius; and on a stone pedestal in the centre of Burgplatz was the Braunschweiger Löwe, emblem of the city. This was a doggy-like lion with a Roman mane of smooth, tight curls, and a posture suggesting it would rather sit and lick its master's hand than do anything of a remotely predatory nature. The Lion of Brunswick (or its Merovingian ancestor) was appropriated by the National Socialists as a symbol of aggression: a pair of sleek, dynamic lions was sculpted by Arno Breker to guard the Löwenbastion on the banks of the Maschsee in Hanover; and two quartets of vicious leaping lions were designed to embellish the towers of the Wehrmacht Oberkommando and New Reichs Chancellery on the Großer Platz in Berlin – buildings which were, of course, never built.

The bells of the cathedral struck eleven as I entered the *Dom*. The walls of the Romanesque nave were painted a pristine white. Columns twisted like sticks of barley sugar supported the Gothic aisles. At the head of the nave was a stone sarcophagus which covered the tombs of the twelfth-century Duke Heinrich of Saxony – known as Henry the Lion – and his consort Mathilde, daughter of King Henry II of England. Their stone effigies rested on top of the tomb, noble and serene. The walls of the choir were painted with thirteenth-century *secco* murals of Christ Pantocrator, the martyrdom of Thomas à Becket and the oldest surviving representation of a German imperial eagle. A crypt beneath the choir contained the metal coffins of princes and princesses of the House of Welf, including that of Caroline of Brunswick, queen consort of King George IV of England. Below this undercroft, directly beneath the sarcophagus of Henry and Mathilde, was another crypt, accessible by means of a narrow flight of steps, which I descended, passing below a round arch whose capital was carved with a snarling lion's head sculpted by Arno Breker in the Nordic style of the Merovingian period. The crypt beneath the crypt was encased in walls of stippled granite blocks, glittering in the gloom. Engraved on the walls were the coats of arms of Lübeck, Lüneburg, Munich and Braunschweig, four cities founded by Henry the Lion; and a pagan sun wheel – a swastika with curved hooks. In the centre of the crypt was a low arched vault illuminated by a deathly orange glow which descended from the shallow dome of the undercroft. On a metal plinth lay two stone coffins which reputedly contained the mortal remains of Duke Henry the Lion and his Plantagenet queen.

After spending some time in this ghoulish subterranean chamber, I felt tainted by the aura of National Socialism and was relieved to resurface into the fresh air of the Burgplatz. I sat outside a café in Platz der deutschen Einheit and watched wedding parties spill out of the grand, neo-Gothic civic buildings of Braunschweig. One group assembled on the steps of the Rathaus to pose for photographs before the happy couple were whisked away in a shiny black Audi limousine. I crossed Bohlweg and had a salad lunch in one of the bistros opposite the Schloss. The neoclassical ducal palace served during the Third Reich as one of Nazi Germany's two *Junkerschulen* (the other being in Bad Tölz in Bavaria), where future SS officers received their military and ideological education. The palace was destroyed in the war, but its shell was rebuilt in 2007 and now forms the spectacular façade of a shopping mall, complete with restored equestrian dukes and a newly forged quadriga of steeds driven by Brunonia, the goddess of the Duchy and Free State of Braunschweig.

There was a smell of hops in the air as I drove north around the ring road, before turning east along Kastanienallee into a colony of Wilhelmine villas gleaming in the sunlight. I walked to the end of Grunewaldstraße and around the back of the Stadtpark until I arrived at a salient of the park known as the Franzsches Feld. There was a smell of newly mown grass and a view across the sloping meadow towards the spires of Braunschweig. This was the venue for some of the earliest demonstrations by the National Socialist German Workers' Party. It came to be known as the "SA-Feld", as it was here that the brown-uniformed troops assembled to hear speeches by their Gruppenführer delivered from a "Rednertribüne" at the top of the slope. On 17 and 18 October 1931, Hitler consecrated the site as "holy ground" by having the entire membership of the SA, some one hundred thousand men, march past. Each individual SA standard was "inseminated" by the "Blood Flag" of the 1923 putsch in a ceremony once described as like "guiding a bull's penis into a cow's vagina". The low, semi-circular stone "pulpit" was still there, occupied by a pair of ruddy-faced drunks awash on a sea of crumpled beer cans. Somewhere in the woods behind the park was a National Socialist *Thingstätte*. I went to explore the gullies and ravines below the trees of the Nußberg, following trails left by mountain bikers. In one bowl I stumbled across a quarter-circle of stone steps and the remains of some concrete bunkers, but was unable to join these up into the contours of an amphitheatre. I returned to the Franzsches Feld and stopped a man who was walking his dog. I showed him the photocopied plan of the *Thingplatz* I had brought with me. He confirmed there was indeed something hidden in the woods and wished me "Viel Spaß" in my quest. I retraced my steps to the depression in the trees and realised that the quarter-circle of steps corresponded to the curve of the amphitheatre on my plan. I descended into the hollow and began to notice the curved outlines of moss-covered steps beneath the dank undergrowth. I reached the bottom of the depression and ascended the opposite side, observing rows of stone terracing that would have been invisible from the top of the bowl. A symmetrical pattern slowly fell into place and, reaching the far side of the hollow, I realised I had traced a path along the axis of the *Thingstätte* from "Einmarsch" to "Ausmarsch".

I drove out of Braunschweig into a forest beyond the village of Riddagshausen and stopped by a small estate of half-timbered buildings with green doors and tiny eyelet windows in their thatched roofs. On the other side of the road a pair of fighting stags, their bronze antlers clashing together, were mounted on a limestone plinth. The sculpture marked the entrance to a Reichsjägerhof built in the 1930s for the Reichsforstmeister Hermann Göring. I followed an avenue through oak, birch and beech trees to an imposing hunting lodge in the style of a Lower Saxon farmhouse, its black and white beams offset by green shutters and doors. Painted in gold lettering across the beams was "Hie gut deutsch Waidwerk alle-wege", which means something like "Here be good old German hunting". The lodge was commissioned by the local Gauleiter and Gaujägermeister, who were keen to ingratiate themselves with the Master of the Reichs Hunt. Göring accepted the lodge as a wedding gift for himself and his bride Emmy Sonnemann at a ceremony on 5 May 1935; but it seems he never stayed here, preferring the comfort of the Stadthotel on his visits to Braunschweig. It is now a kindergarten, and it seemed inappropriate to hang around for long. I returned to the buildings opposite the gate-keeper's lodge and ordered a *Pflaumentorte* and *latte macchiato* in the Gasthof Grüner Jäger. The inn was frequented by the young French writer Marie-Henri Beyle, later known as Stendhal, during his tour of duty with Napoleon's troops in the occupied Duchy of Brunswick from 1806 to 1808. The motive for Beyle's regular visits to the Grüner Jäger had something to do with *chercher la femme*. In 1934–35 the Gasthof and its out-houses were rebuilt in a *völkisch* style which matched the appearance of Göring's hunting lodge.

To the south of Braunschweig is the self-contained garden suburb of Mascherode, now known as "Südstadt". It was built between 1936 and 1939 to house six thousand workers of the German Labour Front employed in the nearby Büssing works, ostensibly to construct com-mercial vehicles, but secretly to manufacture armaments and aeroplane engines for the forthcoming war. I drove up and down streets of one-up, two-down cottages built to a standardised blueprint. Some were red brick, others half-timbered; all were small and neat with tidy, well-maintained gardens: this was middle-class Braunschweig, not working-class Salzgitter. Towering over Welfenplatz (once Robert-Ley-Platz) at the heart of the sub-urb was the former Volksgemeinschaftshaus, an assembly hall designed by Speer in the form of a huge tithe barn built from local Elm sandstone. Cut into the gable above a massive porch were six semi-circular embrasures (reminiscent of those in the towers of the Hindenburg Mausoleum) from where bells may once have pealed. Were it not for the clumsy "Führer balcony" and the eagle and swastika insignia of the Third Reich (now obscured by messy plastering), the community hall would have resem-bled an early Christian hall church. That, of course, was the intention. As Speer himself remarked: "If we add a tower, the church will be complete." This was the prototype of the Volksgemeinschaftshaus, the secular temple where the local community would assemble to worship its leader. "Ein Land. Ein Volk. Ein Führer" – the holy trinity of National Socialism.

I entered Speer's racial church, once hung with fire bowls and sun wheels, to find an Edeka supermarket where I bought a bottle of multi-vitamin fruit juice and a square of Ritter chocolate. The upper floor was a "Roxy" youth club and, again, it was not seemly to linger there. Apparently there remains the outline of a *Reichsadler* that filled the "altar" end of the pseudo-sacral hall, but it is now hidden behind post-war renovation work. The low wing extending from the side of the community hall once housed offices of the DAF, Hitler Youth, NSDAP and an *Ehrenhalle* for the "Toten der Bewegung", a small shrine to commemorate the comrades killed in the putsch of 1923. Now there are nail salons and mobile phone shops. The two remaining sides of Welfenplatz are built in the German equivalent of a mock-Tudor style, which would not look out of place in the Stanmore or Pinner of John Betjeman's *Metroland*. I entered one of the cafés and ordered a cup of tea. "Ein Tee, bitte." The waitress looked at me blankly. I repeated "Ein Tee, bitte" and got no response. I have always had a problem ordering a cup of tea in Germany. It seems I neither spit out the "*T*" forcefully enough, nor stretch my mouth sufficiently widely around the long "*ee*". Sometimes I get served coffee when I asked for tea. The Germans are coffee drinkers and the idea of a strong milky cuppa to revive one's spirits at half past four in the afternoon would be distasteful to any self-respecting *Hausfrau*. Tea is a beverage that only elderly, asthmatic Germans would drink, and even they would expect it to be flavoured with peppermint, rosehip or camomile. I tried again, and this time asked for a "Schwarztee". Five minutes later I was served a glass of lukewarm water and a sachet of hibiscus-flavoured leaves laid neatly across a glass saucer. No milk.

I drove north along Bundestraße 4, also known as the Lower Saxon Asparagus Road. I was back in northern Germany – flat landscape, big sky, fields of barley and maize, silver birch trees by the roadside, villages of half-timbered red-brick farmhouses. In the pine woods between Gifhorn and Uelzen, white camper vans were parked beneath the trees at intervals along the highway. Large African women were seated behind the wheels, curtains opened, waiting for punters. In Lüneburg I sat at a table at the head of Am Sande, the long, sloping high street. The terrace of the Mälzer restaurant was spread out beneath a sixteenth-century guild house of black bricks, its crow-stepped gables inset with medallions and false windows of cream limestone. Burnished by the setting sun at the foot of Am Sande was a tall red-brick church with a slightly off-beam steeple. It was like being in Pomerania again – except that the food was better. I tucked into a *Hamburger Schnitzel*, a thick pork cutlet wrapped in crispy bacon accompanied by two poached eggs and a moraine of *Bratkartoffeln* fried in parsley and spring onion. I washed the meal down with tall glasses of

Weizenbier brewed in the restaurant's own copper vats. Walking back to my hotel along the alley Hinter dem Stützmauer, I noticed a man leaning on the window sill of one of his neighbours, chatting over a cigarette. As I passed, I couldn't help noticing that the neighbour was wearing nothing but a bra and panties; and that her front room was illuminated by some unusually pink light bulbs. I suddenly realised the entire medieval alley was lined with pink- and red-lit boudoirs inhabited by large African girls dressed in white lingerie, which glowed fluorescently against their black skin in the ultra-violet light they used to eroticise their rooms. As I passed, they smiled and called out "Hello". It was unexpected, quaint and rather charming.

In the morning I drove south towards the Lüneburg Heath, through fields of maize and sunflowers, past paddocks of sleek chestnut horses, beneath tunnels of birch trees that arched over the winding roads. In the woods there were piles of felled logs, and triangles of purple sticks marking the sites where deer had been run over. I overtook tractors, combine harvesters and British tanks. Farmers sold pumpkins, blueberries and fresh eggs by the roadside, between villages of half-timbered, red-brick cottages and barns decorated with painted wooden beams capped with carved horses' heads. I stopped for coffee in Ebstorf, where there was a smokehouse and a chemist's decorated with snake symbols. Gardens bloomed with tall, multi-coloured gladioli and everywhere there were *Findlinge* – boulders to mark the names of houses, farms, fire stations, boundary signs and war memorials.

I stopped in Bergen for a coffee. The town was full of cars with British registration plates and shops selling guns, knives and camouflage gear. The owner of the café knew immediately from my accent that I was British. Her waitress was new and I had to wait while her boss taught her how to make a *latte macchiato*. I continued south from Bergen and turned off the main road at a yellow sign marked "Belsen 4km". The village was dominated by a military complex of watchtowers, sentry boxes, radio masts and barracks concealed behind a double row of green mesh fencing and coils of barbed wire. This was the Hohne Station, home of the 7th Armoured Division, known colloquially as the "Desert Rats".

The "Gedenkstätte Bergen-Belsen" lay two kilometres further down the road, hidden inside thick forest. The trees opened out to reveal an expanse of open heath dotted with stands of oak saplings and silver birch. The sandy soil was carpeted with stubble of rough grass. Rectangular mounds raised over low stone walls and covered with heather marked the sites of mass graves. They resembled the funeral pyres of an ancient tribe. At the far end of the clearing were a concrete obelisk and a Wall of Remembrance. Smaller monuments lay scattered over the heath: a wooden cross to commemorate fifteen thousand Poles; a stone pillar in remembrance of thirty thousand Jews; a memorial in a nearby cemetery to forty-eight thousand Russians who were murdered or worked to death while Belsen was still a prisoner-of-war camp. In a small glade at the edge of the forest were a number of commemorative plaques recording the lives of a tiny proportion of the Jews who died here, who came from across Europe, from Pristina and Sarajevo, Łódź, Tarnów and Warsaw, Kežmarok and Debrecen, Salonica, Paris, Hengelo and Den Haag. The final plaque I read told the tragic story of Felice Schragenheim: born on 9 June 1922 in Berlin, she was transported (presumably from Gleis 17) to Theresienstadt at the age of twenty-two. She was later transferred to Auschwitz, where she survived – only to be sent on a death march to the Groß-Rosen concentration camp in Lower Silesia. As the Red Army advanced and the SS retreated, she was sent on a second death march to Belsen where, according to her memorial stone, she died in March 1945, three weeks and one day before the camp was liberated by the 11th Armoured Division of the British Army. The stone records that she was also known as "Jaguar": her brief life and love affair with the German housewife Lilly Wust were immortalised in the film *Aimée und Jaguar*, which I remember seeing in Frankfurt am Main when it was released in 1999.

There were no fences, no watchtowers, no barracks, no crematoria, no gas chambers. In contrast to Mauthausen, Auschwitz or Buchenwald, this was a place to mourn the dead rather than examine the means of mass murder – a cemetery rather than a museum. Here there was only silence, open scrub and a scattering of memorial stones. I walked to the far end of a long, wide swathe of grassland that was once the main street of the concentration camp. All that remained were the ruins of some latrine and sewage pits (in which inmates were routinely immersed), a small reservoir, a disinfection bath and the foundations of Huts 9 and 10. In the last months of the war these huts were overflowing with dead bodies. The living sat or lay among thousands of corpses left rotting in the street or in the woods behind the barrack huts. I stood there alone: there was little to see and nothing to hear except the breeze whispering through the trees and the dry whirr of crickets in the long rye grass.

I followed the northern bank of the River Aller as it meandered through the Lower Saxon plain. This was equestrian and horticultural country: a land of paddocks, stables and barns decorated with horse-head beams; of fields of sunflowers, gardens of pink and purple hollyhocks and endless tubes of polytunnels. I stopped in Verden to look for accommodation, but there was an international show-jumping event on and the few hotels were fully booked. I had a cup of tea in Lugenstein below a hunched red-brick *Dom*, the oldest Gothic cathedral in Lower Saxony. This may have been the site of the Verdener Blutgericht (the Bloodbath of Verden) of 782 AD. The paintings I had admired in Erfurt and Goslar pictured the Christian Franks peaceably subduing the pagan Saxons, but here something more brutal took place. Four and a half thousand Saxons were reputedly massacred in a single day by Charlemagne's Franks. They were apparently slaughtered in cold blood in revenge for the murder of one Frankish lord by the Saxons of the Süntel. The reprisal seems disproportionate to the original crime: the figure of 4,500 may have been a misreading of a Latin numeral – or an early typo – that was handed down through successive generations of scribes as fact. It is quite possible, of course, that a deed of such breathtaking savagery did actually take place here on the water meadows by the confluence of the Weser and the Aller.

Himmler and Rosenberg came to hear about this historical event and realised it presented an ideal opportunity to celebrate the neo-pagan, anti-Christian cult they espoused. They regarded the pagan Saxons as the original ur-Germans, in opposition to the Gallic Christian Franks. They found a twelve-hectare area of woodland north of Verden and decided to surround the open clearing in its centre with four thousand five hundred menhirs, one to represent each of the slaughtered Saxons. The landscape architects Wilhelm Hübotter and Karl Dröge came from Hanover to design the site, which was named Sachsenhain (Saxons' Grove). Himmler ordered local farmers to provide the four and a half thousand boulders, which were positioned by slave labourers in a double row forming a rough rectangle around the field in the centre of the grove. The avenue between the standing stones reached a length of approximately three kilometres. Completed in 1935, Sachsenhain was one of the early projects of

the *Thing* movement. Bonfires were lit in the central meadow to illuminate nocturnal solstice ceremonies and parades of Hitler Youth and SS.
By 1936, however, the *Thing* movement had petered out and the National
Socialist regime wished to distance itself from such pseudo-mystical black
magic. Hitler had shown only fleeting interest in the fate of the Saxons;
once established in power, he saw himself as an imperial figure in the
mould of a Charlemagne.

I entered the "sacred ring" of Sachsenhain and followed a sandy path
between the two rows of small boulders along the western edge of the
grove. The rose bushes planted in the 1930s had been supplanted by
tall trees which formed a tunnel of greenery over the avenues of standing stones. I had been here many years earlier, my curiosity piqued by
a photo-essay entitled "Mystic Germany" in *Stern-Magazin*. It was certainly quite pleasant to spend a summer evening walking beneath the trees
as the last rays of sunlight filtered through the oak leaves, listening to
the crackle of beech mast beneath my feet and the hollow clicking of
woodpeckers overhead – but there was nothing mystical about it. These
were neither real menhirs nor was this the actual site where four thousand five hundred Saxons were supposedly put to the sword. There was a
vague sense of history about the place, but the history was fake. I imagine
that the Verden Tourist Office tries to avoid promoting this preposterous
National Socialist conceit in its suburbs; but it also has to ensure that any
unsuspecting tourist who does wander into the Saxons' Grove does not
depart in the belief that this is an authentic Germanic *Thingstätte* or the
actual site of the bloodbath. To this end it has placed several noticeboards
around the avenues which recount the history of Sachsenhain and the
(ir-)rationale behind its construction. The unwary visitor is further confused by the fact that many of the boulders are engraved with slogans.
The first inscription I came upon, on my first visit to Sachsenhain, read
"Angenommen er lebt" (Assuming he lives), which I quite naturally took
to refer to Adolf Hitler. It was only when the inscriptions began to take on
a more explicitly Christian message – "Weg mit ihm zum Kreuz", "Öffne
die Augen", "Gottes Reich unter uns", "Mit Leiden helfen", "Gib Brot",
"Vergib", "Unsere Schuld" or "Gottes Freude fest halten" – that I realised these were not the carvings of some proto-hippy National Socialists,
but the work of the young evangelists who now inhabited the former
Hitler Youth commune at the head of Sachsenhain; that these inscriptions
were maybe a way of exorcising the Nazi spirit of place, of reclaiming the
"neo-pagan" site for Christianity.

The avenue along the southern edge of Sachsenhain was lined with larger boulders, presumably some of the original Germanic menhirs plundered from their ancient sites. Jutting out into the central clearing were two "chancels" from where SA or SS leaders could address the ranks of their followers in the meadow below. One of the chancels was surrounded by tall standing stones, the other by a low wall of smaller boulders. On my earlier visit to Sachsenhain I remember standing in the apex of the second chancel and noticing the outline of a swastika in the stone directly below me. It was worn with age and covered with a coat of lichen, but it was unmistakably a thick, X-shaped *Hakenkreuz* above a pair of crossed fasces. I made a mental note at the time that this was probably the last remaining swastika visible on a monument in a public place in Germany. This time I couldn't find it. I discovered one stone engraved with some emblem, possibly a Reichs eagle, but it was too worn to decipher. I noticed that three stones had been removed from the centre of the wall, one of them presumably the stone inscribed with the swastika. I wondered whether it had been removed officially, in an attempt to de-Nazify the site; or whether it had been stolen by a Nazi souvenir-hunter. Whatever the motive, the last swastika in Germany had gone.

15

Westphalia

"Himmler's Sacred Realm of Dream Reality"

Night was falling as I arrived in Porta Westfalica. By the time I had checked into my room, the hotel kitchen had closed for the evening. I sat on the terrace and made do with beer and cigarettes. In the darkness below me was the River Weser, flowing north into Lower Saxony through the gorge between Wittekindsberg and Jakobsberg. The hills were silhouetted in black against a sky deepening from turquoise to Prussian blue. Below the crest of Wittekindsberg was the baldachin of the Kaiser Wilhelm Monument. Illuminated with a spectral glow, its crown and splayed pillars floated in the night like the helm of a Saxon warlord; like the disembodied head of a ghost warrior waiting to be borne to Valhalla.

I drove up to the monument the next morning. A bagpiper was performing off-key renditions of "Greensleeves", "Amazing Grace" and the "Ode to Joy". Some of the tourists were humming along to the Beethoven. The base of the Kaiser Wilhelm Monument stands on a semi-circular ring terrace similar to the one at Kyffhäuser, another of the great national monuments designed in the 1890s by Bruno Schmitz. A double flight of steps leads from the ring terrace around a towering socle, its wall engraved with "Wilhelm dem Grossen – die Provinz Westfalen" ("To Wilhelm the Great – from the Province of Westphalia"). At either end of the inscription is a stone shield crested by an imperial crown. The baldachin soars fifty metres above a circular upper terrace, its canopy supported by six buttressed pillars capped by coronets. The dome over the canopy culminates in an imperial crown surmounted by a golden cross. The colossal

Wilhelmine structure of walls, pillars and arches is hewn from Cyclopean blocks of grey-brown sandstone, encrusted with lichen and sinter and blackened by a hundred years of rain and snow.

A further circle of steps converges on the centre of the baldachin, where Kaiser Wilhelm stands atop a hexagonal pedestal. Sculpted in black bronze by Kaspar von Zumbusch, this German caesar is clad in the cuirassier's tunic of the Prussian *Gardes du Corps* beneath a voluminous coronation cloak embroidered with eagles of the Reich. His bald pate is crowned with a victor's laurel wreath. In his left hand he clasps a sabre, while his right arm is raised high in an imperial gesture, as if blessing his people. Framed within Schmitz's baldachin, the bewhiskered warlord surveys his Lower Saxon and Westphalian lands with the calm authority of a Roman emperor. He is the embodiment of the strength of the German fatherland, the unity of the German nation and the immortality of the German Reich.

Leaving the monument, I took a path into the woods along the spine of the Wiehengebirge, a range of hills that forms the northern arm of the Teutoburger Wald. I found myself following the Wittekindsweg, a path named after Widukind (or Wittekind), leader of the pagan Saxon tribes who, in the eighth century, inhabited the area now known as Westphalia. The air was cool beneath a canopy of beech, plane and sycamore. The forest floor fell away on either side, carpeted with woodrush, purple rampion and a thick mulch of russet leaves. I came at length to the Berghotel Wittekindsburg, a neo-Gothic *Gaststätte* built in 1896. At the top of the cliff in front of the hotel was a concrete platform from where hang gliders could launch themselves from the heights of Wittekindsberg. I sat there in the midday heat and listened to the hiss of lorries on the road from Porta Westfalica to Bad Oeynhausen at the foot of the escarpment. The still, brown Weser meandered between fields of green maize and golden wheat. On the far side of the river the pink and white villas of Porta Westfalica snaked up valleys of pine forest into the hills of the Lipper Land, soft and grey in the heat haze. The blades of a wind turbine rotated lazily on a distant breeze; tiny specks of dazzling light marked the presence of solar panels on invisible buildings.

I stopped for a *latte macchiato* and a slice of *Apfelstreusel* in a little café opposite the Hotel Kaiserhof at the foot of Wittekindsberg. The hotel opened in 1890, two years before work began on the construction of the Kaiser Wilhelm Monument. The monument itself was inaugurated on 18 October 1896, a date deliberately chosen to commemorate the victorious Battle of the Nations of 1813. (Both the Hall of Liberation and the Monument to the Battle of the Nations were also inaugurated on 18 October – in 1863 and 1913, respectively). Twenty thousand representatives of war veterans' and other "vaterländische" associations assembled on the ring terrace of the monument to greet Kaiser Wilhelm II. Flags were hoisted and anthems sung in honour of his grandfather. A brass band of no fewer than thirteen hundred trombonists (according to the website *Westfälische Geschichte*) provided a musical accompaniment to the Kaiser's procession around the monument. After the Kaiser had returned to Berlin, three hundred and seventy VIPs enjoyed a banquet in his honour in the Festsaal of the Hotel Kaiserhof.

I decided to drive to Enger to look for some more tangible evidence of the warlord Widukind, who is reputed to be buried in the town. I made the mistake of driving through Bad Oeynhausen where, at the time of my journey, there was a six-kilometre gap in the autobahn network and all the Polish lorries ground to a halt at an interminable succession of traffic lights. It was two weeks after Germany had beaten Argentina in the World Cup Final, and many cars still flew their black-red-gold pennants or had their wing mirrors draped in the national colours.

I turned off the motorway and drove through a landscape of wheat fields towards Enger. I noticed an Autohaus Widukind on the edge of the town; and then a Wittekindstraße (although I soon realised that every town in Westphalia has a prominent Wittekindstraße). I parked in Barmeierplatz and joined the womenfolk of Enger, who were tucking into goblets of ice cream beneath the yellow sunshades of an *Eis-Café* in Königin-Mathilde-Platz. I perused the menu to see whether they offered a Widukind-Becher. They didn't, but, more bizarrely, they did have an ice cream called a Bismarck-Steak. In the end I settled for a cup of tea, which surprised the waiter, but at least he understood my order.

In the middle of Barmeierplatz was a modern Widukindbrunnen. The stone fountain at its core represented the Irminsul, the sacred tree that, according to pagan Saxon belief, held up the world; and the bronze baldachin that surrounded it symbolised a *Knospenkrone*, the Crown of Buds worn by Queen Mathilde, the great-great-great-granddaughter of Widukind. The sculpture on top of the fountain depicted Widukind riding off to the Carolingian imperial residence of Attigny in the Ardennes to be baptised, following his tribe's inevitable defeat by the Franks and their subsequent conversion to Christianity. The fountain as a whole, according to its accompanying information tablet, represented the transition of Widukind and the Saxons from paganism to the Christian faith.

A bell pealed three times: it was a quarter to five. I followed the sound of the chimes into Kirchplatz, a cobbled wynd overhung with houses whose timbered beams were inscribed with folksy maxims such as "Die Zeit eilt, teilt, heilt" ("Time flies, separates, heals") or "Deutsches Haus, deutsches Land, schirm es Gott mit starker Hand" ("German house, German land, may God protect them with strong hand"). A christening was taking place inside the honey-coloured Stiftskirche. I tiptoed up the nave towards the choir, which was dominated by a Late Gothic winged altarpiece emblazoned in scarlet and gold. In the apse behind the altar was a sarcophagus, on which lay the stone effigy of an oval-faced young man; a nobleman of some rank, as he was clad in a robe which still bore traces of scarlet paint, and around his head was the gold band of a *Spangenkrone* – a coronation crown. His right hand was raised in a gesture of blessing, and in his veiled left hand he held a lily-tipped sceptre; the latter a symbol of purity or virtue, the veiled hand a symbol of submission. According to the Latin inscriptions around the tomb, the mournful figure was Widukind. Little is known about the Saxon duke except that he led a defence of the northern German lands against the Franks in the Saxon Wars of the late eighth century. The conflict started in 772 when Charlemagne's forces captured the Saxon stronghold of Eresburg and felled the Irminsul. Unlike most pagan tribes, Widukind's kinsmen resisted the Frankish incursions for many years, fleeing and reforming several times in a concerted strategy of guerrilla warfare. The Bloodbath of Verden in 782 depleted their numbers, and three years later Widukind accepted Frankish rule and the conversion of his pagan tribes to Christianity.

The effigy on the tomb in the Stiftskirche was sculpted in the early twelfth century and remained hidden from public gaze throughout the Middle Ages. Although nobody knew what he looked like, a cult grew up around the image of Widukind as "the first Saxon", the prototypical German. At first, he was represented as a pale-faced, clean-shaven figure. A painting from Lucas Cranach the Younger's studio in the 1560s, however, portrayed the Saxon leader as a fearsome, armour-plated warlord with a luxuriant beard. During the Age of Enlightenment the figure of Widukind disappeared from the German consciousness, resurfacing only in the nineteenth century when burgeoning German nationalism kindled a resurgence of interest in Teutonic heroes from the past. It became fashionable once again to decorate Germany's grand civic and royal buildings with frescoes illustrating the glorious history of the nation. Romantic-Historicist painters such as Alfred Rethel, Hermann Wislicenus and Julius Schnorr von Carolsfeld were commissioned to paint historical murals for the City Hall of Aachen, the Kaiserpfalz in Goslar and the Residenz in Munich. In these cycles, however, the dominant figure is Charlemagne, founder of the Holy Roman Empire of the German Nation. Widukind and his Saxon tribesmen have been relegated to subservient roles and are depicted as elfin, hippy-like figures clothed in bearskins and winged helmets – in contrast to the crozier-wielding bishops and chain-mail-clad warriors of the Frankish army.

The early National Socialists, nevertheless, put a *völkisch* spin on the figure of Widukind, championing him as a racially pure "Sachsenführer" defending the territories of native German tribes against the incursions of Gallic-Christian Franks. Alfred Rosenberg, ideologue of the "Nordic twilight" strand of National Socialism, visited Widukind's tomb in Enger on "Lower Saxony Day" in 1934 and described the pagan chieftain as a "prototype of the Germanic leader and fighter for the Nordic race and their characteristic beliefs". The small town gained an unexpected popularity between 1934 and 1938; but when Hitler annexed Austria and set Germany on course for imperial domination of Europe, Widukind and the pagan Saxons of Sachsenhain were discarded as prototypes of the New Order – Hitler preferred to see himself as a new Charlemagne. Plans were already advanced, however, for a "Widukind-Gedächtnisstätte", a memorial site to be built in the vicinity of the Stiftskirche in Enger, where the pagan warrior was supposedly buried. The SS-Ahnenerbe purchased one of the eighteenth-century houses on the edge of Kirchplatz and restored it in a *völkisch* style. The wooden beams that arched around its door were decorated with folkloric motifs and an *Odal* rune. An inscription carved in letters of gold read: "This building, erected in 1716, was converted to a Widukind Hall of Remembrance in 1938, the year in which Adolf Hitler, against the will of a hostile world, created the Greater German Empire. It exists to inform all Germans about the heroism of the Saxon freedom fighter Widukind." Inside the Hall of Remembrance was a bust of the Saxon chieftain, a wooden pulpit and a pair of standing candelabra. On the bare white walls were inscribed words of Hitler: "Wer seinem Volke so die Treue hielt, soll selbst in Treue nie vergessen sein!" ("He who remains loyal to his people shall always be remembered with loyalty!")

Little changed after the war. The inscription above the door was modified by removing Hitler's name; and his signature was erased from the quotation inside the Hall of Remembrance (although the quotation itself remained). It was not until the 1970s that the Widukind Memorial Hall with its Hitlerian epigram was deemed unacceptable; and another thirty years passed before the present Widukind Museum, which offers an intelligent, objective history of the Saxon warlord and his changing image through the ages, finally opened. The museum has a modern extension, a glass fin that juts over Steinstraße, but the original house has changed little since the 1930s. The sun wheels on the corbels supporting its pitched roof have been lovingly picked out in blue, green, red and yellow against the geometric black and white of its half-timbered walls. The oak entrance door is divided into twelve panels, each featuring one of the runic symbols used by the SS to denote power, victory or sacrifice. The door is framed by a rustic arch carved with traditional peasant motifs – wolves, serpents, eagles and songbirds – and vines which coil around the fauna before flowering into solar crosses and curly swastikas.

There was a farmers' market in the centre of Detmold. Stalls spread out over the Marktplatz and squeezed around the Donop Fountain below the peeled white trunks of a row of plane trees. On the west side of the square was the Erlöserkirche, a Gothic church plastered in white with a triple-tiered slate spire. On the north side was the coralline Rathaus, a stately building whose pompous Doric portico was incongruously undermined by the entrance to a WC positioned prominently beneath its ceremonial double staircase. The farmers' stalls carried mounds of potatoes and onions; piles of fennel, carrots, celery, pointed *Spitzkohl* and bulbous kohlrabi; trays of fleshy *Steinpilze* and erotogenic *Pfifferlinge*; punnets of strawberries, blackcurrants, gooseberries and redcurrants. Mobile butchers and dairies had unfolded their vans beneath the acacias of the Kleiner Marktplatz to reveal displays of cheeses, creams, quark, wurst, *Speck* and salami. I sat outside a café in Lange Straße below Sonntag, a Wilhelmine-Hanseatic department store coloured like a lemon meringue pie. It was the mid-point of a Tuesday morning and the womenfolk of Detmold were gathering in the cafés along Lange Straße for a coffee break during their shopping expeditions. The waiter said "Thank you very much" in English as I paid for my cup of tea.

I walked through a passageway into Schlossplatz, an eighteenth-century English Garden between the Fürstliches Residenzschloss and its outlying stables and carriage houses. I followed gravel paths around immaculate lawns and exotic trees – juniper, gingko and copper beech. I sat on a bench and listened to the sounds of doves cooing in the trees, water gushing from a fountain and the murmur of conversation from a crèche of young mothers who had corralled themselves and their tiny offspring inside a circle of prams and buggies on the grass – even though it was technically *verboten* to walk on the lawns. Bells tolled from the Schloss: four deep peals followed by eleven softer chimes to mark the hour. I followed the sound of the bells to the corner of the park where the Schloss stood. The Princely Residence boasted an imposing medieval round tower surmounted by a bell-shaped turret adorned with four golden clocks and eight spherical finials. The adjoining entrance wing was built in the 1550s in the style of the Weser Renaissance. Like the Schloss of the Fürstenbergs in Donaueschingen, the seat of the Princes of Lippe had seen better days: the beige plasterwork of its walls was wearing thin, and its sandstone gables were grubby with age. Nylon curtains hung limply behind antique wood-framed, single-glazed windows. A pair of ornamental lampposts and two sentry boxes striped in the red and yellow of the former principality stood guard on either side of an archway into the courtyard of the Schloss. I caught a glimpse of gun carriages and receptacles filled with cannonballs on the cobblestones.

In the centre of the park was a bust of Johannes Brahms, long-faced and heavy-bearded even as a young man in his mid-twenties. The composer worked in the autumn months of 1857 to 1859 at the princely court of Lippe-Detmold as choirmaster and piano teacher to Princess Friederike. He was apparently quite lonely during his sojourns in Detmold and spent much of his time taking solitary walks in the Teutoburg Forest to escape the inhibiting etiquette of the court. The bust of Brahms was sculpted in 1936, as was that of Richard Wagner which stands on a stone herm in a small garden opposite the Landestheater. The latter was installed to celebrate the Richard-Wagner-Festwochen held in Detmold from 1935 to 1944. These bijou alternatives to the Bayreuther Festspiele were the brainchild of a music teacher named Otto Daube, who saw an opportunity to establish Detmold as a third "sacred place" of German culture after Bayreuth and Weimar. His endeavours were supported and financed by the local Gauleitung, which pronounced the Festival Weeks as "reichswichtig". The opening festival in 1935 was publicised by means of a poster depicting a montage of the composer, the sword of Hermann the Cherusker and the Hermann Monument in the forest above Detmold.

The poster for the following year's festival did away with Wagner and Hermann and just depicted a sword, oak leaf and swastika. The Festival Week of 1938 was blessed with both the imprimatur of Adolf Hitler (who sent a well-wishing telegram) and the presence of the *grande dame* of Bayreuth, Winifred Wagner, who came to schmooze with the local Gauleiter Alfred Meyer.[16]

Hermann the German stands high above the trees atop a domed monopteros of blackened sandstone on the summit of the Grotenburg. Coated in a patina of verdigris, the copper warrior raises his sword into the sky in a gesture of leadership, a signal to attack. His back is turned to those ascending the avenue up the hill. He faces west, towards the archenemy – Romans, Franks or the French – who will come from the lands across the Rhine.

I made my way up the avenue to Arminius (to give him his correct name). The little we know about him has been gleaned from the annals of Tacitus and other Roman historians; he only became known as Hermann when Martin Luther germanised the written language in the sixteenth century. The statue of the Germanic warlord stands on top of a tall circular structure in the form of a classical temple ringed by ten pillars whose arches overlap to form pointed Gothic niches. Three of these contain inscriptions which once endowed the monument with its patriotic significance. The first is a quotation from Tacitus, in Latin and German, which praises Arminius as "Germany's liberator", an invincible warrior who successfully defended his people against the might of the Roman Empire. The second inscription apologises for the fact that Germany was only subjugated by Napoleon because the German people had been "verwelscht" (become soft or weak like the French or Italians) and disunited. Engraved above a relief of Kaiser Wilhelm I, the third inscription is in rhyming verse:

---

16   Meyer was later appointed Deputy Reichsminister for the Occupied Eastern Territories. He attended the Wannsee Conference of January 1942 on behalf of his superior Alfred Rosenberg. Later that year Meyer proposed that Jewish "Mischlinge" (people of mixed German and Jewish race) in the territories under his administration be treated with the same "measures" as those being taken against "full" Jews. He committed suicide on 11 April 1945.

Der lang getrennte Stämme vereint mit starker Hand,
Der welsche Macht und Tücke siegreich überwand,
Der längst verlorene Söhne heimführt zum Deutschen Reich,
Armin, der Retter ist er gleich.

(He who with strong hand unified separate tribes,
He who conquered French power and malice,
He who returned long-forgotten sons to the German Reich,
He is at one with the saviour Arminius.)

Arminius's left hand rests on a shield engraved with the motto "Treufest"; his right hand raises a sword high into the sky. His left foot tramples on an eagle and a lictorial bundle, symbols of Roman justice and might. He is clad anachronistically in a nineteenth-century notion of what a Germanic hero should look like – a skimpy tunic revealing the musculature of his chest, a low-slung belt, cloak, pixie boots and a helmet winged like a German eagle. There is a swing to his hips, a *contrapposto* which resembles the pose of Michelangelo's *David*. His bearded face bears a likeness to the young Ernst von Bandel, sculptor of the monument.

I bought a ticket and ascended a spiral staircase inside the Kuppelhalle. I emerged onto an ambulatory encircling the exterior of the dome, with its panoramic view over the forested hills of the Teutoburger Wald and, in the valleys below, an uneven patchwork of green woodland, dun-coloured wheat fields and pale villages – all drained of colour behind a veil of drizzle that receded into a silvery grey amalgam of misty hills, watery cloud and colourless sky. Somewhere up here one autumn morning in 9 AD, so it was believed,[17] Arminius and his band of Cherusci and other barbarian tribes ambushed a convoy of three Roman legions and their auxiliaries, who were returning from their forts on the River Weser to their winter quarters along the Rhine. Twenty thousand Roman soldiers were trapped in ravines and gullies in thick forest and were unable to deploy their usual fighting formations. The convoy, which may have reached a length of fifteen kilometres, was picked off century by century, its soldiers slaughtered, their bodies left unburied, their skulls nailed to trees.

---

17 Archaeologists later identified the site of the *Varusschlacht*, as the massacre is known in German, to the north of Osnabrück at the other end of the Teutoburg Forest.

If Widukind is Germany's Alfred the Great and Arminius its Boadicea, then the Externsteine are Germany's Stonehenge. The one obvious difference is that the Externsteine are a natural phenomenon, a wall of thirteen towering rocks which erupted from the forest floor at the end of the Cretaceous Period sixty-five million years ago. Contemporary druids and New Age hippies gather here, as they do at the Wiltshire megalith, to celebrate solstices and equinoxes; although the notion that ancient druids assembled here in heathen times is one that only existed in the feverish imagination of Himmler and his Wotanist acolytes, who excavated the site in the mid-1930s in an attempt to reveal evidence of an ancient tribe of mystical Aryans from whom the *völkisch* Germanists of the Third Reich could claim a line of descent. Pastor Wilhelm Teudt came from this proto-Nazi milieu of paganists, anti-Semites and German nationalists. In the late 1920s he settled in Detmold and founded an Association of Friends of Germanic History which claimed, in the face of all scientific evidence, that the Externsteine were the site of a pre-Christian observatory where star-worshippers assembled. In 1934 the government of Lippe established an Externsteine Foundation which welcomed the Reichsführer SS and executives from the Ahnenerbe onto its committee. Himmler's archaeologists took the site apart, stone by stone, and drained the artificial lake created in the early nineteenth century; but they found nothing to suggest that the Externsteine were the Germanic cultic site they were looking for. They made do with reclassifying a latrine as a "ritual shaft"; a mortise as the "grounding-hole of the Irminsul"; and a Christian niche grave as a "Germanic stone table". They drew up detailed plans to reconstruct the site as a faux-Germanic theme park, with wattle and daub cottages on top of the highest stones and a replica of the Irminsul at the summit of the Tower Rock. In the end all they added was a prosaic wooden gateway bearing the slogan "Haltet Ruhe am Heiligtum der Ahnen!" ("Keep quiet at the shrine of your ancestors!")

The real history of the Externsteine is less fanciful. The rocks must have been used as a retreat in the Early Stone Age, as microliths from this period have been found there. The first written records of the Externsteine date from the twelfth century and suggest that the stones belonged to the Bishopric of Paderborn. They were inhabited by Christian hermits and used as a staging post by abbots and their retinues travelling between monasteries. It was in this century that a network of grottoes was carved out inside the base of the largest rock. An arcosolium modelled on the Tomb of Christ was built at the foot of the cliff. At the top of Tower Rock a High Chamber was constructed, containing an altar set into an arched niche. The most spectacular relic from this period is a relief depicting the Descent from the Cross, carved into the base of the largest stone. Nicodemus has lost his left arm, Joseph of Arimathea his legs and Mary Magdalene her head, but the surviving elements form a stark depiction of the aftermath of the crucifixion. God the Father turns away in pain, while two figures in the netherworld (possibly Adam and Eve) find themselves trapped within the coils of a dragon-like monster. The crooked tree in the centre of the tableau is supposedly a palm, rather than the Irminsul the paganists would have us believe. All the evidence suggests that during the Early Middle Ages the Externsteine were modelled on Golgotha and served as a place of Christian sanctuary and pilgrimage – and not as a temple for sun-worshippers.

By the early sixteenth century the hermits had left and the Externsteine had lost their religious significance. The stones became a refuge for robber bands. In the seventeenth century they were purchased by Count Hermann Adolph of Lippe, who built himself a hunting lodge at the foot of the cliffs. By the early nineteenth century the Externsteine had become a destination for sightseers, their popularity boosted by the verses of Romantic poets and by the growing enthusiasm for landscapes which exemplified something of the German national soul. Princess Pauline of Lippe had the hunting lodge demolished and replaced by some half-timbered *Gasthäuser*. A network of stairs built by her predecessor was extended to form a bridge between the highest rocks, so that visitors could explore the High Chamber and its altar. The Wiembecke stream was dammed to create an artificial lake at the foot of the cliffs, which rounded off the picturesque appearance of the crags in a more romantic manner. Nevertheless, Princess Pauline rather undermined the natural grandeur of the wall of rocks by ordering a road to be built through the gap between the third and fourth stones. The road through the rocks was designated Germany's Bundesstraße 1, and in 1912 a tramline was added. Trams from Detmold to Paderborn halted at a stop near the foot of the cliffs.

I once visited the Externsteine in midwinter. The nineteenth-century hotels and restaurants had long been demolished and the former B1 with its tramline had reverted to a simple *Wanderweg*. Snow dusted the rocks and glazed the trees of the surrounding forest. The lake was frozen and the meadow at the foot of the stones glistened like a sheet of white satin. The Externsteine had recovered their natural lustre. The entrance kiosk was closed and the few visitors were free to pass through the open turnstile

and approach the stones. I started to clamber up a wrought-iron staircase
to a platform at the top of the tallest stone. The steps had frozen into a
helter-skelter of ice. I climbed three-quarters of the way to the top by
gripping a slippery handrail and kicking my boots into the impacted snow
until I could lever myself up to the next step; but I lost my nerve to climb
right to the top once I realised how difficult it would be to get down again.
I tried a second stairway, which led up the third stone towards an iron
bridge, over which one could cross to the High Altar at the top of Tower
Rock; but the way was blocked by an iron door just around the first bend.
I was beginning to feel like Jimmy Page in his role as mystic seeker in the
fantasy sequence from Led Zeppelin's film *The Song Remains the Same.*
That, in turn, made me wonder whether Aleister Crowley ever practised
"magick" atop the towers of the Externsteine. Apparently not, but I later
discovered that a sequence from Kenneth Anger's film *Lucifer Rising* (for
which Page was commissioned to write a soundtrack) was shot at the
Externsteine. The film opens with random images of Stonehenge, Crowley,
pentagrams, flying saucers, erupting volcanoes, swimming tigers, hatch-
ing crocodiles, bare-breasted hippy chicks and a brief shot of Arminius's
raised sword from the Hermann Monument. A stoned Marianne Faithfull
(playing the demon Lilith) rises at dawn from the arcosolium at the foot
of the cliffs and emerges into the sun below the Descent from the Cross.
Followed by five hooded figures bearing firebrands (filmed at night: continuity was not Anger's strong point), she slowly ascends the stairway of
Tower Rock and crosses the bridge to the High Altar, where the oculus in
the rear of the niche metamorphoses into a sun rising over Egypt, where
Lucifer is taking a bath.

I approached Wewelsburg from the south-west. The Schloss sat on a
bluff, high above wooded slopes. The two round towers at the base of
the triangle formed by the castle's walls were capped with slate helmets;
the larger round tower at the apex of the triangle had lost its dome. The
road skirted a meadow, crossed the River Alme and wound up into the
village of Wewelsburg. At the centre of the farmhouses and tithe barns
was the Ottenshof, a half-timbered *Gasthof* adorned with gaily coloured
carvings of flowers, crosses, sun wheels, swastikas, spades and ears of
corn – the last two symbols those of the Reichsarbeitsdienst of National
Socialist Germany. Until it was recently painted over, the bay window of

Haus Saake, opposite the Ottenshof, was embellished with runes, *platt-deutsch* aphorisms and a row of wooden corbels carved into the shapes of prominent public figures of the age in which it was built; one of them had slicked hair and a toothbrush moustache.

I parked beneath a blue-and-white-striped maypole decorated with the emblems of local anglers, pigeon-fanciers, riflemen, war veterans, Catholic women, a Voluntary Fire Brigade, a Choral Society and a brass band. I followed the castle walls until I reached a cobbled square in front of a bridge leading into the Schloss. Opposite the castle was a guardhouse built in the 1930s for the SS Burgmannschaft, which supervised the castle during the Third Reich. I noticed a stone sentry box with its SS runes chiselled out and, below the bridge, a stone corbel dated 1934 carved into the form of a *Neidkopf*, a personification of envy with glaring eyes and screaming mouth. The bridge spanned a dry moat which was wreathed in mist following rain earlier that morning. I crossed the bridge and passed through an archway below an oriel window, in the style of the Flemish Renaissance, whose entablature bore the inscription *Ano Domini 1604* and the quartered shield of the Fürstenbergs, Prince Bishops of Paderborn.

I paid three euros to visit the Historical Museum of the Prince Bishopric, which shared the rooms of the castle with a youth hostel. The first room of the exhibition was in the former entrance hall of the Burghauptmann's apartments during the stewardship of the SS. The room was gutted by fire during the attempted destruction of the castle in April 1945, but a sixteenth-century "Fireplace of the Virtues" and a floor of glazed bricks, patterned with runic motifs from the 1930s, survived the blaze. In one corner of the room were three wicker chairs, carved with *Odal* runes, which came from the dining room of the SS in the southern wing of the castle. Iron lamps wrought into Tree of Life designs were mounted on the walls, which were hung with six paintings from the private collection of Heinrich Himmler: two views of Schloss Wewelsburg from the meadow below the escarpment; an *Alpine Landscape* painted in 1940; a view of the *Ordensburg Schivelbein* in Pomerania; a lithograph of *The Grand Master's Palace of Marienburg*; and an oil painting from 1815 depicting a fire which destroyed the north tower of Wewelsburg Castle that year.

I followed the course of the museum through the south wing to a circular room on the second floor of the south-west tower, where Himmler once had his study. I lingered here to admire a view over rolling farmland and river valleys which had changed little since the 1930s: only a distant motorway viaduct and some wind turbines gave the present perspective a more contemporary aspect. Near the end of the exhibition I came across two German men in the basement adjacent to the north tower. They seemed lost and exasperated, peering through keyholes and pushing against locked doors. Having done the same myself on my first visit to Wewelsburg twenty years earlier, I realised they were searching for an entrance to the north tower. On that occasion I had discovered a flight of steps from the ramparts down into the moat, from where one could walk to the north tower and peer through one of its embrasures into a crypt. In the gloom one could make out a swastika pattern in the vertex of the domed ceiling of the crypt, and an amulet-shaped basin in its floor. This time, however, the stairway down to the moat was locked and a metal fence prevented access to the lower level of the castle. I walked around the ramparts, but found no way of descending into the moat. There were people down there, however, and eventually I realised that access to the moat and north tower lay through a new museum which had opened since my previous visit.

This museum, housing a permanent exhibition entitled "Wewelsburg 1933 – 1945. Cult and Terror Centre of the SS", opened in April 2010 in the renovated guardhouse opposite the entrance to the castle. Its dual function was to provide a history of the castle during its SS stewardship, and to place this local narrative within the broader context of Himmler's Schutzstaffel. The Reichsführer SS first became acquainted with Westphalia-Lippe when he accompanied Hitler on an election campaign for the Diet of Lippe in January 1933. Their hosts Baron Adolf and Baroness Jutta von Oeynhausen enthused about Westphalia as the heartland of Germany – the land of Widukind, Arminius and the Externsteine. Himmler was smitten, and later that year he explored the region around Detmold, visiting the Hermann Monument and the Externsteine in an attempt to find the perfect location for the Reichsführer School SS he intended to found. On 3 November 1933 he discovered Schloss Wewelsburg and immediately ordered his architect Hermann Bartels to draw up plans for the future SS academy. By 1937 Himmler's plans had expanded into a megalomaniac project, in which the castle would function as a centre for the exclusive use of the SS military elite. This was to be Himmler's Camelot, the stage on which Gruppenführer and Obergruppenführer of the SS would enact their roles as the racial and military vanguard of the National Socialist regime. Wewelsburg would be the repository of the death's head rings of fallen SS soldiers and the shields of deceased Gruppenführer. The paladins of the SS would assemble like Knights of the Round Table in the circular chamber at the foot of the north tower.

The second strand of the museum documented the broader history of Himmler's Schutzstaffel, from its inception as a squad of volunteers who provided security for Nazi rallies in Munich beer halls, to a "state within a state" responsible for ancestral heritage, racial hygiene, euthanasia and mass murder. The "cultural" section of the exhibition included copies of magazines such as *Odal – a Monthly for Blood and Soil* or *Nordland – the Manifesto for Racial Action.* Among the books on display were *Volk ohne Raum* ("People without Living Space"), *Adel und Rasse* ("Nobility and Race"), *Die Stimme der Ahnen* ("The Voice of the Ancestors"), *Germanic Holy Sites* (featuring a photograph on the dust jacket of the High Altar at the Externsteine) and *The Cleansing of the Temple of Art: an Art-Historical Broadsheet for the Recovery of German Art in the Spirit of the Nordic Manner.* A jigsaw puzzle published in 1942 illustrated, when complete, a map of "Deutschland" which extended without borders from Amsterdam to Bucharest. On the *volkstümlich* side, there were display cases of breadboards and christening mugs, Harvest Festival crowns and wedding cups, Yuletide lights and Santa's reindeer, all lovingly decorated with runes or perforated with heart shapes. On the *völkisch* side, there were children's schoolbooks depicting Jews as poisonous toadstools with huge noses; and exhibition catalogues which likened the works of Jewish sculptors to Negroid monsters. Officers of the SS, by contrast, were portrayed as knights in shining armour: Gruppenführer Oswald Pohl, for example, was depicted as Parzival in a painting (in the two-dimensional style of a medieval altarpiece) which echoed that by Hubert Lanzinger of Adolf Hitler as *The Flag Bearer.* Most chilling of all was a set of Meissen porcelain figurines fashioned into drummers from the Hitler Youth and cheerleaders from the League of German Girls – artefacts of great delicacy and beauty which had been manufactured to represent branches of a movement characterised by thuggery and zealotry.

The exhibition culminated in a collection of books and compact discs highlighting Wewelsburg's post-war afterlife as a shrine for neo-Nazi occultists. There were books hailing Wewelsburg as a "Grail Castle" or an SS monastery modelled on the Order of the Jesuits. There were works with titles such as *The Spear of Destiny*; *Adolf Hitler, the Last Avatar*; or *Adolf Hitler and the Secrets of the Holy Lance*, most of which ignored the fact that Hitler demonstrated little interest in this esoteric nonsense. The compact discs were those of a black metal band from Russia who had named themselves Wewelsburg, and a German band called Race War who had released a picture disc entitled *Stimme des Blutes* ("Voice of Blood").

The exhibition ended in the former wine cellar of the SS, from where a tunnel led beneath a rampart into the castle moat. It was refreshing to be outside again in the cool summer air. There was a smell of damp vegetation and the sound of rooks cawing in the elm trees above the ramparts. Above the moat rose the castle walls, weathered grey-brown stone webbed with ivy. A small group of visitors had gathered in front of the door to the north tower, which was due to open at 2 pm. I joined them and waited for fifteen minutes, but the door remained locked. I returned to the museum to ask the staff when the north tower would reopen. The receptionist informed me the door would reopen at 3 pm, once a guided tour of the tower had finished. I reported back to the group waiting in the moat, which had in the meantime been joined by a small chapter of Hell's Angels from Sweden.

At 3 pm the door was duly unlocked and we descended into the crypt in the basement of the north tower. A musty odour of cold, damp stone permeated the subterranean chamber. The circular walls curved upwards into a dome whose vertex was decorated with a meander, an ancient Greek ornamental pattern with a swastika at its centre. Four embrasures cut at a slant into the thick walls of the dome threw shafts of murky light which converged on a circular basin of dark limestone, shaped like a pagan amulet, set into the floor of the crypt. In the centre of the unfinished basin was a gas pipe which had been left unstopped, suggesting that an "eternal flame" to commemorate the "martyrs" of the SS was to have been installed as the focal point of the chamber. In the shadows around the edge were twelve low, circular pedestals ranged symmetrically around the hall. The niches once carved into the wall behind them had been filled in. The precise purpose of the crypt is not recorded. Its architecture is that of a Mycenaean burial chamber, and it is presumed that the rotunda was conceived in order to honour the dead of the SS. It has been suggested that the niches and pedestals were designed to hold urns containing the death's head ring of every fallen SS soldier; or that the shields of deceased Gruppenführer were to be ceremonially burned in the basin in the floor.

Immediately above the crypt was the Obergruppenführersaal, an attractive room resembling a medieval lady's bower – or a nineteenth-century stage set for Wagner's *Parsifal*. A circular colonnade of twelve neo-Romanesque arches hewn from green sandstone supported a ceiling of white stucco. Light flooded into the hall from eight tall bay windows fashioned in the National Socialist style. According to a poem written by Wilhelm Jordan to commemorate the "Yule Celebration" (as the Nazis had retermed Christmas) of 1941, the architecture of the Obergruppenführersaal was "romanisch, doch nicht zu kirchlich, mehr profanisch!" ("Romanesque, but not too Christian, more 'profanesque'!") The light from the windows converged on a spidery sun wheel inlaid in green-black marble in the centre of the polished stone floor. The twelve spokes of the wheel were bent into inverse *Sig* runes in a pattern based on a seventh-century Alemannic fibula (or three swastikas superimposed on each other with an extra hook added to the end of each arm). In 1991 a novel entitled *The Black Sun of Tashi Lhunpo* was published under the pseudonym of Russell McCloud. Written by a German author named Stephan Mögle-Stadel, this conspiracy thriller drew together the familiar themes of Tibet, Atlantis and a superhuman race of "Agarthi" who have morphed into the SS and have been initiated into secret rites held in the "Temple of Wewelsburg" – and whose occult powers are still at large. Since its publication, the fibula in the floor of the Obergruppenführersaal has been known as the "Black Sun", and its motif has become a symbol for those benighted souls who pursue an interest in the occult fantasies of the SS. Exhibited in the SS museum were examples of merchandise available from neo-Nazi websites which use the "Black Sun" as their logo: flags, tablecloths, coasters, a wrist watch – and a pair of pink knickers.

In the post-war period Schloss Wewelsburg has served as a paradigm for the Germans' ability (or inability) to come to terms with their National Socialist past. In the aftermath of the war the crypt was to some extent denazified by the installation of a cycle of ten paintings by Jo Glahé, which were hung around the walls between each pedestal. In an Expressionist style reminiscent of Beckmann or Kirchner, the paintings depicted the consequences of Nazism – book burnings, *Kristallnacht*, euthanasia, concentration camps, refugees and bombed-out cities – and served as a memorial to victims of the SS. By the 1970s, however, a younger generation "blessed by the mercy of late birth" had become fed up with feeling guilty for the crimes of their parents. The paintings were removed and destroyed. Debate rumbled on throughout the 1970s and 1980s as to whether the history of Schloss Wewelsburg as the "Holy of Holies" of the SS should be consciously remembered or conveniently forgotten. The latter option was becoming difficult, since the crypt was turning into a shrine visited by occultists, Satanists and neo-Nazis. It was only with the turn of the millennium, and the general feeling that the events of the twentieth century could be safely consigned to "history", that Wewelsburg has been recast as a site where the crimes of the SS can be openly addressed. But Schloss

Wewelsburg remains contradictory. On one hand it is a place to remember the victims of National Socialism; on the other it is the embodiment of the mystique of the SS. Why do visitors come here? My guess is that most come for the occultism.

At Geseke I rejoined Bundesstrasse 1 and followed the road in a straight line to the west. This was the route of the ancient Westphalian Hellweg, the "Bright Way" that connected the Rhine and Weser rivers in pre-Roman times. The landscape was flat, featureless except for multi-cylindered grain silos and cement works coated with white dust. I turned off the B1 in Erwitte and followed directions to a Schloss. Built in 1648, the manor house lay in ornamental parkland at the end of an avenue of linden trees. Ducks swam in its moat and doves cooed from weeping willows that dangled their branches in the brown water. A wall fortified in a fake medieval manner ran alongside a narrow canal linking the Schloss to the centre of Erwitte. The Altstadt was dominated by the Sankt Laurentiuskirche, whose Romanesque tower was dinted with tiny arched windows in the same style as St Cyriakus in Geseke and the *Dom* of Paderborn. Positioned around the grounds of the castle were a number of black-and-white half-timbered buildings which functioned as clinics for physiotherapy, orthopaedics and urology.

In 1935 Schloss Erwitte was converted into the Reichsschulungsburg Erwitte, an educational centre for aspiring young Nazis administered under the auspices of the German Labour Front. It was one of thirteen such colleges, which formed the next level of National Socialist indoctrination below the three elite Ordensburgen at Sonthofen, Crössinsee and Vogelsang. The Schloss was given a makeover by the leader of the DAF architectural office Julius Schulte-Frohlinde, co-architect with Albert Speer of the Volksgemeinschaftshalle I had visited in Braunschweig. Schulte-Frohlinde was a proponent of the *völkisch* idiom of National Socialist architecture, that "healthy, clear German style" which expressed the core values of the German character.

The Schloss is now a four-star hotel. Tables and chairs were set out beneath sunshades on a terrace in front. I went inside and asked whether they were serving tea. The receptionist replied that the kitchen would reopen in half an hour. I walked back through the park, past the half-timbered clinic buildings built in the 1930s to accommodate the teachers, chauffeurs and other staff employed in the Reichsschulungsburg. At the entrance to the grounds was a hall built in a National Socialist style, a smaller version of the Volksgemeinschaftshalle in the Südstadt of Braunschweig. Constructed from the same rough grey-brown stone as Schloss Wewelsburg, the Horst-Wessel-Halle was built in 1938 as a place of worship where the students of the Reichsschulungsburg could assemble to watch propaganda films or participate in ceremonies glorifying the Party and its Führer. In the 1930s the hall was furnished with wooden pews. A pulpit stood below a swastika at the far end of the aisle. Like Speer's community hall in Braunschweig, this was a National Socialist church – with the hooked cross of the Nazis in place of the Christian cross. A large *Reichsadler* remained clamped to the gable above the entrance. Designed by Willy Meller, sculptor of eagles, laurel wreaths and flaming torches for the arenas of the Third Reich, the massive stone bird is perched erect and alert, its wings unfurled like shields and its talons embedded in a laurel wreath now shorn of its swastika.

The door to the Horst Wessel Hall was locked, so I returned to the Schloss. The café had opened and guests had begun to arrive: a local couple meeting for cocktails after work, and a quartet of businessmen – two German, two American – dressed in suits and ties and rattling their luggage trolleys behind them as they exchanged pleasantries. I ordered a pot of tea, spitting out the *T* and stretching my gums around the *ee* so that the rather formal young waiter would not misunderstand my order.

My hotel in the centre of Dortmund looked as if it had been designed by Speer. It was a monolithic block in red brick with white stone colonnades. Its concave façade ended in a tower-like projection which reminded me of the German Pavilion at the Paris International Exhibition of 1937. The interior of the hotel resembled a Romanov take on Ludwig II's Schloss Herrenchiemsee. Its walls were panelled with red-brown marble, veined with white like slices of corned beef. A grand staircase carpeted in scarlet and gold fleur-de-lis led to a mezzanine floor furnished with copper samovars and Ottoman water jugs two metres high. Tasselled armchairs the size of divans were scattered around the lobby, surrounded by antique dressers, Empire commodes and Victorian grandfather clocks. A crystal chandelier hung like a small spaceship from the skylight. The bar was lit by turquoise and purple neon strips, and Led Zeppelin's *Black*

Dog boomed down from a giant video screen. I looked for the Ukrainian prostitutes, but there were none. I spent a few moments leaning out of the window of my suite, looking at the four giant glass *U*s and the digital screens of frothing, bubbling Pilsener beer on the Dortmunder Union tower. When built in 1926–27, the brewery was the city's first skyscraper. Brewing ceased in 1994 and the building is now an arts centre.

I went back down to the lobby for a beer, sinking into one of the Brobdingnagian sofas. I asked the barmaid if she could tell me anything about the history of the hotel. She replied that the building was formerly the administrative headquarters of Brau und Brunnen AG, the largest brewing group in Germany until it became insolvent in 2004, apparently due to the decline in the Germans' propensity for drinking beer. The hotel was intended to open in time for the World Cup in 2006, but its renovation was beset by dodgy finance and it didn't finally open until 2009. The Turkish owner was now serving a jail sentence for tax evasion. The barmaid was on a zero-hour contract.

I crossed Westentor and set off along Westenhellweg, the western half of the long shopping street cutting through the centre of Dortmund. I was back on the Westphalian Hellweg, the ancient salt route from the Weser to the Rhine. It was 8 pm on a Thursday and the shops were pulling down their shutters. I passed Chinese and Turkish takeaways, a "Gold Ankauf" pawn shop and a BvB (Ballspielverein Borussia, commonly known as Borussia Dortmund) fan shop. I soon reached the big department stores of Kaufhof and Karstadt in the city centre. Karstadt was fronted in Hansaplatz by a post-war replica of its original High Wilhelmine façade designed by Wilhelm Kreis; and in the Alter Markt by the sleek, white, post-modern block of Karstadt sports. The streets were crowded with hen parties, football fans sporting the yellow and black of Borussia (even though we were in the middle of July) and tattooed teenage girls in high-street glad rags. Rappers busked to the accompaniment of beat boxes, and junkies with fucked-up faces and greasy ponytails lounged in doorways. After the pastoral idylls of the Lipper Land and the Teutoburger Wald, I returned to city life with mixed feelings.

The Dortmunders were drawn inexorably to the Alter Markt, where cafés and restaurants had spread their tables out beneath the department stores. I circled the marketplace twice before deciding to dine inside Pfefferkorn, a chain restaurant whose interior was fitted out in *alt deutsch* style with wooden tables, red hessian banquettes, oak-panelled walls and mullioned windows. Huge copper lamps were suspended from the ceiling like upside-down bath tubs. A dark green *Kachelofen* stood in one corner, a wooden rocking horse in another. The walls were covered with paintings of grandees from the Age of Enlightenment, dressed like Goethe in frock coats, white silk stockings and broad-brimmed black hats. Every nook was filled with pewter plates or gilded Madonnas. The waitresses were bossy and the clientele was as hefty as the décor – men with barrel chests and women with thighs like tree trunks. At the table next to mine a group of silver-haired gentlemen were holding their bi-annual school reunion, passing around photographs and sharing memories. At another table two couples, the men dressed in black suits and ties, arrived from a performance at the Stadttheater of Franz Lehár's operetta *Der Graf von Luxemburg*. One alcove had been reserved for a party of younger men, who were belting out drinking songs and giving short speeches, which were received with raucous applause. Eight of them were wearing checked plaid shirts, and I wondered whether they were in uniform – maybe they were a convention of Creedence Clearwater Revival fans, for instance – but looking around the restaurant it seemed that German men just liked to wear comfortable, unpretentious checked plaid shirts. I pushed away the brass candlestick and pot of plastic geraniums that encumbered my table and ordered a *Weizenbier* and a *Westfälischer Grünkohl*, a dish which, when it arrived, turned out to be a hunk of pink smoked pork and a *Kohlwurst* resembling a grilled penis lying semi-erect on a bed of soggy green cabbage.

The following morning, I drove south along Ruhrallee towards Hörde and parked by the derelict gasometers and blast furnaces of the former Krupp steelworks. There was a view back to the north towards a television tower and Dortmund's single skyscraper office block. To the west were the yellow cantilevers of Borussia's Westfalenstadion. Directly in front of me was the gargantuan skeleton of a disused steel plant, a decaying Moloch of pipes, cylinders, chimneys, gantries, tanks, boilers, platforms, turbines, girders, shafts, cables and conveyor belts held together by a patina of rust whose particles shimmered like bronze in the midday heat. As I was taking photographs of the industrial dinosaur, a young man approached my car and raised an eyebrow. I shrugged my shoulders and made it clear I was there for the innocent purpose of taking photographs of Phoenix West. I was unsure whether he was a professional rent boy or an office worker in search of a quickie on his lunch break. Judging by the graffiti on a nearby wall ("Ansatz von Hans" – with "Hans" crossed out and replaced by "Paul"), I suspect the former.

Phoenix Ost, the eastern half of the former Krupp domain, had been transformed into a post-modern development of shopping malls and office blocks on the shores of an artificial lake created over the ruins of the steelworks. I drove south into the hills, through Benninghofen and Loh, estates of steelworkers' cottages mass-built in the 1930s and interspersed with high-rise apartment blocks constructed in the 1970s for *Gastarbeiter* from Turkey, Greece and Yugoslavia. In Höchsten I stopped at a chicken grill in the hope of a light, healthy snack for lunch; but the menu consisted only of combinations of *Currywurst, Mettwurst* or *Riesenbockwurst* with *Kartoffelsalat, Kartoffel-Puree, Sauerkraut* or *Rosenkohl*, the latter a mushy pile of pickled red cabbage. The only alternative was lentil soup, so I settled for a coffee and a cigarette. My request for a *latte macchiato* fell on deaf ears and I was served a mug of strong, nutty coffee with a small metal jug of condensed milk and a tube of sweeteners, all neatly presented on an oval wooden tray. Suitably refreshed, I took a left turn in Benninghofer Mark towards Holzen, where the landscape opened out to a vista of forested hills, cornfields and tidy villages. At the foot of the valley was the River Ruhr. On the crest of the next hill was Hohensyburg.

I walked along the crest of the Hohensyburg escarpment, beneath the shade of trees to escape the heat of the sun. Below me the Ruhr widened into the broad curve of the Hengsteysee reservoir, its surface still and brown and covered with a film of green elodea. The forested scarp continued along the northern bank of the lake, interrupted only by the pipes of the Koepchenwerk power station which pumped water up into storage basins in the hills. A girder bridge carried a railway line across the river into an industrial zone of storage tanks, sewage works, recycling plants, printing works and steel mills. Goods trains rumbled over railway tracks and lorries thundered across the viaduct of an autobahn. On the far side of the motorway lay the northern suburbs of Hagen, where church steeples and factory chimneys rose above white apartment blocks glittering in the sunlight. The valleys to the south of the city folded into the wooded hills of the Märkisches Land, which in turn retreated into a smoky heat haze speckled by glints of blazing light from solar panels high up in the hills.

At the end of the ridge was another monument to Kaiser Wilhelm I. As at Kyffhäuser, the emperor was on a bronze steed and rode out from beneath a Gothic arch. Rather than his customary *Pickelhaube*, here he wore a helmet plumed with ostrich feathers, his gruff, crumpled face framed by a pair of flocculent side-whiskers. The tower above the monarch, however, was not, as at Kyffhäuser and Porta Westfalica, one of Bruno Schmitz's imperious Wilhelmine structures. This was a simple sandstone pylon thirty-four metres high, reinforced by buttresses, pierced by four Gothic niches and capped by a heavy attic slab. The Kaiser's paladins Bismarck and Moltke occupied two side niches: both were clad in military greatcoats and spiked helmets; both clutched a sabre in one hand and a rolled-up document in the other. Like the monarch he served, Bismarck had puffy, angry features made more irascible by a walrus moustache; Moltke's face was flinty, tight-lipped and clean-shaven. Below an imperial crown on the front of the tower was the inscription "18 Januar 1871", the date of the Proclamation of the German Reich. At the centre of the high retaining wall below the monument was a blank stone plaque whose inscription had been erased.

The Kaiser Wilhelm Monument which originally stood on the Syberg was designed by Hubert Stier. Its foundation stone was laid on 28 May 1893 and it was unveiled on 30 June 1902. The official commission of the Province of Westphalia to commemorate the Kaiser's reign had been awarded to Bruno Schmitz and Porta Westfalica; but a group of Ruhr industrialists decided to go ahead and erect their own expression of loyalty to Kaiser and Reich on the heights of Hohensyburg. Stier's monument was a sugary, neo-Gothic confection of walls and towers encrusted with turrets, Iron Crosses, Imperial Crowns and eagles of the Reich. As well as Bismarck, Moltke and Kaiser Bill, there were also statues of Crown Prince Friedrich Wilhelm and Prince Friedrich Karl. Even by the bombastic standards of the *Jahrhundertwende,* Stier's monument was overblown: it was described at the time as "zopfig" (plaited or pigtailed).

Thirty years later the National Socialists decided to give the monument a more contemporary look, one in tune with their own architectural style. They hired the Dortmund sculptor Friedrich Bagdons to refashion it. Bagdons had most of the original monument demolished, retaining only the central pylon, which he pared down to a simpler form. The statues of the Hohenzollern princes, the two sons of Kaiser Wilhelm, were removed; and those of the two Prussian generals relocated to positions at the sides of the tower. The original inscription with the dates of Kaiser Wilhelm's life was replaced by one celebrating the date of the founding of the Wilhelmine Reich. A high retaining wall was built around the base of the monument, at the centre of which was a stone plaque engraved with the date 16 March 1935 – that of the reconstructed monument's completion.

In contrast to Porta Westfalica, there are no signboards on the terrace below the Kaiser Wilhelm Monument at Hohensyburg to inform visitors of its history, and no indication that its tower was built during the Third Reich. There seem to be no records of why the regime went to such lengths to reconstruct this particular monument in this uniquely National Socialist Gothic idiom; or to what purpose they intended to use it once it had been rebuilt. They made no significant alterations to other nationalist monuments such as Kyffhäuser, Porta Westfalica or the Monument to the Battle of the Nations. The monument overlooking the Ruhr valley above Hohensyburg remains a curious hybrid – a celebration of the substance of the Second Reich in the style of the Third.

16

Rhineland

"I Heard Those Slinky Sirens Wail – Whoo!"

I arrived in Xanten on the evening of Boxing Day and checked into a hotel on the market square. The temperature was just above zero, but there was no sign yet of any snow. My plan was to buy a set of winter tyres the next morning for the car I had just purchased; and then to follow the route of Siegfried's Rhine Journey from his home town of Xanten to the Nibelung court at Worms.

I woke on Saturday morning to find Xanten – and my new BMW – beneath six inches of snow. I started to phone around the local car dealers and tyre shops, but soon realised they were all closed. The hotel receptionist explained they were probably taking a "bridge" between the Christmas holiday and the weekend. Only the Autohaus Nüsser was open. Herr Nüsser happened to have a new set of 16-inch all-weather tyres he had ordered for a customer who had failed to collect them, so I set out for the industrial zone of Xanten, trying to steer a straight line in the snow and driving gingerly around any roundabouts in first gear. My new vehicle turned out to have 17-inch wheels – one inch larger than my previous cars – and Herr Nüsser was unable to help me. I drove back to the hotel on my summer tyres, requiring a push from some of the good burghers of Xanten after I had inadvertently turned into a pedestrian zone and got stuck trying to perform a three-point turn on the ice.

After a restorative *latte macchiato* in a café on the marketplace, I set off on foot in search of the river. Xanten was originally a Roman colony on the Rhine, second in importance after Cologne, but the river had altered its course over the centuries and the town now lay a few kilometres to its

west. The overnight snow had begun to melt and I found myself walking
on roads wet with slush or paths clogged with mud. A flock of Canada
geese roosting in a field rose in unison as I approached, levitating a few
feet in a clatter of brown wings and black necks – before settling as one
back into the icy furrows. A curve of poplars on an embankment ahead
suggested the river was close. I heard seagulls mewing as they wheeled
above a jetty – and then there was the Rhine, flowing in a wide bow
between snow-clad banks lined with dark trees. There was a restaurant by
a ferry where a handful of diners sat in a post-Yuletide stupor. I ordered
a bowl of chestnut soup with prawns and watched a solitary barge from
Schiedam hugging the western shore as it fought its way upstream. It
was laden with snow-dusted mounds of coal, on one of which the skip-
per's Mercedes was perched at a precarious angle. After lunch I walked
north along the left bank of the river, following the curve of the tow-
path past stands of black trees whose trunks were frosted with a crust
of snow. It was silent, except for the wind and the river lapping at the
moss-coated blocks of stone banked up along the shoreline. Coal-laden
barges ploughed upstream, their prows almost submerged beneath the
grey waters. Massive Belgian flatboats piled high with shipping containers
cruised effortlessly in the opposite direction. Wavering V-shaped formations of geese flew soundlessly overhead, following the course of the river
north.

Back in the centre of Xanten I discovered a museum devoted to
Siegfried, the bumptious hero of the first part of *Das Nibelungenlied*.
The epic poem recounts how the son of Siegmund and Sieglinde, king
and queen of the Netherlands, was raised "in einer rîchen bürge witen
wol bekannt, nîdene bî dem Rîne: diu was ze Sántén genant" ("in a rich
town on the Rhine known far and wide as Xanten"). The collection documented the legend of Siegfried and the history of the Nibelung saga, from
its completion around the year 1200 by an anonymous poet at the court
of Bishop Wolfger von Erla in Passau; through *Sturm und Drang* and
Heinrich Heine's satire of Siegfried as that "clumsy little ogre"; through
Wagner's tedious, male-bonding *Siegfried* (the third opera of the *Ring*
tetralogy) and Fritz Lang's silent movie epic; from Georg Grosz's caricature of *Siegfried Hitler* to the Führer's death, announced on German radio
to the accompaniment of the power chords of Siegfried's Funeral March
from *Götterdämmerung*. In a post-war Germany fearful of national
heroes, Siegfried's image dissolved into kitsch, parody and post-Nazi
irony. His downfall was complete in 1971 when his character (relieved

of its bearskin) starred in an Austrian porn romp entitled *Siegfried und das sagenhafte Liebesleben der Nibelungen* ("Siegfried and the Legendary Love Lives of the Nibelungen").

Missing from the collection was any mention of those modern German artists, such as Salomé or Anselm Kiefer, who have subverted the mythology of Siegfried and Brünhild in an attempt to reveal how Germany's historical obsession with youth, strength, heroism and sacrifice paved the way for the mindless brutality of the Hitler Youth and the SS. Anselm Kiefer's Brünhilde is a shapely model torn from the pages of a 1970s girlie magazine; his Rhineland a riverscape of blackened tree trunks, military installations and funeral pyres, over which hover the phantom outlines of Arno Breker's statues and Wilhelm Kreis's monuments. His 1975 painting *Siegfried Forgets Brünhilde* is a study of absence and memory (or the absence *of* memory) – a wintry field of icy furrows (much like those I had just walked through by the Rhine) receding into a distant, colourless sky. Scrawled up the vertical axis of the painting are the words, barely legible, "Siegfried vergißt Brünhilde".

I woke on Sunday morning to a crisp, icy marketplace beneath a clear blue sky. The Xantener Dom gleamed in the sunlight. Bells tolled from its towers and red flags with gold crosses flew from its spires. I decided to catch a train to Düsseldorf. I walked to the station and waited on the icy crust of the platform, dazzled by a low, bright sun. Cars and buses crunched over the snowbound streets, bringing travellers for the next stopping train to Duisburg. The train departed eight minutes late, due to a most un-German *Lok-Verstörung* (technical problem), and then stopped immediately when the driver had to alight in order to close the level crossing manually. We trundled along embankments, over fields hard and lumpy beneath a thin coat of snow. We passed farms and paddocks where horses were waistcoated against the cold wind. In one field a dog was digging furiously into a molehill: other meadows were covered with battalions of migrating geese. Rows of bare trees ran along roads heading south into the sun. Plumes of smoke trailed from power stations, oil refineries and cement works along the course of the Rhine to the east. Soon the villages were surrounded by warehouses, car workshops, supermarkets and the yellow arches of McDonald's. The single track became a double line and the train picked up speed as we approached Moers.

The urban sprawl grew industrial as we passed pylons, chimneys, water towers, cooling towers, pitheads and disused slag heaps greened by a thin cover of trees. Railway stations named Rheinberg and Rheinhausen indicated the proximity of the river, but we saw only canals and motorways, Volkswagen plants and Bayer chemical works. An incline carried us over allotments where Croatian and Turkish flags flew; past the ruined parapet of a destroyed bridge; and, finally, across the Rhine into Duisburg, a city of docks, wharves, cranes, containers, factories, warehouses and railway sidings.

A freezing wind tore through the concourse of Duisburg station. I found a smoking zone on the platform and lit a cigarette, more in an attempt to keep warm than in a desire to smoke. An express train from Hamburg arrived and I boarded it for the short trip to Düsseldorf. I emerged from the Düsseldorfer Hauptbahnhof into Konrad-Adenauer-Platz and set off along Friedrich-Ebert-Straße, a dreary thoroughfare of 1960s office blocks. The street was empty save for a handful of alcoholics who were smoking and squaring up to each other outside a *döner* kebab shop. I aimed for a red-brick church tower which was the only attractive landmark visible. The Johanneskirche turned out to be a neo-Gothic church consecrated in 1881 as the principal evangelical church of Düsseldorf. It towered over Martin-Luther-Platz. Luther himself was absent, but the spirit of Prussian Protestantism dominated the square. A plumed, caped Kaiser Wilhelm I rode a bronze charger high on a granite pedestal laden with wreaths, garlands, cherubs and eagles. A pair of bas-reliefs set into the sides of the plinth illustrated the fall and rise of Prussia: a Fury strides with scourge and flame over the defeated figure of Germania as, in the background, Queen Louise and her children (one of them the future Kaiser Wilhelm) flee from Napoleon's armies to Königsberg and Memel at the far end of their kingdom; and sixty-five years later a rejuvenated Borussia bows her head to receive the imperial crown from the assembled German states. Germany is defeated, but Prussia rises again. Bismarck is here, stiff and formal in a cuirassier's coat, spiked helmet, riding boots and Iron Cross. Moltke would have been here too, but his statue was destroyed in an air raid in 1943.

I made my way down Bolkerstraße into the heart of Düsseldorf's Altstadt, a depressingly homogenous, stale beer-smelling grid of *Imbisse, Trinkhallen,* lounge bars, sports bars, cocktail bars, nightclubs, *Euro-Diskos, Spielotheke,* head shops, Spanish bodegas, Argentinian steak houses and Belgian waffle shops. There were *Kneipen* for punks, *Kneipen* for Goths, *Kneipen* for heavy metal fans, *Kneipen* for gays and smokers' pubs where men with nicotine-stained hair sat on their own listening to maudlin Country & Western songs. There were breweries where burly, blue-aproned waiters dispensed glasses of reddish-amber *Altbier* from circular copper trays swung from a central handle.

I took refuge in Gut und Gerne, a boutique chocolate shop between Marktplatz and Burgplatz. In the centre of the marketplace, between the wings of the Rathaus, stood an equestrian statue of Johann Wilhelm II (known in Low German as Jan Willem), Kurfürst of the Kurpfalz between 1690 and 1716. The Kurpfalz was a patchwork of lands around Heidelberg and Mannheim on the Middle Rhine, embroiled at the time in a Nine Years' War against Louis XIV of France. Jan Willem decided to move his court to Düsseldorf, capital of the Duchy of Berg which he had inherited from his father. Here the Elector established a glittering court, amassing a huge collection of paintings, notably those of Rubens. Coated in metallic green verdigris, the portly figure of Jan Willem rides forth on his stallion, mace clutched in his right hand. The locks of his long wig flow over an elaborate, multi-plated suit of armour. I was reminded of the golden statue in Dresden of his contemporary August II of Saxony. Jan Willem's stature as the ruler who presided over Düsseldorf's Golden Age matches that of August the Strong in Dresden. The most striking difference between the two Electors is their sexual potency: August sired over three hundred children, whereas Jan Willem died without an heir. He married into the families of the Grand Dukes of Medici and the Holy Roman Emperor, but passed syphilis on to his wives, whose pregnancies either miscarried or bore daughters who failed to survive infancy. His mistress Dorothea von Velen succeeded in bearing him two daughters who successfully survived, but they were pronounced illegitimate and banished from court by Jan Willem's brother, Charles III Philip, when the latter succeeded the former as Kurfürst of the Kurpfalz.

Clustered around the Schlossturm in Burgplatz were a handful of stalls dispensing *Glühwein*, Armagnac, pancakes, potato waffles, Krakauer sausages and Hungarian *Lángos*. Behind the tower was the Rhine again, silvery blue in the sunlight, sweeping in a broad curve between the Oberkasseler Brücke and the Rheinkniebrücke. A bright sun hung low in the sky to the south, softening the outlines of the television tower, Media Harbour and Frank Gehry's Neuer Zollhof. I followed the promenade to the north. The Alter Bastion was planted with plane trees whose branches had been pollarded into rectangular shapes, which lent them the appearance of hat stands. Wrapped in North Face jackets and woolly hats, the Düsseldorfer paraded beneath the trees on their Sunday lunchtime stroll. A young woman strummed Tom Petty's "Free Falling" on a guitar as a Dutch barge, a floating gasworks, pushed upstream.

I continued walking along Joseph-Beuys-Ufer. On the far side of the road were the outer walls of the Ehrenhof, a factory of the arts designed by Wilhelm Kreis for the *GeSoLei* (*Gesundheitspflege, Soziale-Fürsorge und Leibesübungen*) exhibition of 1926, a showcase for the latest German developments in health, hygiene, social welfare and physical education. It was the largest fair of the Weimar Republic, attracting seven and a half million visitors to Düsseldorf. Its showpiece was a Glass Man from Dresden; Kreis was later to move to Dresden and build a permanent Hygiene Museum in the Saxon capital.

I passed through a pair of square stone colonnades and entered the Ehrenhof. Walls of Expressionist brickwork, red striped with diagonals of purple, rested on skirts of cream stone. In the centre of the forum was a low, stone-rimmed basin with a fountain at its centre. Bronze statues stood on terraces in front of the monumental stone porticos leading into the Kunstmuseum and the Kunstpalast: the motto "ARTIBUS" was carved into the architrave of the latter. I recognised the spirit of Leo von Klenze's Königsplatz (before it was contaminated by the Nazis); but the axial plan of the Ehrenhof also reminded me of the Gauforum built ten years later in Weimar.

On the roof above the archway connecting the two art galleries was Arno Breker's reclining *Aurora*, sculpted in 1926 to crown the Ehrenhof and preside over the *GeSoLei* fair. In 2002 Breker's Dawn Goddess was bound in coils of knotgrass by Katinka Bock, a local installation artist. Sponsored by municipal and regional councils to the tune of half a million euros, the installation was designed to open a dialogue about the continued presence on a public building of a work by the infamous National Socialist sculptor. Frau Bock's "wrapping" of *Aurora*, however, failed to take into account that this was an early work by Breker, a sculpture in soft grey *Muschelkalk* inspired by Maillol and Picasso and completed ten years before the sculptor engaged with the Nazi regime.

I entered the church-like foyer of the former Kunstmuseum (now a Glass Museum) and sat on a bench to admire the geometric patterns and colours – amber and black, shot through with shards of turquoise and violet – of the stained-glass windows designed by Jan Thorn Prikker. There was no café there, so I crossed the Ehrenhof into the east wing of the

Kunstpalast, to find myself in a three-storey-high atrium defined by light, white open space. A tall, floaty, tinkly sculptural installation softened the clean lines of the gallery. Black-sweatered culture vultures had collected in a Dallmayr café on the first floor. I queued up behind them and ordered a creamy *Schaumsuppe* seasoned with parsley and chives, and a *Brötchen* flavoured with leek.

At the far end of the Ehrenhof was a Tonhalle designed by Wilhelm Kreis, a Byzantine rotunda of tessellated brickwork ribbed like the grooves of a cogwheel. Peering through its doors, I glimpsed a tunnel of vaulted arches striped with green and maroon tiles, a row of amber wall lamps and tiny squares of turquoise mosaic inlaid in the floor. On the pillars supporting the entrance to the concert hall were bronze busts of Felix Mendelssohn-Bartholdy, Clara and Robert Schumann and Norbert Bürgmüller, a quartet of musicians associated with Düsseldorf. Close to the busts was a plaque quoting words from a play by Heinrich Heine: "Dort wo man Bücher verbrennt, verbrennt man auch am Ende Menschen" ("Where they burn books, they will end up burning people too"). These lines from the play *Almansor* refer to the burning of the Koran by Christian knights after their conquest of Granada; but they assumed a retrospectively prophetic significance when the National Socialists began throwing books onto bonfires one hundred and twelve years later. Books, including those of Heine himself, were burned here, in the Rondel in front of the Tonhalle, as part of a nationwide "Action against the un-German spirit" on the night of 11 April 1933.

I walked through the bare trees and frozen ponds of the Hofgarten and took a tram to Nordpark to see if anything remained of the Schlageter-Denkmal, a monument raised in 1931 to Albert Leo Schlageter, a nationalist hero executed by French occupying forces in 1923. Schlageter served in the First World War and later fought with Freikorps irregulars in Latvia and Silesia. In 1923 he was active in the Rhineland as a saboteur blowing up railway lines and derailing trains used by the French forces. Arrested by the French, he was executed by firing squad on Golzheimer Heath on the northern outskirts of Düsseldorf on 26 May 1923. Designed by Clemens Holzmeister, the Schlageter National Monument was unveiled on 23 May 1931 on the site of his execution. It was the second largest nationalist monument of the Weimar Republic, the largest being the Hindenburg Mausoleum at Tannenberg. Its design, consisting of two stone rings sunk into the ground below a tall steel cross, owed much to the East Prussian memorial. The cross was embedded in a stone altar enclosing a memorial chamber accessible through an arch built into the inside of the outer ring. The surrounding area of heath was laid out as a parade ground for rallies by Freikorps and other paramilitary units, including those of the nascent NSDAP, which was later to lionise Schlageter as one of its own, a "martyr" on a par with Horst Wessel and Wilhelm Gustloff. Schools, streets and a ship were named after him: between 1933 and 1945 the Königsallee in Düsseldorf was known as Albert-Leo-Schlageter-Allee. Plays were written about his exploits and a hundred monuments were dedicated to his memory, some of which still survive. The largest of them all, on Golzheimer Heath, was destroyed by British forces in 1946; but I was curious to find out whether its site still existed. The monument itself was replaced in 1958 by a sculpture of Three Norns commemorating "Opfer des Feldes, der Heimat und des politischen Terrors" ("Victims of Battle, Exile and Political Terror").

A ticket collector entered the tram and asked to see my ticket. He seemed unusually interested in it and asked where I had got on and where I was getting off. I was only travelling four stops and wondered why he was getting so chary about a straightforward single ticket. He eventually explained that the ticket I had purchased was valid for a *Kurzstrecke* of only three stops. I could sense him weighing up whether he should fine me or not. "From where do you come?" "From England." "Na gut, please get out at the next stop and buy a valid ticket next time."

I alighted at Nordpark and followed Edith-Stein-Weg to the east. The low winter sun was setting behind me; ahead of me I saw the Norns silhouetted against a darkening sky. I crossed a bridge over a dual carriageway and descended into a clearing which, judging from its circular shape, must have been the site of the Schlageter Monument. The Three Norns, dark and forbidding, rose up in blocks of black granite from a colossal plinth in the centre of the circle. Engraved on the base of the monument were three inscriptions honouring the dead of the Second World War – soldiers, exiles, political prisoners and victims of the Holocaust. The monument was sculpted in 1958 by Jupp Rübsam, sculptor thirty years earlier of a memorial to the 39th Fusilier Regiment in front of the Tonhalle. Beyond the Norns was an area of the North Cemetery laid out in semi-circular rows of square stone tablets embedded in the ground. They commemorated four thousand Düsseldorfer killed in the war – soldiers, civilians, women, nuns. The sun set, leaving streaks of cold yellow light across a purple sky.

The bus back to the city centre dropped me off opposite the Hauptbahnhof, in front of a building I recognised as a former porn cinema where, forty-two years earlier, Herr Steffner had put me on a sightseeing bus for a tour of Düsseldorf's scenic delights. I sat in the bus while Herr Steffner wandered around the foyer of the cinema, gazing wistfully at the stills and posters advertising the forthcoming erotic attractions.

Herr Steffner was the father of Klaus-Jürgen, a German schoolboy with whom I did an exchange visit in the summer of 1972. The exchange had been arranged by my German teacher "Willi" Renshaw; whose widow was later to become my stepmother. Klaus-Jürgen came to my home town of Reading in May, in time for the final weeks of the school term; and I went to stay with him and his family in Hochdahl in July. Klaus-Jürgen arrived in Reading sporting a powder-blue denim suit and a shiny red boil on his nose. Even worse, he had long hair; but it wasn't the right kind of long hair. It wasn't a fashionably feathered mullet like Rod Stewart's, or a sexy mane of ringlets like Marc Bolan or Robert Plant. It was a bushy, overgrown mop-top: he looked like one of The Monkees. I had cleared his presence at Reading School with my form master and my German teacher, but clearly nobody had informed the headmaster, whose reaction, on spotting the German student in his denim suit and shoulder-length hair amid five hundred boys wearing grey suits, house-colour ties and regulation short-back-and-sides, was to fix Klaus-Jürgen with a glare of basilisk-like intensity, crook his index finger and summon him: "You boy, you, come here, you!" Klaus-Jürgen never recovered from this terrifying introduction to the British educational system.

His experience of life in suburban Reading was not a particularly happy one either. I was at the tail end of my skinhead phase and was embarrassed to be seen with him among my friends at the local youth club: with a haircut like that I could hardly dress him up in braces and Doc Martens. I left him in the care of my father while I sloped off to play football with my mates. Klaus-Jürgen was also someone who would, twenty years later, be known as a "geek": a boy with a fascination for gadgets, for explaining how things worked, for taking things to pieces and putting them back together again. Even thirty years later, when I visited him and his family in Switzerland, he would insist on showing me a new gadget on his Audi or the latest apps on his mobile phone. Paradoxically, Klaus-Jürgen was not into the music all the nerdy boys in the Science stream at Reading School listened to – Genesis, Yes and Pink Floyd – and he was certainly not a devotee of Roxy Music or David Bowie like me and my arty classmates. His tastes were rooted in old-fashioned, blue-collar American blues-rock; in particular Creedence Clearwater Revival, a band who at the time were about as fashionable as flared jeans. Fortunately, he took a liking to British folk rock, and I was able to offload my embarrassing Lindisfarne albums on him, in exchange for some Led Zeppelin singles which were unavailable in Britain. (Whenever I hear "Hey Hey What Can I Do", the charming B-side of Led Zeppelin's "Immigrant Song", I thank Klaus-Jürgen for relieving me of *Fog on the Tyne*.)

So in July I went off to Hochdahl in North Rhine-Westphalia. Hochdahl was a village that had grown into a dormer town for people who worked in Düsseldorf. The Steffners lived in a two-storey apartment which, to a seventeen-year-old who had grown up in a 1930s semi-detached in suburban Reading, was the epitome of Mies van der Rohe modernism. To begin with, their house was upside down: the kitchen and living room were upstairs at street level, whereas the bedrooms were on the garden level below. Instead of walls, there were windows which slid along both sides of the house. The open-plan living room was carpeted in thick, shaggy white pile, a delight to wade through in your bare feet. The bookshelves were white pine, the tables smoked glass, the sofas cream leather and the chairs S-shaped tubes of chrome. For someone brought up in a house with linoleum flooring, Parker-Knoll furniture and black-and-white television, Haus Steffner was Hockneyesque heaven.

Herr Steffner was a quiet, courteous man with body odour, a limp and a slight speech impediment. His wife Ursula was a gorgeous *Hausfrau* straight out of the pages of *Bunte* or *Brigitte*. She had a perfectly oval face, wide hazel eyes, big lacquered hair and a bulging, perma-tanned cleavage which she showed off beneath skin-tight white T-shirts. They were refugees from East Prussia. Horst Steffner came from Eydtkuhnen near the East Prussian–Lithuanian border (now Russian Tschernischevskoj in the Kaliningrad *oblast*). Ursula Steffner (née Juddat, from the Lithuanian Juddatis: her grandfather was a Lithuanian from Insterburg) came from Romeiken, a village near Gumbinnen in the Rominter Heide. These were hamlets in the Rominter Heath which no longer exist: the whole area was depopulated during the war and is now a forgotten wilderness straddling the straight line drawn after the war to form the artificial border between Poland and the Kaliningrad *oblast* of the Soviet Union. Horst was called up for the Wehrmacht and was wounded at the age of nineteen in the Battle of Kharkov. He was hit by shrapnel from a grenade, which shattered his skull and injured his brain. The left side of his body remained partially paralysed for the rest of his life. Everyone else in his unit was killed. Ursula was separated from her parents during the Red Army advance and, at the age of thirteen, was left to fend for herself. She stole bread from the Russians and survived on soup made from pigs' heads as she fled west with her fellow East Prussians. She was reunited with her parents in a refugee camp in Elmshorn, north of Hamburg. Horst, meanwhile, was reunited with his family in a refugee camp in Oldenburg. Because of his injuries, he had to relearn how to speak and write, but eventually served an apprenticeship as a surveyor in a local Public Records Office. He sold his watch and moved to Düsseldorf, where he was employed by the Tiefbauamt as a water and sewage engineer. He had an office in the Wilhelm-Marx-Haus designed by Wilhelm Kreis, and worked his way up to the post of Chief Engineer of North Rhine-Westphalia's sewage treatment plants. Horst and Ursula met at an East Prussian reunion in the Grugahalle in Essen in the early 1950s. They married in 1954 and bought a flat in Racherstraße in the Düsseldorf suburb of Dehrendorf. Klaus-Jürgen was born in 1957 and his sister Ulrike two years later. In 1969 they moved into the brand-new housing estate in Hochdahl-Millrath. Klaus-Jürgen was keen to point out that his parents never looked back. They were refugees from a lost *Heimat*, who never felt entirely at home in West Germany; but, once they had their new apartment, new jobs and new family, they only ever looked forward to their new life. They embodied the *Wirtschaftswunder* of postwar West Germany.

At home in Reading breakfast consisted of milky tea and Scott's porridge oats or Weetabix, depending on the season. Breakfast in Hochdahl was served on white Rosenthal china on the smoked glass and chrome dining table. There were four types of bread (rye, poppy seed, caraway and pumpernickel); wafer-thin slices of Dutch or Swiss cheeses; a selection of ham, salami and wurst (Leberwurst, Blutwurst, Mettwurst and smoky, pink Teewurst which had the texture of salmon mousse); and a cornucopia of tomatoes, cucumbers, pickled gherkins, hard-boiled eggs, jams and honey. Tea (rosehip, hibiscus or orange pekoe) and coffee were served in the Rosenthal china: this would have been the first time I had ever tasted ground coffee; or fresh orange juice, for that matter. There were bowls not only of brown and white sugar, but also sugar crystals which at first I mistook for boiled sweets – or you could just spoon honey into your tea.

The first time I went to Klaus-Jürgen's school, we set off at 6.30 am. I had never been up that early before – it was pitch black outside – nor had

I ever been to school wearing anything other than a grey suit or a school blazer and tie. Going to school clad in a Levi's cord jacket and flared loon pants was a liberating experience which partly compensated for the unearthly hour I had been ordered to get up. Klaus-Jürgen's schoolmates from Hochdahl assembled at the school bus stop, dressed uniformly in denim and wearing brightly coloured satchels high on their shoulders, like the kids you see painted on road signs in urban areas of Germany that ask you to drive voluntarily at a maximum speed of thirty kilometres per hour. The school bus arrived at a quarter to seven and set off for the Städtisches Gymnasium in Haan. Halfway there it broke down and we had to complete our dawn journey to school on foot. Once at the Gymnasium, I was astonished to find boys and girls in the same class, older pupils with long hair – and smoking during breaks. The English lessons embraced language, literature, culture, history and society; in stark contrast to my German lessons at Reading School, where we simply ploughed through *Maria Stuart* or *Der gute Mensch von Sezuan* line by line. (After three years of German tuition at Reading School I could recite entire plays by Schiller or Brecht, but could not string together a single intelligible sentence of colloquial German.)

In the evenings and at weekends (except between 2 pm and 4 pm on Sundays, when it was *verboten* to make any noise which might disturb the neighbourhood) we played table tennis on the patio downstairs by the garden. Ulrike would cry out "Mist!" whenever she mishit a shot. I wasn't sure what she meant by this, and wondered whether she was using the English word "missed", so I began to copy her. Klaus-Jürgen reprimanded me, telling me it was a rude word, although he invariably cried out "Mist, Dreck und Scheiße!" (loosely translated as "poo, crap and shit") whenever he lost a point. Or we would watch television. I remember upsetting Klaus-Jürgen by asking his mother if I could watch a drama on ZDF about doping in athletics (which was topical at the time because the Munich Olympics – one of the most heavily doped Games ever – was about to start) which coincided with his favourite series *Die Zwei* (the German version of *The Avengers*) on ARD.

If I didn't need to go to school, Frau Steffner would take me shopping in Düsseldorf. The big department stores of Kaufhof, Karstadt and Hertie were palaces of elegance and sophistication compared with dowdy old Heelas in Reading; and the exchange rate between the deutschmark and the pound was a ridiculous 11:1 at the time. I bought the two ubiquitous posters (one in lime green, the other in electric blue) which advertised the Munich Olympics; and Frau Steffner bought me the Games mascot, a stripy plastic dachshund named Waldi. Or Herr Steffner would take me to the railway station and buy me a return ticket to Bonn or Cologne. Unfortunately, he failed to explain the difference between a *D-Zug* and an *E-Zug*. On one occasion I found myself hurtling through Hochdahl-Millrath station and not stopping until Wuppertal. Apparently, the *D-Züge* (stopping trains) were listed on the timetable in black and the *E-Züge* (express trains) in red. All I remember of a boat trip down the Rhine was the chemical stink of the river; this, however, was a mere pong compared to the local rivers Düssel, Wupper and Neander, which were open sewers that contaminated the countryside for miles around with waste from the industrial plants of the Ruhr.

It was an idyllic summer, an experience that sowed the seeds of my love of Germany and founded a long and deep friendship, not only between myself and Klaus-Jürgen, but also between his parents and mine. The senior branches of the Steffners and Geoghegans finally met in 1978. It was a proud moment, considering our respective fathers had fought on opposing sides of a war thirty-five years earlier. My father embarrassingly insisted on pronouncing "Hochdahl" with a short rather than long "*o*" (which was understandable, given that "Hochzeit" is pronounced with a short "*o*"). On the other hand Frau Steffner, when addressing my father, kept referring to my mother as "your woman" ("Please ask your woman to come to the table", for example). The word *Frau* means either "woman" or "wife", depending on context.

There was a sad postscript. I recall visiting the Steffners in the early 1980s. Frau Steffner asked after my parents. I was reluctant to break the news that my mother had breast cancer, and was embarrassed at not knowing the words in German. I told her in English, and she understood immediately – "Ach ja, Brustkrebs". Two years later we received a black-edged card from Klaus-Jürgen in the post. His mother had died – from breast cancer. Herr Steffner lost the will to live and died the following year; as did my mother. Of the four parents who had met so joyously six years earlier, only my father remained alive. Klaus-Jürgen sold the family home and went to work for ICI in Middlesbrough. He met a Scots lass and now lives with their four children in Chur, where he runs a company which manufactures polymer mouldings. His sister Ulrike qualified as a doctor, married an architect and settled in Hanover with their children. I never saw her again. I believe she got divorced or had some kind of nervous breakdown, possibly due to the traumatic loss of her parents at such a young age.

Monday morning, and I was back in Xanten. A smattering of snow had fallen during the night and the temperature was one degree above zero. It was finally time to get my winter tyres fitted. The hotel receptionist rang around the local car dealers, many of whom still seemed to be on their Christmas break. A Herr W. phoned back to confirm that he could order the tyres I required and that they would be ready at two-thirty that afternoon. There were some minor details I didn't fully understand on the phone, so I suggested it might be easier if I drove out to the industrial estate to see him in person. Herr W. came out to inspect the car, confirmed he could order the correct size of winter tyre and negotiated a price of 105 euros per tyre, installation included. He asked me in which year the vehicle was manufactured. I replied that it was brand new – and his face fell. He explained that it had been fitted with run-flat tyres, and that it was technically inadvisable and legally impermissible to replace run-flat tyres with regular tyres. Nor could run-flat winter tyres be ordered at short notice; one dealer told Herr W. that he could get hold of a set by the middle of the following week. The only recourse was to approach BMW directly. There was no BMW dealer in Xanten, but Herr W. was kind enough to phone around the local BMW dealers and explain my predicament. BMW in Wesel said they could order the tyres for the following day, but they had no means of fitting them. BMW in Kleve never called back. BMW in Geldern eventually phoned back to say they could order the tyres for one o'clock the following afternoon and fit them – at a price of 205 euros each. I thanked Herr W. for his help: both Herr Nüsser and Herr W. had gone out of their way to assist me, even after it had become clear that this would result in no material gain for them. (I wondered whether my local fitter in Kentish Town would have been so helpful to a stranded foreign motorist.)

It was dusk by the time I arrived back in the centre of Xanten. I checked in for a fourth night at the Hotel Hövelmann and went outside for a cigarette. The marketplace was a sheet of ice which no one seemed to be responsible for gritting. A travelling market of butchers, bakers, florists and greengrocers was closing its shutters and endeavouring to couple trailers to vans. Trees braided with silver and gold Christmas lights sparkled around the square. A carillon pealed from the gable of the Rathaus. I noticed small copper plaques set into the pavement which marked the homes and shops of Jews who once lived and traded here. I walked through St Michael's Gate and entered the *Dom*. Solemn organ music filled the nave and aisles of the cathedral. The Three Magi looked down from grey pillars on a crib and there was a Christmas tree in front of the parish altar. Through the windows of the rood screen I glimpsed fragments of the high altar glittering at the far end of the choir. The walls of the aisles were covered with Gothic carvings – tortured figures of Christ pierced by arrows – and on each of the columns supporting the nave hung a triptych of altar panels: Saint Anthony tempted by a snarling satyr with smooth woman's breasts and the face of a black demon in its crotch; Dionysius holding his own decapitated, yet still mitred, head in his hands. With their slashed silk doublets and frizzy auburn hair, the family of the Virgin Mary portrayed in the altar of St Martin resembled characters in a painting by Cranach; an altar boy in a corner of the painting was the spitting image of Martin Luther. The altar of St Agatha depicted Golgotha as a desert of skulls and bones. Crows circled around a corpse suspended from a tree. A cripple begged St Elizabeth for alms. Clad in a shimmering silver gown, Agatha held a red-hot firebrand in a pair of tongs, as if uncertain what to do with it. Christ on the Cross was relegated to the background of the painting; and on the horizon was the half-built *Dom* of Xanten on the Rhine. As I left the church, I noticed flame-coloured splinters of stained glass in the west window, geometric shards representing the incendiary bombing which destroyed 85% of Xanten at the end of the Second World War.

Morning over the Rhine at Bad Godesberg. A palette of greys: the dull, silvery, flowing grey of the river, as wide here as at Xanten; the auburn-tinted grey of trees on the opposite bank; the soft grey of mist in the valleys; and the darker grey of the Siebengebirge hills. The only colour came from a yellow crane poised above the apartment blocks of Königswinter and from markers at the tips of the breakwaters – red and white on the Königswinter bank, green and white on the Godesberg side. A solitary Dutch barge pushed upstream against the current. Downstream a ferry crossed from Bad Godesberg to Königswinter. On the promenade below the villas of Godesberg, grey figures were walking their dogs.

I was sitting in the breakfast room of the Rheinhotel Dreesen, a wood-panelled salon hung with tapestries and decorated with carvings of woodland and Rhineland deities cavorting in Bacchanalian rites.

The clientele was posh and elderly, the same guests who dined in the white-panelled neoclassical restaurant last night. For dinner I ordered *Rheinische Sauerbraten*, thin slices of meat cooked in a rosehip and burgundy sauce and served with dumplings. The *spécialité de la maison* was that the *Sauerbraten* was *Pferd* rather than the usual *Rind*: tender slices of horse which had a muddy texture and left a bitter aftertaste. I required three glasses of crisp Riesling to clear my palate of the flavour of the equine meat.

The Dreesen was built in 1893–94 in the shape of a white cruise liner moored on the left bank of the Rhine. (It hasn't changed much since: I couldn't sleep in the first room I was allocated because of the noise from antiquated heating pipes. To its credit, the hotel was kind enough to let me change rooms in the middle of the night.) According to a plaque on its riverside wall, the hotel welcomed "worldwide renowned guests", a euphemism perhaps for Adolf Hitler, Josef Goebbels and Sepp Dietrich, who stayed here on the evening of 29 June 1934, before flying off in the middle of the night to slaughter the leadership of the SA in Bad Wiessee. Hitler returned to the Rheinhotel Dreesen a few months later, sailing down the river to address a rally at the fortress of Ehrenbreitstein in support of a German vote in the forthcoming referendum on the future of the Saarland. In September 1938 he based himself in the Dreesen during talks with Neville Chamberlain over the Sudetenland. Their negotiations were acrimonious, but in the evening Hitler's mood changed and he took the British Prime Minister to admire the view over the Rhine, apologising for the fact that the river was hidden in mist. It seems odd to think of National Socialists in the Rhineland. Hitler's axis was Munich–Nuremberg–Weimar–Berlin rather than Düsseldorf–Cologne–Bonn. Compared with Germany further east or further south, there is little evidence in the Rhineland of National Socialist buildings, monuments or concentration camps. Cologne and Bonn are more evocative of post-war Germany; of the Bundesrepublik and the *Wirtschaftswunder*; of democracy rather than autocracy – the Rhineland is the world of Wolfgang Köppen and Heinrich Böll; of Schumann and Beethoven rather than Wagner and Bruckner.

It was the morning of New Year's Eve and, as I left the hotel, I noticed the banqueting hall being decked out for the evening's entertainment – at 138 euros per head for the full Monty. Everything was white: tablecloths, napkins, menus, chairs covered in white satin with white rosettes pinned to their backs. Champagne glasses and chandeliers glittered. Outside it was a damp, bone-chilling morning, but I didn't care: I was fitted out at last with run-flat winter tyres; I was no longer stuck in Xanten; and it was the eve of a new year. I felt as free as Siegfried must have felt at the beginning of his Rhine journey. I slotted the Prelude of *Götterdämmerung* into the CD player and put my foot down on the accelerator.

In fact I left the Rhine and drove up into the Eifel hills towards Vogelsang, the third of the Ordensburgen built during the Third Reich as elite training schools for future leaders of the NSDAP. I climbed above the snowline and took a right turn off the B266 into a long avenue leading to the camp. At first I couldn't get in. The barrier across the entrance should have risen automatically when I pressed the button for a parking ticket, but it was stuck. I pressed an emergency button and spoke to a man inside the camp, who instructed me to lever the barrier out of the socket which held it in place. This proved to be easier said than done. Eventually a burly man in the vehicle behind me came to my assistance, and between the two of us we managed to heave the barrier out of its bracket.

I parked in a field of slush and continued on foot towards the centre of the camp. The two symmetrical wings of the Adlerhof – the original *Burg* built at the centre of Vogelsang in 1934–36 – stretched for two hundred metres across the brow of a steep escarpment. In National Socialist times the west wing contained a library and a reading room. The east wing comprised a restaurant on its lower floor and an auditorium on its upper floor, each capable of accommodating five hundred of the "Junker" being trained at the camp. The auditorium led into an Ehrenhalle, which would have been decked out with tubs of German oak saplings on ceremonial occasions such as "brown weddings", nuptials where the happy couple would pledge their troth not only to each other but also to their beloved Führer. At the far end of the Hall of Honour was a curtained arch which, when opened, led into a tall chamber illuminated by a narrow slit in the north wall of the high tower at the end of the east wing of the Ordensburg. Perched on a wooden console fastened to the wall of this "Kultraum" was a three-metre-high wooden statue, sculpted by Willy Meller, of a *Deutscher Mensch*. His dead eyes raised zombie-like towards the light, and his naked body rippling with a musculature so finely detailed he could have stood in for one of the exhibits in the German Hygiene Museum in Dresden, Meller's *German Man* stood with legs apart, left fist clenched and right arm raised in a gesture halfway between a Roman *adlocutio* and a "Heil Hitler!" salute. Engraved in letters of gold across the face of the console was the word "HIER", which signalled the ritual of commemorating the sixteen National Socialist "martyrs" killed in the Munich putsch of 1923. Their names, mounted in wrought iron on the walls of the shrine (plus those of Albert Leo Schlageter and Horst Wessel), were solemnly read out. On the announcement of each name, the assembled worshippers would reply "Hier".

I negotiated an icy flight of steps down between the barrack blocks where the "Junker" were accommodated. Below me was a grassy slope which banked steeply to a stone amphitheatre embedded in the cliff face. Built in 1936 as a *Thingstätte*, the semi-circular stage could hold the two-hundred-strong male choir of the Ordensburg, an ensemble of some renown who performed at the Nuremberg Rallies of 1936 and 1937. Beneath the grass was the original stone terracing where the rest of the "Junker" would assemble to listen to their colleagues perform choral works such as *Ans Werk*, a "Volkscantata" which sanctified strong limbs and an iron will; or *Ulrich von Hütten*, an oratorio which celebrated a peripatetic sixteenth-century knight lauded by the National Socialists as a warrior for the "German national consciousness".

Immediately below the *Thingstätte* a stone grandstand – a smaller version of the tribune of the Zeppelinfeld at Nuremberg – was built into the slope above a sports stadium. In the wall below its podium were the remains of a relief installed in 1937. Sculpted by Willy Meller from soft red lava, the original ensemble represented seven naked sportsmen lined up beneath the protective wings of an angular *Reichsadler*. Suspended from the eagle's talons was a swastika inside a laurel wreath, which forced the goalkeeper at the centre of the line-up into a crouching position. All seemingly modelled on the same lantern-jawed prototype, the six remaining figures comprised a multi-disciplinary team of shot putter, javelin thrower, discus thrower, boxer, weight lifter and relay runner. Five of them faced the onlooker – full frontal, legs apart, muscles taut, appendages hanging loose. Only the javelin thrower, for some reason, is turned away from the onlooker, displaying a pertly cleaved backside. This, at least, is how the team would have appeared when sculpted by Meller in 1937. In the ensuing years snipers of the Belgian Army, which requisitioned the base after the war, have enjoyed taking pot shots at their heads, hands, knees and genitals. All that remains of them today is a bullet-ridden row of disconnected chests, hips, thighs and shins.

There was more of Willy Meller's statuary hidden beneath the trees to the east of the stadium. I climbed through the woods and emerged into a clearing used by the "Junker" of the Ordensburg for solstice ceremonies. Facing me was Meller's *Fackelträger*, one of the most dramatic relics of National Socialism still in existence in Germany. Attached to a slab of wall ten metres long and six metres high, the Torch Bearer stands naked and erect, full frontal, legs apart. His left hand is clenched into a fist; in his right hand he bears aloft the flaming torch which symbolises the rebirth of the German *Volk* under Adolf Hitler. A cloak swirls around his shoulders, its horizontal sweep counterbalancing the vertical thrust of the Torch Bearer's figure. The statue's once noble face and muscular torso have been ravaged by wind, snow and Belgian bullets, but the vestigial brute power of this Aryan idol remains. The free-standing block of stone to which the *Fackelträger* is attached was built as a "Feuermal", a beacon originally crowned by a long, rectangular fire bowl. The wall below was inscribed in Roman lettering with the words: "IHR SEID DIE FACKELTRÄGER DER NATION. IHR TRAGT DAS LICHT DES GEISTES VORAN IM KAMPFE FÜR ADOLF HITLER." ("You are the torch-bearers of the nation. You carry forth the light of the spirit in the fight for Adolf Hitler.") Four of the sandstone blocks (those inscribed with the words "FACKELTRÄGER" and "ADOLF HITLER") have been removed and replaced with blank white blocks. The "ER" of Hitler's name remains visible, although attempts have been made to deface this toxic pair of letters.

A cold drizzle began to fall. The wind blew sleet through the exposed channels between the barracks and wings of the Adlerhof (Eagles' Courtyard). Vogelsang literally means "birdsong", but the only birds in evidence today were two headless stone eagles which had been dumped, as if nobody knew what to do with them, on a patch of grass by the entrance to the Burgschänke, a beer hall where the "Junker" would spend their evenings. I went to a café in the former Belgian Cinema, but it was closing early for New Year's Eve. The waitress had one portion of pea soup left over from lunchtime, which she agreed to warm up for me.

Iarrived in Rüdesheim after nightfall and checked into the only hotel which was not situated on the Rhine Promenade (and which was therefore out of earshot of the long goods trains which clank along the riverside throughout the night). It was quiet as I walked through a deserted Altstadt. I found an Irish Pub open on the waterfront, although the barman made it clear he was closing at 7 pm and would not reopen until shortly before midnight, after which he would remain open all night in order to celebrate the New Year. Evicted from the Irish Pub at seven, I wandered up Drosselgasse, normally a crowded alley lined with bustling *Weinstuben* and *Weingüter*. Tonight it was empty, every wine tavern shuttered for the evening. I returned to the hotel, at a loss how to spend the remaining hours of 2014. It then occurred to me I could do now what I had planned for the following morning: namely, to walk up to the Niederwald Monument on the edge of the forest above Rüdesheim. I would visit the monument anyway the next day, but walking through the nocturnal vineyards would give me a different perspective – "Germania bei Nacht".

I found a path which led up through the vineyards. The sky was low with cloud and the evening not particularly dark. Rüdesheim fell away below me as I ascended the hillside. I passed an old railway bridge and realised that the path must be following the track of a rack railway line built in the 1880s to transport visitors up to the monument. The path narrowed into a muddy track as I reached the treeline. A neoclassical pavilion loomed out of the night, and soon I reached the ring terrace below the monument.

The forest was silent. Rüdesheim lay below at the foot of the vineyards. On the far side of the river were the lights of Bingen, Ingelheim and an illuminated chapel isolated high in the hills. The Rhine was invisible, a wide, empty black chasm only perceptible because a solitary pleasure boat, with a string of fairy lights above its deck, was cruising noiselessly downstream. To the east of Rüdesheim a chain of lights led away along the Rheingau towards Geisenheim, Oestrich-Winkel and Eltville. In one of these villages, almost exactly eighty-one years earlier, Patrick Leigh Fermor was invited to join the "thirsty and boisterous rump" of a party of young Germans, and ended up the next morning, suffering from a severe hangover, in Mainz.

I, sadly, was on my own on this New Year's Eve – except, of course, for the goddess Germania whose spectral presence had guided me up through the vineyards towards the Niederwald. Illuminated by floodlights set into the floor of the ring terrace, the Niederwald Monument towered over the hillside. In the half-light I could make out an orgy of eagles, archangels, Prussians and Bavarians, Father Rhine and his daughter Mosel; an escalation of plinths and pedestals of ever-decreasing girth piled on top of each other; engraved letters exalting "Deutsches Volk" and "Deutsches Reich". Queening it over all the urns and wreaths and

Iron Crosses was the strapping figure of Germania, the personification of the German nation, her bosom strapped into a breastplate emblazoned with *Reichsadler*, her flowing tresses crowned by a circlet of oak leaves and her formidable thighs concealed beneath a voluminous robe embroidered with eagles, stags, ravens, dragons, swans and all the other fauna of Wagnerian-Teutonic legend. Her left hand wielded a sword of Victory and in her right she bore aloft the *Kaiserkrone*, the Imperial Crown of the new German Reich.

I stumbled back downhill and returned to the tiny room in the annexe of my hotel in order to dry out my clothes. It was now 9 pm, three hours to go before the turning of the year – and I needed to eat. Everywhere in Rüdesheim seemed to be closed, except for three hotels on the riverfront which were the sort of establishment that seeks to attract tour groups of elderly Britons by plastering its windows with photographs of the dishes on offer inside. The only sign of life in Drosselgasse was in Lindwirt, a posh *Weingut* packed with formally dressed burghers tucking into hearty New Year's Eve menus. I tried the door, but it was locked: this was a *Geschlossene Gesellschaft*. I performed another circuit of the centre of Rüdesheim. One *Weinstube* was on the point of closing; another was full of pensioners nodding along to an oompah band. On my way back to the river I passed a *Pfannkuchen* restaurant with a younger, less stuffy clientele. They had tables free and were open until 11 pm. It seemed the perfect place to while away the next two hours. I entered, smiled at the waitress and sat down at an empty table. She informed me that the kitchen had already closed, but that I was welcome to stay for a drink. That left the three tourist restaurants by the river: one was moribund; the second was heaving with coach parties dancing drunkenly to the blast of an over-amplified *Schlager* band; so I settled for the third. It was three-quarters empty: there were a handful of local kids and a few middle-aged couples of the sort who force themselves to go out with each other once a year – and rue the experience. I drank two glasses of wine and ordered a lukewarm potato soup and a stringy *Wiener Schnitzel* with fries. Afterwards I crossed the road and the railway line and sat by the Rhine, smoking a cigarette and wondering what the hell I was doing spending New Year's Eve on my own in a lousy restaurant in a boring, out-of-season tourist trap.

All the pubs were closed and the market square was deserted; there didn't seem to be any focal point where the townspeople would gather to see in the New Year as a community. I returned to my hotel room and watched television in a rather desultory fashion, following the New Year's

celebrations as they crept around the globe. At 11 pm I opened a miniature bottle of *Sekt* from the minibar and toasted the New Year in Ukraine
and Lithuania. At 11.30 I couldn't stand being alone in my room any
longer and wandered outside to smoke my last cigarettes before giving
up for the New Year. I noticed groups of youngsters disappearing into an
alley above the town. I followed them and emerged in the vineyards above
Rüdesheim. I felt rather self-conscious about being on my own among
little knots of revellers strewn along the pathway, and hid myself off the
path among the vines. Midnight arrived. There were loud bangs, cheers
rang out and the sky sparkled with red, gold and silver flashes. Rüdesheim
vanished behind a pall of gunpowder smoke. The church bells tolled for
fifteen minutes. In a cobbled street below, the good burghers of the town
gathered around a bonfire and toasted in the New Year with glasses of
Sekt. Firecrackers continued into the night.

The sun finally broke through the clouds as I drove from Rüdesheim to
Assmannshausen. The Rhine glittered in the light. Railway lines ran along
both banks of the river, frequently disappearing into tunnels crenellated with
mock-Tudor battlements. Medieval keeps and neo-Gothic follies loomed over
crags and bluffs on the left bank. Walled villages of round towers and ruined
chapels lay stretched out below slopes of forests and vineyards. Upstream of
Lorch were two slender islets in the middle of the Rhine which were once
designated a "Toteninsel", an Island of the Dead chosen in 1926 as the site of
a national Reichs Monument to the Fallen of the First World War, a western
counterpart to the Hindenburg Mausoleum in East Prussia.

The river narrowed and the road swung around a headland as it
approached Sankt Goarshausen. I turned off in the village and drove into
the hills above the Lorelei cliff. From the top of the precipice I watched
as a pleasure cruiser chugged upstream, negotiating a course between the
rocks and sandbanks of the twisting green river far below. Machines at
the top of the cliff dispensed souvenir coins or were fitted with loudspeakers which, in exchange for one euro, recited Heinrich Heine's ballad of the
golden-haired siren who lured sailors to their death on the rocks below.
I searched for a machine which might play Roxy Music's "Editions of
You" – "And as I was drifting past the Lor-or-relei, I heard those slinky
sirens wail – whoo!" But there was no Bryan Ferry, no Jerry Hall slink-
ing over turquoise rocks with fins stuck to her ankles. The café at the

top of the cliff was closed, as was the *Freilichtbühne* built in the 1930s as a National Socialist *Thingplatz*. I was familiar with the amphitheatre, having attended an alt-rock Bizarre Festival held there in the summer of 1987. I remember sitting through performances by Julian Cope, The Mission and Iggy Pop. For some reason I decided to give the headline act Siouxsie and the Banshees a miss.

Having abstained from the New Year's Day brunch offered by my hotel in Rüdesheim, I was beginning to feel hungry. I drove back into Sankt Goarshausen for lunch, but every café and tavern was closed. It was the same in Kestert, Kamp-Bornhofen and Filsen. I considered taking the car ferry to Boppard, but that wasn't running either. Eventually I found a mobile *Imbiss* in a car park on the banks of the Rhine in Osterspai. I ordered a coffee and sat in the sun admiring the view over the river. The bare vineyards on the far, south-facing slopes glowed with a tawny light tinged with mauve. I realised this might be my only opportunity to eat some hot food, so I asked for a *Currywurst mit Pommes*. The German national dish duly arrived in its little cardboard tray with corrugated sides. I splashed on mustard and ketchup and stabbed my plastic fork into the curry-powdered sausage. I mulled over the way the Germans insist on pronouncing the French word *pommes* in two distinct syllables with a voiced "*s*". It sounded all wrong. But, then again, English drinkers never pronounce the two umlauts when they order their pints of Löwenbräu.

From Osterspai it was a short drive to Horchheim and thence over the Rhine to Koblenz. I followed signs to the "Deutsches Eck" and parked on the banks of the Mosel. The promenade was thronged with townspeople enjoying the sunshine and the pleasurable feel of New Year's Day. An accordionist played French *chansons* and bells pealed from the towers of the Basilica of St Castor. Canada geese flew in an arrowhead formation overhead, and passengers on the Swiss cruiser *Rhine Princess* yelled New Year's greetings to strollers on the promenade. The confluence of the Rhine and Mosel was marked by four iron mooring posts and the flags of the sixteen federal states, hanging limply around the edge of the headland. At the sharp end of the spit flew the *schwarz-rot-gold* of the national flag. The disposition of the flagpoles took me back to the "Dreiflüsseeck" at Passau, where the flags no longer fly. A cable car crossed the Rhine, carrying tourists up to the fortress of Ehrenbreitstein, Germany's "Wacht am Rhein" high up on the right bank of the river.

Dominating the Deutsches Eck is a black catafalque supporting an equestrian statue of Kaiser Wilhelm I, "like a gigantic cake decoration" according to the writer Kurt Tucholsky, who happened upon the monument in 1930. After Kyffhäuser and Porta Westfalica, this was the third of the great monuments to Wilhelm I designed by Bruno Schmitz in the 1890s. Flanked by a stiff-winged Genius of Victory, the Kaiser sallies forth across the roof of a sarcophagus of blackened granite which, in turn, is raised high upon a massive plinth and surrounded by a colonnade and ring terrace. Sculpted into the face of the socle is an eagle with the wingspan of a stealth bomber swooping over a mass of writhing serpents which, like those on the base of Schmitz's later Monument to the Battle of the Nations, represent Germany's foes. The inscription above the snakes reads "WILHELM DEM GROSSEN", an epithet coined by the Kaiser's grandson Wilhelm II, but one which never really caught on. On the architrave above the hypostyle is a second inscription, taken from a poem entitled *Frühlingsgruß an das Vaterland* by a local poet Max von Schenkendorf, which reads: "NIMMER WIRD DAS REICH ZERSTÖRET, WENN IHR EINIG SEID UND TREU." ("The empire will never be destroyed as long as you are united and loyal.")

The winter sun was sinking, its intense yellow light throwing into relief the stark silhouette of the Prussian warlord and his angelic camp follower. I walked around the rear of the monument and climbed a flight of steps into the interior of the hypostyle supporting the statue. A second flight of steps led to a gallery around the base of the highest plinth, above the pillars which bear the weight of the world's largest equestrian statue. Below me the prow of the Deutsches Eck, like the bows of a great warship, steered a course into the confluence of the Rhine and Mosel – where father was joined with daughter, gold with wine.

17

Hesse

Trespassing on the Past

I was sitting on a bench beneath a row of plane trees along one side of the Kurhausplatz in the centre of Wiesbaden. It was seven o'clock on the evening of Easter Saturday and the sky was darkening from turquoise to indigo. In the centre of a lawn known as the Bowling Green were two fountains, each shaped like three glasses of fizz balanced on top of each other. Water flowed over the rims of the bowls, reminding me of George Best's trick with a pyramid of champagne coupes. Two young women from Italy asked me to take a photo of them against the backdrop of the Neue Kolonnade opposite, where opera-goers were arriving for a performance of *Orpheus and Eurydice* in the Staatstheater. Mercedes-Benz convertibles, silver or black, drew up in front of the Kurhaus, in a wing of which was Käfer's, a swanky bistro I decided to enter for a drink. Its wood-panelled walls were covered with French posters from the 1930s and signed photographs of the celebrities who had dined here. The waiters were wearing tie pins and cufflinks and the *maître d'* sported a winter tan that would have made Franz Beckenbauer look pallid. There was much back-slapping and cheek-kissing as guests arrived for dinner, greeting each other in French or Russian. They were either coming from the casino or going to the opera, and were dressed to the nines in tuxedos or cocktail dresses. I was wearing a turtleneck pullover and an old pair of jeans and felt distinctly self-conscious sitting on my own at the bar. But the barman addressed me as "der Herr" and served me a carafe of peanuts to go with my Aperol Spritz. I tipped him appropriately.

It was here, some twenty years earlier, that I met Brigitte for a drink. We had first encountered each other the previous summer at a Prom Concert in the Royal Albert Hall. I was with a couple of friends. As we entered our box, I noticed a woman in black sitting on her own in the front row. Our eyes met briefly. It wasn't exactly love at first sight; more some kind of mutual recognition. She was wearing a crushed velvet, long-sleeved T-shirt and black hipster trousers. Her dark brown hair was cut into a bob. She had a round face, dark eyes and high cheekbones. I had no idea how old she was. For some reason I sensed she was German. The concert began with the overture to *Tannhäuser*, which I remember the orchestra taking at an excessively slow tempo. After the interval my friends decided we should all change seats and, without even trying, I found myself sitting next to the mysterious stranger. I think she spoke first – with a slight German accent. "Sind Sie deutsch?" I asked. She was. I told her I was going to the Bayreuth Festival later in the summer. "Sind Sie Millionär?" she replied. After the concert I invited her for a drink. We went to a pub in Kensington High Street. She told me she lived in Wiesbaden and was on holiday with her sister. She worked on a television show called *Gesundheit* on ZDF. I didn't quite catch whether she was the presenter or the producer. As we parted, she asked "Treffen wir morgen?"

We arranged to meet at 7 pm outside Hampstead tube station. Neither of us had realised there would be a tube strike the following day. This was the age before the mobile phone, so I had no choice but to wait. Brigitte arrived at 8, having walked from the bus terminus at South End Green. She looked tall and slim in a thigh-length denim jacket. We went for a walk on Hampstead Heath and told each other (in German) about our lives. She had had a *Lebensgefährte* (the German equivalent of a soul mate), but she had suffered a serious illness and they had split up. I had been single for eighteen months at this stage, and told Brigitte that I was "zufrieden" (content) with my life.

I sent her a postcard from Bayreuth and we arranged to meet again on my next business trip to Frankfurt in November. We met in the café-restaurant of the Schirn art gallery, my favourite hang-out when I lived in the city several years earlier. She was wearing a cream raincoat and looked plainer than I remembered her from London. She told me she had joined a choir in Wiesbaden. At some stage I must have said something that annoyed her, for I remember her saying "Willst Du mich verarschen?" ("Are you taking the piss?"), which shocked me slightly. But then she presented me with a homemade video cassette of *Tristan und Isolde* – the same production I had seen in Bayreuth, with Siegfried Jerusalem and Waltraud Meier in the title roles.

We sent each other Christmas cards (hers was handmade) and arranged to meet on my next trip to Germany in February. I was staying overnight in Frankfurt and drove to Wiesbaden to meet her in Käfer's bistro. After a glass of wine she took me on a brief tour of the city centre. It was dark and I remember little of Wiesbaden except the lights along Wilhelmstraße overlooking the Warmer Damm. Brigitte told me that *Gesundheit* was getting good ratings and she was preparing a new series; and that she was thinking of going to the South Pacific for her summer holiday. I drove her back to her apartment in Jahnstraße. She asked me to call her if I was passing through Wiesbaden again at the end of my trip.

My trip finished ten days later in Heidelberg, and I recall sitting in a café wondering whether I should phone Brigitte at short notice or just turn up in Wiesbaden. In the end I decided to do neither and drove home instead. At some stage during the next few weeks I fell in love with her. Maybe it was the look she gave me as we parted in Wiesbaden, or maybe I regretted making the wrong decision in Heidelberg. I sent her a post-card and we arranged to meet one Sunday afternoon in April. I stayed Saturday night in Speyer, walking the streets of the Altstadt in anticipation of our rendezvous the following day. I met Brigitte at her apartment, an *Altbau* on the third floor of a Wilhelmine townhouse near the centre of Wiesbaden. She was dressed in a black roll-neck sweater and white jeans. She looked lithe and feline and told me she had been fasting for Lent. She made me a coffee and showed me around her flat. It had high ceilings and smelled of books. She told me that she had read the complete works of Shakespeare and that she was working on a book in collaboration with an elderly lady who had lived through the Nazi period in Wiesbaden. I asked her about her surname, which sounded Polish or Czech. She replied that her father's family came originally from Silesia. They settled in Haan, the small town near Düsseldorf where Klaus-Jürgen and Ulrike also went to school. She thought that she had also discovered some Jewish blood in her ancestry.

We decided to drive to Frankfurt and go for tea in one of the muse-ums. It was raining when we arrived so we headed for the nearest one, which turned out to be the Post Museum in Sachsenhausen. Over tea and cake she started leafing through the latest issue of *Stern-Magazin*, flicking through the pages until she found the horoscopes at the back. According to my star sign, I would soon find love.

"In wen wirst Du Dich verlieben?" she asked, looking at me rather pointedly.

There was a pregnant pause. She looked at me and tried again. "Wen liebst Du?"[18]

I needed to utter one four-letter word, but it didn't come out. It was my Hugh Grant moment, and it passed. We drove back to Wiesbaden in an awkward silence, listening to Mozart's Clarinet Concerto. The road was wet, and Brigitte told me that I tended to brake very late. Back in Jahnstraße I invited myself up for coffee, but we had run out of things to say to each other. As I left, I tried to kiss her on the lips, but she averted her mouth. I never saw her again.

Easter morning was damp and grey. I set off on foot along Adolfsallee, an avenue of townhouses laid out, according to a bronze plaque at the head of the street, between 1860 and 1890, during the end of the Duchy of Nassau and the beginning of Prussian rule. Wiesbaden was the seat of the Dukes of Nassau until 1866, when it backed the wrong side in the Austro-Prussian War and was annexed by Prussia; an event which turned out to be a blessing in disguise, since the spa city became the summer residence of choice for the Hohenzollerns. I followed gravel paths beneath bare chestnut trees. Birds were singing in the branches. There was a children's playground and a fountain drained and boarded up for the winter. *Gründerzeit* villas rose up on either side of the avenue, fronted by boxy aedicules of fluted columns and voluted capitals. Brass plates affixed to wrought-iron gateways disclosed the offices or studios of beauticians, psychotherapists and tax consultants.

I crossed into Luisenplatz, a square of neoclassical buildings laid out in the French style with geometrical paths, low box hedges and pollarded trees which looked like rows of upturned arms with gnarled fingers splayed and bent. I went for a coffee in Café Degenhardt, a former hairdressing salon redolent of the 1960s with its name in cursive pink neon lettering above its door, and advertisements above the bar for *Kamilleflor* and *Brunetaflor*, "alkali-free shampoos for blondes or brunettes". The café was bustling with young married couples meeting friends for a champagne brunch or a creamy *latte macchiato* heaped with milky foam. At the far

---

18   "Who will you fall in love with? Who do you love?"

end of the square worshippers were spilling out of the Bonifatiuskirche, the principal Catholic church of Wiesbaden. I heard applause inside the church for the choir and musicians who had accompanied Easter Sunday Mass. Outside the church there were beggars on the doors, a priest handing out Easter chocolates and a team of "Street Angels" dispensing food and drink to the vagrants who had collected in Luisenplatz.

I followed Neugasse and Ellenbogengasse, streets lined with chemists, perfumeries, tattoo parlours and shops selling health food, hearing aids and orthopaedic footwear. Above Schlossplatz towered the orange-red brick spires of the evangelical Marktkirche. In the square below the church was a statue of a dashing Wilhelm I, Prince of Orange and Count of Nassau-Dillenburg, resplendent in slashed doublet and hose, garters, embroidered cloak and floppy hat, a dagger in his belt and a razor-sharp rapier sticking out behind him. Known in English as William the Silent, he founded the Independent Netherlands and was assassinated for his Protestant beliefs in 1584.

I crossed Wilhelmstraße into Warmer Damm, a garden landscaped in the English style. Paths of pink gravel wound around lawns still yellow and threadbare from the winter. Coots, mallards and Egyptian geese lay flopped around the edge of a lake in the centre of the park. Rabbits scurried into the undergrowth beneath budding magnolia bushes and cherry trees in the first blossom of spring. Carpets of tiny blue glory-of-the-snow encircled the trunks of oak, chestnut and willow trees, still bare except for fuzzy balls of mistletoe. Rusted, post-industrial sculptures were planted like blades or upturned railway sleepers over the lawns. The graffiti on one read "F**k die Polizei", as if the vandal with the aerosol spray was too coy to spell out the complete F-word in such genteel surroundings. In a grove enclosed by a box hedge stood a white stone statue of Kaiser Wilhelm I, leaning on the trunk of a German oak tree. For once he was bare-headed, bereft of crown, laurel wreath, plumed helmet or *Pickelhaube*. His horse was missing too.

I passed a group of Syrian immigrants huddled around a bench; a bevy of Arabs struggling to keep their hijabs or burqas from flying off in the breeze; two Russian women strolling arm in arm; and some Polish tourists taking photographs of Schiller. The cosmopolitan ambience reminded me of Mariánské Lázně, as did the gentle slope of Wilhelmstraße as it rose towards the grand hotels at the head of the Kurpark. This *mitteleuropäisch* aura was reinforced by the Staatstheater, a stately pile designed by the Viennese architects Fellner & Helmer, whose opera houses more usually adorn Brno, Liberec, Karlový Vary, Rijeka, Oradea, Szeged or Odessa. Euterpe rides across the roof of the theatre in a chariot drawn by a quadriga of panthers; Muses and Fates strum lyres or blow trumpets atop the highest gables; and Calliope sits on a throne at the centre of the tympanum, presiding over a dying Tragedy and a lustful Comedy. In niches on either side of the grand portico are classically robed personifications of Drama, Song, Music and Dance, the latter two headless after being shot at by Americans in the Second World War; and on a pedestal in front of the theatre stands a young Schiller in satin and frills, declaiming his epic verse above masks of Drama and Comedy, and the glum figure of Tragedy with her chin slumped upon her fists.

In a small square between the Vier Jahreszeiten and Nassauer Hof hotels at the far end of Wilhelmstraße, I noticed the green-bronze statue of another German kaiser, set on a marble plinth in the centre of a bed of yellow and purple pansies. I assumed this would be Wilhelm II, the *grand seigneur* who made Wiesbaden fashionable in the 1890s. It turned out to be his father Friedrich III, the kaiser who died of throat cancer after ninety-nine days on the throne. Broad-chested and full-bearded, he stands in military uniform with a tasselled cloak thrown over his shoulder, sabre in one hand and a mace clutched priapically against his thigh in the other. Plaques attached to the plinth record his victories as commander of the German 3rd Army against the French at the Battles of Wörth and Sedan in 1870.

Clouds the hue of a dowager duchess's blue-rinsed hair were piling up above the Kurhaus. Kaiser Friedrich surveyed the colonnades on either side of the Bowling Green, where the triple-tiered fountains continued to cascade their champagne-bowl overflow, the curtains of water now blowing sideways in the stormy wind. I walked beneath the arcade of the Theaterkolonnade and crossed the forecourt of the Kurhaus. Below the Ionic columns of its mighty portico was a bronze plaque commemorating the visits of Goethe and Dostoyevsky to this casino of the gods. In the foyer of the Kurhaus, Apollo and Pallas Athena, Asklepios and Eirene confronted each other across a checkerboard floor of polished black and white stone. In the spandrels above them Neptune, Venus, Diana and Apollo (again) battled centaurs and sea monsters or were transported through the heavens in showers of Klimtian gold. Below the glass cupola ran a circular frieze of nymphs in swirling, diaphanous robes trailing garlands and blossoms. I sat on a banquette beneath the dome and listened to the sound of a Brahms symphony being recorded inside the Friedrich-von-Thiersch-Saal. The marble statues and coffered ceilings reminded me of the Befreiungshalle; but the high-minded ideals of the Bavarian king were missing. This was a Hellenism corrupted by the Hohenzollerns into bling for a royal gambling den.

I took the A66 from Wiesbaden. The autobahn passed an American air base, one of the eight from which a succession of C-54 "Rosinenbomber" kept West Berlin supplied with food during the Soviet blockade of 1948–49. Beyond Wiesbadener Kreuz the road surface lightened and the landscape opened out into farmland criss-crossed by lines of electricity pylons. To the north were the hills of the Taunus; to the south the Odenwald; straight ahead the skyscrapers of Frankfurt am Main. I entered the city along Theodor-Heuss-Allee, a dual carriageway lined with exhibition halls and the office blocks of banks, insurance firms and joint-stock companies. Mega-hotels for trade fair visitors – from the blue moon of the Radisson Blu to the tombstones of the Marriott – towered over City-West. Below the pink granite pencil of the MesseTurm – a post-modern homage to Art Deco New York – was the Europa-Viertel, a brand-new quarter of high-rise hotels and sharp-edged office blocks designed by the Frankfurt studio of Albert Speer (junior) & Partners. I found my hotel at the head of Europa-Allee, a long, straight boulevard bordered by wide, clean, empty pavements and symmetrical cubes of anthracite black or ash grey office blocks. Boasting a Starbucks, a Maredo steak house and a Motel One, the newly laid-out avenue was a twenty-first-century version of the *Prachtstraßen* once designed by Albert Speer (senior) for Germania and the *Führerstädte* of the Third Reich. (These did not include Frankfurt, which was regarded by Hitler as a "New Babylon" run by liberals, Social Democrats and Jews).

In the early evening I set off on foot along Mainzer Landstraße, a shabby thoroughfare of car dealerships, grubby pre-war townhouses and disused office blocks covered with wire netting to prevent their windows being broken. The street corners abutting Platz der Republik were a jumble of taxi offices, internet bureaux, shisha cafés, 24/7 shops, an AIDS help centre and a methadone clinic. Düsseldorfer Straße was lined with two-star hotels and a succession of restaurants – Korean, Vietnamese, Turkish, Malay and Ethiopian. Kids on the corner of Niddastraße sidled up to offer me drugs. I ended up in the subterranean concourse of the

Hauptbahnhof, in a labyrinth of featureless corridors and stairways which connected U-Bahn, S-Bahn and Deutsche Bahn platforms. The shops were closed and the concrete walls splashed with urine. I encountered a team of security guards and then a dozen or so junkies who had spread themselves and their gear – needles, spoons, foil and lighters – over a dead-end stairway. On the upper concourse Easter travellers rushed for trains or queued for takeaway food, while heroin addicts stumbled around the margins of the station – tattooed, emaciated figures shrivelled and crippled from years of abuse.

The fetid smell of the Hauptbahnhof lingered on past the *döner* kebab shops of Münchener Straße and the boarding houses along Moselstraße. Suddenly there was the river – and a stiff breeze from downstream which blew all the sleaze away. The skyscrapers were behind me and a different Frankfurt lay stretched out along the banks of the Main: a provincial riverscape of trees, towers and churches which had changed little since it was painted in 1858 by Gustave Courbet. Joggers thumped over the Holbeinsteg, negotiating a course between families walking their dogs and vendors selling roasted chestnuts. I followed Holbeinstraße, past turreted neo-Gothic villas and post-modern museum extensions, until I reached Mörfelder Landstraße. From here avenues of tall, Wilhelmine townhouses, each one plastered in off-white and trimmed with pink-brown sandstone, ran up the Lerchesberg towards the woods which skirted the city.

I was on my way to meet friends in Sachsenhausen, but first I wanted to take a nostalgic look at the area where I once lived. My home for two and a half years was an apartment in a modern block in Ziegelhüttenweg. At the head of the street was Ziegelhüttenplatz, a stepped concrete plaza built in the 1970s. The chemist, optician, supermarket and OBI hardware store were still there, but my branch of Deutsche Bank and my travel agency had gone. (I remember how my travel agent used to intone my surname into the phone whenever she booked a return flight to London for me: "Gustav Emil Otto Gustav Heinrich Emil Gustav Anton Nordpol". I always found it amusing that the Germans couldn't think of a name beginning with the letter N.) The supermarket was posh in the late 1980s: it sold kiwi fruit (which had not yet reached the British market); Cambozola cheese (Germany's answer to Gorgonzola); and bread stuffed with *Kümmel* (caraway seeds) – and the girl in the bakery fancied me. It has since gone downmarket, rebranded as a branch of HIT. On the pavements stood the same *Litfaßsäulen*, those timeless symbols of German continuity. They were even advertising some of the same bands I had heard twenty-five years earlier. I remember seeing Iggy Pop in Offenbach in 1989, thinking he was getting on a bit then; and now here he is again, still going strong a quarter-century later. As are a version of The Sweet (I saw a different line-up performing in Frankfurt twenty-five years ago); and I first listened to Udo Lindenberg as a student over forty years ago.

I walked around the car park and garden at the rear of Ziegelhüttenweg 17–19, peering up at the second-floor apartment where I used to live. I remembered the communal washing machines in the basement and the woman who pinned up a notice accusing the other tenants of stealing her knickers from a clothes line (it wasn't me: I also lost some boxer shorts); and the corpulent, indolent young man in the flat below me who reminded me of Diego Maradona: he drove a flashy black Opel Manta B and had a miserable Brazilian girlfriend. In the evenings I would sit on my balcony and watch the C-130 Hercules transport planes of the US Air Force taking off from the Rhein-Main Air Base on the south side of Frankfurt Airport. They were heavy, propeller-driven machines which looked like airborne whales. They lumbered so slowly into the air I was worried they would stall and belly-flop onto the apartment blocks at the top of Lerchesberg.

I continued up Ziegelhüttenweg, past the pizza parlour and the printing works, over the level crossing and into the *Schrebergärten*, the allotments where I would go on summer evenings to drink a *Weißbier* in one of the little homespun bars that flew the flags of Eintracht Frankfurt and the Bundesrepublik. On the opposite side of the street was the Kissel-Siedlung, an estate of boxy apartment blocks built after the war to house refugees from the Silesian or Bohemian cities after which the estate's streets were named: Breslau, Beuthen, Liegnitz, Aussig, Gablonz, Karlsbad and Teplitz-Schönau (now Polish Wrocław, Bytom and Legnica and Czech Ústí nad Labem, Jablonec nad Nisou, Karlový Vary and Teplice). The old German names were still painted in Gothic script on the walls of the houses.

I retraced my steps back towards Schweizer Straße at the heart of Wilhelmine Sachsenhausen, through streets of tall townhouses painted or plastered in myriad shades of brown and cream. I arrived at Adolf Wagner to find that Gabi had cried off with flu and that Andreas was hobbling away down the street, as he had to start a new job in a post office sorting centre at 7 am the next day. Justine and I found a table at the back of the *Äpfelwein* tavern, at which we were soon joined by a family from Saxony. The restaurant was noisy and full of tourists – half German, half foreign. I found it surprising that so many tourists were here in Sachsenhausen on Easter Sunday; my hotel in the Europa-Viertel was empty. Justine explained that Frankfurt received millions of one-night tourists: Germans who stayed overnight before catching a plane; and foreigners who stayed one night before setting out on a tour of Germany.

It was difficult to determine whether Adolf Wagner was still an authentic apple wine inn or whether it had become a parody of itself, a caricature of a *völkisch* tavern which catered exclusively for tourists and trade fair visitors. The air conditioning and touch screens didn't quite sit right with the wooden beams, mullioned windows and smoky paintings of eighteenth-century Frankfurt: post carriages racing past tollbooths on the banks of the Main; or groups of broad-beamed men in waistcoats and flat caps sitting around trestle tables smoking pipes and pouring glasses of *Ebbelwoi* from *Bembel*, the ubiquitous jugs of grey earthenware patterned with blue fruit- or vine-related motifs. Justine and I decided to forgo the obligatory hors d'oeuvre of *Handkäse mit Musik* (oily translucent cheese served with chopped onion sprinkled with caraway seeds) and avoid the traditional main course of *Schweinshaxe*. We ordered *Frankfurter Schnitzel* which, when it arrived, looked and tasted no different from *Wiener Schnitzel*. The meat was accompanied by *Bratkartoffeln* and *Grüne Soße*, a Hessian delicacy of cold sauce, made from seven herbs, which has an aftertaste of gooseberries and was apparently relished by Goethe. By the time it came to pay the bill I had lost count of the number of glasses of *Ebbelwoi* I had drunk. Fortunately, the waiter had been ticking them off on my beer mat. As we left, I noticed an anthropomorphic *Bembel* with arms and legs scurrying off beneath a table. It may have been in a painting.

Walking back over Untermainbrücke, I was struck by how spectacular Frankfurt could appear by night. I had forgotten the skyscrapers of Mainhattan and was looking down along the river bank, admiring the soft lamplight along Untermainufer and the Gothic spires of the Saalhof, Alte Nikolaikirche and Kaiserdom. I was suddenly aware of a massive, almost subliminal presence above me. Looking up, I could identify a yellow neon circle here, a slash of white neon there, a green triangle, a red letter *S* – the emblems of the biggest German banks floating high in the night. Then slowly, imperceptibly, the shapes of their towers detached themselves from the sky, forming a vast wall of steel and glass, barely visible in the darkness. In a vain attempt to sober up, I stopped for an espresso in the café of the Komödie Theater, after which I found myself in the Taunusanlage, a strip of parkland inhabited by statues of Schiller and

Heine and ghostly vagrants asleep on benches or plunging their arms into waste bins in search of discarded beer bottles.

A canyon of pink and purple neon beckoned from Taunusstraße. Knots of young Arabs shuttled between *Spielhallen* and *Spielotheken*; track-suited East Europeans shuffled around the entrances of the Double D Eros-Center and Dolly Buster's XXX Internet Lounge; skinny prostitutes sat smoking with their pimps in the vestibules of Eros Land and Sex Inns. Solitary men stood around street corners watching and waiting. Along Elbestraße the windows of the *Gründerzeit* townhouses were ablaze with neon: symmetrical patterns of blue, green, red and pink light. Neon hearts above the doorways, red lanterns above the windows, strips of white light across the balconies. Light flashing from streetlamps, car headlights, mobile phones and cigarette lighters. The corner of Weserstraße and Niddastraße stank of excrement and urine. A crowd of twenty or thirty heroin addicts had gathered around a needle exchange, some slumped across the pavement with blood on their feet, others agitated and high on stimulants. A user arrived on a bicycle, riding down the street firing the same question: "Wer hat Isch? Wer hat Isch?" I walked down Niddastraße, through the centre of the old fur trade. Young North Africans – dealers and their look-outs – were hanging around below the arches at the end of the street. On the corner of Moselstraße I encountered a pair of furtive Ethiopians who fell silent and looked at me questioningly as I passed them. I remember thinking how ironic it was that all these sleazy streets were named after idyllic German rivers.

Easter Monday. A low, grey sky discharged a fine, relentless drizzle over Frankfurt. I noticed a group of bedraggled demonstrators carrying a couple of multi-coloured flags emblazoned with the slogan "PACE". There were only eleven of them, yet they warranted a police escort of three motorcyclists and one van. I followed them along the top end of Mainzer Landstraße, a canyon of glass and steel with the silver aluminium skyscraper of Dresdner Bank on one side and on the other the twin towers of Deutsche Bank, those cloven glass polygons tinted silver-blue which reflect the colours of the sky. On a bright day the crystalline towers dissolve into the blue ether; today they were an opaque grey. The demonstrators came to a halt in Opernplatz, in front of the temple dedicated during the Wilhelmine Renaissance to "Dem Wahren Schoenen Guten". They stood around for a while, seemingly at a loss what to do, as if waiting for comrades who had failed to turn up. The three motorcyclists removed their helmets and shook out their long blonde hair, maybe wondering why they had been called out on a bank holiday morning for such an inconsequential demonstration.

I wandered down "Freßgass" and went into Starbucks for a coffee. Twenty minutes later the demonstration marched past. It had grown in size to around one hundred participants and was now policed by five motorcyclists and five vans, all flashing blue lights. At the head of the march were militants from the Kurdistan Workers' Party, bearing red-starred flags and banners which criticised the German government for its support of Turkey in the ongoing refugee crisis. Following the PKK was a motley crew of communists, trade unionists, pacifists, human rights campaigners, anti-racists, anti-capitalists and supporters of immigrants and asylum seekers. It seemed as if anyone could join in as long as they possessed a banner, anorak and knapsack, and didn't mind trudging through the shopping streets of Frankfurt on a wet Easter Monday morning.

I caught up with the protest march in the Römerberg, where the crowd had swelled to around a thousand. The historic heart of Frankfurt was a kaleidoscope of brightly coloured umbrellas and banners. The PKK and peaceniks had been joined by Christian groups, freethinkers and campaigners against NATO, arms exports and night flights. All the different factions had coalesced into a single *Ostermarsch* which filled the square. Grizzled 68ers posed for journalists; and women in their late fifties, still dressed in a punk uniform of leather jacket and ripped jeans, were handing out leaflets denouncing the escalation of conflict in the Middle East or criticising the participation of the Bundeswehr in the "so-called War against Terror". The tone of the protest was earnest and well-meaning: there were ripples of polite applause for arguments propounded by a woman from Pax Christi, who addressed the crowd from a stage in front of the faux-Gothic façade of the Römer city hall, below the golden statuettes of Charlemagne, Ludwig the Bavarian, Friedrich Barbarossa and Maximilian II; below the single- and double-headed eagles of the Reich and the Holy Roman Empire; beneath the flags of Frankfurt, the Federal Republic of Germany and the European Union – a panoply of capitalist-imperialist hegemony which represented almost everything the demonstrators in the square below were protesting against.

On the opposite side of the Römer were the "Six Sisters", a row of houses built in the 1950s and 1960s to replicate the *Fachwerkhäuser* of the Altstadt razed to the ground in the war. Half-timbered with red, maroon and black beams and decorated with gilded corbels, their ground floors have now been given over to cafés, restaurants and souvenir shops. The wares of the latter, protected from the drizzle under plastic sheeting, amounted to little except *Bembel*-related kitsch and scarves, bags and T-shirts stamped with "Deutschland" or "Eintracht Frankfurt". The city is not an easy sell for tourist merchandise. Its attributes are banking, finance, insurance, trade fairs and a mediocre Bundesliga football club. It is a hub of international travel, prostitution, substance abuse and vagrancy. None of this translates easily to a T-shirt. Yanis Varoufakis probably has one reading: "I went to Frankfurt to secure a ninety-billion-euro loan from the European Central Bank, and all I got was this lousy T-shirt."

The speeches were winding down and the demonstration was beginning to degenerate into a cacophony of Socialist marching songs blaring from tinny, hand-held loudspeakers. I decided to go and have lunch in order to escape the din. The restaurants in the Römerberg served the same fare I had dined on the previous evening in Adolf Wagner. I went to the Schirn Kunsthalle, the modern art gallery whose café I had frequented when I used to live in Frankfurt, but it was closed. I noticed there was a café inside the Steinernes Haus, a fifteenth-century patrician's house which now belonged to the Frankfurter Kunstverein. I squeezed onto the end of a table and ordered a bowl of celery and red lentil soup. The bistro was full of protestors from the Römerberg; it seemed that none of the crusty old peaceniks had any scruples about repairing to a *schickimicki* art club café for their lunch.

By early afternoon the rain had abated and I returned to the Römerberg. The loudspeakers had been packed away and the bulk of the demonstrators had dispersed, returning the square to the gold-painted men who stood on crates pretending to be statues. Chinese tourists were taking selfies in front of the Gerechtigkeitsbrunnen, a fountain around a statue of the goddess Justitia spouting jets of water from her orifices. (It is alleged that when the Holy Roman Emperors were crowned in Frankfurt and proceeded to the Römer for their coronation banquets, red wine would flow from one of her breasts and white wine from the other.) The freethinkers remained, distributing leaflets from their stand. I asked for one in English, but their freethinking philosophy was confined to the German language. A solitary singer remained, belting out revolutionary songs to the accompaniment of a battered guitar. A handful of 68ers stayed on to guzzle glasses of apple wine and reminisce about Daniel Cohn-Bendit and the good old days.

It started to rain again and I decided to visit the Kaisersaal, the Imperial Chamber where the Holy Roman Emperors were elected, and then wined and dined after they had been crowned in the nearby Kaiserdom. A baroque portal in a courtyard behind the Römer led up to an antechamber, where I paid an entrance fee of three euros for the privilege of being the sole visitor to the Kaisersaal. Gutted by bombs in 1944, the Imperial Chamber was rebuilt after the war and reopened in 1955. Its plain wooden walls were hung with paintings of every German emperor from Charlemagne to Franz II. It resembled the boardroom of a typical German GmbH of the *Wirtschaftswunder* era. This particular firm was a sprawling multi-national which, for over one thousand years, granted its subsidiaries licence to govern and regulate themselves, even to compete with one another. Having expanded through merger and takeover it found itself, by the turn of the nineteenth century, bloated and no longer fit for purpose; easy prey for a new breed of political predator. Napoleon attempted a hostile takeover; Bismarck sold off the non-profitable parts of the remaining business in order to strengthen its core assets; Hitler finally brought the firm to bankruptcy. Painted in Gothic-arched panels between 1838 and 1853, fifty-two life-sized portraits of the chairmen of the board line the walls of the post-war Kaisersaal: Carolingians, Ottonians, Salians, Saxons and Hohenstaufens clad in robes and chain mail, clutching swords, spears, maces, orbs and the ubiquitous black-eagled banner; Habsburgs in suits of gold armour; Spaniards saturnine in ermine and black velvet; Austrians effete in powdered wigs, waistcoats, breeches and frock coats. At the head of the chamber is the company's founder, Karl der Große, universally known as Charlemagne, seated on the golden throne of Aachen with a sword laid across his knees and a multi-tiered crown on his head – dark, long-haired and full-bearded like a Byzantine patriarch. Only Wenceslaus IV (known as "the Idle") lets the sartorial magnificence of the Imperial side down. Dressed as a Bohemian poacher, he (according to the guidebook) "possessed no statesmanlike tendencies, was moody, short-tempered and given to excessive drinking". (So the Czechs haven't changed much.) Each portrait was accompanied by a Latin proverb or electoral slogan encapsulating the essence of the ruler concerned. I was intrigued to find out what Rudolf II's epigram might be: "Alchemist, Occultist, Pornographer", perhaps? It turned out to be "Fulget Caesaris astrum" ("The star of the emperor burns brightly").

Back on the waterfront pods were falling from a row of honey locust trees and pleasure boats were drawing up beneath the Eiserner Steg.

Max Beckmann painted the iron footbridge in 1922 in a compressed, Expressionist style. His work depicts a crane on the quay in the fore-ground, tugs and barges on the yellow river, smoking factory chimneys in the background and electricity cables across a pale gold sky. The Church of the Three Kings rises in red, orange and yellow verticals on the far bank, a brightly coloured counterpoint to the girder bridge, which almost leaps out of the painting like an iron dragon. Almost one hundred years later the riverscape is pastoral-suburban rather than industrial: a row of trees, an island with a post-modern mill house used as an art gallery, a terrace of low-rise, pastel-coloured, post-war apartment blocks and the church, looking much the same as it does in Beckmann's painting. Further upstream are the twisted glass skyscrapers of the European Central Bank and the red-brick tower, crenellated in gold, of the Main-Plaza hotel complex, a post-modern take on the Wilhelm-Marx-Haus designed by Wilhelm Kreis in the 1920s.

I left the river and walked north towards Börneplatz, an area now occupied by a bland customer service centre which belongs to Frankfurt's public utilities company. It was once Judenmarkt, the Jewish marketplace at the centre of Judengasse, the first ghetto in Europe, established in 1462 in order to segregate Frankfurt's Jews from its Christian population. The street ran in an arc from Konstablerwache to the Main, following the curve of the medieval city walls. By 1600 it constituted the largest Jewish population of any European city. During the nineteenth century Frankfurt's Jewish community was gradually assimilated into bourgeois society and its more affluent denizens moved to new residential areas in the Westend and Nordend. Judengasse remained a picturesque slum of half-timbered houses until it was demolished in the 1870s. In 1882 a new synagogue was erected in Börneplatz. It too was painted by Beckmann, in 1919, at the centre of a claustrophobic, hallucinatory cityscape, its pink walls askew and its turquoise cupola distended.

The appearance of the service centre brought back memories of the protests around Börneplatz in 1987, the year I arrived to live in Frankfurt and read about the controversy in the local press. When excavation had begun on the site earlier that year, bulldozers unearthed the foundations of five houses and two *mikveh* (ritual baths) which once formed part of Judengasse. The city authorities wanted to forge ahead and destroy these remains in order to build their customer service centre over them. This, however, was the first occasion on which post-war Germany had been confronted with the ruins of a historical Jewish community. A protest movement was founded in order to persuade the city to halt its demolition work and preserve these ruins, the last material traces of an entire society. As the Jewish journalist and critic Ludwig Börne himself had written one hundred and fifty years earlier: "Where the dead are silent, the living stones speak all the more loudly." In the end a compromise was reached whereby the authorities agreed to reconstruct some of the surviving foundations of Judengasse in the basement of their new service centre, and the ruins would form the basis of a new Judengasse Museum. It later transpired that the bulldozers had also uncovered remains of the Börneplatz Synagogue, which had been destroyed by the Nazis on *Kristallnacht*; but that the city authorities had kept quiet about this until it was too late to re-excavate the site.

In 1996 a memorial site which recognised the Jewish identity of Börneplatz was unveiled. Hidden behind the customer service centre is an empty square strewn with hard, rough, grey stones, which reminded me of the surface of Buchenwald concentration camp. In the centre of the square is a cube built from slabs of pink sandstone which may once have been gravestones from the adjoining Jewish Cemetery. Planted among the stones is a geometrical orchard of plane trees, pruned so severely that their trunks and branches resemble dry, dead bones. At the edge of the site is a sheaf of street signs recording the naming and renaming of Judenmarkt and Judengasse (the latter was renamed Börnestraße in 1885, re-renamed Dominikanergasse by the National Socialists in 1935, before reverting to Börnestraße in 1978, by which time it no longer existed, having been obliterated, like the rest of the Altstadt, in the Second World War). A marble tablet on the rear wall of the customer service centre reads: "Here stood the Börneplatz Synagogue which was destroyed by Nazi criminals on the 9th day of November 1938."

At the back of the memorial site is the rear wall of one of Europe's oldest Jewish cemeteries. The graveyard was consecrated in the thirteenth century and remained in use until 1818, by which time it contained six and a half thousand gravestones. A wall leads around to the front of the cemetery in Battonnstraße. Embedded in the wall are twelve thousand small metal blocks, each of which bears a pebble and the name of a Jew deported from Frankfurt to a concentration camp and subsequently murdered. Each of these Hirsches, Isaacs, Kochs and Jakobs was born some time between 1860 and 1938, but the date of their death is left blank: it is left to the viewer to insert 1942. The place of death, however, is recorded – Minsk, Riga, Łódź, Theresienstadt, Auschwitz. The cemetery was closed. Through the locked gate I glimpsed piles of baroque tomb-stones, aslant and covered with lichen. Most of the graveyard was empty, two-thirds of the tombs having been smashed to pieces in 1942 in order to recycle the stone for air-raid shelters and bunkers. Fifty trees were also chopped down, and in August that year the cemetery was bombed. Lined up around the walls were some ancient tombstones which had been trans-ferred to the main Jewish Cemetery for safekeeping during the war. They were returned to the Börneplatz graveyard in the 1950s, but their original sites had been destroyed and it was no longer possible to match grave-stones to graves.

I crossed Kurt-Schumacher-Straße and turned up An der Staufermauer, an alley which followed the course of the medieval city wall through a 1950s housing estate, past a *Spielothek*, a Galician social club, a *Kolonialwaren* shop and a reconstructed arch of the original Staufermauer. I emerged into Konstablerwache, a barren concrete plaza lined with stunted trees and fast-food takeaways. Beggars squatted at the entrance to the U-Bahn, vagrants scavenged in waste bins and teenage drug deal-ers gave you the eye. The streets between the retail highway Zeil and the River Main were functional and utilitarian: anonymous blocks of shops, offices and apartments built during the reconstruction of the city centre in the 1950s. Entering Töngesgasse was like walking into a black-and-white photograph of pawn shops, antiquarian booksellers, smokers' pubs and tattoo parlours. A shop named "Sündige Mode" sold apparel for sex play, most of which was more tasteful than the dowdy dresses on display in the windows of the generic *Damen-Mode* boutiques.

Töngesgasse followed the course of the medieval Staufermauer into Großer Hirschgraben, where I sheltered from the rain in Goethe's birth-place. Rebuilt after the war, the Goethe House was a reconstruction of the home of the writer's parents. His father Johann Caspar was a lawyer and Imperial Councillor who played host to Royal Lieutenant François Théas de Thoranc during the French occupation of Frankfurt in the Seven Years' War. Johann Wolfgang was born on the second floor of the house in 1749 and grew up surrounded by books, paintings and musical instruments. The house was decorated in baroque yellow and neoclassical *bleumourant* and furnished with a puppet theatre, an astrological clock and all manner of fashionable chinoiserie. In 1765 Johann Wolfgang left the family home to study in Leipzig and Strasbourg, returning home occasionally to com-pose early *Sturm und Drang* works such as *Götz von Berlichingen* and *The Sorrows of Young Werther* at a standing desk on the third floor of the house. In 1775 he left Frankfurt for good, accepting an invitation from Duke Carl August von Saxe-Weimar to become a member of his privy council. Adjoining the Goethe House was a Goethe Museum, a collection of paintings and sculptures from the writer's era which embraced Füssli's nightmare visions, Hackert's Arcadian landscapes, Friedrich's Baltic vistas and a copy of Tischbein's famous portrait of the classical Goethe, clad in a white traveller's mantle, reclining on a fallen obelisk as he surveys the ruins of the Campagna di Roma. At the exit to the museum was a *Mädchenakt* by Georg Kolbe, a sculptor designated by Adolf Hitler as one of the "divinely favoured" artists of the Third Reich.

I drove north into the uplands of the Vogelsberg. A baroque gateway led into Kloster Arnsberg, a medieval monastery partially demolished during the secularisation of the early nineteenth century. The cloister garden at its centre had been transformed in 1960 into a place of remembrance for victims of war. It was a peaceful spot, surrounded by high stone walls and the ruins of the Gothic monastery church. A fountain at the centre of the garden was boarded up, and the raised strips of heather which surrounded it were a dry, wintry yellow. Several sandstone crosses had been placed, seemingly at random, along the rows of graves. The four hundred and fifty individuals buried here were commemorated by small iron plaques embedded in the ground. Some were German soldiers – I noticed an SS-Sturmmann and an SS-Rottenführer – but most were civilian victims of Nazi violence. I read some of their names: Marija Belausow, Olga Belikowa, Tamara Dim, Jewgenija Iwinskaja, Tanja Drolischewskaja. They were women from Latvia, Poland, Hungary, Czechoslovakia and the Soviet Union who worked as slave labourers for the Nazi war machine.

Others were nameless: their inscriptions read only "Gestapo-Gefangene Ermordet Hirzenhain 26.3.45". A metal plaque on the monastery wall explained that these graves included the remains of eighty-one women and six men shot by the Gestapo and SS near the labour camp of Hirzenhain on 26 March 1945. Some were women who had been working for several weeks in an *Arbeitserziehungslager* (Work Education Camp) affiliated to the Breuer armaments factory in Hirzenhain; others were inmates from a Gestapo prison in Frankfurt who had been transferred to Hirzenhain in a *Sondertransport* when the American military began to close in on the city. These eighty-seven prisoners were woken in the early hours of the morning and told that they were going to be released. They were marched out of the village to a quiet spot by a wood, where they were executed, their bodies thrown into a freshly dug mass grave. The corpses were discovered two months later, after the war had ended, and were reinterred in a cemetery in Hirzenhain. Only one of the victims, Emilie Schmitz from Luxembourg, was ever identified; the others remain anonymous victims killed almost arbitrarily in the final chaotic days of the war. In 1947 the perpetrators were identified and brought to trial. Their leader, SS-Scharführer Fritsch, was sentenced to life imprisonment. It is not recorded how many accomplices he had. In 1960 the eighty-seven bodies were disinterred and reburied in the garden of remembrance laid out here in Kloster Arnsburg.

Hirzenhain, the scene of the crime, was not far, twenty kilometres away on the southern edge of Vogelsberg. I noticed a sign for a *Gedenkstätte* (place of remembrance) as I approached the village. I turned down a track which ran along the side of a field until it reached a sandstone cross at the edge of a wood. There were green fields, birds singing and woodpeckers hammering away at the winter trees, dead leaves on the forest floor, a stream winding along the foot of the field, and the barns and cottages of a hamlet visible in hills to the south. I wondered whether this was the work of one particular sadist, or whether his accomplices were willing executioners. Was this a specialist death squad bussed in from elsewhere, or a bunch of local farmers who were merely following orders? Were they worried that the women might testify against them after the war, or did they lack the resources to transfer them elsewhere? Or was it just easier to shoot them and forget about them?

Fulda appeared in a pool of light as I drove down from the Vogelsberg massif. A volcanic hill covered with trees rose above the city. A chain of smaller hills, each crowned by a church or monastery, ran south towards the hills of the Rhön, where shreds of rain tore from the belly of a black cloud. The *Residenzstadt* was a clean, tidy city with a remote, upland air, situated in a valley close to the former inner German border. Churches, palaces, seminaries, deaconries and provostries combined to form a *Barockviertel* embellished with fountains and statues of saints and of the prince bishops who ruled Fulda. Presiding over the Baroque Quarter was the Collegiate Church of St Salvator. Hessian-Franconian in its sandstone texture and Jesuit-Habsburg in style, Dientzenhofer's cathedral towered over a semi-circular plaza, an amphitheatre of Siena-like proportions where, in 1980, Pope John Paul II addressed a crowd of over 100,000 worshippers.

A male voice, hidden in the monks' choir behind the high altar, was intoning a psalm as I entered the church. The interior of the *Dom* gleamed with white stucco, black marble and gilded putti. Alabaster statuettes of apostles, prophets, popes and bishops occupied the nave and transept. Spandrels high beneath the dome were illuminated with frescoes which, according to the guidebook, "depict the four evangelists floating on clouds in apocalyptic enrapture". Rising above the high altar was a six-pronged baldachin of black marble, capped by capitals of gold leaf, supporting an entablature on which the Virgin Mary's Assumption into Heaven rose in a coiled mass of gilt clouds and volutes towards a gloriole of sunbeams in the vertex of the chancel. At either end of the transept was an ornate altar of marble and agate, one dedicated to Saint Sturmius (the founder abbot of the monastery) and the other to Saint Benedict (founder of the order to which the Church of St Salvator belongs). On the pillars below the cupola were monuments to the eighteenth-century prince abbots Placidus von Droste, Adolf von Dalberg and Adalbert von Schleiffras. The latter, builder of the baroque cathedral, was commemorated by a flagon-shaped tomb of black marble embellished with delicate alabaster filigree. The lacework on the cuffs, sleeves and bodice of the allegorical figure of Love, who holds a copper relief of von Schleiffras, is finely detailed; as are the knots and folds of the alabaster curtains hanging from the canopy above the abbot. So, too, are the inscriptions and tiny perforations in each of the visored helmets framing his memorial; and the skull and ribs of Death, who reclines on a tasselled, embroidered woolsack at the foot of the tomb. Below the high altar is a crypt containing the sarcophagus of St Boniface, the English missionary who felled the Donar Oak and converted the Saxons to Christianity. After his brutal death (he was stabbed in the forehead by Frisians in the Netherlands), he was laid to rest in the Carolingian monastery built in Fulda over the ruins of a Merovingian palace. The Benedictine basilica which was later constructed over his tomb became the spiritual centre of Catholic Germany, a Rome of the North. The basilica was demolished in the eighteenth century and the present baroque *Dom* erected over its site. It was consecrated in 1712, almost a thousand years after the death of the English monk.

On a terrace high above the Domplatz is St Michael's, a Romanesque burial church capped with two Gothic witches' hats of black slate. On the whitewashed walls of its nave are coloured wooden statuettes of saints and abbesses holding crooks and crosiers, bells and books. An arch at the far end of the nave leads into a Carolingian rotunda of sandstone columns and walls painted with faded red and gold frescoes. The circular colonnade reminded me, for some reason, of the Obergruppenführersaal in Schloss Wewelsburg. Across an arch above the apse flew angels on white saucers, escorting a procession of strange, white, lip-shaped objects through the firmament: St Michael and his angels leading the souls of the Just before the face of Christ, according to the church's booklet. I descended into the crypt below the rotunda, a musty undercroft with an odour of earth, stone and bones. Abbot Eigil, builder of the church, was buried here in 822. There were memorial slabs to the monks Amnichad and Meginbracht from the tenth and eleventh centuries. Around the crypt was a gallery of tiny cells which served as charnel houses. Back upstairs in the rotunda, I read that St Michael's was restored between 1935 and 1938, when many of its Gothic and baroque additions were removed. There seems, however, to have been no sinister motive behind the restoration; no project to transform the church into a National Socialist cult site in the manner of Quedlinburg or Braunschweig – merely a desire to restore its Romanesque purity.

Sheets of rain screened the hills with a fine gauze as I left Fulda and drove up into the Rhön. The Wasserkuppe was hidden beneath low cloud. Above the forests the landscape opened out into moorland of stunted trees, molehills and boulders, bogs covered with sodden yellow sedge. I stopped at a roadhouse on the Schwarzes Moor near the spot where the borders of Hesse, Bavaria and Thuringia converged. I was searching for the location where, twenty-five years earlier, I had been arrested by the Federal Border Police for trespassing on the territory of the GDR. I was living in Frankfurt at the time, and had driven out to the Rhön to have a look at the inner German border fortifications which, in the summer of 1989, were still firmly in place. Erich Honecker had just boasted that "the Wall will still be standing in fifty or even in one hundred years' time – if the reasons for it have not been removed by then". I had parked my car at the end of a track which would once have led into a spur of Thuringian land containing the villages of Frankenheim and Birx, but had since been cut off by the "anti-fascist protection barrier" of the GDR. I had wandered down a grassy slope, past one of the striped stone pillars marking the boundary, until I reached the first metal mesh fence of the border installations. In the distance I could see a village, presumably Frankenheim, on top of the spur of East German land.

It was an uncanny moment. I seemed to be quite alone amidst the rocks and moorland of the Rhön. On the other side of the fence I could make out a trench and the course of the concrete-plated *Kolonnenweg*. I wondered what it would be like to live in Frankenheim, an isolated hill village enclosed on three sides by the Iron Curtain. I reached out to touch the mesh of the fence. All of a sudden, I heard shouts behind me. An officer of the Federal Border Police was yelling at me to return to the road. I had been so wrapped up in the moment I had not heard his car approach. He told me that the official border between the Bundesrepublik and the GDR was marked by the pillar I had walked past, and that I had therefore trespassed on the territory of the German Democratic Republic. He handed me a sheet of paper printed in Bundesgrenzschutz green and proceeded to talk me through it: "Visitors to the border area are exposed to great danger if they, out of ignorance or thoughtlessness, do not heed the course of the border. It is often wrongly assumed that the land between the actual border and the border fortifications of the GDR is no-man's-land. At the border of the GDR there is **no** NO-MAN'S-LAND!!"

The officer demanded to see my documents. I didn't have my passport with me. "Where are you from?"

"Great Britain."

"Where do you live?"

"Frankfurt," I replied, realising immediately how foolish my answer was. I had been living in Frankfurt for two years and had never bothered to register with the authorities and obtain a resident's permit. Being exposed as an illegal alien was a crime worse than trespassing on the territory of the GDR.

"How long have you been living in Frankfurt?"

"Two months," I lied.

"I will have to fine you," he continued, "for trespassing on foreign territory. The officers of the East German Border Troops will have observed your misdemeanour and will issue a complaint against the Federal Border Police unless we are seen to punish you. The fine will be five deutschmarks. Please read the rest of the advice sheet and heed the instructions, should you ever find yourself in the proximity of the border again. And you must register with the authorities within the next month if you wish to remain in the Federal Republic."

Back in the present, after a warming bowl of thick pea and bacon soup, I set off from the roadhouse. The rain lashed sideways as I walked along the track to the former border. After eight hundred metres I came to a turning circle in the road, where I noticed an ancient stone engraved with the letters KB on one side and GSW on the other. It marked the historical border between the Königreich Bayern and the Großherzogtum Sachsen-Weimar. A wooden signboard delineated the course of the former German–German border. This was possibly the spot where I had been arrested all those years before. I could make out the village of Frankenheim in the distance, obscured by a grove of trees I didn't recall from my earlier visit. All that remained of the border was a trench and the remnants of the *Kolonnenweg*, a double track of latticed concrete used by vehicles of the East German border police to patrol the frontier. According to the signboard, the *Staatsgrenze West* performed a three-pronged incursion into Bavarian territory, empty farmland which was presumably not fenced in even though it belonged to the GDR.

I followed the *Kolonnenweg* up a hill to the north-east and, after two hundred metres, came across a ruined watchtower of the standard BT-9 model, of which I had been blissfully unaware during the course of my earlier misdemeanour. Beside the tower was a hillock, seemingly man-made, covered with bushes and boulders. Across the rough flight of steps leading to its peak was a yellow sign on a chain marked "Betreten verboten". I stepped over it and climbed to the top. On the upper platform was a concrete plinth, some railings and two rusted ventilator shafts. The hillock must have served some purpose as a bunker or storage room. I watched a couple of young hikers struggling against the wind and rain as they approached the watchtower from the Thuringian side of the border. They looked at me disapprovingly when they realised my lack of respect for simple rules. A short section of the border fortifications had been left intact, presumably as a sort of mini-museum or unofficial monument to the absurdity of the Iron Curtain. It consisted of a double row of metal mesh fencing of the standard 3.2 metre format, topped by additional strands of barbed wire; two gateways with serrated metal frames; a trench reinforced with concrete panels; a tank-trap half-buried in the ground which, oddly, reminded me of a Christian cross; a disconnected metal grille; and the frieze-like pattern of the concrete *Kolonnenweg*. Several yards in front of the outer fence were the remains of a once brightly striped

East German border post. Now aslant and ravaged by wind and rain, its blackened concrete had been eaten away and its rusted reinforcing rods exposed to the elements.[19]

Returning to Hesse, I followed the valley of the Ulster through Hilders and Tann, crossing back into Thuringia near Geisa. In Vacha, a small walled town on the eastern bank of the River Werra, I noticed a watch-tower, a stretch of concrete wall and a giant green *Ampelmann*. The "Green Man" – an exercise in *Ostalgie*, presumably – had been positioned at the head of the Werrabrücke, a fourteen-arched medieval bridge con-necting Thuringian Vacha with Hessian Philippsthal. In the Middle Ages the Werra formed the boundary between the lands of the abbeys of Fulda and Hersfeld; from 1816 it was the border between the Electorate of Hesse and the Grand Duchy of Saxe-Weimar; and after the Second World War it separated the Occupation Zones of the Soviet Union from those of the United States of America. In 1952 the bridge was cordoned off and the border, which ran along the Werra and over the bridge, was closed. It was a complex section of border to control. The course of the river had to be altered and iron grilles mounted beneath the arches in order to prevent escapees swimming through. A metal mesh fence and watchtower were erected on the bridge itself, and concrete walls (apparently the first to be built along the Iron Curtain) were installed along the river banks to isolate the townspeople of Vacha from the river. A new road had to be built between Vacha and the village of Unterbreizbach (since the old road crossed two kilometres of West German territory), and Haus Hoßfeld, on the opposite bank of the river, was divided in two, one-third of the house walled up and placed out of bounds to its own residents.

For forty years Vacha was a dead-end town with no hinterland, where "undesirable elements" were expelled; where would-be escapees were shot in the river; where the local church superintendent was an "unofficial col-laborator" who informed on his parishioners. The bridge was reopened on the night of 11 November 1989 and much of its fencing dismantled the following day. In 1990 it was designated a "Brücke der Einheit" (Bridge

---

19   In the process of writing this, I discovered some ancient slides of me and three friends on a camping holiday in the Harz Mountains in the spring of 1974. We are in a forest. In the foreground is a white signpost. I can't make out the lettering, but it probably says something like "Halt. Hier Zonengrenze". On the far side of a stream is a black, red and gold concrete pillar marking the border of the GDR. The stream would have been the actual boundary. The photos show us grinning and gurning with our arms wrapped around the GDR marker. Trespassing, once again, on East German territory.

of Unity); but nobody crosses it. It seems that the walls between Hessian Philippsthal and Thuringian Vacha continue to exist in their inhabitants' minds. The watchtower on the bridge (a truncated BT-11 column with an octagonal observation deck) was dismantled in 1997, but a newer watchtower on the Vacha bank (a square BT-9 *Führungsstelle* which coordinated the activities of a chain of watchtowers along the border) had been recently restored and preserved as a museum piece.

The water meadows down to the river were sodden and discoloured from winter rains. Halfway along them ran a sixty-metre segment of concrete wall, of the standard, fourth-generation *Grenzmauer 75* type made from prefabricated plates of concrete topped by a horizontal concrete pipe. This type of wall was normally only used to surround West Berlin: it was odd to find this iconic structure in the rural backwater of Vacha; and even odder to find it still standing. It was in a dilapidated condition: some of its plates had fallen out; it was streaked with grime and graffiti; and the horizontal piping was filthy, broken and coated with moss. It had not been preserved in any way; it should have been demolished years ago with the rest of the border fortifications. For some reason it remained, lurking half-concealed in the undergrowth by the river, a sinister reminder of an ugly past.

18

Franconia

How German Is It

On a Monday morning in late July, I stopped for a late breakfast in Randersacker, a village to the south of Würzburg. I sat at a table outside the Rösner Backstube in the marketplace. Randersacker was a village of *Weinstuben* and *Weingüter*, solid buildings with pointed or cello-shaped gables, vine-clad walls and window boxes overflowing with geraniums. Each tavern had a wrought-iron sign above its door: a coil of vine leaves, a bunch of grapes or a replica of the distinctive Franconian *Bocksbeutel*. Körners Weinstube, built in 1934 according to the date above its garage, had a Madonna and Child sculpted into a niche in its façade and painted on its walls a ladder of high-water marks, the highest of which recorded a flood on 7 February 1909.

Pennants in the red and white colours of Franconia hung limply in the morning heat, above noticeboards advertising next weekend's "Dorffest für Alle", a celebration of twenty-five years of partnership between Randersacker and its twin town Vouvray in France. In the centre of the marketplace was a tall oak tree, a "Kriegserinnerungseiche" commemorating the dead of two world wars; and in the bushes round the edge was an older memorial, a stone monument engraved with a helmet and Iron Cross and embossed with enamel medallions containing sepia photographs of villagers who had sacrificed their lives for the fatherland in the First World War. The fountain in the centre of the square was a recent installation, an old-fashioned bathtub painted in baroque gold. Water poured in from a tap above it and flowed out through a hole in its side. The inscription on a tablet beside it, also painted in gold, read "BALTHASARS BADEWANNE" ("Balthasar's bathtub"). I wondered whether it had anything to do with Balthasar Neumann, architect of the baroque Residenz in Würzburg.

A church bell tolled half past eleven and the tables of the café began to fill up with elderly ladies arriving for their daily *Kaffee und Kuchen*. A school bus arrived and disgorged boys and girls who disappeared, yelling and whooping, satchels high on their shoulders, into the cobbled streets of lime-, lemon- and orange-painted houses up the slopes towards the vineyards combing the hills above the village. I read a notice confirming that the fountain was indeed related to Balthasar Neumann, its gilt and stucco intended to celebrate the baroque imagination of the architect, who owned a vineyard in the village and built the little ochre pavilion with the hipped roof and rococo capitals which stood in a garden opposite the Sparkasse. I left the marketplace and walked down to the river. Swans and geese paddled in the shallows of the Main, beneath willow trees hanging over the Promenade. A Dutch barge from Vreeswijk fought against the current, trying to manoeuvre itself into a straight line in order to navigate the lock of a dam upstream. I caught sight of a truncated stone cone on the crest of a hill above the vineyards. It was once known as the Adolf Hitler Tower.

I drove south from Randersacker and found a road through the vineyards to the Rothberg ridge at the top of the slopes. I parked the car and walked along a track above the highest terrace of vines. There was a cool breeze in the air and birds were singing in the trees. Below me I could hear the snarl of tractors working on the slopes between the vines, and the hum and whine of lorries on the A3 autobahn in the valley below. Small, hard grapes were beginning to form on the vines – Bacchus, Riesling and Spätburgunder, according to the labels on their supporting stakes. I had a panoramic view of the Main, its waters now olive green, flowing between caravan parks and football pitches, market gardens and wineries. As the path curved to the north, I caught a glimpse of Balthasar Neumann's Käppele pilgrimage church and the towers of Festung Marienberg on the left bank.

Eventually I reached a clearing at the top of the hill. The Adolf-Hitler-Turm was in the form of a cone with its top cut off. A narrow ramp led up a shallow embankment to a walled circle at the top of the tower. A signboard at the base of the ramp chronicled its history. The summit of Rothberg was a well-known beauty spot during the Kaiserreich. In the

1920s it became a popular site for the bonfires and solstice ceremonies of youth groups. A stone platform built towards the end of the decade was enlarged in the 1930s into a "Sonnenstuhlturm" (sun-seat tower). It was designated as an "Adolf Hitler Tower" when the National Socialists took power in 1933. Three stone swastikas and the date 1933 were bricked into its walls, and a swastika banner flew from a flagpole erected in its crown. The tower was neither completed (its ramp was intended to have steps) nor officially unveiled, and only two National Socialist ceremonies – to celebrate Hitler's birthday in 1934 and 1936 – were recorded as having taken place here. During the war it was apparently used as an anti-air-craft battery. After the war its swastikas were hacked away and the tower reverted to its former name of Sonnenstuhlturm. I was busy examining the outlines of the hooked crosses, which had been somewhat inexpertly removed, when a man appeared and asked me: "Sind Sie Geocacher?" ("Are you a geocacher?") I had no idea what he meant, and replied that I was just a tourist. I bumped into him later in the crown of the tower and asked what geocaching was. He explained it was based on a website which provided clues to treasure hidden near sites of particular interest. He had observed me with my notebook and camera, and had assumed I was a fellow geocacher. I wished him luck with his treasure-seeking and returned to my car.

I continued south on the B13, following the River Main until I came to Ochsenfurt. I had read about a statue here of a *Bull Tamer* by Willy Meller, sculptor of Reich eagles, torch bearers and Victory goddesses for the arenas and Ordensburgen of Nazi Germany. The *Bull Tamer* had been commissioned for Seebad Prora, the industrial-scale seaside resort by the Baltic coast on the island of Rügen. It represented a naked warrior breaking in a muscular bull. The animal was shorn of its hind legs, since it was designed to stand, as if rearing out of the water, on a plinth in the central pool of the unfinished Festival Square at the centre of the *Kraft durch Freude* resort. The statue was executed in 1939 by the stonemason Wilhelm Ax in Ochsenfurt, but never transported to Prora as construction on the resort was abandoned when war broke out. The bull remained, according to the literature, in a park on the banks of the Main, just below the bridge which carries Bundesstraße 13 over the river to the centre of Ochsenfurt.

I stopped for a *latte macchiato* in the café of a NORMA supermarket and sat outside to survey the scene. There was no sign of Meller's statue on this side of the bridge. I walked beneath the bridge; nothing there either. I noticed a landscaped park on the other side of the river and crossed over. Still no sign of the bull. Then, looking back, I realised the bridge carrying the main road over the river had been demolished, and the bridge I had crossed was the old bridge, now only accessible to pedestrians. The main road bridge was being rebuilt, and the area beneath it was fenced off as a construction site. Assuming this area was now out of bounds, I set off to find the stonemasons where the statue had been executed, in case the bull had been returned there. Finding nothing, I decided to abandon my search and continue south. But driving out of Ochsenfurt I felt a nagging sense of failure in my quest for the beast. Surely it must be here somewhere.

I turned round and drove back into the town. I would take one last look at the bridge and, if there was nothing there, I would go and enquire at the stonemasons. I parked once more outside the supermarket and walked along the river bank towards the demolished bridge. There was nothing to see except a backwater of the Main, a thicket of *Auwald* and a row of fencing around the construction site. I was about to turn back when I realised that the bull was right in front of me. I hadn't noticed it because it was hidden in a cage of scaffolding covered with green netting. It was a monstrous beast, all neck and rump, blackened by damp and freckled with lichen. A fierce Triton gripped one of its horns, pulling the animal's head back in an attempt to tame it. It felt rather poignant to come across this mythical creature, designed as the centrepiece of the "Seebad der 20,000", the "Colossus of Prora", left high and dry on the banks of the sleepy River Main in Ochsenfurt – a bull destined for the raging Baltic, but stranded by the ford of the oxen.

After the pastoral delights of Randersacker and Ochsenfurt, the mean streets of Nuremberg provided a rude awakening. People were rougher and uglier, drivers more aggressive, streets lined with grubby hotels and post-war office blocks. The strip of parkland below Spittlertor was strewn with litter and discarded sleeping bags. Bosnian women pushing children in buggies solicited for money. Pensioners fished in litter bins for empty bottles. Frauentormauer was quiet, its brothels closed for the morning. Ludwigstraße stank of drains and grilled meat. I passed shisha bars, kebab joints and head shops, internet cafés which bought and sold stolen mobile phones. Tattooed men and women smoked cigarettes on street corners. One young man with a top-of-the-range BMW was being questioned by a police officer. The police station, around the corner in Jakobsplatz, was a modern building with a stylised Nuremberg eagle above its entrance. Its site was once the local headquarters of the Gestapo.

I made my way down to the river and pursued a crooked course over bridges and islets, criss-crossing the shallow brown waters of the Pegnitz. A wooden hangman's bridge crossed to the Trödelmarkt, an island preserved in the aspic of the 1970s, where old hippies sat on benches swigging local beer from dark bottles. Ranged around the flea market were a Swiss watch shop, a "Spielzeugkiste" which sold dolls, gonks and rocking horses, a bead shop full of steampunk knick-knacks, a shoe shop specialising in deerskin footwear and a glassware shop with psychedelic lava lamps.

Reaching the Hauptmarkt, I climbed to the terrace of one of the Italian cafés overlooking the square. The bells of the Frauenkirche tolled midday and, to the accompaniment of tinkling chimes, the seven electors of the Holy Roman Empire appeared and rotated around Emperor Charles IV. The mechanical figures were re-enacting the proclamation of the Golden Bull of 1356, a decree which established the procedure of electing a new emperor. It also nominated the Kaiserburg of Nuremberg as the first seat of each new Imperial Diet. Above the arches of the New City Hall was a shield bearing the arms of Nuremberg – a virgin eagle in gold on a field of blue. Flagpoles on the edge of the square flew the red and white colours of Franconia and the sky-blue and white of Bavaria. Red-and-white-striped awnings covered the market stalls in the square below. Here you could buy Franconian strawberries and Nuremberg gingerbread. "Noch etwas Deutsches? Von deutschen Bauern?" ("Something German? From German farmers?") was the urgent cry of one stallholder. Maybe it was because his trailer was sandwiched between traders selling "Spezialitäten" from the Balkans or "Köstlichkeiten" from the Mediterranean. Glittering in the sun in the far corner of the marketplace was the Schöner Brunnen, bright in gold, red and green paint, encircled by prophets, evangelists and, in a dazzling ring of orbs and sceptres around the fountain's base, the same seven electors of the Holy Roman Empire. The entire scene was coloured, of course, by Leni Riefenstahl's film *Triumph of the Will*, whose penultimate scene depicts the Hauptmarkt packed with brass bands and cheering crowds assembled to watch the closing parade of the 1934 Nazi Party

Congress. Accompanied by Göring, Streicher and Hess, Hitler stands on the seat of an open-top Mercedes-Benz at the edge of the square (known at the time as Adolf-Hitler-Platz) and salutes an endless succession of paramilitary organisations as they goose-step their way over Fleischbrücke, eyes-right the Führer and clump up Rathausplatz towards the Kaiserburg.

In the afternoon I walked east through the Südstadt of Nuremberg. I stopped for a coffee in Kopernikusplatz, opposite a decommissioned Kaufhof supermarket whose silver honeycombed façade was now plastered with fly-posters and graffiti. I continued afterwards along Landgrabenstraße, past lottery shops, tattoo parlours, tanning salons and a gun shop. The street signs were in Gothic script and the local pub was named the "Deutscher Michel". Further east, the streets of Galgenhof were lined with falafel bars, kebab shops, shawarma grills and *çiğ köfte* restaurants. Men stood smoking on the pavement outside Greek furriers and Kurdish hairdressing salons. Women, clad despite the heat in black hijabs, browsed in front of Turkish bridal shops and jewellers whose windows were piled high with glitzy bangles. "Any gold bought and sold," they advertised, "teeth included." I passed a shisha wholesaler, a Turkish Airlines travel agency and, rather incongruously, a shop selling Bavarian *Trachten* – girly blouses and dirndls for women; gingham shirts, embroidered jackets and lederhosen for men and boys. Signs in its windows announced it was celebrating its eightieth anniversary, which meant it opened in 1937, just in time for the Party Rally of that year.

Speaking of which, I arrived at the Platz der Opfer des Faschismus. I crossed the road and continued past the Ramada Park Hotel and the Meistersingerhalle, home of the Nuremberg Symphony Orchestra. The path led into parkland, where it was cool beneath the trees, the air fragrant with the smell of lime and roses. An embankment to my left covered the remains of a grandstand at the head of the Luitpoldhain, where Leni Riefenstahl whizzed up and down flagpoles on a lifting mechanism as she filmed the massed ranks of the SA and SS in the arena below.

The fourth day of *Triumph of the Will* opens with a close-up of one of the roc-sized eagles mounted at either end of the grandstand. The camera pans down to the three tiny figures of Hitler, Himmler and Lutze marching over the granite slabs of the "Straße des Führers" towards the nine-arched war memorial at the far end of Luitpoldhain. A second camera tracks back to the grandstand, overhung by three tall swastika banners. A military band in front of the war memorial plays sombre music. Smoke and flames rise from fire bowls on top of the stone blocks surrounding the forecourt of the Ehrenhalle. The three men approach a huge wreath in the centre of the forecourt. They salute the dead. Hitler lays a smaller wreath. The three men return down the avenue formed by columns of stormtroopers. Standards lowered for the remembrance of the dead rise to salute them. A band in front of the grandstand strikes up a fanfare as Hitler ascends the podium.

The standard bearers of the SA march forward and disperse along the wings of the grandstand. Flag bearers from the outer terraces of the arena converge in the central avenue, forming a river of red, white and black which flows through the ranks of brown-shirted SA men. On reaching the grandstand they diverge into serpentine columns which snake back and forth as they fall into line along the terraces between the two giant eagles. To the accompaniment of thunderous marching music the SS arrives, a mass of black-uniformed soldiers goose-stepping over the paving stones. Another fanfare announces Konrad Lutze, the new leader of the SA. In a disconcertingly high-pitched voice he swears an oath of loyalty to the Führer on behalf of the SA. The stormtroopers thrice hail victory. Hitler speaks, absolving the SA from any responsibility for the "dark shadow" that has crossed the National Socialist movement under Ernst Röhm's leadership. The brownshirts hail their Führer. Guns blast the sky as Hitler moves down the line of "Deutschland Erwache" standards, looking intently into the eyes of each standard bearer and briefly pressing each standard against the blood flag of the movement carried by an adjutant behind him. Riefenstahl's film lingers on standards from Mittelfranken, Gotha, Spessart, Paderborn, Dresden-Neustadt, Peine, Bielefeld, Gelnhausen and Gardelegen. The band strikes up the *Horst-Wessel-Lied* and the ceremony is soon over. The stormtroopers disperse and march into the city, where they will continue to parade for several hours through the streets of the Altstadt.

It is difficult to imagine all this today. The temperature was over thirty degrees and no one had dared to venture out into the Luitpoldhain except a couple of shirtless Australian backpackers and two girls in neo-hippy garb, who were rehearsing some kind of Wicca ceremony on the lawn in front of the Ehrenhalle. A strip of grass down the middle of the field had been mown shorter than the rest: it traced the path of what was once known as the "Straße des Führers". At the edge of the field was a broad flight of granite steps covered with moss and weeds – which led nowhere. It was all that remained of the Luitpoldhalle, an exhibition hall and congress centre built in 1906 for cultural and political events. I smiled at a man tearing stickers off the signboards relating the history of the "Reichsparteigelände". He didn't smile back. When he'd gone, I realised the stickers he'd been removing were those of antifascist activist groups – "Antihomophobia Aktion", "Fuck the Alternative für Deutschland", "Fight Sexism", "Cool Kids have no Fatherland". Maybe he was the person who had been scrawling "Nationaler Sozialismus jetzt!" and "Nationaler Widerstand jetzt!" on all the cigarette machines in the neighbourhood.

Seeking to escape the sun's heat, I began a circumambulation of the Congress Hall, the preposterous amphitheatre designed to replace the Luitpoldhalle as the annual venue for "The Opening Day of the Party Congress". I followed a seemingly endless route beneath arches of meticulously assembled blocks of granite. The granite came from over eighty German quarries, each stone personally approved by Hitler, and the blocks were pieced together according to a "stone placement plan" which matched and contrasted stone of different colours and textures in order to provide a variegated veneer to the finished building. The blending of different granites was attractive and the colonnade remained well preserved, but its unending repetitiveness was mind-numbing. After walking a couple of hundred metres, I encountered a Turkish wedding party whose guests had chosen the arcade of the Nazi Congress Hall as a backdrop to the couple's happy day. Not wishing to intrude, I turned back and walked around to the Dutzendteich at the front of the building, and thence into the courtyard at its centre.

The arena inside the Congress Hall was a cauldron of hot, red brick, empty save for lorries, skips and a ring of lock-ups full of pallets, duckboards and fencing stored for the Nürnberger Volksfest, held twice yearly on the grounds outside. The glass "stake" through the Party Rally Grounds Documentation Centre in the north wing protruded over the compound. The south wing belonged to the Nuremberg Symphony Orchestra and housed a Serenadenhof which staged open-air concerts in the summer. If the arcade of granite blocks around the exterior of the Congress Hall expressed the vanity of the Third Reich, the unfinished brickwork of its interior, raw and hot like the inside of a crater, exposed the banality of its megalomania. This was the test of Speer's Theory of Ruin Value, whereby the greatness of a civilisation is measured by the grandeur and aesthetic appeal of its ruins. It failed.

As I left the Congress Hall I caught a brief glimpse, through a break in the trees on the far side of the Dutzendteich, of the prematurely ruined grandstand at the head of the Zeppelin Field. On my way there I stopped for lunch in the beer garden of the Gaststätte Wanner, where I ate in the company of American high school students on an exchange visit to the Reichsstadt-Gymnasium in Rothenburg ob der Tauber. After lunch I continued along the shore of the lake to the arena at the centre of the Party Rally Grounds. To enter the Zeppelin Field I had to negotiate a network of crash barriers and temporary grandstands in the process of being dismantled following a beer-and-fast-cars event there the previous weekend. Speer's grandstand was in a decrepit state, its main tribune a ruin, its steps crumbling, the corridor of its demolished colonnade fenced off because of the danger of collapse. Much of its limestone cladding had deteriorated, exposing rough brickwork beneath. The terracing was streaked with damp, overgrown with weeds and littered with broken bottles and crushed cans. Photographs taken in 1938 may have given the impression that this pristine, altar-like structure with its golden swastikas, scarlet banners and bronze cauldrons would last for a millennium; but it survived only a further seven years before the gilded mega-swastika above its main tribune was blown up by the US Army. Six Party Rallies were held in the Zeppelinfeld between 1933 and 1938. For the first three of these the Reich Labour Service paraded before a temporary wooden grandstand. By 1936 the new Zeppelin tribune had been completed and seventy thousand spectators could be seated on the stone terracing around the arena. By day they would be captivated by the parades of the Reich Labour Service, the war games of the Wehrmacht, the gymnastics exercises of the German League of the Reich for Physical Exercise, and the mass dance performances of the Faith and Beauty movement. By night they would be awestruck by columns of light shooting thousands of metres into the sky to form a brilliant dome.

There was little sense of that wonder on this July afternoon. The steps of the Zeppelin tribune were white hot, the terracing too exposed for anyone to linger there long. Those tourists who braved the heat were drawn inexorably towards the rostrum from where the Führer once addressed his followers. They posed, strutted, thrust their chests out and flexed their hips. One young man contorted himself by trying, in vain, to take a selfie while simultaneously performing a Hitler salute. The field below the grandstand was busy with Polish labourers dismantling fencing, marquees and temporary cabins, taking down scaffolding and loading lorries.

I crossed the arena towards the football stadium, where a few teenagers in the black and maroon kit of 1.FC Nürnberg were kicking a ball around. The Frankenstadion was redeveloped in the 1980s on the site of the old municipal stadium used in the 1930s as the rally ground for "The Day of the Hitler Youth". The sixth day of the Nazi Party Congress was devoted to the blue-eyed boys who would succeed the "old fighters" and carry the torch of the movement into the future: "For you are the flesh of our flesh and the blood of our blood." These words of the Führer are hailed, in Leni Riefenstahl's film, by fifty thousand pubescent voices, which then break into the banner song of the Hitler Youth:

> Uns're Fahne flattert uns voran,
> Uns're Fahne ist die neue Zeit.
> Und die Fahne führt uns in die Ewigkeit,
> Ja, die Fahne ist mehr als der Tod!
>
> (Our flag flutters before us,
> Our flag is the new age.
> And the flag guides us into eternity,
> Yes, the flag is more to us than death!)

On the podium, Hitler and Hess exchange the smirks of two middle-aged men who have just groomed another fifty thousand young boys.

I caught sight of the Veste as I approached Coburg from the south. Its towers and bastions lay sprawled over a hill on the far side of the town. The road to the fortress passed through Neue Heimat, an estate of small family houses built during the 1930s for, I discovered later, "deserving fighters of the SA". They were in the standard *völkisch* style of the Third Reich, with wooden shutters, glass bricks and steep dormer roofs with that little swing outwards at the base of the roof. I imagined a metal boot scraper by the front door, a stack of logs and an accordion playing *Heimatlieder* in the back garden.

There was a sausage stall at the foot of Veste Coburg, where I had a *Currywurst* and a bread roll before climbing the path to the castle. Inside the fortress I visited the wood-panelled rooms where Martin Luther lived between April and October 1530 during the Diet of Augsburg. Outlawed in Catholic Bavaria since the Diet of Worms nine years earlier, the reformer had to remain in Saxony, the state to which Coburg belonged at the time. He had a suite of rooms with a view north towards the Thuringian Forest. The cawing of crows and jackdaws disturbed him at his work, but he still managed to fire off daily missives to his representatives in Augsburg, as well as composing psalms and sermons and working on translations of Aesop's Fables and the Holy Bible.

A portrait of Luther from the studio of Lucas Cranach the Elder hung in the reformer's study. Cranach lived in Veste Coburg during the autumn of 1506, producing woodcuts and murals of hunting scenes for his patron Elector Frederick the Wise. Around thirty works by Cranach were on display in the Steinerne Kemenate of the castle, among them several portraits of the heavy-jowled, square-bearded, ermine-robed Electors Frederick the Wise, John the Steadfast and John Frederick the Magnanimous of Saxony. Cranach was obsessed with *The Suicide of Lucretia*, a subject he painted in almost forty versions. Two of them were on display in the gallery. Both depicted a pale, anguished woman drawing a dagger to her breast, frozen in the split second before it penetrates her skin. Her plain, round face and pinned-up hair indicated a personification of chastity. The painting on display entitled *Dido, the Queen of Carthage,* attributed to the studio of Cranach the Elder, was more suggestive. The queen was wearing a fur-trimmed, gold-coloured robe above a white undergarment which had slipped down to reveal her breasts. She had already plunged the dagger into her chest, yet there was a coquettish tilt to her head and a come-hither expression on her face, which seemed to encourage an erotic response in the viewer. Eve, in Cranach's painting of *Adam and Eve*, had half a bush clamped between her legs in order to protect her pudenda. But her swollen belly, and the vertical gash in the trunk of the Tree of the Knowledge of Good and Evil, suggested things had already gone much further than a single bite of the apple would ordinarily make possible. Cranach's tiny, medallion-like painting of a *Reclining Nymph*, asleep on a river bank between a stag and a beaver, was, according to its description, the first depiction in Germany of a naked woman (or girl, in this case) out of doors.

The Bavarian State Exhibition in the rooms of Veste Coburg was devoted to the theme of the Reformation, this being the five hundredth anniversary of Martin Luther nailing his ninety-five theses to the door of the Schlosskirche in Wittenberg. A panel at the end of the exhibition noted that the annual Reformation Day public holiday (observed in Protestant regions of Germany) was appropriated by the National Socialists for propaganda purposes. Luther was hailed as a man of "urdeutscher Charakter", whose anti-Semitic writings were used, by Himmler among others, to legitimise *Kristallnacht* and the persecution of the Jews. The City of Nuremberg presented a first edition of Luther's *On the Jews and Their Lies* to Julius Streicher on the occasion of his birthday in 1937. Streicher's newspaper *Der Stürmer* described the treatise as the most radically anti-Semitic tract ever published. Luther did indeed advocate burning synagogues, seizing Jewish money and property, enslaving the Jews as forced labourers or expelling them. "We are at fault in not slaying them," he wrote. Luther's apologists argue that the reformer was *mis*appropriated by the National Socialists, as his position on the Jews was religious rather than racial.

Coburg was an early stronghold of National Socialism: the first town to elect a Nazi mayor and a council with a Nazi majority, the first to fly the swastika flag from its town hall and the first to award the freedom of the town to Adolf Hitler – all long before the National Socialists had seized power. Hitler was no stranger to the place. He visited "dear old Coburg", as he described it, on fourteen occasions between 1922 and 1937. His first visit to the "Erste nationalsozialistische Stadt Deutschlands" was in October 1922, for the third "Deutscher Tag" organised by the Deutschvölkischer Schutz- und Trutzbund (German Nationalist Protection and Defiance Federation), a union of right-wing extremists. Hitler had been invited to attend and was expected to bring a handful of his NSDAP followers with him. He turned up at the station with six to eight hundred stormtroopers, almost the entire membership of the SA at the time. The parade had been banned by the local police, but Hitler ignored the ban and commanded his supporters to unfurl their banners, strike up their music and march into the town. Local socialists and communists attacked the parade, but were beaten back by the fists and truncheons of the stormtroopers. The police joined in on the side of the NSDAP and the "reds" were routed. The "March on Coburg" was remembered as a defining moment in the history of the Nazi movement. Ten years later the Coburg Badge, one of the highest decorations awarded by the regime, was struck in commemoration of the brawl. The motto engraved in its wreath read "MIT HITLER IN COBURG 1922–1932". Back in 1922 the exhausted stormtroopers, flushed with victory, dossed down for the night on straw billets in the Altes Schützenhaus, a nineteenth-century gymnasium which I passed on my way into the centre of the town.

I entered the Altstadt through the Judentor and walked up Judengasse, wondering what fate befell the Jews of Coburg. I emerged in the Markt, one of the finest town squares in Germany. The Rathaus displayed a baroque façade of sky blue and pale orange, encrusted with scrolls and garlands. The Stadthaus opposite was built between 1597 and 1601 as a chancellery for Duke Johann Casimir of Saxe-Coburg. Its lucarne gables, edged with carmine sandstone, were topped with obelisks and statuettes of *Landsknechte* bearing pikestaffs. An archway into its courtyard was embellished with the heraldic shield of the duke, supported by two golden lions. Above the shield a trio of crowned, visored helmets sprouted trif-fid-like antennae and a Moor's head wrapped in a turban. In the spandrels above the arch were the yellow, black and green Saxon shield of the House of Wettin (the ancestral dynasty of the Saxe-Coburgs) and the red-and-white-striped Ludovingian lion of Hesse and Thuringia. (Coburg's confusing history has placed it, at various times, as an outpost of Saxony, as the capital of a Thuringian micro-state and, since a plebiscite in 1919, on the northern fringes of Franconia-Bavaria.) On the east side of the marketplace was the Gothic Hof-Apotheke, once known as "Zum gold-enen Strauß" (The Golden Ostrich). The faded murals on the front of the pharmacy depicted the arms of the House of Wettin and a likeness of Cyriakus Schnauß, the apothecary who founded the business in 1543. If you look closely, you can see a tiny relief, the size of a single brick, which illustrates the golden ostrich. Like Dürer and his rhinoceros, the artist had clearly never seen a real ostrich. This bird was a cross between a dragon and a swan, and was in the process of devouring a man. Only the unfortunate fellow's legs remained visible.

Pennants in the colours of the European Union, the Federal Republic, Bavaria and Coburg hung in the still, hot air above the Fountain of the Green Tree in a corner of the square. The town's yellow and white banner was emblazoned with a Negro's head in honour of Coburg's patron saint Mauritius, an Egyptian Moor who is often wrongly portrayed as a black African. The black Moor with his large gold earring was regarded by the National Socialist town councillors of the 1930s as an affront to the racial homogeneity of the nation. They replaced the emblem with a black and yellow sword and shield, with a swastika in the pommel of the sword. Mohrenstraße (Moor's Street) was renamed Straße der SA, but the town's manhole covers, which feature a prominent Moor's head, were left as they were. A statue of Prince Albert in the centre of the square portrays Queen Victoria's consort in the regalia of a Knight of the Garter. In one hand he holds a marshal's baton, in the other an architectural plan for the Crystal Palace exhibition hall. A circle of fountains in the paving stones around him spurted into action at regular intervals, providing temporary relief from the heat for the boys and girls who disported themselves beneath its jets. The smell of *Bratwurst* being grilled over pine cones emanated from a mobile sausage stand. Another van arrived for tomorrow's Saturday market, towing a mobile stall advertising *Pferdewurst*.

On the edge of the Altstadt was the Ehrenburg, a royal palace rebuilt in the early nineteenth century by Karl Friedrich Schinkel in a style which, in Britain, would be termed Jacobethan – a Downton Abbey for the Saxe-Coburgs. A statue of Duke Ernst I of Saxe-Coburg and Gotha, dressed in the uniform of the 7th Prussian Cuirassier Regiment, stood in the middle of a garden at the centre of Schlossplatz. Ernst I fought against Napoleon at the Battle of the Nations, although he is not commemorated by a plaque on the walls of the Befreiungshalle. He was perhaps better known as a "shameless syphilitic rake" who, together with his French mistress, conducted orgies in the ducal residences. Ernst I died in 1844 and was succeeded by his eldest son. Like his father, Ernst II was a military man, fond of shooting rallies, and "a mighty hunter of wine, women and song" whose "lower teeth, like those of a bulldog, protruded far beyond his upper ones". An equestrian statue of the duke stood on the lower slopes of the Hofgarten, overlooking Schlossplatz. With his spiked helmet, bristling moustache and pugnacious jaw line, he looked every inch the caricature of a Prussian Junker.

On the far side of Schlossplatz the audience was arriving for a performance of Schiller's *Wallenstein* trilogy in the Landestheater, one of two identical neoclassical theatres built in Coburg and Gotha during the reign of Duke Ernst I. The one in Gotha was destroyed in the Second World War; this one survived, since Coburg, far removed from major centres of population, was largely untouched by the war. During the Cold War period it found itself backed up against the Iron Curtain, lost in the hinterlands of West Germany. Bypassed by the currents of modern life, Coburg still feels like a throwback to a quieter, slower age. There is something quintessentially German about it – in a traditional, unspoilt, old-fashioned way.

Spread out beneath a canopy of oak and ash trees on the other side of Theaterplatz was the Prinzregenten beer garden, where several hundred Coburgers were celebrating the end of the working week by downing glasses of *Weißbier*, dark Tucher beer or Sylvaner wine. I queued at a counter for the *Tagesgericht* of *Bismarckheringe mit Bratkartoffeln*, which came with chives and onion, swimming in vinegar. I found a bench to sit on, sharing a table with a young couple having a drink with their parents. The girl's white, classical Greek-style shift dress was tied with a cord around her waist, and showed off her tanned limbs. Her face was finely sculpted, with high cheekbones and blue eyes. Her blonde hair was braided into a circlet. I was tempted to ask if she had been in *Triumph of the Will*. For some reason the title of Walter Abish's novel *How German Is It* came to mind. Maybe this was how German it is. Then, as if on cue, one of those travelling journeymen arrived, a middle-aged man dressed in a short black jacket, bell-bottomed black corduroy trousers, black waistcoat, broad-brimmed black hat, lots of buttons and a single gold earring. He had a little bedding roll strapped to his back and carried a walking stick carved into a spiral. He hailed from Kiel and had been "auf der Walz" (on the road) for two *Wanderjahre* – in Romania and Andalusia, among other places. He was now on his way to Schweinfurt, doing odd jobs to pay his way, or doing the rounds of beer gardens in order to collect money for his *Abendbrot*. I gave him a euro and wished him "Gute Reise".

I was "oben". Everyone in Bayreuth understands what that means. People go "nach oben". Up there. To the green hill. The Festspielhaus. I was on the terrace of Wolfgang-Wagner-Platz in front of the Festival Theatre, trying to keep cool beneath the shade of a lime tree. It was early, an hour and a half yet before the curtain rose on *Das Rheingold*. The atmosphere was hushed, as if no one dared raise their voice. People were observing each other, hoping to recognise a celebrity or a familiar face. Some looked twice at me, wondering who I was. I wandered around the terrace, clutching my second glass of prosecco, my stomach full of bubbles, trying not to break wind or stare too pointedly at the stupendous cleavages on display. I was glad I'd decided to wear black tie: it made me feel as if I belonged in this exalted company. The most elegantly dressed Wagnerites were the Japanese, women in sheaths of champagne silk, men in embroidered waistcoats. The worst dressed, myself excepted, were the British, in shapeless suits or rumpled linen jackets. Germans of both sexes and all ages power dressed, exuding authority and entitlement.

Below the terrace was a garden, at the head of which was a bust of Richard Wagner – big, bold, expressive, overly smooth, almost cartoonish.

There were steles around the garden in memory of "silenced voices", singers who for one reason or another had their operatic career at Bayreuth curtailed. Cosima Wagner would not countenance the Master's works being defiled by musicians of "Israelite impurity". Many singers who had performed Wagnerian roles at opera houses in Berlin, Vienna and London were turned down by Bayreuth for being insufficiently "Christian". A later generation of Jewish or homosexual singers, although free to perform at Bayreuth, were confronted, after the rise of National Socialism, with a fate worse than missing a gig at the Festspielhaus.

I returned to the bust of Wagner and read the sign beneath it. The head was sculpted in 1986 by Arno Breker, the celebrated National Socialist whose works I had seen exhibited in Schwerin. Having been successfully denazified after the war, Breker continued to attract noteworthy patrons – the City of Bayreuth, in this case – well into his dotage. The sign read: "Breker and his style were particularly admired by the National Socialist leaders. Described as 'sculpted ethos' and 'the shape of ideology', his work is characteristic of the art of the Third Reich. Nevertheless, he received numerous commissions even after 1945, and primarily sculpted busts of famous personalities." The fact that his sculpture of Wagner towers over a garden dedicated to the memory of singers ostracised by the National Socialists, some of whom were murdered in concentration camps, did not seem entirely appropriate. Nevertheless...

A fanfare from the balcony of the Festspielhaus summoned the audience inside. We assembled in the sloping auditorium, beneath a blue and gold ceiling supported by Corinthian columns. Men commented on the lack of air-conditioning and debated whether to remove their tuxedos; women took selfies before settling onto the hard, wooden seats. The house lights dimmed. Silence.

A long E flat from invisible strings announces the beginning of the world – the primeval sludge at the bottom of the Rhine. The curtain rises on the Golden Motel, a sleazy roadside establishment in 1970s Texas. A trio of white trash hookers sprawl on sun loungers around a cheap suburban pool. Woglinde and Wellgunde get to their feet occasionally to hang a bra or thong on a washing line. Their pimp Alberich, in a beat-up leather jacket and coonskin leggings, is drunkenly attempting to roger Flosshilde as she sings of the gold that glitters and gleams beneath the waters of the Rhine.

The stage rotates to reveal a gas station at which a Mercedes convertible is pulling up. The gods pile out of the car and disport themselves in a boudoir above the diner, followed all the while by a roving cameraman.

An anachronistic sign offering "FREE wi-fi" notwithstanding, the vibe is pure mid-seventies, evocative of *The Man Who Fell to Earth* or retro movies such as *Boogie Nights* and *The People vs. Larry Flint*. Wotan and Loge are Hugh Hefner and Larry Flint, Jr.; Freya and Fricka ageing Playmates or Penthouse Pets. The star of the show is a non-singing actor who plays no part in Wagner's opera; a pill-popping, chain-smoking gofer in a silver bomber jacket who runs the motel and serves in the diner – a Danny DeVito to Mime's Jack Nicholson. After a while I realised that the close-ups on a digital screen above the stage were being filmed in real time by an actor following the action with a camcorder. It was clever, but confusing. Trying to follow a retro-noir movie at the same time as listening to a Wagner opera is a challenge. The cinematic dimension adds an extra layer of *Kunst* to Wagner's *Gesamtkunstwerk*, but too much *Kunst* detracts from the singing.

Another set of non-Wagnerian characters arrive – rent boys in tiny black leather briefs and calf-length cowboy boots, and groupies in Californian bikinis – and spend the rest of the opera jiving in slow motion on the floor of the diner. The video trickery allows Alberich, wearing the *Tarnhelm*, to turn into a real serpent, a python which slithers over blocks of wooden Rheingold. I found this unnecessarily literal. When the gods enter Valhalla, their rainbow bridge is represented by the rainbow flag of the LGBT community. The gentleman from Barcelona sitting next to me whispered: "We are grown-ups now. We don't need this shit. Maybe it was fun in the 1980s to *épater les bourgeois*, but now we would just like to listen to the music." At last the gas station goes dark and the stage is illuminated by a single image on the video screen of the Rhinemaidens swimming through clear blue water (an image borrowed, perhaps, from the cover of Nirvana's *Nevermind* album).

Wagner's power chords reached their climax and the curtain fell. There was some booing, presumably for the theatrical director and stage designer. Curtain calls completed, the house lights came on and the audience relaxed. Body odours filled the auditorium. I was glad to get outside and breathe some fresh air.

Rheingold is relatively short, and it was still light in the Richard-Wagner-Park outside. I visited the second garden below the terrace, where there was a bust of Cosima Wagner on a herm, also sculpted by Arno Breker – smooth, monumental, with Breker's trademark hollowed-out eyes. At the foot of the park I turned into Gontardstraße, a street of detached family houses, each one reminiscent of the villa built for Leni Riefenstahl I had seen in Berlin. Plastered in white, with angular metal porches, wooden doors, metal grilles over the windows, wooden shutters, stone window frames arched in the prescribed National Socialist style, steep tiled roofs with that little swing outwards at the base of the roof – these were pure Third Reich, posh *völkisch* family dwellings. There was a whole estate of them along Gontardstraße, Felix-Mottl-Straße and Heinrich-Schütz-Straße, the name of each street indicated by a sign in Gothic script. I sometimes wonder what it would be like to have lived in Germany in 1937. For a moment, I felt as if I was actually there. Or maybe I had drunk too much prosecco.

T he curtain rises on Act One of *Die Walküre* to reveal Hunding's Hut, a vast barn of wooden beams overlooked by a watchtower. The video screen is now in silent film mode, with Sieglinde as Lillian Gish, fluttering her eyelashes and looking aghast at Siegmund's appearance. On Wotan's arrival the video changes to an early propaganda film about the discovery of oil in the Soviet Union. In Act Two Wotan appears as a Soviet commissar in charge of an agro-industrial collective, a dilapidated factory strewn with oil drums, chains, pipes and primitive food-processing machinery. Numerous non-Wagnerian characters toil in the background, ordered to work at a Stakhanovite pace by the leader of the gods. In Act Three Hunding's Hut has been transformed into an oil rig, complete with nodding donkey and railway track. Judging by the red star above the factory and the Turkic slogans, we were now in Soviet Azerbaijan. I was beginning to figure out a leitmotif running through the production – gas station, oil well, black gold, oil as a contemporary take on Rhine gold as the source of greed and treachery which lies at the heart of the tetralogy. The Ride of the Valkyries lacks its usual ethereal quality – and its horses. An octet of plump chorus girls rushes up and down the gantries of the oil rig. This is no aerial cavalcade, and these are no warrior maidens; but by now it has become apparent that the director is wilfully sabotaging Wagner's big scenes. The nodding donkey is cranked up and trundled along the railway track to the front of the stage, where it begins to dip up and down over the orchestra pit, causing the winding gear in the cage beneath it to rotate. It forms an unusual counterpoint to the tender parting of Wotan and Brünnhilde. I detected some more booing during the curtain calls, directed mainly at the Valkyries.

In the second interval I changed seats with the wife of the gentleman from Barcelona, so that she could sit next to her husband. They had booked late and had been unable to get two seats together. Josep invited me for a glass of champagne on the terrace outside. He was an alpha male Catalan, relaxed and confident in jeans and an open-necked shirt. He ran a factory manufacturing air-conditioning units and pooh-poohed the argument propounded by the Wagner family that the sound of air-conditioning in the Festival Theatre would detract from the audience's enjoyment of the music. His wife Teresa, who spoke German with a thick Catalan accent, merchandised art books in Barcelona galleries. She worked for one of the publishers I used to represent. "It's a small world," she remarked.

Monday morning. A day off from Wagner. I didn't have to go "nach oben". Back to normality. Ordinary people were going about their everyday routines. I walked into the centre of Bayreuth, keeping to the shaded side of the street. I crossed the Roter Main to the Rotmainhalle, a market hall built in 1935. A fresco on the front of the building was the work of Oskar Martin-Amorbach, painter of peasants tilling swastika-shaped furrows in the fields of National Socialism. Here there were fishermen, ploughmen, shepherds and a milkmaid wielding rakes and ploughshares as they brought home the harvest of the Third Reich. I walked through the Mühltürlein into Maximilianstraße, where a double row of plane trees provided some shelter from the midday sun. Working people were having lunch (Wagnerites were still on brunch) beneath the sunshades sprawling over the marketplace. Down the centre of the street were baroque fountains of Neptune and Hercules and a maypole, striped in the red and white of Franconia and decorated with emblems of the town's tradespeople – roofers, carpenters, masons, smiths, car mechanics, locksmiths, plumbers, barbers, tailors, butchers and bakers. Rather disappointingly, there were no musicians or singers. The Reichshof displayed the double-headed eagle of the Holy Roman Empire in a stone plaque above its door; the Mohren-Apotheke had enamel medallions of Moorish heads set into its windows. I wondered whether they had to be removed whenever Hitler was in town. I went into the chemist to buy some dental floss. I didn't know what to ask for in German, so I tried a literal translation: "Zahnfaden" or "Zähnefaden". Then I showed the assistant a piece of thread and mimed pulling it through my teeth.

"Oh, Floss," she said. "Ja, Floss. Genau."

I turned off Maximilianstraße into Kanzleistraße. The main post office, built during the *Kaiser-Zeit*, displayed its original inscriptions – "Post Telegraph Telephon" – from the days when these new-fangled inventions were still spelt with a French "*ph*". I passed the long, flax-coloured range of the baroque chancellery of the margraves, now the seat of the Upper Franconian Government, and a row of sixteenth-century mansions in pink Franconian sandstone with crooked oriels and undulating gables. The Seckendorffer Haus was now a lavender-painted funeral parlour, the Nanckenreuther Haus a tavern which served *Braunbier*. The Lutheran Stadtkirche opposite had twin Gothic towers connected by a stone bridge, a feature borrowed from the Marienkirche in Halle and the Stadtkirche of Wittenberg, and replicated in the fantastical cathedrals painted by Schinkel. The interior of the church was cool and bright, its pristine white walls set off with arches and web vaulting of pink sandstone. Attached to a pillar was a bronze plaque commemorating the removal and destruction, in 2004, of a medieval *Judensau*, one of many such anti-Semitic sculptures which may still be found on the walls of German churches.

Over breakfast in the hotel I read an article on the front page of the *Nordbayerische Kurier* about a new sauna in Bayreuth which thousands of people paid huge amounts of money to visit, in some cases four times in a week. It took me a couple of minutes before I realised it was a spoof. This was the hottest day of the Festspiele. Beneath my tuxedo I was dripping with sweat before I'd even arrived at the Festival Theatre. The auditorium was cool, but had no air-conditioning, and I sat in a cold, clammy shirt throughout the first act of *Siegfried*.

The stage set is a parody of Mount Rushmore, with giant sculpted heads of Marx, Lenin, Stalin and Mao. Siegfried rushes in, towing a bear on a rope behind him. The bear turns out to be the factotum from *Rheingold*. He smears himself in oil. In Act Two we are transported to Berlin Alexanderplatz circa 1989 – S-Bahn, Centrum department store, Minol petrol station, World Clock. The dancers from the gas station in *Rheingold* turn up and try on some new western fashions, until they are chased away by a biotronic crocodile. Maybe this is the dragon. No, Fafnir is in human form and is killed by a hail of bullets from a Kalashnikov. Siegfried then courts and dances with a woodbird dressed for the Rio carnival. In Act

Three we remain in Alexanderplatz. The Wanderer is drinking wine, eating a plate of spaghetti and smoking a cigarette. He stubs his fag out in the pasta and summons Erda. On his command "Hinab! Hinab!" she fellates him. Meanwhile Siegfried discovers Brünnhilde and the heads of the communist dictators light up, as if Brünnhilde's awakening signals a revolution of the proletariat. The opera concludes back in Alexanderplatz, where the passionate duet between the hero and the Valkyrie is upstaged by seven biotronic crocodiles. One of them gobbles down the woodbird, but Siegfried manages to rescue her from the reptile's jaws. He then proceeds to flirt with her and forgets Brünnhilde. By this stage we had rather lost sight of Wagner's leitmotifs – ring, fire, sword and spear, blood and water. It's fine to deconstruct the *Ring*, but it helps if you reconstruct it in a coherent way. The crocodiles got a curtain call. No one booed them.

Götterdämmerung. I was now getting into a routine: rise late; brunch in the hotel; hang out in coffee bars in the town centre; return to the hotel and change into black tie; a glass of prosecco in the hotel lobby; shuttle bus to the Festival Theatre; *Kaffee und Kuchen* in the first interval; a glass of white wine in the second interval; walk back to the hotel for a cold beer and supper (smoked salmon or roast beef with olive oil and remoulade) in the bar; listen to the other guests (a ruddy-faced and slightly sleazy British gentleman wearing a tailored three-piece suit, an elderly New York lesbian, an aristocratic family from Hamburg and a skinny French woman who doesn't touch alcohol) sounding off about Wagner.

The prelude to *Twilight of the Gods* opens with a trio of bag ladies on the streets of New York City. The Norns are practising voodoo with shrunken heads, sticking pins in chickens and examining their entrails, smearing themselves in blood. The threads of fate break and the supremacy of the gods unravels. I timed Act One at two hours plus, during which the humidity in the auditorium must have risen by several degrees. Curtain calls accounted for a further ten minutes. When the doors opened, people were almost trampling on each other in their eagerness to reach some fresh air.

I wandered down to the Richard Wagner Garden, hoping to catch a whiff of breeze coming up through the trees of the park. I was joined on my bench by an elegant woman of uncertain age clad in walnut-brown fishnet stockings and a sheer top which made it obvious, from the back at least, that she wasn't wearing a bra. She expressed dismay at the length of the first act as she had, like me, assumed that Siegfried's disguised seduction of Brünnhilde would take place in Act Two. She worked for an energy company in Essen and extolled the cultural virtues of the Ruhrgebiet, describing theatre and opera performances which, in their raw industrial realism, were the antithesis of the Bayreuther Festspiele. On my own subject of book publishing, she apologised for possessing a Kindle, but told me she occasionally ordered real books from her local independent bookshop in Essen. "The Heinrich-Heine Buchhandlung?" I asked. "Ja, genau," she exclaimed. "Es ist eine kleine Welt." ("It's a small world.")

The gossip in the second interval was whether the director Hans Castorf would turn up for a curtain call, this being the final year of his production. Act Three opens at the entrance to a U-Bahn station (tiled in authentically urinous yellow) in Berlin. There are blood-stained garments on a clothes rack and a black girl talking to a tramp. The audience gasps as the gofer, on the video screen, slashes open a bag of cocaine, rubs his face in it, slices his finger open with a meat knife and smears himself with blood. Dressed in black leather, the Rhinemaidens start throwing the clothes around. Siegfried slaps the black girl and beats up the tramp. Siegfried, Hagen and Gunther dry-hump the Rhinemaidens. Simulated sex and gratuitous violence had become the leitmotifs of this production. I found myself longing for the existential *Ring* productions of Wieland and Wolfgang Wagner – with just the fire, the ring, the empty stage and the curvature of the earth – but hey or "Hoiho! Hoiho hoihe!" we're in the twenty-first century now. Audiences have shorter attention spans; they demand sensation; they want beer, cocaine, Cadillacs, blowjobs and crocodiles. They want globalisation and political correctness – an LGBT Valhalla, a token black girl, Baku, Route 66, Berlin Alexanderplatz and the New York Stock Exchange.

In a scene stolen from Tarantino's *Jackie Brown*, the gofer is thrown into the boot of a car. Siegfried is clubbed to death with a baseball bat. Brünnhilde opens a door in the wings and a real bat flies out and flits around the auditorium. This is neither in Wagner's libretto nor, one assumes, an intended part of Castorf's production. It's a *Fledermaus* which has found itself in the wrong opera. While aurally magnificent, Brünnhilde's immolation is visually as incoherent as the rest of the production. The stage rotates between the Buna Chemical Works in Schkopau and the New York Stock Exchange. Hagen dies on the video screen but remains alive on stage, trying to fish the burning ring out of a flaming brazier. The Rhinemaidens rearrange some paintings on the walls of the Stock Exchange. Brünnhilde pours petrol on everything around her, but fails to set it alight. At the end she wanders off rather aimlessly. No zombie Siegfried. No funeral pyre. No horse. No Rhine. The world doesn't end. Bravos for the singers and musicians. Boos for Hans Castorf, particularly from the mild-mannered man and his mousy wife in the seats next to mine; a couple who had sat in silence for the previous sixteen hours and were now letting rip their disapproval of the blowjobs and crocodiles with booming German boos – "Buh! Buh!" I rushed back to the hotel for a shower.

Finale

The House of Skulls

On Friday morning I drove from Valhalla to Walhalla: from Wagner's hall of dead heroes in Bayreuth to a hall of dead Germans built by King Ludwig I of Bavaria on a hill above the Danube. Walhalla doesn't look anything like Valhalla. Valhalla would be a tithe barn of oak beams decorated with wolf skins and runic inscriptions, peopled by heroic warriors and nubile Valkyries; Göring and Streicher both modelled their country residences on this template. Walhalla looks more like the Parthenon: like an English bank, a French museum or an Italian government ministry. Walhalla is a peripteros, a temple in the ancient Greek style surrounded by a peristyle of Doric columns. It was named by the Swiss historian Johannes von Müller, chosen by Ludwig to advise him on the building of a pantheon to commemorate German men and women of outstanding merit. Müller compiled an initial list of one hundred illustrious Teutons, whose busts would be displayed around the walls of the temple – and included himself.

Ludwig was a Bavarian patriot rather than a German nationalist. The idea of Germany as a nation had lost much of its significance following the dissolution of the Holy Roman Empire in 1806. *Deutschtum* was defined mainly by language: by membership of the German-speaking world. Ludwig's fixation with Germanness had little to do with a unified, centralised nation state. He was no Bismarck, no Hitler. He was fascinated by the diversity of the Germanic world, by a fatherland which embraced Prussians, Austrians, Saxons, Swabians, Rhinelanders, Bohemians, Tyrolese and, beyond the borders of the High German-speaking world, the Dutch and Anglo-Saxons. If the Befreiungshalle above Kelheim was to reflect his nostalgia for the "tribes", the peoples or nations which constituted the Germanic world, then Walhalla, its twin, would celebrate the individuals who made that world great.

Walhalla preceded the Hall of Liberation by two decades. Ludwig conceived the initial idea for a "pantheon of the Germans" in 1807, when the nation was in disarray, its identity obliterated by French hegemony. In 1816 he commissioned his fellow philhellene Leo von Klenze to design a suitable building. The foundation stone was laid on 18 October 1830, an anniversary of the Battle of the Nations which had begun the process of restoring Germany's national identity. Walhalla was unveiled exactly twelve years later on 18 October 1842. The consecration of what was, in effect, Germany's first national monument was not quite the nationwide celebration Ludwig had envisaged. The conservative, papist cabinet of the Bavarian government had vetoed the idea of a national celebration and specifically banned a bust of Martin Luther from taking its rightful place among the ninety-six other busts mounted on the walls of the Hall of Fame in preparation for its grand opening. (Luther was eventually admitted in 1848, following Ludwig's abdication and the demise of Bavaria's ultramontane government.)

The unveiling of Walhalla ended up as a provincial Bavarian affair characterised by some dodgy costumes and clunky verse. Ludwig was greeted on the steps of the monument by a maiden dressed as Germania, who proceeded to address the king with a panegyric replete with references to fame, glory, might, pride, freedom, joy and victory. She bade him accept "die Krone Beharrlichkeit" (the crown of perseverance), echoing the epithet of "beharrlich" (persistent) I had seen engraved on statues of the king in Kelheim and Munich. There followed a procession of thirty-two young women representing the genii of the German states; and a male voice choir who intoned "heroic lays" in praise of "bold victors" and "noble warriors", "German spirit" and "German fame", "German greatness" and the "German fatherland". Ludwig gave a speech in which he repeated lines from the preface of a guide to the *Walhalla-Genossen* he had written in 1829: "Rühmlich ausgezeichneten Teutschen als Denkmal und darum Walhalla, auf daß teutscher der Teutsche aus ihr trete besser als er gekommen", the tortuous syntax of which means something like "Walhalla stands as a monument to the most notably distinguished Germans, from which the German will emerge more German than he was before he entered". On the following day the bards and bigwigs moved upstream to Kelheim, to celebrate the laying of the foundation stone of Ludwig and Klenze's sister monument, the Befreiungshalle.

I entered Walhalla. My first impressions were similar to those I experienced on first entering the Hall of Liberation: marble walls the colour of jellied veal or corned beef; a blue and gold coffered ceiling and a white, gold-starred floor; thrones, candlesticks and statues of winged Victories scattered around the edge. The main difference was in the shape: this was a shoe box, in contrast to the hat box of the Befreiungshalle. Silhouetted against the opisthodomos at the far end of the hall was a statue of Ludwig I as Caesar, seated on a marble throne, his arms resting on a pair of Bavarian lions. Above him was a frieze sculpted by Martin von Wagner, which depicted the history of the Germanic peoples, from their migration from the East to their Christianisation by St Boniface in the Early Middle Ages. On the upper walls were sixty-four marble tablets commemorating the first generation of famous Teutons, those poets and warlords of whom no authoritative likenesses remain: Hermann, Odoaker, Chlodwig, Widekind and Charlemagne; the Anglo-Saxons Hengist, Horsa, Egbert and Alfred the Great; Hildegard of Bingen, Walther von der Vogelweide, Wolfram von Eschenbach, Elizabeth of Thuringia, the anonymous poet of the *Nibelungenlied* and an assortment of Goths, Ostrogoths, Visigoths, Vandals and Batavians. At intervals along the cornice were caryatids, towering Pallas Athenae robed in Bavarian blue and white; sisters of the handmaidens who bear the names of the German peoples around the exterior of the Befreiungshalle. Like the Valkyries in Wagner's *Ring*, they provided a link between the world of men and the realm of the gods, for above them, in the pediments supporting the ceiling, were black and gold bas-reliefs illustrating the rise and fall of the Germanic deities, accompanied by a bestiary of swans, eagles, wolves, serpents and squirrels.

And so to the busts, those white marble likenesses of one hundred and thirty eminent Germans, arranged in two horizontal rows on the walls. The veterans of the upper row were mounted on individual consoles; later scions were lined up on shelves below them. The first faces I recognised belonged to Dürer, Luther, Beethoven, Bach and Wagner. These grandees all have quite distinctive features, and I am more familiar with musicians and artists than I am with rulers and military men. A second scan of the hall revealed Bismarck, Kaiser Wilhelm I (labelled here "Wilhelm der Siegreiche") and Anton Bruckner. I would probably have recognised Frederick the Great, had it not been for the laurel wreath wrapped around his head. And that was it – the sum of my conversance with illustrious

Germans. Bruckner, incidentally, was the only distinguished (honorary) German to be inducted into the Hall of Fame during the Third Reich. Hitler personally visited the monument on 6 June 1937 to unveil the bust of his favourite symphonic composer. He was accompanied by Goebbels, who gave a speech playing down Bruckner's Austrian-Catholic character, claiming him instead as a "shoot of peasant stock", a German "Kantor" in the tradition of Bach.

Thereafter I was reduced to checking the names below the busts in order to identify the faces. Embarrassingly, I had failed to recognise the likenesses of Mozart (who was not wearing his customary wig), Goethe (sculpted here as a young man: I would surely have recognised an older likeness of him), Schubert (not wearing his trademark spectacles), Brahms (here without his usual excess of facial hair) and Einstein (whose hair was too smooth: it was presumably too difficult to sculpt his "mad scientist" look). Schubert was a relatively late entrant, inducted in 1928; Brahms, surprisingly, was a very late inductee, added as recently as 2000. There were a number of royal figures I half-recognised from paintings of Holy Roman Emperors I had seen in Goslar, Frankfurt and Nuremberg: Friedrich I Barbarossa, Henry the Lion, the "Stupor Mundi" Friedrich II, August the Strong of Saxony and Catherine the Great of Russia, who began life as Princess Sophie of Anhalt-Zerbst. Less embarrassingly, I failed to identify Kant, Schiller, Haydn, Erasmus, Copernicus (one in the eye for the Poles), Gutenberg (whom I mistook for Emperor Charles IV on account of his two-pointed beard), Konrad Adenauer and Richard Strauss. I should have recognised Kant as I had seen a copy of his bust, sculpted by Johann Gottfried Schadow, in the tower of the Königsberger Dom.

I vaguely recognised the two most recent inductees to the pantheon: they turned out to be Heinrich Heine and Sophie Scholl. Heine, added in 2010 (he was not the first Jew in Walhalla: Einstein was inducted in 1990), had a deliberate crack running across his face and body in recognition of the fact he was a less than enthusiastic supporter of the Walhalla project at the time of its construction. In fact he satirised it as a "place of skulls" in a poem entitled *Lobgesang auf König Ludwig* ("Eulogy for King Ludwig"). Heine mocked the king as an "Art-Eunuch" surrounded by a "painted seraglio". (Ludwig did indeed commission a pavilion in the Palace of Nymphenburg to be hung with portraits of thirty-six of the most desirable lovelies of Munich.) He ridiculed the king's potted biographies of the *Walhalla-Genossen* as a catalogue of every German fraudster and mountebank "from Teut to Schinderhannes" (Teut being a travelling salesman and Schinderhannes a notorious highwayman). Heine went on to speculate that the "great poet" and "brave hero" Ludwig would be "canonised by the Pope" and "worshipped by apes and kangaroos". Most of the busts in the Hall of Fame confronted the viewer head on, but Heine's face was turned away, as if he wished he were somewhere else. As he unveiled the poet's bust, the President of the Bavarian Academy of Arts remarked that "Heinrich Heine doesn't need Walhalla, but Walhalla needs him".

Rather uncharitably, I couldn't help feeling that Sophie Scholl had been included as a token anti-Nazi and a token female. Apart from Catherine the Great, the only other women I could find were Maria Theresa of Austria and two recent additions: the Carmelite nun Edith Stein, who was murdered in Auschwitz; and the beatified nineteenth-century canoness Karolina Gerhardinger. There was no Königin Luise: she was presumably too Prussian for this Bavarian-Catholic Hall of Fame. I didn't expect to find busts of Ludwig II of Bavaria (too gay), Bertolt Brecht (too GDR) or Adolf Hitler (for obvious reasons), but I was disappointed at the absence of Lucas Cranach the Elder. Caspar David Friedrich and Thomas Mann were presumably too Baltic-Hanseatic, Marx and Engels too left-wing and Rosa Luxemburg too female, too left-wing, too Jewish and too Polish. Helmut Kohl had passed away a couple of weeks earlier, so I guessed his time would come in a couple of decades. (There is a rule that candidates must have been dead for at least twenty years before they can be considered for inclusion in Walhalla.)

Now for the interesting bit. Who on earth were the lawyer Iustus Moeser, the poets Gottfr. Aug. Buerger and Wilhelm Heinse, the scholar Iohann Müller, the "Künstler in Erz" Peter Fischer, Aegidius Tschudi, Goerres, H.S. von Hallwyl, Bruder Nikolaus von der Fluee, Eberhard im Bart, Walther von Plettenberg, Otto de Guerige and Nicolaus Ludewig Graf von Zinzendorf? What had these men achieved that they should be granted membership to this exclusive club – at the expense of, for example, Karl Friedrich Schinkel, Robert Schumann, Georg Hegel, Arthur Schopenhauer, Alexander von Humboldt or the Brothers Grimm?

I looked them up in my *Duden-Lexikon* when I returned home. Justus Möser was an eighteenth-century historian who "represented an organic view of history". He turned against the Enlightenment and the French Revolution in order to further the cause of German nationalism. Gottfried August Bürger was an eighteenth-century poet close to the Göttinger Hain, a circle of patriotic students who sought to free German poetry from the influence of the French Enlightenment and restore a tradition of simple folkloristic verse. Wilhelm Heinse was a poet of the *Sturm und Drang* movement who wrote the "lascivious romance" *Ardinghello oder die glückseligen Inseln*. Johann Müller (not to be confused with the Johannes von Müller who had assisted King Ludwig with the selection) was an astronomer of the German Renaissance, better known as Regiomontanus. Aegidius Tschudi, Bruder Nikolaus von der Flüe and Hans von Hallwyl were all Swiss, which probably explains why I had never heard of them. They were, respectively, a statesman of the Counter-Reformation, a mystic who became patron saint of the Swiss Confederation, and an officer who led the confederates in the Battle of Murten of 1746 against the Burgundians. Hallwyl sounded like a Swiss equivalent of Andreas Hofer, which alerted me to the absence of the Tyrolese freedom fighter from this German pantheon; until I realised Hofer's peasant rebellion was fought against the Bavarian Army which, at the time, was allied with Napoleon. Johann Joseph Görres was a scholar and journalist of the Romantic Movement, a critic of Napoleon (and of Prussia) who advocated a return to a united Germany under the rule of a Kaiser. Like Ludwig I, he was a nostalgist for the Holy Roman Empire. Eberhard im Bart (the Bearded) was a knight of the Order of the Holy Sepulchre who unified the Duchy of Württemberg, founded the University of Tübingen (and expelled all the Jews from his new state). Otto de Guerige turned out to be Otto von Guericke, a seventeenth-century burgomaster of Magdeburg who invented the vacuum pump; Nikolaus Ludwig was a Count of Zinzendorf and Pottendorf, a Pietist who founded the Moravian Church movement; and Wolter von Plettenberg was a Grand Master of the Livonian Order, an autonomous branch of the Teutonic Knights which ventured further up the Baltic coast and settled lands now belonging to Latvia and Estonia. He spent most of his life battling the Russians and, according to Wikipedia, died at the venerable age of eighty-five, sitting in a full suit of armour in a chair in front of a roaring fire.

This left Peter Fischer, whose bust was labelled "Künstler in Erz". I assumed that the "Erz" was an abbreviation of "Erzgebirge", which would render him an "artist in the Ore Mountains". This would be quite plausible, as Caspar David Friedrich painted scenes of the mountain range between Saxony and Bohemia. There was no entry for Peter Fischer in *Duden*. I tried Wikipedia, English and German versions. Nothing there either. I googled him. Nothing. Whoever he was, and whatever his merits, he was deemed more worthy of a place in this pantheon of august Germans than his fellow painters Matthias Grünewald, Albrecht Altdorfer, Cranach and Friedrich. Maybe his paintings of the Saxon-Bohemian uplands were popular in the 1830s, but failed to stand the test of time. Perhaps he was the Jack Vettriano of his age. Or maybe he was a joke, a Nat Tate, a non-existent figure included in order to fool the know-alls.[20]

On leaving the cold marble pallor of Walhalla, the natural colours of the landscape outside seem extraordinarily vibrant and intense – fields of shiny green maize and soft golden barley, shreds of pearly cloud drifting across an azure sky, and the sun sparkling on the surface of the Danube. Altdorfer painted the scene in the 1520s. In *Landschaft an der Donau bei Regensburg* dark conifers cover the rocky hillside beneath a mass of writhing storm clouds. A ploughed field snakes down towards the river, represented by a smudge of silvery light in the distance. Cut back to 2018 and there are logistics centres and recycling plants in the valley below, shopping malls alongside the motorway, a bright red football stadium and a television tower on the hills above Regensburg. A buzzard glides back and forth over the river; businessmen are driving home over a girder bridge; lorries are slowing for a *Stau* on the autobahn; tractors are bringing home the harvest. A group of tourists from northern Germany sit on the steps beside me. They open a bottle of wine.

"Prost."

"Chin-chin."

"Zum Wohl."

Everything is safe, solid, familiar; just as it should be.

"Alles Gute."

"Alles in Ordnung."

---

20 I discovered, after further research, that he was a typo. Peter Fischer was in fact Peter Vischer the Elder, a sculptor from Nuremberg, a contemporary of Dürer. The description "Künstler in Erz" referred to the fact that he worked in bronze, and had nothing to do with the Ore Mountains.

Acknowledgements

The literary inspiration for *The Ruins of the Reich* came initially from a quirky little book entitled *Zum Stolze der Nation* published in the *bibliophilen Taschenbücher* series, and kindly sold to me at trade discount by the Buchhandlung Walther König in Cologne. Written by Helmut Scharf, it documents the great patriotic monuments of nineteenth-century Germany, from Walhalla and the Hall of Liberation to the Monument to the Battle of the Nations.

The bible of National Socialist architecture is Helmut Weihsmann's monumental *Bauen unterm Hakenkreuz*, published in Vienna in 1998. It records every building constructed during the Third Reich, from *Gauforen* and *Thingstätten* to thousands of ordinary housing estates. As I found out to my cost, it gets the location of the Ordensburg "Falkenburg" wrong but, that apart, it is an impressive work.

Wilhelm Kreis was the one architect whose work spanned German history from the Wilhelmine Reich through the Weimar Republic to National Socialism and beyond. His Bismarck towers, department stores, museums, exhibition halls and banks formed a leitmotif to my travels. His megalomaniac projects for Hitler's Berlin and Nazi necropolises remained unrealised. The *catalogue raisonné* of his work published by Klinkhardt & Biermann in 1994 provides a thorough overview of his work.

Arno Breker's sculptures from the Third Reich remain under wraps unless they are displayed at exhibitions which specifically engage with National Socialism, such as the one I visited in Schwerin, whose catalogue *Zur Diskussion gestellt: der Bildhauer Arno Breker* offers a critical appraisal of his work. I encountered his pre-Nazi *Aurora* in Düsseldorf and his post-war busts of Richard and Cosima Wagner in Bayreuth.

On a personal level, I would like to thank Sally Osborn for her editorial work (and for identifying the Cockney Rebel song from which I stole a line), and Ian "Tobe" Moore for designing the maps and cover. The publishers Nicholas Brealey and Ion Mills offered useful advice and contacts, and I am grateful to Bill Godber and his team at Turnaround Publisher Services for taking care of sales and distribution.

Klaus-Jürgen Steffner, Renata Jonenaite and Justine Schmitt contributed ideas which found their way into the narrative. I never got round to reading the book about Alt Rehse published by its mayor Dr Wolfgang Köpp, but I am grateful to him for showing me around his village. Finally, I would like to remember my late brother Christopher, who accompanied me on my first visits to Český Krumlov and Kaliningrad.

Bibliography

Walter Abish, *How German Is It* (London, 1983)

Peter Adam, *The Arts of the Third Reich* (London, 1992)

Karl Arndt, Georg Friedrich Koch and Lars Olof Larsson (eds), *Albert Speer: Architektur* (Frankfurt am Main, 1995)

Oliver August, *Along the Wall and the Watchtowers* (London, 1999)

Fritz Backhaus, Raphael Gross, Sabine Kößling and Mirjam Wenzel, *The Judengasse in Frankfurt*, transl. Adam Blauhut and Michael Foster (Munich, 2016)

Karl Bartsch and Helmut de Boor (eds), *Das Nibelungenlied* (Wiesbaden, 1972)

Bauhaus-Universität Weimar, *Vergegenständlichte Erinnerung: Perspektiven einer janusköpfigen Stadt* (Weimar, 1999)

Vojtěch Blodig, *Terezín in the "Final Solution of the Jewish Question" 1941-1945* (Prague, 2003)

Wulff E. Brebeck, Frank Huismann, Kirsten John-Stucke and Jörg Piron (eds), *Endzeitkämpfer: Ideologie und Terror der SS* (Berlin and Munich, 2011)

Rudolf Conrades (ed.), *Zur Diskussion gestellt: der Bildhauer Arno Breker* (Schwerin, 2006)

Roman Czejarek, *Szczecin in Old Postcards*, transl. Monika Laskowska (Łódź, 2005)

Norman Davies, *Vanished Kingdoms: The History of Half-Forgotten Europe* (London, 2011)

Documentation Centre Party Rally Grounds, *Fascination and Terror* (Nuremberg, 2017)

Jens Malte Fischer, *Gustav Mahler*, transl. Stewart Spencer (London, 2011)

Bruno Flierl, *Schloss – Palast der Republik – Humboldt-Forum. Mitte Spreeinsel in Berlin – ein Ort historischer Brüche* (Berlin, 2009)

Günter Grass, *Crabwalk*, transl. Krishna Winston (London, 2003)

Marie Therese Hug, Prinzessin von Preußen (ed.), *Deutschland, Deutschland über alles: Der deutsche Kampf um Selbstbestimmung* (Munich, 1991)

Volker Kluge, *Olympiastadion Berlin: Rundgang durch das ehemalige Reichssportfeld* (Berlin, 2000)

Volker Knopf and Stefan Martens, *Görings Reich: Selbstinszenierungen in Carinhall* (Berlin, 1999)

Dr Wolfgang Köpp, *Alt-Rehse – Schau auf dieses Dorf* (Blankensee, 1999)

Kai Krauskopf, *Bismarckdenkmäler: Ein bizarrer Aufbruch in die Moderne* (Hamburg and Munich, 2002)

Brian Ladd, *The Ghosts of Berlin: Confronting German History in the Urban Landscape* (Chicago and London, 1997)

Iris Lauterbach, Julian Rosefeldt and Piero Steinle, *Bürokratie und Kult: Das Parteizentrum der NSDAP am Königsplatz in München* (Berlin and Munich, 1995)

Patrick Leigh Fermor, *A Time of Gifts* (London, 1977)

Rudolf Leopold, *Egon Schiele: Landscapes*, transl. John Gabriel (Munich, 2004)

Claudio Magris, *Danube*, transl. Patrick Creagh (London, 1989)

Christopher McIntosh, *The Swan King: Ludwig II of Bavaria* (London, 2003)

Jonathan Meades, "The Devil's Work" (*The Times Magazine*, 29 October 1994).

Sabrina Michielli (ed.), *BZ '18–'45: One Monument, One City, Two Dictatorships*, transl. Peter Brannick (Bolzano, 2016)

Eduard Mörike, *Werke* (including *Historie von der schönen Lau*) (Munich, 1977)

Winfried Nerdinger and Ekkehard Mai (eds), *Wilhelm Kreis: Architekt zwischen Kaiserreich und Demokratie 1873–1955* (Berlin and Munich, 1994)

Gavriel D. Rosenfeld, *Munich and Memory: Architecture, Monuments and the Legacy of the Third Reich* (Berkeley and Los Angeles, 2000)

Jürgen Rostock and Franz Zadniček, *Paradiesruinen: Das KdF-Seebad der Zwanzigtausend auf Rügen* (Berlin, 2006)

Royal Academy of Arts, *Anselm Kiefer* (London, 2014)

Helmut Scharf, *Zum Stolze der Nation: Deutsche Denkmäler des 19. Jahrhunderts* (Dortmund, 1983)

Manfred Scheuch, *Historischer Atlas Deutschland* (Vienna, 1997)

Thomas Schmidt, *Werner March, Architekt des Olympia-Stadions 1894–1976* (Basel, 1992)

Ruth Schmitz-Ehmke, *Die Ordensburg Vogelsang: Architektur, Bauplastik, Ausstattung* (Cologne, 1988)

W.G. Sebald, *Austerlitz*, transl. Anthea Bell (London, 2001)

Nicholas Shakespeare, *Snowleg* (London, 2004)

Stadtgeschichtliches Museum Leipzig, *Völkerschlachtdenkmal* (Leipzig, 2009)

Jan Tabor, *Kunst und Diktatur: Architektur, Bildhauerei und Malerei in Österreich, Deutschland, Italien und der Sowjetunion 1922–1956* (Baden, 1994)

Jürgen Tietz, *Das Tannenberg-Nationaldenkmal* (Berlin, 1999)

The Times Atlas of European History, Second Edition (London, 1998)

Klaus Vogel (ed.), *Das Deutsche Hygiene-Museum Dresden 1911–1990* (Dresden, 2003)

Ian Walker, *Zoo Station: Adventures in East and West Berlin* (London, 1987)

Helmut Weihsmann, *Bauen unterm Hakenkreuz: Architektur des Untergangs* (Vienna, 1998)

Michael Welder, *Reise nach Königsberg: Spurensuche von Litauen in das nördliche Ostpreußen* (Leer, 1990)

Michael Welder, *Reise nach Ostpreußen: Spurensuche zwischen Weichsel und Memel* (Leer, 1992)

Michael Welder, *Reise nach Schlesien: Spurensuche zwischen Annaberg und Zobten* (Würzburg, 2002)

Benedikt Weyerer, *München 1933–1949: Stadtrundgänge zur politischen Geschichte* (Munich, 1996)

Robert S. Wistrich, *Weekend in Munich: Art, Propaganda and Terror in the Third Reich* (London, 1995)